CORPORATE GOVERNANCE IN LESS DEVELOPED AND EMERGING ECONOMIES

RESEARCH IN ACCOUNTING IN EMERGING ECONOMIES

Series Editors: Mathew Tsamenyi, Shahzad Uddin and Shahrokh M. Saudagaran

Recent Volumes:

RESEARCH IN ACCOUNTING IN EMERGING ECONOMIES
VOLUME 8

CORPORATE GOVERNANCE IN LESS DEVELOPED AND EMERGING ECONOMIES

EDITED BY

MATHEW TSAMENYI

Birmingham Business School, University of Birmingham, UK

SHAHZAD UDDIN

Essex Business School, University of Essex, UK

Emerald
JAI

United Kingdom – North America – Japan
India – Malaysia – China

JAI Press is an imprint of Emerald Group Publishing Limited
Howard House, Wagon Lane, Bingley BD16 1WA, UK

First edition 2008

British Library Cataloguing in Publication Data
A catalogue record for this book is available from the British Library

ISBN: 978-1-84855-252-4
ISSN: 1479-3563 (Series)

Awarded in recognition of
Emerald's production
department's adherence to
quality systems and processes
when preparing scholarly
journals for print

INVESTOR IN PEOPLE

CONTENTS

LIST OF CONTRIBUTORS

Adom Adu-Amoah	Ecobank, Accra, Ghana
Orhan Akisik	Isenberg School of Management, University of Massachusetts, Amherst, USA
Chandana Alawattage	University of Aberdeen Business School, Aberdeen, UK
Ali Al-Nodel	College of Economy and Administration, Qassim University, Saudi Arabia
Preye Edward Gesiye Angaye	Department of Accounting, Niger Delta University, Nigeria
Son Dang-Duc	Faculty of Accounting and Auditing, University of Commerce, Hanoi, Vietnam
Susela Devi	Faculty of Business and Accountancy, University of Malaya, Malaysia
Gordon Gao	School of Accounting, Economics and Statistics, Napier University, UK
Simon S. Gao	School of Accounting, Economics and Statistics, Napier University, UK
David Gwilliam	Exeter University Business School, UK
Hafiza Aishah Hashim	Faculty of Management and Economics, Universiti Malaysia Terengganu, Malaysia

Khaled Hussainey   Division of Accounting and
                             Finance, Stirling Management
                             School, Stirling University, UK

Mostafa Kamal Hassan   Department of Accounting,
                             College of Business, University of
                             Sharjah, United Arab Emirates;
                             Faculty of Commerce, Alexandria
                             University, Egypt

Ahmed Kholeif   Essex Business School, University
                             of Essex, UK

Martin Francis Kyeyune   Bournemouth Business School,
                             University of Bournemouth, UK

Pik Kun Liew   Essex Business School, University
                             of Essex, UK

Sudhir C. Lodh   School of Accounting, University
                             of Western Sydney, Australia

Jyoti Devi Mahadeo   School of Public Sector Policy and
                             Management, University of
                             Technology, Mauritius

Neil Marriott   Winchester Business School,
                             University of Winchester, UK

Pru Marriott   Winchester Business School,
                             University of Winchester, UK

Esinath Ndiweni   Cardiff School of Management,
                             University of Wales Institute,
                             Cardiff, UK

Susan Newberry   Faculty of Economics and Business,
                             University of Sydney, Australia

Joseph Mensah Onumah   Department of Accounting,
                             University of Ghana Business
                             School, Legon, Ghana

Peter John Opio   University of East London
                             Business School, University
                             of East London, UK

Hakim Ben Othman   LEFA-IHEC Business School,
                            Carthage, Tunisia

Afzalur Rashid   School of Accounting and Finance,
                            University of Wollongong,
                            Australia

Ronita D. Singh   Faculty of Economics and Business,
                            University of Sydney, Australia

Teerooven Soobaroyen   School of Management
                            and Business, Aberystwyth
                            University, UK

Venancio Tauringana   Bournemouth Business School,
                            University of Bournemouth, UK

Mathew Tsamenyi   Birmingham Business School,
                            University of Birmingham, UK

Shahzad Uddin   Essex Business School, University
                            of Essex, UK

Danture Wickramasinghe   Manchester Business School,
                            University of Manchester, UK

Daniel Zeghal   Telfer School of Management,
                            University of Ottawa, Canada

Tianxi Zhang   Department of Accounting, Antai
                            College of Economics and
                            Management, Shanghai Jiaotong
                            University, China

LIST OF REVIEWERS

Hafez Abdo
Nottingham Trent University, UK

Kamran Ahmed
Latrobe University, Australia

Orhan Akisik
University of Massachusetts, USA

Chandana Alawattage
University of Aberdeen, UK

Omar Al Farooque
University of New England, Australia

Jahangir Ali
Latrobe University, Australia

Ben Ali
University Paris Dauphine, France

Marcia Annisette
York University, Canada

Owolabi Bakre
University of Essex, UK

Bala Balachandran
South Bank University, UK

Bernardo Batiz-Lazo
University of Leicester, UK

Atauar Belal
Aston University, UK

Rebecca Boden
University of Wales Institute, Cardiff, UK

John Brierley
University of Sheffield, UK

Ashley Burrowes
University of Wisconsin, USA

Lesley Catchpowle
Greenwich University, UK

Rajesh Chakraborti
Indian School of Business, India

Chris Cowton
University of Huddersfield, UK

Istemi Demirag
Queen's University of Belfast, UK

Susela Devi
University of Malay, Malaysia

Keith Dixon
University of Canterbury,
New Zealand

Maria Dyball
Macquarie University, Australia

Charles Elad
University of Westminster, UK

Simon Gao
Napier University, UK

George Georgiou
University of Birmingham, UK

Claudia Girardone
University of Essex, UK

Abey Gunasekarage
University of Canterbury,
New Zealand

Rose Hanifa
University of Bradford, UK

Jim Haslam
University of Dundee, UK

Ron Hodges
University of Sheffield, UK

Mohammed Hudaib
University of Essex, UK

Khaled Hussainey
University of Stirling, UK

Aziz Jaafar
Bangor University, UK

Lisa Jack
University of Essex, UK

Kelum Nishanta Jayasinghe
University of Essex, UK

Gregory Jobome
University of Liverpool, UK

Susana Jorge
University of Coimbra, Portugal

Ahmed Kholeif
University of Essex, UK

Naoko Komori
University of Manchester, UK

Piotr Korczak
University of Bristol, UK

Pik Liew
University of Essex, UK

Jinghui Liu
University of Adelaide, Australia

Gregory Liyanarachchi
University of Otago,
New Zealand

Sudhir Lodh
University of Western Sydney,
Australia

Mark Mak
University of Manchester, UK

Musa Mangena
University of Bradford, UK

Keith Maunders
University of Hull, UK

Yuval Milo
London School of Economics, UK

Monir Mir
University of Canberra, Australia

Mahmood Momin
Auckland University of Technology, New Zealand

Stephen Owusu-Ansah
University of Texas-Pan American, USA

Abu Rahaman
University of Calgary, Canada

John Ritchie
University of Durham, UK

Aly Salama
University of Durham, UK

Will Seal
Loughborough University, UK

Rudra Sensarma
University of Hertfordshire, UK

Venancio Tauringana
University of Bournemouth, UK

Hardy Thomas
University of Essex, UK

Chibuike Uche
University of Nigeria, Nigeria

Bob Wearing
University of Essex, UK

Danture Wickramasinghe
University of Manchester, UK

Tomasz Piotr Wisniewski
University of Leicester, UK

Mahbub Zaman
University of Manchester, UK

INTRODUCTION TO CORPORATE GOVERNANCE IN LESS DEVELOPED AND EMERGING ECONOMIES

Mathew Tsamenyi and Shahzad Uddin

ABSTRACT

Purpose of paper – *This paper sets out to introduce the special issue on corporate governance in less developed and emerging economies. It summarises and reflects on themes and findings raised in the papers in the volume.*

Design/methodology/approach – *The findings reported in the paper are based on desk research and review of the papers contained in the volume.*

Findings – *The paper finds that the adoption of appropriate corporate governance systems is becoming a central issue in less developed and emerging economies. Factors such as the 1997 Asian financial crisis, the adoption of international donor led reforms, and the globalisation of capital markets are among the factors that are driving corporate governance reforms in less developed and emerging economies.*

Research limitations/implications – *The pressure from international donors has compelled some less developed and emerging economies to*

Corporate Governance in Less Developed and Emerging Economies
Research in Accounting in Emerging Economies, Volume 8, 1–11
Copyright © 2008 by Emerald Group Publishing Limited
ISSN: 1479-3563/doi:10.1016/S1479-3563(08)08018-3

adopt corporate governance models developed in the West with no modification. The paper argues that while it is imperative for less developed and emerging economies to reform their corporate governance systems, it is important that these systems are adapted to suite the specific needs of individual countries.

Originality/value of *paper – The paper is a summary of studies exploring various corporate governance issues in less developed and emerging economies. The issues addressed in these studies are important to understand corporate governance issues in both the private and public sectors in less developed and emerging economies.*

Over the past decade corporate governance reform has become an important global policy agenda driven by events such as the 1997 Asian financial crisis, major corporate scandals (such as Enron and WorldCom), and the globalisation of capital markets (Ahunwan, 2003; Krambia-Kapardis & Psaros, 2006; Marnet, 2007). In several less developed and emerging economies corporate governance reform is also driven by the adoption of international donor led economic reforms (Vaughn & Ryan, 2006; Tsamenyi, Enninful-Adu, & Onumah, 2007; Okike, 2007; Uddin & Choudhury, 2008). This in particular has made corporate governance reform an essential element of the development agenda promoted by the World Bank (Wolfensohn, 1998; Singh & Zammit, 2006; World Bank, 2002).

Accounting research in less developed and emerging economies in general has over the years been marginalised and labelled esoteric despite most people living in these environments (Alawattage, Hopper, & Wickramasinghe, 2007). This situation has improved over the past decade with the area of corporate governance in particular attracting significant interest (Haniffa & Cooke, 2002; Haniffa & Hudaib, 2006; Ararat & Yurtoglu, 2006; Tsamenyi, et al., 2007; Okike, 2007; Mangena & Tauringana, 2007; Uddin & Choudhury, 2008). These studies are however scattered across both specialist and non-specialist accounting journals making it difficult to tease out common theoretical and policy issues that have emerged from them.

This special issue is motivated by the need to provide a platform for debating both theoretical and practical issues on corporate governance relevant to less developed and emerging economies. The volume will provide a source for practitioners, policy makers, donor agencies, and academics with interest in corporate governance in less developed and emerging economies to draw upon. We believe the special issue is apt given the increasing pressure on some less developed and emerging economies by the World Bank and other international donors to reform their corporate governance systems. It is believed that corporate governance reforms will enhance the accountability of firms and instil investor confidence in these countries. The corporate governance systems recommended to these countries are largely based on those developed in the West (particularly the Anglo-American model). Given that less developed and emerging economies operate under different sets of structural conditions, it is worth exploring the applicability of these Western models to less developed and emerging economies. For example, an empirical question that can be asked is: Do less developed and emerging economies need different corporate governance systems from those pertaining in the developed world?

Answers to this type of question will require studies on corporate governance systems in individual less developed and emerging economies. It may also require comparative studies between developed and less developed countries. Fuller understanding of corporate governance systems in less developed and emerging economies should contribute to the minimisation of the unexpected and unsought consequences of imposed corporate governance framework from the West. This is of paramount practical concern for policy makers, managers, accountants, and others since they are affected by the regulatory regimes and changes of regulations on a daily basis in their working environment.

The seventeen papers in this volume are drawn from all four continents that have less developed and emerging economies. We have seven papers from Africa (Adu-Amoah, Tsamenyi, and Onumah; Angaye and Gwilliam; Hassan; Kholeif; Ndiweni; Soobaroyen and Mahadeo; and Tauringana, Kyeyune, and Opio), seven papers from Asia and the Middle East (Alawattage and Wickramasinghe; Hussainey and Al-Nodel; Dang-Duc, Marriott and Marriott; Gao, Gao, and Zhang; Hashim and Devi; Liew; and Rashid and Lodh), and three papers focusing on a number of less developed and emerging economies drawn from Africa, Asia-Pacific and the Middle East, Eastern and Central Europe, and Latin America (Akisik; Othman and Zeghal; and Singh and Newberry).

The methods adopted are diverse. Seven papers use qualitative methods, nine papers use quantitative methods and one paper adopts a mixture of both qualitative and quantitative methods. The methods adopted reflect the nature and complexities of the issues examined in each paper. A number of the papers have been theorised with authors drawing on theories such as economic agency, political economy, institutional, and legitimacy. The papers in the volume have examined wide ranging issues including disclosure and corporate governance, corporate governance regulatory frameworks, the need to understand corporate governance from the wider socio-cultural context, the influence of international donors on corporate governance practices, and corporate governance in small and medium enterprises.

A number of papers examine corporate governance and disclosure. The paper by Tauringana et al. provides insights into the determinants of timeliness of corporate annual reports. The authors investigate the association between corporate governance mechanisms, dual language reporting (in English and Swahili), and timeliness of annual reports of companies listed on the Nairobi Stock Exchange (NSE) in Kenya. Based on their analysis Tauringana et al. conclude that the timeliness of annual reports is influenced by the proportion of finance experts on the audit committee, frequency of board meetings, and dual language reporting. The finding relating to the dual language of English and Swahili offers new insight into the analysis of disclosure. Hussainey and Al-Nodel investigate the online financial reporting practices of listed firms in Saudi Arabia. The authors report that the majority of the firms in Saudi Arabia use the Internet to communicate some information about corporate governance to their stakeholders. The banking sector was found to have the highest level of corporate governance disclosure while the industry and service sectors have the lowest level of disclosure about corporate governance. Factors such as the nature of control over the sector and the involvement of government in the ownership and management of businesses were found to have significant impacts on online reporting practices. Hussainey and Al-Nodel's paper raises the awareness of the role that the Internet can play in improving financial reporting and corporate governance practices in less developed and emerging economies.

The paper by Kholeif draws on agency theory to examine the effect of CEO duality on corporate performance in Egypt. The role of other corporate governance mechanisms (board size, top managerial ownership, and institutional ownership) as moderating variables in the relationship between CEO duality and corporate performance is also examined. The author concludes that the performance of firms with large boards and low top management ownership is negatively affected by CEO duality and positively affected by institutional ownership. To improve corporate governance the author recommends that the Egyptian Capital Market Authority encourages listed companies to increase top management ownership and reduce board sizes. The paper by Hashim and Devi examines the relationship between board characteristics and ownership structure and earnings quality in Malaysia. The authors report significant association between board tenure and earnings quality, as well as between outside board ownership and family ownership and earnings quality. The paper questions the role of agency theory in explaining the conflicts between the controlling owners and the minority shareholders under conditions of concentrated ownership. This conclusion calls for alternative explanations of corporate governance practices from the traditional agency analysis, an issue raised by some of the other papers in this volume (see for example the papers by Alawattage and Wickramasinghe; and Adu-Amoah, Tsamenyi, and Onumah; and Ndiweni in this volume).

The study of Othman and Zeghal investigates the impacts of country-level attributes (in terms of common law versus civil law) on corporate governance disclosure in selected emerging markets. The authors conclude that common law emerging markets have substantially higher levels of corporate governance disclosure than civil law markets. The authors further reported that corporate governance disclosure is positively associated with the size of the capital market for the entire sample of emerging markets and for the sub-samples of common law and civil law countries. Law enforcement has a strong positive influence on corporate governance disclosure in common law emerging countries but no influence was found for civil law countries. Othman and Zeghal's paper identifies the importance of the legal and institutional environment in shaping corporate governance practices.

The paper by Akisik examines the relationship between the inflow of foreign direct investment (FDI) and its determinants in 27 emerging markets between 1997 and 2005. The paper offers a new insight into the analysis of FDI inflows into emerging markets by focusing on the role of accounting standards and corporate governance. The paper found that the adoption of high-quality accounting standards and effective corporate governance leads to an increase in FDI. Based on this the Akisik concludes that emerging markets can attract FDI by improving the quality of financial reporting and corporate governance.

Some papers offer insights into compliance with or the effect of corporate governance regulations. The paper by Gao et al. examines the effectiveness of China's 2005 shareholding reform in terms of reducing state-owned shareholdings in companies. The authors undertook this analysis by comparing the shareholder structures of 470 listed companies prior to and after the reform. Gao et al.'s focus is to identify the effect of the change in corporate ownership on governance and firm performance. Based on their analysis, the authors argue that the reform was effective in reducing both shareholding concentrations and largest shareholdings. They conclude that the reform had positive impact on corporate performance, suggesting that state-owned shareholdings are harmful to corporate performance. Rashid and Lodh's study investigates the effect of ownership concentration and the imposition of corporate governance on voluntary corporate social disclosures in Bangladeshi firms. The authors argue that the imposition of corporate governance regulation influences the voluntary corporate social disclosure practices of the firms. Rashid and Lodh conclude that there will be no incentives for the companies to provide voluntary social disclosure in the absence of regulation.

The paper by Soobaroyen and Mahadeo uses legitimacy theory to investigate compliance with the corporate governance code in Mauritius. The authors found a reasonable level of compliance with the more visible requirements of the code but observed non-compliance with issues such as the number of company boards being chaired by independent directors, uncertainties on the actual operation of board committees, and the non-disclosure of directors' remuneration. The authors also found that compliance statements were vague, ambiguous, or even inconsistent with the extent of compliance disclosed in the reports. The authors conclude that many of the companies in their sample are adhering selectively with the code to project an image of symbolic compliance. This conclusion supports the argument raised by some of the other papers in this volume for a much broader explanation of corporate governance practices in less developed and emerging economies.

A number of papers identify the importance of social and cultural factors in understanding corporate governance practices. Arguments presented in these papers suggest that for a fuller understanding of corporate governance practices in less developed and emerging economies there is the need to consider the social, cultural, and political contexts of these countries. These social and cultural factors are likely to render imported western corporate governance models unworkable. The paper by Alawattage and Wickramasinghe is very significant in this context as it moves beyond traditional economic theories that have dominated corporate governance analysis. The authors use a political economy framework based on the work of Antonio Gramsci and Karl Polanyi to tease out the changing regimes of governance and the roles of accounting in a Sri Lanka Tea plantation. Alawattage and Wickramasinghe have managed through their analysis to explore the underlying social and political issues embedded in corporate governance practices through different regimes of governance, and argue that each regime requires a different mode of accounting. The authors conclude that the actual governance structures and processes are embedded in broader socio-political structures. How governance systems operate in practice is therefore shaped by the social and political context. In other words, politics rather than accounting determined the operations of the governance systems. The role of social and political relations in corporate governance has also been emphasised in the study of Liew on Malaysia. She identified domestic politics and family relations as influential in the ownership, management, and corporate governance of Malaysian corporations.

The paper by Adu-Amoah, Tsamenyi and Onumah provides empirical evidence on corporate governance practices of Rural Banks in Ghana. These banks are located in the rural areas of Ghana where traditional cultural values dominate. The authors argue that corporate governance practices in the rural banks are embedded in social and political relations thereby questioning the wholehearted adoption of western corporate governance models without any modifications. The implication of this study is that the design and implementation of corporate governance systems in these types of organisations should take into consideration the local social, cultural, and political context. A similar argument has been presented by Ndiweni on corporate governance in Southern Africa. The author locates corporate governance in a social and cultural context. Drawing on the traditional African philosophy of *ubuntu* she argues that *ubuntu* informs corporate practices and influences perceptions on what constitutes '*good*' corporate governance and ethics in Southern Africa. Based on the findings of the study, Ndiweni proposes an alternative corporate governance framework informed by *ubuntu,* communitarianism, and stakeholder theories which will take into account the social and historical context of Southern Africa.

Angaye and Gwilliam's paper provides evidence on the nature and practice of corporate governance in listed companies in Nigeria. The context of the paper is particularly interesting given the economic and political turbulence that Nigeria has experienced over the past three decades. The paper examines the effect of ethnicity, gender, and power relationships on corporate governance practices. Despite the support by the interviewees for the development of corporate governance systems along the lines of those in the developed world, the authors identify inadequacies of the Nigerian governance regulatory infrastructure as an obstacle to such a move. In particular the authors note the lack of mechanisms for implementation and enforcement of corporate governance regulations in Nigeria.

Hassan's paper on public sector reform in Egypt also offers another dimension of social factors in corporate governance. The author draws on institutional theory to examine how internal reporting systems shaped the corporate governance practices in an Egyptian public sector organisation. The paper reports that internal organisational confusion was created as a consequence of the interplay between the new form of corporate governance and the intra-organisational power, routines, and know-how. Hassan's analysis is important because it is one of the few papers that examine the relationship between management accounting and corporate governance (see for instance Seal, 2006).

In terms of the influence of international donors on corporate governance, both the studies of Adu-Amoah et al. in Ghana and Liew in Malaysia identify the influence of the World Bank in corporate governance practices. The study of Adu-Amoah et al. identify that as a result of poor performance and failure of rural banks in Ghana the World Bank through the Central Bank of Ghana recommended Western models of corporate governance to these banks. The authors argue that these models did not operate as expected. Liew's paper examines corporate governance reforms in Malaysia in the aftermath of the 1997 Asian financial crises. She argues that the Malaysian government promoted corporate governance reforms as a way of recovering from the crisis and to satisfy the international financial community. Liew notes that Malaysian companies changed their corporate governance practices predominantly to fulfil the legal requirements enforced by the government and to attempt to recover investor confidence lost during the crisis. The papers by Adu-Amoah and Liew are important that they have both questioned the appropriateness of World Bank imposed systems of corporate governance on less developed and emerging economies.

The studies of Singh and Newberry and Dang-Duc et al. have implications for understanding accounting and corporate governance issues in Small and Medium Enterprises (SMEs). Singh and Newberry examine the appropriateness of applying the International Financial Reporting Standards (IFRS) for SMEs to developing countries. The authors argue that the current standard-setting process does not provide appropriate voice to developing countries. Singh and Newberry recommend that those seeking IFRS for developing countries may need to both devise an acceptable solution and obtain inside access to the standard-setting process to achieve this aim. Dang-Duc et al. provide empirical evidence on how banks use financial information of SMEs in Vietnam. Relying on the views of bank lending officers the authors explore the governance implications of the financial information of the SMEs. Dang-Duc et al. argue that the banks do not rely on accounting information provided by the SMEs in making their lending decisions. This conclusion questions the role of accounting information in SMEs.

While these papers do not provide a coherent account of corporate governance practices in the context of capital market reforms based on Western knowledge in less developed and emerging economies, they are related in many ways. A number of common issues emerged from these studies. First, some papers highlighted the unrealistic assumptions that Western corporate governance models are transferable and applicable in LDCs. There is an underlying assumption that institutions and societies are always homogeneous. The fundamental understanding of policy makers' belief is that a corporate governance model is just a set of techniques so that the main issue for them is how these techniques could be transferred or developed for attaining market and organisational efficiency and, in turn, economic development. These are highly unrealised and ambitious, as shown in some of the papers in the special issue. The mismatch between the reality and assumptions may have resulted in one major practical problem, which is an imbalanced regulatory framework (Uddin & Choudhury, 2008). Policy makers and aid agency officials hold the view that the corporate governance models in the West are unproblematic. Recent research, however, has illustrated that the Anglo-American corporate governance models can be questioned even in the developed countries (Unerman & O'Dwyer, 2004; Reinstein & McMillan, 2004).

Second, many papers in the special issue raised the contextual differences between less developed and Western countries. They argue that corporate governance reforms in LDCs are being formulated, informed by research based on neo-classical assumptions, which often ignore the context within which they operate. This epistemological position masks our understanding of accounting within peculiar societies and sectors (see for instance, Hopper, Tsamenyi, Wickramasinghe, & Uddin, 2007). For example, Anglo-American corporate governance models ignore the effects of family ownership upon accountability and transparency assuming professionalised management and a degree of separation of ownership and control. However, in many countries as reported in some of the papers in this special issue families dominate ownership and management with very different results (Ansari & Bell, 1991). Perfect competitive markets are unlikely to occur in developing countries where weak judicial system and enforcement in capital markets prevail. More often private ownership is concentrated in families with informal linkages to vital external actors and institutions in the social, political, and commercial domains. Thus, there is a strong need to accommodate these complex factors into a broader corporate governance model. These papers further contribute to the more fundamental debate about the effectiveness of structural adjustment programmes, including capital market reforms, in LDCs.

However, we wish to encourage more research on corporate governance, accountability and transparency in less developed and emerging economies. Researchers and policy makers should endeavour to explore suitable corporate governance models for less developed and emerging economies. Rather than considering the fact that local contexts are unproblematic and passive, future studies should open up a new agenda for studying corporate governance issues meaningfully, considering that local contexts are problematic and dynamic. Peculiarities in politics and culture should be fundamental to these studies and researchers should look for alternative frameworks to understand these theoretical deviations from the mainstream political economy and institutionalism. Familial relations in business, historical evidence concerning accounting practices, accounting reporting within small-scale enterprises and internal accountability within families and extended families are important avenues to understand how these traditional societies operate financially. In pursuing these studies, perhaps more intensive studies are needed to understand how corporate governance operates in such a context.

In sum this special issue seeks to promote debates on corporate governance in less developed and emerging economies. The papers in the volume have provided wide ranging empirical and theoretical issues that will have policy implications and also generate future academic debates.

ACKNOWLEDGMENTS

We are greatly indebted to the authors who have contributed papers to the volume. We also acknowledge the various referees for contributing to the success of the volume by doing such a meticulous review within a short notice. We are also grateful to Sarah Kennedy and Vicky Williams of Emerald Group Publishing and Zoë La Roche of Elsevier for their help in bringing this volume to fruition. Special thanks go to Karen Hanson of the University of Birmingham for her administrative support. We also wish to thank Victor Murinde for his encouragement and support in editing the volume. Finally, we thank John Samuels and Richard Briston for giving us the opportunity to edit the volume.

REFERENCES

Ahunwan, B. (2003). *Globalization and corporate governance in developing countries*. New York: Transnational Publishers.

Alawattage, C., Hopper, T., & Wickramasinghe, D. (2007). Introduction to management accounting in less developed countries. *Journal of Accounting and Organizational Change, 3*(3), 183–191.

Ansari, S. L., & Bell, J. (1991). Symbolism, collectivism, and rationality in organizations. *Accounting Organisation and Society*, 549–570.

Ararat, M., & Yurtoglu, B. B. (2006). Corporate governance in Turkey: An introduction to the special issue. *Corporate Governance: An International Review, 14*(4), 201–205.

Haniffa, R., & Cooke, T. E. (2002). Culture, corporate governance and disclosure in Malaysian corporations. *Abacus, 38*(3), 317–349.

Haniffa, R., & Hudaib, M. (2006). Corporate governance structure and performance of Malaysian listed companies. *Journal of Business Finance & Accounting, 33*(7&8), 1034–1062.

Hopper, T., Tsamenyi, M., Wickramasinghe, D., & Uddin, S. (2007). Management accounting in less developed countries: What is known and needs knowing. Paper presented at the Accounting and Subalternity Conference, York University, Toronto, Canada, August.

Krambia-Kapardis, M., & Psaros, J. (2006). The implementation of corporate governance principles in an emerging economy: A critique of the situation in Cyprus. *Corporate Governance: An International Review, 14*(2), 126–139.

Mangena, M., & Tauringana, V. (2007). Disclosure, corporate governance and foreign share ownership on the Zimbabwe stock exchange. *Journal of International Financial Management and Accounting, 18*(2), 53–85.

Marnet, O. (2007). History repeats itself: The failure of rational choice models in corporate governance. *Critical Perspectives on Accounting, 18*, 191–210.

Okike, E. N. (2007). Corporate governance in Nigeria: The status quo. *Corporate Governance: An International Review, 15*(2), 173–193.

Reinstein, A., & McMillan, J. J. (2004). The Enron debacle: More than a perfect storm. *Critical Perspectives on Accounting, 15*, 955–970.

Seal, W. B. (2006). Management accounting and corporate governance: An institutional interpretation of the agency problem. *Management Accounting Research, 17*, 389–408.

Singh, A., & Zammit, A. (2006). Corporate governance, crony capitalism and economic crises: Should the US business model replace the Asian way of "doing business"? *Corporate Governance: An International Review, 14*(4), 220–227.

Tsamenyi, M., Enninful-Adu, E., & Onumah, J. (2007). Disclosure and corporate governance in developing countries: Evidence from Ghana. *Managerial Auditing Journal, 22*(3), 319–334.

Uddin, S., & Choudhury, J. (2008). Rationality, traditionalism and the state of corporate governance mechanisms: Illustrations from a less developed country. *Accounting, Auditing and Accountability Journal, 21*(7), 1026–1105.

Unerman, J., & O'Dwyer, B. (2004). Enron, Worldcom, Andersen et al.: A challenge to modernity. *Critical Perspectives on Accounting, 15*(6/7), 971–993.

Vaughn, M., & Ryan, L. V. (2006). Corporate governance in South Africa: A bellwether for the continent? *Corporate Governance: An International Review, 14*(5), 504–512.

Wolfensohn, J. D. (1998). *"A battle for corporate honesty", The world in 1999*. USA: The Economist Newspaper Limited.

World Bank. (2002). *The future of research on corporate governance in developing and emerging markets*. Unpublished synthesis note of the workshop, World Bank, Washington, DC.

CORPORATE GOVERNANCE, DUAL LANGUAGE REPORTING AND THE TIMELINESS OF ANNUAL REPORTS ON THE NAIROBI STOCK EXCHANGE

Venancio Tauringana, Martin Francis Kyeyune and Peter John Opio

ABSTRACT

Conceptual Paper

Purpose of paper – *The study investigates the association between corporate governance mechanisms (proportion of finance experts on the audit committee, PFAC; frequency of board meetings, FBMG and proportion of non-executive directors, PNED), dual language reporting (DULR) (in English and Swahili) and timeliness of annual reports (TIME) of companies listed on the Nairobi Stock Exchange (NSE) in Kenya.*

Design/methodology/approach – *The data for the analysis is gathered from annual reports of 36 companies listed on the NSE for two financial years ending in 2005 and 2006. Ordinary least square (OLS) is used to determine the association between the corporate governance mechanisms,*

Corporate Governance in Less Developed and Emerging Economies
Research in Accounting in Emerging Economies, Volume 8, 13–37
Copyright © 2008 by Emerald Group Publishing Limited
All rights of reproduction in any form reserved
ISSN: 1479-3563/doi:10.1016/S1479-3563(08)08001-8

DULR and TIME. Company size (SIZE), gearing (GEAR), profit-ability (PROF) and industry (INDS) are used as control variables.

Findings – *The findings suggest that there is a significant negative relation-ship between corporate governance mechanisms (PFAC and FBMG), DURL and TIME. Consistent with extant research, the study also found that SIZE and INDS are significantly associated with TIME. No signi-ficant association is found between PNED, GEAR, PROF and TIME.*

Research limitations/implications – *The findings of the research will help Kenyan policy makers and practitioners in formulating corporate governance policies. However our research is limited, among others, because it focuses on only companies listed on the NSE. The results may therefore not be representative of all companies operating in Kenya.*

Originality/Value of paper – *The value of the paper lies in that the results provide, for the first time, evidence of the relationship between corporate governance mechanisms (PFAC, FBMG and PNED), DURL and timeliness of the annual reports.*

INTRODUCTION

The usefulness and importance of the annual report in developing countries has been well documented (e.g. Naser, Nuseibeh, & Al-Hussaini, 2003; Al-Razeen & Karbahari, 2004). It has also been suggested that the annual report is the most important source of company information for decision making (Marston & Shrives, 1991; Bartlett & Chandler, 1997; Stanton & Stanton, 2002). A key qualitative characteristic that affects the usefulness of the annual report is its timeliness. Timeliness of annual reports (TIME) is important for proper functioning of any capital market (Ashton, Willingham, & Elliot, 1987; Imam, Ahmed, & Khan, 2001; Citron, Taffler, & Uang, 2008). Prior research has shown that 'late' announcement of earnings is associated with 'lower' abnormal returns than is 'early' announcement (Chambers & Penman, 1984; Givoly & Palmon, 1982; Haw, Qi, & Wu, 2000; Ahmed, 2003; Wang & Song, 2006). Delay in the release of information is likely to increase the uncertainties associated with decisions for which the financial statements provide information (Ng & Tai, 1994; Haw et al., 2000; Annaert, De Ceuster, Polfliet, & Campernhout, 2002; Lee, Mande, & Son, 2008).

Despite the developments in internet reporting, TIME remains of parti-cular importance in developing countries, such as Kenya, since information in these markets is limited and has a long-time lag (Errunza & Losq, 1985). Access to more timely information is severely hampered in the case of Kenya due to the limited availability of internet access especially in the rural areas. For example, Oyelaran-Oyeyinka and Adeya (2004) suggest that despite the increase in the use of email and internet facilities in Kenya, the cost and convenience has limited its use. They also cite the slow dial-up connection to the internet as a severe factor that limits the setting up and keeping up of internet facilities. Given the limited access to internet facilities and that interim reports, a timelier source of information, are not required to be audited, we argue that the annual report remains the most important source of reliable company information for most users in Kenya.

The objective of this research is to empirically investigate the association between corporate governance mechanisms (proportion of finance experts on the audit committee, PFAC; frequency of board meetings, FBMG and proportion of non-executive directors, PNED) and dual language reporting (DURL) (in English and Swahili) and TIME on the Nairobi Stock Exchange (NSE), in Kenya.

The focus on corporate governance mechanisms is partly motivated by the growing recognition that corporate governance mechanisms play a central role in the governance of large organisations (Fama & Jensen, 1983; Beekes, Pope, & Yound, 2004) and in particular the paucity of literature on the association between governance and TIME. The recognition has led to a proliferation of research investigating the contribution made by the board of directors as a whole, non-executive directors and audit committees in helping ensure that managers act in the best interest of the shareholders. For example, Mangena and Tauringana (2008) found that a larger board size is associated with better performance in an environment of economic and political uncertainty while Evans and Weir (1995) established that the frequency of board meetings is associated with better performance. Barako, Hancock, and Izan (2006) and Tsamenyi, Enninful-Adu, and Onumah (2007) report a significant association between proportion of non-executive directors and the extent of voluntary disclosure. Other studies also show the effectiveness of audit committee in ensuring greater levels of voluntary disclosure (Mangena & Pike, 2005). Finally, corporate governance mechanisms have been found to have a significant effect on timeliness of incorporation of value relevant information into share prices (Beekes & Brown, 2006; Beekes, Brown, & Chin, 2007) and timeliness of internet reporting (Abdelsalam & Street, 2007). Our study which also investigates the relationship between corporate governance mechanisms and timeliness is the first to focus on the annual report.

The research is also partly motivated by the DULR practice (i.e. English and Swahili) by some NSE listed companies which may also affect TIME. The Companies Act (1978, Chapter 486) states that communication between the company and its members should be in a manner acceptable to both parties, however, financial accounts should be kept in English. NSE listing rules, however, require that if a language other than English is used in the annual report, a translation shall be provided (The Capital Markets Authority, 2002a). Consequently, some NSE listed companies have adopted the practice of reporting in both English and Swahili. The rationale for the practice is embedded in the fact that Swahili is a symbol of national and African heritage while English is internationally acceptable to foreign investors (Abdulaziz, 1991). Moreover, companies are required to reserve 25% of any Initial Public Offers (IPOs) for local investors (The Capital Markets Authority, 2002b), most of whom live in the rural areas and derive their income from agriculture. Owing to low levels of education attainment, such rural-based people are more likely to comprehend annual report messages in Swahili than English. Given that the agriculture sector is the highest contributor to Kenya's Gross Domestic Product (GDP) with 24.5% in 2005/2006 and employing over 80% of the working population (Central Bank of Kenya, 2006), companies, especially large ones, cannot afford to ignore the needs of these potential investors. While the practice of dual reporting may enhance understandability of the annual report message especially among those Kenyans who are more fluent in Swahili than English, we hypothesise that dual reporting may delay the release of the annual report because more time may be required to prepare and publish an annual report in both English and Swahili compared one written in English only.

In addition to the two motivations discussed above, our focus on the three corporate governance mechanisms (PFAC, FBMG and PNED) and DURL contributes to existing literature in a number of ways. First, Okeahalam and Akinboade (2003) emphasize the need to embark on meaningful research on corporate governance in Africa as limited rigorous academic research has been published. None of the few studies that have been published on the role of corporate governance in the last few years using African data has investigated the effect of corporate governance on TIME. For example, Barako et al. (2006) and Tsamenyi et al. (2007) are concerned with effect of corporate governance on the extent of disclosure in Kenya and Ghana respectively, while Mangena and Tauringana (2007) investigate the effect of corporate governance on foreign ownership on the Zimbabwe Stock Exchange.

Second, there is currently no available study on the effectiveness of the three corporate governance mechanism investigated by this study on the

TIME. The current evidence on the effectiveness of the three corporate governance mechanisms relate to other aspects of company performance or reporting. For example, Abbott, Park, and Parker (2000) investigate the impact of finance expertise on financial reporting fraud, Klein (2002) deals with earnings management, Mangena and Pike (2005) with disclosure and earnings restatement was investigated by Lin, Li, and Yang (2006). The relationship between frequency of board meetings and company performance was investigated by Evans and Weir (1995) and Frey (1993) and that between the proportion of non-executive and voluntary disclosure by Barako et al. (2006) and Tsamenyi et al. (2007).

Third, to our knowledge, this is the first time a study has ever investigated the association between DULR and TIME. Investigating this association is important for improving the quality of financial reporting in Kenya because reporting in both English and Swahili may enhance understandability of the annual report message (particularly for those who are more fluent in Swahili than English). Since timeliness and understandability are both qualitative characteristics of useful information, the findings should provide evidence of whether there is a conflict between understandability (due to DULR) and TIME.

Finally, research evidence on the TIME on the NSE is also timely in the wake of the Kenyan Government embarking on the process of transforming the NSE by mobilising domestic savings and attracting foreign capital inflows (Barako et al., 2006). As the NSE assumes increasing importance as a financial centre and a cheaper source of finance (Wagacha, 2001), the quality of the information (measured by its timeliness) assumes greater importance and its scrutiny becomes even more urgent.

The rest of the paper is organised as follows. Corporate reporting and governance in Kenya is briefly discussed in the next section. This is followed by a literature review and hypotheses development; a description of the research design and a presentation of the empirical results. In the final section, conclusions are drawn and the limitations and implications discussed. Future avenues of research in this area are also suggested.

CORPORATE REPORTING AND GOVERNANCE IN KENYA

Corporate governance has attracted considerable attention over the past decades, prompting a proliferation of conceptual and empirical models, and creation of codes of best practices. Despite these divergences, the core issues addressed by corporate governance are the composition of board of director, the roles of nominal directors and the use of independent auditors (Yakasai, 2001) in ensuring greater accountability and improving performance (Cadbury Committee, 1992). Like many other African states, Kenya has made great strides in developing its own corporate governance framework. However, the mechanisms for effective governance are still in their nascent stage. Very little has been undertaken to assess the effectiveness of the governance mechanism in place. This section examines the main governance mechanisms used in Kenya.

The Companies Act

In many respects, Kenya's main corporate reporting framework, the Companies Act, 1978 (Chapter 486, Laws of Kenya) reflects the country's colonial past as it is based, and is substantially the same as, the UK Companies Act 1948 (Ogola, 2000). The Companies Act lays down provisions in respect of accounts and audit (Sections 147–163). For example, the duty to prepare the profit and loss account and balance sheet (Section 148) and contents of group accounts (Section 152). With respect to audits, the Companies Act requires companies to appoint auditors who must be members of the Institute of Certified Public Accountants of Kenya (ICPAK) and meet the criteria for an auditor as laid out in the Accountants Act (1977). The Companies Act further specifies that the auditors' report should appear as an annex to the profit and loss account and balance sheet and prescribes the contents of the auditors' report.

In addition to the requirements of the Companies Act, NSE listed companies are also subject to the requirements of the Capital Market Authority (2002a) listing rules. These requirements relate to public issues and disclosure in prospectus. Regarding TIME, the Capital Market Authority (2002a) listing rules state that every company shall prepare an annual report containing audited annual financial statements within *four months* of the close of its financial year. Further, the rules stipulate that a complete set of financial statements should include the following components: balance sheet; income statement; a statement showing either all changes in equity or changes in equity other than those arising from capital transactions with owners and distributions to owners; cash flow statement and accounting policies and explanatory notes.

The Capital Market Act

The corporate governance guidelines are contained in the Capital Market Act (2002) (Chapter 485A) and cover principles of good corporate governance and best practices by listed companies. In particular, the Act states that 'the board should compose of a balance of executive directors and non-executive directors. Further, the independent and non-executive directors should form at least one-third of the membership board. The Act also requires that the size of the board should not be too large to undermine an inter-active discussion during board meetings or too small such that the inclusion of a wider expertise and skills to improve effectiveness of the board is compromised. In addition, the Act requires the establishment of an audit committee of at least three independent and non-executive directors. The audit committee members are required to have broad business knowledge relevant to the company's business. Finally, the Act tasks the audit committee with reviewing quarterly, half-yearly and year-end financial statements focusing on, among others, the compliance with International Accounting Standards and other legal requirements.

LITERATURE REVIEW AND HYPOTHESES DEVELOPMENT

Literature Review

As discussed before, there is currently no specific research on the association between the corporate governance mechanisms (PFAC, FBMG and PNED), DULR and TIME. Previous research on the three corporate governance mechanisms relate to issues such as the impact of finance expertise on financial reporting fraud (Abbott et al., 2000), earnings management (Klein, 2002), disclosure (Mangena & Pike, 2005) and earnings restatement (Lin et al., 2006); frequency of board meetings on company performance (Evans & Weir, 1995; Frey, 1993) and proportion of non-executive on voluntary disclosure (Barako et al., 2006; Tsamenyi et al., 2007). Only three studies identified have examined the relationship between governance and timeliness. However, the focus of the studies the speed at which information is incorporated into share prices and internet reporting. Beekes and Brown (2006) and Beekes et al. (2007), for example, examined the relationship between governance quality and variables such as timeliness, frequency of disclosure, analysts' earnings forecasts. Their findings, suggest that, among others, value relevant information released by companies with better governance is incorporated into the share price faster. Finally, Abdelsalam and Street (2007) investigated the significance of the association between timely internet reporting and corporate governance characteristics of board experience and board independence. Their findings suggest that boards with less cross directorships, more experience and lower length of service provide timelier internet reporting.

The sole prior study of the effect on DULR relates to the extent of voluntary disclosure (Leventis & Weetman, 2004). The study investigated the relationship between voluntary and dual reporting on the Athens Stock Exchange. Using a sample of 87 companies consisting of 46 companies reporting in Greek only and 41 companies reporting in both Greek and English they found that dual reporting was significantly associated with the extent of voluntary disclosure at 1% level of significance. Since dual reporting entails preparing an annual report in two languages rather than one, we believe that it has the potential to affect TIME.

A number of previous researches, however, exist on the TIME. According to Owusu-Ansah and Leventis (2006) the predominant focus of the timeliness studies has been on developed countries (e.g. Carslaw & Kaplan, 1991; Bamber, Bamber, & Schoderbek, 1993; Soltani, 2002). However, a few studies are based on developing countries (e.g. Abdulla, 1996; Haw et al., 2000; Ahmed, 2003; Leventis & Weetman, 2004). A primary objective of the extant studies is to determine whether an association exists between company specific characteristics and timeliness. For example, company size (Ashton, Graul, & Newton, 1989; Carslaw & Kaplan, 1991; Owusu-Ansah & Leventis, 2006), financial year-end (Davies and Whitred, 1980; Knechel & Payne, 2001; Owusu-Ansah, 2000), gearing (Carslaw & Kaplan, 1991; Owusu-Ansah & Leventis, 2006), auditor type (Gilling, 1977; Carslaw & Kaplan, 1991; Leventis, Weetman, & Caramanis, 2005), extraordinary items (Newton & Ashton, 1989; Ashton et al., 1989; Schwartz & Soo, 1996), industry (Givoly & Palmon, 1982; Bamber et al., 1993; Schwartz & Soo, 1996) and audit opinion (Jaggi & Tsui, 1999; Bamber et al, 1993; Soltani, 2002). As a result of these previous studies, we control for the influence of company specific variables in our investigation.

Hypotheses Development

Corporate Governance Mechanisms
The three corporate governance mechanisms examined in this study are proportion of finance expertise on the audit committee (PFAC), frequency

of board meetings (FBMG) and proportion of non-executive directors (PNED). PFAC is expected to be negatively associated with TIME because a higher proportion of finance experts on the audit committee is more likely to bring pressure to bear on management to release the annual report early. Prior studies, for example, found that capital markets react positively to the appointment of non-executive directors with financial expertise to the audit committees (Defond, Hann, & Hu, 2005) suggesting that finance expertise on the audit committee is perceived by the market as enhancing the quality of financial reporting. Other studies reported a negative relationship between audit committees' financial expertise and financial statements fraud (e.g. Abbott et al., 2000), earnings management (Klein, 2002) and earnings restatement (Lin et al., 2006). This suggests that audit committee financial expertise may alleviate problems of financial fraud, earnings management and earnings restatement, respectively. In addition, the findings of a positive relationship between audit committee financial expertise and extent of disclosure (e.g. Mangena & Pike, 2005) also suggest that audit committee financial expertise is effective in alleviating the problem of information asymmetry.

FBMG is expected to be negatively associated with the TIME. The rationale is that the more the board of directors meets the more frequently it is likely to address problems as they arise and therefore would be quicker in approving the release of annual reports. In the context of the Companies Act, 1978 (Chapter 486), the board of directors needs to approve the annual report before it is published. FBMG has been found to be associated with firm performance. For example, Evans and Weir (1995) suggest that regular meetings allow potential problems to be identified, discussed and avoided and should therefore lead to a superior level of performance and hence higher profitability. Their findings suggest that weekly meetings were associated with superior performance compared to monthly meetings. The influence of FBMG on firm performance was also investigated by Desai (1998) who found that increased number of board meetings was positively related to subsequent firm performance. Vafeas (1999) also found that operating performance of firms improved following years of abnormal board activity in terms of number of board meetings. The improvements were most pronounced for firms with poor prior performance.

Finally, prior research suggest that non-executive directors influence a wide range of board decisions including enhancing firm-value by protecting shareholder interests against managerial opportunism (e.g. Dahya, McConnell, & Travlos, 2007); CEO removal (Weisbach, 1988);

negotiation of tender offer bids (Byrd & Hickman, 1992); voluntary disclosure (Chen & Jaggi, 2000) and resistance to greenmail payments (Kosnik, 1987). Consequently we hypothesize that PNED may also influence the TIME on the NSE. Beekes et al. (2004), for example, investigated whether the influence of non-executive directors extended to the timeliness and conservatism in reported earnings. They found that firms with a higher proportion of non-executive directors adopt a more conservative approach with respect to timeliness of bad news recognition of earnings. Having a greater proportion of non-executive directors has some limitations. For example, non-executive directors may (1) stifle strategic actions of the board (Goodstein, Gautum, & Boeker, 1994), (2) impose excessive monitoring (Baysinger & Butler, 1985), (3) lack business knowledge needed to be effective (Paton & Baker, 1987) and (4) lack true independence (Demb & Neubauer, 1992). The lack of true independence may be of particular concern in developing countries due to scarcity of a large pool of professionals with business experience to undertake the role of non-executive directors. Given the opposing views of the possible effectiveness of PNED, the direction of the relationship between PNED and TIME is not predicted. Based on the above discussion the following hypotheses will be tested:

H$_1$. The proportion of finance experts on the audit committee (PFAC) is negatively associated with TIME on the NSE.

H$_2$. Frequency of board meetings (FBMG) is negatively associated with TIME on the NSE.

H$_3$. Proportion of non-executive directors (PNED) is associated with TIME on the NSE.

Dual Language Reporting
The Companies Act (1978, Chapter 486) requires that correspondence between the company and its members should be done in a manner acceptable to both parties but financial accounts should be kept in English. The NSE listing rules further require that if a language other than English is used in the annual report, a translation shall be provided (The Capital Markets Authority, 2002a). Consistent with Capital Market Authority (2002a) some companies listed on the NSE choose to report in both English and Swahili. For the purpose of this research we coded annual reports reporting in English and Swahili (1) and those reporting in English only (0). We expect the relationship between DULR. and timeliness to be positive.

This is because the preparation of annual reports in two languages is more onerous and time consuming than those in one language. For example, dual reporting may require more time and implies further costs such as preparation and design costs (Leventis & Weetman, 2004). Further delays may be encountered in making sure that the translation is both technically and culturally correct (Le Searc'h & Klotz, 1999). Finally, we also expect that more time will be required for auditors to check the accounts in Swahili and English compared to those in English only. It can, therefore, be hypothesised that:

H₄. Dual language reporting (DULR) is positively associated with TIME on the NSE.

Control Variables
The influence of company specific variables on timeliness has been investigated by a myriad of studies before (e.g. Davies & Whitred, 1980; Ashton et al., 1987; Henderson & Kaplan, 2000; Soltani, 2002; Owusu-Ansah & Leventis, 2006). The influence of company size has featured in many studies and has been mostly found to be negatively associated with TIME. For example, Jaggi and Tsui (1999) and Owusu-Ansah (2000) reported a significant negative association between size and TIME. Gearing has also been linked to timeliness because high gearing increases the probability of company failure that in turn increases the probability of the auditor being sued. This gives the auditor incentive to perform more work to minimise the possibility of a successful lawsuit. This is likely to extend the time required to complete the audit (Carslaw & Kaplan, 1991). Previous studies such Jaggi and Tsui (1999), Simnett, Aitken, Choo, and Firth (1995) and Owusu-Ansah and Leventis (2006) found no significant relationship between gearing and TIME.

Further, previous research on the association between profitability and timeliness is based on the premise that if a firm releases its earnings report earlier than expected, its share price rises, on average, while if the report is late its share price declines (e.g. Chambers & Penman, 1984; Kross & Schroeder, 1984). Longer period of time is also required to audit earnings reports reflecting bad news, delaying their disclosure relative to those containing good news (Givoly & Palmon, 1982). A significant inverse relationship was reported by Courtis (1976) and Henderson and Kaplan (2000). However, Davies and Whitred (1980) and Ashton et al. (1987) found that profitability was not significantly associated with audit delay. Finally, we also control for industry based on previous research findings. We classify our companies, consistent with Ashton et al. (1989), into 'financial' industry (banks and insurances companies) and 'non-financial' industry. According to Bamber et al. (1993) banks are expected to report early because their accounting systems are centralised and automated, and banks hold little inventory or fixed assets. Financial companies have been found to have shorter audit periods than non-financial (e.g. Ashton et al., 1987, 1989). Bamber et al. (1993) found that banks reported significantly earlier than other industries. However, Ng and Tai (1994) did not find any significant association. Based on the preceding arguments it can be hypothesized that:

H_5. Company size (SIZE) is negatively associated with TIME on the NSE.

H_6. Gearing (GEAR) is positively associated with TIME on the NSE.

H_7. Profitability (PROF) is negatively associated with TIME on the NSE.

H_8. The 'financial' services INDS companies listed on the NSE release their annual reports significantly earlier than 'non-financial' INDS companies.

RESEARCH DESIGN

The Data

The data used consists of the latest two annual reports of NSE listed companies. At the time of data collection, May 2007, the total population of companies listed on the NSE was 48. Owing to the small population all companies were considered for investigation. The main criteria used for the sampling of the companies was that the company must have been listed for the past two years and have available two latest annual reports. Forty-four companies matched the criteria and the annual reports were gathered through a letter to each company and in some cases the annual reports were collected in person. In the end a total of 36 companies provided a complete set of two annual reports which amounts to about 82% of the companies that met the main criteria. Corporate governance, dual reporting and company specific control variables and the timeliness were all collected from the annual reports.

The Model

The following ordinary least square (OLS) regression model was used to investigate the influence of corporate governance mechanisms on timely reporting behaviour of the 72 pooled companies (36 companies over two years) in our sample.

$$TIME_j = \beta_0 + \beta_1 PFAC_i + \beta_2 BMNG_i + \beta_3 PNED_i + \beta_4 DULR_i$$
$$+ \beta_5 SIZE_i + \beta_6 GEAR_i + \beta_7 PROF_i + \beta_8 INDS_i + e_i$$

All the variables used in the regression model are defined in Table 1.

RESULTS AND DISCUSSION

Descriptive Analysis

The TIME frequency of the release of the annual report by sampled companies is presented in Table 2 for 2005, 2006 and pooled. The table shows that for 2005, 91.66% of the companies reported within the regulatory time of 120 days (four months) as required by the Capital Market Authority (2002a). For the year 2006 the frequency analysis shows

Table 1. Definition of Variables Included in the Multiple Regression Model.

Symbol	Variable Description	Acronym and Expected Sign
–	Time measured by number of days between financial year-end and the date of release of company's audited annual financial statements	TIME (?)
β_1	The proportion of financial experts on the audit committee (measured by number of directors with finance background on the audit committee) divided by the total number of directors on the audit committee	PFAC (−)
β_2	Frequency of board meetings found by dividing number of times the board met in one calendar year by 12 months	FBMG (−)
β_3	The proportion of non-executive directors to total directors of the company	PNED (?)
β_4	Dual language reporting; '1' if the company used both English and Swahili to present its annual report and accounts; '0' if English only	DUAL (+)
β_5	Natural log of year-end capital employed	SIZE (−)
β_6	Ratio of long-term debt to long-term debt plus equity	GEAR (+)
β_7	Profitability measured by profit before interest and tax divided by capital employed	PROF (−)
β_8	Industry; 1 if the company belongs to the 'non-financial' industry; 0 if it belongs to the 'financial' industry	INDS (?)

Table 2.   TIME of NSE listed Companies.

Publication Lead-Time (TIME)	Frequency			Percentage			Cumulative Percentage		
	2005	2006	Pooled	2005	2006	Pooled	2005	2006	Pooled
0–30	0	0	0	0.00	0.00	0.00	0.00	0.00	0.00
31–40	1	2	3	2.78	5.56	4.17	2.78	5.56	4.17
41–50	3	4	7	8.33	11.11	9.72	11.11	16.67	13.89
51–60	12	10	22	33.33	27.77	31.95	44.44	44.44	44.44
61–70	5	2	7	13.88	5.56	9.72	58.32	50.00	55.56
71–80	3	5	8	8.33	13.88	11.11	66.65	63.88	66.67
81–90	3	4	7	8.33	11.11	9.72	74.98	74.99	76.39
91–100	2	3	4	5.56	8.33	5.55	80.54	83.32	81.94
101–110	2	1	3	5.56	2.78	4.17	86.10	86.10	86.11
111–120	2	1	3	5.56	2.78	4.17	91.66	88.88	90.28
121–130	2	2	4	5.56	5.56	5.55	97.22	94.44	95.83
131–140	0	1	1	0.00	2.78	1.39	97.22	97.22	97.22
141–150	0	0	0	0.00	0.00	0.00	97.22	97.22	97.22
151–160	1	0	1	2.78	0.00	1.39	100.00	97.22	98.61
161–170	0	1	1	0.00	2.78	1.39	100.00	100.00	100.00
Total	36	36	72	100.00	100.00	100.00	100.00	100.00	100.00

that 88.88% of the companies met the deadline. These statistics suggest that for 2005, three companies or 8.34% released their annual report after the regulatory deadline of 120 days. In 2006, 4% or 11.12% also missed the regulatory deadline to publish their financial statements.

Table 2 also reveals that a total of 44.44% of the companies in 2005 and 2006 published their financial statements before 60 days had elapsed since the financial year-end. The figures in the table also show that the greatest number of companies publish their annual reports between 51 and 60 days. For example, in 2005 a third of the companies (33.33%) reported within that period whilst in 2006 the percentage of companies reporting during the same period is lower at 28%.

The descriptive statistics of the TIME, corporate governance mechanisms, DULR and company-specific control variables are presented in Table 3. The TIME descriptive statistics show that the mean number of days taken to publish the financial statements in 2006 (panel B) was 76.47 days compared to 74.50 days in 2005 (panel C). There are also differences in the minimum and maximum days taken to publish the financial statements over the two years. For example, the minimum for 2006 is 35 days compared to 33 days for 2005. Further, the statistics also reveal that the maximum number of days taken to release the financial statements was 170 days for 2006 compared to 153 days for 2005. Reporting times are trending towards the laggardly.

Table 3. Descriptive Statistics for Dependent and Independent Variables.

Descriptive Statistics	TIME	PFAC	FBMG	PNED	DULR	SIZE (KSH'mil)	GEAR	PROF	INDS
Panel A – Pooled data (N = 72)									
Mean	75.49	.2660	.3504	.7368	.61	7966.54	.5750	.1830	.6944
Std. Dev	28.89	.1572	.1392	.1492	.491	13886.34	.3094	.2383	.4639
Minimum	33.00	.0000	.17	.20	0	21.00	.07	−.56	.00
Maximum	170.0	.8	1.0	.92	1	57040.00	2.00	.98	1.00
Panel B – 2006 data (N = 36)									
Mean	76.47	.2592	.3481	.7289	.61	7966.54	.5750	.1830	.6944
Std. Dev	28.89	.1572	.1392	.1492	.491	13886.34	.3094	.2383	.4671
Minimum	35.00	.0000	.17	.20	0	21.00	.07	−.56	.00
Maximum	170.0	.8	1.0	.92	1	57040.00	2.00	.98	1.00
Panel C – 2005 data (N = 36)									
Mean	74.50	.2728	.3528	.7447	.61	8026.36	.5897	.1683	.6944
Std. Dev	28.22	.1614	.1412	.1510	.494	13478.50	.3454	.2397	.4672
Minimum	33.00	.11	.17	.20	0	21.00	.08	−.56	.00
Maximum	153.0	.80	1.0	.92	1	49770.00	2.00	.98	1.00

The statistics suggest that, on average, there was a two-day delay in releasing financial statements in 2006 compared to 2005. To find out if the delay was not influenced by a small number of companies taking unusually long time to report the medians for both years were calculated. The results show that the median for 2006 is 72.5 days compared to 64 days for 2005 days. This again confirms that the companies appear to be taking longer to report in 2006 compared to 2005.

Despite these findings, TIME on the NSE compares favourably with some developing countries. For example, Jaggi and Tsui (1999) reported a mean audit delay of 105 days in respect of Hong Kong, while Imam et al. (2001) reported a mean delay of 5.86 months in Bangladesh. Recently, Owusu-Ansah and Leventis (2006) reported a mean of 113.26 days for the release of financial statements in Greece.

Multivariate Analyses

Table 4 presents the correlation analyses results of the dependent and independent variables. Correlation analysis is important as a first step in

Table 4. Pearson Correlations between Dependent and Independent Variables.

	TIME	PFAC	FBMG	PNED	DULR	SIZE	GEAR	PROF	INDS
TIME	1.000								
PFAC	−.365**	1.000							
FBMG	−.31**	−.171	1.000						
PNED	−.014	−.350**	.221	1.000					
DULR	−.487**	.339**	.260*	−.099	1.000				
SIZE	−.502**	.297*	.089	−.115	.430**	1.000			
GEAR	.087	−.056	.145	.309	−.132	.297*	1.000		
PROF	−.199	.274*	.005	.127	.303**	−.280*	.017	1.000	
INDS	.072	−.112	−.269*	−.138	−.282*	−.356**	−.455***	−.322**	1.000

**Correlation is significant at the 0.01 level (2-tailed).
*Correlation is significant at the 0.05 level (2-tailed).

identifying the nature of the relationship between the dependent and independent variables. It is also important for the detection of any high correlations between independent variables so as to avoid the problem of multicollinearity. According to Field (2005) high levels of co-linearity increase the probability that a good predictor of the outcome will be found non-significant and rejected from the model.

The problem lies, however, in determining what represents a high value. For some, a high r is anything above ± 0.500; for others it is anything around ± 0.600 (Eastman, 1984). However, if correlation coefficient is less than ± 0.800 it does not seem to offer a serious threat to regression results (see Farrar & Glauber, 1967; Judge, Griffiths, & Hill, 1985). As can be seen from Table 4, the highest correlation among independent variables is between gearing (GEAR) and industry (INDS) at −.455 and DULR and size (SIZE) which is .430. These correlation co-efficients are low and considered not to cause serious problems with multicollinearity. The results also show a significant correlation at 1% between TIME and PFAC, FBMG, DURL and SIZE.

The OLS multiple regression results of the association between corporate governance mechanisms and DULR on TIME on the NSE are presented in Table 5. The F-statistic is significantly different from zero, suggesting that a subset of the independent variables does explain the variation in timeliness about its mean. The results in Table 5, as indicated by the value of the R-squared adjusted, indicates the model explains 41.9% of the variation in TIME.

Table 5. Pooled OLS Regression Model Estimates of TIME.

R	R^2		Adjusted R^2	Std. Error of the Estimate
.696	.485		.419	22.01295

	Sum of squares	df	Mean square	F	Significance
Regression	28728.091	8	3591.011	7.411	.000
Residual	30527.895	63	484.570		
Total	59255.986	71			

	Unstandardised Coefficients		Standardised Coefficients	t	Significance	Collinearity Statistics	
	B	Std. error	Beta			Tolerance	VIF
(Constant)	190.060	23.535		8.076	.000		
Corporate governance mechanisms[a]							
PFAC	−56.240	20.164	−.306	−2.789	.007	.679	1.473
FBMG	−50.179	21.576	−.242	−2.326	.023	.757	1.321
PNED	−37.438	20.729	−.194	−1.806	.076	.707	1.414
Dual language reporting[b]							
DULR	−16.385	6.643	−.278	−2.466	.016	.642	1.558
Control variables[c]							
SIZE	−13.371	3.859	−.377	−3.465	.001	.691	1.446
GEAR	−10.579	11.643	−.113	−.909	.367	.527	1.899
PROF	−2.180	14.074	−.018	−.155	.877	.607	1.648
INDS	−20.156	8.278	−.324	−2.435	.018	.463	2.161
Average							1.615

[a,b,c]All variables are as defined in Table 1.

The coefficient estimates for corporate governance mechanisms (PFAC and FBMG) are all statistically significant. These results confirm our hypotheses one and two. DULR is also significantly associated with timeliness at the 5% level of significance which is consistent with our fourth hypothesis although the direction is contrary to our prediction. Consistent with hypotheses five and eight the SIZE and INDS variables are also significantly associated with TIME although the sign of the relationship in respect of industry is contrary to that predicted. The results in Table 5, however, suggest that corporate governance mechanism (PNED) and the control variables, GEAR and PROF, are not significantly associated with TIME by companies listed on the NSE. These results indicate that our third, sixth and seventh hypotheses are not supported.

The negative and significant coefficient on the PFAC variable suggests that companies with a higher proportion of finance experts on their audit committee release their annual reports early. This is consistent with the notion that finance experts are aware of the importance of the annual report being released on time and may put some pressure on management to have the annual report released timely after the end of the financial year. The results are consistent with previous studies on the effectiveness of proportion of finance experts on different aspects of financial reporting, e.g. Abbott et al. (2000) and Klein (2002) on minimising financial statements fraud and earnings management respectively and Mangena and Pike (2005) on increasing voluntary disclosure.

The significant negative relationship between FBMG and TIME indicates that companies which hold meetings frequently publish their annual reports earlier. The result is consistent with the suggestion that boards which meet more frequently are likely to approve the release of the annual reports sooner compared to those meeting less frequently. This is consistent with similar findings in respect of effectiveness of board meetings in improving financial performance (e.g. Desai, 1998; Vafeas, 1999) and higher audit assurance (e.g. Carcello, Hermanson, Neal, & Riley, 2002).

The significant negative association between DURL and TIME suggests that companies that report in both Swahili and English are timelier than those that report only in English. The finding is contrary to our prediction that dual reporting companies may delay publishing their annual report because more time may be require to prepare an annual reporting written in both English and Swahili than one in English only. However, given that companies are required to reserve 25% of any IPOs for local investors (The Capital Markets Authority, 2002b) most of who live in the rural areas, more likely to comprehend annual report messages in Swahili than English, and have limited internet access, the early release of annual reports in dual language is probably an attempt by management of such companies to legitimise the companies activities (Stanton & Stanton, 2002) or impression management (Ewen, 1988; Leary & Kowalski, 1990). The early release of dual language annual reports also suggest that there is no conflict between timeliness and understandability (as a result of dual reporting).

The significant negative relationship between SIZE and TIME reported in Table 4 is consistent with previous research results by Schwartz and Soo (1996), Henderson and Kaplan (2000) and Jaggi and Tsui (1999). However, the result contradicts that reported by Simnett et al. (1995) and Owusu-Ansah and Leventis (2006). Finally, the results of a significant negative relationship between INDS and TIME suggest that financial services companies on average report later than 'non-financial companies'. Despite the significance of the results, the sign of the relationship is contrary to the one predicted in the hypothesis.

Additional Analyses

We tested for the robustness of our model for hetroscedasticity, multicollinearity, undertook the probability plot procedure and tested for the effect of outliers on our results with the Cook's distance procedure (Cook, 1977). These results, not reported here, indicate no problems with our model, except those relating to multicollinearity diagnostics, in Table 4. The general guideline regarding the variance inflation factor (VIF) is that if it is greater than 10 then there is cause for concern (Myers, 1990). If the average VIF is substantially greater than one then the regression may be biased (Bowerman & O'Connell, 1990). Tolerance of below .2 indicates a potential problem (Menard, 1995). As can be seen from the results in Table 4, the VIF is not greater than 10, the average VIF is 1.12 and tolerance levels are all above .2 which suggests that there is no serious problem with multicollinearity.

SUMMARY, CONCLUSION AND LIMITATIONS

This study has investigated the relationship between corporate governance mechanisms (PFAC, FBMG and PNED), DULR and TIME of annual reporting on the NSE. The study covered two years (2005 and 2006) and was based on the companies' annual reports. SIZE, GEAR, PROF and INDS were used in the study as control variables. The results suggest that on average, the time taken to release annual reports in 2005 was 74.5 days and was 76.47 days in 2006. The study also found (using the pooled data for 2005 and 2006) that corporate governance mechanisms (PFAC and FBMG) and DURL are negatively associated with TIME of annual reports on the NSE. The results PFAC are consistent with Abbott et al. (2000) in respect of financial statements fraud and Klein (2002) in respect of earnings management. The negative relationship between FBMG and TIME suggest that frequency of board meetings is an effective corporate governance mechanism in ensuring TIME. This is consistent with previous research in respect of the effectiveness of FBMG in respect of company performance (Evans & Weir, 1995; Vafeas, 1999). Finally, the significant negative relationship between DURL and TIME suggests that despite companies having to report in both Swahili and English, their annual reports are still timelier than those that report in English only.

The conclusion from the study is that corporate governance mechanisms (PFAC and FBMG) are effective while PNED is not, in improving the TIME on the NSE. Another conclusion is also that DURL does not conflict with TIME. These results have policy implications for preparers of annual reports and the Kenyan regulatory authorities especially the NSE. First, since PFAC is associated with TIME of annual reports the NSE may to make it more explicit in the Capital Market Act (2002, Chapter 485A) the proportion of finance experts required on the audit committee since currently the Act simply requires audit committee to have 'broad business relevant to the company business'. Second, The NSE exchange may also wish to monitor the frequency of board meeting with the view of encouraging those companies that meet less frequently to increase the frequency of such board meetings since it impacts on the timely release of annual reports. Finally, the finding that DULR is associated with timelier annual reporting suggests that the regulatory authorities need to encourage other companies currently not reporting in two languages to adopt DULR. This will increase the utility of the annual report information since this will lead to annual reports that are both understandable to a wider audience and timelier.

The reported results should be interpreted in the light of a number of limitations. First, owing to a small number of companies, it was not possible to include in the model many possible explanatory variables of TIME on the NSE. This may explain why the study could only explain 41.9% of the variation in TIME. Second, the investigation is limited to companies listed on the NSE and the results may therefore not be representative of all companies operating in Kenya. Third, due to data limitation (small number of companies listed on the NSE) it was not possible to explain the variation for each of the two years under investigation resulting in having to run a multiple regression on a pooled data over the two years. Fourth, despite finding that PNED has no influence on TIME, it is not possible to say with a degree of certainty why this is the case. Future studies may need to ascertain why non-executive directors are not effective in ensuring timely release of the annual report. Finally, the study uses publicly available data to investigate the relationship between corporate governance mechanisms and timeliness. It is possible that other techniques such as surveys and personal interviews may suggest other influences which are not publicly available.

ACKNOWLEDGMENTS

The authors are, respectively, Senior Lecturer in Accounting and Finance & PhD Student, Centre for Finance & Risk, Bournemouth University and Senior Lecturer of Strategy, University of East London. We would like to acknowledge our gratitude to Dr Musa Mangena (Bradford University School of Management) and the two anonymous reviewers. However, any errors and omissions of fact or mistakes in interpretation remain solely our responsibility.

REFERENCES

Abbott, L. J., Park, Y., & Parker, S. (2000). The effects of audit committee activity and independence on corporate fraud. *Managerial Finance, 26*(11), 55–67.

Abdelsalam, O. H., & Street, D. L. (2007). Corporate governance and the timeliness of corporate internet reporting by UK listed companies. *Journal of International Accounting, Auditing and Taxation, 16*, 111–130.

Abdulaziz, M. H. (1991). East Africa (Tanzania and Kenya). In: J. Cheshire (Ed.), *English around the World: Sociolinguistic perspectives* (pp. 391–401). Cambridge: Cambridge University Press.

Abdulla, J. Y. A. (1996). Timeliness of Bahraini annual reports. *Advances in International Accounting, 9*, 73–88.

Accountants Act. (1977). *The Accountants Act 1977 (Chapter 531)*. Nairobi: Government Printers.

Ahmed, K. (2003). The timeliness of corporate reporting: A comparative study of South Asia. *Advances in International Accounting, 16*, 17–43.

Al-Razeen, A., & Karbhari, Y. (2004). Annual corporate information: Importance and use in Saudi Arabia. *Managerial Auditing Journal, 19*(1), 117–133.

Annaert, J., De Ceuster, M. J. K., Polfliet, R., & Campernhout, G. V. (2002). To be or not to be ... too late: The case of Belgian semi-annual earnings announcements. *Journal of Business Finance and Accounting, 29*(3/4), 477–495.

Ashton, R. H., Graul, P. R., & Newton, J. D. (1989). Audit delay and the timeliness of corporate reporting. *Contemporary Accounting Research, 5*(2), 657–673.

Ashton, R. H., Willingham, J. J., & Elliot, R. K. (1987). An empirical analysis of audit delay. *Journal of Accounting Research, 25*(2), 275–292.

Bamber, E. M., Bamber, L. S., & Schoderbek, M. P. (1993). Audit structure and other determinants of audit report lag: An empirical analysis. *Auditing: A Journal of Practice & Theory, 12*(1), 1–23.

Barako, D. G., Hancock, P., & Izan, H. Y. (2006). Factors influencing corporate disclosure by Kenyan companies. *Corporate Governance, 14*(2), 107–125.

Bartlett, S. A., & Chandler, R. A. (1997). The corporate report and the private shareholder: Lee and Tweedie 20 years on. *British Accounting Review, 29*, 245–261.

Baysinger, B. D., & Butler, H. N. (1985). Corporate governance and the board of directors: Performance effects of changes in board composition. *Journal of Law, Economics and Organisations, 1*(1), 101–124.

Beekes, W., & Brown, P. R. (2006). Do better governed Australian firms make more informative disclosures? *Journal of Business Finance & Accounting, 33*(3/4), 422–450.

Beekes, W, Brown, P. R., & Chin, G. (2007). Do better governed firms make more informative disclosures? Canadian Evidence. Available at SSRN: http://ssrn.com/abstract=881062

Beekes, W. P., Pope, P., & Yound, S. (2004). The link between earnings timeliness, earnings conservatism and board composition: Evidence from the UK. *Corporate Governance: An International Review, 12*(1), 47–59.

Bowerman, B. L., & O'Connell, R. T. (1990). *Linear statistical models: An applied approach* (2nd ed.). Belmont, CA: Duxbury.

Byrd, J. W., & Hickman, K. A. (1992). Do outside directors monitor managers? Evidence from tender offer bids. *Journal of Financial Economics, 32*, 195–222.

Cadbury Committee. (1992). *Report of the committee on the financial aspects of corporate governance.* London: Gee and Company.

Capital Market Act. (2002). *Guidelines on corporate governance practices by public listed companies in Kenya.* (Chapter 485A). Kenya: Capital Markets Authority.

Capital Markets Authority. (2002a). *The Capital Markets (Securities) (Public Offers, Listing and Disclosure) Regulations,* Legal Notice No. 60, May 3, 2002 (Kenya Gazette Supplement No. 40).

Capital Markets Authority. (2002b). *The Capital Markets Act,* Legal Notice No. 134, August 2, 2002 (Chapter 485A).

Carcello, J. V., Hermanson, D. R., Neal, T. L., & Riley, R. A., Jr. (2002). Board characteristics and audit fees. *Contemporary Accounting Research, 19*(3), 365–384.

Carslaw, C. A. P. N., & Kaplan, S. E. (1991). An examination of audit delay: Further evidence from New Zealand. *Accounting and Business Research, 22*(85), 21–32.

Central Bank of Kenya. (2006). *Annual report.* Nairobi: Central Bank of Kenya.

Chambers, A., & Penman, S. (1984). Timeliness of reporting and the stock price reaction to earnings announcement. *Journal of Accounting Research, 22*(1), 21–47.

Chen, C. J. P., & Jaggi, B. (2000). Association between independent non-executive directors, family control and financial disclosures in Hog Kong. *Journal of Accounting and Public Policy, 19*, 285–310.

Citron, D. B., Taffler, R. J., & Uang, J. (2008). Delays in reporting price-sensitive information: The case of going concern. *Journal of Accounting and Public Policy, 27*, 19–37.

Companies Act. (1978). *The Companies Act 1978.* Laws of Kenya (Chapter 486). Nairobi: Government Printers.

Cook, R. D. (1977). Detection of influential observations in linear regression. *Technometrics, 19*(1), 15–18.

Courtis, J. K. (1976). Relations between timeliness of corporate reporting and corporate attributes. *Accounting and Business Research, 6*(25), 45–56.

Dahya, J., McConnell, J., & Travlos, N. G. (2007). The Cadbury Committee, corporate performance and top management turnover. *Journal of Finance, 57*(1), 461–483.

Davies, B., & Whitred, G. P. (1980). The association between selected corporate attributes and timeliness in corporate reporting: A further analysis. *Abacus, 16*(1), 48–60.

Defond, M., Hann, R. N., & Hu, X. (2005). Does the market value financial expertise on audit committees of boards of directors? *Journal of Accounting Research, 43*(2), 153–193.

Demb, A., & Neubauer, F. F. (1992). *The corporate board: Confronting the paradoxes.* Oxford: Oxford University Press.

Desai, A.B. (1998). *A study of the relationship between changes in the corporate governance mechanism, CEO turnover, and performance in declining firms.* Unpublished Ph.D. thesis, The University of Memphis, Memphis, TN.

Eastman, B. (1984). *Interpreting mathematical economics and econometrics.* London: Macmillan.

Errunza, V. R., & Losq, E. (1985). The behaviour of stock prices on LDC markets. *Journal of Banking and Finance, 9*(4), 561–575.

Evans, J., & Weir, C. (1995). Decision processes, monitoring, incentives and large firm performance in the UK. *Management Decision, 33*(6), 32–38.

Ewen, S. (1988). *All consuming images: The politics of style in contemporary culture.* New York: Basic Books.

Fama, E., & Jensen, M. C. (1983). Separation of Ownership and Control. *Journal of Law and Economics, 26*, 301–325.

Farrar, D., & Glauber, R. (1967). Multicollinearity in regression analysis: A problem revisited. *Review of Economics and Statistics, 49*(1), 92–107.

Field, A. (2005). *Discovering statistics using SPSS for windows* (2nd ed.). London: Sage Publications.

Frey, B. S. (1993). Does monitoring increase work effort? The rivalry with trust and loyalty. *Economic Inquiry, 21*(4), 663–670.

Gilling, D. M. (1977). Timeliness in corporate reporting: Some further comment. *Accounting and Business Research, 8*(29), 34–36.

Givoly, D., & Palmon, D. (1982). Timeliness of annual earnings announcements: Some empirical evidence. *The Accounting Review, 57*(3), 486–508.

Goodstein, J., Gautum, K., & Boeker, W. (1994). The effect of board size and diversity on strategic change. *Strategic Management Journal, 15*(3), 241–250.

Haw, I., Qi, D., & Wu, W. (2000). Timeliness of annual report releases and market reaction to earnings announcements in an emerging capital market: the case of China. *Journal of International Financial Management and Accounting, 11*(2), 108–131.

Henderson, B. C., & Kaplan, S. E. (2000). An examination of audit report lag for banks: A panel data approach. *Auditing: A Journal of Practice and Theory, 19*(2), 159–174.

Imam, S., Ahmed, Z. U., & Khan, H. S. (2001). Association of audit delay and audit firm's international links: Evidence from Bangladesh. *Managerial Auditing Journal, 16*(3), 129–133.

Jaggi, B., & Tsui, J. (1999). Determinants of audit report lag: Further evidence from Hong Kong. *Accounting and Business Research, 30*(1), 17–28.

Judge, G. G., Griffiths, W. E., & Hill, R. C. (1985). *The theory and practice of econometrics* (2nd ed.). New York: John Willey & Sons.

Klein, A. (2002). Audit Committee, board of directors characteristics, and earnings management. *Journal of Accounting and Economics, 33*, 375–400.

Knechel, R. W., & Payne, J. L. (2001). Additional evidence on audit report lag. *Auditing: A Journal of Practice and Theory, 20*(1), 137–146.

Kosnik, R. D. (1987). Greenmail: A study of board performance in corporate governance. *Administrative Science Quarterly, 32*, 163–185.

Kross, W., & Schroeder, D. (1984). An empirical investigation of the effect of quarterly earnings announcement timing on stock returns. *Journal of Accounting Research, 22*(1), 153–176.

Le Searc'h, M., & Klotz, A. (1999). Corporate translation: Handle with care. *Business and Economic Review, 45*(2), 12–15.

Leary, M. R., & Kowalski, R. M. (1990). Impression management: A literature review and two component model. *Psychological Bulletin, 107*, 34–37.

Lee, H., Mande, V., & Son, M. (2008). A comparison of reporting lags of multinational and domestic firms. *Journal of International Financial Management and Accounting, 19*(1), 28–56.

Leventis, S., & Weetman, P. (2004). Impression management: Dual language reporting and voluntary disclosure. *Accounting Forum, 28*, 307–328.

Leventis, S., Weetman, P., & Caramanis, C. (2005). Determinants of audit lag: Some evidence from the Athens Stock Exchange. *International Journal of Auditing, 9*, 45–58.

Lin, J. W., Li, J. F., & Yang, J. S. (2006). The effect of audit committee performance on earnings quality. *Managerial Auditing Journal, 21*(9), 921–933.

Mangena, M., & Pike, R. (2005). The effect of audit committee shareholding, financial expertise and size on interim financial disclosures. *Accounting and Business Research, 35*, 327–349.

Mangena, M., & Tauringana, V. (2007). Disclosure, corporate governance and foreign ownership on the Zimbabwe Stock Exchange. *Journal of International Financial Management and Accounting, 18*(2), 53–85.

Mangena, M., & Tauringana, V. (2008). *Corporate boards, ownership structure and firm performance in an environment of severe political and economic uncertainty.* A paper presented to the European Accounting Association. Rotterdam: Erasmus University.

Marston, C. L., & Shrives, P. J. (1991). The use of disclosure indices in accounting research: A review article. *British Accounting Review, 23*(3), 195–210.

Menard, S. E. (1995). *Applied logistic regression analysis.* Thousand Oaks, CA: Sage university paper series on quantitative applications in social sciences, 07-106, Sage.

Myers, R. (1990). *Classical and modern regression with applications* (2nd ed.). Boston, MA: Duxbury.

Naser, K., Nuseibeh, R., & Al-Hussaini, A. (2003). Users' perceptions of the various aspects of the Kuwaiti corporate reporting. *Managerial Auditing Journal, 18*(6/7), 599–617.

Newton, J. D., & Ashton, R. H. (1989). The association between audit technology and audit delay. *Auditing: A Journal of Practice and Theory, 8*, 22–37.

Ng, P. P. H., & Tai, B. Y. K. (1994). An empirical examination of the determinants of audit delay in Hong Kong. *British Accounting Review, 26*(1), 43–59.

Ogola, J. J. (2000). *Company Law* (2nd ed.). Nairobi: Focus Publications Ltd.

Okeahalam, C. C., & Akinboade, O. A. (2003). *A Review of corporate governance in Africa: Literature, issues and challenge.* Washington, DC: Global Corporate Governance Forum.

Owusu-Ansah, S., & Leventis, S. (2006). Timeliness of corporate annual financial reporting in Greece. *European Accounting Review, 15*(2), 273–287.

Owusu-Ansah, S. (2000). Timeliness of corporate financial reporting in emerging capital markets: Empirical evidence from the Zimbabwe Stock Exchange. *Accounting and Business Research, 30*(3), 241–254.

Oyelaran-Oyeyinka, B., & Adeya, C. N. (2004). Internet access in Africa: Empirical evidence from Kenya and Nigeria. *Telematics and Iinformatics, 21*, 67–81.

Paton, A., & Baker, J. C. (1987). Why won't directors rock the boat? *Harvard Business Review, 65*(6), 10–18.

Schwartz, K. B., & Soo, B. S. (1996). The association between auditor changes and reporting lags. *Contemporary Accounting Research, 13*(1), 353–370.

Simnett, R., Aitken, M., Choo, F., & Firth, M. (1995). The determinants of audit delay. *Advances in Accounting, 13*, 1–20.

Soltani, B. (2002). Timeliness of corporate and audits reports: Some empirical evidence in the French context. *The International Journal of Accounting, 37*, 215–246.

Stanton, P., & Stanton, J. (2002). Corporate annual reports: Research perspectives used. *Accounting, Auditing and Accountability Journal, 15*(4), 478–500.

Tsamenyi, M., Enninful-Adu, E., & Onumah, J. (2007). Disclosure and corporate governance in developing countries: Evidence from Ghana. *Managerial Auditing Journal, 22*(3), 319–334.

Vafeas, N. (1999). Board meeting frequency and firm performance. *Journal of Financial Economics, 53*(1), 113–142.

Wagacha, M. (2001). Kenya's capital market: To list or not list – A survey of enterprise attitudes. Unpublished discussion paper, Institute of policy Analysis and Research, Nairobi.

Wang, J., & Song, L. (2006). Timeliness of annual reports of Chinese listed companies. *Journal of Chinese Economics and Business Studies, 4*(3), 241–257.

Weisbach, M. (1988). Outside directors and CEO turnover. *Journal of Financial Economics, 20*, 431–460.

Yakasai, A. G. (2001). Corporate governance in a third world country with particular reference to Nigeria. *Corporate Governance, 9*(3), 238–253.

CORPORATE GOVERNANCE ONLINE REPORTING BY SAUDI LISTED COMPANIES

Khaled Hussainey and Ali Al-Nodel

ABSTRACT

Purpose – *This paper examines the extent to which Saudi listed companies report online information about their corporate governance practice in light of the guidance issued by the Saudi Arabian Capital Market Authority (SACMA), thereafter.*

Methodology – *We adopted a content analysis approach, accordingly a corporate governance disclosure index is developed to analyse the content of every company's website.*

Findings – *We found that the majority of Saudi listed companies utilise the Internet to communicate some information about corporate governance to their stakeholders. We also found that the level of online reporting of corporate governance varies between sectors. In particular, the paper revealed that the banking sector has the highest level of corporate governance disclosure compared with other sectors. On the other side, companies in the industry and service sectors provide very little information about corporate governance on their websites. The results suggest that the nature of control over the sector, the involvement of government in the ownership and management of businesses and some social assumptions*

Corporate Governance in Less Developed and Emerging Economies
Research in Accounting in Emerging Economies, Volume 8, 39–64
Copyright © 2008 by Emerald Group Publishing Limited
ISSN: 1479-3563/doi:10.1016/S1479-3563(08)08002-X

could have an impact on companies' decision to disclose online information about their corporate governance in developing countries.

Practical implications – *The importance of investigating online reporting of corporate governance in Saudi Arabia emerges from the fact that SACMA published a guidance in 2006 that recommends the disclosure of corporate governance information by Saudi listed companies. Therefore, it would be worthwhile informing SACMA about the extent of compliance with the guidance of corporate governance. This is essential taking into consideration two facts: first, the recent remarkable growth of the Saudi stock market which was accompanied by significant increase in the demand for additional information by stakeholders; second, the recent increase of the utilisation of the Internet by companies for disclosure purposes worldwide. Further, the results of this research study could add to our limited knowledge about the practice of corporate governance in developing countries.*

Originality/value – *This paper contributes to the limited literature on disclosure practices in developing countries in general and in Saudi Arabia in particular. Our review of the literature revealed that there is no study to date on online disclosure of corporate governance in Saudi Arabia and very limited research has been carried out in developing countries in general. This is important taking into consideration environmental factors of developing countries, which could bring different sight in the issue of the disclosure of corporate governance.*

1. INTRODUCTION

This study is an attempt to assess the extent to which Saudi listed companies voluntarily communicate corporate governance information over the Internet to their stakeholders. It also explores the extent to which online reporting of corporate governance varies between Saudi listed companies according to their sectors.

This research is motivated by a number of observations. First, Saudi Arabian Capital Market Authority (SACMA) issued a guidance that recommends all listed companies to disclose corporate governance information to the public. Therefore, it would be worthwhile informing SACMA about the extent to which listed companies comply with the new guidance and the potential factors that explain differences in companies' compliance. Second, research on corporate governance in the business environment of developing countries in general and in that of Saudi Arabia in particular is limited. The review of the literature suggests that not only there are few papers researching the issue of corporate governance but also all of them approach the issue by describing the state of corporate governance from an official regulation perspective or from a perspective of what should the practical applications of the principles of corporate governance be.

Finally, researching the utilisation of the Internet to report information about corporate governance is meaningful taking into consideration arguments such as that online reporting is more comprehensive than any other source of reporting, provides companies with opportunities to voluntarily disclose timely information, gives companies more flexibility in terms of the nature and quantity of the reported information and helps companies to decrease the cost of disclosure. The results of this research should give insight about the position of companies in developing countries in the utilisation of the Internet to communicate with their stakeholders.

A corporate governance disclosure index is developed to analyse the content of every company's website to identify whether corporate governance information is disclosed or not. We found that the majority of Saudi listed companies use the Internet to communicate with their stakeholders. Our findings also suggest that the level of online reporting of corporate governance varies between sectors. In particular, we found that the banking sector has the highest level of corporate governance disclosure compared with other sectors. On the other side, companies in the industry and service sectors provide very little information about corporate governance on their websites. The results suggest that the nature of control over the sector, the involvement of government in the ownership and management of businesses, and some social assumptions could have an impact on companies' attitude to disclose online information about their corporate governance in developing countries.

The paper is organised as follows. Section 2 provides a background on the context of corporate governance in Saudi Arabia. Section 3 reviews the literature of corporate governance and online reporting, particularly in the region. Sections 4 and 5 describe the research methodology and data. Section 6 reports the descriptive analyses and the main findings. Section 7 concludes the findings and suggests lines for further research.

2. CORPORATE GOVERNANCE PRACTICE IN SAUDI ARABIA

As this paper aims to assess the extent to which Saudi listed companies voluntarily communicate corporate governance information over the

Internet with their stakeholders, this section provides a general description of the environment of the Saudi businesses practices. This description is important in understanding the Saudi practice of corporate governance in general, and for placing the findings of this study within its context, as well as other environments with similar characteristics.

Several environmental factors affect Saudi businesses practices and it is difficult for this research to deal in detail with all these factors. Instead, it will consider some of the most important environmental factors, as suggested by the literature. The main environmental factors that are more related to the practice of corporate governance and will be discussed in this section are some aspects of the political, economical and social systems. The discussion of these environmental factors will be followed by a discussion of the 1965 Company Law that regulates the practice of Saudi businesses and the guidance of corporate governance issued by SACMA in 2006.

The environment of the Saudi business practice possesses some characteristics of free market found in the western countries, but differs in some critical aspects. The early stage of the political, economical and social developments in the country makes the environment of the Saudi business practices significantly different from that of the developed countries and most similar to that of the developing countries in general and that of the middle eastern countries in particular.

The political system of Saudi Arabia is a monarchy, headed by the King. The Basic Law of Government, which was introduced in 1992, is considered to be the constitution of Saudi Arabia (Economist Intelligence Unit, 2003). There are three legislative bodies, within the political system, which have the authority to initiate and/or approve policies, regulation or rules: the Council of Ministers, the Consultative Council and various individual Ministries. There are also various groups or parties influencing major political issues and the development of regulations. The main influencing groups are the royal family, Islamic scholars, state officials, tribal leaders and businessmen; all of whom have different interests and different powers depending on the importance of the issue to their interests and affairs (Al-Amari, 1989; Al-Rumaihi, 1997; Aba-Alkhail, 2001; Economist Intelligence Unit, 2003; Al-Nodel, 2004).

As an Islamic country, the legal system of Saudi Arabia is derived from Islamic law (Shariah; Alqur'an Alkareem and Sunna Alsharifah), and coded laws for a number of specific fields, such as commerce, tax and labour. Al-Amari (1989) reported that Islamic law prevails in legal disputes and in case of conflictions.

Saudi society is heavily influenced by its Arabic heritage and Islamic values (Al-Rumaihi, 1997; Aba-Alkhail, 2001; Al-Nodel, 2004). The only practicing religion in the country is Islam, all Saudis are Muslim, and the country is considered to be the centre of most Muslims. Al-Rumaihi (1997) described Saudi society as characterised by the impact of the personality and power of particular individuals and the role of family and friend relationships over regulations, privilege given to personal relationships over tasks and the existence of a high level of secrecy. The country's strongest income and political system enable the government to have an impact on the life of Saudis, such as education, health and life style. The country's 2006 GDP, GDP growth rate and Nominal Per Capita are presented in Table 1.

The economy of Saudi Arabia is an oil-based economy whereas government exercises strong controls over major economic activities. It possesses 25% of the world's proven petroleum reserves, ranks as the largest exporter of petroleum and plays a leading role in OPEC. Worldwide oil prices and production volumes strongly affect Saudi economy. Since the discovery of oil in 1938, oil revenue represents the biggest contribution to the economy. In 1990s, it accounted for around 35% of nominal GDP, about 75% of government revenues and 85% of export receipts (Economist Intelligence Unit, 2003). Table 2 presents the country's budgetary revenues, expenditures and net surplus (or deficit) for the last three years.

Table 1. Saudi GDP, GDP Growth Rate and Nominal
Per Capita in 2006.

GDP Growth at constant prices of 1999 (billion US $)	213.04
GDP growth	4.3%
Nominal per capita (2004)	$ 16,744

Source: Wikipedia website (2008).

Table 2. Saudi Arabia Budgetary Revenues, Expenditures and Net
Surplus or Deficit 2005–2007.

	Annual Government Budgeting (Estimates) Million Saudi Riyals ($1 = 3.75 SR)						
	Total revenues	Oil revenues		Non-oil revenues		Total expenditures	(Deficit)/Surplus
	Amount	Amount	%	Amount	%	Amount	Amount
2005	280,000	220,000	79	60,000	21	280,000	0
2006	390,000	320,000	82	70,000	18	335,000	55,000
2007	400,000	330,000	83	70,000	17	380,000	20,000

Source: SAMA (Saudi Arabian Monetary Agency) annual report (2007).

Due to the increase of the importance of oil, as worldwide commodity, in the 1970s, the country observed unprecedented increase in its income, which in turns led to developments in different aspects of the country's businesses practices such as establishments of joint-stock companies, developments of structures of companies and issuance of regulations for businesses and professional (Basher & Sadorsky, 2006).

Nevertheless, the current business practice of Saudi companies is still much beyond that of the developed countries. Noticeable features of the current practice of Saudi companies are the domination of family businesses, the deep involvement of the government in the private sector and the existence of a number of foreign-owned and controlled companies based on joint venture agreements with domestic companies.

The domination of family businesses type in Saudi Arabia is argued by Al-Nodel (2004). He explained that joint-stock companies represent only 1.14% of the total number, and account for less than 40% of the total capital of the registered businesses. The explanation for the domination of family businesses type in Saudi Arabia was given by Al-Rehaily (1992) who argued that the increases in world oil prices and Saudi production of oil during the 1970s, reaching its peak in 1980, created a significant number of middle-class people who were motivated to establish their own business. Some of these businesses have grown up significantly all over the country, but the ownership-structure of these businesses is still dominated by families.

The existence of a number of foreign-owned and controlled companies based on joint venture agreements with domestic companies and the involvement of government in businesses represent another significant feature of the Saudi private sector (Presley, 1984; Aba-Alkhail, 2001). Al-Rehaily (1992) asserted that foreign investors mostly use joint venture form to carry out business within Saudi Arabia. In this regard, Presley (1984, p. 27) stated:

> The identification of the private sector in Saudi Arabia is not as straightforward as it is in many other countries. It is complicated by two important features: by the operation of a great number of private foreign-owned and controlled companies working in the country, the majority in joint venture agreements with domestic companies and, second, by the partial involvement of the government in many industries, making the division between public and private sectors difficult to define.

The 1965 Company Law regulates the practice of businesses in Saudi Arabia (Ministry of Finance and National Economy, 1983). It sets conditions for establishing businesses, describes the legal framework for businesses and requires the publication of annual financial statements audited by an independent party (see also Al-Rehaily, 1992; Aba-Alkhail, 2001; Al-Nodel, 2004). In other words, articles of the 1965 Company Law sets conditions for several aspects of businesses such as legal frameworks through which business companies can be established, the registration requirements, minimum capital to be maintained, number of partners, number of directors, accounts, the annual audit of the accounts and so on. Shinawi and Crum (1971) asserted that the origin of the 1965 Saudi Company Law goes back to the British Companies Act of 1948. Kahlid (1983) reported a similarity between the 1965 Saudi Company Law and the UK acts issued in 1948, 1967 and 1976. It is difficult for this research to discuss all the aspects of the 1965 Company Law; however, the legal frameworks of businesses and the reporting requirements that are set by the 1965 Company Law will be discussed in short.

With respect to the legal frameworks of businesses, the 1965 Company Law provides several legal frameworks through which businesses can be established such as general partnership, joint venture, joint-stock company, limited liability company and cooperative company.[1]

The 1965 Company Law also sets the reporting requirements of businesses. It requires the issuance of a balance sheet, a profit and loss account and a report on the company's operations and financial position every fiscal year. It further stipulates that all corporations and limited liability companies must issue annual financial statements audited by an independent auditor licensed to practice by the Saudi Ministry of Commerce and Industry.

The stock market of Saudi Arabia is under development. In 1984, the Royal Decree No. 81230 was issued as an attempt to officially regulate the stock exchange (Abdeen & Dale, 1984; El-Sharkawy, 2006). Under this Royal Decree, the Saudi Arabian Monetary Agency (SAMA), thereafter, was given actual control over the stock exchange through national commercial banks.

The significant change was in 2003 when the SACMA, which took responsibility of controlling the exchange of Saudi stocks from SAMA, was established (Ramady, 2005). This was accompanied by the use of an inclusive electronic stock exchange system called *TADAWUL* that enabled online trading of stocks, electronic investment accounts instead of manual traditional accounts and access of easy and more information about listed companies and the market (Ameinfo, 2006). This period observed significant changes with respect to the number of listed companies or market value. Table 3 compares some key numbers of the Saudi stock market between 1996 and 2005.

Table 3.   Key Figures of Saudi Stock Market between 1996 and 2005.

Year	No. of Transactions (Thousands)	Traded Stock (Million)	Market Value ($ Million)	Index
1996	284	138	46	1,531
1997	460	314	59	1,958
1998	377	295	43	1,413
1999	438	528	61	2,029
2000	498	555	68	2,258
2001	605	692	73	2,430
2002	1,034	1,736	75	2,518
2003	3,763	5,566	157	4,438
2004	13,320	10,298	306	8,206
2005	46,607	12,281	650	16,713

Source: TADAWUL (2006).

Due to the sharp decrease of the Saudi stock market in 2006 which resulted in a loss of about 45% of its market value, dropping its index to 11,141.04 at the end of 2006 as compared to about 20,100.40 for the same period of 2005, resulting in a significant loss for Saudi investors, SACMA intensified its efforts to provide fairness in the trading of the Saudi stocks. Among these efforts was the issuance of the guidance of corporate governance for listed companies.

The guidance provides recommendations of the criteria for the best corporate governance practice that listed companies should counsel. It has covered to some extent the main five principles issued by the Organization for Economic Co-operation and Development (OECD), which are the rights of shareholders, the equitable treatment of shareholders, the role of stakeholders in corporate governance, disclosure and transparency and the responsibility of the board of directors.

Under the SACMA guidance of corporate governance, listed companies are required to report to SACMA about their compliance with the criteria of corporate governance or reasons for incompliance if any. The reporting contains, for example, the board of directors' functions, responsibilities, formation, committees of board of directors, audit committee, nomination and remuneration committee, meetings of the board and remuneration and indemnification of board members.[2]

Finally, it should be noted that SACMA asserts that the criteria for the best corporate governance practice mostly constitutes the guiding principles for all listed companies unless any other regulations, laws or rules require such requirements.

3. LITERATURE REVIEW: CORPORATE GOVERNANCE AND ONLINE REPORTING

Although corporate governance has been the subject for an extensive research in developed countries,[3] limited research has been carried out to investigate the issue of corporate governance in business environment of developing countries. Furthermore, those limited studies approach this issue describe the state of corporate governance from an official perspective or from a perspective of what should the practical applications of the principles of corporate governance be.

For example, Al-Motairy (2003) explored the state of corporate governance practices in Saudi Arabia. He reviewed different regulations of business and profession in the country such as the company law, stock market law, foreign investment law and other professional regulations. He concluded that there is a vital need for (1) a review of these regulations to reflect the current practices of corporate governance, (2) the issuance of guidance for best practices for management and financial affair in corporations and (3) the establishment of an organisation to accelerate the adoption of best practices of corporate governance.

Similarly, Fouzy (2003) evaluated the practices of corporate governance's principles in Egypt. He recognised the development in Egyptian official regulations toward the application of best practices of corporate govern-ance. He then argued that in practice Egyptian companies do not meet these developments enough.

Another example is a study by Oyelere and Mohamed (2005) that investigated the practices of corporate governance in Oman and how it is being communicated to stakeholders. They recommended enhanced regula-tion and communication for the Omani stock market to keep pace with the international developments.

Finally, a research paper by the Center for International Private Enterprise (CIPE) (2003) examined the corporate governance practice in four Middle Eastern countries (Egypt, Jordan, Morocco and Lebanon). It found that corporate governance practice is approached differently by each country depending on the sophistication of the financial market in the country. It further provided several recommendations to improve the application of the principles of corporate governance in the region as a whole.

The conclusion of these research studies is that a better regulation of the corporate governance in the region is critical in order to increase the public confidence in the regional financial markets. We further argue that a communication of such corporate governance to the interested parties is important, as well as the regulations itself since the aims of the regulations would not be approached unless the fundamentals of corporate governance practice are communicated to stakeholders whose confidence is important for the development of regional financial markets. One modern and effective device of disclosure of corporate governance information to stakeholders is the Internet.

A review of the literature suggests that online reporting of financial information was the subject of most research investigating regional companies' utilisation of the Internet to report information to stakeholders such as in Egypt (Mohamed, 2002; Metwali, 2003; Al-Deesty, 2004; Aly, Simon, & Hussainey, 2008); Jordon (Al-Htaybat & Napier, 2006); Saudi Arabia (Tawfik, 2001; Al-Jaber & Mohamed, 2003; Al-Saeed, 2006); Oman (Oyelere & Mohamed, 2005) and GCC Countries (Ismail, 2002). For the purpose of this research, we will review the key articles that are related to the online reporting in Saudi Arabia.

Tawfik (2001) surveyed 69 joint-stock companies in Saudi Arabia. He found that only six companies use the Internet for reporting of financial information. He also revealed that information about companies' products was the most common information available on Saudi companies' websites.

Al-Jaber and Mohamed (2003) compared the Internet reporting in three regional countries (Egypt, Saudi Arabia and Kuwait). They found that there are some variations in the online reporting practices among these countries. They also found that companies' products were the main concern for online reporting by these countries, whereas financial information was the second type of information reported on the Internet. They concluded that regional companies are still beyond in the use of the Internet to report their financial information, in comparison to companies in western countries due to the nature of the technology development in the region.

Recently, Al-Saeed (2006) explored the practices of the online reporting by 46 Saudi companies from 3 sectors: industry, cement and agriculture. He found that only 40 companies have websites, and companies from the cement sector were the better off with respect to the use of the Internet for reporting financial information. He also found that company' size and profitability were significant factors in determining Saudi companies' use of the Internet reporting. With respect to the content of the online reporting, he asserted that general information about the company and its products were the most frequently reported information.

To conclude, describing the state of corporate governance, whether from the official regulation perspective or from the perspective of what should the practical applications of the principles of corporate governance be, would not provide sufficient evidence about the corporate governance practice in the region. The communication of such corporate governance to the interested parties is crucial since the aim of the regulations is to increase the public confidence in financial markets. This would not be approached unless the fundamentals of corporate governance practice are communicated to stakeholders. One important disclosure mechanism for effectively communicating corporate governance information to stakeholders is Internet. Unfortunately, the utilisation of Internet to communicate information about companies' corporate governance practice to stakeholders is under researched, particularly in developing countries. Therefore, our study aims to answer the following research questions:

1. To what extent do Saudi companies use the Internet to communicate with their stakeholders regarding their corporate governance practice?
2. To what extent does the online disclosure on corporate governance information vary between sectors?

4. RESEARCH METHODOLOGY

To examine the extent to which Saudi listed companies report corporate governance information online, we used the content analysis approach to identify the types of information appears in companies' websites. The rationales of using this approach are: first, it enables us to search directly at the most current information on the websites, hence, to look at a central aspect of social communication. Second, it relies on the most efficient and common media of communication between companies and the public. It also allows both quantitative and qualitative analyses. To explain, it allows identifying the content of every website qualitatively then calculating the disclosure score for each company to perform quantitative analyses. Finally, it enables us to cover all Saudi listed companies, which would be difficult by using another method such as interviews.

We carefully reviewed corporate governance disclosure literature to select disclosure items that Saudi companies might disclose online. The key articles we reviewed include Andersson and Daoud (2005), Oyelere and Mohamed (2005) and Aksu and Kosedag (2006). Reviewing these articles gave us a list of disclosure items. To select our final list of the disclosure index, we compared this list of items with those items recommended by SACMA corporate governance regulations. This allowed us to crease a disclosure index applicable to Saudi companies. Table 4 shows our disclosure index.

Once the final list of corporate governance disclosure items was identified, we used the un-weighted scoring approach in creating the disclosure scores for each company in our sample. Disclosure scores were calculated as follows. First, an appropriate score was allocated to the company if its website contained a particular piece of information. These scores represent the partial scores. In other words, we allocated a score of 1 for the presence of a corporate governance disclosure item and a score of 0 otherwise.[4] Second, individual scores were then aggregated into a total index, which summarises the overall quantity in a single number.

Since our paper used a disclosure index to measure the extent of corporate disclosure, which was not amenable to be measured directly, we used two methods to cross-check/validate the disclosure scoring process.

First, because the companies' websites were visited between October 2005 and January 2006, these websites were revisited after a short period of time. In particular, companies' websites were revisited again in March 2006 and June 2006 as a validity check. The resulting corporate governance disclosure score for each company from the second and third time phase coincided exactly with those calculated at the first time round. In the case of companies whose websites were under construction, it was confirmed that they were still under construction up to the end of June 2006. This provided assurance of stability of the coding method used in our paper. Second, all companies' websites were independently coded by the first researcher and the second researcher. The correlation between the results produced by the first and second authors was above 95%.

5. DATA

Data is collected from Saudi listed companies' websites between October 2005 and January 2006. Our preliminary sample was based on all Saudi companies listed in the Saudi Stock Market in January 2006. At that time, the total number of companies listed in the Saudi Stock Market was 77 representing 8 sectors: agriculture, services, cement, industrial, banks, electrical, telecommunication and insurance.

We used $TADAWUL^5$ website (http://www.tdwl.net) and Google website (http://www.google.com) to access every company's website. We deleted some companies from our analysis for a number of reasons. First, we deleted companies that have no website (11 firms). Second, we deleted one

Table 4. Corporate Governance Disclosure Index.

1. Board of Director	2. Nomination Committee
Chairman	Chairman of the committee
Name (picture, gender)	Members of the committee
Age	Principles of composition
Main education	Responsibilities and tasks
Work experience	Number of meetings per year
Responsibilities and tasks	Other
Salary and compensation	3. Compensation Committee
Other	Chairman of the committee
Chief Executive Officers (CEO)	Members of the committee
Name (picture, gender)	Principles of composition
Age	Responsibilities and tasks
Main education	Number of meetings per year
Work experience	Other
Responsibilities and tasks	4. Executive Committee
Salary and compensation	Chairman of the committee
Other	Members of the committee
Finance Director	Principles of composition
Name (picture, gender)	Responsibilities and tasks
Age	Number of meetings per year
Main education	Other
Work experience	5. Audit Committee
Responsibilities and tasks	Chairman of the committee
Salary and compensation	Members of the committee
Other	Principles of composition
Non-Executive Directors (NED)	Responsibilities and tasks
Name (picture, gender)	Number of meetings per year
Age	Other
Main education	6. Other committees
Work experience	Chairman of the committee
Responsibilities and tasks	Members of the committee
Salary and compensation	Principles of composition
Other	Responsibilities and tasks
The Board's Secretary	Number of meetings per year
Name (picture, gender)	Other
Age	7. Internal Control System
Main education	Aims
Work experience	Procedures
Responsibilities and tasks	Other
Salary and compensation	8. Key Shareholders and Ownership Structure
Other	9. Other Corporate Governance Issues

Table 5. The Sample.

Sector	No. of firms	%	Accessible Firms	%
Agriculture	9	11.6	7	10.9
Services	18	23.4	12	18.8
Cement	8	10.4	7	10.9
Industrial	28	36.4	24	37.5
Banks	10	13	10	15.6
Electrical	1	1.3	1	1.6
Telecommunication	2	2.6	2	3.1
Insurance	1	1.3	1	1.6
Total	77	100	64	100

company that has a website under construction. Finally, we deleted another company that has a restricted website. This reduced our sample to 64 companies (Table 5).

6. DESCRIPTIVE ANALYSIS AND MAIN FINDINGS

The descriptive analysis suggests that the majority of Saudi companies use the Internet to communicate corporate governance information to their stockholders. It also shows a variation in corporate governance online reporting practice among sectors. In particular, it reveals that banks have the highest level of online reporting of corporate governance information. The correlation between the level of corporate governance online disclosure and the banking sector type is statistically significant. The results are discussed in detail below.

6.1. Companies' Utilisation of the Internet to Report Corporate Governance

Table 6 shows the disclosure score for each company in our sample. It describes that the majority (71%) of Saudi listed companies (46 companies) are disclosing online information about their corporate governance, in comparison to (28.1%) Saudi companies (18 companies) that are not disclosing any information about their corporate governance on their website. Ten of these companies are from the industrial sector, six from the service sector and one company from each of the cement and

Table 6. Disclosure Scores.

Sector/Firms	Disclosure Scores	Sector/Firms	Disclosure Scores
Agriculture		*Industrial*	
NADEC	5	SABIC Co.	8
Hail Agricultural	8	Al-Ahsa	No website
Saudi Fishers Co.	3	Almarai Company	15
Qassim Agriculture Co.	No website	Alujain	20
TABUK Agricultural	5	National Metal	No website
Bishah Agriculture	No website	Nama Co.	0
Ash-Sharqiyah	4	SIDC	4
Al Jouf Development Co.	2	Saudi Ceramics Co.	0
Gazadco Development	4	Nat. Indus. Co.	3
Services		National Gypsum	0
SIEC	0	Sahara Petro.	0
Ahmed H. Fitaihi	Under construction	Saudi Advanced	5
Al Mawashi Al Mukairish	No website	S. A. Fertilizers	No website
Al-Baha Investment &	No website	S. A. Refineries	No website
Development Co.			
Arriyadh Development	2	S. A. Amiantit	0
Aseer Trading, Tourism	No website	Saudi Cable	0
Saudi Hotels & Resort	0	SPIMACO	1
Saudi Automotive	0	Gasco	0
Jarir Marketing Co.	0	Filling & Packing	0
Makkah Construction &	12	Saudi Industrial	0
Development Co.			
SAPTCO	5	Arabian Pipes Co.	1
Thimar Co.	5	Food Products Co.	1
Tihama Advertising,	0	N. Co. for Glass	1
Saudi Land Transport Co.	Restricted website	Saudi Chemical	6
Taibah Investment	7	Zamil Industrial	25
Saudi Real Estate Co.	0	Saudi Ind. Invest.	3
The National Shipping Co.	10	SAVOLA	8
Tourism Enterprise Co.	No website	Saudi Dairy	0
Cement		*Banks*	
Yanbu Cement Co.	7	Riyad Bank	3
Tabuk Cement Co.	1	Bank Aljazira	21
EPCC	8	Saudi Investment	5
Saudi Cement Co.	0	Saudi Hollandi	2
Yamama Cement Co.	4	SABB	6
Qassim Cement Co.	3	Arab National	20
Southern Province Cement	No website	SAMBA	4
Arabian Cement Co.	2	Al Rajhi Bank	6
Telecommunication		Banque Saudi	6
Etihad Etisalat Co.	0	Bank Albilad	9
Saudi Telecom	6	*Insurance*	
Electrical		Cooperative Insurance	5
Saudi Electricity	4		

telecommunication sectors. The range of disclosure scores for companies that are disclosing online information about their corporate governance is between 1 and 25. Of these companies, four companies in the industrial sector and one in the cement sector have the lowest disclosure score.

With respect to the nature of the corporate governance information that is more frequently reported by the majority of companies is detailed information about the names of the board of directors and information about ownership. Companies with disclosure scores between 6 and 8 provide detailed information about names of the board of directors, managers' team, number of board meetings and detailed information about remuneration of the board of directors. For companies with disclosure scores greater than 8, we observe that these firms provide more detailed information about corporate governance and some provide it in more formal expression. For example, looking at Bank Aljazira Annual Report 2005 which is available online at the bank website, one can observe a comprehensive corporate governance information been reported.[6]

Only three companies in our sample have supplied an identified section entitled *"corporate governance"* in their websites. One of these is an industrial company, Zamil Industrial Investment Co., and the others are related to the Banking sector (Bank Aljazira and National Arabic Bank). These companies have the highest disclosure scores (20–25 corporate governance items).

The rest provide information about their corporate governance either in the *"About us"* section or in the company online annual report. For example, one can see the names of directors in the first two pages of the annual report for these companies, while their remuneration appears in the income statement.

6.2. *Variations between Sectors*

Table 7 shows the descriptive analysis for all sectors. It reveals that the minimum corporate governance disclosure score is between 0 and 2, while the maximum is between 4 and 25. The banking sector has the highest mean (8.2) and median (6) disclosure scores compared with other sectors. This is due to the fact that all banks report at least one piece of corporate governance information and Bank Aljazira and Arab National Bank have the highest disclosure scores in this sector as well as among the whole listed companies.

Table 7. Descriptive Analysis.

Sector	No. of Firms	Minimum	Maximum	Mean	Median
Banks	10	2	21	8.2	6
Services	18	0	12	3.4	1
Agriculture	9	2	8	4.4	4
Cement	8	0	8	3.6	3
Industrial	28	0	25	4.2	1
Electrical	1	4	4	4	4
Telecommunication	2	0	6	3	3
Insurance	1	5	5	5	5

The insurance sector has the second highest mean (5) and median (5) disclosure scores. The possible explanation for these highest scores for the insurance sector is that the insurance sector is under direct control of SAMA, similar to banks, so such tight control might play roles in enforcing insurance companies to disclose online information about their corporate governance.

The agriculture sector with a mean of 4.4 and a median of 4 comes as the third highest disclosing sector of information about their corporate governance. There are two main factors that could have an influence on the agriculture sector's online disclosure of corporate governance. First, the long establishment of the sector in the country is likely to have helped agricultural companies to better apply the requirements of corporate governance. Second, the similarity of the companies in the agriculture sector with regard to their size and capital structure could also create incentives for them to disclose online information about their corporate governance. This is evident by the relatively low variation among companies in this sector, as Table 6 suggests the minimum corporate governance disclosure score for the agriculture sector is 2 and the maximum is 8, representing the lowest variation within each sector.

On the other side, service and industry sectors have the lowest means (3.4 and 4.2) and medians (1 and 1) disclosure scores compared with other sectors, respectively. This is supported by the fact that the 2 sectors contain significant number of companies with disclosure score of zero, 10 companies in the industry sectors and 6 companies in the service sector as shown in Table 6. The possible explanations for these results are the nature of the capital structure and the deep involvement of government within these sectors.[7]

In fact, significant numbers of companies in the industry and service sectors are small in terms of their capital and shareholders. For example,

Jarir Marketing Co, Tihama Advertising and SIEC from the service sector and Saudi Ceramics Co., Filling & Packing and Saudi Dairy from the industry sector have an average of SR 228,000,000 in capital and an average of 22,800,000 shareholders which are small, in comparison to the averages of the Saudi stock market of about SR 650,000,000 in capital and 65,000,000 shares. The impact of companies' capital structure on their attitude to report information to their stakeholders has also been suggested by the literature (Al-Saeed, 2006).

Another possible explanation for the reluctance of companies in service and industry sectors to disclose online information about their corporate governance is the deep involvement of Saudi government in the ownership and management of some companies in these two sectors. This is evident by the participation of the Saudi government in the ownership and management of companies such as Saudi Automotive in the service sector and SABIC Co., Gasco and SPIMACO in the industry sector. The deep involvement of the Saudi government in the private sector has also been affirmed by several researchers such as Presley (1984), Al-Rehaily (1992) and Aba-Alkhail (2001).

Finally, the cement, telecommunication and electrical sectors have relatively moderate scores with respect to their willingness to disclose online information about their corporate governance as shown in Table 7. No significant observation can be suggested for companies that fall in these three sectors.

Table 8 states the correlation analysis between disclosure score and the eight sectors in our sample. It suggests that the banking sector has a positive correlation with disclosure scores and this correlation is significant at the 5 percent level. However, other sectors have insignificantly negative or positive correlations with disclosure scores. This is consistent with the descriptive analysis reported above and suggests that Saudi sector types are linked with the reporting patterns of corporate governance information.

6.3. Discussion of the Results

The majority of Saudi listed companies utilise Internet to report online information about their corporate governance, they, however, differ with respect to the quantity, and nature of the information reported and the method of reporting from very little and informal to sophisticated, formal and extensive reporting. The most frequent piece of information reported by

Table 8. Correlation Analysis.

Sector	CG Disclosure
Banks	0.28**
	(0.024)
Services	–0.10
	(0.412)
Agriculture	–0.06
	(0.657)
Cement	–0.07
	(0.603)
Industrial	–0.01
	(0.928)
Electrical	–0.01
	(0.913)
Telecommunication	–0.05
	(0.679)
Insurance	0.01
	(0.944)

The significance levels (two-tail test) are: *, 10%; **, 5%; ***, 1%.

most companies relates to the personnel involved in the company whether in the company's management or ownership.

The reporting of personnel involved in the management or own significant shares of the company is likely due to the nature of Saudi society which is characterised by the impact of the personality and power of particular individuals, and the role of family and friend relationships over regulations, and privilege given to personal relationships over tasks (Al-Rumaihi, 1997).

In this type of environment, companies are more likely to be motivated to report the piece of corporate governance information that relates to personnel involved in the company rather than that relates to policies, regulations and laws because information about personnel is more understandable, believable and appreciable by the Saudi society than the information about policies, regulations or laws.

The results also suggest an existence of variations between sectors with respect to their online reporting of corporate governance information. It reveals that banks are the most willing Saudi businesses to report online information about their corporate governance; in contrast companies of industry and service sectors are the least willing businesses to report information about their corporate governance.

The expansion of Saudi banks, the use of new technologies and the regulations and guidance on banks corporate governance from the 1990s till now are the potential factors that drive Saudi banks to extensively use Internet as a disclosure mechanism for communicating corporate governance information to their stakeholders. This finding is in line with the suggestion of the literature. Previous studies have suggested that corporate governance in the banking sector in developing countries is an extremely important issue (Arun & Turner, 2004).

To explain, Saudi stock market is still underdeveloped and Saudi banks have been (are still) the key player in the Saudi financial system as they are considered the most important source of finance for the majority of individuals and companies, and the main depository for the economy's savings (G-20, 2005). At the beginning of the 1990s the Saudi banks had expanded their branches, introduced stronger management methods and new technologies, raised new capital, improved their profitability and set aside large provisions for doubtful accounts (G-20, 2005).

Regulators, also, intensified their efforts to better control this sector. Accordingly, a number of regulations have been issued to ensure that this important sector is effectively directed and controlled. The main purpose of these regulations and requirements is to organise and control the relationships and responsibilities between the board, management, shareholders and other relevant stakeholders within a legal and regulatory framework (Al-Sayari, 2007). Examples of these regulations include the "Powers and Responsibilities of the Board of Directors of Commercial Banks in Saudi Arabia" issued in 1981; the guidance document issued in 1996 on the role of the Audit Committee of the Board and the circular "Qualifications and Requirements for Appointments to Senior Positions in Banks licensed in Saudi Arabia" which is issued in 2004.

In contrast, factors such as the deep involvement of government in management and ownership, the nature of capital structure and the size of some companies in the service and industry sectors could have influenced the concern of the management of these sectors' companies to utilise Internet to report information about their corporate governance.

The deep involvement of Saudi government in the private sector presents an important feature of the context of Saudi businesses practices (see, e.g., Presley, 1984; Aba-Alkhail, 2001; Al-Nodel, 2004). This is particularly observable in some energy and petrochemical companies (industry sector) and some transportation and real estate companies (service sector).

This involvement of government in the ownership of these companies could provide the management of these companies negotiable power with stakeholders such as financier or shareholders that exceed the power or advantages of online communication of information about corporate governance practice. This is reasonable taking into consideration the nature of the development in the country with respect to its political and economical systems and the existence of a high level of secrecy (Al-Rumaihi, 1997).

7. SUMMARY AND CONCLUSION

The study aims to explore the extent to which Saudi listed companies report corporate governance information online. It also examines the extent to which corporate governance online reporting varies between sectors. A content analysis approach was used to examine the content of each company's websites. Based on a list of corporate governance disclosure items, we identified the disclosure score for each company. We also identified the mean and median disclosure scores for each sector and carried out a correlation analysis for each sector type with the reporting score for each sector.

This study concludes that the aspects of the Saudi society, as suggested by the literature (see, e.g., Al-Rumaihi, 1997), have an influence over the type of voluntarily reported information about corporate governance. It argues that the majority of Saudi companies utilise the Internet to communicate corporate governance information to their stockholders. They, however, differ with respect to the quantity and nature of the information reported and the method of reporting from very little and informal to sophisticated, formal and extensive reporting. The most frequent piece of information reported by most companies relates to the personnel involved in the company whether in the company's management or ownership. This is more likely due to the social aspects of Saudi society that is characterised by the impact of the personality and power of particular individuals and the role of family and friend relationships over regulations and privilege given to personal relationships over tasks (Al-Rumaihi, 1997). In this type of environment, information about personnel is more understandable, believable and appreciable by the society than information about policies, regulations or laws.

The study also shows a variation in corporate governance online reporting practice among sectors. It suggests that some environmental factors such as the nature of control and the deep involvement of the government in the management and ownership could have different impacts on the attitude of companies to report online information about their corporate governance. In particular, our findings show that banking sector has the highest level of online corporate governance information. The correlation between the level of corporate governance online disclosure and the banking sector type is statistically significant. These results are in line with the suggestion of the literature as the banking sector is an extremely important device of the economic growth and is the most important source of finance for the majority of companies; therefore, it is more regulated than any other sector and has more incentives to report their corporate governance online.

The involvement of the government in some business, on the other side, could provide some safeguard or protect that could make companies' management less willing to report corporate governance information online in developing countries, particularly which are in an early stages of political and economical systems.

The main limitation of the study is that we did not cover the whole market so the sample may not be representative of the population of Saudi companies. This, however, is justified by the nature of the study, which relied on the availability of companies' websites. So companies that are not included in our study are more likely to have either no website, with a website under construction or the access to the information in their website is restricted. This is evident by checking the type of companies, which are not included. We found that these companies are in general small and less likely to use the online reporting. Nevertheless, a study with a large number of companies is needed for future research.

Our study focuses on corporate governance online reporting practice by Saudi listed companies and the extent to which this practice varies between different sectors. However, beside sector type, there are other determinants of corporate disclosure such as the intention to raise external finance, firm size, profitability, listing/cross listing, gearing and auditor type need an extensive investigation. So, it would be interesting to examine the determinants of corporate governance online reporting of Saudi companies. This study also suggested some impact of social assumptions on corporate governance disclosure; therefore, we believe that investigating such assumptions in an extensive research using a different research method and/or in a different environment is worthwhile. It is also interesting to examine the economic consequences of this type of reporting, for example, the extent to which corporate governance reporting provides value-relevant information for investors.

NOTES

1. General partnership is a form of business formulated when two or more persons are engaged in business and they are jointly and severally liable for business

debts. A joint venture is an association of two or more persons where third parties are not aware of the association. Joint-stock company is the regular form of corporation, with capital divided into equal shares without naming shareholders, who are liable only to the extent of the value of their shares. Limited liability company is composed of at least 2 but no more than 50 partners liable for the company's debt, each to the extent of his or her contribution to the company's capital stock. Cooperative company is a form of business that might be formed between a joint-stock company and a limited liability company to carry out a specific cooperative purpose.

2. Detailed information about these regulations is discussed in the following articles (SACMA, 2006): Article 9: Disclosure in the Board of Directors' Report; Article 10: Main Functions of the Board of Directors; Article 11: Responsibilities of the Board; Article 12: Formation of the Board; Article 13: Committees of the Board; Article 14: Audit Committee; Article 15: Nomination and Remuneration Committee; Article 16: Meetings of the Board; Article 17: Remuneration and Indemnification of Board Members.

3. Examples include the United Kingdom (see, for example, Demirag, 1998; Ezzamel & Willmott, 1993; Writer, 2001; Vinten, 2001), the Netherlands (Groot, 1998) and Canada (Elloumi & Gueyie, 2001). Other researchers compared corporate governance practice between developed countries. For instance, Vinten (2000) compared corporate governance practice between the United Kingdom and the United States. Another comparative study is Charkham (1994), which found significant differences in the corporate governance practices in five countries: Japan, Britain, France, the United States and Germany.

4. Our paper focuses on the presence or absence of certain information on companies' websites. It does not measure the qualitative dimension of the corporate governance issue, which refers to the meaningfulness of corporate governance disclosure; the quality of corporate governance and the effectiveness of corporate governance. This is because Saudi companies are still at an early stage of implementing corporate governance regulations and we find it very difficult – at the current stage – to gain further information about the quality of corporate governance through other research methods like questionnaires and interviews.

5. *TADAWUL* is a semi-governmental organisation responsible for executing stock exchange.

6. Such as Application of internal controls, Application of transparency policy, Number of board meetings, Board responsibilities, Number of NEDs and CEO in the board, Name of the chairman of the board, and number of meetings attended, Names of members of the board and number of meetings attended, Name of the CEO, Executive committee – number of members, Executive committee – responsibilities, Number of Executive committee meetings per year, Names of members attended the Executive committee – number of meetings previously attended, Remuneration of attending committee meeting – member, Remuneration of attending committee meeting – CEO, Audit committee – chairman, Audit committee – responsibilities, Audit committee – number of members, Audit committee – number of independent members, Audit committee – number of meetings, Names of members attended audit committee meeting and the number of meetings previously attended, Internal control procedures.

7. This paper does not intent to hypothetically test the factors that could affect Saudi listed companies' attitude to report information about their corporate governance, however, that does not prevent us from logically referring to them as explanations for our findings as long as they are suggested by the context of Saudi businesses or the literature.

REFERENCES

Aba-Alkhail, K. (2001). *Regulating the auditing profession in Saudi Arabia: the formulation of early auditing standards.* PhD Thesis, University of Essex, Essex, UK.

Abdeen, A., & Dale, S. (1984). *The Saudi financial system in the context of western and Islamic finance.* Chichester, UK: Wiley.

Aksu, M., & Kosedag, A. (2006). Transparency and disclosure scores and their determinants in the Istanbul stock exchange. *Corporate Governance, 14*(4), 277–296.

Al-Amari, S. (1989). *The development of accounting standards and practices in the Kingdom of Saudi Arabia.* PhD Thesis, University of Glasgow, Glasgow, UK.

Al-Deesty, M. (2004). Accounting and auditing on the Internet between practice and expectations: Comparative empirical study for large Egyptian and American companies. *Egyptian Journal of Commerce Studies* (4), 1–36.

Al-Htaybat, K., & Napier, C. (2006). *Online corporate financial reporting in developing countries: The case of Jordan.* BAA Annual Conference, Portsmouth University, Portsmouth, UK.

Al-Jaber, N., & Mohamed, F. (2003). *Disclosing financial reports on the internet: A survey of Egypt, Saudi and Kuwait.* Working paper No. 61, King Saud University, Al-Qassim, pp. 1–30.

Al-Motairy, O. (2003). Implementing corporate governance in Saudi Arabia. *Arab Journal of Administrative Sciences, 10*(3), 281–305.

Al-Nodel, A. (2004). *The business risk audit approach: International dissemination and the impact of a business orientation on auditors' perceptions of risks.* PhD Thesis, University of Manchester, Manchester, UK.

Al-Rehaily, S. (1992). *The evolution of accounting in Saudi Arabia: A study of its relevance to the social & economic environment.* PhD Thesis, University of Hull, Hull, UK.

Al-Rumaihi, J. (1997). *Setting accounting standards in a non-western environment with special reference to the Kingdom of Saudi Arabia.* PhD Thesis, University of Dundee, Dundee, UK.

Al-Saeed, K. (2006). Measurement of the degree of disclosure in Internet website: An application on Saudi joint-stock companies. *Riyadh News Paper*, September 28.

Al-Sayari, H. (2007). Corporate governance for banks in the Kingdom of Saudi Arabia. *BIS Review* (83), 1–3.

Aly, D., Simon, J., & Hussainey, K. (2008). *Determinants of corporate disclosure and transparency: Evidence from Egypt.* Working Paper, University of Gloucestershire, Cheltenham, UK.

Ameinfo. (2006). Middle east finance and economy; will the Saudi stock market boom continue? http://www.ameinfo.com/fn/ (accessed on 30th September 2006).

Andersson, M., & Daoud, M. (2005). *Corporate governance disclosure by Swedish listed corporations,* Master Thesis, JÖNKÖPING International Business School, Jönköping, Sweden.

Arun, T. G., & Turner, J. D. (2004). Corporate governance of banks in developing economies: Concepts and issues. *Corporate Governance, 12*(3), 371–377.

Basher, S., & Sadorsky, P. (2006). Oil price risk and emerging stock markets. *Global Finance Journal, 17*, 224–251.

Center for International Private Enterprise (CIPE). (2003). *Regional corporate governance: Recommendations in corporate governance.* Working Group of Middle East and North Africa, http://www.cipe-arabia.org/search.asp (accessed on 20th September 2006).

Charkham, J. (1994). *Keeping good company: A study of corporate governance in five countries.* Oxford: Oxford Press.

Demirag, I. (Ed.) (1998). Short termism, financial systems, and corporate governance. In: *Studies in managerial and financial accounting: Special issue on corporate governance, accountability, pressures to perform; An international study* (Vol. 8, pp. 7–24). Stamford, UK: JAI Press.

Economist Intelligence Unit Limited. (2003). *Country profile 2003: Saudi Arabia.* http://www.eiu.com (accessed on 10th February 2006).

Elloumi, F., & Gueyie, J. (2001). Financial distress and corporate governance: An empirical analysis. *Corporate Governance, International Journal of Business in Society, 1*(1), 15–23.

El-Sharkawy, H. (2006). Historical years in Saudi stocks. *Al-Jazirah Newspaper*, September, No. 12413.

Ezzamel, M., & Willmott, H. (1993). Corporate governance and financial accountability: Recent reforms in the UK public sector. *Accounting, Auditing, and Accountability Journal, 6*(3), 109–132.

Fouzy, S. (2003). *Evaluation of corporate governance in the Arab Republic of Egypt.* The Egyptian Centre for Economic Studies, Working Paper No, 82, pp. 1–39.

G-20. (2005). *Institution Building in the Financial Sector.* Communication Development Incorporated, Washington. http://www.g20.org/G20/webapp/publicEN/publication/further/doc/20050922_institution_building.pdf (accessed on 22nd May 2008).

Groot, T. (1998). The impact of performance pressures on R & D management in the Netherlands. In: I. Demirag (Ed.), *Studies in managerial and financial accounting: Special issue on corporate governance, accountability, pressures to perform; An international study* (Vol. 8, pp. 163–184). Stamford, UK: JAI Press.

Ismail, T. H. (2002). An empirical investigation of factors influencing voluntary disclosure of financial information on the Internet in the GCC Countries. http://www.ssrn.com/abstract = 420700

Kahlid, T. M. (1983). Financial audit: Comparative study about the responsibility of an external auditor in the Kingdom of Saudi Arabia and the United Kingdom. *Proceedings of the second accounting conference on accounting development*, King Saud University, Riyadh.

Metwali, T. (2003). Financial reporting on the Internet: A study on the Egyptian business environment. *Egyptian Journal of Commercial Studies, 1*, 273–321.

Ministry of Finance and National Economy. (1983). *The companies law of 1965.* Riyadh, Saudi Arabia: Government Press.

Mohamed, F. (2002). Financial reporting on the Internet: A survey of Egyptian, Saudi Arabian, and Kuwaiti companies. *Journal of Financial and Commercial Studies, 3*, 203–227.

Oyelere, P., & Mohamed, E. (2005). *A survey of Internet reporting of corporate governance practices by companies listed in Oman.* The 2nd Annual International Accounting Conference, Istanbul, Turkey, November.

Presley, R. (1984). *A guide to the Saudi Arabian economy.* London: Macmillan Press.

Ramady, M. (2005). *The Saudi Arabian economy: Policies, achievements and challenges.* New York, USA: Springer.

Saudi Arabian Capital Market Authority (SACMA). (2006). Criteria of the best practices of corporate governance. http://www.cma.org.sa/cma%5Far/ (accessed on 15th September 2006).

Saudi Arabian Monetary Agency (SAMA). (2007). http://www.sama.gov.sa/ (accessed in 20th September 2007).

Shinawi, A., & Crum, W. (1971). The emergence of professional public accounting in Saudi Arabia. *International Journal of Accounting Education and Research, 6*(2), 103–110.

Tadawul. (2006). http://www.tadawul.com.sa/wps/portal/!ut/p/_s.7_0_A/7_0_49I (accessed on 29th September, 2006).

Tawfik, M. S. (2001). The electronic distribution of business reports and the extent of need for re-organization of its financial aspect: An evaluation study of variable interpretive factors in banking sector. *Journal of Public Administration Institute, 41*(1), 107–162.

Vinten, G. (2000). Corporate governance the need to know. *Industrial and Commercial Training, 32*(5), 173–178.

Vinten, G. (2001). Corporate governance and the sons of Cadbury. *Corporate Governance: International Journal of Business in Society, 1*(4), 4–8.

Wikipedia website. (2008). http://www.Wikipedia.com (accessed on 10th July 2008).

Writer, N. (2001). Turnbull 2000: Corporate governance and the financial sector. *Balance Sheet, 9*(2), 20–23.

CEO DUALITY AND ACCOUNTING-BASED PERFORMANCE IN EGYPTIAN LISTED COMPANIES: A RE-EXAMINATION OF AGENCY THEORY PREDICTIONS

Ahmed Kholeif

ABSTRACT

Purpose – *This paper aims at re-examining the predictions of agency theory with regard to the negative association between CEO duality (i.e. the Chief Executive Officer, CEO, serves also as the board chairman) and corporate performance. It also examines the role of other corporate governance mechanisms (board size, top managerial ownership and institutional ownership) as moderating variables in the relationship between CEO duality and corporate performance.*

Methodology/approach – *This paper uses the financial statements for the year 2006 of most actively traded Egyptian companies to examine these predictions of agency theory. Moderated Regression Analysis is used to analyse the empirical data.*

Corporate Governance in Less Developed and Emerging Economies
Research in Accounting in Emerging Economies, Volume 8, 65–96
Copyright © 2008 by Emerald Group Publishing Limited
ISSN: 1479-3563/doi:10.1016/S1479-3563(08)08003-1

Findings – *The findings indicated that the hypothesized relationships between CEO duality, the moderating variables and corporate performance have changed. For companies characterized by large boards and low top management ownership, corporate performance is negatively affected by CEO duality and positively impacted by institutional ownership.*

Research limitations/implications – *A limitation of this study is the use of accounting-based performance measures because of the expected earnings management behaviours by CEOs.*

Practical implications – *The Egyptian Capital Market Authority should adopt a reform programme to encourage Egyptian listed companies to modify their governance structures by increasing top management ownership and reducing board sizes before incorporating the new governance rules into the listing requirements.*

Originality/value of paper – *The paper contributes to the literature on corporate governance and corporate performance by introducing a framework for identifying and analysing moderating variables that affect the relationship between CEO duality and corporate performance.*

1. INTRODUCTION

In recent years, the Anglo-American system of corporate governance has received increasing attention because of a series of shocking financial scandals and corporate failures, including Enron, WorldCom, Tyco International, Global Crossing, Quest Communications, Adelphia Communications, ImClone, Xerox, HealthSouth and Royal Ahold (Coles, McWilliams, & Sen, 2001; Eighme & Cashell, 2002; Klein, 2002; Tipgos & Keefe, 2004; Agrawal & Chadha, 2005; Davidson, Stewart, & Kent, 2005; Parker, 2005; Seal, 2006; Balgobin, 2008; Bauer, Frijns, Otten, & Tourani, 2008; Omran, Bolbol, & Fatheldin, 2008). These corporate crashes refer to the failure of existing corporate governance practices in predicting and preventing corporate failures. At the heart of the Anglo-American corporate governance system is an agency problem that agents (e.g. managers) will not act to maximise the returns to principals (e.g. shareholders) unless corporate governance mechanisms are implemented to narrow the divergence of interests between shareholders and managers (Jensen & Meckling, 1976). However, the effectiveness of these mechanisms depends critically on the ability of the board of directors to detect managerial mistakes (Donaldson & Davis, 1991). This body is in place to represent and safeguard the interests of shareholders. It monitors and controls managerial actions on behalf of shareholders by setting strategic policies and goals.

According to agency theory, the interests of shareholders are safeguarded only where different people occupying the two positions of the Chief Executive Officer (CEO) and the chairman of the board of directors (Rhoades, Rechner, & Sundaramurthy, 2001). Molz (1988) asserts that firms whose have one individual who serves as both chairman and chief executive officer/managing director (CEO duality) are considered to be more managerially dominated. Mak and Li (2001) argue that when a single individual wears the hats of both the CEO and chairman of the board (unitary leadership structure), managerial dominance is greatly enhanced since that individual is more aligned with management than with stockholders. This means that CEO duality (i.e. the CEO serves also as the board chairman) is negatively associated with corporate performance. For example, 8 of the above 10 recent scandals had board chairs who were also CEO, including Enron, Tyco International, Quest Communications, Adelphia Communications, ImClone, Xerox, HealthSouth and Royal Ahold. However, empirical evidence is mixed with respect to this prediction of agency theory. Some scholars found that non-executive board chair is positively associated with corporate performance (e.g. Berg & Smith, 1978; Rechner & Dalton, 1991; Daily & Dalton, 1994). Other scholars found that executive-chaired boards are significantly associated with higher corporate performance (e.g. Donaldson & Davis, 1991; Finkelstein & D'Aveni, 1994; Lin, 2005). Still others suggest that no significant difference in corporate performance between executive and non-executive chaired boards (e.g. Chaganti, Mahajan, & Sharma, 1985; Molz, 1988; Baliga, Moyer, & Rao, 1996; Abdullah, 2004).

The prevalence of agency theory in the corporate governance literature is ascribed by Daily, Dalton, & Cannella (2003, p. 372) to two factors as follows. 'First, it is an extremely simple theory, in which large corporations are reduced to two participants – managers and shareholders – and the interests of each are assumed to be both clear and consistent. Second, the notion of humans as self-interested and generally unwilling to sacrifice personal interests for the interests of others is both age old and widespread.' From this perspective it is assumed that the main purpose of internal and external corporate governance mechanisms is to provide shareholders with some reassurance that managers will try to achieve outcomes that are in the shareholders' interests. In corporate governance research governance mechanisms are conceptualised as deterrents to managerial self-interest (Shleifer & Vishny, 1997).

The present paper seeks to re-examine the predictions of agency theory with regard to the negative association between CEO duality and corporate performance in the context of a developing country, Egypt. It also examines other corporate governance mechanisms such as board size, top managerial ownership and institutional ownership that moderate, and possibly change, the relationship between CEO duality and corporate performance. Thus this paper uses Moderated Regression Analysis (MRA) as this technique is the most appropriate form of analysis when the relationship between dependent and independent variables is conditional on the values assumed by other variables (Baron & kenny, 1986; Russell & Babko, 1992; Dunk, 1993; Hartmann & Moers, 1999; Smith, 2003). MRA assumes that the effect of one independent variable (e.g. CEO duality) on the dependent variable (e.g. corporate performance) depends on the level of one or more other independent variables (e.g. board size, top management ownership and institutional ownership). In particular, Sharma, Durand, and Gur-Arie's (1981) framework for identification and analysis of moderator variables will be used.

The empirical data used in this paper is based on the financial statements for the year 2006 of most actively traded companies in the Egyptian stock market as reported by the Egyptian Market Authority. The Egyptian context is particularly important because the Anglo-American model of corporate governance has recently been adopted in Egypt. The Egyptian Institute of Directors, with support from the World Bank, the International Finance Corporation and the Ministry of Foreign Trade, has created a code, guidelines and standards of corporate governance that are based on the corporate governance principles of the Organization of Economic Co-operation and Development (OECD). So this study could highlight the effectiveness of the Anglo-American model of corporate governance in Egypt.

The remainder of this paper is organised in five sections. In the next section, existing practices and recent developments of CEO governance in Egypt are described. Then, study hypotheses based on agency theory are developed. This is followed by details of the research method employed in this study. The paper then analyse the empirical data. This is followed by the discussion of the findings and the implications for theory and policy. The final section provides some conclusions.

2. THE CEO GOVERNANCE IN EGYPT: CRITICISMS AND RECENT DEVELOPMENTS

The World Bank and the International Monetary Fund utilise the OECD principles of corporate governance (i.e. the rights of shareholders, the equitable treatment of shareholders, the treatment of stakeholders, disclosure and transparency and the duties of board members) to assess and produce reports on the corporate governance institutional frameworks and practices in individual countries (Mallin, 2007). In February 2004, they prepared a report that benchmarked the Egyptian corporate governance against the OECD principles of corporate governance. The report identified several weaknesses in the Egyptian corporate governance practices. This section focuses on describing the existing practices and recent improvements in CEO governance rules in Egypt.

2.1. Description of Existing Egyptian CEO Governance Practices

The existing practices of CEO governance in Egyptian companies are as follows:

1. *Board structure and independence*
   Egyptian companies have one-tier board structure.[1] This means that one single board comprising executive and non-executive directors. This form of board structure is predominant in countries such as the UK, the USA and the majority of EU Member States (Mallin, 2007). However, there are no rules that govern the board structure from executive or non-executive directors in Egypt. The 2002 listing rules introduced the concept of 'non-executive director' for the first time but the concept of the 'independent board member' is not clearly applied in Egypt. In most Egyptian companies, there is no clear separation between the board of directors and the executive management. The board of directors does not include independent members, nor does it form *ad hoc* committees to consider assigned subjects.

2. *Chairman and chief executive officer*
   In Egypt, the chairman is often also the CEO. The board member responsible for the executive management is sometimes called the managing director or the chief executive officer. This means that there is CEO duality. The CEO is responsible for the running of the board as well as the running of the company's business. This duality exists in some other countries. In Australia, only a small percentage of large companies have CEO duality (Donaldson & Davis, 1991). However, about 80% of large US companies have CEOs are also the chairman (Kesner & Dalton, 1986; Dalton & Kesner, 1987; Dahya & Travlos, 2000). Dahya and Travlos (2000) found that CEO duality in US companies changed from 76.8% in 1985 to 81.7% in 1995. In fact, the

two roles should not be combined and carried out by one person, as this
would give an individual too much power.

3. *Board size and appointments to the board*

In Egypt, the board of directors consists of an odd number of members,
with a minimum of three members. Board members must be shareholders
or represent the participating companies which are shareholders with the
exception of two members (as a maximum) who are chosen because they
are 'experts in the field'. The annual general assembly elects directors on
the board for a period of three renewable years, sets their remuneration
and can remove them if necessary. Election conditions include the
ownership of a minimum number of shares as indicated in the company's
statutes (with the exception of the two experts). These shares will be kept
as qualification shares until the expiry of the board's term and the
ratification of the last annual financial statements by the annual general
assembly. Directors must submit a CV, including a list of companies
with which they have been associated during the previous three years.
An employee cannot be appointed before having served at least two years
with the company. A recent Prime Ministerial decree mandates that
directors may serve on a maximum of two boards, but CEOs should only
serve on one board with the exception of directors who owns at least 10%
of the company's share capital. If the company experiences losses, board
members cannot be re-appointed.

4. *The board meeting and the functions of the board of directors*

In Egypt, the board holds its meetings at the request of its chairman or
two-thirds of its members. The board meeting is considered valid if the
number of attendees is not less than half of its members plus one,
provided the number of attendees is not less than three board members.
However, there is no disclosure of board meeting attendance. The board
of directors has the responsibility for supervising the implementation of
the company's objectives as decided by its general assembly. The board
is responsible to the shareholders. The functions of the board of
directors include: inviting the shareholders to meet, investing the
company's funds, requesting loans, appointing executive managers and
submitting financial statements and board reports to the general
assembly meeting. According to the World Bank–International Monetary Fund (IMF) report on the observance of standards and codes, the
boards of most Egyptian companies do not yet play a central and
strategic role, and their functions are not clearly distinguished from
those of management. They most often lack independence from
controlling shareholders and from management. Boards do not have
the responsibility for monitoring governance practices, or for overseeing

disclosure and communications, although board members are liable for false statements.

2.2. Recent Improvements in CEO Governance Rules

In October 2005, the Egyptian Institute of Directors, with support from the World Bank, the IMF and the Ministry of Foreign Trade, has developed a code, guidelines and standards of corporate governance that are based on the corporate governance principles of the OECD. The 'new' Egyptian code of corporate governance consists of a set of guidelines and standards related to the following:

1. General assembly,
2. Board of directors,
3. Internal audit department,
4. External auditor,
5. Audit committee,
6. Disclosure of social policies and
7. Avoiding conflict of interest.

This 'new' Egyptian code has introduced a number of improvements in CEO governance. For example, the board of directors should include a majority of non-executive directors and it is preferred that the two posts of the chairman and the CEO should not be held by the same person. However, these 'new' governance principles are neither mandatory nor legally binding. So it is less likely to have a real impact on existing corporate governance practices in Egypt. Currently, the Egyptian Capital Market Authority is working on a proposal to incorporate the Egyptian code of corporate governance into the listing requirements. This means that in the near future the 'new' governance rule is going to be mandatory. This paper examines the impact of these 'new' rules of corporate governance on practice.

3. AGENCY THEORY AND HYPOTHESES DEVELOPMENT

In the last decades of the twentieth century, agency theory became the dominant force in the theoretical understanding of corporate governance and it still informs research on this area (Jensen & Meckling, 1976; Fama & Jensen, 1983; Eisenhardt, 1989; Phan & Yoshikawa, 2000; Clarke, 2004; McCarthy & Puffer, 2008). Because of the separation of finance and management in modern large corporations and the self-interested utility-maximising individuals, agency theory suggests that there is an agency problem between shareholders (principals) and the CEO (agents). The relationship between shareholders and the CEO will inevitably be problematic as managerial actions depart from those required by shareholders to maximise their returns and shareholders attempt to prevent their CEO from maximising their utility. From this point of view, corporate governance essentially concerns the constraints that are applied to minimise the opportunistic behaviours of the CEO and, therefore, reduce the agency problem. To align managerial incentives with the interests of stockholders, various corporate governance mechanisms can be used to control these behaviours. In this paper, I examine the agency problem caused by CEO duality and a number of corporate governance mechanisms that minimise this problem, mainly top managerial ownership, board size and institutional ownership. I argue that top management ownership, board size and institutional ownership have a moderating effect in the relationship between CEO duality and corporate performance (see Fig. 1). The following sections develop the study hypotheses based on agency theory.

3.1. CEO Duality and Corporate Performance

A major corporate governance mechanism that minimises managerial opportunism is the board of directors. This body, in theory, is in place to safeguard the interests of the company's shareholders and provides a monitoring of managerial actions on behalf of shareholders by setting strategic policies and goals (Mallin, 2007). This protection will occur more fully where board chairman is independent of executive management. The CEO is primarily responsible for initiation and implementation of strategic decisions, while the board has the responsibility for ratifying and monitoring decisions taken by the CEO. An implicit assumption of agency theory is that CEO is an inherently opportunistic agent who will capitalise

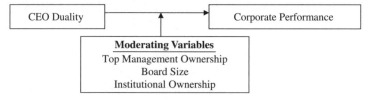

Fig. 1. Moderating Variables in the Relationship between CEO Duality and Corporate Performance.

on every chance to maximise personal welfare at the expense of share-holders.

Where the CEO is board chairman, the role of the board as an internal monitoring and control mechanism is compromised. Agency theory proposes that when the CEO also serves as board chairman, then board monitoring and control are weakened and the interests of the shareholders will be sacrificed to a degree in favour of executive management, that is, there will be managerial opportunism such as higher levels of executive compensation, adoption of 'poison pills' and payment of greenmail (Levy, 1981; Dayton, 1984; Davis, 1991; Rechner & Dalton, 1991; Pi & Timme, 1993; Brickley, Coles, & Terry, 1994). This suggests a negative relationship between CEO duality and firm performance. Hence, I offer the following hypothesis (alternate form):

H1. CEO duality is negatively related to corporate performance.

3.2. Interaction of Top Management Ownership and CEO Duality

An agency problem exists when the CEO has established goals which conflict with that of shareholders. Such problem is more likely to occur when the CEO has little or no financial interest in the outcome of his decisions (Jensen & Meckling, 1976; Fama & Jensen, 1983). This is often the norm, as the CEO of many large companies is typically not the majority shareholder. Consequently, the CEO is more likely to pursue strategies which maximise his personal welfare at the expense of shareholders and minimise his personal risk (Boyd, 1995).

An implication of agency theory is that where CEO duality is retained, shareholder interests could be safeguarded by aligning the interests of the CEO and the shareholders by suitable incentive schemes for the CEO. Such schemes typically include plans whereby the CEO obtains shares, perhaps at a reduced price, thus aligning financial interests of the CEO with those of shareholders (Morck, Shleifer, & Vishny, 1988). Where there is CEO duality, the presence of top management ownership will align the interests of the CEO with shareholders (Barnhart & Rosenstein, 1998). Thus based on agency theory predictions, I expect that high top management ownership with CEO duality is likely to give rise to high corporate performance, as posited below (alternate form):

H2. As top management ownership increases, CEO duality positively affects corporate performance.

3.3. Interaction of Board Size and CEO Duality

According to agency theory, coordination/communication problems and agency problems increase as board size becomes larger. Coordination/ coordination problems, on the one hand, arise from the fact that it would be more difficult for the company to arrange board meetings and for the board to reach a consensus as a board increases in size. This suggests that larger boards are less efficient and slower in making their decisions. For example, Bantel and Jackson (1989) suggest that small sized boards are more efficient. On the other hand, agency problems result from dysfunctional norms of behaviour in board meetings. Lipton and Lorsch (1992) suggest that directors on the board normally do not criticise the policies of the CEO or hold candid discussions about corporate performance. John and Senbet (1998) argue that while the board's monitoring capacities increase as the number of directors on the board increases, this benefit may be offset the cost and inefficiencies that are often associated with large groups.

With larger boards, the cost to any director of not exercising diligence in controlling and monitoring the decisions taken by the CEO falls in proportion to the total number of directors on the board. Jensen (1993) argues that when a board has more than seven or eight directors, the board of directors is less likely to function effectively and are easier for the CEO to control. With CEO duality, it becomes clear that the CEO will acquire a wider power base and locus of control, thereby leading to a lower level of corporate performance (assuming that CEO is an inherently opportunistic agent) (Yermack, 1996; Eisenberg, Sundgren, & Wells, 1998; Hermalin & Weisbach, 2003; Bennedsen, Kongsted, & Nielsen, 2007; Cheng, 2008). For instance, Yermack (1996) finds that firm valuation is negatively associated to board size. Hence, I posit that high corporate performance will be associated with small board size and CEO duality. This association is consistent with the view that both coordination/communication problems and agency problems become more severe as a board grows larger. Based on this logic, I develop the following hypothesis (alternate form):

H3. As board size increases, CEO duality negatively affects corporate performance.

3.4. Interaction of Institutional Ownership and CEO Duality

Agency theory argues that in the modern large corporation, share ownership is widely held, which makes effective coordination among shareholders difficult and expensive, making the CEO the de facto policymaker. Thus CEO actions are more likely to depart from those required to maximise shareholder returns. In agency theory terms, there is an agency problem which is the extent to which returns to shareholders fall below what would be if shareholders exercised direct control of the company. The CEO has more inside information than shareholders who therefore face a moral hazard problem because the value of managerial strategic decisions may be difficult to determine fully. In the case of CEO duality, these problems are exaggerated. However, these agency problems are minimized when there is ownership concentration, especially in the case of institutional investors. Where institutional investors are the largest holders of shares in companies, taking into account the voting power associated with their shareholdings, their approval or otherwise of strategies of the CEO can be critical factors in shaping how a company is managed and run (Chung, Michael, & Jeong-Bon, 2002; Mallin, 2002). In addition, institutional investors have more access to inside information like the CEO (Burns, 2001; Cross, 2004). Thus they can closely control decisions and actions taken by the CEO and limit the power of the CEO, especially when CEO and chairman positions are combined (Chaganti & Damanpour, 1991). This suggests that high institutional ownership with CEO duality is likely to be associated with high corporate performance, as posited below (alternate form):

H4. As institutional ownership increases, CEO duality positively affects corporate performance.

4. RESEARCH METHODOLOGY

4.1. Sample Selection and Data Collection Method

The annual Disclosure Book issued by Cairo and Alexandria Stock Exchanges (CASE) was the main source of data. This book identifies the most active listed companies in Egypt and contains a complete data on board characteristics, ownership structure, corporate performance and other related variables. The sample used in this study was based on the 50 most active Egyptian companies in July 2007. These companies cover 15 industries. The banks and the other financial institutions were deleted from the sample because of their huge debt structure which is very much different from the other firms, leaving 40 firms in the sample. The use of secondary data based on the financial statements of the most active

Egyptian companies is due to data availability and reliability because these are required by law and are issued by the Egyptian Capital Market Authority. The most recent year (2006) was selected to reflect the impact of recent developments in corporate governance in Egypt on corporate performance.

4.2. Measurement of Dependent, Independent and Moderating Variables

4.2.1. Dependent Variables: Corporate Performance Variables
The dependent variable in this study is accounting-based performance. Previous studies on corporate governance and corporate performance have used accounting measures such as return on assets and return on equity (Muth & Donaldson, 1998; Erhardt, Werbel, & Shrader, 2003). The present paper uses return on assets and return on equity to measure corporate performance because the former mainly reflect operating results and the latter reflect capital structure decisions. Return on assets (ROA) is measured by net profit after tax divided by total assets. Regarding return on equity (ROE), it is measured by net profit after tax divided by shareholders equity.

4.2.2. Independent and Moderating Variables
The main independent variable in this study is CEO duality. A dummy variable is used as a proxy for CEO duality. This variable takes the value of 1, if the CEO also served as board chairman and 0 if there are different people occupying the two positions of CEO and board chairman. The moderating Variables examined in this study are board size, managerial ownership and institutional ownership. The board size is measured based on the total number of directors serving on a company's board. Managerial ownership is measured by the proportion of shares owned by top management divided by total number of shares. Finally, institutional ownership is measured by the ratio between shares owned by institutional investors and total number of shares.

5. DATA ANALYSIS AND FINDINGS

5.1. Descriptive Statistics

Table 1 reports some descriptive statistics for all dependent and independent variables. With regard to accounting-based performance, there is a wide

Table 1. Descriptive Statistics of Dependent and Independent Variables.

		Descriptive Statistics			
	N	Minimum	Maximum	Mean	Standard deviation
Return on assets	40	−0.0813	0.3555	0.101008	0.1002988
Return on equity	40	−0.3554	0.9397	0.209575	0.2218939
CEO duality	40	0	1	0.78	0.423
Top management ownership	40	0.0000	0.6627	0.065593	0.1547256
Board size	40	5	24	11.00	4.231
Institutional ownership	40	0.0034	0.9175	0.474593	0.3037503
Valid N (listwise)	40				

deviation between firms. The minimum and maximum reported ROA are −8% and 35.6%, respectively. The mean ROA is 10% with a standard deviation of 0.1003. ROE appears relatively stronger with a minimum of −35.5% and a maximum of 94%. While the mean ROE is 21%, the standard deviation is 0.222. For 78% of firms in the sample, the same person holds both the CEO and the board chairman positions. This figure is close to that reported in previous works. For example, CEO duality is 78.7% in Rechner and Dalton (1991), 76% in Donaldson and Davis (1991) and 80.94% in Brickley, Coles, and Jarrell (1997). This suggests that avenue for agency problems emanating from conflict of interest are exaggerated.

In most of the firms in the sample, top management appears not to have significant ownership with a mean of 6.6% and a standard deviation of 0.155. While the maximum top management ownership is 66.3%, the minimum top management ownership is 0%. As previously suggested, top management ownership is important as it may be a mechanism that aligns the divergence in interests with shareholders (Jensen & Meckling, 1976). Of the firms in the sample, the mean board size is 11 members with a standard deviation of 4.231. The minimum board size is 5 members and the maximum board size is 24 members. This suggests that firms in Egypt have relatively large board sizes. This is not good for corporate performance according to researchers such as Jensen (1993) and Lipton and Lorsch (1992) who argue that large board sizes are less effective for corporate performance. Finally, the mean institutional ownership is 47.5% with a standard deviation of 0.304. The minimum institutional ownership is 0.34% and the maximum institutional ownership is 92%. This implies that institutional investors in Egypt might have a significant impact on corporate performance as expected by researchers such as Salancik and Pfeffer (1980) and Chaganti and Damanpour (1991).

5.2. Moderated Regression Results

Sharma et al. (1981) proposed a framework for identifying and analysing moderating variables, as depicted in Fig. 2. According to this framework, MRA is applied by examining three regression equations for equality of the regression coefficients. For example, if we assumed three variables; Y (dependent variable), $X1$ (independent variable) and $X2$ (moderator variable).

(1) $Y = a + b1\ X1$
(2) $Y = a + b1\ X1 + b2\ X2$
(3) $Y = a + b1\ X1 + b2\ X2 + b3\ X1\ X2$

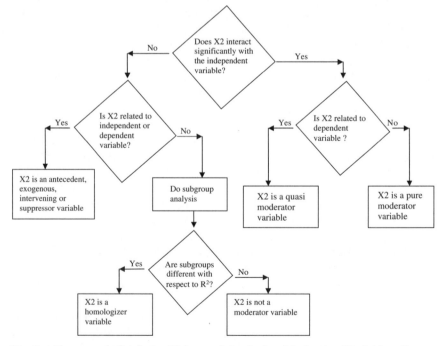

Fig. 2. Framework for Indentifying and Analysing Moderator Variables. *Source:* Adapted from Sharma et al. (1981, p. 297)

If Eqs. 2 and 3 are not significantly different (i.e. $b3 = 0$; $b2 \neq 0$), $X2$ is not a moderator variable but simply an independent variable. For $X2$ to be classified as a pure moderator variable, Eqs. 1 and 2 should not be different but should be different from Eq. 3 (i.e. $b2 = 0$; $b3 \neq 0$). For $X2$ to be a quasi moderator, Eqs. 1, 2 and 3 should be different from each other (i.e. $b2 \neq b3 \neq 0$). The following sections use this framework to test research hypotheses.

5.2.1. Hypothesis 1

To test the first hypothesis, a simple regression analysis was used to analyse the hypothetical negative relationship between CEO duality and corporate performance. The results, presented in Table 2, indicated that CEO duality significantly and negatively affected corporate performance as measured by ROE (p-value $= 0.086$)[2] but this relationship is not statistically significant when using ROA as a measure of corporate performance (p-value $= 0.149$). This gives us mixed evidence. These results are not uncommon in other research on CEO duality and corporate performance (e.g. Daily & Dalton, 1992; Brickley et al., 1997). This issue might be resolved when considering the moderating effect of other corporate governance variables.

5.2.2. Hypothesis 2

I also hypothesised that corporate performance may be influenced by the interaction of top management ownership and CEO duality. Test results (Table 3) indicated no significant interaction between top management ownership and CEO duality relative to ROA (p-value $= 0.786$) and ROE (p-value $= 0.894$). By examining the correlation between CEO duality,

Table 2. The Results of the First Hypothesis Test.

	Coefficient	Value	Standard Deviation	t-Statistics	p-Value
Dependent Variable: ROA					
Constant	A	0.144	0.033	4.361	0.000
CEO duality	b1	−0.055	0.037	−1.471	0.149
Dependent Variable: ROE					
Constant	A	0.321	0.072	4.460	0.000
CEO duality	b1	−0.144	0.082	−1.762	0.086

$R^2 = 0.054$; Adjusted $R^2 = 0.029$; $F(1, 38) = 2.165$; p-value $= 0.49$.
$R^2 = 0.076$; Adjusted $R^2 = 0.051$; $F(1, 38) = 3.106$; p-value $= 0.086$.

Table 3. The Interaction between CEO Duality and Top Management
Ownership.

	Coefficient	Value	Standard Deviation	t-Statistics	p-Value
Dependent Variable: ROA					
Constant	A	0.162	0.043	3.724	0.001
CEO duality	b1	−0.069	0.048	−1.448	0.156
Management ownership	b2	−0.086	0.132	−0.649	0.520
CEO duality × management ownership	b3	−0.087	0.319	−0.273	0.786
Dependent Variable: ROE					
Constant	A	0.358	0.095	3.761	0.001
CEO duality	b1	−0.174	0.04	−1.674	0.103
Management ownership	b2	−0.176	0.290	−0.607	0.548
CEO duality × management ownership	b3	−0.094	0.700	−0.134	0.894

$R^2 = 0.074$; Adjusted $R^2 = -0.003$; $F(3, 36) = 0.957$; p-value $= 0.423$.
$R^2 = 0.089$; Adjusted $R^2 = 0.014$; $F(3, 36) = 1.178$; p-value $= 0.332$.

top management ownership, ROA and ROE (Table 4), it became clear that
top management ownership was neither a moderator variable nor another
independent variable as it had a significant negative correlation with
CEO duality (the main independent variable). This suggested that top
management ownership might be an antecedent, extraneous, intervening or
suppressor variable (Rosenberg, 1968). Additional analyses were performed
to identify the role played by top management ownership in the relationship
between CEO duality and corporate performance.

First, I hypothesised that top management ownership may be an
intervening variable which comes between the independent variable
(CEO duality) and the dependent variable (corporate performance). Three
conditions should be met: (1) CEO duality predicts corporate performance,
(2) CEO duality predicts top management ownership and (3) top management ownership predicts corporate performance.

From Table 2 above, the first condition was partially met. The relationship between CEO duality and corporate performance was moderately
significant when corporate performance was measured by ROE but
was insignificant when using ROA as a measure of corporate performance.
With regard to the second condition, Table 5 showed a significant negative
association between CEO duality and top management ownership

Table 4. The Correlation between CEO Duality, Managerial Ownership, ROA and ROE.

		\multicolumn{4}{c}{Correlations}			
		Return on assets	Return on equity	CEO duality	Top management ownership
Return on assets	Pearson correlation	1	0.805**	−0.232	0.001
	Significance (2-tailed)		0.000	0.149	0.995
	N	40	40	40	40
Return on equity	Pearson correlation	0.805**	1	−0.275	0.039
	Significance (2-tailed)	0.000		0.086	0.813
	N	40	40	40	40
CEO duality	Pearson correlation	−0.232	−0.275	1	−0.504**
	Significance (2-tailed)	0.149	0.086		0.001
	N	40	40	40	40
Top management ownership	Pearson correlation	0.001	0.039	−0.504**	1
	Significance (2-tailed)	0.995	0.813	0.001	
	N	40	40	40	40

**Correlation is significant at the 0.01 level (2-tailed).

Table 5. The Results of Testing the Second Condition.

Dependent Variable: Top Management Ownership

	Coefficient	Value	Standard deviation	t-statistics	p-value
Constant	A	0.209	0.045	4.624	0.000
CEO duality	B1	−0.185	0.051	−3.601	0.001

$R^2 = 0.254$; Adjusted $R^2 = 0.235$; $F(1, 38) = 12.968$; p-value = 0.001.

(p-value = 0.001). The third condition was not met as the results of analysis presented in Table 6 were not significant at conventional significant levels. Thus top management ownership failed to be an intervening variable.

Table 6.   The Results of Testing the Third Condition.

	Coefficient	Value	Standard Deviation	t-Statistics	p-Value
Dependent Variable: ROA					
Constant	A	0.165	0.041	3.985	0.000
Management ownership	b1	−0.101	0.119	−0.849	0.401
CEO duality	b2	−0.074	0.044	−1.694	0.099
Dependent Variable: ROE					
Constant	A	0.361	0.091	3.990	0.000
Management ownership	b1	−0.192	0.261	−0.738	0.465
CEO duality	b2	−0.180	0.095	−1.885	0.067

$R^2 = 0.072$; Adjusted $R^2 = 0.022$; $F(2, 37) = 1.435$; p-value $= 0.251$.
$R^2 = 0.089$; Adjusted $R^2 = 0.040$; $F(2, 37) = 1.807$; p-value $= 0.178$.

Next, I hypothesised that top management ownership may be an antecedent variable. It comes before the independent variable (i.e. the CEO duality) in the sequence. According to Rosenberg (1968), the antecedent variable does not explain away the relationship between the independent and dependent variables but clarifies the influences which preceded this relationship. Three conditions should be met:

1. All three variables – antecedent, independent and dependent – must be related.
2. When the antecedent variable is controlled, the relationship between the independent and the dependent variable should not vanish.
3. When the independent variable is controlled, the relationship between the antecedent variable and the dependent variable should disappear.

None of these conditions were met. The correlation only existed between CEO duality and top management ownership, presented in Table 4 above. Furthermore, when the effect of top management ownership was controlled in Table 7, the relationship between CEO duality and corporate performance persisted (a moderate significant relationship at the 0.10 level). The third condition was not met as there was not any relationship between top management ownership and corporate performance as presented in Table 4 above. The results of these tests confirmed that top management ownership is not an antecedent variable.

Then, I hypothesised that top management ownership may be an extraneous variable. A variable is considered extraneous if it is logically prior to both the independent and dependent variables and if it is controlled, the relationship cancels out. However, as explained earlier in Table 4 above,

Table 7. The Partial Correlation between CEO Duality and Corporate Performance (the Effect of Top Management Ownership was Controlled).

		Correlations			
Control variables			Return on assets	Return on equity	CEO duality
Top management ownership	Return on assets	Correlation	1.000	0.806	−0.268
		Significance (2-tailed)		0.000	0.099
		df	0	37	37
	Return on equity	Correlation	0.806	1.000	−0.296
		Significance (2-tailed)	0.000		0.067
		df	37	0	37
	CEO duality	Correlation	−0.268	−0.296	1.000
		Significance (2-tailed)	0.099	0.067	
		df	37	37	0

top management ownership was only associated with CEO duality and was not related to ROA and ROE. In addition, the relationship between CEO duality and corporate performance did not disappear when top management ownership was controlled, as presented in Table 7 above. Thus we concluded that top management ownership was not an extraneous.

This left us with one more possibility that top management ownership may be a suppressor variable. A suppressor variable is one which may intercede to cancel out, reduce or conceal a true relationship between two variables (Rosenberg, 1968). The theoretical significance of suppressor variables is evidence. If one tests a hypothesis based upon a theory but finds that the relationship is weak or absent, one may conclude that the theory is defective or erroneous. However, the theory may be sound, and the data, if properly analysed, may support it. In the context of this paper, the weak relationship between CEO duality and corporate performance may be due to the intrusion of a third variable, top management ownership. In fact, after controlling on top management ownership, the negative correlation between CEO duality and corporate performance as well as the significance level increased (compare Tables 4 and 7 above). So the relationship between CEO duality and corporate performance improved when controlling the effect of top management ownership. This means that top management ownership is a suppressor variable that weakens the relationship between CEO duality and corporate performance and conceals its true strength.

5.2.3. Hypothesis 3

Hypothesis 3 focused on how the interaction between board size and CEO duality may affect corporate performance. Table 8 indicated that the interaction between board size and CEO duality did not affect corporate performance measured by ROA (p-value = 0.485) and ROE (p-value = 0.652). The correlation between CEO duality, board size, ROA and ROE (Table 9) showed that no significant correlation between board size and other variables. According to Sharma et al.'s (1981) framework, board size either is a homologizer variable[3] or is not a moderator variable. It seems that board size has the characteristics of the homologiser variable. To confirm this, I first divided the sample at 8 members[4] into small and large boards. Then, I regressed corporate performance measures (ROA and ROE) on the control variable (board size) and CEO duality. Table 10 indicates that for large boards, CEO duality significantly and negatively affected ROA (p-value = 0.039) and ROE (p-value = 0.034) and the model explained 14.3% of the variation in ROA and 15% of the variation of the variation in ROE. Table 10 also indicates that for small boards, CEO duality positively impacted ROA and ROE and the model explained just 0.2% of the variation in corporate performance but the results were not significant at conventional levels. This resulted in concluding that sub-groups (large vs. small boards) were different with respect to R^2 and board size was a homologiser variable.

Table 8. The Results of the Third Hypothesis Test.

	Coefficient	Value	Standard Deviation	t-Statistics	p-Value
Dependent Variable: ROA					
Constant	A	0.023	0.105	0.216	0.830
CEO duality	b1	0.012	0.116	0.106	0.916
Board size	b2	0.013	0.010	1.215	0.232
CEO duality × board size	b3	−0.008	0.011	−0.705	0.485
Dependent Variable: ROE					
Constant	A	0.222	0.237	0.934	0.356
CEO duality	b1	−0.032	0.262	−0.123	0.903
Board size	b2	0.010	0.023	0.441	0.662
CEO duality × board size	b3	−0.011	0.025	−0.455	0.652

$R^2 = 0.123$; Adjusted $R^2 = 0.050$; $F(3, 36) = 1.686$; p-value = 0.187.
$R^2 = 0.081$; Adjusted $R^2 = 0.004$; $F(3, 36) = 1.056$; p-value = 0.380.

Table 9. The Correlation between CEO Duality, Board Size, ROA and ROE.

	Correlations				
		Return on assets	Return on equity	CEO duality	Board size
Return on assets	Pearson correlation	1	0.805**	−0.232	0.196
	Significance (2-tailed)		0.000	0.149	0.226
	N	40	40	40	40
Return on equity	Pearson correlation	0.805**	1	−0.275	−0.039
	Significance (2-tailed)	0.000		0.086	0.809
	N	40	40	40	40
CEO duality	Pearson correlation	−0.232	−0.275	1	0.172
	Significance (2-tailed)	0.149	0.086		0.289
	N	40	40	40	40
Board size	Pearson correlation	0.196	−0.039	0.172	1
	Significance (2-tailed)	0.226	0.809	0.289	
	N	40	40	40	40

**Correlation is significant at the 0.01 level (2-tailed).

Table 10. The Relationship between CEO Duality and Corporate Performance (the Effect of Board Size was Controlled).

Board Size		Large (Members > 8)		Small (Members ⩽ 8)	
Corporate performance		ROA	ROE	ROA	ROE
Coefficient					
Constant	Value	0.200	0.411	0.073	0.210
	Standard Deviation	0.046	0.101	0.033	0.089
CEO duality	Value	−0.109	−0.245	0.006	0.016
	Standard Deviation	0.051	0.110	0.043	0.115
R^2		0.143	0.150	0.002	0.002
Adjusted R^2		0.112	0.120	−0.122	−0.122
p-value		0.039	0.034	0.891	0.894

5.2.4. Hypothesis 4

In Hypothesis 4, I expected that the interaction between CEO duality and institutional ownership may influence corporate performance. Test results (Table 11) indicated that the interaction between institutional ownership and CEO duality was not significant relative to ROA (p-value $= 0.404$) and ROE (p-value $= 0.205$) but the model as a whole was significant

Table 11. The Results of the Fourth Hypothesis Test.

	Coefficient	Value	Standard Deviation	t-Statistics	p-Value
Dependent Variable: ROA					
Constant	A	0.057	0.045	1.268	0.213
CEO duality	b1	−0.041	0.055	−0.758	0.454
Institutional ownership	b2	0.236	0.093	2.520	0.016
CEO duality × institutional ownership	b3	−0.091	0.108	−0.844	0.404
Dependent Variable: ROE					
Constant	A	0.112	0.099	1.123	0.269
CEO duality	b1	−0.067	0.121	−0.551	0.585
Institutional ownership	b2	0.569	0.207	2.751	0.009
CEO duality × institutional ownership	b3	−0.308	0.238	−1.291	0.205

$R^2 = 0.314$; Adjusted $R^2 = 0.257$; $F(3, 36) = 5.497$; p-value $= 0.003$.
$R^2 = 0.313$; Adjusted $R^2 = 0.256$; $F(3, 36) = $; p-value $= 0.003$.

(p-value $= 0.003$) and explained 31% of the variation in corporate performance. By examining the correlation between CEO duality, institutional ownership, ROA and ROE (Table 12), it became clear that institutional ownership was not a moderator variable as it had a significant positive correlation with both ROA and ROE. This simply suggested that institutional ownership was just another independent variable. By removing the interaction between CEO duality and institutional ownership from the regression model, the significance level of the model was improved (p-value $= 0.001$) and the model still explained 30% of the variation in ROA and 28% of the variation in ROE, as presented in Table 13.

6. DISCUSSION

In this study, I investigated the predictions of agency theory with regard to the negative association between CEO duality and corporate performance. I hypothesized that board size, top managerial ownership and institutional ownership were moderating variables which might moderate, and possibly change, the relationship between CEO duality and corporate performance.

Table 12. The Correlation between CEO Duality, Institutional
Ownership, ROA and ROE.

		Correlations			
		Return on assets	Return on equity	CEO duality	Institutional ownership
Return on assets	Pearson correlation	1	0.805**	−0.232	0.443**
	Significance (2-tailed)		0.000	0.149	0.004
	N	40	40	40	40
Return on equity	Pearson correlation	0.805**	1	−0.275	0.393*
	Significance (2-tailed)	0.000		0.086	0.012
	N	40	40	40	40
CEO duality	Pearson correlation	−0.232	−0.275	1	0.191
	Significance (2-tailed)	0.149	0.086		0.238
	N	40	40	40	40
Institutional ownership	Pearson correlation	0.443**	0.393*	0.191	1
	Significance (2-tailed)	0.004	0.012	0.238	
	N	40	40	40	40

**Correlation is significant at the 0.01 level (2-tailed).
*Correlation is significant at the 0.05 level (2-tailed).

Table 13. The Results of the Fourth Hypothesis Test (without
Interaction).

	Coefficient	Value	Standard Deviation	t-Statistics	p-Value
Dependent Variable: ROA					
Constant	A	0.082	0.033	2.461	0.019
CEO duality	b1	−0.078	0.033	−2.347	0.024
Institutional ownership	b2	0.167	0.046	3.613	0.001
Dependent Variable: ROE					
Constant	A	0.197	0.075	2.632	0.012
CEO duality	b1	−0.190	0.075	−2.556	0.015
Institutional ownership	b2	0.337	0.104	3.252	0.002

$R^2 = 0.301$; Adjusted $R^2 = 0.263$; $F(2, 37) = 7.951$; p-value $= 0.001$.
$R^2 = 0.281$; Adjusted $R^2 = 0.242$; $F(2, 37) = 7.232$; p-value $= 0.002$.

To accomplish this objective, I used the data of 40 most active non-financial
Egyptian listed companies. I examined two accounting-based performance
metrics: ROA and ROE. Sharma et al.'s (1981) framework was used to
identify and analyse moderating variables.

I predicted that CEO duality would be negatively associated with corporate performance because when the CEO also serves as board chairman, then board monitoring and control are weakened and the interests of the shareholders will be sacrificed to a degree in favour of executive management. Research findings suggested that one of the two performance metrics (ROE) moderately supported this hypothesis. This was a preliminary finding as I expected that other corporate governance mechanisms may moderate, and possibly change, the relationship between CEO duality and corporate performance.

In addition, I investigated the interactive effect of top management ownership and CEO duality on corporate performance. I did not find a significant interaction between top management ownership and CEO duality for the two performance measures (ROA and ROE). Then, I concluded that top management ownership was not a moderator variable. By examining the correlation between top management ownership and other variables (CEO duality, ROA and ROE), I found that top management ownership had a significant negative relationship with CEO duality. This resulted in excluding the possibility that top management ownership might be another independent variable. I conducted a number of analyses to identify the role played by top management ownership into the relationship between CEO duality and corporate performance. As a result of these analyses, I also excluded the possibilities that top management ownership might be an intervening variable, an antecedent variable or an extraneous variable. I concluded that top management ownership was a suppressor variable which may intercede to cancel out, reduce or conceal a true relationship between CEO duality and corporate performance and should be controlled.

I also examined the interactive effect of board size and CEO duality on corporate performance. I found that no significant interaction between board size and CEO duality for both corporate performance measures (ROA and ROE). Furthermore, there was no significant correlation between board size and other variables (CEO duality, ROA and ROE). Additional analysis revealed that board size was a homologiser variable. This type of moderating variable should be controlled as it influences the strength of the relationship between CEO duality and corporate performance, does not interact with CEO duality, and is not significantly related to either CEO duality or corporate performance.

Last not least, I investigated the impact of the interaction between institutional ownership and CEO duality on corporate performance. The results indicated that the interaction between institutional ownership and

CEO duality was not significant relative to corporate performance measures (ROA and ROE). The correlation between institutional ownership and other variables (CEO duality, ROA and ROE) suggested that institutional ownership was not a moderator variable but was just another independent variable as it had a significant positive correlation with corporate performance.

As a result of my findings, the hypothesized relationships between the independent variable (CEO duality), the moderating variables (top management ownership, board size and institutional ownership) and the dependent variable (corporate performance) have changed (see Fig. 3). I found that board size was the only moderating variable (a homologizer variable), top management ownership was a suppressor variable, and institutional ownership was another independent variable.

To test this new model, I controlled the effects of board size[5] and top management ownership[6] on the relationship among CEO duality, institutional ownership and corporate performance. The results, presented in Table 14, indicated that the new regression model as a whole explained 45.2% of the variation in ROA (p-value $= 0.001$) and 38.6% of the variation in ROE (p-value $= 0.002$). R^2 improved sharply when comparing these results with those reported in Tables 2 and 13. So the new model is better in explaining the variation in corporate performance. This means that for companies characterized by large boards and low top management ownership, corporate performance is negatively affected by CEO duality and positively affected by institutional ownership. This conclusion is consistent with other research such as Daily and Dalton (1994) and Brickley et al. (1997).

The findings of this paper confirmed the predictions of agency theory with regard to the negative impact of CEO duality on corporate performance.

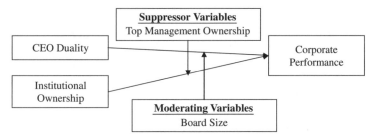

Fig. 3. The New Relationships between CEO Duality, Other Corporate Governance Mechanisms and Corporate Performance.

Table 14. The Relationship among CEO Duality, Institutional
Ownership and Corporate Performance (the Effects of Board Size and
Top Management Ownership were Controlled).

	Coefficient	Value	Standard Deviation	t-Statistics	p-Value
Dependent Variable: ROA					
Constant	A	0.119	0.055	2.191	0.038
CEO duality	b1	−0.123	0.047	−2.594	0.016
Institutional ownership	b2	0.197	0.058	3.427	0.002
Dependent Variable: ROE					
Constant	A	0.270	0.126	2.143	0.042
CEO duality	b1	−0.280	0.110	−2.554	0.017
Institutional ownership	b2	0.365	0.133	2.742	0.011

$R^2 = 0.452$; Adjusted $R^2 = 0.408$; $F(2, 25) = 10.312$; p-value $= 0.001$.
$R^2 = 0.386$; Adjusted $R^2 = 0.337$; $F(2, 25) = 7.863$; p-value $= 0.002$.

This paper examined the role of top management ownership, board size and institutional ownership as potential corporate governance mechanisms that might intervene and possibly change the relationship between CEO duality and corporate performance. Owing to low management ownership and large board sizes, these two governance mechanisms failed to control the opportunistic behaviours of CEOs. The only effective governance mechanism was institutional ownership. The Egyptian Capital Market Authority should consider the governance characteristics of Egyptian listed companies before enforcing any governance rules. Failing to do so will lead to loose coupling or decoupling. The Egyptian Capital Market Authority should adopt a reform programme to encourage Egyptian listed companies to modify their governance structures by increasing top management ownership and reducing board sizes before incorporating the new governance rules into the listing requirements.

This study contributed to the literature on corporate governance and corporate performance (e.g. Yermack, 1996; Gompers, Ishii, & Metrick, 2003; Klapper & Love, 2004; Bauer et al., 2008) by introducing a framework for identifying and analysing moderating variables that affect the relationship between CEO duality and corporate performance. It also highlighted the fact that the 'new' corporate governance principles that have recently been introduced to the Egyptian stock exchange market are still not effective as most Egyptian companies have large boards, low top management ownership and CEO duality.

The findings of this study open new directions for future research. Firstly, other corporate governance mechanisms such as outside directors, independent auditors, internal auditors, audit committees and ownership structure may influence the relationship between CEO duality and corporate performance. There is a great potential for future studies to investigate these relationships. For example, if there are more outside non-executive directors, who have incentives to develop reputation as experts in decision control, on a board it will become more effective because non-executive directors are more capable of checking and monitoring managers and reducing agency problems (Fama & Jensen, 1983; Mak, 1996). Ownership concentration is a main characteristic that distinguishes between the Anglo-American model of corporate governance and the Continental European model of corporate governance. Ownership concentration is also another important factor that should be considered in future research. Under high ownership concentration, conflicts of interest are not between managers and shareholders, but between large and small shareholders (Morck et al., 1988; Shleifer & Vishny, 1997)[7].

Secondly, there can sometimes be a kind of reverse causality between CEO duality and financial performance, at least in cross-sectional studies – namely that, when performance is good, duality is tolerated by investors, but when performance is poor, it is harder for CEOs to defend duality or other less favoured governance arrangements. This reverse relationship represents another future research opportunity[8]. Third, the framework for identifying and analysing moderating variables is a valuable tool that should be used in other corporate governance research as well as other accounting research. Finally, a limitation of this study is the use of accounting-based performance measures because of the expected earnings management behaviours by CEOs (Beasley, 1996; Healy & Wahlen, 1999; Burgstahler & Eames, 2003; Bradbury, Mak, & Tan, 2006), taking into account the weaknesses in corporate governance structures in the Egyptian listed companies. Future research should use market-based measures or combine accounting-based measures with market-based measures.

7. CONCLUSION

Egypt is currently moving towards adopting the Anglo-American model of corporate governance. This study focuses on the issue of CEO duality and its negative impact on corporate performance. It draws on agency theory to interpret and make sense of the empirical data. According to agency theory, the interests of shareholders are safeguarded only where different people occupying the two positions of the CEO and the chairman of the board of directors. This implies that CEO duality (i.e. the CEO serves also as the board chairman) is negatively associated with corporate performance. However, empirical evidence is mixed with respect to this prediction of agency theory. This paper aims at re-examining the predictions of agency theory with regard to the negative association between CEO duality and corporate performance using the financial statements for the year 2006 of most actively traded companies in the Egyptian stock market. It also examines the role of other corporate governance mechanisms (board size, top managerial ownership and institutional ownership) as moderating variables in the relationship between CEO duality and corporate performance. Moderated Regression Analysis is used to analyse the empirical data. The findings indicated that the hypothesized relationships between CEO duality, the moderating variables (top management owner-ship, board size and institutional ownership) and corporate performance have changed. It was found that board size was the only moderating variable (a homologiser variable), top management ownership was a suppressor variable and institutional ownership was simply another independent variable. For Egyptian companies characterized by large boards and low top management ownership, corporate performance is negatively affected by CEO duality and positively impacted by institutional ownership. Some research opportunities that extend this paper were introduced.

NOTES

1. This differs from two-tier board structure that consists of a supervisory board and an executive board of directors. The supervisory board oversees the direction of the business while the management board is responsible for the running of the business (Mallin, 2007).

2. A moderate significant relationship at the 0.10 level.

3. Homologiser variable is a type of moderators which influences the strength of the relationship, does not interact with the independent variable, and is not significantly related to either the independent or dependent variable. In such a situation, the error term is posited to be a function of the moderator variable.

4. The selection of 8 members was based on Jensen's (1993) assumption that when a board has more than seven or eight directors, the board of directors is less likely to function effectively and are easier for the CEO to control.

5. I focused only on large boards (members > 8) as most Egyptian companies have large board sizes (30 out of 40 companies).

6. I focused only on low top management ownership as mot Egyptian companies in the sample have low management ownership (36 out of 40 companies). In this regard, top management ownership is low when top management owns less than 20% of the company's total number of shares. The selection of this percentage is based on the assumption that 20% or more gives the owner the ability to exercise significant influence over operating and financial policies of the company.

7. Thanks to one of my anonymous reviewers for refereeing to the important role of outside directors and ownership concentration as moderator variables.

8. Thanks to my other anonymous reviewer for this research opportunity.

REFERENCES

Abdullah, S. (2004). Board composition, CEO duality and performance among Malaysian listed companies. *Corporate Governance*, *4*, 47–61.

Agrawal, A., & Chadha, S. (2005). Corporate governance and accounting scandals. *Journal of Law and Economics*, *48*(2), 371–406.

Balgobin, R. (2008). Global governance practice: The impact of measures taken to restore trust in corporate governance practice internationally. *Journal of Corporate Governance*, *7*(1), 7–21.

Baliga, B., Moyer, C., & Rao, R. (1996). CEO duality and firm performance: What's the fuss? *Strategic Management Journal*, *17*, 41–53.

Bantel, K. A., & Jackson, S. E. (1989). Top management and innovations in banking: Does the composition of the top team make a difference? *Strategic Management Journal*, *10*, 107–124.

Barnhart, S., & Rosenstein, S. (1998). Board composition, managerial ownership and firm performance. *The Financial Review*, *33*, 1–16.

Baron, R., & kenny, D. (1986). The moderator-mediator variable distinction in social psychological research: Conceptual, strategic and statistical considerations. *Journal of Personality and Social Psychology*, *51*(6), 1173–1182.

Bauer, R., Frijns, B., Otten, R., & Tourani, A. (2008). The impact of corporate governance on corporate performance: Evidence from Japan. *Pacific-Basin Finance Journal*, *16*(3), 236–251.

Beasley, M. (1996). An empirical analysis of the relation between the board of director composition and financial statement fraud. *The Accounting Review*, *71*, 443–465.

Bennedsen, M., Kongsted, H., & Nielsen, K. (2007). The causal effect of board size in the performance of small and medium-sized firms. *Journal of Banking and Finance*, *1*, 1–12.

Berg, S., & Smith, S. (1978). CEO and board chairman: A quantitative study of dual vs. unity board leadership. *Directors and Boards*, *3*, 34–39.

Boyd, B. (1995). CEO duality and firm performance: A contingency model. *Strategic Management Journal*, *16*, 301–312.

Bradbury, M., Mak, Y., & Tan, S. (2006). Board characteristics, audit committee characteristics and abnormal accruals. *Pacific Accounting Review*, *18*(2), 47–68.

Brickley, J., Coles, J., & Jarrell, G. (1997). Leadership structure: Separating the CEO and chairman of the board. *Journal of Corporate Finance*, *3*, 189–220.

Brickley, J., Coles, J., & Terry, R. (1994). Outside directors and the adoption of poison pills. *Journal of Financial Economics, 35*, 371–390.

Burgstahler, D., & Eames, M. (2003). Earning management to avoid earnings decreases and losses. *Journal of Accounting and Economics, 24*, 99–126.

Burns, T. (2001). Implications of information technology on corporate governance. *International Journal of Law and Information Technology, 9*(1), 21–38.

Chaganti, R., & Damanpour, F. (1991). Institutional ownership, capital structure and firm performance. *Strategic Management Journal, 12*, 479–491.

Chaganti, S., Mahajan, V., & Sharma, S. (1985). Corporate board size, composition and corporate failure in retailing industry. *Journal of Management Studies, 22*, 400–417.

Cheng, S. (2008). Board size and the variability of corporate performance. *Journal of Financial Economics, 87*, 157–176.

Chung, M., Michael, F., & Jeong-Bon, K. (2002). Institutional monitoring and opportunistic earning management. *Journal of Corporate Finance, 8*(1), 33–45.

Clarke, T. (2004). *Theories of corporate governance: The philosophical foundations of corporate governance.* London: Routledge Taylor and Francis Group.

Coles, J., McWilliams, V., & Sen, N. (2001). An examination of the relationship of governance mechanisms to performance. *Journal of Management, 27*(1), 23–55.

Cross, S. (2004). Corporate governance, information technology and the electronic company in the United Kingdom. *Information and Communication Technology Law, 13*(2), 117–128.

Dahya, J., & Travlos, N. G. (2000). Does the one man show pay? Theory and evidence on the dual CEO revisited. *European Financial Management, 6*, 85–98.

Daily, C., & Dalton, D. (1992). The relationship between governance structure and corporate performance in entrepreneurial firms. *Journal of Business Venturing, 7*(5), 375–386.

Daily, C., Dalton, D., & Cannella, A. (2003). Corporate governance: Decades of dialogue and data. *Academy of Management Review, 28*(3), 371–382.

Daily, C. M., & Dalton, D. R. (1994). Bankruptcy and corporate governance: The impact of board composition and structure. *Academy of Management Journal, 37*, 1603–1617.

Dalton, D., & Kesner, I. (1987). Composition and CEO duality in boards of directors: An international perspective. *Journal of International Business Studies, 28*, 33–42.

Davidson, R., Stewart, T., & Kent, P. (2005). Internal governance structures and earnings management. *Accounting and Finance, 45*, 241–247.

Davis, G. (1991). Agents without principles? The spread of the poison pill through the intercorporate network. *Administrative Science Quarterly, 36*, 583–613.

Dayton, N. (1984). Corporate governance: The other side of the coin. *Harvard Business Review, 62*, 34–37.

Donaldson, L., & Davis, J. (1991). Stewardship theory or agency theory: CEO governance and shareholder returns. *Australian Journal of Management, 16*, 49–64.

Dunk, A. (1993). The effect of budget emphasis and information asymmetry on the relation between budgetary participation and slack. *The Accounting Review, 68*(2), 400–410.

Eighme, J., & Cashell, J. (2002). Internal auditors' roles in overcoming the financial reporting crisis. *International Auditing, 17*, 3–10.

Eisenberg, T., Sundgren, S., & Wells, M. (1998). Larger board size and decreasing firm value in small firms. *Journal of Financial Economics, 48*, 113–139.

Eisenhardt, K. (1989). Making fast strategic decisions in high-velocity environments. *Academy of Management Journal, 32*, 543–576.

Erhardt, N., Werbel, J., & Shrader, C. (2003). Board of directors diversity and firm financial performance. *Corporate Governance: An International Review, 11*, 102–111.

Fama, E., & Jensen, C. (1983). Separation of ownership and control. *Journal of Law Economics, 26*, 301–325.

Finkelstein, S., & D'Aveni, R. (1994). CEO duality as a double-edged sword: How boards of directors balance entrenchment avoidance and unity of command. *Academy of Management Journal, 37*, 1079–1108.

Gompers, P., Ishii, J., & Metrick, A. (2003). Corporate governance and euity prices. *Quarterly Journal of Economics, 118*(February), 107–155.

Hartmann, F., & Moers, F. (1999). Testing contingency hypotheses in budgetary research: An evaluation of the use of moderated regression analysis. *Accounting, Organisations and Society, 24*(4), 291–315.

Healy, P., & Wahlen, J. (1999). A Review of the earning management literature and its implications for standard setting. *Accounting Horizons, 13*(4), 365–383.

Hermalin, B., & Weisbach, M. (2003). Boards of directors as an endogenously determined institution: A survey of the economic literature. *Federal Reserve Bank of New York Policy Review, 9*, 7–26.

Jensen, M. (1993). The modern industrial revolution, exit and the failure of internal control systems. *Journal of Finance, 48*(July), 831–880.

Jensen, M., & Meckling, W. (1976). Theory of the firm: Managerial behaviour, agency costs and ownership structure. *Journal of Financial Economics, 3*, 305–360.

John, K., & Senbet, L. W. (1998). Corporate governance and board effectiveness. *Journal of Banking and Finance, 22*, 371–403.

Kesner, I., & Dalton, D. (1986). Boards of directors and the checks and (Im)balances of corporate governance. *Business Horizons, 29*(5), 17–23.

Klapper, L., & Love, I. (2004). Corporate governance, investor protection, and performance in emerging markets. *Journal of Corporate Finance, 10*, 703–728.

Klein, A. (2002). Audit committee, board of director characteristics, and earnings management. *Journal of Accounting and Economics, 33*(August), 375–400.

Levy, L. (1981). Reforming board reform. *Harvard Business Review, 59*, 166–172.

Lin, Y. (2005). Corporate governance, leadership structure and CEO composition: Evidence from Taiwan. *Corporate Governance: An International Review, 13*, 824–835.

Lipton, M., & Lorsch, J. (1992). A modest proposal for improved corporate governance. *Business Lawyer, 59*(November), 59–77.

Mak, Y. T. (1996). The voluntary use of outside directors by initial public offering firms. *Corporate Governance, 4*, 94–106.

Mak, Y. T., & Li, Y. (2001). Determinants of corporate ownership and board structure: Evidence from Singapore. *Journal of Corporate Finance, 7*, 235–256.

Mallin, C. (2002). Corporate governance, institutional investors and socially responsible investment. *Corporate Governance: An International Review, 10*, 1–3.

Mallin, C. (2007). *Corporate governance* (2nd ed.). New York: Oxford University Press.

McCarthy, D., & Puffer, S. (2008). Interpreting the ethicality of corporate governance decisions in Russia: Utilising integrative social contracts theory to evaluate the relevance of agency theory norms. *Academy of Management Review, 33*(1), 22–31.

Molz, R. (1988). Managerial domination of boards of directors and financial performance. *Journal of Business Research, 16*, 235–249.

Morck, R., Shleifer, A., & Vishny, R. (1988). Management ownership and market valuation: An empirical analysis. *Journal of Financial Economics, 20*(March), 293–315.

Muth, M., & Donaldson, L. (1998). Stewardship theory and board structure: A contingency approach. *Corporate Governance: An International Review, 6*, 5–28.

Omran, M., Bolbol, A., & Fatheldin, A. (2008). Corporate governance and firm performance in Arab equity markets: Does Ownership concentration matter? *International Review of Law and Economics, 28*(1), 32–45.

Parker, L. (2005). Corporate governance crisis down under: Post-Enron accounting education and research inertia. *European Accounting Review, 14*(2), 383–394.

Phan, P., & Yoshikawa, T. (2000). Agency theory and Japanese corporate governance. *Asia Pacific Journal of Management, 17*(1), 1–27.

Pi, L., & Timme, S. (1993). Corporate control and bank efficiency. *Journal of Banking and Finance, 17*, 515–530.

Rechner, L., & Dalton, D. (1991). CEO duality and organizational performance: A longitudinal analysis. *Strategic Management Journal, 12*, 155–160.

Rhoades, D., Rechner, P., & Sundaramurthy, C. (2001). A meta-analysis of board leadership structure and financial performance: Are "two heads better than one? *Corporate Governance: An International Review, 9*, 311–319.

Rosenberg, M. (1968). *The logic of survey analysis.* New York: Basic Books, Inc.

Russell, C., & Babko, P. (1992). Moderated regression analysis and likert scales: Too coarse for comfort. *Journal of Applied Psychology, 77*(3), 336–342.

Salancik, C., & Pfeffer, J. (1980). Effects of ownership and performance on executive tenure in US corporations. *Academy of Management Journal, 23*, 635–664.

Seal, W. (2006). Management accounting and corporate governance: An institutional interpretation of the agency problem. *Management Accounting Research, 17*(4), 389–408.

Sharma, S., Durand, R., & Gur-Arie, O. (1981). Identification and analysis of moderator variables. *Journal of Marketing Research, 18*(3), 291–300.

Shleifer, A., & Vishny, R. W. (1997). A survey of corporate governance. *Journal of Finance, 52*, 737–783.

Smith, M. (2003). *Research methods in accounting.* London: SAGE Publications.

Tipgos, M., & Keefe, T. (2004). A comprehensive structure of corporate governance in post-Enron-corporate America. *CPA Journal, 74*(12), 46–51.

Yermack, D. (1996). Higher market valuation of companies with a small board of directors. *Journal of Financial Economics, 40*(February), 185–212.

BOARD CHARACTERISTICS, OWNERSHIP STRUCTURE AND EARNINGS QUALITY: MALAYSIAN EVIDENCE

Hafiza Aishah Hashim and Susela Devi

ABSTRACT

Purpose – *The relationship between the board characteristics (i.e. board independence, CEO duality, board size, board meeting and board tenure) and the ownership structure (i.e. managerial ownership, family ownership and institutional ownership) and earnings quality is examined.*

Design/methodology/approach – *Data from 280 non-financial companies listed on Bursa Malaysia's Main Board for the year 2004 is used.*

Findings – *Significant association was found between board tenure and earnings quality. In addition, a positive significant association was found between outside board ownership and family ownership and earnings quality. However no significant relationship was found between board of directors' independence and earnings quality.*

Research limitations/implications – *The association between audit committees' characteristics and earnings quality was not examined. An examination of the impact of ownership structure on boards of directors and audit committees is warranted. An investigation of the impact of the*

Corporate Governance in Less Developed and Emerging Economies
Research in Accounting in Emerging Economies, Volume 8, 97–123
Copyright © 2008 by Emerald Group Publishing Limited
All rights of reproduction in any form reserved
ISSN: 1479-3563/doi:10.1016/S1479-3563(08)08004-3

ownership structure on earnings quality in Malaysia using separate test on family-controlled and non-family-controlled firms is suggested.

Practical implications – *The appropriateness of policy directives requiring majority independent directors may be considered by policy makers.*

Originality/value – *The conflict of interest between outside shareholders and managers in a diffused ownership support the agency theory. However, utility of agency theory to explain the conflicts between the controlling owners and the minority shareholders where ownership concentration is prevalent is limited. Whilst demonstrating the dominant impact of ownership structure on earnings quality in Malaysia the study calls for alternative explanations of corporate governance practices in different institutional settings.*

1. INTRODUCTION

The Asian financial crisis in the late 1990s as well as the highly publicized scandals in the United States revealed the critical need for firms in both developed and developing countries to improve corporate governance practices and to regain investors' confidence in the integrity of accounting numbers. Erosion in financial reporting quality has raised troubling questions about various aspects of corporate governance. Consequently most Asian countries[1] have been proactive in improving and strengthening corporate governance systems. Malaysia introduced the Malaysian Code on Corporate Governance (MCCG) (2000) outlining the principles and best practices for corporate governance. The Malaysian Code was fully implemented in January 2001 with a revamp of the listing requirements of the Kuala Lumpur Stock Exchange.[2] The Revamped Listing Requirements represent a major milestone in corporate governance reform,[3] creating an environment that demands higher standards of conduct and a higher quality of disclosure from corporate governance participants in Malaysia.

However, developing countries in Asia face problems in strengthening corporate governance. Bhattacharyay (2004) highlights seven key problems including (1) excessive government intervention; (2) highly concentrated ownership structure; (3) weak external discipline in the corporate sector; (4) weak legal systems and regulatory framework; (5) lack of quality information; (6) lack of investors' protection; and (7) lack of a developed capital market that undermines the effectiveness of the corporate governance mechanism employed in Asia. Contrary to the conflict of interest between outside shareholders and managers in a diffused ownership, such as that commonly found in the United Kingdom and the United States, the agency problem centres around conflicts between the controlling owners and minority shareholders in Asia, where the ownership concentration is prevalent (Claessens & Fan, 2002). The concentrated ownership creates agency conflicts between controlling owners and minority shareholders, which are difficult to mitigate through the traditional functions of a board of directors (Fan & Wong, 2003). The tightness of ownership allows self-interested behaviour of managers to go unchallenged, internally by the board of directors and externally by takeover markets, as the controlling owners, who are often also the managers, gain effective control of a corporation and have the power to determine how the company is run and may expropriate the minority shareholders' wealth. Thus, this study contributes to this ongoing debate. The objective of this study is to examine the relationship between one aspect of the internal governance mechanisms – the board characteristics, namely, the board independence, CEO duality, board size, frequency of board meetings and board tenure, and ownership structure and earnings quality of Malaysian listed corporations.

There are four motivations for this study. First, while there is extensive literature that discusses the role of the ownership structure in corporate governance around the world (Shleifer & Vishny, 1997; La Porta, Lopez De Silanes, & Shleifer, 1999), there is scarcity of prior research that empirically examines the relationship between the ownership structure and financial reporting outcomes in the context of a developing country. Except for prior studies that examine the relationship between the ownership structure and performance (see, e.g. Bathala & Rao, 1995; Mitton, 2002; Ng, 2005; Vethanayagam, Yahya, & Haron, 2006), little is known about the relationship between ownership structure and financial reporting quality, especially on the earnings quality issues in less-developed economies.

Second, given the conflicting theoretical viewpoints regarding the relationship between family ownership and agency costs, this study seeks to investigate whether the existence of family board members on the board provides incentives to reduce or create agency costs in the Malaysian context. Some argue that family-controlled firms reduce agency costs as they carry along their family name and reputation into the business while others argue that family-controlled firms create agency costs by extracting private benefits at the expense of minority shareholders (Bartholomeusz & Tanewski, 2006).

Third, recent literature acknowledges the importance of the institutional investors in corporate monitoring to protect minority shareholder's interests. Institutional investors in Malaysia have emerged as a powerful constitution with a significant role in corporate governance. The establishment of the Minority Shareholder Watchdog Group (MSWG) that represents the five largest institutional funds in Malaysia, that is, the Employee Provident Fund (EPF), *Lembaga Tabung Angkatan Tentera*[4] (LTAT), *Lembaga Tabung Haji*[5] (LTH), Social Security Organization (SOCSO) and *Permodalan Nasional Berhad*[6] (PNB), to monitor and deter abuses by company insiders shows the Malaysian government's commitment to encourage shareholder activism in Malaysia. Prior studies that examine the role of institutional investors from the perspective of financial reporting quality are limited (Velury & Jenkins, 2006) and this paper is the first to investigate the impact of institutional ownership on earnings quality in the Malaysian environment.

Fourth, prior studies linking institutional features and financial reporting quality in the East Asian market are cross country studies (Fan & Wong, 2002; Leuz, Nanda, & Wysocki, 2003; Boonlert-U-Thai, Meek, & Nabar, 2006). However, findings of cross country studies have been questioned for limited sample size, endogeneity problems, noisy variables and severe omissions of correlated variables (Gul, 2006). Since different countries have different levels of investor protection, legal enforcement and ownership structure, it is important to acknowledge these factors when discussing earnings quality in different countries that are based on different socio-economic (Boonlert-U-Thai et al., 2006; Lo, 2007) to provide a more meaningful earnings quality study.

The remainder of the paper is organized as follows. Section 2 discusses the relevant literature to develop research hypotheses. Section 3 explains the sample selection, research method and variable measurement. Section 4 discusses the research results. Section 5 identifies additional potential issues for future research and concludes.

2. LITERATURE REVIEW AND HYPOTHESIS DEVELOPMENT

One of the most important functions that corporate governance can play is to ensure the quality of the financial reporting process (Cohen, Krishnamoorthy, & Wright, 2004). Watts and Zimmerman (1978, p. 113) state that '*one* function *of financial reporting is to constrain management to act in the shareholders' interest*'. Given the increasing complexity of business today, more comprehensive information is required by investors to make their investment decisions. McKinsey and Company (2002) survey on corporate governance issues, found that the majority of investors agree that corporate governance is of great concern and that strengthening the quality of accounting disclosure should be top priority. Majority of institutional investors are willing to pay a high premium for companies with good corporate governance, averaging 12–14% in North America and Western Europe, 20–25% in Asia and Latin America and over 30% in Eastern Europe and Africa. The survey further evidences that the majority of the respondents (i.e.71%) state that accounting disclosure is the most important factor impacting their investment decisions and 52% of the respondents identify improving financial reporting quality as the governance priority for policymakers.

Bushman and Smith (2001) note that publicly reported accounting information can be used as important input information in various corporate governance mechanisms. The importance of corporate governance mechanisms to improve financial reporting quality is widely acknowledged (see Cohen et al., 2004, for a comprehensive discussion) and good governance helps reduce the risk of financial reporting problems. Hermanson (2003, p. 44) notes: '*Good governance goes in-hand with reduced risk of financial reporting problems and other bad accounting outcomes*'. Evidence of the association between poor governance and poor financial reporting quality including earnings manipulation, financial restatements and fraud is extensive (see, e.g. Beasley, 1996; Dechow, Sloan, & Sweeney, 1996; Peasnell, Pope, & Young, 2000; Klein, 2002; Kao & Chen, 2004; Davidson, Goodwin-Stewart, & Kent, 2005). These early studies focus mainly on the role of boards as a monitoring tool and the contribution of non-executive directors in enhancing the quality and integrity of accounting information. Cohen et al. (2004) discuss the corporate governance mosaic and financial reporting quality. They identify two mechanisms: internal, comprising board of directors, audit committee, internal auditors, external auditors and management; and external, comprising courts and legal system, regulators, financial analysts, stock exchanges, legislators and stockholders. This study focuses on one aspect of the internal mechanism, the Board of Directors.

Furthermore, Li (1994) argues that the differences in corporate governance across countries emerge as a result of the variations in the ownership structure. An understanding of the effects of various ownership structures is vital to explaining the corporate governance and control process of firms under different institutional arrangements and national contexts. Mitton (2002) finds that firm-level differences in variables, related to corporate governance of five East Asian countries, i.e. Indonesia, Korea, Malaysia, Philippines and Thailand, had a strong impact on firm performance during the 1997–1998 financial crisis. Specifically, firms with higher disclosure quality, higher outside ownership concentration and less diversified operations revealed greater stock performance during the crisis. Hence, this suggests that in countries with weak legal protection of minority shareholders, at least some power to protect minority shareholder interests lies at the firm level, where those with higher disclosure quality and transparency, a more favourable ownership structure and less diversified operations appear to provide protection to the minority shareholder during the crisis (Mitton, 2002).

In Malaysia, one-man or family run companies (Halim, 2001) and significant government equity holdings (Abdullah, 2006) distinguish the ownership pattern of Malaysian companies and may complicate the effectiveness of corporate governance mechanisms. Large ownership or ownership concentration where controlling shareholders have more than 50% ownership is common in Malaysia and may contribute to deficiencies in the corporate governance system employed (Thillainathan, 1999). World Bank (2005) reports that about 85% of companies in Malaysia have owner-managers; the post of CEO, chairman of the board or vice-chairman belongs to a member of the controlling family or a nominee; and large shareholders typically owning more than 60% of shares. Companies with extensive individual and family owners and managers tend to discourage professionalism, encourage non-compliance and facilitate false accounting as well as result in a severe conflict of interest (Halim, 2001). Thus, the following discussion focuses on the board characteristics and ownership structure literature to develop hypotheses on its relation to financial reporting quality.

2.1. Board Characteristics

2.1.1. Board Independence
Advocates of the agency theory believe that boards comprising of a majority of outside directors reduces agency conflicts as they provide an effective monitoring tool for the board (Fama & Jensen, 1983). They argue that the inclusion of outside directors[7] increases the boards' ability to be more

efficient in monitoring the top management and ensures there is no collusion with top managers to expropriate stockholder wealth as they have an incentive to develop their reputation as experts in decision control. Normally, outside directors are expert managers from other large organizations and with their expertise, independence, objectivity and legal power, outside directors become potentially powerful governance mechanisms to mitigate agency costs and protect shareholders wealth (Li, 1994).

The independent directors must be solely outside directors who have no other relationship with the companies except being on the board of directors. For Malaysian companies, 'independent director' is defined in Chapter 1 of the Listing Requirements of the Kuala Lumpur Stock Exchange (KLSE) as '*independent of management and free from any business or other relationship which could interfere with the exercise of independent judgment or the ability to act in the best interests of an applicant or listed issuer*'. The KLSE Listing Requirements 2001 also include '*independence from concentrated and holdings of shares*' in their definition of director's independence. The MCCG views that good corporate governance rests firmly with the board of directors and the Code requires one third of the board to be comprised of independent non-executive directors in order to provide independent judgment to the decision process.

Efficient monitoring by non-executive directors, who are free from managerial influence, improves the quality of financial information (Higgs Report, 2003). A number of studies in developed countries report that a higher proportion of independent non-executive directors on the board is associated with higher financial reporting quality (Beasley, 1996; Dechow et al., 1996; Peasnell et al., 2000; Klein, 2002; Davidson et al., 2005). As outside members do not play a direct role in the management of the company, their existence may provide an effective monitoring tool to the board and thus produce higher quality financial reports (Peasnell et al., 2000). However, evidence from countries with a highly concentrated ownership structure is inconclusive. On one hand, Kao and Chen (2004) and Jaggi, Leung, and Gul (2007) find significant negative evidence between earnings management and the presence of a higher proportion of outside directors in Taiwan and Hong Kong. This suggests that the inclusion of a larger proportion of outside members on the board of directors provides better oversight of management to mitigate earnings management activity. On the other hand, Park and Shin (2004) fail to find empirical support of an association between earnings management and board independence in Canada, where the ownership structure is highly concentrated and a large block holder controls the public traded firms.

Further, Abdullah and Mohd Nasir (2004) and Abdul Rahman and Mohamed Ali (2006) do not find any significant association between independence of boards and earnings management in Malaysia. Furthermore, Jaggi et al. (2007) finds an insignificant relationship between proportions of non-executive directors and accrual quality in high family ownership samples of Hong Kong listed companies, which suggests that the monitoring effectiveness of independent directors is reduced in family-controlled firms. Because of these conflicting results, Malaysian evidence is re-tested in this study and it is hypothesized that:

H_1. Board independence is positively associated with earnings quality.

2.1.2. CEO Duality

In addition to the requirement of a well-balanced board, the MCCG (2000) recommends the separation of the role between Chairman and CEO. This is to avoid a considerable concentration of power if the two roles are carried out by one individual. The separation of the position of CEO and Chairman provides essential check and balance over management's performance. However in the case of CEO duality, the Code recommends that strong independence elements must be induced (MCCG, 2000).

The supporters of role separation between the CEO and chairman believe that combining the two positions compromises a board's independence (Coombes & Wong, 2004). They contend that the board's principal role is to oversee the company's management and the role of the CEO is to manage the company well, thus protecting the shareholders' interest. This is well supported in the agency theory that suggests splitting the two jobs is desired to make the board more independent. Nevertheless, advocates of stewardship theory suggest a combination of the CEO and chairman to enhance the decision process and implement the company's objectives with the minimum interference from the board (Lin, 2005). The combination of the two roles facilitates decision-making and helps a board stay better informed about company matters without a confusion of accountability (Coombes & Wong, 2004).

While arguments for separating the roles between the chairman and the CEO roles are more persuasive, existing empirical analyses yield mixed results of the impact of role duality on financial reporting quality. Kao and Chen (2004), Xie et al. (2003), Davidson et al. (2005) and Abdul Rahman and Mohamed Ali (2006) do not find an association between CEO duality and earnings management activity. However, Abdul Rahman and Haniffa (2005) reveal significant relationship between role duality and performance for pooled data from year 1996 to 2000 for a Malaysian sample. Surprisingly, their study shows a gradual decrease in percentage of separation role of Chairman and CEO from 1996 to 2000 although the MCCG (2000) recommends a separation role to ensure balance and authority. Despite this conflicting result, it is hypothesized that:

H$_2$. Firms with a separation role between the Chairman and the CEO are likely to have greater earnings quality.

2.1.3. Board Size

Another important characteristic that affect financial reporting quality is board size (Beasley, 1996; Xie et al., 2003; Kao & Chen, 2004). Jensen (1993) posits that smaller boards provide better controlling function than larger boards. In addition, Kao and Chen (2004) suggest that larger board size will weaken the functioning of the board due to difficulty in achieving efficient communication between board members.

Beasley (1996) confirms that as board size decreases, the likelihood of financial statement fraud also decreases. Kao and Chen (2004) and Abdul Rahman and Mohamed Ali (2006) find a positive association between board size and the extent of earnings management. Larger board size increases earnings management as they are unable to monitor the management effectively compared to a smaller size board. Coordinating and processing problems becomes more difficult when the boards are too large and larger board size is likely to have free riding by individual directors (Abdul Rahman & Mohamed Ali, 2006).

Contradictory to Beasley (1996) and Kao and Chen (2004), Xie et al. (2003) support that larger board may be better in preventing earnings management compared to smaller boards as larger boards may be more likely to have independent directors with corporate and financial expertise. They evidence significant negative association between larger board size and the level of discretionary accruals and suggest that larger number of experienced directors helps to prevent earnings management.

In Malaysia, the MCCG (2000) recommends that the impact of size on the effectiveness of the board must be considered, but does not recommend any specified number. Based on both arguments, the direction of board size is indeterminate in this study and it is hypothesized that:

H$_3$. The size of boards of directors is associated with earnings quality.

2.1.4. Board Meeting Frequency

Xie et al. (2003) argue that boards that meet more often could reduce earnings management activity as they are able to allocate more time on issues such as earnings management while boards that seldom meet are unlikely to focus on these issues. Boards that meet more are expected to have lower earnings management and therefore report higher quality earnings compared to boards that seldom meet. They found a negative association between level of earnings management and the meeting frequency of the board and suggest that board activity provides effective monitoring mechanisms of corporate financial reporting.

In Malaysia, the Malaysian Institute of Chartered Secretaries and Administrators (MAICSA) has issued guidelines on the board meeting through its best practice guide, *A Guide to Annual General Meeting* and *The Company Secretary: A Reference Kit* (Zulkafli et al., 2005). Further, MCCG (2000) recommends that the board meet regularly and disclose the number of board meetings held a year together with details of attendance of each individual director. This disclosure enables shareholder to identify whether the board is in control and directors are committed in doing their work. Even though the desired number of meetings required for board to be effective is not stated, the Code recommends that less than four times a year of meetings is not a good indicator that the board is still in control (MCCG, 2000). It is hypothesized that:

H₄. Board meetings are positively associated with earnings quality.

2.1.5. Board Tenure

There are two conflicting views on the impact of director tenure on board effectiveness (Vafeas, 2005). On one hand, it is argued that more experienced directors have greater knowledge about the firm's operation that enable them to exercise better decision control compared to less experienced directors. On the other hand, given the directors have served the firm for quite a long time, their independence is compromised as they become more likely to befriend management and hence be less critical about the quality of financial reports (Vafeas, 2005). Beasley (1996) suggests that the ability of boards to monitor management effectively is consistent with the increased number of years they serve. He finds negative and significant association between the number of years of board service for outside directors and the likelihood of financial statement fraud. Since there are two conflicting arguments, the direction of the next hypothesis is indeterminate:

H$_5$. Board tenure is associated with earnings quality.

2.2. Ownership Structure

2.2.1. Managerial Ownership

While having independent directors appears to be critical for the effectiveness of the board's monitoring function, the extent of shareholding held by management may affect control over the board. Jensen and Meckling (1976) theorize as management ownership increases, their interests will be more closely aligned with owners and the need for intense monitoring by the board should decrease. Bathala and Rao (1995) argue that the role of outside board members is less critical for firms with a higher proportion of inside ownership. Their study shows that higher proportions of insider ownership held by inside board members helps to closely align the managerial and shareholder interests, thus reducing the need for intense monitoring by external board members.

While Bathala and Rao (1995) focus on inside member's ownership, Beasley (1996) studies the effect of outside director's ownership and financial statement fraud. He observes a significant negative relationship between outside directors' ownership and the likelihood of financial statement fraud, suggesting that a higher level of ownership held by outside directors does help reduce the likelihood of financial statement fraud. Additionally, Peasnell, Pope, and Young (2005) investigates managerial share ownership as the intervening variable and posit that the constraining association between earnings management and the proportion of outside directors will be more prominent when the level of managerial share ownership is low. The demand for non-executive directors is lower in companies where the level of managerial ownership is high as shareholders let the management run the companies (Peasnell, Pope, & Young, 1998).

Given the 'closely-knit' ownership of Malaysian companies, Abdullah (2006) investigates the influence of management and non-executives interest on financial distressed firms of an 86-matched sample of distressed and non-distressed companies for the period 1999–2001. He fails to find an association between board independence and CEO duality on firm value, however, he finds a significant association between management interests and firm value at the lower level and higher level of ownership.

Pergola (2005) argues that Beasley's (1996) study does not distinguish between the inside and outside stock ownership to see the impact of management's ability to negate board effectiveness. Therefore, in this study the influence of managerial ownership on earnings quality is investigated separately for inside and outside board ownership. The hypotheses are:

H₆. Inside board ownership is positively associated with earnings quality.

H₇. Outside board ownership is positively associated with earnings quality.

2.2.2. Family Ownership

La Porta et al. (1999) reviews the corporate ownership structure of 27 countries around the world and reveals that except in economies with very good shareholder protection such as the United States, families or the state typically control firms in countries with poor shareholder protection.

Bartholomeusz and Tanewski (2006) find that family firms have lower proportions of independent directors, a higher proportion of 'grey' directors and a greater combination of roles between CEO and Chairman compared to the non-family-controlled firms in an Australian study. In Hong Kong, however, Ng (2005) finds that at a relatively low level of family ownership (16.86% and below), managers, who are normally the professional managers, entrench their interests with the companies as their shareholdings are not substantial and tend to maximize their interest. However, at a wide spectrum of medium level of ownership (16.86–63.17%), the results show that family managers align their interests with the companies and the performance is improved with greater ownership concentration. Again when family managers gain a relatively high level of ownership beyond (63.17%), they become so powerful and entrench their interests with the companies to the detriment of the minority shareholders' interest. In a similar environment, Similarly, Jaggi et al. (2007) note that outside directors monitoring effectiveness is reduced in family-controlled firms, which results in a lower quality of reported earnings in Hong Kong.

Haniffa and Cooke (2002) find a negative significant association between the proportion of family members on the board and the extent of voluntary disclosures by Malaysian companies. The presence of many family members as board members may result in less demand for voluntary disclosure as they have better access to inside information. Additionally, Mohd Ghazali and Weetman (2006) report similar findings between family domination and the extent of voluntary disclosure after the 1997 financial crisis. They argue that family-owned companies remain secretive even after the corporate governance reform, which suggests they preserve a tradition inherited from the past and resist attempts to change their attitudes towards greater voluntary disclosure at the point of regulatory change. Since there are two different theoretical viewpoints on the role of family ownership and agency costs, the direction of the next hypothesis is indeterminate:

H8. Family ownership is associated with earnings quality.

2.2.3. Institutional Ownership

To date, institutional investors' participation has emerged as an important force in corporate monitoring serving as a mechanism to protect minority shareholder's interest (Daily, Dalton, & Cannella, 2003). The significant increase in the institutional investors' shareholdings has led to the formation of a large and powerful constituency which plays a significant role in corporate governance.[8]

Involvement of institutional investors may improve corporate governance practices by mitigating the problems associated with conflict between controlling owners and minority shareholders in Asian firms (Claessens & Fan, 2002). Institutional investors are able to diligently monitor as they have the resources, expertise and stronger incentives to actively monitor the actions of management and prevent managers' opportunistic behaviour (Wan Hussin & Ibrahim, 2003). Owning substantial shareholdings makes it difficult to sell shares immediately at the prevailing price, and therefore, the institutional investors have greater incentives to closely monitor companies with high free cash flow (Chung, Firth, & Kim, 2005). Mitra and Cready (2005) observe that active monitoring from the institutional investors also helps to prevent managerial opportunistic reporting behaviour and improves the quality of governance in the financial reporting process.

Abdullah (1999) is the first to examine the relationship between institutional shareholdings and accounting earnings quality (measured by earnings response coefficient) and finds evidence that the presence of institutional investors leads to lower earnings quality. He argues that Malaysian institutional investors prefer short-term investments rather than long-term achievement thereby inevitably causing their decision to dispose of their substantial shareholdings to dramatically depress the market share price and supporting the 'myopic investor' hypothesis. However, although findings by Abdullah (1999) may have been appropriate at that time, recent capital market development initiatives[9] have encouraged greater institutional investors' participation as corporate monitoring. Institutional investors in Malaysia nowadays have become a very large and powerful constitution, playing a very significant role in corporate governance to protect minority shareholder's interest.[10] Abdul Wahab, How, & Verhoeven (2007) find that institutional investors use corporate governance practice as a measuring tool for their investment decisions, suggesting that firms with better corporate governance practices attract higher institutional ownership from institutional investors. For this study it is hypothesized that:

H9. Institutional ownership is positively associated with earnings quality.

3. METHODOLOGY

3.1. Sample Selection

At the end of 2005, there were 649 financial and non-financial companies listed on Bursa Malaysia's Main Board. Due to different statutory requirements, all banks, insurance and unit trust companies were excluded from the population of interest. In addition, utilities companies were also excluded from the population of interest because they possess different incentives and opportunities to manage earnings (Peasnell et al., 2000; Abdul Rahman & Mohamed Ali, 2006). After eliminating 55 financial companies and 2 utilities companies, the sample size is reduced to 592 non-financial companies. As there are strict data requirements for the accrual quality estimation (to calculate earnings quality measure for year 2004, 7 years complete accounting data is required, $t = 1999\text{--}2005$), the sample is further reduced to 426 non-financial companies. 8 companies belonging to industries with less than 10 observations were also eliminated from the analysis.[11] Earnings quality accounting data is obtained from the Perfect Analysis Database and any missing financial data was collected manually from respective annual reports. Information pertaining to boards of directors and ownership was obtained from annual report disclosures. Further, 138 companies were excluded as the required financial and corporate governance data was not available, resulting in a final sample of 280 non-financial companies with complete data for earnings quality, board characteristics and ownership.

3.2. Regression Model

This study used a linear multiple regression analysis to test the association between the dependent variable of earnings quality and the independent variables: board independence, CEO duality, board size, board meetings, board tenure, managerial ownership, family ownership and institutional ownership.

$$EQ = \beta_0 + \beta_1 BIND + \beta_2 CEODUAL + \beta_3 BDSIZE + \beta_4 BDMEET$$
$$+ \beta_5 BDTENURE + \beta_6 INSOWNS + \beta_7 OUTOWNS + \beta_8 FAMILY$$
$$+ \beta_9 INSTITUTIONAL + \beta_{10} LGSIZE + \beta_{11} ROA + \varepsilon$$

Where, EQ is measured by accrual quality based on modified Dechow and Dichev (2002) model[12], BIND is the number of independent NEDs/total number of board members, CEODUAL equals 1 if the roles of the chairman and CEO are combined and 0 otherwise, BDSIZE the total number of directors on the board of the company, BDMEET the total number of board meetings, BDTENURE the average number of years of board service of independent non-executive directors on the board of the company, INSOWNS the percentage of shares held by inside board members including executive directors and non-independent non-executive directors, OUT-OWNS the percentage of shares held by independent non-executive directors, FAMILY the proportion of family members to total number directors on the board, INSTITUTIONAL the proportion of shares owned by institutional investors to total number of shares issued, LGSIZE the log of total asset, ROA the ratio of net income to total assets and ε the error term.

Consistent with prior studies, this study includes firm size and return on assets as control variables in the regression model. The log of total assets is used to measure firm size and to control for the firm size effect (Jaggi et al., 2007) and return on assets was used to control firms with different performance (Abdul Rahman & Mohamed Ali, 2006).

3.3. Earnings Quality Variable

The modified Dechow and Dichev (2002) accrual quality model as used in Francis, LaFond, Olsson, and Schipper (2005) is used to measure earnings quality. This is considered as a better proxy for earnings quality (Jaggi et al., 2007). This measure is based on the observation that accruals map into cash flow realizations and regardless of managerial intent, the accrual quality is affected by the measurement error in accruals. In Dechow and Dichev (2002) the estimated residuals from firm-specific regressions of working capital accruals on past, present and future cash flow from operation capture total accruals estimation error by management and are viewed as an inverse measure of earnings quality. For a more complete characterization of the relationship between accruals and cash flow, Francis et al. (2005) extend the Dechow and Dichev (2002) accrual quality model by including two additional variables, i.e. change in revenue and property, and plant and equipment (PPE). McNichols (2002) opine that combining Dechow and Dichev (2002) model and Jones (1991) model variables significantly increases the explanatory power of the accrual quality model.

$$\frac{\Delta \text{TCA}_{j,t}}{\text{Assets}_{j,t}} = \varphi_{0,j} + \varphi_{1,j} \frac{\text{CFO}_{j,t-1}}{\text{Assets}_{j,t}} + \varphi_{2,j} \frac{\text{CFO}_{j,t}}{\text{Assets}_{j,t}}$$

$$+ \varphi_{3,j} \frac{\text{CFO}_{j,t+1}}{\text{Assets}_{j,t}} + \varphi_{2,j} \frac{\Delta \text{REV}_{j,t}}{\text{Assets}_{j,t}} + \varphi_{2,j} \frac{\text{PPE}_{j,t}}{\text{Assets}_{j,t}} + v_{j,t}$$

Where, $\Delta \text{TCA}_{j,t}$ is the firm js total current accruals in year t, $= (\Delta \text{CA}_{j,t} - \Delta \text{CL}_{j,t} - \Delta \text{Cash}_{j,t} + \Delta \text{STDEBT}_{j,t})$; $\Delta \text{CA}_{j,t}$ the firm js change in current assets between years $t-1$ and t; $\Delta \text{CL}_{j,t}$ the firm js change in current liabilities between years $t-1$ and t; $\Delta \text{Cash}_{j,t}$ the firm js change in cash between years $t-1$ and t; $\Delta \text{STDEBT}_{j,t}$ the firm js change in debt in current liabilities between years $t-1$ and t; $\text{Assets}_{j,t}$ the firm js average total assets in year t and $t-1$; $\text{CFO}_{j,t}$ the firm js net cash flow from operation in year t; $\Delta \text{REV}_{j,t}$ the firm js change in revenue in year $t-1$ and t and $\text{PPE}_{j,t}$ the firm js gross value of PPE in year t.

For each firm-year, the above equation is estimated cross-sectionally for all firms (minimum 10 firms within each industry groups) using rolling 7-year windows. These estimations yield 5 firm- and year-specific residuals, $v_{j,t}$, $t = t-4, \dots t$, which form the basis for the accrual metric. Accrual Quality $_{j,t} = \sigma(v_{j,t})$, is equal to the standard deviation of the firm js estimated residuals. Larger standard deviations of residuals correspond to poorer accrual quality and vice versa. Following DeFond, Hung, and Trezevant (2007) the standard deviation score is multiplied by -1 so that a higher score indicates higher earnings quality (EQ).

4. RESULTS AND DISCUSSIONS

4.1. Descriptive Statistics

Table 1 presents the descriptive statistics of the variables used in the regression tests. The mean and median of earnings quality is −0.752 and −0.5361, respectively. On average, 41.4% of directors are independent non-executive directors, which suggest a domination of inside directors in the majority of Malaysian listed companies. Although MCCG (2000) requires companies to have at least one third of the board comprising of independent non-executive directors, 13.2% of the companies do not fulfill the requirements of the Code. For CEO duality, 85% of companies choose to separate chairman and CEO. Similar to Abdul Rahman and Mohamed Ali (2006), the average board size of Malaysian companies is eight directors. The board meeting range from 1 to 12 meetings per year with an average meeting of 5 times a year. The average length of tenure for independent directors serving in companies in Malaysia is 5.6 years with a maximum value of 28 years.

Independent non-executive directors in Malaysia only hold a small percentage ownership ranging from 0% to 7.76%, while executive directors and non-independent non-executive directors hold up to 82.18%. In terms of family domination, the proportion is varied from 0% to about 71%, with

Table 1. Descriptive Statistics for Dependent and Independent Variables.

	Mean	Median	Std. Deviation	Minimum	Maximum
EQ	−0.752	−0.5361	0.70375	−4.86	−0.06
BIND	0.4141	0.375	0.11143	0.25	0.86
CEODUAL	0.15	0	0.35771	0	1
BDSIZE	7.925	8	2.04906	4	16
BDMEET	5.28	5	1.7243	1	12
BDTENURE	6.5	5.6	4.4140	0.08	28.25
INSOWNS	27.8207	29.185	23.37277	0	82.18
OUTOWNS	0.2915	0	0.88237	0	7.76
FAMILY	0.1893	0	0.21178	0	0.71
INSTITUTIONAL	5.707	3.005	7.96399	0	67.83
LGSIZE	8.7441	8.675	0.54647	7.28	10.42
ROA	0.0347	0.0377	0.1852	−1.6	2.01

an average proportion of family members of about 18.93%. There are almost equivalent numbers in terms of family- and non-family-controlled firms in the sample where 50.4% have no family members sitting on the corporate board while 49.6% have at least two or more family members sitting on the corporate board. The percentage of institutional shareholdings for the sample ranges from 0% to 67.83%, with average shareholdings of about 3%.

To examine the correlation between the independent variables, a Pearson product moment correlation (r) was computed. The overall correlations among the explanatory variables were relatively low and below 0.5. The correlation matrix confirms that multicollinearity is not a problem in this study (Table 2).

4.2. Multivariate Analysis

Table 3 presents the results of the multivariate regressions used to test the hypotheses stated earlier. The multiple regression model tested in this study reported a high F-value (significant at the 0.01 level).

In the model tested, the coefficient for board independence was not significant. This finding is however consistent with prior studies in Malaysia by Che Ahmad, Ishak, and Abd Manaf (2003), Abdullah (2004), Abdul Rahman and Mohamed Ali (2006) and Vethanayagam et al. (2006). Che Ahmad et al. (2003) suggest that in respect of diversification strategy, the presence of independent directors does not seem to influence the decision process. This may be either because they do not have contact with the daily operation of the firm or that they have limited qualifications and are merely appointed based on the relationship with the CEO of the firm. Abdul Rahman and Mohamed Ali (2006) and Vethanayagam et al. (2006) also argue that Malaysian independent directors lack expertise, skills and knowledge to understand financial reporting details which explains their insignificant findings concerning the relationship between board independence and the accounting issues they examine. Perhaps, the most important issue addressed by Vethanayagam et al. (2006) is that the domination of inside directors on the board in Malaysia raises questions regarding the quality and accountability of independent directors when some independent directors are not truly independent of management.

This study finds significant association between board tenure and earnings quality at the traditional 5% significance level. The longer span of time the independent directors serve in the firms gives them the ability to effectively

Table 2. Correlations among Variables.

	EQ	BIND	CEODUAL	BDSIZE	BDMEET	BDTENURE	INSOWNS	OUTOWNS	FAMILY	INSTITUTIONAL	LGSIZE	ROA
EQ	1											
BIND	-.047	1										
CEODUAL	-.024	.081	1									
BDSIZE	.002	-.235**	-.053	1								
BDMEET	.041	.093	-.018	-.079	1							
BDTENURE	.181**	.084	.037	.045	-.091	1						
INSOWNS	.021	-.122*	.126*	.038	-.217**	-.002	1					
OUTOWNS	.085	.042	.097	.162**	-.069	.164**	.144*	1				
FAMILY	.224**	-.228**	.119*	.156**	-.182**	.095	.477**	.154**	1			
INSTITUTIONAL	.105	-.033	-.013	.211**	.010	.112	-.151*	.002	-.039	1		
LGSIZE	.099	.120*	-.026	.228**	.306**	.254**	-.216**	-.075	-.121*	.252**	1	
ROA	-.066	.036	.057	.068	.000	.121	-.052	.054	-.021	.147*	-.032	1

**Significant at 0.01 level; *significant at 0.05 level.

Table 3. Regression Results.

	Predicted Sign	T	Sig
(Constant)		−2.298**	0.023
BIND	+	−1.176	0.241
CEODUAL	−	−1.667*	0.097
BDSIZE	?	−1.874*	0.062
BDMEET	+	1.392	0.165
BDTENURE	+	2.256**	0.025
INSOWNS	+	−0.619	0.536
OUTOWNS	+	2.919***	0.004
FAMILY	+	3.251***	0.001
INSTITUTIONAL	+	1.676*	0.095
LGSIZE	+	1.365	0.174
ROA	+	−0.925	0.356
Adjusted R^2	0.1066		
F-Statistics	3.4937***		
N	280		

The reported t-statistics are White-adjusted values to control for heteroscedasticity.
***Significant at 0.01 level; **significant at 0.05 level; *significant at 0.1 level.

monitor the management which results in higher financial reporting quality. Other board characteristics, CEO duality, and board size and earnings quality are also significantly related but at 10% level. Abdul Rahman and Mohd Haniffa (2005), too find that companies with separate board leadership structure are more likely to contribute to the higher quality earnings. However this finding does cast doubts on the appropriateness of the MCCG (2000) recommendation for role separation.

In respect of managerial ownership, this study fails to find any significant relationship between inside board ownership and earnings quality. However, it finds a positive and highly significant association between outside board ownership and earnings quality at a 1% level. This suggests that outside director ownership create incentives for the independent directors to be more associated with the company and be more involved in their oversight functions in monitoring the quality of financial reports. The finding supports agency theory (Jensen & Meckling, 1976) that suggests substantial shareholdings by outside board members should provide greater incentives for them to monitor the management.

In the case of family ownership, interestingly, this study finds a positive significant association between family ownership proxied by the proportion of family members on the board to the total number of directors and earnings quality. The family control board is found to be highly significant at 1% level. This supports the notion that the presence of family members reduces agency costs as they have greater expertise concerning the firm's operations to effectively monitor the firm's activities. A discussed ealier, The World Bank Report (2005) shows that the majority of shares (67.2%) in Malaysia are in family hands and family firms are growing to the second generation, which supports the view that family firms reduce agency costs as they strive to maximize the long-term wealth of their firms in order to protect their family's name and reputation.

Consistent with expectations, this study finds a positive significant association between institutional ownership and earnings quality but at a 10% level. The result suggests institutional investors are likely to actively monitor their investments due to the large amount of wealth they invested (Velury & Jenkins, 2006). However, this finding raises questions as to the level of involvement of institutional investors in improving corporate governance practices as well as financial reporting quality in Malaysia. The effectiveness of the MSWG in encouraging shareholder activism and its impact on the financial reporting quality in Malaysia require further investigation.

With respect to the control variables, only firm size is associated with earnings quality. Firm size is positively related to earnings quality suggesting that larger firms are more closely scrutinized than smaller firms (Park & Shin, 2004) and thereby motivating them to report higher quality earnings compared to the smaller firms.

5. CONCLUSION, LIMITATIONS OF THE STUDY AND SUGGESTIONS FOR FUTURE RESEARCH

This paper examines the relationship between one of the internal corporate governance mechanisms, the board characteristics, namely board independence, CEO duality, board size, frequency of board meeting and board tenure; and the ownership structure (i.e. managerial ownership, family ownership and institutional ownership) and the financial reported earnings quality in Malaysia. It is shown that firms with longer average tenure of independent directors, evidence higher earnings quality. The study also reveals that outside board ownership and family ownership play a significant role in constraining quality of reported earnings. The substantial shareholdings by outside directors as well as the presence of a higher proportion of family members on the corporate board is shown to enhance the reported earnings quality of firms. However, no significant association is found between board independence and earnings quality. Consequently, this raises concerns of the appropriateness of policy directives that call for majority independent directors when there is a scarcity of qualified independent directors. Further, given the fact that family-controlled firms are dominant in Asian corporations, the findings of this study supports calls to address the implementation of corporate governance mechanisms that are most apt for the institutional context of a given country.

The objective of the study is confined to examining the characteristics of the board of directors as one aspect of the internal corporate governance mechanism. Another key component of this internal mechanism is the audit committee (Cohen et al., 2004). However in this study, the audit committee independence was not included because prior studies in the Malaysian context suggest the existence of multicollinearity problem between board independence and audit committee independence. In the Malaysian context it is noted that because of a lack of sufficiently qualified independent directors, the same independent directors serve on both the board of directors and audit committees. Furthermore, Abdul Rahman and Mohamed Ali (2006) show there is no association between audit committee characteristics and financial reporting quality. It was observed that audit committee members have yet to perform their role in the monitoring process.

The findings of this study warrant further investigation of the impact of the ownership structure in determining the earnings quality in Malaysia. Since this study finds a highly significant relationship between family-controlled firms and earnings quality, future research might investigate the relationship between corporate governance mechanisms and its effect on family-controlled and non-family-controlled firms. Furthermore, the correlations among variables, as presented in Table 2, reveal that the family board control variable is correlated with all the test variables in this study. A separate test on family-controlled and non-family-controlled firms might give a more comprehensive overview of the role of corporate governance in countries with a concentrated ownership structure in the hands of family members such as in East Asian countries. Interestingly, too, whilst this study shows a positive significant association between family ownership and earnings quality, it would be useful to see if the effectiveness of internal corporate governance mechanisms such as boards of directors and audit committees are impacted by ownership structure. In this study, the association between audit committees and financial reporting quality was not examined as explained earlier because of the existence of multicollinearity problem between board independence and audit committee independence. The impact of ownership structure on AC effectiveness and the association with earnings quality will further enhance the findings from this study.

NOTES

1. See, for example, Malaysian Code on Corporate Governance (2000), Singapore Code of Corporate Governance (2001), Thailand Code for Best Practice for Directors of Listed Companies (2002), Bangladesh Code of Corporate Governance (2004), Hong Kong Corporate Governance Code (2004) at http://www.micg.net/code.htm

2. Now known as Bursa Malaysia.

3. Public listed companies in Malaysia were mandated to include in their annual report the statement of corporate governance, a statement of internal control, composition of the board of directors, composition of audit committee, quorum of audit committee and any additional statements by the board of directors.

4. Army Savings Board.

5. Pilgrimage Savings Board.

6. National Equity Board.

7. Fama and Jensen (1983, p. 20) contend that outside directors signal to internal and external markets for decision agents that (1) they are decision experts, (2) they understand the importance of diffuse and separate decision control and (3) they can work with such decision controls system.

8. Example, in the United States, the California Public Employees' Retirement System (CalPERS) has been active in seeking greater director independence and in firms in which they invest their fund, CalPERS request that firms have a majority of independent directors sitting on the board and even identifies the lead directors for the post of chairman and imposes age limits on directors (Daily et al., 2003). In the United Kingdom, institutional investors own between 65 and 75% of the UK stock market which suggests the prominent role that institutional shareholders can play as an agent to governance systems (Mallin, 2003). In fact, Hermes Investment Management, which is owned by and is principal fund manager for British Telecom (BT) Pension schemes, manages over 75 billion euro representing equity investments in over 3,000 companies worldwide and is the largest institutional investor in the United Kingdom (Lee, 2003).

9. The introduction of Capital Market Master Plan (CMP) by the Securities Commissions is to chart the direction of the Malaysian capital market for the next 10 years. 10 out of 152 recommendations dealing with the development of the institutional and regulatory framework for the capital market from 2001 to 2010 focus specifically on the issues of corporate governance. Corporate governance becomes a key strategic thrust of the CMP and one of the important recommendations by CMP is a mandatory disclosure on the state of compliance with the MCCG (2000).

10. Subsequent to the introduction of MCCG (2000), the government has established the Minority Shareholder Watchdog Group (MSWG) to encourage

independent and proactive shareholder participation in listed companies in Malaysia. MSWG has become the think-tank and resource centre that acts as an effective check and balance mechanism on behalf of the minority shareholders to deter abuses from the majority shareholders. This non-profit organization represent the five largest institutional funds in the country including the Employee Provident Fund (EPF), Lembaga Tabung Angkatan Tentera (LTAT), Lembaga Tabung Haji (LTH), Social Security Organization (SOCSO) and Permodalan Nasional Berhad (PNB).

11. Industries with less than 10 observations are excluded to ensure efficiency in accruals model estimation (Jones, 1991).

12. Modified Dechow and Dichev (2002) model is explained in Section 3.3.

REFERENCES

Abdul Rahman, R., & Haniffa, R. M. (2005). The effect of role duality on corporate performance in Malaysia. *Corporate Ownership and Control, 2*(2), 40–47.

Abdul Rahman, R., & Mohamed Ali, F. H. (2006). Board, audit committee, culture and earnings management: Malaysian evidence. *Managerial Auditing Journal, 21*(7), 783–804.

Abdul Wahab, E. A., How, J. C. Y., & Verhoeven, P. (2007). Institutional investors, corporate governance and firm performance in Malaysia. *2nd Journal of Contemporary Accounting and Economic Symposium Proceedings*, Universiti Sains Malaysia, Malaysia, pp. 1–53.

Abdullah, S. N. (1999). *The role of corporate governance and ownership structure on accounting earnings quality*. Unpublished PhD Dissertation. Universiti Utara Malaysia.

Abdullah, S. N. (2004). Board composition, CEO duality and performance among Malaysian listed companies. *Corporate Governance, 4*(4), 47–61.

Abdullah, S. N. (2006). Board structure and ownership in Malaysia: The case of distressed listed companies. *Corporate Governance, 6*(5), 582–594.

Abdullah, S. N., & Mohd Nasir, N. (2004). Accrual management and the independence of the board of directors and audit committees. *IIUM Journal of Economics and Management, 12*(1), 49–80.

Bartholomeusz, S., & Tanewski, G. A. (2006). The relation between family firms and corporate governance. *Journal of Small Business Management, 44*(2), 245–267.

Bathala, C. T., & Rao, R. P. (1995). The determinants of board composition: An agency theory perspective. *Managerial and Decision Economics, 16*(1), 59–69.

Beasley, M. S. (1996). An empirical analysis of the relation between the board of director composition and financial statement fraud. *The Accounting Review, 71*(4), 443–465.

Bhattacharyay, B. N. (2004). Strengthening corporate governance in developing countries in Asia: Prospects and problems. In: *Corporate governance: An international perspective* (pp. 1–12). Malaysia: Malaysian Institute of Corporate Governance Publication.

Boonlert-U-Thai, K., Meek, G. K., & Nabar, S. (2006). Earnings attributes and investor-protection: International evidence. *The International Journal of Accounting, 41*, 327–357.

Bushman, R. M., & Smith, A. J. (2001). Financial accounting information and corporate governance. *Journal of Accounting and Economics, 32*, 237–333.

Che Ahmad, A., Ishak, Z., & Abd Manaf, N. A. (2003). Corporate governance, ownership structure and corporate diversification: Evidence from the Malaysian listed companies. *Asian Academy of Management Journal, 8*(2), 67–89.

Chung, R., Firth, M., & Kim, J. B. (2005). Earning management, surplus free cash flow and external monitoring. *Journal of Business Research, 58*, 766–776.

Claessens, S., & Fan, J. P. H. (2002). Corporate governance in Asia: A survey. *International Review of Finance, 3*(2), 71–103.

Cohen, J., Krishnamoorthy, G., & Wright, A. (2004). The corporate governance mosaic and financial reporting quality. *Journal of Accounting Literature, 23*, 87–152.

Coombes, P., & Wong, S. C. Y. (2004). Chairman and CEO – One job or two? *The McKinsey Quarterly*, 43–47.

Daily, C. M., Dalton, D. R., & Cannella, A. A., Jr. (2003). Corporate governance: Decades of dialogue and data. *Academy of Management Review, 28*(3), 371–382.

Davidson, R., Goodwin-Stewart, J., & Kent, P. (2005). Internal governance structures and earnings management. *Accounting and Finance*, 1–27.

Dechow, P. M., & Dichev, I. D. (2002). The quality of accruals and earnings: The role of accrual estimation errors. *The Accounting Review, 77*(Suppl.), 35–59.

Dechow, P. M., Sloan, R. G., & Sweeney, A. P. (1996). Causes and consequences of earnings manipulation: An analysis of firms subject to enforcement actions by the SEC. *Contemporary Accounting Research, 13*(1), 1–36.

DeFond, M., Hung, M., & Trezevant, R. (2007). Investor protection and the information content of annual earnings announcements: International evidence. *Journal of Accounting and Economics, 43*, 37–67.

Fama, E., & Jensen, M. (1983). Separation of ownership and control. *Journal of Law and Economics, 26*(2), 301–325.

Fan, J. P. H., & Wong, T. J. (2002). Corporate ownership structure and the informativeness of accounting earnings in East Asia. *Journal of Accounting and Economics, 33*, 401–425.

Fan, J. P. H., & Wong, T. J. (2003). Do external auditors perform a corporate governance role in emerging markets? Evidence from East Asia. *Malaysian Accounting Review, 2*(1), 13–45.

Francis, J., LaFond, R., Olsson, P. M., & Schipper, K. (2005). The market pricing of accrual quality. *Journal of Accounting and Economics, 39*(2), 295–327.

Gul, F. (2006). Auditors' response to political connection and cronyism in Malaysia. *Journal of Accounting Research, 44*(5), 931–963.

Halim, R. (2001). My say: Malaysian corporate governance: The solution. *The Edge Daily*, July 2. Retrieved on August 2, 2005, from http://www.theedgedaily.com/cms

Haniffa, R. M., & Cooke, T. E. (2002). Culture, corporate governance and disclosure in Malaysian corporations. *ABACUS, 38*(3), 317–349.

Hermanson, D. R. (2003). Does corporate governance really matter? What the research tells us. *Internal Auditing, 18*(2), 44–45.

Higgs Report. (2003). *Good practice suggestions from the Higgs Report*. London: Financial Reporting Council.

Jaggi, B., Leung, S., & Gul, F. A. (2007). *Board independence and earnings management in Hong Kong firms: Some evidence on the role of family ownership and family board control*. Working Paper. Department of Accounting and Information System, Rutgers University, New Jersey, USA.

Jensen, M. C. (1993). The modern industrial revolution, exit and failure of internal control system. *The Journal of Finance, 48*, 831–880.

Jensen, M. C., & Meckling, W. H. (1976). Theory of the firm: Managerial behavior, agency costs and ownership structure. *Journal of Financial Economics, 3*(40), 305–360.

Jones, J. J. (1991). Earnings management during import relief investigations. *Journal of Accounting Research, 29*(2), 193–228.

Kao, L., & Chen, A. (2004). The effects of board characteristics on earnings management. *Corporate Ownership & Control, 1*(3), 96–107.

Klein, A. (2002). Audit committee, board of director characteristics and earnings management. *Journal of Accounting and Economics, 33*, 375–400.

La Porta, R., Lopez De Silanes, F., & Shleifer, A. (1999). Corporate ownership around the world. *The Journal of Finance, 54*(2), 471–517.

Lee, P. (2003). The need for and value of good governance: An institutional investors' view. In: *Selected issues in corporate governance: Regional and country experiences* (pp. 11–20). New York and Geneva: United Nations Conference on Trade and Development.

Leuz, C., Nanda., D., & Wysocki, P. D. (2003). Earnings management and investor protection: An international comparison. *Journal of Financial Economics, 69*, 505–527.

Li, J. (1994). Ownership structure and board composition: A multi-country test of agency theory predictions. *Managerial and Decision Economics, 15*, 359–368.

Lin, Y. F. (2005). Corporate governance, leadership structure and CEO compensation: Evidence from Taiwan. *Corporate Governance, 13*(6), 824–835.

Lo, K. (2007). Earnings management and earnings quality. *Journal of Accounting and Economic*, doi.10.1016/j.jacceco.2007.08.002

Malaysian Code on Corporate Governance (MCCG). (2000). *Finance Committee on Corporate Governance*. Kuala Lumpur: Securities Commission.

Mallin, C. (2003). The relationship between corporate governance, transparency and financial disclosure. In: *Selected issues in corporate governance: Regional and country experiences* (pp. 1–10). New York: United Nations Conference on Trade and Development.

McKinsey & Company. (2002). *Global investor opinion survey: Key findings*. London: McKinsey & Company.

McNichols, M. F. (2002). Discussion of the quality of accruals and earnings: The role of accruals estimation errors. *The Accounting Review, 77*(Suppl.), 61–69.

Mitra, S., & Cready, W. M. (2005). Institutional stock ownership, accrual management and information environment. *Journal of Accounting, Auditing and Finance, 20*(3), 257–286.

Mitton, T. (2002). A cross-firm analysis of the impact of corporate governance on the East Asian financial crisis. *Journal of Financial Economics, 64*, 215–241.

Mohd Ghazali, N. A., & Weetman, P. (2006). Perpetuating traditional influence: Voluntary disclosure in Malaysia following the economic crisis. *Journal of International Accounting, Auditing and Taxation, 15*, 226–248.

Ng, C. Y. M. (2005). An empirical study on the relationship between ownership and performance in a family-based corporate environment. *Journal of Accounting, Auditing and Finance*, 121–146.

Park, Y. W., & Shin, H. H. (2004). Board composition and earnings management in Canada. *Journal of Corporate Finance, 10*, 431–457.

Peasnell, K. V., Pope, P. F., & Young, S. (1998). A new model board. *Accountancy, 122*(1259), 91.

Peasnell, K. V., Pope, P. F., & Young, S. (2000). Accrual management to meet earnings targets: UK evidence pre and post Cadbury. *British Accounting Review, 32*, 415–445.

Peasnell, K. V., Pope, P. F., & Young, S. (2005). Board monitoring and earnings management: Do outside directors influence abnormal accruals? *Journal of Business Finance & Accounting, 32*(7&8), 1311–1346.

Pergola, T. M. (2005). Management entrenchment: Can it negate the effectiveness of recently legislated governance reform? *The Journal of American Academy of Business Cambridge, 6*(2), 177–183.

Shleifer, A., & Vishny, R. W. (1997). A survey of corporate governance. *The Journal of Finance, 52*, 737–783.

The World Bank Report. (2005). *Report on the Observance of Standards and Codes (ROSC) – Corporate Governance Country Assessment Malaysia*, June 1–38. Retrieved on April 15, 2007, from http://www.worldbank.org/ifa/rosc_cg.html

Thillainathan, R. (1999). Corporate governance and restructuring in Malaysia – A review of markets, mechanisms, agents and the legal infrastructure. Paper prepared for the joint World Bank and OECD Survey of Corporate Governance. Organisation for Economic Co-operation and Development. Available online at http://www.oecd.org/dataoecd/7/24/1931380.pdf

Vafeas, N. (2005). Audit committees, board and the quality of reported earnings. *Contemporary Accounting Research, 22*(4), 1093–1122.

Velury, U., & Jenkins, D. S. (2006). Institutional ownership and the quality of earnings. *Journal of Business Research, 59*, 1043–1051.

Vethanayagam, J., Yahya, S., & Haron, H. (2006). Independent non-executive directors, managerial ownership and firm performance in Malaysian public listed companies. In: *Proceeding Symposium on Accountability, Governance and Performance*. Griffith University, Available online at http://www.griffith.edu.au/school/gbs/afe/symposium/2006/

Wan Hussin, W. N., & Ibrahim, M. A. (2003). Striving for quality financial reporting. *Akauntan Nasional* (March), 18–24.

Watts, R. L., & Zimmerman, J. L. (1978). Towards a positive accounting theory of the determination of accounting standards. *The Accounting Review, 53*(1), 112–134.

Xie, B., Davidson, W. N., III., & DaDalt, P. J. (2003). Earnings management and corporate governance: The role of the board and the audit committee. *Journal of Corporate Finance, 9*, 295–316.

Zulkafli, A. H., Abdul-Samad, M. F., & Ismail, M. I. (2005). *Corporate governance in Malaysia*, pp. 1–18. Retrieved August 2, 2005, from http://www.micg.net/research.htm

A STUDY OF CORPORATE GOVERNANCE DISCLOSURE AND ITS COUNTRY-LEVEL DETERMINANTS IN THE EMERGING MARKETS

Hakim Ben Othman and Daniel Zeghal

ABSTRACT

Purpose – *This study examines country-level attributes that impact on Corporate Governance Disclosure (CGD) depending on the emerging market country's legal system.*

Methodology/approach – *We evaluate CGD level using 749 annual reports (year ended 2006) in 57 emerging market countries. We develop a CGD determinants model that compares differences in country level attributes between common law and civil law emerging market countries. Our model builds on a multiple regression and assumes interaction between the origin of the legal system and country-specific attributes.*

Findings – *Common law emerging markets have substantially higher levels of CGD than civil law ones. CGD is positively associated with the size of the capital market for the entire sample of emerging markets and for the sub-samples of common law and civil law countries.*

Corporate Governance in Less Developed and Emerging Economies
Research in Accounting in Emerging Economies, Volume 8, 125–155
Copyright © 2008 by Emerald Group Publishing Limited
All rights of reproduction in any form reserved
ISSN: 1479-3563/doi:10.1016/S1479-3563(08)08005-5

Law enforcement also has a strong positive influence on CGD in common law emerging countries, whereas it has no influence on CGD in civil law emerging countries.

Practical implications – *Providing CGD levels for emerging markets helps to a better understanding of the corporate governance characteristics that prevail in each country. Decision makers (international investors, market authorities, standard setters, etc.) should be aware of how country level attributes may interact with the legal system (common law or civil law) to influence CGD.*

Originality of the paper – *This is one of the few papers to present evidence of the impact of country level attributes on CGD. This study contributes to identifying the attributes that influence CGD with reference to common law and civil law emerging markets.*

1. INTRODUCTION

In the last decade, corporate governance practices and their disclosure are getting an increasing importance in financial academic literature and professional circles all over the world. Our objective in this study is to examine country level attributes that impact on corporate governance disclosure depending on the emerging market country's legal system.

Several financial crises have marked emerging economies such as Russia, Brazil, and South East Asia during 1997–1998. These crises had a devastating impact not only on the economies of the affected countries but also on other emerging countries perceived to be similarly situated (Mathieson, Richards, & Sharma, 1998; Johnson, Boone, Breach, & Friedman, 2000). Although such crises were linked to capital flow from these countries causing a substantial decline in currencies and asset prices, experts argue that these crises may have been directly attributable to widespread poor corporate governance in emerging economies (Vaughn & Ryan, 2006). Consequently, the quality of corporate governance in developing economies came under close scrutiny (Malherbe & Segal, 2001). A number of international rating agencies and investment banks are working on governance rankings for emerging markets. Governance rankings have been produced by Deutsche Bank for Latin American countries, by Deminor Ratings for European countries, and by Credit Lyonnais Securities Asia (CLSA) for Asian countries. Standard and Poor's has entered the governance ranking market and is producing rankings for both developed and emerging markets.

A recent study by the McKinsey Consulting Group has shown that investors in certain emerging market countries would pay a significant premium for shares in a company with "good" corporate governance, as opposed to investing in one with a similar financial performance but with poor corporate governance (Rose, 2003). Similarly, in Canada, Bujaki and McConomy (2002) found that investors are increasingly basing their investment decisions on companies' corporate governance records and are willing to pay more for shares of well-governed companies than for shares of poorly governed companies with comparable financial results. Lee (2001) and Newby (2001) also report that 'poor' corporate governance is seen as risky, while 'good' corporate governance is seen as a sign of strength.

Indeed, multiple corporate governance systems may be implemented within a company. However, disclosure on existing corporate governance systems and how these are processed is not always made mandatory by the capital market authority or commercial law. In the context of emerging economies where information sources are mostly limited to annual reports, the company's outsiders (minor shareholders) may know about corporate governance practices only if these are disseminated in annual reports. Meanwhile, we observe that performance reporting is no longer restricted to financial disclosures (income statement, balance sheet, funds-flow statement, performance information, etc.). Annual reports are increasingly providing non-financial information including a significant section on corporate governance practices.

Corporate Governance Disclosure (henceforth CGD) provides a description of corporate governance characteristics for companies. This type of disclosure helps, therefore, to convey valuable information to many decision makers and allows them to assess the appropriateness and effectiveness of each firm's corporate governance system. More specifically, CGD reduces asymmetries between insiders (managers and major shareholders) and outsiders (minor shareholders). Therefore, agency costs are reduced and firms with 'good' corporate governance are valued more highly (Durnev & Kim, 2005). Further, at a country level, CGD may attract international investors and investment banks and make capital markets trustworthy.

Previous literature has addressed corporate disclosure as a broad issue and concentrated on wealthy economies (Lang & Lundholm, 1993; Meek, Roberts, & Gray, 1995; Maher & Andersson, 2000). A number of recent papers attempted to examine the issue of corporate disclosure also broadly in some emerging markets (Hong Kong: Gul & Leung, 2004, Ho & Wong, 2001;

Singapore: Eng & Mak, 2003; Malaysia: Haniffa & Cooke, 2002; Indonesia: Tabalujan, 2002; Bangladesh: Ahmed, 1996; Taiwan: Chen, Kao, Tsao, & Wu, 2007). These studies were exclusively interested in firm-level attributes that may determine non-disclosure based corporate governance mostly measured by the CIFAR (1995) index or the Botosan (1997) index[1]. Very few studies have focused on CGD itself. Bujaki and McConomy (2002) and, more recently, Aksu and Kosedag (2006) investigated CGD determinants for firms listed, respectively, on the Toronto Stock Exchange and on the Istanbul Stock Exchange. Nevertheless, both of these studies were limited to only one country, and consequently, CGD determinants were essentially confined to firm-level attributes such as firm characteristics and agency costs proxies. Although Patel, Balic, and Bwakira (2002) explored CGD as captured by the Transparency and Disclosure (T&D) score developed by S&P's across 19 emerging markets, their study was limited simply to a description of the CGD level for these 19 emerging markets and did not seek to identify CGD determinants in emerging markets.

Thus, it would appear that little attention has focused on an analysis of CGD across different countries. No attempt, to our knowledge, has been made to identify the country-level attributes of CGD for a comprehensive sample of emerging markets. In this study, we ask how emerging market countries deal with disclosure on corporate governance with reference to their particular environments. Which country level attributes influence disclosure on corporate governance in emerging markets? Does the origin of their legal system, either a common law system inherited from former British colonizers, or a civil law system inherited from continental European (France, Spain, Portugal, etc.) colonizers, justify differences between CGD levels and their country-specific attributes across emerging market countries? Our objective is then to focus on the role of country-level attributes in explaining CGD in common law and civil law emerging market countries.

It is noteworthy that emerging market countries have a variety of distinguishing features that may influence CGD and, within their different environments, companies may indeed operate differently. Hence, CGD is a function of the environmental context in which annual reports are produced. International accounting literature (e. g. Gray, 1988; Nobes & Parker, 2000) argues that common law countries have socio-economic environments that encourage full disclosure, whereas civil law countries have socio-economic environments marked with secrecy and uncertainty avoidance which limit the level of disclosure observed in such countries. In this regard, the legal approach developed by (La Porta, Lopez-de-Silanes,

Shleifer, & Vishny, 1997; La Porta, Lopez-de-Silanes, Shleifer, & Vishny, 1998; La Porta, Lopez-de-Silanes, Shleifer, & Vishny, 2000; La Porta, Lopez-de-Silanes, & Shleifer, 2006) highlights that investor protection is higher for common law countries and enhances the development of financial markets. We concentrated our work on country-specific attributes (investor protection, law enforcement, and capital market size) expected to affect the level of CGD differently across emerging countries depending on the origin of their legal systems.

This paper extends the work of Patel et al. (2002) by investigating country level attributes of CGD within a significantly larger and more representative sample of emerging markets. We have the advantage of calculating CGD levels as captured by T&D items developed by Standard and Poor's. T&D has been reported to be objective compared to the CLSA composite that partly relies on subjectivity (Durnev & Kim, 2005). The T&D score is based on 98 items that "*are meant to be global in relevance* and not reflecting a specific country or regional approach to corporate governance" (Patel, Balic, & Bwakira, 2003). This enhances international corporate governance comparisons, particularly among emerging countries. We also integrate recent measures developed by Kauffmann, Kraay, and Mastruzzi (2007)[2] to assess some country level attributes (e.g. law enforcement and voice and accountability). Such indicators are useful for broad cross-country comparisons of governance (Kauffmann et al., 2007).

Using a comprehensive sample of 57 countries with emerging markets based on 749 companies followed by S&P's at the year ended 2006, our results collectively indicate that CGD level is substantially higher for common law emerging countries than for civil law ones. We also found that CGD is substantially determined by the size of the capital market for both common law and civil law emerging markets. However it is highly influenced by law enforcement only in common law emerging markets.

Shedding light on corporate governance disclosure and its country-level determinants in emerging markets is potentially useful for a number of organizations and decision makers, including specialized financial institutions (e.g. rating agencies, investment banks), international investors, as well as market authorities and standard setters.

The paper proceeds as follows. The next section presents the background and develops the hypotheses for the study. The research design is described in Section 3. Results are discussed in Section 4, followed by conclusions in Section 5.

2. BACKGROUND AND HYPOTHESES DEVELOPMENT

International accounting literature generally argues that financial reporting is largely influenced by the environment found in different countries. A particular company's disclosure practice is the result of an interactive process among a number of environmental factors (Cooke & Wallace, 1990). Hofstede (1984) developed four dimensions of culture that differ across countries: uncertainty avoidance, individualism, power distance, and masculinity. It is commonly accepted that disclosure levels within a given country are mostly affected by the degree of uncertainty avoidance. Uncertainty avoidance measures the extent to which people feel threatened by unknown situations and an uncertain future. This is expressed in a need for formality, predictability, and prescriptive rules. Gray (1988) relied upon cultural differences proposed by Hofstede to explain international differences in accounting practices (including disclosure). He developed four distinguishable accounting values which are linked to cultural values: statutory control versus professionalism, uniformity versus flexibility, conservatism versus optimism, and secrecy versus transparency. Then, he extended his analysis by demonstrating that the first two contrasting values relate to authority and enforcement while the second two contrasting values relate to measurement and *disclosure*. In this respect, managers in countries with strong uncertainty avoidance are expected to be more secretive, which would provide an environment less favorable to extensive disclosure.

Moreover, Gray (1988) pointed out that cultural values have institutional consequences in the form of legal systems, the nature of capital markets, etc. More specifically, the cultural dimension of strong uncertainty avoidance and the accounting value of secrecy have shaped the disclosure environment in civil law countries. In contrast, the disclosure environment in common law countries emerged from the cultural dimension of weak uncertainty avoidance and the accounting value of transparency that prevail in such countries. Civil law countries prefer confidentiality and the restriction of disclosure of information about the business only to those who are closely involved with its management and financing. Conversely, common law countries are more transparent, open and adopt a publicly accountable approach. Furthermore, it has been recently demonstrated that country-level variables are the most important determinant of a firm's governance disclosure. Only country-level variables have been reported to matter for less-developed countries, while firm characteristics have almost no influence on CGD (Doidge, Karolyi, & Stulz, 2007). Therefore, CGD is determined by country-level attributes.

2.1. Legal Origin and its Implications for CGD: Main Hypotheses

The French and continental civil traditions (Germany, Spain, Portugal, etc.) as well as the British common law traditions have spread around the world through a combination of conquest, imperialism, outright borrowing, and more subtle imitation (La Porta et al., 1998). Nobes (1998) stressed that colonial inheritance is probably a major explanatory factor for the general system of financial reporting in many countries outside Europe. Within emerging countries, laws are not written from scratch, but rather inherited (transplanted) – voluntarily or otherwise – from former colonizers with which they maintain significant economic and business relations. Most emerging market countries inherited their legal system from the colonial era. For instance, former French colonies have a civil law legal origin and represent the French legal family, whereas former British colonies have mostly a common law legal origin and represent the British legal family. North (1988) argues that Britain has better institutions than does France. According to his view, former British colonies are likely to inherit better institutions than former French colonies with positive ramifications on financial development (Beck, Demirgüç, & Levine, 2003).

The most basic prediction of the legal approach is that investor protection encourages the development of financial markets. Investor protection includes not only shareholder rights written into the laws and regulations but also the effectiveness of their enforcement (La Porta et al., 2000). Legal systems both through anti-director rights written into laws (de jure) and their legal enforcement (de facto) represent key forces of investor protection and may provide a favorable environment to higher CGD. The extent to which property rights are enforced is important for economic growth (Acemoglu & Johnson, 2005). Poor respect of investor protection would make it less valuable to invest in corporate governance and its disclosure since controlling shareholders who are more likely to be expropriated by the state gain less from investing in corporate governance and its disclosure (Doidge et al., 2007). Law enforcement is based on the efficiency of the judicial system, the rule of law, and the control of corruption (La Porta et al., 1998; Leuz, Nanda, & Wysocki, 2003; Boonlert-U-Thai et al., 2006). La Porta et al. (1997, 1998, 2000, 2006) demonstrated, among other things, that law and its enforcement vary across countries (and legal families) and greater investor protection increases investor's willingness to provide financing. Hence, we considered investor rights, law enforcement and capital market size as country-specific attributes that would impact on CGD and vary with the legal origin (common law, civil law) of emerging countries.

2.1.1. Investor Rights

Managers may use their power to divert corporate wealth to them-selves, without sharing it with the other investors (Djankov, La Porta, Lopez-de-Silanes, & Shleifer, 2007). Expropriation takes various forms such as excessive compensation, transfer pricing, self-serving financial transac-tions (e.g. outright theft of corporate assets, directed equity issuance, personal loans to directors). To address this problem, laws protecting investor rights play a crucial role in controlling directors. Anti-director rights are key measures that protect investors against their expropriation by directors. Such laws provide a favorable legal environment to CGD even though laws pertaining to investor protection differ across emerging countries. In this regard, it has been established that anti-director rights are substantially higher in English legal origin countries than in civil law origin ones (Djankov et al., 2007).

> The first hypothesis we test is that disclosure on corporate governance increases with the level of anti-director rights in emerging markets. However, we expect that the influence of anti-director rights on CGD is more likely to be significant in common law emerging countries than in civil law ones.

2.1.2. Law Enforcement

La Porta et al. (1998, 2006) provided evidence that law enforcement is sharply higher in common law countries than in civil law ones. According to Leuz et al. (2003), the variables pertaining to law enforcement are the following developed by La Porta et al. (1998): efficiency of the judicial system, rule of law and the corruption index. However, Kauffmann et al. (2007) provide very recent measures of regulatory quality, rule of law and control of corruption which are based on the aggregation of a large number of individual data sources. These data sources consist of surveys of firms and individuals, as well as the assessments of the commercial risk rating agencies, non-governmental organizations, and the number of multilateral aid agencies, non-governmental organizations, and a number of multilateral aid agencies and other public sector organizations (Kauffmann et al., 2007).

2.1.2.1. Regulatory Quality. According to Kauffmann et al. (2007), the regulatory quality of the judicial system in a given country is considered as the ability of the government to formulate and implement sound policies and regulations that permit and promote private sector development.[3] Klapper and Love (2004) have demonstrated a positive relationship between the quality of country level legal systems and the average of firm-level governance indices within each country of the 14 emerging markets considered in their study.

2.1.2.2. Rule of Law. Based on Kauffmann et al. (2007) and La Porta et al. (2006), the rule of law in a given country is considered as the extent to which agents have confidence in and abide by the rules of society, and in particular the quality of contract enforcement, the courts, etc. (World Bank, 2007, A decade of measuring the quality of governance, p. 3). The rule of law includes perceptions of the incidence of both violent and non-violent crime, the effectiveness and predictability of the judiciary, and the enforceability of contracts (Boonlert-U-Thai, Meek, & Nabar, 2006).

2.1.2.3. Control of Corruption. Kauffmann et al. (2007) and La Porta et al. (2006) consider the control of corruption in a given country as the extent to which public power is exercised for private gain, including both petty and grand forms of corruption as well as "capture" of the state by elites and private interests. (World Bank, 2007, A decade of measuring the quality of governance, p. 3).

> This is the second hypothesis of our study. Disclosure on corporate governance increases with law enforcement. However, we expect that law enforcement is more likely to have a significant influence on CGD in common law emerging countries than in civil law ones.

2.1.3. Importance of Equity Markets
Capital markets are considered one of the key factors in a country's economic development because of its role in the optimal allocation of resources among the different economic sectors and among firms within each sector. In developed capital markets, the pressures exerted by investors are important; investors require quality financial information and more disclosure to make optimal choices when they analyse investment opportunities (Gray, McSweeney, & Shaw, 1984; Adhikari & Tondkar, 1992). Countries with successful stock markets mandate that shareholders receive the information they need and the power to act – including both voting and litigation – on this information (Djankov, et al., 2007).

Accordingly, it has been demonstrated that financial disclosures by firms listed on stock exchanges can be influenced by total market capitalization (Adhikari & Tondkar, 1992; Salter, 1998), and also by the disclosure requirements of stock exchanges (Jaggi & low, 2000, p. 503). Doupnik and Salter (1995) argued that a strong equity market is generally associated with better production and disclosure of sophisticated information.

> The third hypotheses we test is that disclosure on corporate governance increases with market capitalization in emerging countries. However, because of the relatively higher size and strong equity capital markets in common law origin countries compared to civil law ones (Nobes, 1998), we expect that the influence of the capital market size on CGD is more likely to be significant in emerging common law countries than in civil law ones.

2.2. Control Variables

In the following, we discuss hypotheses related to control variables.

2.2.1. Level of Economic Development

Economic conditions are major determinants in the development of a country's accounting and financial system. More specifically, Adhikari and Tondkar (1992) established that a country's level of economic growth has a positive effect on the development of accounting systems and practices.[4] In countries where the level of economic growth is relatively high, the social function of accountancy as an instrument of measurement and communication is of considerable importance. Business and economic activities will reach a size and complexity that require a sophisticated, high-quality corporate disclosure practices. Where information plays a critical role (Abdolmohamadi, Rhodes, & Tucker, 2002; Nobes, 1998), the accounting system and corporate disclosure will undergo significant changes in response to demands of the changing economic conditions of a more dynamic business environment. Belkaoui (1983) supports that the higher the level growth of income, the better the adequacy of reporting and disclosure.

These arguments lead us to think that the decision by some emerging countries to disclose information on their corporate governance systems is associated with economic development. We expect that disclosure on corporate governance increases with the level of economic development of emerging markets.

2.2.2. Degree of External Economic Openness

Foreign investors, international credit rating agencies, multinational corporations, and world financial institutions represent external pressure and may potentially influence companies' disclosure on corporate governance in emerging markets. Cooke and Wallace (1990) introduced the relevance of including external environmental factors in trying to understand corporate disclosure. One of these factors is the degree of outside economic openness. According to these authors, the more a country's economy is open to the outside world, the more the country will be exposed to diverse international investors and capital providers' pressures (Zeghal & Mhedbi, 2006). Such pressures could lead corporations in emerging economies to further disclosure on their corporate governance systems. Hence, we expect that disclosure on corporate governance increases with the degree of external economic openness of emerging markets.

2.2.3. Voice and Accountability

Belkaoui (1983) suggests that political freedom influences corporate disclosure as a large practice. Political freedom can be assessed as the extent to which citizens are able to participate in selecting their government, as well as freedom of expression, freedom of association, and free media, which are captured by voice and accountability (Kauffmann et al., 2007).

Indeed, societies that support more information are likely to support free media including active financial press and free circulation of newspapers. In this case, financial community may have more influence to require more CGD. Companies may respond to this desire for reassuring investors by increasing the amount of information about CGD.

Bushman, Pitroski, and Smith (2004) used average rank of the countries media development (print and television) between 1993 and 1995 as a proxy for the intensity of information dissemination in a country. Cooke and Wallace (1990) and Archambault and Archambault (2003) considered newspapers are a significant source of information. Dyck and Zingales (2004) demonstrated that a high level of diffusion of the press is negatively related to benefits of control. These authors used newspapers printings as a proxy for the influence of the press in a society. However, Kauffmann et al. (2007) provided voice and accountability as a more comprehensive proxy that captures among other things media and press freedom. Therefore, we expect that disclosure on corporate governance increases with voice and accountability in emerging markets.

2.2.4. Accounting Systems

Many researchers support the adoption of international standards. They argue that harmonization of international accounting enhances the quality of financial information, improves the comparability of accounting information in the international milieu, facilitates financial operations on international scale, and thus contributes to a better globalization of capital markets (Taylor, Evans, & Joy, 1986). Peavy and Webster (1990) underline that the adoption of international standards, especially by developing countries, contributes considerably to strengthening integration and competitiveness in the financial markets. According to Wolk, Francis, and Tearney (1989), international accounting harmonization is beneficial for developing countries, especially with emerging markets, because it provides them with better prepared standards as well as the best quality accounting framework and reporting practices.

Chamisa (2000) studied the question of the usefulness of IAS for developing countries. Using a case study in Zimbabwe, he analyzed the impact of the adoption of IAS standards on the accounting practices of listed companies. He found that these standards have a particular importance for developing countries with an emerging capital market.

More recently, Zeghal and Mhedbi (2006) established that developing countries with Anglo-American culture, mostly former British colonies, are more willing to adopt IFRS-IAS standards than developing countries belonging to other cultures.

Since countries adopting international accounting standards (IFRS) are more likely to have higher quality reporting standards, we expect that disclosure on corporate governance increases with IFRS adoption.

3. METHODOLOGY

Our research design helps explain where we obtained data, how we operationalized the dependent and independent variables, and the form of analysis being undertaken to test the hypotheses.

3.1. Sample Selection

The key issue about data is that they cover primarily large and liquid companies that may have exposure to international capital markets. These corporations are selected and followed, among other things, by international credit agencies which are mostly interested in large firms with liquid securities. We collected data about companies followed by Standard and Poor's (S&P) and included in their S&P/IFC Emerging Markets Indices. We chose S&P's since these indices cover many more countries than do CLSA or the FTSE Institutional Shareholder Services (ISS) (Doidge et al., 2007). In our sample, all companies must be domiciled in an emerging market (S&P/IFCG) or a lesser developed global frontier market (S&P/IFCG Frontier) and are among the most actively traded securities in the market. Our sample construction begins with the list of companies indicated on the Global Industry Standard (GIC's) for the emerging Markets Database. We collected the latest full annual reports essentially from the web sites of these companies (year ended 2006). Companies those do not have a web site, or those have a web site and do not provide annual reports, have been contacted by regular mail and we obtained further few annual reports. Moreover, following Doidge et al. (2007), we retain countries for which rated firms are fewer than 5. For example, we include Lebanon for which only three companies are rated and Ivory Coast for which only one company is rated. We check to see if the results reported below differ when excluding such countries and find that doing so makes little difference. This left us with a sample of 947 companies from 57 emerging markets.

3.2. Empirical Model

To test for the importance of environmental factors on CGD in emerging markets, we consider country-level attributes that may affect CGD disclosure internationally. We develop a CGD determinants model that takes into consideration differences in country-level attributes between common law and civil law emerging countries. First, our model builds on regressions tested over the total sample of emerging countries with interactive variables for each group of common law and civil law emerging countries. Next, our model is tested separately on sub-samples of common law and civil law emerging countries. However, we exclude investor protection (INV) in the second step of multivariate analysis because of data limitation on this variable, which reduces substantially the size of sub-samples and, consequently, the degree of freedom of the model.[5]

$$\text{SCORE}_j = + a_{1j}\text{INV\_ORIGIN}_j + a_{2j}\text{ENF\_ORIGIN}_j + a_{3j}\text{CM\_ORIGIN}_j$$
$$+ a_{4j}\text{INV}_j + a_{5j}\text{ENF}_j + a_{7j}\text{CM}_j + a_{8j}\text{ECO}_j + a_{9j}\text{FDI}_j$$
$$+ a_{10j}\text{VOICE}_j + a_{11j}\text{IFRS}_j + \varepsilon_j$$

3.2.1. CG Disclosure Measurement: SCORE

$SCORE_j$ denotes the CGD level of country j for the year ended 2006. We calculate a country level disclosure on CG based on the T&D score developed by S&P's. We base the S&P score on the information firms provide in their annual reports. More specifically, the approach to scoring items is dichotomous in that an item scores one if disclosed and zero if it is not. To ensure the judgement of relevance is not biased, the entire annual report is read before any scoring is made. Hence, T&D score is measured by searching company annual reports for the information of 98 possible items broadly divided into the following sub-categories:

(a) Ownership structure and investor relations (28 items)
(b) Financial transparency and information disclosure (35 items)
(c) Board management structure and process (35 items)

The scores for each item are added and equally weighted to derive a final score for each company. The 98 data items are unweighted to reduce subjectivity.[6] The score for each company k is calculated as follows:

$$SCORE_k = \frac{\sum_{i=1}^{N} X_{ik}}{N}$$

where N is the total number of items expected to be disclosed for firm j. N is equal to 98.

X_{ik} is equal to 1 if item i is disclosed for firm k, and 0 if not disclosed.

The scores for companies examined from each country are averaged to obtain the country's disclosure score. The country's disclosure score, $SCORE_j$, represents aggregation at a country level of CGD practices observed in annual reports of listed domestic firms. Data for all 98 items that make up T&D score were directly and manually extracted from 749 annual reports for the year ended 2006, which consisted in an extensive hand collection.

3.2.2. Measurement of Independent Variables

The unit of analysis for independent variables in this study is the nation state, and data are collected mainly from publications produced by the World Bank. This was in order to test the environmental dependency of CGD practices.

3.2.2.1. Test Variables

INV_ORIGIN: INVESTOR RIGHTS*ORIGIN. This is an interactive variable to test for the impact of investor rights (INV) on CGD according to the origin of the legal system for the whole sample of emerging markets.

Legal origin: ORIGIN. ORIGIN$_j$ acts as a dummy variable. It takes a value of one if the emerging country j has a common law legal system, zero if the emerging country has a civil law legal system.

Common law emerging countries may have English as an official language (Frank, 1979), or if their history have been marked by a strong tie with United Kingdom or the United States (Nobes, 1998), such as having been a past colony, or being a member of the commonwealth. On the other hand, civil law emerging countries are mostly former Continental European (France, Spain, Portugal, Germany, etc.) colonies.

Investor rights: INV. INV$_j$ denotes investor rights of country j. This variable is measured as an index aggregating anti-director rights that the company law or commercial code in a country recognizes. The index is initially developed by La Porta et al. (1997, 1998), then revised by Djankov et al. (2007). We use this revised index which is formed by adding 1 when: (1) the country allows shareholders to mail their proxy vote; (2) shareholders are not required to deposit their shares prior to the General Shareholders' Meeting; (3) Cumulative voting is allowed; (4) an oppressed minorities mechanism is in place; (5) the law listing rules explicitly mandate or set as a default rule that shareholders hold the first opportunity to buy new issues of stock; or (6) when the minimum percentage of share capital that entitles a shareholder to call for an extraordinary Shareholders' meeting is less than or equal to 10% (the sample median). The index ranges from 0 to 6. The source of the data is the commercial laws of the various countries.

ENF_ORIGIN: ENFORCEMENT*ORIGIN. This is an interactive variable to test for the impact of law enforcement (ENF) on CGD according to the origin of the legal system for the whole sample of emerging markets.

Law enforcement: ENF. ENF$_j$ denotes law enforcement of country j for the year ended 2006. Following Leuz et al. (2003), we build and aggregate measure of the variables pertaining to law enforcement but use those developed by Kauffmann et al. (2007). We measure law enforcement (ENF) as the mean score (index) across the assessment of regulatory quality, rule of law, and control of corruption corresponding to 2006 year end.[7]

CM_ORIGIN: CAPITAL MARKET SIZE*ORIGIN. This is an interactive variable to test for the impact of the capital market size on CGD according to the origin of the legal system for the whole sample of emerging markets.

Importance of equity markets: CM.   The size of emerging capital markets (CM_j) is measured by the average stock market capitalization of country j during the last five years 2002–2006 (source: World Development Indicators, 2007, World Bank).

3.2.2.2. Control Variables

Level of economic development: ECO.   The variable (ECO_j) is measured by the rate of the gross domestic product (GDP) per person of country j for the year ended 2006 (source: World Development Indicators, 2007, World Bank).

Degree of external economic openness: FDI.   This variable (FDI_j) is measured by the rate of net inflows Foreign Direct investment, divided by the GDP of country j, for the year ended 2006. FDI is essential to the growth and viability of an emerging market economy (Nenova, 2004). International investors and capital providers are, in most cases, a major source to support high-quality disclosure on corporate governance systems in emerging markets (source: World Development Indicators, 2007, World Bank).

Voice and accountability: VOICE.   We use the measure of this variable ($VOICE_j$) from Kauffmann et al. (2007) corresponding to country j year ended 2006.

Accounting systems: IFRS.   Pacter (2007) reports in http://www. iaspplus.com (Deloitte) four classes of countries: IFRS not permitted for domestic listed companies, IFRS permitted for domestic listed companies without being mandatory, IFRS required for some domestic listed companies (e.g. financial institutions in United Emirates), and IFRS required for all domestic listed companies. We refer to Pacter's classification of the 57 emerging countries in our sample according to IFRS. However, we simplify this classification and distinguish between countries requiring the adoption of IFRS for all domestic listed companies and those permitting or not allowing the adoption of IFRS.[8] $IFRS_j$ adoption at a country level is measured by a dummy variable that takes the value of one if the country j requires IFRS for all domestic listed companies, 0 otherwise (year ended 2006).

4. RESULTS

4.1. Descriptive Statistics and Univariate Analysis

Table 1 reports the distribution of 57 emerging countries and 749 companies by geographic area and presents descriptive statistics pertaining to the T&D score for the year ended 2006.

The average percentage of T&D score for the entire sample is 0.423. The maximum possible score is 0.833 and is from Asia (China). However, the sharply high level of disclosure of Chinese companies followed by S&P is most likely the result of their decision to conform to the listing and disclosure standards in London and Hong Kong, rather than the domestic norm in China. By "bonding themselves to the disclosure standards of the most demanding financial markets, many emerging market issuers may be wishing to signal that their management, governance, and transparency practices are at a world class, and not just a regional level." (Patel et al., 2002).

Nevertheless, it is noteworthy that many emerging markets (India, Malaysia, Thailand, Turkey, Jordan, Israel, etc.) show CGD scores comparable to those reported by S&P for developed European markets in Patel et al. (2003) study. The presumption that only industrialized countries report high levels of CGD, while the developing world suffers from uniformly poor governance disclosure is not still true.

The sample distribution by geographic area shows that the average of T&D score is comparatively and respectively higher for emerging countries from Asia (0.485), Africa (0.462), MENA (0.438), Latin America (0.327), and Europe (0.308). Africa reports a relatively higher T&D score than MENA, Latin America and European emerging countries, yet this may be due to the sharply high average T&D score for South Africa (0.532) among African emerging countries. Mauritius also shows relatively high T&D scores because of some large companies implementing high standards of disclosure (e.g. Shell, Rogers) that are listed on Mauritius stock exchange.

Table 2 gives descriptive statistics for the independent variables for the total sample of emerging markets.

Table 3 presents descriptive statistics and univariate tests on the dependent and independent variables for separate sub-samples of common law and civil law emerging countries. Panel A provides descriptive statistics and univariate difference of continued variables, whereas panel B reports univariate difference of the discrete variables. Most entries in the table are descriptive and self-evident. As expected, the mean of T&D score (SCORE)

Table 1. Distribution of T&D Score for Emerging Markets at
the End of 2006.

Region	Country	No. of Countries	No. of Companies	Mean	Standard Deviation	Minimum	Median	Maximum
Africa		9	85	0.462	0.116	0.059	0.464	0.678
	Botswana		5	0.466	0.058	0.369	0.488	0.523
	Ghana		4	0.342	0.137	0.142	0.386	0.452
	Ivory Coast		1	0.059	–	–	0.059	–
	Kenya		14	0.397	0.082	0.190	0.422	0.488
	Mauritius		5	0.521	0.118	0.309	0.571	0.583
	Namibia		2	0.357	0.050	0.321	0.357	0.392
	Nigeria		9	0.386	0.080	0.261	0.404	0.523
	South Africa		35	0.540	0.085	0.226	0.559	0.678
	Zimbabwe		10	0.427	0.057	0.309	0.440	0.500
Asia		13	248	0.485	0.165	0.119	.0.511	0.833
	Bangladesh		10	0.308	0.058	0.238	0.297	0.404
	China		35	0.580	0.111	0.261	0.595	0.833
	India		40	0.524	0.105	0.273	0.529	0.761
	Indonesia		10	0.502	0.140	0.190	0.511	0.678
	Korea		35	0.426	0.123	0.297	0.419	0.697
	Malaysia		30	0.653	0.079	0.476	0.660	0.797
	Pakistan		15	0.357	0.080	0.202	0.369	0.464
	Philippines		20	0.367	0.139	0.083	0.392	0.702
	Singapore		10	0.613	0.141	0.261	0.648	0.750
	Sri Lanka		14	0.522	0.101	0.333	0.511	0.654
	Taiwan		10	0.444	0.157	0.154	0.470	0.630
	Thailand		15	0.565	0.085	0.392	0.559	0.702
	Vietnam		4	0.190	0.055	0.119	0.196	0.250
Europe		13	107	0.308	0.150	0.071	0.285	0.750
	Bulgaria		6	.0174	0.056	0.107	0.172	0.238
	Croatia		9	0.297	0.160	0.130	0.250	0.678
	Czech Republic		5	0.647	0.066	0.583	0.642	0.750
	Estonia		5	0.252	0.065	0.178	0.261	0.321
	Hungary		5	0.328	0.148	0.142	0.345	0.488
	Latvia		6	0.246	0.035	0.190	0.244	0.297
	Lithuania		5	0.261	0.102	0.119	0.309	0.357
	Poland		20	0.226	0.086	0.071	0.232	0.416
	Romania		5	0.276	0.118	0.095	0.285	0.392
	Russia		25	0.399	0.138	0.190	0.369	0.630
	Slovak Republic		5	0.261	0.116	0.166	0.261	0.452
	Slovenia		9	0.337	0.093	0.166	0.380	0.416
	Ukraine		2	0.077	0.025	0.059	0.0773	0.095

Table 1. (*Continued*)

Region	Country	No. of Countries	No. of Companies	Mean	Standard Deviation	Minimum	Median	Maximum
Latin		9	93	.327	.110	.119	.321	.702
America[a]	Argentina		7	0.384	0.186	0.130	0.321	0.702
	Brazil		20	0.311	0.087	0.130	0.309	0.440
	Chile		20	0.361	0.103	0.178	0.363	0.547
	Colombia		1	0.333	–	–	0.333	–
	Jamaica		14	0.341	0.103	0.154	0.357	0.476
	Mexico		20	0.288	0.101	0.119	0.267	0.583
	Peru		6	0.248	0.110	0.130	0.208	0.416
	Trinidad and Tobago		3	0.436	0.083	0.357	0.428	0.523
	Venezuela		2	0.333	0.033	0.309	0.333	0.357
MENA		13	216	0.438	0.133	0.059	0.434	0.738
	Bahrain		15	0.452	0.075	0.345	0.452	0.559
	Egypt		9	0.403	0.095	0.250	0.392	0.559
	Israel		36	0.543	0.114	0.285	0.571	0.702
	Jordan		8	0.572	0.097	0.392	0.571	0.738
	Kuwait		32	0.378	0.042	0.309	0.375	0.500
	Lebanon		3	0.369	0.066	0.297	0.380	0.428
	Morocco		9	0.294	0.136	0.107	0.250	0.476
	Oman		15	0.538	0.091	0.261	0.559	0.654
	Qatar		6	0.378	0.033	0.333	0.380	0.428
	Saudi Arabia		12	0.388	0.086	0.238	0.398	0.559
	Tunisia		19	0.212	0.074	0.059	0.214	0.357
	Turkey		40	0.519	0.070	0.392	0.535	0.642
	UAE		12	0.370	0.078	0.238	0.357	0.523
Total		57	749	0.423	0.157	0.059	0.428	0.833

[a]Ecuador is dropped due to unavailability of annual reports.

is statistically higher for common law emerging countries than for civil law ones. Common law emerging countries are mostly former British colonies and maintain privileged economic relations with developed Anglo-American countries (UK, US, Australia, etc.). CGD in emerging countries seems to be influenced by the level of transparency and disclosure prevailing in the business environment of their former colonizers and main economic partners. In this regard, Saudagaran and Biddle (1992) provided evidence that the disclosure requirements and expectations in Anglo-American developed economies (e.g. US, UK, Canada) are higher than in Continental European economies (e.g. France, Germany, Switzerland). Even though due to the increasing role of capital markets, common standards for

Table 2. Descriptive Statistics on Independent Variables Related to CGD Determinants Model for the Total Sample of Emerging Markets.

Variable	N	Mean	Standard Deviation	Minimum	Q1	Median	Q3	Maximum
Independent variables								
INV	41	3.402	1.205	0.000	3.000	3.750	4.000	5.000
ENF	57	0.074	0.702	−1.760	−0.373	0.100	0.640	1.990
CM	57	0.547	0.495	0.045	0.205	0.339	0.695	2.103
ECO	57	8052.292	9355.052	382.886	1879.094	5521.491	9610.956	51283.380
FDI	57	0.043	0.041	0.001	0.017	0.030	0.056	0.217
VOICE	57	−0.060	0.789	−1.660	−0.62	−0.110	0.57	1.15

N is the number of emerging countries. INV, Investor rights; ENF, law enforcement level; CM, market capitalization to GDP ratio; ECO, GDP per Capita; FDI, foreign direct investment to GDP ratio; and VOICE, voice and accountability level.

disclosure in developed countries are becoming more widespread, we still find substantial differences in CGD practices between common law and civil law emerging economies.

Similarly, capital market size (CM) and investor protection (INV) are substantially higher in common law emerging markets. This result is consistent with the findings of La Porta et al. (1998). Moreover, the GDP per capita (ECO) is, on average, more important than in civil law emerging markets. However, Voice and accountability (VOICE) shows higher levels in civil law emerging markets. This may be due to the European countries considered in our sub-sample of civil law emerging economies (e.g. Poland, Czech Republic, Hungary, etc.) which benefit from relatively higher standards of freedom of expression essentially after they integrated the European Union.

Foreign direct investment (FDI) in panel A and the degree of IFRS adoption (IFRS) in panel B report no significant difference between common law and civil law emerging countries. This result with respect to the IFRS adoption requirement is inconsistent with our prediction that common law emerging countries are more willing to use IFRS than civil law ones. It should be noted, however, that we calculated T&D scores for the year ended 2006. Since the adoption of IFRS has been mandatory since 2005 for consolidated accounts for all companies listed on European stock markets, this substantially increased the number of European civil law emerging countries requiring IFRS (Bulgaria, Czech Republic, Estonia, Hungary, Poland, Romania, Latvia, Lithuania, Slovenia, etc.).

Table 3. Comparison of Variables between the Two Groups of Emerging Countries.

Dependent Variable	Emerging Countries	N	Mean	Standard Deviation	Median	t-Statistic (p-Value)
Panel A: Distributional statistics and univariate difference of dependent and independent variables for 22 Common law and 35 Civil law emerging countries						
SCORE	Common law	22	0.451	0.096	0.431	3.348
	Civil law	35	0.340	0.134	0.333	*(0.000)****
Independent variables						
INV	Common law	13	4.384	0.506	4.000	4.244
	Civil law	28	2.946	1.165	3.000	*(0.000)****
ENF	Common law	22	0.111	0.831	0.103	0.314
	Civil law	35	0.051	0.620	0.100	*(0.377)*
CM	Common law	22	0.810	0.585	0.686	3.480
	Civil law	35	0.381	0.345	0.269	*(0.000)****
ECO	Common law	22	11041.400	13503.97	5580.433	1.960
	Civil law	35	6173.425	4700.855	5521.491	*(0.027)***
FDI	Common law	22	0.036	0.035	0.025	0.890
	Civil law	35	0.046	0.042	0.035	*(0.811)*
VOICE	Common law	22	−0.295	0.667	−0.355	1.809
	Civil law	35	0.086	0.833	0.270	*(0.037)***

Independent Variable	Emerging Countries	N	Mean Proportion	z-statistic (p-value)
Panel B: Univariate difference of independent discrete variables for 22 Anglo-American and 35 Euro-continental emerging countries				
IFRS	Common law	22	0.409	1.194
	Civil law	35	0.571	*(0.883)*

N is the number of emerging countries. SCORE denotes the CGD level of by country; INV, investor rights; ENF, law enforcement level; CM, market capitalization to GDP ratio; ECO, GDP per capita; FDI, foreign direct investment to GDP ratio; VOICE, voice and accountability level; and IFRS, IFRS adoption.

** Significance at the 0.05 level (p-value <0.05).
*** Significance at the 0.01 level (p-value <0.01).

4.2. Multivariate Analysis

Table 4 presents regression results of the CGD determinants model we tested over the sample of emerging countries. Table 5 provides additional results from separate analyses for common law and civil law emerging countries.

Table 4. Regressions of SCORE on Test and Control Variables Based on the Total Sample of Common Law and Civil Law Origin of Emerging Countries[a].

Variable	Coefficient Estimate (*p*-Value)
Panel A: Total sample of emerging countries	
INTERCEPT	0.317
	(0.001)***
INV_ORIGIN	0.037
	(0.027)**
ENF_ORIGIN	0.059
	(0.276)
CM_ORIGIN	−0.137
	(0.130)
INV	−0.007
	(0.710)
ENF	0.030
	(0.551)
CM	0.181
	(0.009)***
ECO	0.000
	(0.250)
FDI	−1.422
	(0.048)**
VOICE	−0.069
	(0.060)*
IFRS	0.018
	(0.682)
N	41
Breusch–Pagan test for heteroscedasticity $\chi^2(1)$	2.27
Prob $> \chi^2$	0.1322
Man VIF	3.51
Fisher $F(10, 29)$	3.90
Prob $> F$	(0.0018)***
R^2 adjusted	0.4201

The total sample of 57 emerging countries is reduced to 41 due to data missing for the explanatory variable investor rights INV.

The *p*-values are reported in parentheses below coefficient estimates.

*Significance at the 0.10 level (*p*-value < 0.10).

**Significance at the 0.05 level (*p*-value < 0.05).

***Significance at the 0.01 level (*p*-value < 0.01).

[a]The CGD determinants model is presented as follows:

$$\text{SCORE}_j = a_0 + a_1 \text{INV\_ORIGIN}_j + a_2 \text{ENF\_ORIGIN}_j + a_3 \text{CM\_ORIGIN}_j + a_4 \text{INV}_j$$
$$+ a_5 \text{ENF}_j + a_7 \text{CM}_j + a_8 \text{ECO}_j + a_9 \text{FDI}_j + a_{10} \text{VOICE}_j + a_{11} \text{IFRS}_j + \varepsilon_j$$

SCORE denotes the CGD level by country. INV_ORIGIN, interactive variable INV*ORIGIN; where ORIGIN is a dummy variable that takes the value of one if the country's legal origin is common law legal system, 0 otherwise; ENF_ORIGIN, interactive variable ENF*ORIGIN. CM_ORIGIN: interactive variable CM*ORIGIN; INV, Investor rights; ENF, law enforcement level; CM, market capitalization to GDP ratio; ECO, GDP per Capita; FDI, foreign direct investment to GDP ratio; VOICE, voice and accountability level; IFRS, IFRS adoption.

Table 5. Regressions of SCORE on Test and Control Variables Based on Separate Samples of Common Law and Civil Law Emerging Countries[a].

Variable	Coefficient Estimate (*p*-Value)	Coefficient Estimate (*p*-Value)
	Panel A: Sub-sample of Common law emerging countries	Panel B: Sub-sample of Civil law emerging countries
INTERCEPT	0.454	0.247
	(0.000)***	*(0.001)***
ENF	0.120	0.034
	(0.002)***	*(0.561)*
CM	0.074	0.199
	(0.036)**	*(0.009)****
ECO	−0.000	0.000
	(0.007)***	*(0.500)*
FDI	−0.224	−0.793
	(0.657)	*(0.173)*
VOICE	−0.021	−0.045
	(0.460)	*(0.301)*
IFRS	−0.029	0.054
	(0.449)	*(0.319)*
N	22	35
Breusch–Pagan test for heteroscedasticity $\chi^2(1)$	0.21	0.64
Prob > χ^2	*(0.6436)*	*(0.4246)*
Mean VIF	1.88	2.02
Fisher $F(6, 14)$; $F(6, 22)$	3.91	2.16
Prob > F	*(0.014)***	*(0.078)**
R^2 adjusted	0.4543	0.1695

We exclude investor protection, INV, because of data limitation on this variable, which reduces substantially the size of sub-samples and, consequently, the degree of freedom of the model. For both common law and civil law emerging countries sub-samples, when taking in account the independent variable INV, the Fisher statistic is not significant and the sample size is reduced respectively from 22 to 11 and from 35 to 29, which alters the degrees of freedom of the regressions. The *p-values* are reported in parentheses below coefficient estimates.

*Significance at the 0.10 level (*p*-value<0.10).

**Significance at the 0.05 level (*p*-value<0.05).

***Significance at the 0.01 level (*p*-value<0.01).

[a]The CGD determinants model tested separately over sub-samples of Common law and Civil law emerging markets is presented as follows:

$$\text{SCORE}_j = a_0 + a_1\text{ENF}_j + a_2\text{CM}_j + a_3\text{ECO}_j + a_4\text{FDI}_j + a_5\text{VOICE}_j + a_6\text{IFRS}_j + \varepsilon_j$$

SCORE denotes the CGD level of by country. ENF, law enforcement level; CM, market capitalization to GDP ratio; ECO, GDP per Capita; FDI, foreign direct investment to GDP ratio; VOICE, voice and accountability level; IFRS, IFRS adoption.

The Breusch–Pagan test statistic for heteroscedasticity is not statistically significant in Table 4 and Table 5 (panels A and B) suggesting no heteroscedasticity pertaining to our CGD determinants model.

The variance Inflation Factor (VIF) was calculated to assess the extent of any multicolinearity problem. All VIF factors for independent variables are less than 10. Mean VIF is 3.51 for the model with interactive variables for the entire sample of common law and civil law emerging countries (Table 4). Mean VIF is respectively 1.88 and 2.02 for our model tested separately over samples of common law and civil law emerging countries (Table 5). According to Neter, Wasserman, and Kunter (1983), the VIF indicates a problem of multicollinearity if the factor exceeds 10. Thus, the mutlicollinearity does not appear to be a problem in our model.

Tables 4 and 5 show that the variables of the regression model are globally significant. The Fisher test statistic is significant at a level of 1% (Table 4), 5% (panel A) and 10% (panel B) in Table 5. R^2 adjusted is 0.4201 for the total sample of emerging countries and it is comparatively higher for common law emerging countries (0.4543) than for civil law emerging countries (0.1695). Overall, the CGD determinants model developed is shown to provide a reasonably good explanation of CGD level.

Consistent with our predictions, Table 4 exhibits a significantly higher influence of investor protection, INV, on CGD for common law emerging markets than for civil law ones. The interactive variable INV_ORIGIN shows a positive and significant coefficient at a 5% level. Moreover, the coefficient of the variable CM is positive and statistically significant at a level of 1% for the entire sample (Table 4), which indicates that the CM size affects positively and substantially the level of CGD for the emerging countries considered as a whole.

The interactive variable ENF_ORIGIN reports no statistically significant coefficient, suggesting that there is no substantial difference of the effect of law enforcement, ENF, on CGD between common law and civil law countries. However, Table 5 (panel A) outlines that law enforcement, ENF, does have a sharply significant influence at a 1% level on CGD within common law emerging countries, whereas law enforcement ENF has no influence on CGD within civil law emerging countries.

Although the interactive variable CM_ORIGIN shows no different influence of CGD between common law and civil law emerging markets, the size of CM affects significantly CGD at a level of 1% for the entire sample of emerging markets. Similarly, Table 5 highlights that CGD is substantially influenced by the size of CM for separated sub-samples of common law and civil law emerging markets.

Nevertheless, control variables exhibit no relationship with CGD (Table 5). The level of economic development, ECO, external economic openness, FDI, voice and accountability, VOICE, and IFRS adoption seem to exert no direct influence on CGD when tested separately over subsamples of common law and civil law emerging countries. These findings corroborate those obtained by Belkaoui (1983) who found no influence of economic, political and civil indicators on reporting and disclosure over a sample of 55 developed and less developed countries.

5. CONCLUSION

The purpose of this paper is to investigate environmental factors that have the potential of influencing CGD at a country level across a large sample of emerging markets. This study outlines major differences between common law and civil law institutional factors and assesses their implications on CGD level.

We collected annual reports of 749 companies followed by S&P/IFC from 57 countries classified by S&P's as emerging markets for the year ended 1996. Based on the 98 items of T&D score developed by S&P's, we calculated the score for each company, then the average CGD score by emerging country. We built a CGD determinants model that accounts for differences in country-level attributes between common law and civil law emerging countries.

Findings provide evidence, as hypothesized, that the level of CGD is substantially higher for common law emerging countries than for civil law ones. As argued by La Porta et al. (1998), civil law countries have mostly lower protection for investors than common law countries. In civil law emerging markets, laws offer weak shareholder protection. It might, thus, be costly for companies to adopt different provisions in their corporate charters because it will be difficult for investors and judges to understand non-standard contracts. Therefore, companies in countries with overall weak legal environments may not have much flexibility to improve their own investor protection and, consequently, civil law countries report lower corporate governance indices. Again, as hypothesized, on average. CGD is, indeed, significantly determined by law enforcement in common law countries, whereas this country level attribute has almost no influence on CGD in civil law countries. Considering the global sample of common law and civil law emerging markets, we conclude that investor protection outlines a significantly higher influence of on CGD for common law emerging markets than for civil law ones. It has been hypothesized that capital market size was likely to be more significant in emerging common law countries. However, the capital market size has a substantial effect on CGD in both common law and civil law emerging markets. This suggests that the capital market is taking a more active and supportive role in enhancing CGD in civil law emerging countries.

Our results are potentially important for international decision makers including specialized financial institutions and international investors as well as for the emerging countries concerned. Market regulators as well as standard setters would better understand specific factors that may promote CGD in common law and civil law emerging markets. We believe that CGD will continue to be a rich field of empirical enquiry. Research on CGD determinants in different environments can only stand to enrich researcher's understanding of how emerging countries cope with disclosure on corporate governance in their specific legal environment.

NOTES

1. CIFAR index is an index of financial disclosure developed by the Center for International Financial Analysis Research since 1995. Botosan (1997) index is based on the three following components of items: background information, performance information, and non-financial information.

2. Daniel Kauffmann and Aart Kraay, with the assistance of Pablo Zoido-Lebaton and Massimo Mastruzzi initiated a long standing research program of the World Bank Institute and the Research Department of the World Bank since 1996. They have compiled and measured the quality of governance in over 209 countries, based on 33 data sources produced by 30 different organizations worldwide. Hence, the idea that governance cannot be measured becomes a fallacy. Given the wide range of indicators now available, World Governance Indicators are transparent and precise about the degree of imprecision in the data. Falling short of total precision does not detract from usefulness and relevance of the data. Many meaningful comparisons are feasible (*in* "Measuring Decade Quality of the Governance", World Bank, 2007, p. 3).

3. World Bank (2007), "Measuring Decade Quality of the Governance", p. 3. Available at http://www.worldbank.com

4. Also financial literature seems to indicate that accounting affects economic growth through its effects on financial sector. Accounting disclosure practices contribute to reducing uncertainty and asymmetry, which helps to reassure investors and creates a trustworthy economic environment. The capital market will efficiently channel funds toward the right investment opportunities and, thus, stimulate growth opportunies. See Ndubizu (1992), Larson and Kenny (1995), and Kang and Pang (2005).

5. For both common law and civil law emerging countries sub-samples, when taking in account the independent variable INV, the Fisher statistic is not significant (p-value is respectively 0.628 and 0.361) and the sample size is reduced respectively from 22 to 11 and from 35 to 29, which alters the degrees of freedom of the regressions.

6. Many researchers have considered unweihgted scores as the norm in annual report studies (e.g. Cooke, 1989a, 1989b; Archambault & Archambault, 2003).

7. Law Enforcement should be derived from a principal component analysis of the covariance matrix of the three variables: regulatory quality, rule of law and control of corruption. However, we calculated Law Enforcement as the mean of the three above variables because we observed substantially high correlations between these variables (see correlation matrix), determinant is very close to zero, KMO is 0.756 > 0.700, and component score coefficients for these variables are very similar (see component score coefficient, Appendix).

8. We also considered IFRS dummies as follows: IFRS0 receives 1 if the country does not permit IFRS for domestic listed companies, 0 otherwise; IFRS1 receives 1 if the country permits IFRS for some domestic companies, 0 otherwise; IFRS2 receives 1 if the country requires IFRS for some domestic listed companies, 0 otherwise; IFRS3 receives 1 if the country requires IFRS for all domestic listed companies, 0 otherwise. However results did not change and IFRS has no impact on CG disclosure. Moreover, the use of a larger number of variables to control for IFRS adoption reduces the degree of freedom given the limited number of country-level observations. Therefore, we opted for only one dummy variable for IFRS adoption as defined above.

ACKNOWLEDGMENTS

We thank the editors and two anonymous reviewers for their helpful comments and suggestions. We acknowledge the helpful comments made by the participants at the European Accounting Association meeting 2008 in Rotterdam. We are grateful to the CGA-Accounting Research Centre at the University of Ottawa and LEFA Laboratory at IHEC Carthage for their support. We would like to thank Miss Hanen Saadouli, Miss Hounaida Mersni, and Miss Meriem ElOun for their research assistance.

REFERENCES

Abdolmohamadi, M., Rhodes, J., & Tucker, R. (2002). The influence of accounting and auditing on a country's economic development. *Review of Accounting and Finance, 1*, 42–53.
Acemoglu, D., & Johnson, S. (2005). Unbundling institutions. *Journal of Political Economy, 113*(5), 949–995.

Adhikari, A., & Tondkar, R. H. (1992). Environmental factors influencing accounting
    disclosure requirements of global stock exchanges. *Journal of International Financial
    Management and Accounting, 4*, 75–105.
Ahmed, K. (1996). Disclosure policy choice and corporate characteristics: A study of
    Bangladesh. *Asia-Pacific Journal of Accounting, 3*(1), 183–203.
Aksu, M. H., & Kosedag, A. (2006). Transparency and disclosure scores and their determinants
    in the Istanbul stock exchange. *Corporate Governance: An International Review, 14*(4),
    277–296.
Archambault, J. J., & Archambault, M. E. (2003). A multinational test of determinants of
    corporate disclosure. *The International Journal of Accounting, 38*, 173–194.
Beck, T., Demirgüç, A., & Levine, R. (2003). Law and finance: Why does legal origin matter?
    Journal of Comparative Economics, 31, 653–675.
Belkaoui, A. (1983). Economic, political, and civil indicators and reporting and
    disclosure asequacy: Empirical investigation. *Journal of Accounting and Public Policy,
    2*, 207–219.
Boonlert-U-Thai, K., Meek, G. K., & Nabar, S. (2006). Earnings attributes and investor
    protection. *The International Journal of Accounting, 41*, 327–357.
Bujaki, M., & McConomy, B. J. (2002). Corporate governance: Factors influencing voluntary
    disclosure by publicly traded Canadian firms. *Canadian Accounting Perspectives, 1*(2),
    105–139.
Bushman, R. M., Pitroski, J. D., & Smith, A. (2004). What determines corporate transparency?
    Journal of Accounting Research, 42(2), 207–252.
Chamisa, E. (2000). The relevance and observance of the IASC standards in developing
    countries and the particular case of Zimbabwe. *The International Journal of Accounting,
    35*(2), 267–286.
Chen, A., Kao, K. L., Tsao, M., & Wu, C. (2007). Building a corporate governance index from
    the perspectives of ownership and leadership for firms in Taiwan. *Corporate Governance:
    An International Review, 15*(2), 251–261.
Cooke, T. E. (1989a). Disclosure in the corporate annual report of Swedish companies.
    Accounting and Business Research, 16(Spring), 113–122.
Cooke, T. E. (1989b). Voluntary corporate disclosure by Swedish companies. *Journal of
    International Financial Management and Accounting, 1*(2), 171–195.
Cooke, T. E., & Wallace, R. S. O. (1990). Financial disclosure regulation and its environment:
    A review and further analysis. *Journal of Accounting and Public Policy, 9*, 79–110.
Djankov, S., La Porta, R., Lopez-de-Silanes, F., & Shleifer, A. (2007). The law and economics
    of self dealing. *Journal of Financial Economics, 88*, 430–465.
Doidge, C., Karolyi, G. A., & Stulz, R. M. (2007). Why do companies matter so much for
    corporate governance. *Journal of Financial Economics, 86*, 1–39.
Doupnik, T., & Salter, S. (1995). External environment, culture, and accounting practice:
    A preliminary test of a general model of international accounting development.
    International Journal of Accounting, 30(3), 189–202.
Durnev, A., & Kim, H. (2005). To steal or not to steal: firm attributes, legal environment, and
    valuation. *Journal of Finance, 60*, 1461–1493.
Dyck, A., & Zingales, L. (2004). Private benefits of control: An international comparison.
    Journal of Finance, 59(2), 537–600.
Eng, L. L., & Mak, Y. T. (2003). Corporate governance and voluntary disclosure. *Journal of
    Accounting and Public Policy, 22*, 325–345.

Frank, W. G. (1979). An empirical analysis of international accounting principles. *Journal of Accounting Research* (Autumn), 103–121.

Gray, S. J. (1988). Towards a theory of cultural influences on the development of accounting systems internationally. *Abacus, 24*, 1–15.

Gray, S. J., McSweeney, L. B., & Shaw, J. C. (1984). *Information disclosure and multinational corporations.* London, England: Wiley.

Gul, F., & Leung, S. (2004). Board leadership, outside directors' expertise and voluntary corporate disclosures. *Journal of Accounting and Public Policy, 23*, 351–379.

Haniffa, R. M., & Cooke, T. E. (2002). Culture, corporate governance and disclosure in Malaysian corporations. *Abacus, 38*(3), 317–349.

Ho, S. S. M., & Wong, K. S. (2001). A study of the relationship between corporate governance structures and the extent of voluntary disclosure. *Journal of International Accounting, Auditing & Taxation, 10*, 139–156.

Hofstede, G. (1984). Cultural dimensions in management and planning. *Asian Pacific Journal of Management*, 83–94.

Jaggi, B., & Low, P. L. (2000). Impact of culture, market forces, and legal system on financial disclosures. *The International Journal of Accounting, 35*, 495–519.

Johnson, S., Boone, P., Breach, P., & Friedman, A. (2000). Corporate governance in Asian financial crisis. *Journal of financial Economics, 58*, 141–186.

Kang, T., & Pang, Y. H. (2005). Economic development and the value-relevance of accounting information: A disclosure transparency perspective. *Review of Accounting and Finance, 4*(1), 5–31.

Kauffmann, D., Kraay, A., & Mastruzzi, M. (2007). *The worldwide governance indicator project: answering the critics.* World Bank Policy Research Working Paper No. 4149, Washington, DC.

Klapper, F., & Love, I. (2004). Corporate governance, investor protection, and performance in emerging markets. *Journal of Corporate Finance, 10*, 703–728.

La Porta, R., Lopez-de-Silanes, F., & Shleifer, A. (2006). What works in securities laws? *Journal of Finance, 61*, 1–32.

La Porta, R., Lopez-de-Silanes, F., Shleifer, A., & Vishny, R. W. (1997). Legal determinants of external finance. *Journal of Finance, 52*, 1131–1150.

La Porta, R., Lopez-de-Silanes, F., Shleifer, A., & Vishny, R. W. (1998). Law and finance. *Journal of Political Economy, 106*, 1113–1155.

La Porta, R., Lopez-de-Silanes, F., Shleifer, A., & Vishny, R. W. (2000). Investor protection and corporate valuation. *Journal of Financial Economics, 58*(1–2), 3–27.

Lang, M., & Lundholm, R. (1993). Cross-sectional determinants of analyst ratings of corporate governance disclosures. *Journal of Accounting Research, 31*(2), 246–271.

Larson, R. K., & Kenny, S. Y. (1995). An empirical analysis of international accounting standards, equity markets, and economic growth in developing countries. *Journal of International Financial Management and Accounting, 6*(2), 130–157.

Lee, J. (2001). Corporate governance-and why you need it. *Asiamoney, 12*(9), 24–26.

Leuz, C., Nanda, D., & Wysocki, D. (2003). Earnings management and investor protection: An international comparison. *Journal of Financial Economics, 69*, 505–527.

Maher, M., & Andersson, T. (2000). *Convergence and diversity of corporate governance regimes and capital markets.* Oxford: Oxford University Press.

Malherbe, S., & Segal, N. (2001). Corporate governance in South Africa. OECD Development Center Online. Available at: http://www.oecd.org

Mathieson, D., Richards, A., & Sharma, S. (1998). Financial crisis in emerging markets. *Finance and Development*, *38*, 3–7.

Meek, G. K., Roberts, C. B., & Gray, S. J. (1995). Factors influencing voluntary annual report disclosures by US, UK and continental European multinational corporations. *Journal of International Business Studies*, *26*, 555–572.

Ndubizu, G. A. (1992). Accounting disclosure methods and economic development: A criterion for globalizing capital markets. *The International Journal of Accounting*, *27*(2), 151–163.

Nenova, T. (2004). How is corporate governance relevant in low income countries? Available at http://rru.worldbank.org/Discussions Topics/ Topic44.aspx

Neter, J., Wasserman, W., & Kunter, M. (1983). *Applied linear regression models*. Boston: Richard D. Irwin, Inc.

Newby, A. (2001). New rules of good behaviour. *Euromoney*, *389*(September), 44–59.

Nobes, C. (1998). Toward a general model of the reasons for international differences in financial reporting. *Abacus*, *34*(2), 162–186.

Nobes, C., & Parker, R. (2000). *Comparative international accounting*. Essex, England: Pearson Education Ltd.

North, D. (1988). Institutions, economic growth and freedom: an historical introduction. In: M. A. Walker (Ed.), *Freedom democracy and economic welfare*. Vancouver: Fraser Institute.

Pacter, P. (2007). http://www.iasplus.com, Deloitte.

Patel, S., Balic, A., & Bwakira, L. (2002). Measuring transparency and disclosure at firm-level in emerging markets. *Emerging Market Review*, *3*, 310–324.

Patel, S., Balic, A., & Bwakira, L. (2003). Transparency and disclosure study: Europe. S&P Report.

Peavy, D. E., & Webster, S. K. (1990). Is GAAP the gap to international market? *Management Accounting*, *72*, 31–35.

Rose, R. (2003). *JSE responsibility index to measure non-financial risks* (October, 16, p. 17). South Africa: Business Day (South Africa) Limited.

Salter, S. B. (1998). Corporate financial disclosure in emergent markets: Does economic development matter? *The International Journal of Accounting*, *33*(2), 211–234.

Saudagaran, S. M., & Biddle, G. C. (1992). Financial disclosure levels and foreign stock exchange listing decisions. *Journal of International Financial Management and Accounting*, *13*(3), 106–148.

Tabalujan, B. S. (2002). Family capitalism and corporate governance of family controlled listed companies in Indonesia. *University of New South Wales Law Journal*, *25*(2).

Taylor, M. E., Evans, T. G., & Joy, A. C. (1986). The impact of IASC accounting standards on comparability and consistency of international reporting practices. *International Journal of Accounting Education and Research*, *22*, 1–9.

Vaughn, M., & Ryan, L. V. (2006). Corporate governance in South Africa: A bellwether for the continent. *Corporate Governance: An International Review*, *14*(5), 504–512.

Wolk, H. I., Francis, J. R., & Tearney, M. G. (1989). *Accounting theory: A conceptual and institutional approach*. Boston: PWS-Kent Publishing Company.

World Bank Institute. (2007). *A decade of measuring the quality of governance-governance matters 2007* (Available at http://www.govindicators.org). Development Research Group.

World Development Indicators. (2007). The World Bank, Wasington, USA. Available at http://publications.worldbank.org/online

Zeghal, D., & Mhedbi, K. (2006). An analysis of the factors affecting the adoption of international accounting standards by developing countries. *The International Journal of Accounting*, *41*, 373–386.

APPENDIX. PRINCIPAL COMPONENT ANALYSIS OF THE RULE OF LAW, REGULATORY QUALITY, AND CONTROL OF CORRUPTION

Correlation Matrix

		RL	RQ	CC
Correlation	RL	1.000	0.882	0.947
	RQ	0.882	1.000	0.869
	CC	0.947	0.869	1.000
Significance (1-tailed)	RL		0.000	0.000
	RQ	0.000		0.000
	CC	0.000	0.000	

RL, Rule of law; RQ, regulatory quality; CC, Control of Corruption.
Covariance Matrix[a]
[a]Determinant = 0.003 The variables are dependent: good.

KMO and Bartlett's Test[a]

Kaiser–Meyer–Olkin measure of sampling adequacy		0.756
Bartlett's test of sphericity	Approximtely χ^2	210.933
	df	3
	Significance	0.000

[a]Based on correlations.

Component Score Coefficient Matrix[a]

	Component
	1
RL	0.356
RQ	0.347
CC	0.333

RL, Rule of law; RQ, regulatory quality; CC, Control of Corruption.
Extraction Method: Principal Component Analysis.
Component Scores.
[a]Coefficients are standardized.

ACCOUNTING STANDARDS, CORPORATE GOVERNANCE, AND FOREIGN DIRECT INVESTMENTS: THE EXPERIENCE OF EMERGING MARKET ECONOMIES

Orhan Akisik

ABSTRACT

Purpose: *The purpose of this paper is to examine the relationship between the inflow of foreign direct investment (FDI) into emerging market economies and its determinants between 1997 and 2005 from a new perspective emphasizing the role of accounting standards and corporate governance.*

Methodology: *The study covers 27 emerging market and transition economies that are classified into three groups: Asian, Central and Eastern European, and Latin American. Considering the possible endogeneity in studies on corporate governance, Generalized Two-Stage Least Squares (G2SLS) and Generalized Method of Moments (GMM) estimation techniques are used in this study.*

Findings: *Results indicate that the adoption of high quality accounting standards and effective corporate governance lead to an increase in FDI.*

Corporate Governance in Less Developed and Emerging Economies
Research in Accounting in Emerging Economies, Volume 8, 157–187
Copyright © 2008 by Emerald Group Publishing Limited
ISSN: 1479-3563/doi:10.1016/S1479-3563(08)08006-7

I conclude that, in order to attract more FDI, emerging market countries should improve the quality of financial reporting and corporate governance in addition to improving their macroeconomic indicators.

Originality: *This is, to my knowledge, the first study that aims to explore the association of FDI with accounting standards and corporate governance.*

Research limitations: *Difficulty in obtaining data constitutes the major limitation in international accounting research, in general, and in this study, in particular. Therefore, some emerging market countries are necessarily excluded from the study.*

1. INTRODUCTION

This paper aims to explore the association of foreign direct investment (FDI) inflow into emerging market countries with accounting standards and corporate governance between 1997 and 2005.

One of the striking developments over the past three decades that affected world economies profoundly has been the increasing volume of financial capital flows across countries (Cooper, 1999). Despite the fact that a variety of financial capital flows exists, there is a significant preference among countries to attract more FDI.[1] Both developed and developing countries have been competing to increase their shares of FDI inflows since economic and financial globalization enabled free movement of capital.

FDI has a number of advantages over portfolio investments: First, FDI is considered as less threatening to financial stability than portfolio investment since it is unlikely to leave host countries in an economic crisis. Second, FDI, in addition to financial capital, includes non-financial benefits provided by multinational corporations (MNCs) into host countries.[2] For example, physical capital, technology, know-how, and new management techniques refer to these benefits, which are desperately needed by developing countries (Jackson, 2007; De Mello, 1999; Bergsman & Shen, 1995). Third, FDI through MNCs is regarded as a vehicle that enables host countries to integrate with the rest of the world (Jackson, 2007). These are the major arguments that stress the importance of FDI both for developed and emerging market countries.[3]

FDI undertaken by MNCs is primarily directed to two main regions: South-East Asia and Latin America. In South-East Asia, China is the largest recipient of FDI, whereas, in Latin America, Argentina, Brazil, and

Mexico receive the largest portion of FDI (Barclay, 2000, p. 1; Bergsman, 2000, p. 266).

Although emerging market countries have been steadily increasing their shares of the world total since the beginning of 1990s, FDI is still largely attracted by developed economies.[4] Among the major shortcomings that prevent emerging market countries from attracting more FDI are low human resource development, low productivity, high inflation, inadequate infrastructure, small market size, political instability, and corruption. In addition to these, the lack of good financial reporting standards along with an ineffective corporate governance system has recently been recognized in explaining the inadequacy of FDI in emerging market countries (Preobragenskaya & McGee, 2003; Rueda-Sabater, 2000).

Some prior studies have examined the relationship of foreign portfolio investments with accounting standards and corporate governance (e.g. Chipalkatti, Quan, & Rishi, 2006). Nevertheless, there is no study – to my knowledge – that determines the effect of accounting standards and corporate governance on FDI in emerging market countries.[5]

In this study, I attempt to fill this gap by examining FDI inflows into emerging market countries from a new perspective emphasizing the role of accounting standards and corporate governance, in addition to macroeconomic variables.

Recognizing the possible endogeneity between FDI and corporate governance, I use Generalized Two-Stage Least Squares (G2SLS) and Generalized Method of Moments (GMM) estimation techniques in the study.

The study makes important contributions to international accounting literature in several respects. First, my empirical tests provide strong evidence that FDI inflow is closely associated with high quality accounting standards and corporate governance. This is an important finding for emerging market countries seeking to increase their shares of FDI in world total. Both high quality accounting standards and effective corporate governance system lead to an increase in FDI. Second, my analysis provides evidence that IFRS and US-GAAP are regarded as high quality accounting standards by investors, justifying the efforts of regulatory organizations to develop a uniform, high quality set of accounting standards. Third, I find that code law system has a significant effect on corporate governance structure in emerging market countries.

The conclusions that have been drawn are important for a number of groups including investors, creditors, governments, accounting standard setters, and capital markets regulators.

The paper is designed as follows. Section two examines some prior studies on FDI and corporate governance in emerging market countries. In section three, the methodology is discussed. Section four is about empirical analysis, and in section five, concluding remarks take place.

2. FDI INFLOWS, CORPORATE GOVERNANCE, AND ACCOUNTING STANDARDS IN EMERGING MARKET COUNTRIES: AN OVERVIEW

FDI has become a major source of economic growth for many emerging market countries (Alfaro, Chanda, Kalemli-Ozcan, & Sayek, 2004a; Foreign Direct Investment for Development-Maximising Benefits, Minimising Costs, OECD, 2002). Benefits of FDI for this group of countries may be evaluated at both microeconomic and macroeconomic levels. The micro-economic benefits of FDI result mainly from technological and organiza-tional capabilities acquired by host countries through MNCs (Borensztein, De Gregorio, & Lee, 1998).

At the macroeconomic level, FDI may contribute to maintaining external balance by financing current account deficits in host countries (Chudnovsky & López, 1999). Many authors view FDI as a major source of external financing since 1990s, especially in developing countries, whose domestic savings have usually been insufficient (Calderón, Loayza, & Serven, 2004; Santiso, 2003, p. 55).[6]

Prior studies on emerging markets provide evidence that FDI is primarily related to market size and labor cost in host countries.[7] For instance, China, India, Brazil, Argentina, and Mexico are very likely to continue to attract FDI thanks to their large domestic markets and export potential in the near future.

In addition to macroeconomic variables, the role of institutional factors, such as political stability, adequate infrastructure, and effective legal framework[8] has been emphasized in many recent studies on FDI in emerging market countries (Bevan, Estrin, & Meyer, 2004; Bevan & Estrin, 2004; Berglöf & Pajuste, 2005, p. 175; Baniak, Cukrowski, & Herczynski, 2002; Garibaldi, Mora, Sahay, & Zettelmeyer, 2001; Hausman & Fernández-Arias, 2000; Meyer, 1995; Schneider & Frey, 1985).

Table 1 shows FDI inflows into Asian, Central and Eastern European, and Latin American emerging market countries between 1997 and 2006. For the Asian group, except for the slowdown in 1998, 2001, and 2002, it is

Table 1. FDI Inflows – Emerging Market Countries (US$ Billion).

Groups	1997	1998	1999	2000	2001	2002	2003	2004	2005	2006
Asian	94.97	85.18	102.74	138.90	99.57	83.96	88.46	137.58	160.77	96.95
CEEC	19.58	21.26	24.26	26.38	27.45	28.32	26.17	54.99	66.36	36.61
Latin	58.02	61.00	79.36	72.74	62.18	42.49	34.08	53.16	59.35	30.03
Total	172.57	167.43	206.36	238.02	189.20	154.76	148.72	245.73	286.48	163.59

Source: IMD World Competitiveness (2007).

observed that FDI inflows rose in this period. In particular, there is a considerable increase in FDI inflows in the period of 2002 through 2005. One major determinant of this increase has been the rapid economic growth rate that spurred the market-seeking FDI. Although FDI inflows increased in the entire region in 2005, individual economies achieved different performances.

For example, FDI inflows into China and Hong Kong continued to grow while they declined in Korea and Taiwan. Thailand and Indonesia recorded 164% and 177% increases in FDI inflows in 2005, respectively.[9]

These enormous increases result not only from extensive cross-border mergers and acquisitions (M&As), but also from greenfield investments following the structural reforms that strengthened the economic structures and provided confidence for investors (World Investment Report, 2006, chap. 2, p. 52). Structural reforms including the passing of securities and accounting laws, mandates for greater corporate transparency and codes of corporate governance have considerably improved the financial reporting environment in Asian countries since the 1990s (Roche, 2005, p. 47; White Paper on Corporate Governance in Asia, 2003).[10]

Preobragenskaya and McGee (2003) argue that one of the major factors that adversely affect the ability of many developing countries in attracting FDI is the lack of credible financial information. In order to eliminate this shortcoming and to gain credibility, a number of emerging market economies in South-East Asian and Central European regions have already adopted IFRS as a set of high quality accounting standards.[11] However, the adoption of high quality accounting standards can only be regarded as a first step, but not sufficient for establishing a well-developed financial reporting infrastructure that would produce credible financial information. Financial statements that are prepared in compliance with the adopted high quality financial reporting standards would fairly present the results of operations if an effective corporate governance structure exists (Mueller, 2006; Imhoff, 2003; Principles of Corporate Governance, 2002; Kothari, 2000).

In this context, sustainability of economic growth in Asian countries through outward-looking policies and their continued success in attracting FDI depend largely on the existence of well-functioning financial markets and efficient corporate governance systems, which ensure that firms are successfully managed to increase their values to the shareholders (Nam, Kang, & Kim, 2001, p. 88).[12] Many authors stress the importance of an effective corporate governance system in attracting FDI on appropriate conditions (Leuz & Wysocki, 2006; Gillan & Starks, 2003; Rajan & Zingales, 1998).[13] Both developed and developing countries need to enhance the quality of corporate governance if they really want to increase their shares of FDI inflows (Berglöf & Pajuste, 2005; Bishop, 2002; Garibaldi et al., 2001; Rueda-Sabater, 2000).[14]

As seen in Table 1, FDI inflows into Central and Eastern European transition countries increased remarkably in 2004 and 2005, reaching nearly $67 billion. Both greenfield investments and M&As account for the increase in FDI inflows in this period (World Investment Report, 2006, chap. II, p. 85). In the process of privatizations of state-owned enterprises, comprehensive incentive packages including tax rebates along with regulations that support market economies are offered to foreign investors. Privatizations require the establishing of an effective corporate governance system to protect the shareholders' rights. In the transition to a market economy, all Central and Eastern European countries experienced corporate governance problems when they established their capital markets. Companies that relied on foreign capital to finance their business activities had to improve their corporate governance systems (Mejstřik & Mejstřik, 2007, p. 66; Bedõ & Ozsvald, 2007, p. 136).

The Latin American emerging market countries group includes the six largest economies in the region. Although FDI inflows into Latin America decreased from 1999 to 2003,[15] they started rising again in 2004 and 2005 as a result of strong economic growth and soaring commodity prices.[16] In 2005, FDI inflows into Latin America and Caribbean increased to $104 billion, including investments in offshore centers. Besides strong economic growth, current account surplus resulting from a rise in foreign demand for commodities is another factor that caused the surge in FDI inflows, thereby leading to an increase in profits of foreign companies. Reinvested profits are one of the major components of FDI inflows in Latin American countries since 2003. Considering the fact that corporate governance in Latin America has become an essential tool for attracting FDI and maintaining the sustainability of economic growth, Latin American countries have committed themselves to improve codes of corporate governance

(Corporate Governance in Latin America, New Thoughts for a New Century, 2000; Agosin & Pastén, 2003; Apreda, 1999; White Paper on Corporate Governance in Latin America, OECD, 2003).

Important points of the discussion above in this section may be summarized as follows:

Although market size and labor cost still remain as major elements, emerging market countries have recently recognized the important role of institutional factors in determining the amount of FDI. Both forms of FDI – M&As and greenfield investments – are positively affected by structural reforms that include new securities and accounting laws, and good corporate governance and legal systems. Structural reforms are expected to improve the financial reporting environment. The lack of credible financial information is emphasized as one of the major factors that adversely affect the ability of emerging market economies to attract FDI. Nevertheless, that has not been empirically tested yet.

The common characteristic of these studies is that they do not examine the effect of accounting standards and corporate governance together on FDI empirically.

3. METHODOLOGY

This study attempts to identify the relationship between FDI inflows and their determinants from a new perspective in 27 emerging market countries between 1997 and 2005. Emerging market countries are broken down into three groups; Asian, Central European, and Latin American.[17] Countries in these groups have been continuously attracting FDI since the 1990s (Lipsey, 1999).

The main idea of this paper is that factors that have an impact on FDI inflows are more diverse today than earlier as a consequence of globalization. Accordingly, it may be inadequate to attempt to explain FDI inflows just by taking into account of standard macroeconomic variables, such as market size, per capita income growth, labor cost, and openness of economies. In addition to these factors, high quality accounting standards, good corporate governance, and an effective legal system that enable the enforceability of contracts have become crucial in attracting FDI inflows in recent years.

In order to test the validity of these relationships, I develop two hypotheses as follows.

3.1. Development of Hypotheses

3.1.1. Foreign Direct Investment and High Quality Accounting Standards

It has been argued that the lack of credibility of financial reporting systems would adversely affect the ability of emerging market countries in attracting FDI (e.g. Saudragan & Diga, 1997). Without having an effective financial reporting system that provides investors with reliable and true information, emerging market countries are unlikely to attract more FDI. As a result, a number of emerging market countries has recently enhanced their efforts to improve financial reporting systems in order to increase their bargaining power in attracting FDI.

There are two major sets of financial reporting systems that are considered highly credible by users: US Generally Accepted Accounting Principles (US-GAAP) and IFRS.[18] Although US-GAAP are still widely used in the world, it is observed that there has been an increasing tendency to use IFRS. Besides EU member countries that require listed companies to use IFRS since January 1, 2005, some developed and emerging market countries, such as Australia, New Zealand, China, and Hong Kong have voluntarily adopted IFRS or adapted them to their domestic accounting standards (Chorafas, 2006, p. 61; Hung & Subramanyam, 2004).

Financial reporting, which requires the use of high quality accounting standards – IFRS or US-GAAP – is expected to increase FDI inflows in emerging market countries. It is, therefore, hypothesized in the alternative form that:

Hypothesis 1. There is a positive relationship between FDI inflows and high quality accounting standards in host countries.

3.1.2. Foreign Direct Investment and Corporate Governance

Would the adoption of high quality foreign accounting standards or their convergence with domestic accounting standards be considered as adequate to attract FDI? Probably, it would not because an effective corporate governance system is also regarded as important as high quality accounting standards. An effective corporate governance system would lead not only to an increase in FDI by protecting the rights of minority shareholders against the owners and managers of firms (Bishop, 2002), but also provide confidence that is necessary for an efficient functioning of market economies. This is very crucial for lowering cost of capital (Principles of Corporate Governance, 2004, p. 11, OECD).

Emerging market countries have recently taken important steps in improving their corporate governance systems, considering the fact that a good corporate governance system is crucial for attracting more FDI.

However, it may be argued that FDI would also lead to an improvement in corporate governance system of host countries to the extent that MNCs could introduce advanced managerial techniques, including corporate governance principles. For example, Yudaeva, Kozlov, Melentieva, and Ponomareva (2003) find that, in Russia, majority foreign-owned firms are more efficiently managed and have minimal corporate governance problems. In contrast to their findings, Kogut and Macpherson (2003, p. 203) provide evidence that corporate governance in developing countries may not be improved by majority-owned FDI, no matter what type of FDI it is. Instead, they argue that minority investors could play an important role in improving the corporate governance system (Kogut & Macpherson, 2003, pp. 208–209).[19]

These contradictory views will form the basis of my second hypothesis. It is, therefore, hypothesized that:

Hypothesis 2. There is a positive relation between FDI inflow and corporate governance, which may run in both ways.

4. EMPIRICAL ANALYSIS

4.1. Data and Models Used

Data used in the study except for those concerning accounting standards and legal framework have been obtained from the World Competitiveness Yearbook, 2007. The World Competitiveness Yearbook has been published by the International Institute for Management Development (IMD) in Switzerland since 1989 and provides comprehensive economic, social, managerial, and legal statistics on national economies, which are based on data released by the IMF, the World Bank, and UNCTAD (see Table 2).

I compiled data on accounting standards from two different sources:

- IAS Plus – Use of IFRS for Reporting by Domestic Listed and Unlisted Companies by Country and Region and
- Use of IAS around the World[20]

Considering the fact that both US-GAAP and IFRS are high quality international accounting standards,[21] I created a dummy variable to

Table 2. List of Variables: Description, Notations, and Expected Signs.

Description of Variables	Measure	Notation	Expected Sign
Foreign direct investment inflow	Natural logarithm of FDI inflow (US$billion)	ln FDI	
High quality accounting standards	Dummy variable	ACCST	+
Market size	Natural logarithm of GDP at purchasing power parity (US$billion)	ln GDP	+
Openness of economy	Natural logarithm of share of export in GDP	ln EXPGDP	+
Inflation rate	Natural logarithm of GDP deflator	ln GDPDEFL	−
Effectiveness of corporate governance	Natural logarithm of corporate governance index	ln CORPGOV	+
One-year lagged foreign direct investment inflow	Natural logarithm of one-year lagged FDI inflow (US$billion)	ln FDI_LAG	+
Common-law system	Dummy variable	ENG	+
French code-law system	Dummy variable	FRENCH	+/−
German code-law system	Dummy variable	GERMAN	+/−
Effectiveness in controlling of corruption	Natural logarithm of control of corruption index	ln CONTRCORR	+

measure accounting quality using the following method. First, all of the countries are classified into three groups as follows:

- Countries that require the use of IFRS and/or US-GAAP,
- Countries that allow the use of IFRS and/or US-GAAP, and
- Countries that require only the use of domestic accounting standards.

Second, they are classified further as countries with high quality accounting standards and countries with low quality accounting standards.

High quality accounting standards: Countries that require or allow the use of IFRS or US-GAAP: ACCST = 1
Low quality accounting standards: Countries that require the use of domestic accounting standards: ACCST = 0

In order to measure the effect of corporate governance on FDI inflows, I use a composite index which is the simple average of the following indexes of corporate governance mechanism by IMD:[22]

• Credibility of managers in society (*credibility of managers is prevalent in society*),
• Effectiveness of corporate boards in management of companies (*corporate boards do supervise the management of companies effectively*), and
• Adequacy and implementation of accounting and auditing practices (*auditing and accounting practices are adequately implemented in business*).

These indexes are based on executive opinion surveys and are each scored from 0 to 10. Accordingly, my corporate governance composite index takes on values between 0 and 10.

It is the CEO and senior management that run day-to-day business operations of companies. They are also responsible for identifying and developing strategic plans to achieve long term goals. In addition, senior management is responsible to insure that financial reporting system produces reliable financial information for decision makers. Both CEO and senior management are expected to operate the company with integrity and due care. They should never put their personal interests before those of shareholders and investors (Principles of Corporate Governance, 2002). Prevalence of credible managers, who run companies in an ethical manner, complying with rules and regulations, will contribute to the effectiveness of the corporate governance system in society. In practice, effective corporate governance rests upon the presence of an effective corporate board. Millstein (1995, p. 451) argues that the corporate board is the focal point of the corporate governance; it hires, compensates, and evaluates CEO and senior management.

In addition to adequacy, effective implementation of accounting standards depends largely on the ability of the corporate board and its internal audit committee. Implementation of high quality accounting standards is as important as their adequacy for an effective corporate governance system. Many developing countries have recently adopted IFRS in order to attract FDI. However, adoption of IFRS would be insufficient without implementing them effectively. Effective implementation requires a well-developed and effective internal control system, and well-educated and experienced accountants.

Corporate governance is closely associated with the effectiveness of legal system, which is primarily classified as common law and code law. Prior research documents that common law countries protect investors' rights better than code law countries do (La Porta, Lopez-de-Silanes, Shleifer, & Vishny, 1998). In this study, both common law (ENG) and code law (FRENCH and GER) are used as instrumental variables to measure the impact of legal system on corporate governance.

One of the major problems that studies on corporate governance should deal with is endogeneity (Renders & Gaeremynck, 2006). To address the possible endogeneity of corporate governance, I estimate both G2SLS and GMM for panel data using the following model.

G2SLS IV:

$$\ln FDI_{it} = \alpha_0 + \alpha_1 \ln GDP_{it} + \alpha_2 \ln EXPGDP_{it} + \alpha_3 \ln GDPDEFL_{it}$$
$$+ \alpha_4 ACCST_{it} + \alpha_5 \ln CORPGOV_{it} + u_{it}$$

First Stage G2SLS Regression:

$$\ln CORPGOV_{it} = \beta_0 + \beta_1 \ln GDP_{it} + \beta_2 \ln EXPGDP_{it} + \beta_3 \ln GDPDEFL_{it}$$
$$+ \beta_4 ACCST_{it} + \beta_5 \ln FDI\_LAG_{it} + \beta_6 ENG_{it} + \beta_7 FRENCH_{it}$$
$$+ \beta_8 GERMAN_{it} + \beta_9 \ln CONTRCORR_{it} + \varepsilon_{it}$$

The model establishes a relation between FDI and its determinants that include ACCST and CORPGOV in addition to macroeconomic variables. As noted in the introduction section of the study, I expect a positive association of ACCST and CORPGOV with FDI.

In the first stage G2SLS regression, CORPGOV is regressed on GDP, EXPGDP, GDPDEFL, ACCST, and instrumental variables FDI_LAG, ENG, FRENCH, GER, and CONTRCORR. Estimation results using this model are presented in the following section of the study.

4.2. Empirical Results

Table 3 presents 27 emerging market countries, which are classified into Asian, Central and Eastern European and Latin American groups. The Latin American group includes the six largest economies in the region.

In Tables 4 through 7 descriptive statistics – number of observations, mean values and standard deviations – for dependent and independent variables for all countries and country groups are presented.

ACCST has a mean value of 0.43 for all available observations, which may be interpreted that almost the half of emerging market countries have adopted high quality accounting standards. Across country groups, the value of this variable ranges from 0.15 in Latin American countries to 0.82

Table 3. Emerging Market Countries.

Asian Group	Central and Eastern European Group	Latin American Group
China	Bulgaria	Argentina
HongKong	Czech Republic	Brazil
India	Estonia	Chile
Indonesia	Greece	Colombia
Korea	Hungary	Mexico
Malaysia	Poland	Venezuela
Philippines	Romania	
Singapore	Russia	
Taiwan	Slovakia	
Thailand	Slovenia	
	Turkey	

Table 4. Descriptive Statistics.

Variable	N	Mean	Standard Deviation
Panel A: All available observations, 1997–2005			
Dependent variable:			
FDI	238	1.23	1.35
Independent variables:			
ACCST	243	0.43	0.50
CONTCORR	162	3.94	0.53
CORPGOV	185	1.71	0.17
FDI_LAG	237	1.23	1.35
ENG	234	0.19	0.39
EXPGDP	236	3.48	0.76
FRENCH	234	0.42	0.50
GDP	240	5.66	1.28
GDPDEFL	243	5.19	1.47
GERMAN	234	0.35	0.48

in Central and Eastern European countries, meaning that there has been a significant preference in the latter to use high quality accounting standards even before IFRS became mandatory starting in 2005 in EU countries. CORPGOV variable has nearly the same value across country groups, ranging from 1.60 in Central and Eastern European countries to 1.78 in Asian countries group. For all observations, ENG that represents common law system takes a value of 0.19, indicating that the code law (FRENCH and GERMAN) system is widespread in emerging market countries.

Table 5. Descriptive Statistics.

Variable	N	Mean	Standard Deviation
Panel B: Asian Countries, 1997–2005			
Dependent variable:			
FDI	85	1.68	1.33
Independent variables:			
ACCST	90	0.18	0.38
CONTCORR	60	3.94	0.60
CORPGOV	72	1.78	0.14
FDI_LAG	84	1.67	1.34
ENG	90	0.50	0.50
EXPGDP	90	3.85	0.80
FRENCH	90	0.20	0.40
GDP	90	6.28	1.19
GDPDEFL	90	4.91	0.44
GERMAN	90	0.30	0.46

Table 6. Descriptive Statistics.

Variable	N	Mean	Standard Deviation
Panel C: Central and Eastern European Countries, 1997–2005			
Dependent variable:			
FDI	99	0.50	1.21
Independent variables:			
ACCST	99	0.82	0.39
CONTCORR	66	4.06	0.39
CORPGOV	65	1.60	0.15
FDI_LAG	99	0.52	1.21
ENG	90	0.00	0.00
EXPGDP	92	3.45	0.64
FRENCH	90	0.30	0.46
GDP	96	4.93	1.20
GDPDEFL	99	5.46	2.20
GERMAN	90	0.60	0.49

However, it is observed that there is a strong preference in Asian countries to adopt common law system. Hong Kong, India, Malaysia, Singapore, and Thailand are common law countries. In contrast to Asian group, both Central and Eastern European countries and Latin American countries have code law system.[23]

Table 7. Descriptive Statistics.

Variable	N	Mean	Standard Deviation
Panel D: Latin American Countries, 1997–2005			
Dependent variable:			
FDI	54	1.87	0.95
Independent variables:			
ACCST	54	0.15	0.36
CONTCORR	36	3.74	0.56
CORPGOV	48	1.75	0.15
FDI_LAG	54	1.84	0.98
ENG	54	0.00	0.00
EXPGDP	54	2.91	0.48
FRENCH	54	1.00	0.00
GDP	54	5.95	0.85
GDPDEFL	54	5.17	0.57
GERMAN	54	0.00	0.00

Table 8 presents Pearson correlations matrix among dependent and independent variables. FDI variable is highly correlated with FDI_LAG, GDP, CORPGOV, and ENG. A high correlation between FDI and GDP suggests that FDI is mainly of market-seeking type, consistent with the arguments made in Section 2. There is a positive correlation between FDI and CONTRCORR though it is weak ($\rho = 0.04$). By contrast, the correlation between CONTRCORR and CORPGOV is very strong ($\rho = 0.39$), implying that an increase in the ability of emerging market countries to control corruption would improve corporate governance system. CORPGOV is also highly correlated with ENG ($\rho = 0.38$). This may suggest that countries with common law system have more efficient corporate governance system than do countries with code law system. In contrast to my expectation, FDI is negatively correlated with ACCST.

A strong positive correlation exists between FDI_LAG and CORPGOV ($\rho = 0.20$).[24]

It is noteworthy that there is a strong negative correlation ($\rho = -0.3402$) between ACCST and CORPGOV reflecting a trade-off between these two variables.

A strong positive relationship exists between CORPGOV and EXPGDP, which represents the openness of economies ($\rho = 0.2172$). More specifically, an increase in openness is associated with good corporate governance. This appears plausible because open economies, which are economically

Table 8. Pearson Correlations Matrix, 1997–2005.

	FDI	ACCST	CONTRCORR	CORPGOV	FDI_LAG	ENG	EXPGDP	FRENCH	GDP	GDPDEFL	GERMAN
FDI	1.0000										
ACCST	-0.1112	1.0000									
CONTRCORR	0.0444	0.0292	1.0000								
CORPGOV	0.1990	-0.3402	0.3946	1.0000							
FDI_LAG	0.1863	-0.2932	-0.1437	0.2005	1.0000						
ENG	0.2359	-0.2345	0.2596	0.3834	0.1274	1.0000					
EXPGDP	0.0330	0.0232	0.2581	0.2172	0.0285	0.4510	1.0000				
FRENCH	-0.0943	-0.1587	-0.3760	0.1097	0.1411	-0.4179	-0.5249	1.0000			
GDP	0.5544	-0.2401	-0.3636	-0.0758	0.1668	0.0134	-0.4477	0.0516	1.0000		
GDPDEFL	-0.1106	0.1772	-0.0925	0.0773	-0.0047	-0.1359	-0.1222	0.2316	0.0330	1.0000	
GERMAN	-0.1188	0.2812	0.3125	-0.3615	-0.2234	-0.3550	0.1724	-0.6231	-0.1527	-0.0623	1.0000

integrated with the rest of the world, need to have an effective corporate governance system in order to lure foreign investors.

Table 9 presents regression results based on G2SLS and GMM estimation techniques.[25]

In Regression 1 that reports the results of G2SLS random effect model, all the variables are highly significant. Consistent with my hypotheses, FDI is positively strongly related to ACCST and CORPGOV, indicating that high quality accounting standards and good corporate governance lead to an increase in FDI. The overall model explains a significant amount of the variation in FDI ($R^2 = 0.34$). Among the control variables are GDP, EXPGDP, and GDPDEFL major determinants of FDI.

Regression 2 presents the first stage estimation of random effect model, in which CORPGOV is used as a dependent variable. Results indicate that main variables of interest, ACCST and FDI_LAG, are not significant determinant of CORPGOV. It appears that GER is the only legal system that is significant. CONTRCORR is positively strongly related to CORPGOV, meaning that an increase in the ability of emerging market countries to control corruption improves CORPGOV.[26]

Regression 3 reports the results of the G2SLS fixed effect estimation model. As with Regression 1, all the variables are again highly significant, and the model captures a significant portion of the variation in FDI ($R^2 = 0.34$). The strength of this model is that it enables the researcher to test the endogeneity using Davidson–McKinnon test. The result indicates that there is endogeneity between FDI and CORPGOV.[27]

Regression 4 presents the results of first stage estimation of fixed effect model. In contrast to Regression 2, FDI_LAG is significant and appears to lead to an improvement in CORPGOV. As in Regression 2, GER and CONTRCORR are strongly related to CORPGOV.

Finally, Regression 5 presents the results of GMM estimation technique, which is used to control the heteroskedasticity.[28]

In addition to the adjusted coefficient of determination (adj. $R^2 = 0.14$), this model reports three statistics, which test the validity of the instruments selected. All of these statistics yield highly significant results, indicating the suitability of the model. Kleinbergen-Paap rk LM statistic is a test of under-identification that determines whether the excluded instruments are correlated with the endogenous variable. The null hypothesis that the equation is under-identified is rejected, meaning that selected instruments are relevant.[29] Hansen J-statistic is a test of over-identification of all instruments. The results indicate that the joint hypothesis that the instruments are relevant, that is, uncorrelated with the error term, and that

Table 9. Regression Results

G2SLS IV : $\ln \text{FDI}_{it} = \alpha_0 + \alpha_1 \ln \text{GDP}_{it} + \alpha_2 \ln \text{EXPGDP}_{it} + \alpha_3 \ln \text{GDPDEFL}_{it}$
$+ \alpha_4 \text{ACCST}_{it} + \alpha_5 \ln \text{CORPGOV}_{it} + u_{it}$

First Stage G2SLS : $\ln \text{CORPGOV}_{it} = \beta_0 + \beta_1 \ln \text{GDP}_{it} + \beta_2 \ln \text{EXPGDP}_{it}$
$+ \beta_3 \ln \text{GDPDEFL}_{it} + \beta_4 \text{ACCST}_{it}$
$+ \beta_5 \ln \text{FDI\_LAG}_{it} + \beta_6 \text{ENG}_{it} + \beta_7 \text{FRENCH}_{it}$
$+ \beta_8 \text{GER}_{it} + \beta_9 \ln \text{CONTCORP}_{it} + \varepsilon_{it}$

	(1)	(2)	(3)	(4)	(5)
	G2SLS (RE)	G2SLS (RE)	G2SLS (FE)	G2SLS (FE)	GMM (FE)
CORPGOV	5.112***		4.982***		5.422***
	(1.13)		(1.15)		(1.14)
GDP	0.796***	0.029**	0.795***	0.022	0.759***
	(0.10)	(0.015)	(0.11)	(0.015)	(0.087)
EXPGDP	0.416***	0.080***	0.438***	0.071**	0.363**
	(0.15)	(0.022)	(0.16)	(0.023)	(0.18)
GDPDEFL	−0.160**	−0.000	−0.153**	0.000	−0.154***
	(0.068)	(0.008)	(0.068)	(0.008)	(0.059)
ACCST	0.898***	−0.023	0.874***	−0.027	0.998***
	(0.26)	(0.029)	(0.26)	(0.030)	(0.26)
FDI_LAG		0.012		0.016*	
		(0.009)		(0.009)	
ENG		0.029		0.025	
		(0.070)		(0.070)	
FRENCH		0.100		0.083	
		(0.071)		(0.073)	
GER		−0.121**		−0.128**	
		(0.064)		(0.065)	
CONTCORR		0.174***		0.170***	
		(0.028)		(0.028)	
CONSTANT	−13.06***	0.554**	−12.93***	0.644**	
	(2.03)	(0.213)	(2.10)	(0.223)	
Observations	130	130	130	130	130
Number of year	6				6
R^2	.				0.21
R-overall	0.333		0.337		
R-within	0.316		0.256		
R-between	0.731		0.722		
R-adj	.		.		0.142
Waldtest	79.36	120	264.6		
Kleinbergen-Paap					26.50

Table 9.   (*Continued*)

	(1)	(2)	(3)	(4)	(5)
	G2SLS (RE)	G2SLS (RE)	G2SLS (FE)	G2SLS (FE)	GMM (FE)
p-value					0.0000714
Hansen-Jstat					5.352
p-value					0.253
Davidson-McKinnontest				6.019	
p-value				0.016	
Endogeneitytest					14.127
p-value					0.0002

Standard errors in parentheses.***p<0.01, **p<0.05, and *p<0.1.
Notes: Dependent variables are inflow of FDI in US billion dollars and CORPGOV. With the exception of ACCST, ENG, FRENCH, and GER all the variables are in natural logarithms. Estimations (2) and (4) are first stage results. RE and FE are abbreviations for random and fixed effect, respectively. Standard errors are robust with a correction of heteroskedasticity. Instrumented: CORPGOV; Included Instruments: GDP, EXPGDP, GDPDEFL, ACCST; Excluded Instruments: FDI_LAG, ENG, FRENCH, GER, and CONTRCORR.

the excluded instruments are correctly excluded from the estimated equation is accepted (*p*-value = 0.25). Finally, C-statistic tests the endogeneity. The null hypothesis that the variable is exogenous is rejected, meaning that CORPGOV is an endogenous variable (*p*-value = 0.0002).

Table 10 presents the results of G2SLS estimation technique based on random effect (RE) and fixed effect (FE) models for country groups. Regression results show that main explanatory variables, ACCST and CORPGOV are highly significant in both RE and FE models for Asian and Latin American groups. However, they turn out to be insignificant for Central and Eastern countries group. The only variables that are significant for this group are GDP and EXPGDP, suggesting that FDI is of market-seeking type and positively related to the export capability of countries.

The legal system instruments appear to have different effects on CORPGOV. For Asian group, only FRENCH is highly significant and has a positive effect on CORPGOV. ENG has a positive sign, though not significant. For this country group, GERMAN is dropped. For Central and Eastern European countries group, ENG is dropped indicating that the countries in this group have entirely French or German code-law systems. French and German code-law systems yield mixed results; FRENCH is positively related to CORPGOV though it is not significant. On the other

Table 10. Regression Results

$$\text{G2SLS IV}: \ln \text{FDI}_{it} = \alpha_0 + \alpha_1 \ln \text{GDP}_{it} + \alpha_2 \ln \text{EXPGDP}_{it} + \alpha_3 \ln \text{GDPDEFL}_{it} + \alpha_4 \text{ACCST}_{it} + \alpha_5 \ln \text{CORPGOV}_{it} + u_{it}$$

$$\text{First Stage G2SLS}: \ln \text{CORPGOV}_{it} = \beta_0 + \beta_1 \ln \text{GDP}_{it} + \beta_2 \ln \text{EXPGDP}_{it} + \beta_3 \ln \text{GDPDEFL}_{it} + \beta_4 \text{ACCST}_{it} + \beta_5 \ln \text{FDI\_LAG}_{it} + \beta_6 \text{ENG}_{it} + \beta_7 \text{FRENCH} + \beta_8 \text{GER} + \beta_9 \ln \text{CONTRCORR}_{it} + \varepsilon_{it}$$

	(1)	(2)	(3)	(4)	(5)	(6)	(7)	(8)	(9)
	RE_ASIA	RE_ASIA	FE_ASIA	RE_CE	RE_CE	FE_CE	RE_LATIN	RE_LATIN	FE_LATIN
CORPGOV	3.919**		3.374*	-2.715		-4.984	4.440***		4.247***
	(1.72)		(1.77)	(2.55)		(3.27)	(1.44)		(1.36)
GDP	0.917***	0.052	0.998***	0.852***	0.030	0.756***	1.362***	-0.095*	1.423***
	(0.29)	(0.03)	(0.36)	(0.18)	(0.041)	(0.21)	(0.24)	(0.036)	(0.22)
EXPGDP	0.944**	0.092**	1.126**	0.892***	0.134*	0.640*	0.278	-0.108	0.648*
	(0.43)	(0.04)	(0.52)	(0.26)	(0.078)	(0.34)	(0.33)	(0.681)	(0.33)
GDPDEFL	-0.190	-0.019	-0.256	0.0173	-0.000	0.0484	-0.435	0.117**	-0.338
	(0.33)	(0.035)	(0.34)	(0.080)	(0.016)	(0.091)	(0.27)	(0.056)	(0.24)
ACCST	1.403***	-0.037	1.275***	0.136	-0.024	-0.0335	1.099**	0.113	0.923**
	(0.43)	(0.037)	(0.49)	(0.66)	(0.084)	(0.76)	(0.52)	(0.112)	(0.47)
FDI_LAG		0.011			-0.020			0.011	
		(0.008)			(0.017)			(0.023)	

	(1)	(2)	(3)	(4)	(5)	(6)	(7)	(8)
ENG	0.032							
	(0.033)							
FRENCH	0.167**				0.045			0.876**
	(0.078)				(0.235)			(0.458)
GER					−0.327*			
					(0.183)			
CONTRCORR	0.265***				0.276*			0.296***
	(0.043)				(0.149)			(0.075)
CONSTANT	−14.23***	0.073	−14.13**	−2.710	0.072	2.264	−12.84***	−14.46***
	(4.71)	(0.445)	(5.49)	(4.78)	(0.75)	(6.44)	(3.67)	(3.73)
Observations	49	49	49	45	45	45	36	36
Number of year	6	6	6	6	6	6	6	6
R^2								
R-overall	0.607		0.614	0.465		0.329	0.613	0.603
R-within	0.619		0.627	0.504		0.361	0.677	0.670
R-between	0.428		0.395	0.0290		0.428	0.136	0.0142
R-adj								
Waldtest	70.45	142	218.6	40.29	22	55.08	51.65	370.3

Standard errors in parentheses. *** <0.01, ** $p<0.05$, and * $p<0.1$.

Notes: Dependent variables are inflow of FDI in US billion dollars and CORPGOV. With the exception of ACCST, ENG, FRENCH, and GER all the variables are in natural logarithms. Estimations (2), (5), and (8) are first stage results. RE and FE are abbreviations for random and fixed effect, respectively. Instrumented: CORPGOV; Included Instruments: GDP, EXPGDP, GDPDEFL, ACCST; Excluded Instruments: FDI_LAG, ENG, FRENCH, GER, and CONTRCORR.

hand, GERMAN is significant, but has negative sign, implying that there is a negative association between German code-law system and CORPGOV in Eastern and Central European countries. Finally, for Latin American countries, FRENCH has a strong positive impact on CORPGOV. ENG is dropped because there is no country in this group that has been identified by common-law system.

Overall, the results are consistent with my hypotheses that the adoption of high quality accounting standards and a good corporate governance mechanism supported by an effective legal system are essential for emerging market countries to attract more FDI (Alfaro, Kalemli-Ozcan, & Volosovych, 2004b).

5. CONCLUSIONS

Although FDI inflows have been steadily increasing since 1950s, the increase in its growth rate has become more striking over the past three decades in consequence of globalization. Since then, both developing and developed economies have been competing with each other in order to attract FDI. What makes FDI more attractive than other types of capital flows is a number of non-financial benefits provided by MNEs that are considered a crucial vehicle for maintaining economic development in host countries.

In this study, I used the G2SLS and GMM estimation techniques in examining FDI inflows from the viewpoint of accounting standards and corporate governance.

My finding, which FDI is strongly and positively associated with high quality accounting standards and good corporate governance, is important for a number of groups including investors, governments, accounting standard setters, and capital markets regulators.

In addition to the groups mentioned above, these findings are also useful for emerging market countries seeking to increase their shares of FDI in world total. Both the use of high quality accounting standards – IFRS and US-GAAP – and good corporate governance practices would lead to an increase in FDI inflow.

My analyses suggest that there could be a bi-directional relationship between FDI and corporate governance in the overall sample for fixed effect model.

Besides contributions, the study has some constraints. First, it covers a relatively short period of time, resulting in a small sample size. Therefore, economic benefits from adopting of high quality accounting standards and good corporate governance practices might not have been fully reflected in the results. Second, as in many international studies, I have got some difficulties in obtaining complete data. Therefore, some developing countries have been excluded from the sample. Third, corporate governance index has been constructed using only three variables. In fact, there is a variety of factors that could have an influence on corporate governance.

A future study that would focus on the characteristics of relationship between FDI and corporate governance in different emerging countries groups may be interesting.

NOTES

1. According to OECD, an ownership of 10% or more of ordinary shares or voting power of a corporation is called direct investment (Benchmark Definition of Foreign Direct Investment, OECD, 1999). Besides direct investments, foreign aid, commercial loans, and portfolio investments are other types of capital flows. The share of foreign aid in total capital flows has been continuously declining since 1960s (Bergsman & Shen, 1995). Commercial loans, which were considered as a major source of capital flows in 1970s, became trivial after financial crises of 1980s.

2. There is not a single definition of MNC on which everybody agrees. One definition refers to a firm that operates and controls income-generating activities in more than one country (Dunning, 1973).

3. In this paper, the term "developing country" is interchangeably used with "emerging market country". Emerging market countries account for approximately 80% of world population. One major characteristic of emerging market countries is that they are in a transitional phase, moving from developing to developed market economies. Former Soviet Republic and Eastern Bloc countries, China, and Mexico constitute examples for emerging market countries (Mody, 2004; Bond, 1970).

4. Growing domestic markets, low costs of production and extensive privatizations of state-owned enterprises have been the major impetus for attracting FDI, especially into a small number of emerging market economies in Latin America and Asia (Pugel & Lindert, 2000, p. 630; Foreign Direct Investment and Technology Transfer in India, United Nations, New York, 1992).

5. Both accounting standards and corporate governance owe their increasing importance mainly to the development of capital markets in consequence of globalization. Global accounting standards are considered as a major factor among others that enables the functioning of capital markets efficiently by facilitating the transfer of idle funds across countries smoothly. It is observed that many emerging market countries have recently accelerated their efforts either to adopt International Financial Reporting Standards (IFRS) or to adapt them to their domestic accounting standards, following the decision of EU that requires the use of IFRS for listed companies in preparing of financial statements starting in 2005. Corporate governance is another major factor that influences investment decisions in emerging market countries considerably (Gibson, 2003). Poor corporate governance, which

adversely affects both the development of capital markets and economic growth, has been blamed for financial crises in emerging market countries (Johnson, Boone, Breach, & Friedman, 2000).

6. Portfolio investments are also important in financing economic growth; however, they are regarded as volatile and risky as evidenced by financial crises that shook some of the Asian and Latin American countries in 1980s and 1990s. It is widely believed that portfolio investments and short-term bank loans would lead to financial crises if they were not effectively managed. Currency crises of 1990s in Asian and Latin American countries are said to have resulted from portfolio investments that left these countries suddenly as a result of changes in interest rates (Evans, 2002; Bergsman, 2000; Reinhardt, 1999).

7. There are a number of studies that examine the relationship of FDI with market size and labor cost. For example, Schmitz and Bieri (1972), Agarwal (1980), Kravis and Lipsey (1982), Schneider and Frey (1985), Wang and Swain (1995), and Billington (1999) have established a link between FDI and market size, which is measured by GDP or per capita GDP. For studies that examine the relationship between FDI and labor cost (see e.g. Schneider & Frey, 1985; Culem, 1988).

8. Effectiveness rather than extensiveness of legal framework is crucial for attracting FDI. In other words, legal infrastructure, even if it improves the shareholder rights, will not be sufficient to lure foreign investors as long as written legal rules are not effectively applied (Pistor, Raiser, & Gelfer, 2000).

9. Another regional economy that needs to be addressed here is India that maintained economic and political stability over this period. In 2005, FDI inflows in India exceeded $6 billion as a result of high growth rates of the economy and stock market.

10. "Perhaps most spectacular in its drive to reform has been China, despite its huge size and large number of corporate scandals ... There can be little doubt that China has made more progress in improving corporate governance in the last decade than other countries have achieved in a century" (Roche, 2005, p. 66).

11. Although Preobragenskaya and McGee (2005) regard the lack of credible financial reporting information as an obstacle for attracting FDIs, they do not make any further explanation as to which form of FDIs – M&As or greenfield investments – is more sensitive to financial reporting quality. Nor do they examine the effect of accounting standards on FDI empirically.

12. A number of Asian countries have improved non-financial disclosure and now require that listed companies disclose corporate governance practices and structures (White Paper on Corporate Governance in Asia, 2003, p. 45).

13. Corporate governance does not have a single and universally accepted definition. Rather, it is defined in many different ways by authors. According to one definition, corporate governance is a set of relationships between a company's shareholders, its board of directors, and its management (White Paper on Corporate Governance in Asia, 2003, p. 12; Roche, 2005, p. 4; Colley, Doyle, Logan, & Stettinius, 2005; Gillan & Starks, 2003; La Porta, Lopez-de-Silanes, Shleifer, & Vishny, 2000; Monks & Minow, 1995, p. 1). Shleifer and Vishny (1997) define corporate governance as a mechanism that ensures that investors in corporations get a return on their investments.

14. For example, in order to attract more FDI, China adopted a reform package to improve legal framework, corporate governance, and financial reporting

standards in the 1980s (Zhang, 2001). One major reason of this is that investors do not always purchase all of the shares of acquired companies. In other words, both forms of FDI – greenfield investments and M&As – may result in either wholly foreign owned or partly foreign owned investments. About 30% of acquisitions in developing countries aim to acquire minority interests, for which good corporate governance is considered very important (Bishop, 2002; Claessens & Fan, 2002; Claessens, Djankov, & Lang, 2000).

15. Garcia-Herrera and Santabarbara (2005) argue the effect of China on Latin American countries as one of the largest recipients of FDI. They conclude that, in recent years, FDI inflows into China might have adversely affected FDI in some Latin American countries such as Mexico and Colombia.

16. Latin American countries experienced different performances in FDI inflows. For example, FDI inflows declined in Brazil, Mexico, and Chile, three major economies in the region, in 2005 while they increased in Argentina due to high economic growth. On the other hand, FDI inflows into Colombia increased threefold as a result of cross-border acquisitions of local firms (World Investment Report, 2006, chap. II).

17. See Table 3 for the list of emerging market country groups included in this study.

18. Although financial reporting systems and financial reporting standards are synonymously used (Bhattacharyya, 2006), these do not have the same meaning. Financial reporting systems are more comprehensive than financial reporting standards since they additionally cover some institutional factors.

19. The validity of this argument may be suspected because high concentration of ownership in Asian corporations would have a deterrent impact on minority shareholders since it increases the risk of expropriating their rights by controlling shareholders (Claessens & Fan, 2002; Claessens et al., 2000). In general, high ownership concentration refers to poor protection of minority shareholders (La Porta et al., 1998; LeFort & Walker, 2000). Ownership structure of companies in emerging market countries is different than that of companies in Anglo-Saxon countries, such as the US and the UK. In both countries, ownership structure is widely dispersed. For example, shares of ownership by three largest shareholders in 10 largest private non-financial firms in the US and UK are 20% and 19%, respectively. However, in Asian countries except for South Korea and Taiwan, it ranges from 49% (Singapore) to 58% (Indonesia) (La Porta et al., 1998; Capaul, 2003; Stulz, 2005).

20. http://www.iasplus.com/country/use.ias.htm; http://bodurtha.georgetown.edu/IAS_39/FAS-IAS/use_of_ias_around the world

21. Tarca (2004) suggests that both US-GAAP and IAS be named as international accounting standards. In general, both US-GAAP and IFRS are considered high quality accounting standards. The idea is supported by a survey conducted by KPMG on 509 large companies whose headquarters are located in one of 17 European countries. The countries also include Switzerland and Norway in addition to 15 member countries of EU. Over a quarter of respondents report that they consider changing the basis of preparing their financial statements in the short-run. A majority of respondents want to adopt IAS while another 29% want to adopt US-GAAP. More than 50% of respondents rated US-GAAP as being high-quality standards. The majority of the other half rated IAS as being high quality standards while few

respondents rated either GAAP as being poor quality standards (Global Financial Reporting, IAS or US GAAP? European Survey, KPMG: April, 2000).

22. The corporate governance index is the same as was used by Akisik and Pfeiffer (2007).

23. In Asian group, China, Korea, and Taiwan have German code law system. Indonesia and The Philippines are identified with French code law system.

24. A positive correlation does not mean that changes in one variable will necessarily cause changes in the other variable. There could be a one-, or two-way relation between these variables.

25. I conducted the Hausman test in order to determine if there is endogeneity. The null hypothesis that OLS is an appropriate estimation technique is rejected (p-value $= 0.024$), indicating that CORPGOV is endogeneous.

26. When I run this regression using ENG as the only legal instrument, untabulated results show that CORPGOV turns out to be strongly positively related to FDI_LAG, ENG, and CONTRCORR instruments. This may suggest that, besides CONTCORR, FDI_LAG and ENG are crucial determinants of CORPGOV.

In Stata, Sargan–Hansen statistic computes the test of over-identifying restrictions. Untabulated results of this statistics suggest that the null hypothesis that the instruments are uncorrelated with the error term should be accepted (p-value $= 0.5095$).

27. In Stata, Davidson–McKinnon test that is an augmented form of Hausman test computes exogeneity for a fixed-effect regression model via instrumental variables. A rejection of null hypothesis means that the variable tested is endogenous and instrumental variables techniques should be used in analysis. In my analysis, null hypothesis is rejected (p-value $= 0.0151$), indicating that CORPGOV is endogenous.

28. Generalized Method of Moments (GMM) estimation technique has been introduced by L. Hansen (Baum, Schaffer, & Stillman, 2007).

29. An instrumental variable must have two properties: (1) it must be exogenous, that is, uncorrelated with the error term of the structural equation; (2) it must be partially correlated with the endogenous variable. Finding a variable with these two properties is usually challenging" Wooldridge (2006, p. 540).

ACKNOWLEDGMENTS

I am grateful to Michael Ash, Christopher F. Baum, Peter Ireland, Bernard Morzuch, Suleyman Ozmucur, Ray J. Pfeiffer Jr., Pinar Uysal, Erinc Yeldan, and three anonymous referees for their valuable comments and suggestions.

REFERENCES

Agarwal, J. P. (1980). Determinants of foreign direct investment: A survey. *Weltwirtschaftliches Archiv, 116*(4), 739–773.

Agosin, M. R., & Pastén, E. H. (2003). *Corporate governance in chile*. Central Bank of Chile, Working Papers, No. 209.

Akisik, O., & Pfeiffer, R. J. Jr. (2007). *Globalization, US foreign investments and accounting standards*. Working Paper, November, Isenberg School of Management, University of Massachusetts-Amherst.

Alfaro, L., Chanda, A., Kalemli-Ozcan, S., & Sayek, S. (2004a). FDI and economic growth: The role of local financial markets. *Journal of International Economics*, *64*, 89–112.

Alfaro, L., Kalemli-Ozcan, S., & Volosovych, V. (2004b). *Capital flows in a globalized world: The role of policies and institutions*. Working Paper, December, 17–18, Prepared for the NBER Conference on International Capital Flows.

Apreda, R. (1999). *Corporate governance in Argentina – New developments through 1991–2000*. Working Paper. Available at http://www.cema.edu.ar/publicaciones/download/documentos/154.pdf

Baniak, A., Cukrowski, J., & Herczynski, J. (2002). *On determinants of foreign direct investment in transition economies*. Working Paper, December. Available at http://www.cerge.cuni.cz/pdf/gdn/RRCII_41_paper_01.pdf

Barclay, L. A. A. (2000). *Foreign direct investment in emerging economies – corporate strategy and investment behaviour in the Caribbean*. London and New York: Routledge Studies in International Business and the World Economy.

Baum, C. F., Schaffer, M. E., & Stillman, S. (2007). Enhanced routines for instrumental variables/generalized method of moments estimation and testing. *The Stata Journal*, *7*(4), 465–506.

Bedõ, Z., & Ozsvald, E. (2007). Corporate governance and ownership concentration on the Budapest stock exchange. In: B. Dallaga & I. Iwasaki (Eds), *Corporate restructuring and governance in transition economies* (pp. 135–155). Studies in Economic Transition, Great Britain: Palgrave Macmillan.

Benchmark Definition of Foreign Direct Investment, OECD. (1999). 3rd Edition. Available at http://www.oecd.org/dataoecd/10/16/2090148.pdf

Berglöf, E., & Pajuste, A. (2005). *What do firms disclose and why? Enforcing corporate governance and transparency in central and Eastern Europe*. Working Paper, Stockholm School of Economics: Stockholm, Sweden.

Bergsman, J. (2000). Is there competition for foreign direct investment? In: L. Sawers, D. Schydlowsky & D. Nickerson (Eds) *Emerging financial markets in the global economy* (pp. 261–272). Singapore: World Scientific.

Bergsman, J., & Shen, X. (1995). Foreign direct investment in developing countries: Progress and problems. *Finance & Development*, *32*(4), 6–8.

Bevan, A. A., & Estrin, S. (2004). The determinants of foreign direct investments into European transition economies. *Journal of Comparative Economics*, *32*, 775–787.

Bevan, A. A., Estrin, S., & Meyer, K. (2004). Foreign investment location and institutional development in transition economies. *International Business Review*, *13*, 43–64.

Bhattacharyya, A. K. (2006). Do we need national accounting norms? *Business Standard*, *26*(October). http://www.business-standard.com/economy/storypage.php

Billington, N. (1999). The location of foreign direct investment: An empirical analysis. *Applied Economics*, *31*, 65–76.

Bishop, B. (2002). Investment and corporate governance in East Asia. *CIPE Feature Service*, http://www.cipe.org

Bond, R. R. (1970). Emerging nations and emerging institutions. *The International Journal of Accounting Education and Research, 6*(1), 83–90.

Borensztein, E., De Gregorio, J., & Lee, J.-W. (1998). How does foreign direct investment affect growth? *Journal of International Economics, 45*(1), 115–135.

Calderón, C., Loayza, N., & Serven, L. (2004). *Greenfield foreign direct investment and mergers & acquisitions: Feedback and macroeconomic effects.* World Bank Policy Research Working Paper, No. 3192.

Capaul, M. (2003). *Corporate governance in Latin America.* Whither Latin American Capital Markets, LAC Regional Study, Background Paper, Chief Economist Office, Latin America and the Caribbean Region, World Bank.

Chipalkatti, N., Quan, L. V., & Rishi, M. (2006). *Portfolio flows to emerging capital markets: do corporate transparency and public governance matter?* Working Paper, Seattle University.

Chorafas, D. N. (2006). *IFRS, fair value and corporate governance-the impact on budgets, balance sheets and management accounts.* CIMA Publishing.

Chudnovsky, D., & López, A. (1999). *Globalization and developing countries: Foreign direct investment and growth and sustainable human development. Paper prepared for the UNCTAD/UNDP Global Programme on Globalization, Liberalization and Sustainable Development.* http://www.fund-cenit.org.ar/publicpdf/globalization.pdf

Claessens, S., Djankov, S., & Lang, L. H. P. (2000). The separation of ownership and control in East Asian corporations. *Journal of Financial Economics, 58,* 81–112.

Claessens, S., & Fan, J. P. H. (2002). Corporate governance in Asia: A survey. *International Review of Finance, 3*(2), 77–103.

Colley, J. L., Jr., Doyle, J. L., Logan, G. W., & Stettinius, W. (2005). *What is corporate governance?* The McGraw Hill Co.

Cooper, R. N. (1999). Should capital controls be banished? *Brookings Papers on Economic Activity, 1,* 89–125.

Corporate Governance in Latin America, New Thoughts for a New Century. (2000). Available at http://www.oecd.org/dataoecd/56/55/1922332.pdf

Culem, C. G. (1988). The locational determinants of direct investments among industrialised countries. *European Economic Review, 32*(4), 885–904.

De Mello, L. R., Jr. (1999). Foreign direct investment-led growth: Evidence from time series and panel data. *Oxford Economic Papers, 51,* 133–151.

Dunning, J. H. (1973). The determinants of international production. *Oxford Economic Papers, 25,* 289–336.

Evans, K. (2002). *Foreign portfolio and direct investment.* Global Forum on International Investment – Attracting Foreign Direct Investment for Development, OECD, Shanghai, December 5–6.

Foreign Direct Investment and Technology Transfer in India. (1992). *United Nations center on transnational corporations.* United Nations: New York.

Foreign Direct Investment for Development – Maximising Benefits. Minimising Costs, Overview, OECD, 2002.

Garcia-Herrera, A., & Santabarbara, D. (2005). *Does China have an impact on Foreign direct investment to Latin America.* Working Paper No. 517, Banco De Espana.

Garibaldi, P., Mora, N., Sahay, R., & Zettelmeyer, J. (2001). What moves capital to transition economies? *IMF Staff Papers,* Special Issue, Vol. 48. Available at http://www.imf.org/External/Pubs/FT/staffp/2001/04/pdf/garibald.pdf

Gibson, M. S. (2003). Is corporate governance ineffective in emerging markets? *Journal of Financial and Quantitative Analysis, 38*(1), 231–250.

Gillan, S. L., & Starks, L. T. (2003). *Corporate governance, corporate ownership, and the role of institutional investors: A global perspective.* Working Paper Series 2003-01, John Weinberg Center for Corporate Governance, University of Delaware. http://www.lerner.udel.edu/ccg/

Global Financial Reporting, IAS or US-GAAP? *European Survey*, KPMG, April, 2000.

Hausman, R., & Fernández-Arias, E. (2000). *Foreign direct investment: Good cholesterol?* Working Paper No. 417, 26 March, Inter-American Development Bank Research Department.

Hung, M., & Subramanyam, K. R. (2004). Financial statement effects of adopting accounting standards: The case for Germany. *Review of Accounting Studies, 12*(4), 623–657.

Imhoff E. A. Jr. (2003). *Accounting quality, auditing and corporate governance.* Working Paper, University of Michigan Business School.

Jackson, J. K. (2007). Foreign direct investment: Current issues. *CRS Report for Congress, Foreign Affairs, Defense, and Trade Division, Congressional Research Services*, http://fpc.state.gov/document/organization/84930.pdf

Johnson, S., Boone, P., Breach, A., & Friedman, E. (2000). Corporate governance in the Asian financial crisis. *Journal of Financial Economics, 58*, 141–186.

Kogut, B., & Macpherson, J. M. (2003). Direct investment and corporate governance – Will multinational corporations 'Tip' countries toward institutional change? In: P. K. Cornelius & B. Kogut (Eds), *Corporate governance and capital flows in a global economy* (pp. 183–215). New York: Oxford University Press.

Kothari, S. P. (2000). The role of financial reporting in reducing financial risks in the market. *Proceedings, Federal Reserve Bank of Boston* (pp. 89–112). Available at http://www.bos.frb.org/economic/conf/conf44/cf44_6.pdf

Kravis, I. B., & Lipsey, R. E. (1982). The location of overseas production and production for exports by US multinational firms. *Journal of International Economics, 25*, 201–223.

La Porta, R., Lopez-de-Silanes, F., Shleifer, A., & Vishny, R. (1998). Law and finance. *Journal of Political Economy, 106*(6), 1113–1155.

La Porta, R., Lopez-de-Silanes, F., Shleifer, A., & Vishny, R. (2000). Investor Protection and Corporate Governance. *Journal of Financial Economics, 58*, 3–27.

Lefort, F., & Walker, E. (2000). Ownership and capital structure of Chilean conglomerates: Facts and hypotheses for governance. *Revista ABANTE, 3*(1), 3–27.

Leuz, C., & Wysocki, P. (2006). *Capital-market effects of corporate disclosures and disclosure regulation.* Research Study, Commissioned by the Task Force to Modernize Securities Legislation in Canada.

Lipsey, R. E. (1999). *The role of foreign direct investment in international capital flows.* Working Paper, No. 7094, NBER, April, http://www.nber.org/papers.w7094

Mejstřik, K., & Mejstřik, M. (2007). Corporate governance, ownership concentration and foreign direct investment in the Czech Republic. In: B. Dallago & I. Iwasaki (Eds), *Corporate restructuring and governance in transition economies* (pp. 65–90). Studies in Economic Transition, Great Britain: Palgrave Macmillan.

Meyer, K. E. (1995). Foreign direct investment in the early years of economic transition: A survey. *Economics of Transition, 3*(3), 301–320.

Millstein, I. M. (1995). The state of corporate governance, Appendix-1. In: R. A. G. Monks & N. Minow (Eds), *Corporate governance* (pp. 445–464). Cambridge, MA: Blackwell.

Mody, A. (2004). *What is an emerging market?* IMF Working Paper, September. Available at http://www.imf.org/external/pubs/ft/wp/2004/wp04177.pdf

Monks, R. A. G., & Minow, N. (Eds). (1995). *Corporate governance.* Blackwell Business.

Mueller, D. C. (2006). The anglo-saxon approach to corporate governance and its applicability to emerging markets. *Corporate Governance, 14*(4), 207–219.

Nam II, C., Kang, J., & Kim, J.-K. (2001). Comparative corporate governance trends in Asia. In: *Corporate governance in Asia – A comparative perspective.* OECD, pp. 85–119.

Pistor, K., Raiser, M., & Gelfer, S. (2000). Law and finance in transition economies. *Economics of Transition, 8*(2), 325–368.

Preobragenskaya, G. G., & McGee, R. W. (2003). *The Role of International Accounting Standards in Foreign Direct Investment: A Case Study of Russia.* Working Paper presented at the 13th International Conference of the International Trade and Finance Association, 28–31 May, Vaasa, Finland.

Preobragenskaya, G. G., & McGee, R. W. (2005). *Accounting and financial system reform in a transition economy: A case study of Russia.* Springer.

Principles of Corporate Governance. The business roundtable – An association of chief executive officers committed to improving public policy, May, 2002.

Principles of Corporate Governance, OECD. (2004).

Pugel, T. A., & Lindert, P. H. (2000). *International economics* (11th ed.). McGraw-Hill.

Rajan, R. G., & Zingales, L. (1998). Financial dependence and growth. *American Economic Review, 88*(June), 559–586.

Reinhardt, C. M. (1999). Capital flows to developing countries: Implications for saving and investment. Comment and discussion. *Brookings Papers on Economic Activity, 1,* 170–180.

Renders, A., & Gaeremynck, A. (2006). *Corporate governance and performance: Controlling for sample selection bias and endogeneity.* Working Paper, Katholieke Universiteit Leuven, Department of Accountancy, Finance and Insurance (AFI), http://www.econkuleu-ven.be/eng/tew/academic/afi/pdfs/AFI_0606.pdf

Roche, J. (2005). *Corporate Governance in Asia.* London and New York: Routledge Taylor & Francis Group.

Rueda-Sabater, E. J. (2000). Corporate governance and the bargaining power of developing countries to attract foreign investment. *Corporate Governance, 8*(2, April), 117–124.

Santiso, J. (2003). *The political economy of emerging markets – actors, institutions and financial crises in Latin America.* Palgrave Macmillan.

Saudragan, M., & Diga, J. D. (1997). Financial reporting in emerging capital markets: Characteristics and policy issues. *Accounting Horizons, 11*(2, June), 40–65.

Schmitz, A., & Bieri, J. (1972). EEC tariffs and U.S. direct investment. *European Economic Review, 3,* 259–270.

Schneider, F., & Frey, B. S. (1985). Economic and political determinants of foreign direct investment. *World Development, 13*(2), 161–175.

Shleifer, A., & Vishny, R. W. (1997). A survey of corporate governance. *The Journal of Finance, 52*(2, June), 737–783.

Stulz, R. M. (2005). Corporate governance and financial globalization. *NBER Reporter,* pp. 13–15.

Tarca, A. (2004). International convergence of accounting practices: choosing between IASs and US GAAP. *Journal of International Financial Management and Accounting, 15*(1), 60–91.

Wang, Z. Q., & Swain, N. J. (1995). The determinants of foreign direct investment in transforming economies. *Weltwirtschaftliches Archiv, 131*(2), 359–382.

White Paper on Corporate Governance in Asia, OECD. (2003). Avaiable at http://www.oecd.org/dataoecd/48/55/25778905.pdf

White Paper on Corporate Governance in Latin America, OECD. (2003). Avaiable at http://www.oecd.org/dataoecd/25/2/18976210.pdf

Wooldridge, J. M. (2006). *Introductory econometrics – A modern approach*. Thomson South-Western, 3rd edition.

World Competitiveness Yearbook. (2007). *International Institute for Management Development (IMD)*. Geneva: World Competitiveness Yearbook.

World Investment Report. (2006). *United Nations conference on trade and development*. New York and Geneva: United Nations.

Yudaeva, K., Kozlov, K., Melentieva, N., & Ponomareva, N. (2003). Does foreign ownership matter? *Economics of Transition, 11*(3), 383–409.

Zhang, K. H. (2001). How does foreign direct investment affect economic growth in China. *Economics of Transition, 9*(3), 679–693.

CORPORATE GOVERNANCE REFORM AND FIRM PERFORMANCE: EVIDENCE FROM CHINA

Simon S. Gao, Gordon Gao and Tianxi Zhang

ABSTRACT

Purpose – *The purpose of this study is to empirically evaluate the effectiveness of China's 2005 shareholding reform and investigate the relationship of the changes of state-owned shareholdings and the largest shareholdings with corporate performance.*

Methodology/approach – *This study uses a sample of 470 listed firms that were subject to China's 2005 shareholding reform with data from 2004 and 2006. First, we examine whether the reform has reduced state-owned shareholdings measured by ownership concentration and the largest shareholdings through comparing shareholder structures of the reformed listed companies prior to and after the reform. Second, regression analysis was used to explore the relationship between the change of ownership concentration and largest shareholdings and corporate performance of Chinese listed firms.*

Findings – *This study reveals the effectiveness of the shareholding reform as both ownership concentration and largest shareholdings decrease. This*

Corporate Governance in Less Developed and Emerging Economies
Research in Accounting in Emerging Economies, Volume 8, 189–209
ISSN: 1479-3563/doi:10.1016/S1479-3563(08)08007-9

study presents evidence suggesting a positive impact of China's 2005 shareholding reform on corporate performance and endorsing the notion that state-owned shareholdings are detrimental to corporate performance.

Research limitations – *ROE is used as a measure of corporate performance, which is influenced by the rules of accounting standards and corporate behavior.*

Originality/value – *This study provides empirical evidence on the effectiveness of China's shareholding reform and shows a positive relation between the reduction of ownership concentration and corporate performance. This is the first study to examine this relation using the cases of Chinese listed companies. The findings have implications to regulatory bodies, public listed firms and investors in China in terms of corporate governance and shareholding configuration.*

1. INTRODUCTION

Following the Berle and Means' (1932) essay, there have been a significant body of studies that has examined the relationships between corporate ownership, governance and firm performance (e.g., Bhagat & Bolton, 2008; Tam & Tan, 2007; Sánchez-Ballesta & García-Meca, 2007). While the complex relationships have been identified, the empirical results reveal some mixed results.

The agency-based literature argues that the separation of ownership and control has an adverse on the value of a firm as information asymmetry between owners (principals) and managers (agents) is exploited by management. The monitoring of agents' actions is influenced by how principals are organized in terms of the existence of a large number of small owners and a few large controlling shareholders. Large shareholders invest in information and monitor managers more effectively than a large number of small-dispersed owners (Shleifer & Vishny, 1986). There is a considerable amount of research on the effects of ownership structure on firm performance. However, the empirical results in this field are often conflicting and inconsistent (Sánchez-Ballesta & García-Meca, 2007). Economists generally presume state ownership as being detrimental to corporate performance (Boycko, Shleifer, & Vishny, 1996; Shleifer & Vishny, 1997; Estrin, 2002). Political interference through state ownership is usually at the expense of corporate profitability (Boycko et al., 1996) as politicians may use their control to deliberately transfer resources of firms to their political supporters (Shleifer & Vishny, 1997). The literature also shows that private ownership is preferable to state ownership because the state has a 'grabbing hand' that extorts companies for the benefits of politicians and bureaucrats at the expense of corporate wealth (Boycko et al., 1996; Shleifer & Vishny, 1997). Estrin (2002) observes that, even if the government is not corrupt, the firms under the control of the state cannot concentrate on profit maximization, because the state has political and economic objectives.

Corporate governance proponents have frequently claimed that good governance has a positive impact on firm performance (Bhagat & Bolton, 2008; Gompers, Ishii, & Metrick, 2003). Several authors have constructed variables that evaluate corporate governance practices and found that higher corporate governance scores are associated with higher stock returns and better firm performance (e.g., Bai, Liu, Lu, Song, & Zhang, 2004; Drobetz, Schillhifer, & Zimmermann, 2004). However, a recent study by Bhagat and Bolton (2008) finds none of the governance measures (e.g., management ownerships, board independence, CEO-Chair duality, etc.) are correlated with future stock market performance of the firms.

Most of the above studies were based on the developed economies. Little has been known as to whether the complexity relationships between corporate ownership, governance and firm performance are also held in the developing economies. This study aims to present empirical evidence as to the effectiveness of China's recent shareholding reform and whether the reform has contributed to China's corporate performance. The findings are expected to enhance our knowledge concerning the relationships between state shareholding and corporate performance. In this study, we address two research questions. First, we examine whether China's 2005 shareholding reform has reduced state ownership measured by ownership concentration and the largest shareholdings by means of comparing the shareholder structures of reformed listed companies prior to and post the reform. Second, we investigate whether the change of state-owned shareholdings is positively related to the improvement of firm performance. Our empirical evidence supports this positive relation. Overall, this study presents evidence consistent with the notion that state-owned shareholding is detrimental to corporate performance.

The organization of the paper is as follows. Section 2 provides a brief review of the literature on corporate governance. Section 3 presents a background of China's listed companies, corporate governance and the 2005 shareholding reform. Section 4 describes the hypotheses and research methods, including sample and data. Section 5 reports the empirical results. The final section concludes the paper highlighting the contribution and limitations.

2. LITERATURE REVIEW

Corporate governance is an assurance to guarantee the interests of investors (Shleifer & Vishny, 1997) and it is a system to protect interests of investors from expropriation by the insiders (La Porta, Lopez-de-Silanes, Shleifer, & Vishny, 2000). The term 'governance' derives from the Latin word 'gubernance', meaning to 'steer'. Corporate governance is the system by which business corporations are steered and controlled, involving the distribution of rights and responsibilities among different participants in the corporations and specifying rules and procedures for making decisions on corporate affairs.

Berkowitz, Pistor, and Richard (2003) believe that corporate governance is a must to the operation, management and sustainable development of modern businesses as it aims at promoting corporate fairness, transparency and accountability. Dennis and McConnell (2003) document that corporate governance is the set of mechanisms – both institutional and market based – that induce the self-interested controllers of a company to make decisions that maximize the value of the company to its owners. Recent studies of corporate ownership have found that, outside of the United States and the United Kingdom, diffuse ownership is relatively uncommon and most corporations are controlled by large shareholders. Claessens, Djankov, and Lang (2000) find that cross-holding and pyramidal ownership is common among Asian economies. The literature generally shows that the listed firms have better corporate governance and better performance and market valuation (e.g., La Porta, Lopez-de-Silanes, Shleifer, & Vishny, 1998; La Porta, Lopez-de-Silanes, Shleifer, & Vishny, 1999; Claessens, Djankov, Fanand, & Lang, 2002; Faccio and Lang, 2002).

Agency theory presumes that human behavior is opportunistic and self-serving in nature; therefore, the fundamental function of the board of directors is to control managerial behavior and ensure top managers act in the interests of shareholders. The agency approach to corporate governance attempts to provide answers to the key question of 'how can shareholders ensure that non-owner managers pursue their interests' (Allen & Gale, 2001). The degree of ownership concentration affects the nature of contract, creating agency problems. Jensen and Meckling (1976) theorize that when ownership is diffused, agency problems arise from the conflict of interests between top managers and outside shareholders. When ownership is concentrated, the nature of the agency problems shifts away the tension between top managers and outside shareholders to the conflict between the large shareholders and minority shareholders. This is because concentrated ownership can give the large shareholders more discretionary powers of using firm's resources to serve their own interests at the expense of other shareholders. When the large shareholders gain dominance in the control rights, they could expropriate the minority shareholders to pursue their own benefits. Expropriation of minority shareholders by controlling shareholders can take a variety of forms, including such as excessive executive compensation, loan guarantees of and transfer pricing between related companies, dilutive share issues, etc., which was commonly termed as *'tunneling'* (La Porta et al., 2000). The primary agency problems have therefore broadened from mitigating the agency conflicts between firm managers and diffuse shareholders (Jensen & Meckling, 1976; Bae, Kang, & Kim, 2002) to protecting minority shareholders from expropriation by controlling shareholders and their management team (Shleifer & Vishny, 1997).

Under agency theory, two categories of mechanisms are available to address the conflict between shareholders and managers, and between controlling shareholders and minority shareholders. *Internal* mechanisms include the ownership structure, the board of directors, managerial compensation, financial transparency and adequate information disclosure. *External* mechanisms include an active market for corporate control, the proper legal framework and competition. Without effective internal control and outside monitoring, large shareholders are more likely to commit frauds and make 'tunneling' much easier. A number of studies (e.g., Bae et al., 2002; Bertrand, Mehta, & Mullainathan, 2002) analyze how tunneling affects a firm's value. Fama and Jensen (1983) document that increased ownership concentration decreases financial performance because it raises the firm's cost of capital as a result of decreased market liquidity or decreased diversification opportunities on behalf of the investors. Obviously, the most important issue to address the agency problem in large corporations is to restrict expropriation of minority shareholders by controlling shareholders (La Porta et al., 1998).

Corporate governance in China has also received much attention (e.g., Qian, 1995, 1996; Lin, Chen, & Tang, 2001; Liu & Lu, 2003). A number of studies have attempted to investigate the impact of state ownership on corporate governance (e.g., Cho, 1998; Xu & Wang, 1999; Zhang, Zhang, & Zhao, 2001; Schipani & Liu, 2001; Tian, 2001; Bai et al., 2004). While most of the studies find state shares played a negative role in China's corporate governance, Tian (2001), examining the relation between the ownership structure and market valuation of Chinese listed firms, finds that the impact of government ownership on stock market valuation is non-linear. It deteriorates a firm's performance when government ownership is small, but improves a firm's performance when government ownership gets significantly larger. He also finds that the effect of the shareholding of the largest shareholder is non-linear with a U-shaped relationship between a firm's market value and the proportion of shares held by the largest shareholder. Several other studies have examined the impact of governance mechanisms on the performance of Chinese listed firms. Bai et al. (2004) provide an analysis of the impact of various governance mechanisms on firm market valuation and show evidence that the degree of concentration of shares held by other large shareholders (i.e., excluding the largest one which are mainly the state or state agents) positively affects the market value of a firm. The next section provides a background of the development of China's listed companies, corporate governance and the 2005 shareholding reform.

3. CHINESE LISTED COMPANIES AND THE SHAREHOLDING REFORM

After three decades of the economic reform, the ownership structure of Chinese companies has changed. Under the reform, unprofitable small and medium-size State-owned Enterprises (SOEs) were privatized or merged. Large SOEs were converted into shareholding companies with limited liabilities and among them a selected few were listed on China's two stock exchanges. The Chinese stock market was organized by the government as a vehicle for its SOEs to raise capital and improve operating performance (Green, 2003). In China 78% of listed companies belong to certain groups whose parent firms are serving as the controlling shareholders. Parent firms can easily tunnel the resources out of the listed entities. Numerous anecdotes illustrate how the controlling shareholders of listed firms expropriate the minority shareholders and tunnel firm resources.

It has been widely accepted that the restructuring of SOEs is the key to the success of the Chinese economy, despite SOEs still comprise a significant share of industrial output (Allen, Qian, & Qian, 2005). Chinese companies, especially SOEs, have benefited substantially from the rapid growth in public listing and the general public enthusiasm for the equity market. The number of listed companies on the Shanghai and Shenzhen Stock Exchanges had risen from 14 in 1991 when the stock market began to 1434 in 2006 and the total market capitalization aggregated to approximately RMB 8,940.4 billion (US$1224.7 billion) in 2006, as shown in Table 1.

The equity ownership in a Chinese listed firm appears in five different forms, including state-owned shares, legal-person shares, employee shares, tradable A-shares and B-shares which are only available to foreign investors

(Balsara, Chen, & Zheng, 2007). Due to restrictions in the market capacity when offering shares to the public, the percentage of shares available to the open market has been relatively low. After the offering, more than half of available shares are held by those 'promoters/issuers' who are either state-owned shareholders (e.g., government institutions) or state-controlled shareholders (e.g., SOEs). This enables the 'promoters/issuers' to remain control of the company (Chen, Lee, & Rui, 2001). Based on the regulations, state-owned shares and legal entity shares held by the promoters/issuers are not traded on China's open markets. China's effort to reap the benefits of privatization, while retaining public ownership in listed companies, is an interesting experiment (Chen et al., 2001; Zhang & Zhao, 2004). The preservation of state-owned and legal-person shares was largely attributed to the communist authority's long-term policy of maintaining the state control over companies. The authority imposes a strict segmentation on the stock market to prevent private and foreign investors from acquiring controlling interests in Chinese listed companies (Chen et al., 2001).

The ownership of Chinese listed companies is highly concentrated and the average number of shares owned by the top 10 largest shareholders is 56.49% (Chen, Ke, & Isaac, 2007). The single largest shareholder owns on average 41% of the total outstanding shares, both non-transferable state shares and/

Table 1. Listed Companies in China and Market Capitalization.

Year	No. of Listed Firms	Total Market Cap (RMB: b)	Market Cap/ GDP (%)	Tradable Shares (%)	A-Share (%)	B-Share (%)	H-Share (%)	Non-Tradable Shares (%)
1993	183	3,531	10.20	n/a	n/a	n/a	n/a	n/a
1994	291	3,690.61	7.89	n/a	n/a	n/a	n/a	n/a
1995	323	3,474.28	5.94	n/a	n/a	n/a	n/a	n/a
1996	530	9,842.38	14.50	n/a	n/a	n/a	n/a	n/a
1997	746	17,529.25	23.54	n/a	n/a	n/a	n/a	n/a
1998	851	19,505.6	24.90	n/a	n/a	n/a	n/a	n/a
1999	949	26,741.17	32.26	35.40	27.13	4.44	3.83	64.60
2000	1,088	48,090.9	53.77	35.62	29.46	2.87	3.29	64.38
2001	1,154	43,522.2	45.37	34.76	25.27	3.11	6.38	65.24
2002	1,224	38,329.13	37.43	34.66	25.69	2.84	6.13	65.34
2003	1,287	42,578	36.49	35.3	26.7	2.72	5.88	64.70
2004	1,377	37,056	27.14	36.00	27.84	2.76	5.40	64.00
2005	1,381	32,430	17.79	38.20	29.90	2.86	5.44	61.80
2006	1,434	89,404	42.69	37.84	22.16	1.54	14.14	62.16

Source: China Annual Statistics Yearbook 2002 and Year 2002–2006 data from CSRC (2007), http://www.crsc.gov.cn

or legal-person shares (Chen et al., 2007). State shareholders dominate in Chinese public listed companies. Of these companies 31% are controlled by the state as the majority controlling shareholder with more than 50% stake, and over 40% of these listed companies have the state holding of more than 10% stakes (Faccio & Lang, 2002). Only about one third of equity shares of Chinese listed companies are traded predominately on the two domestic exchanges. Limited numbers of firms have a very small amount of shares traded on overseas stock markets (e.g., Hong Kong, Singapore). This multi-form of equity ownership reflects a very unique phenomenon of China's corporate shareholding structure, which brings about some distinctive problems that China's corporate governance system requires to tackle. For example, the split shareholding structure has substantially distorted the pricing mechanism in China's stock market and added more uncertainty to investors. The structure puts individual investors in an inferior position in terms of influencing corporate policies and disposing of the firms' profits and assets.

There are many problems caused by the splitting-share structure among the Chinese listed companies. For example, concentrated ownership structure leads 'insider control' of corporate affairs. Despite its majority ownership, the state often does not exercise real control over its companies. It is the insider-managers that predominantly control the listed companies. Managers are typically controlled and supported by the Communist Party and their ministerial associates. The controlling authorities have no incentive to select the best managers to ensure companies profitable and efficient because of other interests and political motives. The government and the Communist Party establishment can exercise a critical influence on a company's affairs. Jian and Wong (2003) provide evidence that group-controlled firms in China are more likely to use 'connected transactions' to manipulate earnings and tunnel firm value. Examining the associated transactions between the listed firms and their controlling shareholders (i.e., the state), Cheung, Jin, Rau, and Stouraitis (2005) find evidence that the controlling shareholders extract value from the listed firms; the median value loss for these firms represents 34% of the value of the associated transaction. They also find that the minority shareholders in firms conducting associated transactions with SOEs end up significantly worse off than those in firms conducting associated transactions with non-SOEs.

In contrast to developed markets, China's securities market is primarily made up of individual investors and there is a lack of institutional investors (Chen, Firth, & Gao, 2002; Chen et al., 2007). These individual investors are segregated and they have very limited power. Consequently it is the state shareholders holding non-tradable shares actually control over the public listed companies. The dominance of state shareholders in Chinese listed companies has led to problematic corporate governance practices, significant related-party transactions and, at times, marginalization of individual shareholders' interests (Chen et al., 2007). The corporate governance system adopted by Chinese listed firms can be best described as a control-based model, in which the controlling shareholders (in most cases, the state) closely control over the listed firms through concentrated ownership and 'management friendly boards' (Fan, Wong, & Zhang, 2005). There is generally a lack of timely disclosure of accounting information. Indeed, the continuing success of Chinese economy and stock market development depends on the effectiveness with which their corporate governance systems can protect investor interest, particularly the minority investors' interest.

In February 2004, China's State Council issued the Guidelines on Promoting Reform, Opening-up and Steady Development of China's Capital Market. After a year-long formulation of detailed rules, the shareholding structure reform officially started on April 29, 2005, when the Chinese stock market regulator announced a trial reform of splitting state shares for four domestic listed companies. In June 2005 the regulator required other 42 listed companies to participate in the reform. The main purpose of China's shareholding reform was to improve shareholding structure and corporate performance of Chinese listed firms. The general guidelines of the reform include: (1) non-tradable shareholders should compensate tradable shareholders as the precondition of floating their shares on stock exchanges; (2) non-tradable shares will be locked-up for 12 months after the individual company's reform scheme takes effect and non-tradable shareholders cannot sell more than 5% of their stakes within another 12 months and (3) the companies should obtain the approval of reform schemes from at least two-thirds of tradable shareholders before implementation. To make all their shares tradable, listed companies undergoing reform have to offer additional shares or funds to private investors as compensation for potential losses in the value of their portfolios when the state-owned shares hit the market. The reform has been viewed by the regulator and investors as vital for China's capital market to function as an open and fair market for both majority and minority public shareholders. More than 80% of Chinese firms listed domestically have completed state shareholding reform by the mid-2006.

It is widely claimed that China's reform of the shareholding structure of listed companies will improve liquidity of domestic stock markets and Chinese listed companies' corporate governance and performance. So far there has been no empirical evidence showing that China's shareholding reform has changed the shareholding structure of Chinese listed companies and improved corporate performance. This study attempts to provide empirical evidence.

4. HYPOTHESES AND RESEARCH METHODS

4.1. Hypotheses

China has a much higher ownership concentration of the state than any country observed in either developed or other emerging markets (Claessens et al., 2000). The high percentage of the state ownership is attributed by the fact that the majority of Chinese listed companies were evolved from state-owned or state-controlled enterprises. As noted in the preceding section, the 2005 reform under the Chinese government's plan aims to reduce both the level of ownership concentration and the largest shareholder's holding in the companies. This reform has been claimed successful. The first objective of this study is to provide evidence as to whether the shareholding reform had reduced the proportion of the top 10 shareholdings and the largest shareholding in Chinese listed companies. Therefore, the following hypotheses are proposed:

H1. The proportion of the top 10 shareholdings in Chinese listed companies is different between prior to and after the shareholding reform.

H2. The proportion of the largest shareholdings in Chinese listed companies is different between prior to and after the shareholding reform.

Agency theory is built on the notion that separation of ownership and control potentially leads to self-interested behaviors by managers as both shareholders (i.e., the principal) and managers (i.e., the agents) are depicted as utility maximizers (Jensen & Meckling, 1976). However, when owner-ship is concentrated, the nature of the agency problems shifts away the tension of managers and outside shareholders interests to conflicts between the large shareholders and minority shareholders (Jensen & Meckling, 1976). This is because concentrated ownership can give the large shareholders more discretionary powers of using firm's resources to serve their own interests at the expenses of other minority shareholders and corporate interest. Moreover, increased ownership concentration would expect to decrease financial performance because it raises the firm's cost of capital as a result of decreased market liquidity or decreased diversification opportunities on behalf of the investor (Fama & Jensen, 1983). As noted by La Porta et al. (1998), the most important agency problem in large corporations is that of restricting expropriation of minority shareholders by controlling shareholders. In the case of Chinese listed companies, the controlling shareholders are mostly the state and state-controlled establishments. Because the state has interests beyond the corporate goal as noted previously, reducing state ownership would expect to direct increasing resources and management energy towards business activities, thus leading to the improvement of corporate performance, which would benefit minority shareholders. While the agency-based literature argues that the separation of ownership and control has an adverse on the value of a firm and firm performance, the empirical results in this field are often conflicting and inconsistent (Sánchez-Ballesta & García-Meca, 2007). The second objective of this study is to provide evidence in respect of a relationship between the reduced ownership concentration and the largest shareholding and corporate performance with a view to addressing whether the shareholding reform is effective, leading to the improvement of corporate performance of Chinese listed companies. Therefore, the following hypotheses are proposed:

H3. There is a positive relation between the reduced ownership concentration and corporate performance.

H4. There is a positive relation between the reduced largest shareholding and corporate performance.

4.2. Samples

Our sample consists of 470 Chinese companies listed on the Shanghai and Shenzhen Stock Exchanges, which were subject to the 2005 shareholding reform. Initially, we consider all A-share companies listed on the two stock exchanges that were subject to the shareholding reform in 2005 and filed their 2006 audited financial reports, totaling over 800 firms. For the purpose of this study, we then include only companies with available information of their large shareholdings (including top ten and the largest shareholders and their holdings) in the annual reports of 2004 and 2006.

To test the effects of ownership concentration on corporate performance, we further limit our sample size to only manufacturing companies with a view to eliminating the industrial effect on the different levels of corporate performance. Manufacturing has the largest number of firms in the sample. In this case, our sample includes 97 manufacturing firms.

4.3. Variables

Table 2 lists variables and their definitions. The change of ownership concentration (ΔTOPTEN) is defined as a control variable. ΔROE represents the changes of corporate performance from 2004 to 2006. ROE (Return on Equity) is used to approximate corporate performance. In accounting literature, earnings and ROE have been empirically shown as significant variables in explaining stock price and firm performance (e.g., Ball & Brown, 1968; Kothari & Zimmerman, 1995; Barth, Beaver, & Landsman, 1998; Burgstahler & Dichev, 1997; Collins, Maydew, & Weiss, 1997; Zhang et al., 2008). In the models, we also consider some commonly used control variables, including company size, leverage and fixed assets (e.g., Kapopoulos & Lazaretou, 2007).

5. EMPIRICAL RESULTS

Table 3 provides the descriptive statistics of the sample companies. Our first set of tests on the changes of ownership concentration and the largest shareholdings involves a comparison of means in the whole observed sample. The empirical results of the *t*-test are listed in Table 4. Both H1 and H2 are supported by the test results. The results show both changes of ownership concentration and the largest shareholding are statistically significant at the 1% significant level, suggesting that after the shareholding reform ownership concentrations in these sampled companies decrease. On average it decreases 7.226%. The interval of its difference is from −7.997% to −6.455% with the 95% confidence level. Similarly, the largest shareholdings also decrease significantly. On average it decreases 6.786% with the interval of its difference being from −7.656% to −5.925% with the 95% confidence level.

We also test the hypothesis that the shareholding changes after the reform is positively associated with corporate performance measured by ROE. A regression model is adopted to test the relationship between shareholding

Table 2. Definition of Variables.

TOPTEN	The proportion of top 10 shareholdings of A-share reformed companies (which reformed either in 2005 or 2006) listed on the Shanghai and Shenzhen stock exchanges.
ΔTOPTEN	The change of ownership concentration is measured as the change of top 10 shareholdings; i.e., the proportion of top 10 shareholdings by the end of 2006 are subtracted by the proportion of top 10 shareholdings by the end of 2004.
TOPONE	The proportion of the largest shareholding of A-share reformed companies (which reformed either in 2005 or 2006) listed on the Shanghai and Shenzhen stock exchanges.
ΔTOPONE	The change of the largest shareholding is measured as the proportion of the largest shareholding by the end of 2006 subtracted by the proportion of largest shareholding by the end of 2004.
ΔROE	The change of ROE refers reformed company's 2006 ROE is subtracted by its 2004 ROE.
SIZE	Company size is measured by company total book value assets in 2004.
LEVER	Financial leverage ratio 2004, measured by company total liabilities over total assets in 2004.[a]
FIXED	Fixed assets ratio 2004 – measured by company's fixed assets over total assets in 2004.

[a]We use total liabilities instead of long-term liabilities because our sample covers a variety of firms in different sectors; whose debts structure can be different. Total liabilities would eliminate the differences caused by debts configuration. We did not use debt to equity as the ratio of financial leverage because a substantial part of equity capital in Chinese firms was non-tradable and therefore the valuation of such equity was problematic.

concentrations and corporate performance. The model is presented as follows and the empirical results are shown in Table 5.

$$\Delta ROE = \alpha + \beta_1 \Delta TOPTEN + \beta_2 SIZE + \beta_3 LEVER + \beta_4 FIXED + \varepsilon$$

The Pearson correlation tests reveal that the relation between company size (SIZE) and the change of corporate performance (ΔROE), and the relation between financial leverage (LEVER) and the change of corporate performance (ΔROE) are insignificant. We therefore eliminate these two explanatory variables (SIZE and LEVER) from the original linear-regression model. The linear-regression equation is then adjusted as below:

$$\Delta ROE = \alpha + \beta_1 \Delta TOPTEN + \beta_2 FIXED + \varepsilon$$

The empirical results of the adjusted regression analysis are listed in Table 6.

Table 3. Descriptive Statistics.

	Sample No	Minimum	Maximum	Mean	Standard Deviation
Panel A – All Sample 470					
ROE (%) (2004)	470	−96.95	34.88	6.76	12.74
ROE (%) (2006)	470	−61.19	44.34	9.08	9.23
ΔTOPTEN	470	−71.62	40.34	−7.23	8.52
ΔTOPONE	470	−61.31	62.81	−6.79	9.51
Panel B – Only Manufacturing Companies					
ΔROE	97	−12.35	28.44	1.00	7.71
ΔTOPTEN	97	−24.81	3.70	−9.93	6.15
SIZE	97	19.37	23.87	21.04	.83
2004 LEVER	97	7.28	78.40	43.92	15.81
2004 FIXED	97	10.13	85.90	40.28	18.14

Table 4. Test Results of Changes of Ownership Concentration and Largest Shareholdings.

	T Value	No.	Significant (2-tailed)	Mean Difference	95% Confidence Interval of the Difference	
					Lower	Upper
ΔTOPTEN	−18.405	470	.000	−7.226	−7.997	−6.455
ΔTOPONE	−15.493	470	.000	−6.786	−7.646	−5.925

Table 6 shows that the relation between ownership concentration (ΔTOPTEN) and the change of corporate performance (ΔROE) is significantly positive. This means corporate performance increases as the ownership concentration decreases.[1] The empirical results support H3, suggesting that the positive impact of ownership concentration (ΔTOPTEN) on corporate performance. The shareholding reform had reduced the ownership concentration of reformed companies; which might have led to the increase of their ROE in 2006. This result is, however, different from the findings of Kapopoulos and Lazaretou (2007) in the case of Greece where empirical findings suggest that a more concentrated ownership structure positively relates to higher firm profitability. The difference between the two results is probably due to the fact that in China the ownership concentration of shares is largely in the hand of the state and governmental agents,

Table 5. The Correlation of Ownership Concentration.

		ΔROE	ΔTOPTEN	SIZE	LEVER	FIXED
ΔROE	Pearson Correlation	1				
	Sig. (2-tailed)	–				
ΔTOPTEN	Pearson Correlation	.236*	1			
	Sig. (2-tailed)	.019	–			
SIZE	Pearson Correlation	−.110	−.066	1		
	Sig. (2-tailed)	.280	.516	–		
2004 LEVER	Pearson Correlation	.108	.009	.472**	1	
	Sig. (2-tailed)	.288	.927	.000	–	
2004 FIXED	Pearson Correlation	−.216*	−.156	.380**	.273**	1
	Sig. (2-tailed)	.032	.122	.000	.006	–

**Significant at the 0.01 level (2-tailed); *significant at the 0.05 level (2-tailed).

whereas in Greece it is a few individual shareholders holding the majority of controlling shares. We also did the similar tests of the change of holdings of largest shareholders on corporate performance. We explore the relation between the changes of largest shareholdings and corporate performance by using the estimated equation of a regression model as below:

$$\Delta ROE = \alpha + \beta_1 \Delta TOPONE + \beta_2 SIZE + \beta_3 LEVER + \beta_4 FIXED + \varepsilon$$

Table 7 contains the correlations of test results. The Pearson correlations reveal the relations between company size (SIZE) and the change of corporate performance (ΔROE), and between financial leverage (LEVER) and corporate performance (ROE) are insignificant. As well, we eliminated these two explanatory variables (SIZE) and (LEVER) from the original linear-regression model and adjust the model as below:

$$\Delta ROE = \alpha + \beta_1 \Delta TOPONE + \beta_2 FIXED + \varepsilon$$

The empirical results of the regression analysis are listed in Table 8.

From Table 8, we find the relation between the changes of the largest shareholdings (ΔTOPONE) and the change of corporate performance (ΔROE) is significantly positive. This means corporate performance increases as the largest shareholding reduces. Similarly, the test shows a negative relation between the company fixed assets ratio (FIXED) and the change of corporate performance (ΔROE).

The above empirical results confirm H4 that there is a positive impact of the change of largest shareholdings on corporate performance. It probably

Table 6.   Empirical Results.

Panel A: Dependent Variable: ΔROE; *a*; Predictors (Constant); FIXED; ΔTOPTEN

R	R^2	Adjusted R^2	Std Error of the Estimate	Durbin-Watson
.297	.088	.069	7.440	2.013

Panel B: ANOVA *F*-Test of Ownership Concentration

	Sum of Squares	Df	Mean Squares	F value	Sig.
Regression	514.827	2	257.414	4.649	.012
Residual	5,313.991	95	55.351		
Total	5,828.745	96			

Panel C: The Coefficients of Ownership Concentration

	Un-Standardized Coefficients		Standardized Coefficients	T Value	Sig.
	Beta	Std. error	Beta		
Constant	6.714	2.068		3.244	.002
ΔTOPTEN	.261	.124	.207	2.098	.037
FIXED	−.075	.041	−.181	−1.849	.065

suggests that the largest shareholdings of Chinese listed companies have reduced effectively after the reform, which reflects in the increase of corporate performance. Overall, the results could suggest a positive impact of the shareholding reform on corporate performance.

6. CONCLUSIONS

This study examines the effectiveness of China's 2005 shareholding reform and the relationships between the changes of state-owned and the largest shareholdings and corporate performance. The empirical result reveals the effectiveness of the shareholding reform as both ownership concentration and the largest shareholdings decrease. The result also confirms the positive effect of the changes of state-owned shareholdings, reflected in both the reduction of ownership concentration and the largest shareholding of the state, towards corporate performance. Overall, our empirical results are consistent with both theoretical and our predictions.

Table 7. The Correlations of the Changes of Largest Shareholdings.

		ΔROE	ΔTOPONE	SIZE	2004 LEVER	2004 FIXED
ΔROE	Pearson Correlation	1.000				
	Sig. (2-tailed)	–				
ΔTOPONE	Pearson Correlation	.232*	1.000			
	Sig. (2-tailed)	.021	–			
SIZE	Pearson Correlation	−.111	−.314**	1.000		
	Sig. (2-tailed)	.279	.001	–		
2004 LEVER	Pearson Correlation	.108	−.084	.473**	1.000	
	Sig. (2-tailed)	.287	.395	.000	–	
2004 FIXED	Pearson Correlation	−.214*	−.244*	.381**	.271**	1.000
	Sig. (2-tailed)	.031	.013	.001	.005	–

**Significant at the 0.01 level (2-tailed); *significant at the 0.05 level (2-tailed).

Table 8. Empirical Results.

Panel A: Dependent Variable: ΔROE; *a*; Predictors (Constant); FIXED; ΔTOPONE

R	R^2	Adjusted R^2	Std Error of the Estimate	Durbin-Watson
.284	.081	.061	7.470	2.050

Panel B: ANOVA *F*-Test of the Largest Shareholdings

	Sum of Squares	Df	Mean Squares	F value	Sig.
Regression	471.722	2	235.860	4.225	.016
Residual	5,357.025	95	55.803		
Total	5,828.745	96			

Panel C: The Coefficients (*a*) of the Largest Shareholdings

	Un-standardized Coefficients		Standardized Coefficients	T value	Sig.
	Beta	Std. error	Beta		
(Constant)	5.756	1.922		2.995	.003
ΔTOPONE	.211	.114	.190	1.896	.062
FIXED	−.073	.042	−.167	−1.671	.097

Our findings contribute to the literature in at least three ways. First, we provide empirical evidence on the effectiveness of China's shareholding reform. Second, we show the shareholding reform in China has reduced the proportion of ownership concentration and there is a positive relation between the reduction of ownership concentration and corporate performance. This can possibly be explained with the agency model that following the shareholding reform, the conflicts between the state-owned shareholding, or the controlling shareholder (as the 'agent') and the minority shareholders (as the 'principal') have been lessened, which could lead to the improvement of corporate performance. This is the first study, as far as we are aware, to directly examine this relation using the cases of Chinese listed companies. Third, our findings have implications to regulatory bodies, public listed firms and investors in China in terms of corporate governance and shareholding configuration.

However, our study is also subject to some limitations. We used ROE as a measure of corporate performance, which is clearly influenced by the rules of accounting standards and corporate behavior in presenting financial statements. We cannot exclude the possibility that some firms might have altered their accounting figures in order to seek objectives beyond the corporate aim. The future research could use alternative measures of corporate performance, particularly market value indicators. Also, our study examines only Chinese listed companies. As with any study using only one country to study the influences of shareholding changes on corporate performance, it is possible that our results do not generalize to other countries. This suggests that it would be interesting for future researchers to undertake similar studies across countries.

NOTE

1. The test results also reveal a negative relation between the company's fixed assets ratio (FIXED) and the change of corporate performance (ΔROE). The explanation of this relationship is beyond the scope of this paper.

ACKNOWLEDGMENT

The authors are grateful to the two anonymous reviewers and the guest editors for their valuable comments and suggestions on the prior version of the paper.

REFERENCES

Allen, F., & Gale, D. (2001). Do financial institutions matter? *Journal of Finance, 56,* 1165–1175.

Allen, F., Qian, J., & Qian, M. (2005). Law, finance, and economic growth in China. *Journal of Financial Economics, 77,* 57–116.

Bae, K., Kang, J., & Kim, J. (2002). Tunneling or value added: Evidence from mergers by Korean business groups. *Journal of Finance, 57,* 2695–2740.

Bai, C.-E., Liu, Q., Lu, J., Song, F., & Zhang, J. (2004). Corporate governance and market valuation in China. *Journal of Comparative Economics, 32,* 4519–4616.

Ball, R., & Brown, P. (1968). An empirical evaluation of accounting income numbers. *Journal of Accounting and Economics, 6,* 159–178.

Balsara, N. J., Chen, G., & Zheng, L. (2007). The Chinese stock market: An examination of the random walk model and technical trading rules. *Quarterly Journal of Business & Economics, 46*(2), 43–63.

Barth, M., Beaver, W., & Landsman, W. (1998). Relative valuation roles of equity book value and net income as a function of financial health. *Journal of Accounting and Economics, 25,* 1–34.

Berkowitz, D., Pistor, K., & Richard, J. F. (2003). Economic development, legality, and the transplant effect. *European Economic Review, 47,* 165–195.

Berle, A. A., & Means, G. C. (1932). *The modern corporation.* New York: MacMillan.

Bertrand, M., Mehta, P., & Mullainathan, S. (2002). Ferreting out tunneling: An application to Indian business groups. *Quarterly Journal of Economics, 117,* 121–148.

Bhagat, S., & Bolton, B. (2008). Corporate governance and firm performance. *Journal of Corporate Finance, 14,* 257–273.

Boycko, M., Shleifer, A., & Vishny, R. (1996). A theory of privatization. *The Economic Journal, 106,* 309–319.

Burgstahler, D., & Dichev, I. (1997). Earnings, adaptation and equity value. *The Accounting Review, 72,* 187–215.

Chen, G., Firth, M., & Gao, N. (2002). The information content of concurrently announced earnings, cash dividends, and stock dividends: An investigation of the Chinese stock market. *Journal of International Financial Management and Accounting, 13*(2), 111–124.

Chen, G. M., Lee, B., & Rui, O. (2001). Foreign ownership restrictions and market segmentation in China's stock markets. *Journal of Financial Research, 24*(1), 133–155.

Chen, J., Ke, Q., & Isaac, D. (2007). Board characteristics as corporate governance mechanisms. In: J. Chen & S. Yao (Eds), *Globalization, Competition and Growth in China* (pp. 15–40). London: Routledge.

Cheung, Y.-L., Jin, L., Rau, R., & Stouraitis, A. (2005). Guanxi, Political Connections, and Expropriation: The Dark Side of State Ownership in Chinese Listed Companies, Mimeo.

China Annual Statistics Yearbook. (2002). Beijing: National Bureau of Statistics of China.

Cho, M. (1998). Ownership structure, investment, and the corporate value: An empirical analysis. *Journal of Financial Economics, 47,* 103–121.

Claessens, S., Djankov, S., Fanand, J., & Lang, L. (2002). Disentangling the incentive and entrenchment of large shareholdings. *Journal of Finance, 57,* 2741–2771.

Claessens, S., Djankov, S., & Lang, L. (2000). The separation of ownership and control in East Asia corporations. *Journal of Financial Economics, 58,* 81–112.

Collins, D., Maydew, E., & Weiss, J. (1997). Changes in value relevance of earnings and book value over the past forty years. *Journal of Accounting and Economics, 24,* 39–67.

CSRC (China Securities Regulatory Commission). (2007). www.csrc.gov.cn

Dennis, D. K., & McConnell, J. J. (2003). International corporate governance. *Journal of Financial and Quantitative Analysis*, *38*, 1–36.

Drobetz, W., Schillhifer, A., & Zimmermann, H. (2004). Corporate governance and expected stock returns: Evidence from Germany. *European Financial Management*, *10*(2), 267–293.

Estrin, S. (2002). Competition and corporate governance in transition. *Journal of Economic Perspectives*, *16*, 101–124.

Faccio, M., & Lang, L. (2002). The ultimate ownership of western European corporations. *Journal of Financial Economics*, *65*, 365–395.

Fama, E., & Jensen, M. (1983). Separation of ownership and control. *Journal of Law and Economics*, *26*, 301–329.

Fan, J. P. H., Wong, T. J., & Zhang, T. (2005). The emergence of corporate pyramids in China. *CEI Working Paper Series* No. 2005-16, Hitotsubashi University, Japan.

Gompers, P. A., Ishii, J. L., & Metrick, A. (2003). Corporate governance and equity prices. *Quarterly Journal of Economics*, *118*(1), 107–155.

Green, S. (2003). China's capital market: Better than a casino. *World Economics*, *4*(4), 37–54.

Jensen, M., & Meckling, W. (1976). Theory of the firm: Managerial behaviour, agency costs and ownership structure. *Journal of Financial Economics*, *3*, 305–360.

Jian, M., & Wong, T. J. (2003). Earnings management and tunneling through related party transactions: Evidence from Chinese corporate groups. Working paper, Hong Kong University of Science and Technology, Hong Kong.

Kapopoulos, P., & Lazaretou, S. (2007). Corporate ownership structure and firm performance: Evidence from Greek firms. *Corporate Governance: an International Review*, *15*(2), 144–158.

Kothari, S., & Zimmerman, J. (1995). Price and return models. *Journal of Accounting and Economics*, *20*, 155–192.

La Porta, R., Lopez-de-Silanes, F., Shleifer, A., & Vishny, R. (1998). Law and finance. *Journal of Political Economy*, *106*, 1113–1155.

La Porta, R., Lopez-de-Silanes, F., Shleifer, A., & Vishny, R. (1999). Corporate ownership around the world. *Journal of Finance*, *54*, 471–517.

La Porta, R., Lopez-de-Silanes, F., Shleifer, A., & Vishny, R. (2000). Investor protection and corporate governance. *Journal of Finance*, *58*, 3–28.

Lin, Z. J., Chen, F., & Tang, Q. (2001). Corporatisation and corporate governance in China's Economic Transition. *Economics of Planning*, *34*, 5–35.

Liu, Q., & Lu, J. Z. (2003). Earnings management to tunnel: Evidence from China's listed companies. EFMA 2004 Basel Meetings Paper. Available at SSRN: http://ssrn.com/abstract = 349880 or DOI: 10.2139/ssrn.349880

Qian, Y. (1995). *Reforming corporate governance and finance in China, corporate governance in transitional economy*. Washington, DC: The World Bank.

Qian, Y. (1996). Enterprise reform in China: Agency problems and political control. *Economics of Transition*, *4*, 427–447.

Sánchez-Ballesta, J. P., & García-Meca, E. (2007). A meta-analytic vision of the effect of ownership structure on firm performance. *Corporate Governance: An International Review*, *15*(5), 879–892.

Schipani, C., & Liu, J. (2001). Corporate governance in China: Then and now. Working Paper No. 407, William Davison Institute.

Shleifer, A., & Vishny, R. (1986). Large shareholders and corporate control. *Journal of Political Economy*, *96*, 461–488.

Shleifer, A., & Vishny, R. (1997). A survey of corporate governance. *The Journal of Finance*, *52*(2), 737–783.

Tam, O. K., & Tan, M. G. (2007). Ownership, governance and firm performance in Malaysia. *Corporate Governance: An International Review*, *15*(2), 208–222.

Tian, L. (2001). Government shareholding & the value of China's modern firms. Working Paper No. 395, William Davidson Institute.

Xu, X., & Wang, Y. (1999). Ownership structure and corporate governance in Chinese stock companies. *China Economic Review*, *10*, 75–98.

Zhang, A., Zhang, Y., & Zhao, R. (2001). Impact of ownership and competition on the productivity of Chinese enterprises. *Journal of Comparative Economics*, *29*, 327–346.

Zhang, J., Zhang, T., & Zhang, X. (2008). Corporate governance, performance and management turnover: An empirical analysis of Chinese listed companies. Paper presented at the 8th International Business Research Conference, March, Dubai.

Zhang, Y., & Zhao, R. (2004). The valuation differential between class A and B shares: Country risk in the Chinese stock market. *Journal of International Financial Management & Accounting*, *15*(1), 44–59.

THE INFLUENCE OF OWNERSHIP STRUCTURES AND BOARD PRACTICES ON CORPORATE SOCIAL DISCLOSURES IN BANGLADESH

Afzalur Rashid and Sudhir C. Lodh

ABSTRACT

Purpose – *This study examines the influences of ownership concentration and the imposition of regulation on corporate governance (especially appointments of independent outside directors into the board) on voluntary corporate social disclosures (CSD) practices in Bangladesh.*

Design/methodology/approach – *CSD indices are developed using content analysis in terms of different attributes reported in the sample companies' annual reports. Consistent with earlier studies, a checklist of items is constructed to assess the extent of CSD in annual reports. A two-stage least square (2SLS) regression analysis is used to examine the extent of the influences on CSD practices due to differing ownership structures and changed board compositions upon a notification of good corporate governance principles by the regulatory body in Bangladesh. To compare the differences on CSD practices before and after the imposition*

Corporate Governance in Less Developed and Emerging Economies
Research in Accounting in Emerging Economies, Volume 8, 211–237
Copyright © 2008 by Emerald Group Publishing Limited
All rights of reproduction in any form reserved
ISSN: 1479-3563/doi:10.1016/S1479-3563(08)08008-0

of regulation two periods (pre-notification from 2004 to 2005 and post-notification from 2006 to 2007) are considered for the analysis.

Findings – *The results show that although ownership structures have small influence on CSD practices, but the imposition of regulation on good corporate governance can significantly influence such practices.*

Practical implications – *This suggests that without regulation (imposed or otherwise) companies have no incentives to provide voluntary social disclosures in annual reports in a developing country context.*

Original/value of paper – *This study contributes to the literature on the practices of CSD in the context of developing countries. As well, this study supports the theory of pro-regulation on corporate governance.*

INTRODUCTION

"Corporate social disclosures" (CSD) has become increasingly prominent issue in the social accounting and corporate governance literature. There is a host of studies conducted on CSD practices in the context of developed countries including Australia and New Zealand (Guthrie & Mathews, 1985; Guthrie & Parker, 1989; Hackston & Milne, 1996; Deegan & Gordon, 1996; Deegan & Rankin, 1996; Hall, 2002); United States (Ernst & Ernst, 1978); Western Europe (Dierkes, 1979; Rey, 1980; Adams, Hills, & Roberts, 1998) and Japan (Yamagami & Kokubu, 1991; Stanwick & Stanwick, 2006). The literature shows that in developed countries there is an increased awareness about CSD practices among different stakeholders. However, some literature has linked ownership structure and firm performance (Morck, Shleifer, & Vishny, 1988; Han & Suk, 1998; Short & Keasey, 1999; Xu & Wang, 1999; Yammeesri & Lodh, 2004; Sheu & Yang, 2005; Yammeesri, Lodh, & Herath, 2006). However, none of these studies examined the associations between CSD practices, ownership concentration and imposed regulation of corporate governance practices.

The literature on voluntary CSD is divided into two divergent theoretical underpinnings: from market-driven *self-regulation* (in a Milton Friedman's economic rationality sense), to *pro-regulation*. This study investigates whether ownership concentration and the imposition of regulation on corporate governance practices, including a change of board composition, influence voluntary CSD practices in developing countries. For example, Milton Friedman believed that the responsibility of business is to make profits and belongs *solely* to the individual outside the business community. Being a supporter of the free-market perspective, he adopted the purely agency theory perspective (Jensen & Meckling, 1976) and believed that any attempt to satisfy stakeholders, other than shareholders, is misguided (Solomon, 2007). However, such ideas of market-driven self-regulation are debated vigorously. It is argued that business has the responsibility to preserve the environment for continued profits; to become socially responsible and to have the basic sense to "clean up the mess" they made (Solomon & Martin, 2004, p. 171). Therefore, there is an increased concern about whether corporate entities are acting in a socially responsible manner. Accordingly, CSD practices have received an increasing amount of attention from academics, government, professional bodies, industries and corporations (Perera, 2007; Ghazali, 2007). CSD practices are seen as providing a solution to improved accountability for societal issues and have become an international issue (for example, global warming and climate change) (Cheney, 2001; Hall, 2002).

Following the recent high incidence of corporate collapses around the world (in particular, the collapses of Enron, WorldCom and HIH Insurance); corporate governance reforms have emerged in several countries. A cause of these collapses has been alleged to the ethical consequence, rather than simply auditing failure (Parker, 2005; Gordon, 2007; Perera, 2007). This has given rise to the imposition of regulation and/ or good corporate governance principle guidelines by several developed countries, for example, introduction of Sarbanes-Oxley Act, 2002 in United States, Higgs Report, 2003 and Smith Report, 2003 in United Kingdom and CLERP 9 in Australia.

Mathews (1984, p. 204) defines CSD in the corporate social and environmental research arena as:

> voluntary disclosure of information both qualitative and quantitative, made by organizations to inform or influence a range of audiences. The qualitative disclosures may be financial or non-financial terms.

Gray, Owen, and Maunders (1987) define CSD or triple bottom line reporting as:

> the process of communicating the social and environmental effects of organizations' economic actions to particular interest groups within society and to society at large. (p. ix)

The World Business Council for Sustainable Development (WBCSD, 2000, p. 10) proposed a broader understanding of the concept, emphasizing the balance between sustainable economic development as well as working with employees, their families, the local community and society at large to improve their quality of life.

The emergence of CSD can be traced back to the early 1960s and 1970s in industrialized countries. In the last two decades or so, following the growing criticisms of industries by external pressure groups, the issue of good corporate governance has become a prominent global agenda (Burke, 1984; Yamagami & Kokubu, 1991). Various influential standards and guidelines exist in developed countries, including Global Reporting Initiatives (GRI), ISO 14000, AA1000 and the International Standard on Assurance Engagements (ISAE) 3000. An important question remains whether such disclosures are occurring in developing countries. It is considered to be a new phenomenon in developing countries and law does not require such disclosures to be made; even though the need for them is acute (Gray, Owen, & Adams, 1996).

Milne (2007) argues that social research accounting "should concentrate on the extent of disclosure, relationship between disclosure and other variables (e.g., industry size and market capitalization), the audit of disclosures and view of participants" (p. 50). He further argues that other than disclosure practices, there are numerous studies that also have analyzed the relationships on various firm characteristics over the last two decades.

In the context of developing countries, there are several studies conducted on CSD practices (Singh & Ahuja, 1983; Teoh & Thong, 1984; Andrew, Gul, Guthrie, & Teoh, 1989; Savage, 1994; Hegde, Bloom, & Fuglister, 1997; Belal, 2001; Imam, 2000; Haniffa & Cooke, 2002; Haniffa & Cooke 2005; Kuasirikun & Sherer, 2004; De Villiers & Van Staden, 2006). However, CSD in the context of Bangladesh were studied by Belal (2001) and Imam (2000). Most of these studies examined the extent of CSD, rather than examine the relationship between CSD practices and corporate governance attributes. This study, therefore, investigates whether ownership concentration and the imposition of regulation on corporate governance practices (including a change of board composition) influences voluntary CSD practices in a developing country context in Bangladesh.

The remainder of this paper is organized as follows. The second section outlines the background literature and theoretical framework on CSD practices. The third section illustrates the context of CSD practices in Bangladesh. The method and hypotheses are developed in the subsequent section. A note on data collection and research method is outlined in fifth section. Empirical results are interpreted in the following section. A conclusion is drawn in the final section.

BACKGROUND LITERATURE ON CSD PRACTICES

The issue of business social responsibilities and to what extent businesses should make social disclosures has been debated for over the last few decades (Milne, 2007). Numerous theories have dominated CSD research. A few of these theoretical underpinnings are discussed below.

Market-Driven Forces and Regulation

This perspective suggests that the market or economic forces will motivate managers to provide information (such as, CSD) even in the absence of regulation (Deegan, 2006). The market forces will lead corporations to provide socially oriented information that may influence the share price and returns, and will be in line with modern management (Mathews, 1995). Contrary to this view, the pro-regulation perspective suggests that regulation is required and the market might not always work in the best interest of society:

> Over the years there have been many arguments and debates over the necessity for regulation. Those who believe in the efficacy of markets argue that regulation is not necessary as market forces will operate to best serve society and optimise the allocation of resources. However, there are many who point out that markets do not always operate in the best interests of societies, so some form of intervention in the form of regulation is necessary. (Gaffikin, 2005, p. 1)

Stakeholder Theory

The concept of CSD has been alleged to arise consistent with stakeholder theory, and the suggestion that companies should disclose environmental and social issues in addition to their financial reporting (Solomon, 2007, p. 250). This perspective suggests that financial matters should not be the only consideration – there are moral obligations that should never be abandoned whatever the circumstances that an organization faces (Solomon & Martin, 2004). Therefore, rather than maximize the interest of the share-holders only, stakeholder theory suggests that the interest of the wider community involved in corporations (such as employees, customers and suppliers, communities and even the environment) is to be satisfied (Freeman, 1984; Blair, 1995; Stovall, Neill, & Perkins, 2004). Compliance of such obligation (or social responsibility) ranges from profit maximization to social awareness and community service (Lantos, 2001).

Social Contract, Accountability and Organizational Legitimacy

Corporate social responsibility also arises to provide greater accountability, which can be considered a social contract in a legitimacy sense. This assumes that corporations act within the bounds and norms of society (Mathews, 1995; Gray, Owen, & Maunders, 1998). According to De Villiers and Van Staden (2006, p. 763), "corporations will do whatever they regard as necessary in order to preserve their image of a legitimate business with legitimate aims and methods of achieving it". Therefore, it is expected that corporations in developing countries will publish voluntary social and environmental information to ensure legitimacy.

This study is conducted with a *pro-regulation* perspective. It assumes that companies will not make any CSD voluntarily.

THE CORPORATE SOCIAL DISCLOSURE CONTEXT IN BANGLADESH

Bangladesh is a developing country in Asia. The population of Bangladesh during the year ended 30th June 2007 was approximately 141.8 million, making it the 8th most populous nation in the world and one of the most densely populated, with more than 961 people per square kilometer (Index of Economic Freedom, 2008). Therefore, living standards are increasing concerns in Bangladesh. Moreover, due to increased industrialization and growing foreign investment there are some adverse impacts on the environment. The river Buriganga, on the bank of which the capital city Dhaka stands, became "clinically dead" as most of the industries are either on its banks (Belal, 2001) or the industrial waste ultimately flows in it. Due to industrialization, industries occupy cultivable fertile lands and industries dispose of wastes to the nearby fertile lands (causing the loss of fertility) and the waterways. However, there are neither active external pressure groups nor regulations requiring firms to make such disclosure. Foreign investors may not consider investing in Bangladesh companies that are not socially and ethically responsible (Belal, 2001). A reason is that most of the foreign investor companies are already exposed to CSD for their reporting environment and see it primarily as an acculturated issue. Therefore, CSD is an increased concern in Bangladesh.

Corporate Governance Regulation in Bangladesh

The United Kingdom Cadbury Report (Cadbury, 1992) defined corporate governance as "the system by which companies are directed and controlled" (p. 15).

Corporate governance also provides the structure through which objectives of the company are set, and the means of attaining those objectives and monitoring performance are determined. Corporate Law Reform Program (CLERP) (1997) defines corporate governance as:

> the rules and practices put in place within a company to manage information and economic incentive problems inherent in a separation of ownership from control in large enterprises. It deals with how, and to what extent, the interest of various agents involved in the company are reconciled and what checks and incentives are put in place to ensure that managers maximise the value of the investment made by shareholders ... (p. 62)

Corporate governance suffers from being a multi-level concept which differs between country (or economy) and individual levels. However, following on the high degree of corporate collapses and scandals around the world over this decade, the corporate watchdog, the Securities and Exchange Commission of Bangladesh (SECB) announced the "Corporate Governance Notification 2006" for the listed firms on the Bangladeshi Stock Exchanges. This notification is probably the first published comprehensive set of corporate best practices governance guidelines in Bangladesh, and is a milestone of the corporate sector in Bangladesh. It requires compliance with the "board size" (which is 5–20 members) and position of "independent" or "non-shareholder" directors in the board (which is at least 10% of the total board members or minimum one). This independent or non-shareholder directors should not have a significant material interest in the firms.

Following the announcement of "Corporate Governance Notification 2006" for Bangladeshi firms, a number of companies immediately adopted (either fully or partly) such practices to maintain their images. However, such a notification does not require companies to report CSD. Even the Companies Act 1994, which guides corporate financial reporting in Bangladesh, does not require CSD to be reported in the disclosure documents or corporate annual reports. Companies which adopted the notification to change the board structure they made most of CSDs through the "Reports from the Board of Directors". No other form of disclosures, such as brochures, press releases, reporting on the web pages and separate social reports are to be found in the Bangladesh corporate sector. Most of the CSD reports are in the form of qualitative statements. Although the "Corporate Governance Notification 2006" does not require by law that companies should make social disclosures in Bangladesh, it can be assumed that the firms which adopted the corporate governance best practices are making CSD to maintain their organizational legitimacy. We believe that this is done to improve accountability and social awareness to wider stakeholders.

HYPOTHESES

Ownership Concentration and CSD Hypothesis

Due to the separation of ownership and control in modern corporations, there is a conflict of interest between the principal (owners) and the agent (management). The corporate ownership structure is one of the most important factors shaping the corporate governance system of any country. Ownership structures play an important role in determining a firm's objectives, shareholders' wealth and how managers of a firm are disciplined (Porter, 1990; Yammeesri & Lodh, 2004; Yammeesri et al., 2006). Further, ownership structures play an active role as a good monitor in countries where investor protection is weak (Shleifer & Vishny, 1997; La Porta, Lopez-de-Silanes, Shleifer, & Vishny, 1998; La Porta, Lopez-de-Silanes, Shleifer, & Vishny, 2000) and both the legal protection and some forms of concentrated ownership are essential elements of good corporate governance (Shleifer & Vishny, 1997; La Porta et al., 1998).

The corporate control mechanisms in Bangladesh are mostly insider oriented, including high family ownership concentration. That is, the core investors own significant stakes of shares (also known as *ownership control* approach, see for example Xu & Wang, 1999) and, in general, are the board of directors. The spread of share ownership in public limited companies in Bangladesh is not wide and the economic power of businesses is concentrated in dominant shareholder groups. A few shareholders account for a significant portion of total share value. There is evidence of a small ownership concentration by foreign investors, government and institutional investors. However, most public companies in Bangladesh are controlled mainly by founding sponsors/directors who are family members, leading to a very high degree of ownership concentration and control. Representatives of these concentrated owners hold positions on the company board and in management.

In Bangladesh, institutional investors comprise of banks, insurance companies, pension funds, provident funds and mutual funds. They hold power over a substantial amount of invested capital and demand strong performance and transparent corporate governance. These institutional investors have a professional interest in developing the firm's corporate governance (Nandelstadh & Rosenberg, 2003), and can identify key indicators in determining performance in the emerging market. This is because they prefer to work inside the firms to change policies of firms in their portfolio (Baysinger & Butler, 1985, p. 107; Gibson, 2003). Therefore, it is assumed that corporate ownership concentration can influence the firm's voluntary CSD. The following hypothesis is developed:

H₁. There is a significant relationship between the corporate ownership structures and CSD reporting.

Board Composition and CSD Hypothesis

The corporate board plays an important role in determining the primary and dominant internal corporate governance mechanisms. Following on the "Stakeholder Theory", the board will extract successful firms' operations due to prestige concern in the professions and communities (Zahra & Pearce II, 1989) and will provide information and employ comparative resources in enhancing firm's performance (Gopinath, Siciliano, & Murray, 1994). One of the requirements of the "Corporate Governance Notification 2006" in Bangladesh is the appointment of outside independent directors to the board. The view is that such outside independent directors should have advance qualifications, expertise and experience. Thereby, they can effectively influence the board's decision and ultimately can add value to the firm (e.g., Fields & Keys, 2003) and wider community. Of course, any of these outside independent directors will not have enough inside operational information about the firm.

The Corporate Governance notification neither provided any legislative definition on independent directors nor any legislative requirements for their qualifications and guidelines for appointing them into the board. As a result, outside independent directors can be appointed in Bangladesh because of a close relationship with the family, existing board members or a large shareholder. The UK Tyson Report 2003 recommends the appointment of non-executive directors with diversity in background, skills and experience to enhance board effectiveness and improve stakeholders' relationship.

However, given the limitation on the appointment of independent directors, it is assumed there is a moral pressure for outside independent directors to respect the good governance principles advanced through launching the notification. Therefore, such an introduction of independent directors in the board structure may have some influence on the CSD practices in Bangladesh. The following hypothesis is developed:

H_2. The board composition including the representation of outside independent directors can significantly influence the CSD reporting.

RESEARCH METHOD

Sample Selection

The sample companies were selected from the listed companies on the Dhaka Stock Exchange. The data is collected from the annual reports of these selected companies for the financial years 2003–2004 and 2004–2005 (for pre-corporate governance notification), and 2005–2006[1] and 2006–2007 (for post corporate governance notification). The sample is constructed on the basis of a company's highest market capitalization (e.g., Guthrie & Parker, 1990; Belal, 2001) and compliance with the "Corporate Governance Notification 2006", in particular, companies which appointed independent directors. There were 239 listed companies as of 30 June 2006. Following the declaration of the "Corporate Governance Notification 2006", only a few companies adopted those guidelines and appointed independent directors. The companies which did not comply with such a requirement were excluded from the sample. Further, the companies for which market capitalization is less than BDT[2] 50 million were also excluded from the sample. It was assumed that these companies had little role in environmental sustainability exposure. After complying with all of the above considerations, 21 companies were selected.[3] The digitalized soft and hard copies of companies' annual reports were collected from the library of the Dhaka Stock Exchange. The sample consists of variety of industries: Cement, Ceramic, Engineering, Food and Allied, Fuel and Power, Pharmaceuticals and Chemicals, Service and Real Estate, Tannery Industries, Textile and Miscellaneous.

Dependent Variable

CSD indices represent the dependent variable. It is measured in terms of different attributes reported in the company's annual reports (see Appendices A, B and C). Content analysis has been used commonly to measure a CSD in annual reports (Adams et al., 1998; Ernst & Ernst, 1978; Guthrie & Mathews, 1985; Milne & Adler, 1999). Content analysis codifies the text (or content) of a piece of writing into various groups (or categories) depending on selected criteria (Weber, 1985). Following on the identified coding, quantitative scales are derived to permit further analysis (Milne & Adler, 1999). Content analysis assumes that the extent of disclosure can be taken as some indication of the importance of an issue to the reporting entity (Krippendorff, 1980). Content analysis requires objectivity and the specification of variables so that any item can be judged consistently as falling (or not falling) into a particular category (Guthrie & Mathews, 1985).

Consistent with earlier studies on Corporate Social Responsibility (e.g., Haniffa & Cooke, 2002; Haniffa & Cooke, 2005; Ghazali, 2007), a checklist containing 20 items (shown in Appendices A and B) was constructed to assess the extent of CSD in annual reports of the sample companies. A dichotomous procedure was applied whereby a company is awarded a 1 if an item included in the checklist is disclosed, otherwise a 0 is awarded. The CSD index was derived by computing the ratio of actual scores awarded to the maximum score attainable (20) by that company (Ghazali, 2007). More specifically, similar to Haniffa and Cooke (2005), the CSD index was calculated using the following equation:

$$\text{CSD}_i \text{ Index} = \frac{\sum_{t=1}^{nj} X_{ij}}{n_j}$$

where, CSD_i index is the Corporate Social Disclosure index for ith firm, n_i the number of items expected for ith firm, where $n \leqslant 20$ and $X_{ij} = 1$, if jth items are disclosed for firm i, otherwise 0.

Independent Variables

The independent variables are ownership concentration and board composition. Consistent with some prior corporate governance studies (Morck et al., 1988; Short & Keasey, 1999; Demsetz & Villalonga, 2001; Yammeesri & Lodh, 2004; Yammeesri et al., 2006), this study defines the ownership structures as the percentage of shares held by different ownership categories. A variable, DIR, representing the percentage of shares held by directors/sponsors; INST, representing the percentage of shares held by institutions and LB, representing the percentage of shares held by the largest block holders is considered. Similarly, consistent with some other corporate governance studies (e.g., Rechner & Dalton, 1986; Zahra & Stanton, 1988), board composition, BC, refers to the percentage of seats held by the outsiders or independent directors.

Control Variables

Four control variables (company size, profitability, company age and debt) are considered. Company size is considered to be an important factor in voluntary CSD and larger companies are more sensible towards CSD (Guthrie & Mathews, 1985); larger companies are subject to greater scrutiny by various interested groups (Haniffa & Cooke, 2005; Ghazali, 2007). Company size is considered as the natural log of market capitalization (Ghazali, 2007). Therefore, a variable LnMC is considered. Ghazali (2007) argues that companies make more disclosures to signal performance. It is assumed that the firms performing well may try to expose its organizational legitimacy and may make increased social disclosure. Thus, this study considers ROA as the profitability measure to examine firms' performance that may influence the CSD. Consistent with Yammeesri et al. (2006) and Yammeesri and Lodh (2004), a variable ROA is calculated by dividing earnings before interest and taxes (EBIT) by closing assets. The firms listed for a longer period will be sensible towards more disclosure as well. Therefore, a variable AGE is considered for the number of years a firm is listed on the stock exchange. Moreover, debt is an important instrument. It enables voluntary CSD to indicate the creditors that management is less likely to bypass their covenant claim (Haniffa & Cooke, 2005). Consistent with Haniffa and Cooke (2005) and Yammeesri et al. (2006), a variable DEBT is considered as the ratio of total debt to total assets.

EMPIRICAL RESULTS

Tables 1, 2 and 3 provide the descriptive statistics of the selected variables for pre-notification (2003–2004 and 2004–2005), post-notification (2005–2006

Table 1. Descriptive Statistics of the Samples (Pre-Notification Period for 42 Observations).

Variables	Mean	Median	Stdev	Min	Max	Skew	Kurt	Bera-Jarque	Prob
CSD	0.143	0.125	0.097	0.000	0.350	0.348	2.001	2.594	0.273
Director share ownership (DIR)	0.451	0.440	0.175	0.010	0.800	−0.324	3.414	1.036	0.596
Institutional share ownership (INST)	0.183	0.150	0.161	0.000	0.570	0.686	2.685	3.472	0.176
Largest block holders (LB)	0.391	0.345	0.205	0.050	0.760	0.242	1.921	2.446	0.294
Board composition (BC)	0.014	0.000	0.052	0.000	0.250	3.678	15.224	356.169	0.000
LnMC	6.859	6.570	1.331	4.490	10.000	0.457	2.569	1.786	0.409
ROA	0.097	0.085	0.057	0.020	0.240	0.865	3.080	5.244	0.073
AGE	2.807	2.890	0.411	2.080	3.370	−0.436	1.846	3.664	0.160
DEBT	0.336	0.330	0.200	0.000	0.760	0.178	1.951	2.147	0.342

Note: stdev, standard deviation; skew, skewness; Kurt, kurtosis; Bera-Jurque for normality test.

and 2006–2007) and combined pre- and post-notification (2003–2004 to 2006–2007) periods, respectively.

The descriptive statistics include the mean, median, standard deviation, minimum, maximum, skewness, Kurtosis, Bera-Jarque for normality test and respective probabilities. Results reveal that the mean for CSD dependent variable has increased from 14.3% (pre-notification in Table 1) to 24.4% (post-notification in Table 2). The mean for the directors share ownership (DIR) independent variable has declined slightly from 45.1% to 44.3%. The mean for institutional share ownership (INST) independent variable has increased from 18.3% to 20.3% after the notification. The mean for the largest block holders (LB) independent variable has declined slightly from 40.6% to 39.5%. The mean for the board composition (BC) independent variable has increased from 1.4% to 16.2%. The mean market capitalization (LnMC) control variable has increased from 6.859 to 7.057. The mean for performance or profitability (ROA) control variable has increased from 9.70% to 12.10%. The mean for age of companies (AGE) control variable has increased slightly. The mean for debt (DEBT) control variable has declined from 33.6% to 32.8%. These statistics show that after the corporate governance notification, board composition (BC) with independent directors has increased significantly for the sample companies in Bangladesh. All other control variables have a slight increase as well except debt which has declined.

Table 2. Descriptive Statistics of the Samples (Post-Notification Period for 38 Observations).

Variables	Mean	Median	Stdev	Min	Max	Skew	Kurt	Bera-Jarque	Prob
CSD	0.244	0.250	0.163	0.000	0.550	0.213	1.876	2.348	0.309
Director share ownership (DIR)	0.443	0.430	0.185	0.010	0.800	−0.210	2.963	0.290	0.865
Institutional share ownership (INST)	0.203	0.170	0.180	0.000	0.590	0.778	2.628	4.164	0.125
Largest block holders (LB)	0.406	0.330	0.212	0.050	0.760	0.188	1.738	2.820	0.244
Board composition (BC)	0.162	0.170	0.052	0.080	0.330	1.470	6.294	31.669	0.000
LnMC	7.057	6.960	1.421	4.320	9.540	0.168	1.927	2.054	0.358
ROA	0.121	0.110	0.058	0.020	0.240	0.204	2.203	1.302	0.521
AGE	2.931	2.996	0.368	2.303	3.434	−0.379	1.790	3.313	0.191
DEBT	0.328	0.350	0.228	0.000	1.130	1.006	4.967	12.868	0.002

Note: stdev, standard deviation; skew, skewness; Kurt, kurtosis; Bera-Jurque for normality test.

Table 3. Descriptive Statistics of All Samples (Pre- and Post-Notification Periods for 80 Observations).

Variables	Mean	Median	Stdev	Min	Max	Skew	Kurt	Bera-Jarque	Prob
CSD	0.193	0.200	0.141	0.000	0.550	0.654	2.628	6.166	0.046
Director share ownership (DIR)	0.447	0.440	0.180	0.010	0.800	−0.268	3.140	1.024	0.599
Institutional share ownership (INST)	0.195	0.150	0.169	0.000	0.590	0.747	2.717	7.712	0.021
Largest block holders (LB)	0.395	0.330	0.205	0.050	0.760	0.242	1.865	5.078	0.079
Board composition (BC)	0.085	0.085	0.091	0.000	0.330	0.551	2.278	5.779	0.056
LnMC	6.951	6.685	1.378	4.320	10.000	0.321	2.180	3.613	0.164
ROA	0.109	0.100	0.058	0.020	0.240	0.503	2.428	4.469	0.107
AGE	2.868	2.944	0.396	2.079	3.434	−0.462	1.950	6.518	0.038
DEBT	0.337	0.345	0.211	0.000	1.130	0.671	3.877	8.571	0.014

Note: stdev, standard deviation; skew, skewness; Kurt, kurtosis; Bera-Jurque for normality test.

Table 4.   Mean Difference Tests between Pre-Notification and Post-Notification Periods.

	CSDI	DIR	INST	LB	BC	LnMC	AGE	ROA	DEBT
t-tests	−13.51	0.20	−0.18	−0.16	−12.65	−0.63	−1.46	−1.98	6.99
Probability	0.00	0.42	0.25	0.44	0.00	0.27	0.07	0.03	0.00

From Tables 1, 2 and 3, it shows that most of the variables are normally distributed except for the institutional share ownerships (INST), age of companies (AGE) and debt (DEBT) variables at 5% level. Also, the descriptive statistics do not reveal any sign of heteroscedasticity in the sample data and therefore all the variables can be considered for the analysis. Although the volatilities (standard deviations) for all the variables have been increased for the post-notification periods, but for the CSD variable a significant increase is revealed.

Mean difference tests has also been carried out, as shown in Table 4. It shows that the mean difference tests between two sample periods – pre- and post-notifications periods. It reveals that CSD, BC (board composition) and ROA (return on assets) variables have been increased significantly at least 5% level during the post-notification periods. And, debt has been reduced in the post-notification period at least at 1% level.

For performing statistical tests, there is a necessity to meet the criteria for multicolinearity. It refers to high correlations among the independent variables or it is a condition when the independent variables are significantly correlated with one another. When the high degree of correlation is found among the independent variables, these variables must be removed. The correlation matrix between variables is presented in Tables 5, 6 and 7 for pre-notification, post-notification and all samples, respectively. These tables show that there is no strong correlations between the variables as the coefficients are less than 0.75. Therefore, the multicolinearity assumption is met for the all the selected variables.

Model for Analysis

Following model is developed to conduct the empirical analysis and to test the hypotheses:

$$\text{CSD}_{it} = \alpha + \beta_1 \text{DIR}_{it} + \beta_2 \text{Inst}_{it} + \beta_3 \text{LB}_{it} + \beta_4 \text{BC}_{it} + \beta_5 \text{LnMC}_{it} + \beta_6 \text{ROA}_{it} + \beta_7 \text{Age}_{it} + \beta_8 \text{Debt}_{it} + \varepsilon_{it}$$

Table 5. Correlation Matrix for Pre-Notification Period: 2003–2004 and 2004–2005.

	CSDI	DIR	INST	LB	BC	LnMC	AGE	ROA	DEBT
CSDI	1.00								
DIR	−0.27	1.00							
INST	−0.07	−0.34	1.00						
LB	−0.05	0.47	−0.19	1.00					
BC	−0.12	0.32	−0.10	0.34	1.00				
LnMC	0.50	0.24	−0.31	0.45	0.21	1.00			
AGE	0.03	0.27	−0.13	0.60	0.21	0.18	1.00		
ROA	0.12	0.49	−0.18	0.28	−0.14	0.45	0.11	1.00	
DEBT	0.06	−0.39	0.43	−0.48	−0.13	−0.38	−0.12	−0.08	1.00

Table 6. Correlation Matrix for Post-Notification Period: 2005–2006 and 2006–2007.

	CSDI	DIR	INST	LB	BC	LnMC	AGE	ROA	DEBT
CSDI	1.00								
DIR	0.22	1.00							
INST	−0.26	−0.35	1.00						
LB	0.32	0.41	−0.20	1.00					
BC	0.18	0.57	−0.01	0.39	1.00				
LnMC	0.65	0.21	−0.22	0.44	−0.01	1.00			
AGE	0.33	0.29	0.00	0.61	0.17	0.25	1.00		
ROA	0.67	0.26	−0.28	0.38	0.28	0.46	0.28	1.00	
DEBT	0.03	−0.10	0.09	−0.40	−0.12	−0.46	−0.04	0.06	1.00

Table 7. Correlation Matrix for All Samples: 2003–2004 to 2006–2007.

	CSDI	DIR	INST	LB	BC	LnMC	AGE	ROA	DEBT
CSDI	1.00								
DIR	0.02	1.00							
INST	−0.14	−0.34	1.00						
LB	0.16	0.44	−0.20	1.00					
BC	0.34	0.24	0.03	0.22	1.00				
LnMC	0.57	0.22	−0.25	0.44	0.12	1.00			
AGE	0.24	0.27	−0.05	0.60	0.24	0.22	1.00		
ROA	0.48	0.36	−0.21	0.32	0.22	0.46	0.22	1.00	
DEBT	0.04	−0.24	0.25	−0.44	−0.07	−0.42	−0.08	−0.01	1.00

where, CSD_{it} is the CSD index for ith firm at time t, DIR_{it} the percentage of shares held by directors/sponsors for ith firm at time t, $Inst_{it}$ the percentage of shares held by institutions for ith firm at time t, LB_{it} the percentage of shares held by the largest block holders for ith firm at time t, BC_{it} the percentage of seats held by outside independent directors for ith firm at time t, $LnMC_{it}$ the natural log of market capitalization for ith firm at time t, ROA_{it} the return on assets for ith firm at time t, Age_{it} the number of years firm is listed in the stock exchange for ith firm at time t, $Debt_{it}$ the ratio of total debt to total assets for ith firm at time t, α the constant, β_i the regression coefficient for ith item and ε_{it} the error term for ith firm at time t.

The above model is regressed through E-Views 6.0 statistical software and by using two-stage least square (2SLS) regression analysis.

It should be noted that model containing simultaneous equation is through instrumental variables in general. However, maximum likelihood estimates could also be a possible alternative, which provides efficient results. In the above model, the exogenous regressors Z_{ij} (all the first lag of the control variables, viz., $LnMC_{i(t-1)}$, $ROA_{i(t-1)}$, $Age_{i(t-1)}$ and $Debt_{i(t-1)}$) are the instrumental control variables. In our analysis, no endogeneity problem occurred as we have used 2SLS regression by using instrumental control variables which have automatically eradicated such a problem. The problem of endogeneity may be relevant if the parameters are estimated by using an OLS (Ordinary Least Square) regression in the context of time series analysis. In this study, we have used data for four years periods pooling from different organizations and, therefore, this problem is not applicable.

Table 8 represents the 2SLS regression analysis for pre-notification (2003–2004 and 2004–2005); post-notification (2005–2006 and 2006–2007) and combined (all samples) for both pre- and post-notification periods (from 2003–2004 to 2006–2007). Results for the pre-notification show that except for the market capitalization variable, LnMC, all other variables are not associated with the CSD variable. This indicates that the practice of making voluntary social disclosures was not significant prior to the notification of the change of corporate governance practices in Bangladesh.

Regression results for the post-notification reveal a significant positive relationship between the board composition and CSD ($p < .10$ level). The ownership concentration by family directors is also found to be associated with CSD after the imposition of the corporate governance notification ($p < .10$ level). This indicates that the practice of making voluntary social disclosures have become significant after the notification of the change of corporate governance practices in Bangladesh.

Table 8. Influence of Ownership Structures and Board Compositions on CSD for Pre-Notification, Post-Notification and Combined (Pre- and Post-Notifications) Periods.

	Coefficients		
	Pre-notification	Post-notification	Combined pre-post-notifications
Constant	−0.213	−0.704***	−0.386***
	(−1.561)	(−3.696)	(−3.355)
Director share	−0.148	−0.137	−0.170**
ownership (DIR)	(−1.394)	(−1.101)	(−2.257)
Institutional share	−0.027	−0.131	−0.090
ownership (INST)	(−0.297)	(−1.208)	(−1.244)
Largest block	−0.095	−0.112	−0.102
holders (LB)	(−0.957)	(−0.874)	(−1.212)
Board composition (BC)	−0.255	0.807*	0.452***
	(−0.856)	(1.787)	(3.492)
LnMC	0.053***	0.079***	0.059***
	(4.156)	(4.682)	(5.588)
ROA	−0.097	0.727*	0.542***
	(−0.295)	(1.838)	(2.261)
AGE	0.033	0.079	0.054
	(0.834)	(1.321)	(1.480)
DEBT	0.072	0.226**	−0.149**
	(0.834)	(2.272)	(2.225)
Adjusted R^2	0.470	0.707	0.563
S.E. of regression	0.341	0.627	0.514
F-statistic	3.656*	8.760*	11.437*
S.D. dependent variables	0.249	0.143	0.193
Second-stage SSR	2.437	2.252	2.055

The t-tests are presented in the parentheses. Significant at *** 1% level; ** 5% level; * 10% level.

Similarly, when the sample observations both for pre- and post-notification periods are combined, a significant positive relationship is revealed between board composition and CSD ($p < .01$). The ownership concentration by family directors is also found to be associated with CSD after the imposition of the corporate governance notification ($p < .10$ level). The positive association between ROA and CSD practices reveals that the well-performing firms are trying to expose its organizational legitimacy and making increased social disclosures. The significant positive relationship between the DEBT and CSD indicates the creditors are less likely to bypass their covenant claim. The overall regression results indicate that there has been a significant increase of CSD after the imposition of regulation (voluntary or otherwise) to appoint the outside independent directors in the corporate board in Bangladesh.

IMPLICATIONS OF THIS STUDY FOR DEVELOPING COUNTRIES

Although it is not common for companies to have increased CSD reporting in developing countries, this study provides an evidence of greater awareness of such practices following the imposed regulations. Improved CSD practice has occurred as a consequence of the announcement of the Corporate Governance Notification 2006, in Bangladesh. Before this was announced, companies' managements were dominated (mostly) by family shareholders. Representatives of family shareholders held the position in the company board who might not have urged for CSD to comply with organizational legitimacy and accountability to wider community. Outside directors might have played a role in changing the attitudes of the family owners towards improved CSD practices in a developing country context.

LIMITATIONS OF THIS STUDY

The data are collected from a large number of observations of different corporate entities. Those data ignore underlying differences in organizations: in no two organizations are the same (Deegan, 2006). The small sample size may not be representative as there is no control on the sample due to non-compliance of corporate governance best practices by a large number of firms in Bangladesh.

CONCLUSION

Although it is necessary to evaluate the quality and the reliability of the information presented in corporate annual reports, the study identified that the imposition of good corporate governance control mechanism influence corporate voluntary disclosure practices. Results show that corporate ownership structures have little influence on CSD practices, but board composition does have a greater influence on such practices in the context of a developing country, such as in Bangladesh.

This study supports the neo-institutional perspective of pro-regulation. This suggests that without regulation, there are no incentives for companies to provide voluntary social disclosure, especially in a developing country context. Therefore, the regulatory body can consider requiring the companies to make a minimum level of compulsory disclosure.

A further study can be carried out by increasing the analysis period from two years to a few more years for the period of post "Corporate Governance Notification 2006" in Bangladesh, which will allow to increase the sample size as the more firms will adopt the notified good corporate governance principles.

NOTES

1. The annual reports for 2005–2006 for the selected companies were prepared after the notification and therefore it is assumed that there is an implication of 'corporate governance notification' on ownership structures and board compositions.
2. The name of Bangladesh currency – Bangladesh Taka.
3. A total of 80 observations were made depending on the availability of annual reports for the sample companies.

ACKNOWLEDGMENT

We acknowledge the helpful comments on earlier drafts of this paper by Professor Russell Craig, Dr Girijasankar Mallik, participants at the British Accounting Association Annual Conference 2008 and the two anonymous reviewers of this journal.

REFERENCES

Adams, C. A., Hills, W. Y., & Roberts, C. B. (1998). Corporate social reporting practices in Western Europe: Legitimizing corporate behavior? *British Accounting Review, 30*(1), 1–21.

Andrew, B. H., Gul, F. A., Guthrie, J. E., & Teoh, H. Y. (1989). A note on corporate social disclosure practices in developing countries: The case of Malaysia and Singapore. *British Accounting Review, 21*(4), 371–376.

Baysinger, B. D., & Butler, H. N. (1985). Corporate governance and the board of directors: Performance effects in board composition. *Journal of Law, Economics and Organization, 1*(1), 101–124.

Belal, A. R. (2001). A study of corporate social disclosures in Bangladesh. *Managerial Auditing Journal, 16*(5), 274–289.

Blair, M. M. (1995). *Ownership and control: Rethinking corporate governance for the twenty first century*. Washington, DC: Brooking Institute.

Burke, R. C. (1984). *Decision making in complex times: The contribution of a social accounting information system*. Canada: Society of Management Accountants in Canada.

Cadbury, A., Sir. (1992). *Committee on the financial aspects of corporate governance*. United Kingdom: London Stock Exchange.

Cheney, G. (2001). Creating a corporate conscience: New role of non-financial reports. *Accounting Today, 15*(7), 3–4.

Corporate Law Reform Program (CLERP). (1997). *Directors' duties and corporate governance: Facilitating innovation and protecting investors*. Proposal for Reform: Paper No. 3, AGPS, Canberra.

Deegan, C. (2006). *Financial accounting theory*. Sydney, Australia: McGraw Hill.

Deegan, C. M., & Gordon, B. (1996). A Study of the environmental disclosure practices of Australian corporations. *Accounting and Business Research, 26*(3), 187–199.

Deegan, C. M., & Rankin, M. (1996). Australian companies report environmental news objectively? An analysis of environmental disclosures by firms prosecuted successfully by the environmental protection authority. *Accounting, Auditing and Accountability Journal, 9*(2), 50–67.

Demsetz, H., & Villalonga, B. (2001). Ownership structure and corporate performance. *Journal of Corporate Finance, 7*(3), 209–233.

De Villiers, C., & Van Staden, C. J. (2006). Can less environmental disclosure have a legitimizing effect: Evidence from Africa. *Accounting, Organizations and Society, 31*(8), 763–781.

Dierkes, M. (1979). Corporate social reporting in Germany: Conceptual development and practical experience. *Accounting, Organization and Society, 4*(1–2), 87–107.

Ernst and Ernst. (1978). *Social responsibility disclosure: 1978 survey*. Cleveland, Ohio: Ernst and Ernst.

Fields, M. A., & Keys, P. Y. (2003). The emergence of corporate governance from Wall St. to Main St.: Outside directors, board diversity and earnings management, and managerial incentive to bear risk. *The Financial Review, 38*(1), 1–24.

Freeman, R. E. (1984). *Strategic management: A stakeholder approach*. Boston: Pitman.

Gaffikin, M. J. (2005). *Regulation as Accounting Theory*. Working Paper # 09. School of Accounting and Finance, University of Wollongong, Wollongong.

Ghazali, M. (2007). Ownership structure and corporate social responsibility reporting: Some Malaysian evidence. *Corporate Governance: An International Journal of Business in Society, 7*(3), 251–266.

Gibson, M. S. (2003). Is corporate governance ineffective in emerging markets? *Journal of Financial and Quantitative Analysis, 38*(1), 231–250.

Gopinath, C., Siciliano, J. I., & Murray, R. L. (1994). Changing role of the board of directors: In search of a new strategic identity. *The Mid-Atlantic Journal of Business, 30*(2), 175–185.

Gordon, I. M. (2007). The challenge for social accounting. In: R. Gray & J. Guthrie (Eds), *Social accounting, mega accounting and beyond: A Festschrift in Honor of M. R. Mathews.* United Kingdom: The Centre for Social and Environmental Accounting Research, St. Andrews.

Gray, R., Owen, D., & Adams, C. (1996). *Accounting and accountability: Changes and challenges in corporate social and environmental reporting.* London: Prentice-Hall.

Gray, R., Owen, D., & Maunders, K. (1987). *Corporate social reporting: Accounting and accountability.* London: Prentice-Hall.

Gray, R., Owen, D., & Maunders, K. (1998). Corporate social reporting: Emerging trends in accountability and the social contract. *Accounting, Auditing and Accountability Journal, 1*(1), 6–20.

Guthrie, J. E., & Mathews, M. R. (1985). Corporate social accounting in Australia. In: L. Preston (Ed.), *Research in corporate social performance and policy* (Vol. 7, pp. 251–277). Greenwich, CT: JAI Press.

Guthrie, J. E., & Parker, L. D. (1989). Corporate social reporting: A rebuttal of legitimacy theory. *Accounting and Business Research, 19*(76), 343–352.

Guthrie, J. E., & Parker, L. D. (1990). Corporate social disclosure practice: A comparative international analysis. *Advances in Public Interest Accounting, 3,* 159–176.

Hackston, D., & Milne, M. J. (1996). Some determinants of social and environmental disclosures in New Zealand companies. *Accounting, Auditing and Accountability Journal, 9*(1), 77–104.

Hall, J. A. (2002). *An exploratory investigation into the corporate social disclosure of selected New Zealand companies.* Discussion Paper # 211, School of Accountancy, Massey University, New Zealand.

Han, C., & Suk, D. (1998). The effect of ownership structure on firm performance: Additional evidence. *Review of Financial Economics, 7*(2), 143–155.

Haniffa, R. M., & Cooke, T. E. (2002). Culture, corporate governance and disclosure in Malaysian corporations. *Abacus, 38*(3), 317–349.

Haniffa, R. M., & Cooke, T. E. (2005). The impact of culture and governance on corporate social reporting. *Journal of Accounting and Public Policy, 24*(5), 391–430.

Hegde, P., Bloom, R., & Fuglister, J. (1997). Social financial reporting in India: A case. *The International Journal of Accounting, 32*(2), 155–172.

Imam, S. (2000). Corporate social performance reporting in Bangladesh. *Managerial Auditing Journal, 15*(3), 133–141.

Index of Economic Freedom. (2008). *Bangladesh: Present and past score.* The online version available at http://www.heritage.org/ (accessed on February 2008). Washington, DC: The Heritage Foundation.

Jensen, M. C., & Meckling, W. J. (1976). Theory of the firm: Managerial behavior, agency costs and ownership structure. *Journal of Financial Economics, 3*(4), 305–360.

Krippendorff, K. (1980). *Content analysis: An introduction to its methodology.* New York: Sage.

Kuasirikun, N., & Sherer, M. (2004). Corporate social accounting disclosure in Thailand. *Accounting, Auditing and Accountability Journal, 17*(4), 629–660.

La Porta, R., Lopez-de-Silanes, F., Shleifer, A., & Vishny, R. W. (1998). Law and finance. *Journal of Political Economy, 106*(6), 1113–1155.

La Porta, R., Lopez-de-Silanes, F., Shleifer, A., & Vishny, R. W. (2000). Investor's protection and corporate governance. *Journal of Financial Economics, 58*(1), 3–27.

Lantos, G. P. (2001). The boundaries of strategic corporate social responsibility. *Journal of Consumer Marketing, 18*(7), 595–630.

Mathews, M. R. (1984). A suggested classification for social accounting research. *Journal of Accounting and Public Policy, 3*, 199–221.

Mathews, M. R. (1995). Social and environmental accounting: A practical demonstration of ethical concern? *Journal of Business Ethics, 14*, 663–671.

Milne, M. J. (2007). The international and cultural aspects of social accounting. In: R. Gray & J. Guthrie (Eds), *Social accounting, mega accounting and beyond: A Festschrift in Honor of M. R. Mathews*. St Andrews, United Kingdom: The Centre for Social and Environmental Accounting Research.

Milne, M. J., & Adler, R. W. (1999). Exploring the reliability of social and environmental disclosures content analysis. *Accounting, Auditing and Accountability Journal, 12*(2), 237–256.

Morck, R. K., Shleifer, A., & Vishny, R. W. (1988). Management ownership and market valuation: An empirical analysis. *Journal of Financial Economics, 20*(1–2), 293–315.

Nandelstadh, A. V., & Rosenberg, M. (2003). *Corporate governance and firm performance: Evidence from Finland*. Working Paper Number 497. Swedish School of Economics and Business Administration, Stockholm.

Parker, L. R. (2005). Corporate crisis down under: Post-Enron accounting education and research inertia. *European Accounting Review, 14*(2), 383–394.

Perera, H. (2007). The international and cultural aspects of social accounting. In: R. Gray & J. Guthrie (Eds), *Social accounting, mega accounting and beyond: A Festschrift in Honor of M. R. Mathews*. St Andrews, United Kingdom: The Centre for Social and Environmental Accounting Research.

Porter, E. (1990). *The competitive advantage of nations*. New York: Free Press.

Rechner, P. L., & Dalton, D. R. (1986). Board composition and shareholders wealth: An empirical assessment. *International Journal of Management, 3*(2), 86–92.

Rey, F. (1980). Corporate social reporting and performance in France. In: L. Preston (Ed.), *Research in corporate social performance and policy* (Vol. 2, pp. 291–325). JAI Press, CT.

Savage, A. A. (1994). Corporate social disclosure practices in South Africa: A research note. *Social and Environmental Accounting, 14*(1), 2–4.

Sheu, H. J., & Yang, C. Y. (2005). Insider ownership structure and firm performance: A productivity in perspective study in Taiwan's electronics industry. *Corporate Governance: An International Review, 13*(2), 326–337.

Shleifer, A., & Vishny, R. W. (1997). A survey of corporate governance. *The Journal of Finance, 52*(2), 737–783.

Short, H., & Keasey, K. (1999). Managerial ownership and performance of firm-evidence from UK. *Journal of Corporate Finance, 5*, 79–101.

Singh, D. R., & Ahuja, J. K. (1983). Corporate social responsibility in India. *The International Journal of Accounting, 18*(2), 151–169.

Solomon, J. (2007). *Corporate governance and accountability*. United Kingdom: Wiley.

Solomon, R. C., & Martin, C. (2004). *Above the bottom line: An introduction to business ethics* (3rd ed.). Southbank: Thomson Wadsworth.

Stanwick, P., & Stanwick, S. (2006). Corporate environmental disclosures: A longitudinal study of Japanese firms. *Journal of American Academy of Business, 9*(1), 1–7.

Stovall, O. S., Neill, J. D., & Perkins, D. (2004). Corporate governance, internal decision making and the invisible hand. *Journal of Business Ethics*, *51*(2), 221–227.

Teoh, H. Y., & Thong, G. (1984). Another look at corporate social responsibility and reporting: An empirical study in a developing country. *Accounting, Organizations and Society*, *9*(2), 189–206.

Weber, R. P. (1985). *Basic content analysis, sage university paper series on quantitative applications in the social sciences*. Series # 07-049. Beverly Hills, CA: Sage.

World Business Council for Sustainable Development (WBCSD). (2000). *Corporate social responsibility: Making good business sense*. http://www.wbcsd.org/web/publications/csr2000.pdf (accessed on 9th December 2007).

Xu, X., & Wang, Y. (1999). Ownership structure and corporate governance in Chinese stock companies. *China Economic Review*, *10*, 75–98.

Yamagami, T., & Kokubu, K. (1991). A note on corporate social disclosure in Japan. *Accounting, Auditing and Accountability Journal*, *4*(4), 32–39.

Yammeesri, J., & Lodh, S. C. (2004). Is family ownership a pain or gain to firm performance? *Journal of American Academy of Business*, *4*(1–2), 263–270.

Yammeesri, J., Lodh, S. C., & Herath, S. K. (2006). Influence of ownership structure and corporate performance pre-crisis: Evidence from Thailand. *International Journal of Electronic Finance*, *1*(2), 181–199.

Zahra, S. A., & Pearce, J. A., II. (1989). Board of directors and corporate financial performance: A review and integrative model. *Journal of Management*, *15*(2), 291–334.

Zahra, S. A., & Stanton, W. W. (1988). The implications of board of directors' composition for corporate strategy and performance. *International Journal of Management*, *5*(2), 229–236.

APPENDIX A. CSD CHECKLIST STATUS PRE-ADOPTION OF CORPORATE GOVERNANCE NOTIFICATION

	Disclosure Items	Number of Companies Disclosed	Percentage Disclosed	Rank
1	Community involvement in general	9	42.86	1
2	Charitable donation	1	4.76	8
3	Community program (health and education)	3	14.29	6
4	Environmental protection	0	0	0
5	Energy savings	0	0	0
6	Number of employees	3	14.29	6
7	Employee relations	8	38.09	2
8	Employee welfare	1	4.76	8

APPENDIX A. (*Continued*)

	Disclosure Items	Number of Companies Disclosed	Percentage Disclosed	Rank
9	Employee education	2	9.52	7
10	Employee training	6	28.57	4
11	Employee profit sharing	0	0	0
12	Occupational health and safety	2	9.52	7
13	Types of products disclosed	7	33.33	3
14	Product quality and improvements	6	28.57	4
15	Product safety	1	4.76	8
16	Discussion of marketing network	4	19.05	5
17	Focus on customer service	1	4.76	8
18	Customer award/ratings received	0	0	0
19	Value added statement	8	38.09	2
20	Value added data/ratio	4	4.76	8

APPENDIX B. CSD CHECKLIST STATUS POST-ADOPTION OF CORPORATE GOVERNANCE NOTIFICATION

	Disclosure Items	Number of Companies Disclosed	Percentage Disclosed	Rank
1	Community involvement in general	10	47.62	2
2	Charitable donation	0	0	12
3	Community program (health and education)	5	23.81	7
4	Environmental protection	0	0	12
5	Energy savings	0	0	11
6	Number of employees	6	28.57	6
7	Employee relations	8	38.10	4
8	Employee welfare	2	9.52	10
9	Employee education	4	19.05	8
10	Employee training	7	33.33	5
11	Employee profit sharing	0	0	12
12	Occupational health and safety	3	14.29	9

APPENDIX B. (*Continued*)

	Disclosure Items	Number of Companies Disclosed	Percentage Disclosed	Rank
13	Types of products disclosed	9	42.86	3
14	Product quality and improvements	11	52.38	1
15	Product safety	1	4.76	11
16	Discussion of marketing network	6	28.57	6
17	Focus on customer service	3	14.29	9
18	Customer award/ratings received	0	0	12
19	Value added statement	8	38.10	4
20	Value added data/ratio	5	23.81	7

APPENDIX C. SPECIFIC WORDING COUNTED IN CONTENT ANALYSIS

	Disclosure Items	Specific Wording Counted
1	Community involvement in general	If there are wordings, such as "recognizing the importance of community".
2	Charitable donation	If the company provided aid to the schools, colleges, educational and religious institution.
3	Community program (health and education)	If the company organized any blood donation program. Adopting adult literacy program.
4	Environmental protection	Initiatives taken to protect the environment in general; less emission of carbon; not polluting the air and water.
5	Energy savings	If the company used the energy efficient machinery, lamps.
6	Number of employees	Company disclosed the number of employees, helping the society in reducing the unemployment.
7	Employee relations	If the company recognized the employee relations in general; maintaining good understanding between the employees.
8	Employee welfare	If the company provided employee residence, welfare to the family members.

APPENDIX C. (*Continued*)

	Disclosure Items	Specific Wording Counted
9	Employee education	If the company recognition of employee education, provided support for education.
10	Employee training	If the company provided employment specific training.
11	Employee profit sharing	If the company is allowed the employee profit sharing in general, profit bonus, etc.
12	Occupational health and safety	Company took the precautionary measures in the workplace; proving OHS training in the workplace; available measure to cope with an accident.
13	Types of products disclosed	Types of products disclosed in general.
14	Product quality and improvements	Recognizing product quality, initiatives taken for improvements.
15	Product safety	Explanation of product safety in general.
16	Discussion of marketing network	Discussion of marketing and distribution network in general.
17	Focus on customer service	Customer service in general.
18	Customer award/ratings received	Recognition in the form of award received.
19	Value added statement	The company disclosed the value added statement in general.
20	Value added data/ratio	The company disclosed the value added data/ratio in general.

SELECTIVE COMPLIANCE WITH THE CORPORATE GOVERNANCE CODE IN MAURITIUS: IS LEGITIMACY THEORY AT WORK?

Teerooven Soobaroyen and Jyoti Devi Mahadeo

ABSTRACT

Purpose of this paper – *This study investigates compliance with the corporate governance code in an African developing economy (Mauritius).*

Methodology/approach – *We examine the annual reports of 41 listed companies to assess the extent of compliance with the code and to analyze the wording of compliance statements. We also carry out in-depth semi-structured interviews with selected company directors to understand the reasons for compliance (or non-compliance).*

Findings – *Initial findings indicate a reasonable level of compliance with the more visible requirements of the code but noteworthy non-compliance also emerges, particularly in relation to the low number of company boards being chaired by independent directors, to uncertainties on the actual operation of board committees, and to the widespread non-disclosure of directors' remuneration. Furthermore, compliance statements were found to be vague, ambiguous, or even inconsistent with the extent of compliance disclosed in the reports. We believe these are indications that many of*

Corporate Governance in Less Developed and Emerging Economies
Research in Accounting in Emerging Economies, Volume 8, 239–272
Copyright © 2008 by Emerald Group Publishing Limited
All rights of reproduction in any form reserved
ISSN: 1479-3563/doi:10.1016/S1479-3563(08)08009-2

the companies are adhering selectively with the code to project an image of symbolic compliance. Our in-depth follow-up interviews with directors largely confirm this behaviour of selective compliance.

Research implications – *We suggest that the pursuit of legitimacy as an operational resource – rather than efficiency-led rationales – emerges as a potential theoretical explanation for the adoption of the corporate governance code in Mauritius.*

Originality /value of paper – *We bring evidence on how the corporate governance code is being understood and rationalized in a developing economy. We rely on a combination of annual report disclosures, compliance statements, and interview data to investigate corporate governance compliance.*

INTRODUCTION

Over the last two decades, corporate governance codes have been the subject of increasing interest worldwide as it is believed they contribute to better organizational outcomes, board effectiveness and efficiency, and greater investor confidence. The adoption of corporate governance code is now viewed as a central criterion by institutional investors, the World Bank, the Organisation for Economic Co-operation and Development (OECD), and the International Monetary Fund, e.g. refer to Krambia-Kapardis and Psaros (2006. p. 127) and Rueda-Sabater (2000). However, there is an ongoing research debate as to whether such benefits do actually occur (Burton, 2000; Mallin, 2001; Monks, 2001; Daily, Dalton, & Cannella, 2003; Bauer, Guenster, & Otten, 2004; Mueller, 2006; Markarian, Parbonetti, & Previts, 2007) and whether the requirements from corporate governance codes were becoming too bureaucratic (Moxey, 2004) and inappropriate to deal effectively with corporate malpractices (Marnet, 2007). In addition, other authors such as Yakasai (2001), Claessens and Fan (2002), and Buchanan (2007) question the application of 'Western' codes in developing or non-Western environments.

The debate is fuelled by a number of country studies that have reported instances of diverse, piecemeal, selective, and symbolic corporate governance adoption, e.g. refer to Ow-Yong and Guan (2000), Pellens, Hillebrandt, and Ulmer (2001), Hussain and Mallin (2002), Solomon, Wei Lin, Norton, and Solomon (2003), Tsipouri and Xanthakis (2004), Berglöf and Pajuste (2005), Krambia-Kapardis and Psaros (2006), MacNeil and Li (2006), Qu and Leung (2006), and Tsamenyi, Enninful-Adu, and Onumah (2007). Whilst these studies offer a number of reasons to explain their findings, they rarely go beyond country-level environmental factors. There is little attempt at interpreting the findings at the micro (i.e. company) level and for instance, studies seldom consider the perceptions of the actors involved in the actual adoption of the codes. We therefore contend that further research at this micro level may be useful in deepening our understanding of the diverse 'behaviours' in corporate governance adoption. Admittedly, a key characteristic of corporate governance codes has been on making them less prescriptive, less legally enforceable and more flexible.[1] The 'comply or explain' approach in several countries is an acknowledgement that companies will claim 'adoption' of the code in a different way, allegedly in relation to factors such as size, ownership structure or industry. However, MacNeil and Li (2006, p. 486) argue that the benefits of such flexibility may be overstated.

Informed by the above, we seek to assess the extent of compliance with the corporate governance code in Mauritius using annual report disclosures and subsequently analyze the factors underlying the reasons for such compliance by relying on the views of company directors. There are several motivations for this study set in the context of an African developing economy. Firstly, the extant literature largely adopts an agency and rather universalistic perspective towards corporate governance adoption and its benefits, e.g. refer to Laing and Weir (1999) and Pension Investment Research Consultants (2004). We contend that the anecdotal evidence (e.g. from Ow-Yong & Guan, 2000; Tsipouri & Xanthakis, 2004) on the piecemeal and selective nature of compliance with corporate governance codes appears to contradict this perspective. We are drawn to the possibility that whilst claiming to comply with the 'philosophy' of the corporate governance code, companies may be selectively implementing some requirements of the code more for legitimacy reasons than purely for profit-maximising ones. Although this has been initially suggested by Burton (2000, p. 195), Aguilera and Cuervo-Cazurra (2004, p. 424) and Qu and Leung (2006), empirical findings (from the last two mentioned studies) remain inconclusive.

Secondly, the case of Mauritius is a notable example since Rossouw (2005, p. 95) considers it to be one of the few African nations that has made significant progress in corporate governance adoption although there has not been any study of its actual implementation. The formal adoption of the code was a fairly recent event, thereby allowing for an exploration of the corporate governance issues within Mauritius' current socio-economic and political context. This context is dominated by declining competitiveness and foreign direct investment (FDI), a tightly knit family-held business community being pressured to open up and innovate, the need for more ethical business and less corrupt behaviour, and a current political agenda aimed at '*democratizing*' the economy. We believe these are contextual features that are also equally relevant to many Sub-Saharan African developing economies.

Additionally, there is a dearth of corporate governance studies in Africa (Tsamenyi et al., 2007, p. 319; Okike, 2007, p. 174) in spite of the increasing interest on the role of corporate governance in African economies, e.g. refer to Rossouw (2005), Vaughn and Ryan (2006), Okike (2007) and El-Mehdi (2007). Corporate governance is gathering further prominence on the continent, following the establishment of the African Peer-Review Mechanism (APRM), an initiative by the African Union and the New Partnership for Africa's Development (NEPAD). African nations (including Mauritius) have recently engaged into a self-assessment exercise and programmed actions towards improving governance (including corporate governance). These findings and experiences will be disseminated to other African nations in support of policy changes.

Finally, none of the studies reviewed have adopted a dual approach to data collection to assess the in-depth motivations at company level by both relying on annual reports and on directors' opinions.[2] Although surveys (e.g. as in Hussain & Mallin, 2002; Solomon et al., 2003) have been used to gather views from large cross-sectional samples, there is little opportunity to flesh out issues that might emerge from initial responses. As a result, we argue it is critical to document how directors interact with, and rationalize about, the adoption of the corporate governance code in their respective companies.

The remainder of the paper is structured as follows: the next section briefly presents the implications of the legitimacy theory in the corporate governance literature. Then, the context of Mauritius and the research methods are presented. The findings are subsequently explained and analyzed in relation to previous corporate governance studies. Lastly, the implications and relevance of the findings are discussed with particular reference to the legitimacy perspective.

LEGITIMACY THEORY AND RELATED CONCEPTS

The concept of legitimacy is a popular one in management and administrative research (Suchman, 1995) and a similar set of arguments (encompassed in the term 'legitimacy theory'[3]) is frequently invoked to explain social and environmental disclosures in annual reports, e.g. refer to Woodward, Edwards, and Birkin (1996), O'Donovan (2002) and Deegan (2002). Essentially, organizations adopt practices to maintain or enhance their legitimacy in society, i.e. if the company adopts a certain corporate governance requirement (say, an audit committee), then the organization is viewed by society (e.g. the public, government, shareholders, investors) as a 'professional' and 'efficient' one, although the actual benefits of having such a committee might be insignificant. In the words of Tolbert and Zucker (1983, p. 26), the adoption of the practice *'fulfils symbolic rather than task-related requirements'*. As argued by Aguilera and Cuervo-Cazurra (2004), it does not mean that every practice is purely adopted either for efficiency or legitimating reasons, but rather that these two seemingly mutually exclusive motivations both compete with and complement each other (p. 424). Current evidence on the links between corporate governance adoption and organizational legitimacy is not widespread and not yet conclusive, e.g. refer to Aguilera and Cuervo-Cazurra (2004) and Qu and Leung (2006). In both cases however, we question whether it would have been possible to capturing a 'legitimacy variable' solely from secondary data sources or from annual report disclosures.

The concept of legitimacy is itself open to further elaboration and analysis, as reviewed extensively in Suchman (1995). For instance, legitimacy can be depicted strategically, as an operational resource that organizations extract from their cultural environments and employ in pursuit of their goals. There is thus an assumption of a high level of managerial control over the legitimating process, with '... *managers favouring the flexibility and economy of symbolism as opposed to the more substantive responses preferred by the organization's constituents'* (Suchman, 1995, p. 576). However, other researchers examine legitimacy beyond this strategic 'managerial-led' perspective and assert that legitimacy is not merely an operational resource but is also a set of constitutive beliefs influencing the entire fields or sectors of organizational life (e.g. Oliver, 1991; Elsbach, 1994). In this respect, Suchman (1995) adds:

> *In a strong and constraining symbolic environment, a manager's decisions often are constructed by the same belief systems that determine audience reactions. The distinction between symbolic and substantive outcomes fades into insignificance when one considers, managers, performance measures, audience demands as being both the products and producers of larger, institutionalized cultural frameworks.* (Suchman, 1995, pp. 576–577)

However, rather than considering the above views as being competing ones, we believe it is more appropriate to be led by both perspectives since real world organizations face both strategic operational challenges as well as institutional constitutive pressures (Suchman, 1995). Furthermore, Suchman (1995) also examines the three broad types of organizational legitimacy which rely on slightly different 'dynamics', namely (a) *pragmatic legitimacy*, which rests on the self-interested calculations of an organization's most immediate audiences – often involving a critical resource (financial) dependence between the organization and audience, (b) *moral legitimacy*, which rests not on judgements about whether a given activity (e.g. disclosing executive remuneration) benefits the evaluator, but rather on judgements about whether the activity is '*the right thing to do*' – in turn reflecting beliefs about whether the activity effectively promotes societal welfare, as defined by the audience's socially constructed value system and (c) *cognitive legitimacy*, which goes beyond evaluation and self-interest, and involves an affirmative backing, or a mere acceptance, of the organization based on some taken-for-granted cultural account (pp. 578–582).

In conclusion, we consider the possibility that requirements contained within a corporate governance code are selectively complied with primarily for legitimating purposes, in response to a wide set of organizational, political and socio-economic factors. We therefore need to consider the nature of these factors that are applicable to companies in Mauritius.

COUNTRY CONTEXT

Mauritius, a former French and British colony, is an island covering a land area of about 719 sq miles (1860 km^2). The population consists of about 1.25 million people of African, European, Indian and Chinese descent. There is a very strong affinity to the ethnic roots, ancestral languages, cultures and/or religious affiliation, locally referred to as 'communities'. In relation to countries located in Sub-Saharan Africa, Mauritius has performed generally well in terms of economic growth, education, health and living standards, with a per capita income of US$5,450 (World Bank, 2006). More recently however, an economic slowdown is observed, due to the dismantlement of various preferential trade agreements (especially in sugar and textile export), declining FDI and increasing global competition.

A World Bank Report on the Observance of Standards and Codes (ROSC) by Fremond and Gorlick (2002) concluded that the ownership structure of listed companies in Mauritius remained dominated by a small group of family-owned companies (pp. 1–2). In addition, these family-owned holding companies typically own a variety of different enterprises that have little, if any cross-synergies and might therefore be more viable as separate operations. Many of the companies' asset values are high-due to large landholdings – but the earnings generated are relatively low, and the ROSC document contended that adopting the corporate governance code could help in *'unlocking shareholder value'* (p. 15). The continued influence of family-driven management also leads to a high level of opacity in the running of private sector companies. At the same time, the business community has come under intense scrutiny following major fraud cases in three listed companies which involved some of their directors and senior managers. Thus, the Mauritian government saw the introduction of a corporate governance code as a timely development in response to both international and national expectations.

Initially, there was some resistance and stone-walling amongst share-holders and directors during the consultation stage.[4] Some of them perceived that some of the requirements of the corporate governance code were mismatched to the local 'realities' and were asking for too much private information to be disclosed publicly. In Mauritius, there appears a perception that particular ethnic groups are excluded from business sectors whilst others thrive as a result of their business networks and easier access to financing. These aspects are acknowledged in the code as '... *prejudicial behaviour patterns that have evolved in corporate Mauritius*' (National Committee on Corporate Governance, 2004, p. 8). This issue has remained a potent one, as one of the main political parties (now in power) successfully campaigned on the need to *'democratize'* the economy, i.e. to reduce the influence of the 'few families', whilst the losing party was perceived to have been 'too close and sympathetic' to private sector demands. As a result, we are mindful of the fact that compliance with the corporate governance code in Mauritius may reflect some of these 'local' realities. However, evidence in support of this expectation remains to be uncovered and we rely on a dual approach to collect the relevant data.

RESEARCH METHODS

As mentioned in the introduction, we rely on a dual approach to examine the compliance with the corporate governance code. After presenting our arguments for selecting listed companies, we explain how we analyze corporate governance disclosures in the company reports. Secondly, we present the procedures adopted for the follow-up interviews with company directors.

Company Sample

The code issued by the National Committee on Corporate Governance (2004) required all listed companies, banks/financial institutions, large public and private (unquoted) companies and state-owned corporations to 'comply or explain' with the code as from the financial year starting July 2004. In view of the national and international profile of listed companies[5] and the fact that almost all the studies reviewed concentrate on listed companies, we focus our attention on this particular category. A total of 41 companies are on the Stock Exchange of Mauritius' (SEM) Official List with a total market capitalization of about US$2.4 billion (SEM Factbook, 2006). We requested annual reports for financial years ending on or before 31st December 2005 and all the 41 reports were made available for analysis.[6]

Corporate Governance Disclosures

In analyzing these annual report disclosures, we focus on a selection of 13 corporate governance items to assess how many companies comply (or not) with the specific requirements of the code in Mauritius. These will be presented under five headings namely board leadership, board composition, board committees, board and committee activity, and compliance statements and remuneration disclosures. This selection is based on corporate governance items researched in previous studies and these items are generally viewed as crucial to the development of better corporate governance in companies, e.g. refer to Laing and Weir (1999), Ow-Yong and Guan (2000), Pension and Investment Research Consultants (2004) and Krambia-Kapardis and Psaros (2006). The statistics showing attendance at board and committee meetings are also compiled to assess the actual operation of boards. The specific requirements of the code being analyzed are outlined in Table 1 and for ease of reference these are combined with the findings from the annual reports.

As opposed to other corporate governance studies (e.g. Patel, Balic, & Bwakira, 2002; Aksu & Kosedag, 2006) that rely solely on dichotomous (one/zero) procedures and overall compliance scores, our assessment of 'compliance' is not focused entirely on instances where companies achieve either full (one) or nil (zero) compliance with the various requirements of the code. The reasons for our approach are as follows. Firstly, the 'comply or explain' policy provides an inherent and rather substantial element of flexibility for companies, possibly leading to varying interpretations of the

Table 1. Compliance with the Corporate Governance Code-Evidence from 41 Listed Companies.

Specific Requirements from the Mauritius Code	Findings from Annual Reports Disclosures	N = 41	%
Board Leadership (2 items)			
A1: The titles, functions and roles of chairperson and CEO must be kept separate (Section 2.5.4)	A1: Number of companies complying with Section 2.5.4	36	87.8
	Number of companies not complying, all explained by the fact that the company does not have a CEO on the board	5	12.2
A2: The Chairperson must be an Independent Non-Executive Director (INED) elected by his or her fellow directors (Section 2.5.5)	A2: Number of companies complying with Section 2.5.5	7	17.1
	Number of companies not complying, as explained by the following circumstances or reasons for non-compliance:	34	82.9
	Chair is a Non-Executive Director (NED)	29	70.7
	Chair is a NICB (Non-Independent Chairperson of the Board)	3	7.4
	Chair is not categorised as Non-Executive or Independent Director	2	4.8
Board Composition (3 items)			
B1: All companies should have at least two independent directors on their boards (Section 2.2.2)	B1: Number of companies complying with Section 2.2.2	26	63.4
	Number of companies not complying, including three companies having only one independent director	15	26.4
B2: All boards should have at least two executives as members (Section 2.2.3)	B2: Number of companies complying with Section 2.2.3	22	53.7
	Number of companies not complying, including five companies where the Board is only made up of non-executive directors	19	46.3
B3: The board should have an appropriate balance of Executive, NED and INEDs (Section 2.2.1)	B3: The proportion of independent non-executive directors appointed to the board, expressed as a percentage of the Board is as follows:		
	Between 0–25%	13	31.7
	Between 25–50%	11	26.8
	>50%	5	12.2

Table 1. (*Continued*)

Specific Requirements from the Mauritius Code	Findings from Annual Reports Disclosures	N = 41	%
Board Committees (1 item)			
C1: All companies should have at a minimum, an audit and a corporate governance committee (Section 3.5)	C1: Number of companies complying with Section 3.5	35	85.4
	Number of companies not complying, including two companies having instituted an audit committee but not a corporate governance committee	6	14.6
Board and Committee Activity (3 items)			
D1: The board should meet at least quarterly (Section 3.6)	D1: Number of companies complying with Section 3.6	30	73.2
	Number of companies not complying, as explained by the following circumstances or reasons for non-compliance:	11	26.8
	The board has met at least once during the financial year	4	9.8
	Frequency of Board Meetings not disclosed	7	17.0
D2 and D3: The number of times in the year the board (D2) and committees met (D3), plus attendance details for directors must be disclosed (Section 8.4)	D2: Number of companies complying with Section 8.4 (Board Meetings)	34	82.9
	D3: Number of companies complying with Section 8.4 (Committee Meetings)	25	61.0
Compliance Statements and Remuneration (4 items)			
E1: There should be a compliance statement in the annual report (Section 8.4)	E1: Number of companies complying with Section 8.4	34	82.9
E2: Companies should include a transparent Statement of Remuneration Philosophy (Section 2.8.1)	E2: Number companies complying with Section 2.8.1	21	51.2
E3: Companies should disclose in their annual reports details of remuneration paid to each director (Section 2.8.2)	E3: Number of companies complying with Section 2.8.2.	9	22.0
E4: The corporate governance report must include details of related party transactions (Section 8.4)	E4: Number of companies complying with Section 8.4	7	17.1

code's requirements and bearing in mind that compliance with the corporate governance code is rarely certified by an independent party. We therefore contend that a dichotomous approach to the measurement of compliance with the corporate governance code may not be entirely appropriate. Secondly, the reliance on overall (and equally weighted) scores does not account for the qualitative importance of one particular requirement in the code relative to other requirements, e.g. the adoption of a split between the CEO and Chairman vs. the adoption of a policy for directors' appraisal. Furthermore, a cross-country comparison of overall disclosure scores (e.g. as in Patel et al., 2002) does not inform us as to which of the more important requirements of the corporate governance code have been complied with.

Therefore, we rely on the approaches used by Krambia-Kapardis and Psaros (2006) and Alves and Mendes (2004) whereby we examine compliance with the key corporate governance items separately and also investigate (where relevant) the instances of non-compliance as evidence of the diverse behaviours in the adoption of the corporate governance code. Finally, whilst the annual report disclosures allow us to gather factual information on actual corporate governance adoption, a second task has been to analyze the intended meanings conveyed by the so-called compliance statements as a reflection of the company's declared intentions relating to the code. To our knowledge, there has been little attention paid to compliance statements in the corporate governance literature, e.g. refer to MacNeil and Li (2006).

Follow-Up Interviews

We carried out semi-structured interviews with a selection of company directors using an interview checklist (Appendix 1). An analysis of the company's disclosures was carried out prior to the interview, thereby ensuring a personalized approach to the questions. One of the main difficulties has been in securing participation to the interviews, due to the directors' reluctance to participate in such studies. After several cancellations, 9 interviews materialized and although this is a relatively small sample, we believe we at least succeeded in interviewing a diverse set of respondents from different sectors, age groups, gender, professional backgrounds and board roles. Appendix 2 provides the relevant details on the interviewed directors, who coded throughout the paper as quotes from Director A, Director B, etc. The interviews (duration of 60–90 min) were tape-recorded or handwritten. In presenting the findings from the interviews, we emphasise on the diversity of views and attitudes expressed rather than consider how many directors concurred (or not) to particular statements. Whilst the interviews allowed for the discussion of a wider range of aspects relating to corporate governance, we focus on the directors' views we see as more pertinent to the findings from the annual report disclosures.

FINDINGS AND ANALYSIS

Overall Compliance with the Code

Firstly, we present an overall picture of how companies complied with the corporate governance code based on the disclosures. These are summarized in Table 1 and the subsequent sections will consider in detail the surveyed items and where relevant, interview extracts will be provided.

The annual report disclosures appear to indicate a positive move towards adopting the corporate governance code but there seems little evidence of a high or even full compliance with the surveyed items amongst the majority of listed companies. Although it would be difficult to quantify the extent of compliance in this study relative to other countries, the proportion of companies fully complying (5 companies or 12%) with the code in Mauritius is higher than the proportion of companies reported in other country studies (e.g. 3% in Cyprus, by Krambia-Kapardis & Psaros, 2006). During the interviews, directors expressed very different opinions on whether the code had to be legally or voluntarily complied with. For example,

> By now, listed companies should have complied with at least 95% of the code's requirements and then indicate or explain when explain what they intend to do with the remaining rules. It is perhaps ok for other [unlisted] companies not to comply but still they have to explain. (Director A)

> it is a code and not law so you cannot enforce. If I don't comply I explain. It is up to the market to judge ... The most important thing is that it's only a code, so you cannot force people to implement.... (Director B, similar argument by Director I)

> Well all companies cannot abide by the Code at once. All this needs an adaptation time. It is not something that should be rushed into. A steady and careful introduction of the Code is better, rather than seeing all companies abiding by it on paper and in reality they are not able to put it into practice. (Director H)

These statements can be interpreted as being symptomatic of the issues associated with having a Code based on a 'comply or explain' approach.

The flexibility inherent in the corporate governance code (MacNeil & Li, 2006) can be interpreted as the code being voluntary and therefore there is no need to comply (Krambia-Kapardis & Psaros, 2006, p. 137) or crucially, one can decide which aspect to comply with. For example, Director B refers to listing rules which required the adoption of the code but clearly asserts that it is not legally required and should be more market driven. However, Director A seems to believe that all listed companies should already be complying. Finally, Director H appears to favour a relatively phase-by-phase approach (this was not provided for in the code) and suggests that a symbolic compliance with the code will occur if companies are 'forced' to adopt the code at once.

In addition, the directors put forward their own views on the motivations for complying with the corporate governance code. For example, many of the directors concur with the mainstream argument that adopting the code will be primarily beneficial in improving reputation, thereby attracting foreign investment and improving its standing amongst employees:

> The code will have a positive influence on foreign investment. Mauritius will be perceived as a country which means serious business. (Director F, similar statement by Director E)

> Foreign investors will compare their return to the return which they have in their home country ... Foreign investors believe that local companies have potential of growth. Also, they believe that the legal framework in Mauritius is ok-this perception is right as we are not a 'Banana Republic'. (Director B, similar statement by Director A)

> If a company abides by the code it will be viewed positively by its employees and potential employees. Employees will believe in the good running of the organisation. (Director G)

Interestingly however, little mention is made of the potential functional 'benefits' of the corporate governance code for the company, e.g. in terms of organizational outcomes, board effectiveness and efficiency. In contrast to the above views, some directors challenge the notion that corporate governance adoption will have some use for companies. For example,

> I do not believe in theory. I believe in good practice. We are not here to steal we are here to manage the company and we are doing everything for that and that is enough. Everything has to be 100% transparent [but within the company]. The rest do not matter. We can write huge corporate governance reports of 50 pages but then no one believes in all of that. (Director D)

This last statement indeed reflects the view amongst some of the interviewed directors that the corporate governance code is a new form of bureaucratic regulation with questionable positive consequences for companies. In particular, the positive contributions of independent non-executive directors (INEDs) are rarely mentioned. This is elaborated in the next section.

Board Leadership and Composition

With respect to the separation between the CEO and the Chairperson of the Board, it is noted that all applicable (i.e. where the CEO is a member of the Board) listed companies have complied with this requirement. This is a very satisfactory performance, given the United Kingdom's own experience (92% in Pension Investment Research Consultants, 2004, p. 489). However, only 7 companies (17%) have nominated an independent non-executive director (INED) to act as Chairperson. Whilst the code (2004, p. 22) implicitly allows for non-executive directors (NEDs) to chair the board, most of the companies convey the message that the Board may not be operating independently from the influence of executives and that a proper balance of power/authority has yet to be achieved, e.g. refer to Ow-Yong and Guan (2000, p. 128) and Krambia-Kapardis and Psaros (2006, p. 136). This is acknowledged in the case of three companies, who explicitly report having a *'Non-Independent Chairperson of the Board'* – a non-existent term in the corporate governance code.

In relation to board composition, we also find a mixed picture. According to the code, companies are expected to have a Board consisting of at least 2 INEDs and 2 Executive Directors. Only 63.4% of the companies have reported that they have at least two Independent Directors and 53.7% have at least two Executive Directors on their Boards. On average, INEDs made up 33.2% of a board but the proportion of INEDs per company board varied widely from 9.1% to 70%. Since the code only calls for an 'appropriate' balance between the three categories of directors, we argue that listed companies in Mauritius have interpreted this requirement in a rather liberal way. Similar findings have been observed in Alves and Mendes (2004) and Krambia-Kapardis and Psaros (2006). INEDs are viewed as critical actors in the corporate governance agenda, specifically in their roles as chairs of the audit, remuneration and corporate governance committees (Solomon et al., 2003). In at least one third of the surveyed companies, an insufficient proportion of INEDs signals uncertainty as to the balance of power within the board, suggesting that their existence on some boards can be viewed as being more symbolic than substantive. From the interviews, there were indeed views expressed on the role and availability of independent directors. For example,

> I tend not to agree 100% with this idea [i.e. independent directors]. I believe that the best persons to defend the interest of the company are the shareholders. If I am a big shareholder of the company, I will defend the interest of the company more than an independent director. At the end of the day, when we declare dividends, these will go in my pocket. Whereas the independent directors, they do not care. (Director G)

> It was not easy to find people who are really independent. Not only independent, but people who will bring value to the Board. Finding independent people is good but finding someone who is independent and who will bring value to the Board this is not easy. Now even if you recruit someone who is not totally independent and it is disclosed and discussed, I do not see any problem with that. (Director I)

As in the case of Director I, other directors seem to conclude that a certain level of 'fudging' is inevitable and therefore acknowledge that the notion of a truly independent director is unworkable in the Mauritian context. In fact, Monks (2001, p. 144) similarly challenged this very notion of independence in that every independent director will feel personally beholden to those who have appointed him/her. He therefore (Monks, 2001, p. 147) contended that the carefully crafted definitions of independence included in corporate governance merely create an appearance that is disconnected from reality. Finally, Director G (and to a lesser extent, Director I) question the wisdom of having independent directors and whether they can effectively contribute to the board. Likewise, Laing and Weir (1999, p. 463) stated that simply aiming to have an acceptable number of INEDs on the board may create inertia problems as these directors struggle to understand the business, thereby slowing the decision-making process and the board's effectiveness.

Board Committees and Committee Meetings

In relation to the establishment of committees, companies are expected to have at least an audit and a corporate governance committee. A majority (35) of companies do meet this requirement. However, we find little evidence on the level of activity by these committees. 34 companies disclosed information on board meetings but only 25 of them provided data regarding committee meetings. This absence (or lack of consistency in the provision) of information raises the possibility that these committee structures do not operate. Faced with similar evidence, Krambia-Kapardis and Psaros (2006, p. 134) also conclude that not much will be gained if audit or corporate governance committees are *'tokenistic'* and do not meet regularly.

Other respondents emphasised on different uses they perceived from the committees. For example, during one interview, Director C recounted a situation where the audit and corporate governance committees were used pre-emptively to approve the award of an important contract, thereby bypassing normal tendering procedures. We believe this may reflect a socially and informally led perception on the role of the corporate governance code as opposed to the perspective that these committees should operate as control mechanisms (rather than *ex-ante* authorization ones). From the 'story', one can also interpret the managing director's actions as a politically motivated one – as he seeks to implicate non-executive directors in an executive decision – in order to avert potential blame in the future. Thus, whilst the annual report disclosures accurately display 'compliance' with the code's requirements (in this case, the setting up of committees), we find indications that the relevant structure (i.e. audit and corporate governance committees) is being 'subordinated' to the prevailing business culture. Furthermore, the critical comments on the role of independent directors (Director G and I) made in the previous section are indicative of the absence of 'function' some executive directors see in the audit and corporate governance committees, given the fact that these committees are composed (and led) in majority by INEDs.

Executive Remuneration and Directors' Interests

The last sub-heading in Table 1 provides information on the disclosure of executive remuneration and directors' interests. There is a relatively low level of disclosure observed for remuneration-related information. Only 21 of the companies (51%) have provided a statement of remuneration philosophy in their reports with many providing general and relatively uninformative statements. Whilst this may be indicative of a genuine difficulty in appreciating what is meant by 'remuneration philosophy', only 9 companies (22%) have provided detailed remuneration figures (per director) and even fewer (7) have disclosed details on related-party transactions involving directors. One listed company specifically addressed the issue in its annual report, stating it has complied with the code, except for the disclosure of directors' remuneration because *'the Board believes that it is not desirable in the local context to do so and shall comply at an appropriate time. The Committee/Board will review this on an annual basis'*

(Company #36). The fact that several government officials are directors of this company indicates that these concerns are not purely originating from the private sector. In addition, the following interview extracts testify the significant unease of directors regarding remuneration disclosures:

> I know a company in which the Managing Director has accepted to abandon a share of his remuneration when he realised that it will be known. What this means is that the directors of companies start to realise that they will have to explain and they cannot carry on giving figures just like that. This will force directors to be more careful and not to exaggerate. (Director C)

> But why does the code asks for such disclosure? Is it for transparency? But what kind of transparency, why do those reading the report need such information? If shareholders require it they may make a request for it. I believe it [public disclosure] can do a lot of harm. (Director E)

> The code asks for the disclosure of the salaries of individual directors and we think that it will come. We believe that it is useful information but it all depend to what use it is being used. Company #25 has not disclosed but Company #19 – another company where I am a board member – has done so. (Director I)

A few directors do appreciate the increased transparency as being (firstly) beneficial to all directors (i.e. creating a local market for executives) and as being a part of the evolution towards international practices. However, most interviewees conveyed deep concerns as to the social and political consequences of such disclosures. For example, it is feared that these could attract unwanted attention not only from politicians, legislators, trade unions and the media, but also from shareholders and lenders who may not have been privy to the exact details of the remuneration packages. In this respect, Burton (2000, p. 201) contends there might be a dose of pragmatism involved as to how companies decide to apply corporate governance requirements to avoid potentially negative consequences. However, one may also argue that fear of such 'social consequences' is irrational and imaginary (as suggested by one of directors). Indeed, we have not yet found any evidence of a public 'backlash' in the media in reaction to the detailed executive remuneration information published in the annual reports of a few companies. As previously highlighted in the context section, directors and companies in Mauritius may have perceived social and political pressures which persuade them to keep a rather discreet profile regarding their remuneration and other business interests they are involved in. Such pressures appear to be less of an issue in the United Kingdom and in some emerging economies (e.g. Cyprus in Krambia-Kapardis & Psaros, 2006).

However, not a single company in Qu and Leung's (2006) recent study of listed companies in China disclosed executive remuneration data.

So far, we have presented indications of a selective and symbolic mindset amongst Mauritian companies in relation to the adoption of some of the requirements of the corporate governance code. This is consistent with Ow-Yong and Guan's (2000) comments that some companies appear to *pay lip service or comply with the form and not the spirit* of corporate governance codes (p. 130). We identify the following key factors to be of critical importance in influencing a selective compliance with the code namely: a varied understanding of the 'comply and explain' requirement: the corporate governance code being viewed primarily as a way to attract investors; attitudes that are critical of independent directors and board committees; and the perceived social consequences of executive remuneration disclosure. However, further evidence of symbolic compliance emerges from the analysis of compliance statements.

Statements of Compliance

According to the Code of Corporate Governance (2004, p. 18), companies must state in their annual reports the extent of their compliance with the code and must identify and give reasons for areas of non-compliance. From Table 1 (last sub-heading), 7 of the 41 (17%) companies did not actually provide a statement, although they did provide evidence of compliance with some of the corporate governance items. Whilst the provision of a compliance statement is a straightforward disclosure requirement, our reading of the remaining 34 company statements reveals a more varied, nuanced, ambiguous, and occasionally clearly inconsistent assessment of the company's adoption to the corporate governance code. We identify three main categories of statements and examples of such statements are provided in Table 2 (Panels A, B and C).

Firstly, with regards to providing a clear statement of compliance (or identify specific exceptions), 9 companies provided such a statement but in effect, only three of them fully complied with all the surveyed corporate governance items. Amongst the other six companies, there were two particular glaring examples of differences between the 'rhetoric' of the compliance statement and the substantive information in the disclosures, as detailed in Panel A. One initial interpretation is that two of these companies referred to their board's opinion in complying *in all material aspects* to the code. However, this notion of materiality in the adoption of the code is not

Table 2. Examples of "Compliance" Statements.

Panel A: Examples of Statements Stating Full Compliance	Corporate Governance Requirements Not Complied with
The Company is committed to sound Corporate Governance practice guided by the Corporate Governance report for Mauritius issued in 2003. The Board of Directors has always believed in the good practice of corporate governance and therefore complied with the Code of Principles of Good Corporate Governance framework from its inception (#4)	No detailed remuneration disclosures; no evidence of existing audit and corporate governance committees; no information on who are the independent directors
Compliance Statement: The Board is of the opinion that the company now complies with the requirements of the Code of Corporate Governance in all material respects (#40)	No statement of remuneration philosophy; no detailed remuneration disclosures; no information on number of board/committee meetings; no information on directors' attendance at board/committee meetings

Panel B: Examples of Statements 'Suggestive' of Compliance	Corporate Governance Requirements Not Complied with
The company is committed to the principles and practice of good Corporate Governance. Company's policies and practices will where necessary be modified to comply with the Code (#30)	No statement of remuneration philosophy; no detailed remuneration disclosures; no information on who are the independent directors; no information on number of board/committee meetings; no information on directors' attendance at board/committee meetings
The Company is committed to the highest standard of business integrity, transparency, and professionalism in all activities to ensure that the activities within the company are managed ethically and responsibly to enhance business value for all stakeholders. As an essential part of this commitment, the board endeavours to comply with the Code of Corporate Governance for Mauritius (#3)	No statement of remuneration philosophy; no detailed remuneration disclosures; no corporate governance committee set up; no information on actual number of (Audit) sub-committee meetings; no specific director disclosures relating to related-party transactions

Table 2. (*Continued*)

Panel C: Examples of Statements 'Debating' on Compliance	Corporate Governance Requirements Not Complied with
The Board considers Corporate Governance as a matter of priority that requires more attention than merely establishing the steps to be taken to demonstrate compliance with legal, statutory, regulatory or listing requirements. It is fully aware of the contribution that good corporate governance provides to the company in terms of growth, financial stability and performance. Issues of governance will continue to receive the Board and its committees' consideration and attention during the years ahead (#41)	No statement of remuneration philosophy; no detailed remuneration disclosures; no corporate governance committee set up; no information on who are the independent directors
The Board of Directors has set up an Audit Committee and a Corporate Governance committee to implement the requirements of the Code gradually, bearing in mind that this should be a leverage to enable us to further enhance shareholder value, and that the key to good corporate governance is to seek an appropriate balance between performance and conformance (#13)	No statement of remuneration philosophy; no detailed remuneration disclosures; no information on who are the independent directors; no information on actual number of sub-committee meetings

specified and is also not certified by any independent party (e.g. external auditors).

Secondly, differences can be noted from the other 25 companies' statements, whereby some are suggestive of compliance without providing any information on items being not complied with. In this respect, the words 'comply' or 'compliance' is regularly used together with 'committed' or 'commitment' to the code but no explicit statement of compliance (or lack thereof) is made. Panel B provides two examples of this. Finally, some of above-mentioned 25 companies do not provide as such a statement of, or mention, compliance. They rather provide a discursive statement on the need to balance compliance to rules and adherence to higher principles, such as shareholder value, high governance standards etc. In some cases, this may appear to reflect dissensions within the board (or from the company as a whole) on the need to comply with the detailed aspects of the corporate governance. Two examples, labelled as the 'Debating companies', are shown in Panel C. Finally, it is also noted a few companies (#39, #33, #20 and #17) fully complied with the surveyed corporate governance items but did not actually provide a statement of compliance. One of the directors explained this decision:

> Yes, I purposefully did not include the statement. I tried to abide by the code as much as possible but as a precaution I preferred to avoid stating it. (Director F)

During some of the interviews, the issue of the wording (or absence) of the statements of compliance emerged. For example, Director C acknowledged the issue (for Company #37) stating:

> Yes this is true, there were no details. At the time when our last report was prepared we had not yet finalised our procedures ... We have preferred to include a general sentence. We are now more prepared for the next report, so I think there should not be comments like this. (Director C)

In both cases however, the directors reflect a motivation by the companies to project (or at least imply) compliance in the annual reports, even if Director F took an over-precautionary 'legalistic' perspective in not providing any compliance statement. Hence, the findings from this section are that a majority of companies provided statements which were either (i) too general to project a clear image as to their actual extent of compliance or (ii) at odds with their actual extent of adoption. Also, we argue that this ambivalence towards the corporate governance code is echoed in the 'statements of compliance' formulated by the so-called Debaters (as detailed in Table 2, Panel C) and is indicative of a resistance within the board to a more substantive compliance to the corporate governance code. In our review of previous research, there has been little interest in the 'discourses' of compliance statements and there is therefore little opportunity to compare the above findings with other studies, except to a study of UK non-compliers (MacNeil & Li, 2006). They state that UK non-compliers provide extremely brief and uninformative disclosures to explain the reasons for non-compliance (p. 489).

In conclusion, the combination of annual report and interview convincingly demonstrates the companies' behaviours in selectively and symbolically complying with the corporate governance code. We now assess these findings in relation to the legitimacy perspective and particularly in view of Suchman's (1995) conceptualisations.

SELECTIVE COMPLIANCE WITH THE CORPORATE GOVERNANCE CODE: A LEGITIMIZING BEHAVIOUR?

Arguably, the various instances of a 'disconnect' between the 'reality' and 'appearance' of corporate governance compliance do inform us of the prevailing mindsets in Mauritian boardrooms and the interviews show some of the influences of the social context in decisions regarding compliance with the corporate governance code. We also find indications that directors re-interpret the code's requirements and operate it in line with their existing business culture, i.e. companies may adopt the code, but do not use it in the way it was intended. At the same time nonetheless, directors are all too aware of the implications of adopting the code as a way to enhance the companies' reputation to attract foreign investment and to appease local concerns regarding their business practices. Faced with these multiple realities and demands, listed companies in Mauritius appear to have consciously adopted the corporate governance code on a selective and piecemeal basis. In consideration of these empirical findings and conclusions, we contend that the combined evidence from annual reports, compliance statements and interviews provides a rich enough dataset to highlight some of the linkages that emerge between our data on corporate governance adoption in Mauritius and the tenets of legitimacy theory.

Firstly, we observe the directors diverse interpretations of the 'comply or explain' approach and the perceived flexibility in adopting only some of the requirements set out in the corporate governance code. As mentioned by

Suchman (1995, p. 576), legitimacy is principally viewed as an operational resource that needs to be 'managed'. The interviews point to companies and directors displaying a high level of control and understanding on the implications in adopting the corporate governance code, with preferences for the *flexibility and economy* of symbolism as opposed to a substantive implementation and change to the board processes. For instance, independent directors are appointed to the board but not necessarily in sufficient numbers to allow for a constructive balance of power. In addition, people are appointed for the mere reason that they appear independent but they are not necessarily competent and experienced enough to contribute effectively to the board. In parallel, audit and corporate governance committees are constituted but the absence of truly independent directors to chair these committees jeopardizes the committees' mandates in overseeing the activities of company executives. Finally, there is a case where the audit and corporate governance committees were used to justify executive decisions. Hence, the functional 'benefits' of this specific corporate governance structure (i.e. audit committee) appear to be secondary (or perhaps even minimal or irrelevant). The practice is being 'subordinated' to the prevailing business culture and even used to further political agendas within the company/board. Thus, from the point of view of the companies, the prevailing view appears to be more about setting up convenient displays of 'good' corporate governance (e.g. nominating independent directors and setting up audit and corporate governance committees) which are sufficiently flexible and symbolic to claim that the 'prize' of compliance with the corporate governance code has been achieved. Hence, we contend that the pursuit of legitimacy by symbolically complying with the corporate governance code appears to be more in line with the pursuit of a strategic operational resource that companies seek to extract from their cultural environments (Suchman, 1995).

Secondly, this preference for the flexibility and economy of symbolism is made more apparent from the compliance statements whereby companies actively seek to convey an *impression* of compliance with the code rather than provide a concrete assessment of how far they have actually adopted the corporate governance code. This is through the use of use of selective meanings, vague statements and the leaving of such matters to interpretation. In this respect, a study by Page and Spira (2005) sheds some light on this 'gap' between the statements of compliance and the actual extent of compliance. Although their study focused on the various definitions and understandings of auditor independence in professional standards, the authors contend that the *conservation of ambiguity* (p. 302) in these definitions provide interest groups with room to manoeuvre and enable a consensus to be reached amongst groups who may have differing objectives. Ambiguity can be said to exist where a message is capable of multiple interpretations, where a single form of words encompasses multiple substances of meaning (Page & Spira, 2005, p. 301).

Transposed to our findings, the corporate behaviour of using vague, seemingly contradictory or inconsistent statements may be perceived as a reflection of this need to conserve this ambiguity. Furthermore, the quotation by Director F is particularly reminiscent of Page and Spira's (2005) discussion on the conservation of ambiguity, where the director perceives a benefit in not explicitly acknowledging compliance. Based on the arguments by Page and Spira (2005), the widespread use and conservation of 'ambiguity' in the compliance statements can be seen as an attempt at (i) retaining control and flexibility in the adoption of the corporate governance code's requirements, and (ii) satisfying the competing views within the board,. At the same time, companies seek to convey a symbolic 'public' message that compliance has been achieved. Hence, we view this relatively widespread reliance on ambiguity as additional evidence in support of the preferences by some directors for the flexibility and economy of symbolism when it comes to 'adopting' the corporate governance code.

Thirdly, the predominant view from the directors on the role of the corporate governance code suggests that its adoption is primarily driven by a strategic motive to attract investors and (to a lesser extent) to improve the company's standing vis-à-vis existing and potential employees. The apparent benefits of the corporate governance code in attracting FDIs in developing economies are well documented, e.g. refer to Rueda-Sabater (2000). This in fact had been the central argument of the Mauritian government in imposing the corporate governance code to improve the country's competitiveness in relation to other African developing economies. However, little mention is made of the actual or potential functional 'benefits' of the corporate governance code, e.g. in terms of organizational outcomes, board effectiveness and efficiency. For example, the possible benefits of having more productive discussions and debates on the board are not mentioned by at all by the interviewed directors. In contrast, some directors envisage that adopting the code would be well perceived by employees and would improve employees' (as opposed to the Board's) productivity. Hence, we interpret this as an indication that the symbolic and selective compliance with the corporate governance code appears to be motivated by the *pragmatic form of legitimacy*. Indeed, directors selectively comply with the code by relying on the self-interested calculations of the company's most immediate audiences (Suchman, 1995, p. 578) – which are perceived in this case to be primarily foreign investors and to a lesser extent, employees.

It is also important to note that local shareholders (or even local bankers) are not explicitly viewed by most directors as being part of the company's most 'immediate audiences' in the context of adopting the corporate governance code. This seems to suggest that the closely inter-connected business community in Mauritius (which includes local shareholders, directors and financial providers) does not necessarily 'confer' legitimacy based on whether the organization complies or not with the corporate governance code. However, we cannot conclusively consider this claim in this research and this possibility could be studied further by interviewing directly these company stakeholders.

Finally, the socio-economic and political context plays an important part in how companies and directors re-interpret and rationalize about the implications of the corporate governance code. The tightly connected business network in Mauritius has long favoured informal and private relationships and for example, some of the interviewed directors saw the formal requirement to appoint independent directors on the board as being a threat to their existing network and business relationships. Furthermore, many directors view the publication of executive disclosure and related-party interests as a potentially embarrassing and somewhat peripheral aspect in relation to the adoption of other requirements of the corporate governance code. Most companies and directors do acknowledge that this information has to be disclosed to shareholders – but only if it is carried out in a discreet way. In parallel, this reluctance to discuss one's personal income is not confined to private sector companies and there are indications that Mauritian society in general is reticent to discuss openly about the wealth of individuals. Hence, there is a strong belief in the 'wisdom' of not providing such disclosures in the annual report in case they 'unsettle' stakeholders. Drawing on Suchman's conceptualisations (1995) it can be argued that directors view such behaviour as the '*right thing to do*' in demonstrating their 'sensitivity' to the local society. The act of providing less information would maintain societal welfare, as defined by the audience's socially constructed value systems (Suchman, 1995, p. 579). Thus, we suggest this reflects a *moral form of legitimacy*, whereby directors do not comply with certain requirements of the code, in recognition of their judgements and perceptions on the impact this disclosure may cause amongst the organization's stakeholders.

As rightly pointed out by Suchman (1995, p. 579), the seemingly altruistic undertone described above does not necessarily render moral legitimacy entirely interest free. Indeed, organizations often put forward self-serving claims of moral propriety and support these claims with hollow symbolic gestures, such as the disclosure of 'compliance statements', whilst avoiding to address the more substantive and substantial requirements of the corporate governance code. Furthermore, it is acknowledged that a different interpretation of the above may lie in Suchman's (1995) and Elsbach's (1994) understanding of the institutional approach (as opposed to the strategic approach) to legitimacy. As mentioned previously, legitimacy may not be 'merely' a resource to be managed but is also a set of constitutive beliefs shared by actors and audience alike. For instance, in the specific case of the remuneration-related information, the managers' decision not to disclose (or use symbolic disclosures) is constructed by the same belief systems that shape audience reactions, i.e. what are the possible social consequences if people knew about the directors' remuneration? This could thus be suggestive that the selective and symbolic adoption of the corporate governance codes may be influenced by 'deeper' legitimacy dynamics than initially suggested in Aguilera and Cuervo-Cazurra (2004) and Qu and Leung (2006).

CONCLUSION

We sought to examine the extent of compliance with the corporate governance code in Mauritius by analyzing the annual report disclosures of listed companies. We subsequently investigated the likely motivations for compliance using follow-up interviews with company directors. The analysis of annual report disclosures first showed some compliance with some of the key requirements of the corporate governance code and where feasible, these were compared to previous experiences in other countries.

We also identified seemingly deliberate instances of non-compliance from the companies' annual reports, e.g. chairperson's status and actual level of independence, the number of INEDs appointed in company boards, attendance statistics at committee level, remuneration and related-party disclosures. We argue that listed companies in Mauritius may have adopted the corporate governance code selectively and symbolically whilst seeking to convey an image of 'good' compliance with the code. This evidence was greatly reinforced by the analysis of compliance statements, which were at best vague and uninformative or at worst contradictory in relation to the company's actual level of compliance with the code. The disclosure evidence is crucially corroborated by the 'discourses' of the compliance statements and by interviews with company directors. In our opinion, the analysis of disclosures and the in-depth follow-up interviews of directors do largely confirm the symbolic motivations (rather than efficiency-led) motives underlying the companies' behaviours towards adopting the corporate governance code.

In view of the above, we examine the data in light of the implications of legitimacy theory (e.g., Tolbert & Zucker, 1983; Suchman, 1995; Aguilera & Cuervo-Cazurra, 2004). Although legitimacy motivations were already suggested in the corporate governance literature (Aguilera & Cuervo-Cazurra, 2004; Qu & Leung, 2006), we believe the data convincingly suggests a link between the selective compliance with the corporate governance code in Mauritius and the dynamics of organizational legitimacy. Consequently, we propose that the pursuit of a *pragmatic* and a *moral* form of legitimacy, rather than the expectation of efficiency rewards, is at the centre of the companies' motives towards adopting the corporate governance code. The evidence thus indicates that the companies have been implementing the code but the dominant thinking is one which (i) privileges a selective interpretation of the code's requirements, (ii) seeks to rationalize the use of corporate governance structures (e.g. audit committee) to fit the local business practices and (iii) is mindful of the country's 'realities', in view of the perceived sensitivity of the social context to remuneration disclosures. The implications are in contrast with findings suggesting that corporate governance practices may be converging world-wide due to efficiency-led motivations, e.g. reduced cost of capital and better transparency (Markarian et al., 2007).

In summary, this study contributes to the literature in providing a 'micro' perspective to the implementation of a corporate governance code in an African developing country, and it brings persuasive evidence of an 'organizational behaviour' of selective compliance with the corporate governance code. Furthermore, we see organizational legitimacy as a credible theoretical perspective in examining the companies' disclosures and the directors' attitudes in relation to the so-called adoption of, and compliance with, the corporate governance code. Finally, the study demonstrates the need for 'unpacking' the societal context in which the corporate governance code is being implemented and the relevance of assessing the attitudes and perceptions of the decision-makers, rather than solely replying on annual report disclosures.

NOTES

1. One notable exception to this regulation regime is the case of the United States. Indeed, the Sarbanes-Oxley Act in 2002 has caused radical changes to the enforcement and scrutiny of both company directors and auditors, effectively leading to a legally enforced corporate governance code.

2. Alves and Mendes (2004) used a combination of close-ended questionnaire surveys and annual report disclosures, but there is no information to suggest that the survey respondents were company directors.

3. In the literature, there is a diverse use of terms to refer to the concept of legitimacy. For example, one refers to a legitimizing behaviour or to the adoption of practices for legitimating reasons or legitimation purposes.

4. One of the authors was present during the consultations between directors and the national corporate governance committee. As a result, these comments are based on the debates occurring at that time.

5. According to the SEM Factbook (2006), the degree of foreign activity in the local stock market (based on turnover) represented about 20% of the total turnover for 2005.

6. The companies' names are not included in this study and a serial number (#1, #2, ..., #41) is used throughout the paper to identify each company. This was necessary to ensure the anonymity and participation of the directors in subsequent interviews.

ACKNOWLEDGMENT

We wish to acknowledge the comments made by participants at the 5th International Conference on Corporate Governance, Birmingham (July 2007). We also thank the editors and the reviewers for their useful suggestions. Finally, we also express our appreciation to Brian Guest for his valuable help in finalizing this paper.

REFERENCES

Aguilera, R. V., & Cuervo-Cazurra, A. (2004). Codes of good governance worldwide: What is the trigger? *Organization Studies, 25*(3), 415–443.

Aksu, M., & Kosedag, A. (2006). Transparency and disclosure scores and their determinants in the istanbul stock exchange. *Corporate Governance: An International Review, 14*(4), 277–295.

Alves, C., & Mendes, V. (2004). Corporate governance policy and company performance: The portuguese case. *Corporate Governance: An International Review, 12*(3), 290–301.

Bauer, R., Guenster, N., & Otten, R. (2004). Empirical evidence on corporate governance in Europe: The effect on stock returns, firm value and performance. *Journal of Asset Management, 5*(2), 91–104.

Berglöf, E., & Pajuste, A. (2005). What do firms disclose and why? Enforcing corporate governance and transparency in central and Eastern Europe. *Oxford Review of Economic Policy, 21*(2), 1–20.

Buchanan, J. (2007). Japanese corporate governance and the principle of internalism. *Corporate Governance: An International Review, 15*(1), 27–35.

Burton, P. (2000). Antecedents and consequences of corporate governance structures. *Corporate Governance: An International Review, 8*(3), 194–203.

Claessens, S., & Fan, J. P. H. (2002). Corporate governance in Asia: A survey. *International Review of Finance, 3*(2), 71–103.

Daily, C. M., Dalton, D. R., & Cannella, A. A. (2003). Corporate governance: Decades of dialogue and data. *Academy of Management Review, 28*(3), 371–382.

Deegan, C. (2002). Introducing the legitimising effect of social and environmental disclosures – a theoretical foundation. *Accounting, Auditing and Accountability Journal, 15*(3), 282–311.

El-Mehdi, I. K. (2007). Empirical evidence on corporate governance and corporate performance in Tunisia. *Corporate Governance: An International Review, 15*(6), 1429–1441.

Elsbach, K. D. (1994). Managing organizational legitimacy in the California cattle industry: The construction and effectiveness of verbal accounts. *Administrative Science Quarterly, 39*, 57–88.

Fremond, O., & Gorlick, W. (2002). Report on the Observance of Standards and Codes (ROSC), Corporate Governance Country Assessment for Mauritius, World Bank. Available at http://go.worldbank.org/QLG0F5ZKO0

Hussain, S. H., & Mallin, C. (2002). Corporate governance in Bahrain. *Corporate Governance: An International Review, 10*(3), 197–210.

Krambia-Kapardis, M., & Psaros, J. (2006). The implementation of corporate governance principles in an emerging economy: A critique of the situation in cyprus. *Corporate Governance: An International Review, 14*(2), 126–139.

Laing, D., & Weir, C. M. (1999). Governance structures, size and corporate performance in UK firms. *Management Decision, 37*(5), 457–464.

MacNeil, I., & Li, X. (2006). Comply or explain: Market discipline and non-compliance with the combined code. *Corporate Governance: An International Review, 14*(5), 486–496.

Mallin, C. (2001). Corporate governance and the bottom line. *Corporate Governance: An International Review, 9*(2), 77–78.

Markarian, G., Parbonetti, A., & Previts, G. J. (2007). The convergence of disclosure and governance practices in the world's largest firms. *Corporate Governance: An International Review, 15*(2), 294–310.

Marnet, O. (2007). History repeats itself: The failure of rational choice models in corporate governance. *Critical Perspectives on Accounting, 18*, 191–210.

Monks, R. A. G. (2001). Redesigning corporate governance structures and systems for the twenty first century. *Corporate Governance: An International Review, 9*(3), 142–147.

Moxey, P. (2004). *Corporate Governance and Wealth Creation*, ACCA Occasional Papers, No. 37, December.

Mueller, D. C. (2006). The Anglo-Saxon approach to corporate governance and its applicability to emerging markets. *Corporate Governance: An International Review, 14*(4), 207–219.

National Committee on Corporate Governance. (2004). *Report and Code on Corporate Governance for Mauritius*, Ministry of Finance and Economic Development, Port-Louis.

Okike, E. N. (2007). Corporate governance in Nigeria: The status quo. *Corporate Governance: An International Review*, *15*(2), 173–193.

Oliver, C. (1991). Strategic responses to institutional processes. *Academy of Management Review*, *16*, 145–179.

Ow-Yong, K., & Guan, C. K. (2000). Corporate governance codes: A comparison between Malaysia and UK. *Corporate Governance: An International Review*, *8*(2), 125–132.

O'Donovan, G. (2002). Environmental disclosures in the annual report: Extending the applicability and predictive power of legitimacy theory. *Accounting, Auditing and Accountability Journal*, *15*(3), 343–371.

Page, M., & Spira, L. F. (2005). Ethical codes, independence and the conservation of ambiguity. *Business Ethics: A European Review*, *14*(3), 301–316.

Patel, S., Balic, A., & Bwakira, L. (2002). Measuring transparency and disclosure at firm level. *Emerging Markets Review*, *3*(4), 325–337.

Pellens, B., Hillebrandt, F., & Ulmer, B. (2001). Implementation of corporate governance codes in German practice – an empirical analysis of the DAX 100 companies. *Betriebs-Berater*, *56*, 1243–1250.

Pension Investment Research Consultants. (2004). *Corporate governance annual review*. London: PIRC.

Qu, W., & Leung, P. (2006). Cultural impact on chinese corporate disclosure: A corporate governance perspective. *Managerial Auditing Journal*, *21*(3), 241–264.

Rossouw, G. J. (2005). Business ethics and corporate governance in Africa. *Business and Society*, *44*(1), 94–106.

Rueda-Sabater, E. J. (2000). Corporate governance and the bargaining power of developing countries to attract foreign investment. *Corporate Governance: An International Review*, *8*(2), 117–124.

Solomon, J. F., Wei Lin, S., Norton, S. D., & Solomon, A. (2003). Corporate governance in Taiwan: Empirical evidence from Taiwanese company directors. *Corporate Governance: An International Review*, *11*(3), 235–248.

Stock Exchange of Mauritius. (2006). *Market Factbook*. Available at http://www.semdex.com/market_fbook.htm (retrieved on January 15, 2008).

Suchman, M. C. (1995). Managing legitimacy: Strategic and institutional approaches. *Academy of Management Review*, *20*(3), 571–610.

Tolbert, P. S., & Zucker, L. G. (1983). Institutional sources of change in the formal structure of organizations: The diffusion of civil service reform 1880–1935. *Administrative Science Quarterly*, *28*, 22–39.

Tsamenyi, M., Enninful-Adu, E., & Onumah, J. (2007). Disclosure and corporate governance in developing countries: Evidence from Ghana. *Managerial Auditing Journal*, *22*(3), 319–334.

Tsipouri, L., & Xanthakis, M. (2004). Can corporate governance be rated? Ideas based on the Greek experience. *Corporate Governance: An International Review*, *12*(1), 16–28.

Vaughn, M., & Ryan, L. V. (2006). Corporate governance in South Africa: A bellwether for the continent? *Corporate Governance: An International Review*, *14*(5), 504–512.

Woodward, D. G., Edwards, P., & Birkin, F. (1996). Organizational legitimacy and stakeholder information provision. *British Journal of Management*, *7*, 329–347.

World Bank. (2006). *Mauritius Data Profile*. Available at http://www.worldbank.org/mauritius (retrieved on December 18, 2007).

Yakasai, A. G. A. (2001). Corporate governance in a third world country with particular reference to Nigeria. *Corporate Governance: An International Review*, *9*(3), 238–253.

APPENDIX 1. INTERVIEW CHECKLIST

Interview Preamble

1. Objective of the interview: Our study is on understanding the implementation of corporate governance (CG) codes in Mauritian companies and organizations. Technically, they were due to start implementation as from financial year ending 30 June 2005.
2. Although we have a wide interest in the implementation of CG as a whole package, we have decided to focus on what we believe are key features of CG and disclosures in the annual reports.
3. Our data collection includes the publicly available annual reports of companies and interviews with directors to better understand the process of decision. Our aim is not too single out any company or organization or person in terms of whether they are implementing CG or not. As such, no reference will be made to specific company/organizations or to individual directors. The interview is strictly confidential and whilst we may use direct quotations to illustrate some of our research findings, no direct or indirect reference will be made to the person or organization concerned.

Context

An initial and first review of about 20 major companies in Mauritius indicates a very low level of implementation in the first financial year, as indicated by the annual report disclosures. Some companies have actually mentioned their continuing efforts to achieve compliance in later years whereas others have remained silent.

Questions

(a) What are your initial comments on this level of implementation?
(b) Do you believe there has been or will be an impact on foreign investors' confidence in local companies after such a level of low level of implementation to the code?
(c) Do you think implementation of the code will help?
(d) How was the adoption and implementation phase in 2004–2005? Was it a difficult/easy process? Were there any specific members of the board who took responsibility for the implementation?

(e) According to you and your experience in this company, what do you consider to be the main challenges to achieving CG implementation as per the CG code?

(f) Technically, one may argue that regulators may take action if companies do not eventually implement the CG. Has there been such issues been raised by the authorities, auditors and shareholders etc?

(g) Based on your experience as a CEO and director of other companies, what is your experience in finding independent non-executive directors?

(h) In terms of committee set up and board composition, have there been major changes and how was it experienced?

(i) Your company annual report mentions <Statement of compliance in the annual report>. According to you, what does this statement seek to communicate?

(j) Coming to the more specific issue of remuneration, benefits and interests, what importance do you personally attach to the fact that company must have a defined remuneration philosophy, and policy for directors? Is it a key part to CG implementation? If yes/no, why?

(k) Furthermore, what importance do you attach to the public disclosure of individual directors' remuneration, interests and benefits? Is it a key part of the CG implementation? If yes/no, why?

(l) What are the general views expressed by other directors in the Board on the fact that your remuneration, interests and benefits need to be disclosed?

(m) According to you, is there a specific aspect(s) of the Mauritian environment that may (or has) inhibited/slowed down the CG implementation?

APPENDIX 2. DETAILS OF INTERVIEWED DIRECTORS

Director	Position in Listed Companies	Membership of Board Committees	Academic/Professional Background
A	#39 – Chief Executive Officer #16 – Non-Executive Director #15 – Non-Executive Director #23 – Non-Executive Director	None	Economics
B	#14 – Independent Director	Member of the audit committee	Qualified accountant
C	#28 – Chief Executive Officer #37 – Non-Executive Director #19 – Independent Non-Executive Director	Chairman of corporate governance committee (#37) Member of the audit and risk committee (#37) Member of the corporate governance and audit committees (#19)	Banker
D	#9 – Executive Director	None	Businessman
E	#15 – Executive Director	None	Engineering
F	#27 – Director and Company Secretary	None	Qualified accountant

APPENDIX 2. (*Continued*)

Director	Position in Listed Companies	Membership of Board Committees	Academic/Professional Background
G	#12 – Non-Executive Director	Chairman of the corporate governance committee (#34)	Economics and qualified accountant
	#34 – Director	Member of the audit committee (#35)	
	#35 – Director and Company Secretary		
H	#6 – Director	Chairman of the corporate governance committee (#40)	Management
	#40 – Director	Member of the corporate governance committee (#35 and #32)	
	#17 – Non-Executive Director		
	#35 – Non-Executive Director		
	#33 – Non-Executive Director		
	#32 – Non-Executive Director		
I	#25 – Independent Director	Chairman of the corporate governance (#25)	Business administration and accounting
	#19 – Executive Director		

Note: Numbers (e.g. #32) refer to the listed company's serial number.

CHANGING REGIMES OF GOVERNANCE IN A LESS DEVELOPED COUNTRY

Chandana Alawattage and Danture Wickramasinghe

ABSTRACT

Purpose – *This paper examines the changing regimes of governance and the roles of accounting therein in a less developed country (LDC) by using Sri Lanka tea plantations as a case. It captures the changes in a chronological analysis, which identifies four regimes of governance: (a) pre-colonial, (b) colonial, (c) post-colonial and (d) neo-liberal. It shows how dialectics between political state, civil state and the economy affected changes in regimes of governance and accounting through evolving structures, processes and contents of governance.*

Methodology – *It draws on the works of Antonio Gramsci and Karl Polanyi to articulate a political economy framework. It provides contextual accounts from the Sri Lankan political history and case data from its tea plantations for the above chronological analysis.*

Findings – *The above four regimes of governance had produced four modes of accounting: (a) a system of rituals in the despotic kingship, (b) a system of monitoring and reporting to absentee Sterling capital in the despotic imperialism, (c) a system of ceremonial reporting to state capital in a politicised hegemony and (d) good governance attempts in a*

Corporate Governance in Less Developed and Emerging Economies
Research in Accounting in Emerging Economies, Volume 8, 273–310
Copyright © 2008 by Emerald Group Publishing Limited
ISSN: 1479-3563/doi:10.1016/S1479-3563(08)08010-9

politicised hegemony conditioned by global capital. We argue that political processes and historical legacies rather than the assumed superiority of accounting measures gave shape to governance regimes. Governance did not operate in its ideal forms, but 'good governance' initiatives revitalised accounting roles across managerial agency to strengthening stewardship rather than penetrating it into the domain of labour controls. Managerial issues emerged from contradictions between political state, civil state and the economy (enterprise) constructed themselves a distinct political domain within which accounting had little role to play, despite the ambitious aims of good governance.

Originality – *Most accounting and governance research has used economic theories and provided ahistorical analysis. This paper provides a historically informed chronological analysis using a political economy framework relevant to LDC contexts, and empirically demonstrates how actual governance structures and processes lay in broader socio-political structures, and how the success of good governance depends on the social and political behaviour of these structural properties.*

INTRODUCTION

Accounting (and finance) researchers have been busy studying governance from corporate governance perspectives. Using economic theories and scientific methodologies, they explored the relationships between governance systems and capital market dynamics. Unintentionally, important questions such as how these systems evolve under historical and political conditions and what systemic characteristics they produce have been largely unanswered. Consequently, accounting in governance has been conceived to be functional and systemic errors have been thought of as fixable through alternative initiatives. Policy makers for less developed countries (LDCs) have been inspired by this view. New concepts of governance have been introduced, especially for public sector organisations. The 1990s good governance initiative with vested roles for accounting is one example. It was assumed that budgeting, accounting and reporting systems could root out inefficiencies, improve economic efficiency, prevent corruption, and promote policy analysis and debate (World Bank, 1992).

World Bank views were often welcomed by LDC policy makers with little suspicion. It was assumed that good governance initiatives would be unproblematic and development could be boosted (Jenkins, 2002;

Turner & Hulme, 1997). Accounting was conceived to be constitutive for devising better governance mechanisms. What they neglected was contextual conditions which abate the potential effects of these initiatives (Leftwich, 1993). Instead, it was believed that accounting rather than contextual idiosyncrasies has to be made operable for the realisation of development goals. We argue that these assumptions are superficial, as the roles of accounting in respective regimes of governance are conditioned by their historical legacies and political processes.

This paper offers a longitudinal analysis on the regimes of governance in Sri Lankan tea plantations and accounting roles therein. We draw on the works of Antonio Gramsci and Karl Polanyi and provide data from the Sri Lankan political history and tea plantations. We focus on how dialectics between political state, civil state and the economy give form to changing regimes of governance and how each of these regimes presents distinct structures, processes and contents. We argue that political processes and historical legacies rather than the assumed superiority of accounting measures gave shape to governance regimes.

The paper is structured as follows. Section 2 reviews the connection of developmental discourses and governance systems with accounting and development. Section 3 articulates a framework, using Gramsci and Polanyi. Sections 4, 5 and 6 illustrate changing regimes of governance: pre-colonial, colonial, post-colonial and neo-colonial. It pinpoints how these changes are related to dialectics between economy, polity and society and how accounting roles perform therein. Section 7 concludes the paper.

GOVERNANCE, ACCOUNTING AND DEVELOPMENT

It has already been said that research in governance is dominated by corporate governance studies (Dann & DeAngelo, 1983; DeAngelo & Rice, 1983; Linn & McConnell, 1983). Most studies have explored capital market dynamics and taken agency theory (AT) perspectives as their epistemological stance. Research settings have been chosen from data bases so that political and historical dimensions have not been seen over statistical analyses (see Chua, 1986). This resulted in a flood of research and reviews which showed 'positive' relationships between governance, accounting and auditing (e.g., Latham, 1999; Zaman, 2001). Little research has seen the relationships between governance and accounting from historical, social and political perspectives, except for the works by Ezzamel and Willmott (1993) and Giroux and McLelland (2003).

We discern that governance and accounting are perpetually intercon-nected: when we study governance, we would see how accounting is embedded there, and when we study accounting, we would understand how governance conditions accounting's roles. Accounting interacts with those who govern and determines the types of calculative practices demanded by respective regimes of governance (Miller, 2001), and accounting reproduces a particular form of governability and accountability by deploying such practices (Munro, 2004). Histories, cultures and politics can shape the nature of this interconnectedness. Cultural political economy approaches rather than AT perspective can make sense of such relations (Wickramasinghe & Hopper, 2005; Wickramasinghe, Hopper, & Rathnasiri, 2004).

We also see that governance and related accounting roles are reflected in development discourses. For instance, when the 1970s neo-liberal economic policies brought ideological frameworks for the mobilisation of global capital (Faulks, 1999), a set of development discourses such as structural adjustment programme, economic liberalisation and privatisation had emerged to present some challenges for the then existing governance structures in LDCs. Often, the implementation of these programmes was difficult due to the dysfunctions of accounting and governance structures (World Bank, 1989; Uddin & Hopper, 2003; Wickramasinghe et al., 2004; Wickramasinghe & Hopper, 2005). The good governance agenda then emerged for promoting accountability, transparency, and democratisation and development (Potter, 2000; Jenkins, 2002; Minogue, 2002; Overseas Development Administration, 1993; World Bank, 1992).[1]

Policy makers, however, had taken for granted the essential cohabitation of economy, polity and society, which is a precondition for good governance. They neglected the historical factors that (dis)enable that cohabitation. As we see later in the paper, actual governance structures and processes lay in broader socio-political structures, and the success of good governance depends on the social and political behaviour of these structural properties.

DIALECTICS IN GOVERNANCE: POLITY, SOCIETY AND ECONOMY

We argue for a broader concept of governance by locating it in its structural, political and historical context. Governance is located in broader structures – economic and social relations – where we understand how exploitation and subjugation by one (e.g., capital and elites) over the other (e.g., labour and the mass) are organised across social stratifications. Governance is also located in politics where we can understand how conflicting interests and power relations operate. Further, governance is located in historical dynamics: the above structures are the result of complex historical dialectics, events and accidents. Above all, the structural formation of governance has to be a recurring ontology for conceiving the broader concept of governance. According to Gramsci (1971, 1978) and Polanyi (1957), we identify three structural forces which reshape changing regimes of governance: the political state, civil society and the market economy.

Governance contains three main elements: structures, processes and contents. Structures include capital, labour, markets, organisations, and their regulatory mechanisms. Processes connect the structures with agents: management control and forms of accountability are such processes. Contents are rules, regulations, laws, technologies and similar mundane practices, including different forms of accounting. The success of the collective functioning of these elements, however, is subject to the dialectics between the structural forces mentioned earlier.

Dialectical approaches mostly come from Marxist and post-Marxist perspectives. According to Cooper, Taylor, Smith, and Catchpowle (2005, p. 957), a dialectical analysis involves three principles: totality, change and contradictions. As we see later, these principles are dialectical only if they function together. Totality is the social world with its various social, political and economic institutions, and their interrelations. Thus, the constituent elements of the total have to be understood with an understanding of their relations to each other and to the totality. The principle of contradiction is presented as inherent antagonisms between market economy, civil state and political state, which lead to changes in governance systems through the cycles of crisis–solutions–crisis (see also Neimark & Tinker, 1986). It can thus be argued that governance is a historically temporal, negotiated order between theses structural forces.

Gramsci's analysis of hegemony (Gramsci, 1971, 1978) and Polanyi's (1957) views on (great) transformation (see also Burawoy, 2003) are useful here. In its simplistic form, hegemony concerns the construction of consent and the exercise of leadership by the dominant group over subordinate groups. In its complex form, this deals with issues such as the elaboration of political projects (such as good governance), the articulation of interests, the construction of social alliances and the deployment of state strategies (Joseph, 2002). Thus, hegemony is a diffused social order, informed by all social, political, cultural and intellectual forces (Williams, 1960), which can be reflected in a broader structure of governance.

Nevertheless, neo-Marxist analyses of hegemony have their own limitations when they are imported to understand the governance of economic enterprises. This is because hegemonic analyses are rather macro than micro. To understand governance systems within business enterprises, a microanalysis of hegemony is also necessary. Although the hegemonic perspective provides a useful framework to capture a macro historical context within which governance structures change, a mere dialectical analysis between market economy, political state and the civil society would never provide a complete picture of governance, including therein the roles of accounting. This is where accounting researchers have to extend political analysis to integrate those micro-organisational factors. As shown in Fig. 1, we bring in those factors by elaborating the dynamic links between the wider macro forces of governance and the interdependencies between governance *structures, processes and contents.*

While the relationships between *processes, structures and contents* define the nature of governance regimes, the historical convergence and divergence

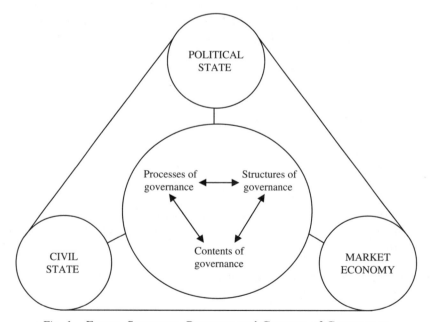

Fig. 1.   Forces, Structures, Processes and Contents of Governance.

of political state, civil state and market economy can articulate the dynamics of changes in these regimes. In colonial epochs, for example, the political state and the market economy would harmonise and make the civil society powerless, which result in a despotic mode of governance where coercion would become the governing principle. In post-colonial epochs, on the other hand, the civil society would be empowered through various political processes, and consent over coercion would become the governing principle.

The relationship between governance and accounting is rather empirical and path-dependent. In a broader sense, as noted, accounting is part of *contents*, and acts as technology which makes governance possible at mundane levels. Accounting is diverse and can render multiple modes of calculative practices possible serving diverse purposes ranging from mere economic efficiency (Johnson & Kaplan, 1987) and the subjugation of labour (Hopper & Armstrong, 1991) to governing at a distance through numbers (Miller & O'Leary, 1987; Miller, 2001). In our framework, accounting's role is historically contingent upon the accountability relations articulated within different governance regimes. Accountability, being conceived as the social context that enable 'giving and demanding of reasons for conduct' (Roberts & Scapens, 1985, p. 447), constitutes a governing *process* within which accounting is deployed, be it functional or dysfunctional. In this sense, accountability is embedded in structural precursors of the social system and enables certain incumbents of the social system to provide and receive 'accounts', which can take various forms, depending upon the multiplicities of social relations within which accountability is embedded. As will be seen below, the governance regimes of Sri Lankan plantations evolved from colonial to post-colonial and neo-colonial regimes forming historically specific structures, processes and contents which gave rise to historically specific accountability relations and accounting forms therein. These historical governance phases are summarised in Table 1, which provides a route map for the remainder of the paper.

Now, how do we place our analysis vis-à-vis existing literature on governance and accounting? Broadly speaking, there are two streams of accounting research, which try to position accounting within governance. The first draws on neo-classical economic extensions, especially AT and transaction cost economics (TCE). This literature is quite diverse which, nevertheless, confines their analysis to different issues arising from the same source: the 'agency problem'. As a theoretical framework, AT provides accounting researchers with a theoretical lens through which an organisation is seen as a hierarchy of 'potentially' dysfunctional agency relationships

Table 1. Regimes of Governance and Accounting.

Transition	Forces of Governance	Regime	Structure	Process	Content	Accounting
Pre-colonial	Convergence of political state, civil state and economy in feudal governance	Despotic under kingship	System of caste as division of work and governing hierarchy	Aristocracy as legitimacy of appropriation of surplus, jurisdiction and control of social mobility	Rituals as social programmes to control individuals, families, castes and society	System of rituals regarding direct monitoring of performance and appropriations
Imperialism and colonisation						
Colonial	Bifurcation of colonial economy and state from native civil society	Despotic under imperialism	Mercantile capitalism subsumed under feudal mode of production	Colonial bureaucracy as mobiliser of mercantile capital and administrator of imperial jurisdiction	Ordinance, rules, regulations, and administrative and financial codes articulated with pre-colonial rituals	System of monitoring of plantation economy and reporting to absentee Sterling capital
Nationalism and nationalisation						
Post-colonial	Convergence of political state and civil society to surrender colonial economy	Hegemonic under political society	State capitalism as anti-imperialist mode of production subsumed under crony capitalism	Political patronage as mechanism of revitalising political society	Rules, regulations, and administrative and financial codes subsumed under political patronage	Ceremonial practice to mask crony capitalism and to legitimise political patronage
Neo-liberalism and privatisation						
Neo-colonial	Revitalising economy subject to hegemony	Hegemonic under global capital	Market capitalism subsumed under global capital and hegemony	Market mechanisms and corporate bureaucracies partially liberated from hegemony	Rules, regulations, and administrative and financial codes subsumed under managerial ideologies of global capital and hegemony	System of transparency, accountability, democratisation, prevention of frauds and corruption, etc., conditioned by hegemony

with divergence of interests and imperfect information, which necessitate a system of governance. Incentive schemes, performance measurement and various responsibility accounting systems are then conceived to be the key elements of governance and their existence is theoretically legitimised as a means to mitigate the 'agency problem'. In that sense, accounting researchers have deployed AT, according to Lambert (2001), to address two fundamental questions. How does governance (i.e., features of information, accounting and compensation systems) affect the agency problem? And how does the existence of the agency problem affect the design and structure of governance?

TCE (Williamson, 1975, 1991), as an extension to classical AT, has also been popular among accounting researchers to analyse dynamics of governance structures. TCE offers a more explicit theory of governance based on Williamson's (1975, 1991) 'discriminating alignment hypothesis', which asserts a change towards transaction cost minimising alignment between alternative governance structures (i.e., market, hierarchy and hybrid) and the attributes of transactions (i.e., frequency, complexity and asset specificity). Accounting researchers have recently tested this proposition and offered more alternatives (Spekle, 2001; Covaleski, Dirsmith, & Samuel, 2003; van den Bogaard & Spekle, 2003). For instance, Spekle (2001) extended the three generic governance structures of TCE to nine different archetypes. In this line of thought, accounting and control systems are seen as defining characteristics of hierarchical and hybrid forms of governance (vis-à-vis market) that determine their intrinsic capacity for administrative controls and co-ordinated adaptation (see Williamson, 1991).

One of the fundamental problems with these neo-classical economic perspectives of governance is that they are confined to the narrow space between agent and principal. The issues of governance have never been seen beyond the contractual relationship between these two supposedly rational economic actors, and their analyses have always been apolitical. As a result, they provide us with a limited epistemological capacity unable to capture dynamics beyond ownership and stewardship. Being locked in the agency relationships across formal organisational hierarchy up to the shareholders, these theoretical frameworks ignore wider institutional settings (those of civil and political states), which historically determine the evolution of governance structures. This ignorance has significant implications when it comes to post-colonial contexts where many large-scale industries have a history of colonialism, nationalisation and (re)privatisation, which have endogenised the civil and political states in the governance structures and processes.

The second stream is Foucauldian accounting research. Researchers of this hue are fundamentally different from the above neo-classical economic extensions not only in their source of theoretical inspiration, but also in their focus and ontology: their ontology is post-structuralist and their focus is on the 'technologies of government', which are

> humble and mundane mechanisms which appear to make it possible to govern: techniques of notation, computation and calculation; procedures of examination and assessment; the invention of devices such as surveys and presentation forms such as tables; the standardization of systems for training and the inculcation of habits; the inauguration of professional specialisms and vocabularies; building design and architectural forms – the list is heterogeneous and is, in principle, unlimited. (Miller & Rose, 1990, p. 8)

Drawing on Foucault's conception of 'governmentality', these researchers attempt to show how 'technologies of government' *indirectly* link the conduct of individuals and organisations to political objectives through 'actions at a distance'. Their main assertion is that individuals, organisations and economies are made governable through these mundane mechanisms, which reproduce 'governmentalities': a disposition toward panoptic conceptions of the society within which everyone is under persistent surveillance for discipline (see Miller & O'Leary, 1987; Miller & Rose, 1990; Neu & Heincke, 2004). These analyses are politically rich as they line up the 'technological' evolution of governance with the evolution of capitalism into a 'disciplinary society' (see Foucault, 1979; Hopper & Macintosh, 1993).

We appreciate this political nature of the analyses, and also agree with the disciplinary effect of those 'technologies of governance'. We also celebrate the pervasiveness of governance across economic and political fields. However, we have certain reservations on these analyses where, especially due to their post-structuralist ontology, the conception of governance has been reduced to mere micro-political exercise of power for discipline, and governance has become discipline through technologies. As a result, as in the case of neo-classical economic extensions of governance, these post-structuralist analyses also ignore the wider political structures and the structural distribution of power.[2] For them, as a result, governance cannot exist in their structural forms.

As has already been mentioned, our framework is structural and acknowledges the pre-existence of structural categories not simply as social categories, but as institutions and structures of power. We see that power exists in these social categories (structures): it is their contradictions and cohabitations which form historically distinct governance structures. As in the case of Foucauldians, we also acknowledge the significance of 'technologies of governance' (which we label 'contents of governance') as mundane instruments through which governance is made possible but, for us, their inventions and deployments are contingent upon the structural properties and processes of governance. Thus, governance is more than deployment of technologies for discipline. It is a hegemony constructed through political alliances between structurally antagonistic parties, and materialised through mundane processes and contents of governance.

PRE-COLONIAL GOVERNANCE: GOVERNANCE THROUGH CASTE RITUALS

The pre-colonial Sri Lanka was a centralised kingship state and economy was subsumed by the kingship state and its ritualistic apparatuses of governance. The structure of governance was a well-defined caste system. On the one hand, the caste system was a system of work division: different castes were chartered with specific occupations or professions. On the other hand, it is a governance structure as castes were hierarchically arranged from the lowest to the highest of landed aristocracy and the king (see Pieris, 1956). The subject of governance was castes and their interactions, not enterprises, because economic activities were organised within castes.

The processes and contents of governance were inscribed in the structure of castes. Governance processes are sort of *habitus* (Bourdieu, 1990) – a system of structured, structuring dispositions. They are partly ideological and partly practical as they provide a set of widely accepted cultural norms according to which power to command and control the social order is distributed. In the pre-colonial epoch, this was embedded in the legitimation of aristocracy by which the system of supervision, jurisdiction and control was in place. Within established ideological frameworks of traditions, members of the aristocracy (higher order castes) were entrusted with the social power to interfere, and judged the legitimacy of collective and individual actions of others in almost all realms of their lives. Coupled with the overall caste system, aristocratic processes determined the heredity of work, ritualised the labour process, appropriated the surplus value, maintained jurisdictions and controlled the social mobility (see Pieris, 1956).

Rituals were the main content of the governance. Production, exchange, domination and exploitation were inscribed in various social and religious rituals (see Seneviratne, 1978). In conjunction with structures and processes, these rituals controlled individuals, families and the whole society (de Silva,

2001). The measurement of performance and the appropriations of surplus were ritualistic. The determination, payment and collection of rent were caste rituals. The performance of economic activities were monitored by the upper castes and criteria of monitoring and controls were also rituals (see Pieris, 1956). That said, performance itself was the maintenance of rituals rather than meeting explicit output targets. Despotism, often characterised by physical punishment, was directed against the avoidance or violation of rituals.

Accounting was inscribed in rituals. Especially in a pre-literate society, where gramocentric documentations and recordkeeping were virtually absent, accounting took the form of oral testimonies and ritual ceremonies (*cf.* Hooper & Kearins, 1997). For example, 'harvesting' was a ritual ceremony where collective labour performed the harvesting activities in front of the physical presence of aristocratic loads. The measurement of output was an intrinsic element of these ritual ceremonies; the paddy harvest, for example, was initially filed into a unit of measurement called '*goyam kole*', which was a customarily a man's-height pile of un-grained paddy. The grained paddy was measured in '*kurunies*', a unit of measurement represented by a wooden cube of a man's forearm-length (*riyana*). Although such measurement rituals never aimed at exact precision and accuracy, there happened to be a reasonable consistency across village constituencies, mainly due to the fact that such wooden boxes of measurements are produced and supplied by the carpenter caste according to their traditional norms of production. Thus, it was the measurement in the physical presence of aristocrats (e.g., *gam vidanye*, the village chief), which constituted account-ing. Beyond this physical observation inscribed in ritual ceremonies, upward reporting in the aristocratic hierarchy was mainly oral testimonies. Power to provide such oral testimonies and their credibility were determined by the relative position of individuals in the caste-based aristocratic hierarchy.

COLONIAL GOVERNANCE: ARTICULATING FEUDAL GOVERNANCE WITH IMPERIALISM

Imperialism penetrated into the feudal society in two major arenas. The first was the transformation of kingship into the colonial state, and the second was the emergence of a plantation-based mercantile economy. However, the emergence of a colonial state did not result in the dissolution of pre-colonial feudal governance but incorporated it to serve the objectives of colonial mercantilism. For example, in 1801, Dundas, Colonial Secretary, in an instructional paper to Governor Sir Frederick North, stated that '(t)he sward must be exclusively ours, and the civil government in all its branches must be virtually ours – but through the medium of its ancient native organs' (quoted in de Silva, 1953). 'Ancient native organs' were mobilised into the colonial civil government by placing native elite caste members in the provincial governance.

Economically, the extension of colonial capitalism was partial. The feudal relations of production and appropriations, by and large, continued to prevail. The majority of the native peasantry did not dissolve and integrated into the emerging plantation economy. Unlike the Enclosure Movement in the West, which provided the initial impetus for the proletarianisation of peasantry, the expansion of plantations did not evict vast masses of peasants from their lands. The expansion of plantations occurred at the cost of primeval forests rather than the muddy and low latitude lands where peasant farming was pervasive. The colonial state did not try any extra-economic measures to push peasantry out from their traditional agriculture into the state-sponsored plantations. Instead, necessary labour was imported from the neighbouring India and ghettoised with plantations, creating a separate ethnic category now known as 'plantation Tamils'. As a result, temple lands and *nindagam* (chieftain villages) remained as specifically pre-capitalist enclaves in the non-plantation sphere of the economy, only partially entwined with the colonial mercantile economy (Jayawardena, 2000; Roberts, 1997).

Thus, the colonial episode of Sri Lankan history resulted in a bifurcation of governance in two distinct directions. First, mercantile capitalism coupled with the colonial bureaucratic apparatus formed the plantation and its associated services such as transportation, ports, banking, insurance and management agencies of British absentee capital. Secondly, feudalism coupled with archaic land aristocracy pervaded the rest of the economy. In the case of the former, the principal apparatus of governance was the official class of planters, who were both the administrative officers of the colonial state, on one hand, and the principal investors in the emerging plantations, on the other. The class of native feudal aristocrats governed the non-plantation peasantry. In neither case did there exist a strong civil state. Civil societies consisted of fragmented village communities aligned with kinship and caste identities, on one hand, and enslaved immigrant Indian labourers in plantations, on the other, both of which lacked political consciousness and organisations to check the expansion of their counterparts: the colonial political state and the mercantile economy. The plantation mode of economy was a compilation of Sterling capital, Ceylon land and Indian labour. Given the virtual absence of a strong civil society and the capture of the colonial political state by the mercantile economy, its *regime of governance* was despotic, where coercion prevailed over consent: the source of power was militant imperialism coupled with feudal aristocracy (Jayawardena, 2000).

The colonial *structure* of governance consisted of a set of interrelated political and economic institutions. The colonial state was placed at the top of the governing hierarchy as the supreme governing body, which was, in turn, responsible to British citizens who contributed to the absentee Sterling capital through the mechanism of the London Stock Market. However, as we will discuss later, economic monitoring and direction of the plantations were in the hands of so-called agency houses.

The *processes* of colonial governance were dual: state bureaucracy and the corporate administrative hierarchies. State bureaucracy was fundamentally military and jurisdictional. Corporate bureaucracy was arranged through the processes of 'agency houses'. The general framework of agency consisted of an agency house in London, another agency house in Colombo and plantation superintendents.[3] The control responsibilities along the agential relationships were such that the superintendents were responsible for managing the labour process, the Colombo agency managed the plantation and the London agency managed the plantation company (de Silva, 1982).

The *contents* of colonial governance were largely legislative (ordinance, rules, regulations and administrative and financial codes) and operationalised through the agency houses. As the management agent of the plantation, Colombo agency houses were entrusted with a series of managerial, secretarial and other related functions (see Table 2). In supervising and monitoring the plantation activities, the Colombo agency houses used what was called the visiting agent system, according to which a plantation expert visited the plantation two or three times a year. After each visit, the visiting agent submitted a report to the agency house covering everything pertaining to cultivation, manufacture, labour, staff, maintenance of buildings and factory machinery, costs of operations and development work. The visiting agent was an inspector, reporter, adviser, scrutiniser and policy maker all rolled into one (de Silva, 1982). His report was studied by agency house executives who made their own comments on the contents of the report and their recommendations. Instructions were then sent to the superintendent of the respective plantation to implement the recommendations. A copy or a summary of this report was sent to the directors of the plantation company in London for their information. Furthermore, this visiting agent was heavily involved in the budgeting process (so-called 'estimates') of the plantation. Draft 'estimates' were sent

Table 2. Functions of Agency Houses.

1. Estate Management
   (a) Budgetary control, including the framing and the responsibility for adherence to revenue and capital budgets;
   (b) Cultivation advice, including the consideration of advice which is obtained from Visiting Agents and the Research Institutes;
   (c) The manufacturing advice given to estates in which the advice obtained by the Agency Houses from their own tasters and brokers play a part; and
   (d) The responsibility for recruitment and disciplinary control of staff including the Superintendent/ Manager. Though there is a delegation of powers to the manager on some matters at the estate level, there is an ultimate control exercised by the Agency Houses.

2. Secretarial and Accounting Services
   (a) Maintenance of records;
   (b) The use of accounts as a means of financial control including giving advice on policy to estate-owning principals, the keeping of accounts for these principals including the operation of the bank accounts and dealings with the bank;
   (c) The granting of credit to principals;
   (d) The procurement of estate supplies for principals;
   (e) Advice on taxation;
   (f) The handling of Exchange Control matters relating to shipment of teas to the London Auctions, remittances of dividends and Head Office expenses in respect of sterling companies and of dividends to non-resident shareholders of rupee companies;
   (g) Acting as insurance agents for principals;
   (h) Acting as shipping agents for principals with responsibility for shipping estate produce to the London Auctions, as well as having the other responsibilities of Shipping Agents;
   (i) Services connected with arrangements for the transport, storage and sale of estate produce;
   (j) Services rendered as directors on Boards of rupee companies, which are principals of the Agency House.
   (k) Procurement of consultancy services for estates, mainly in regard to engineering and legal problems; and
   (l) The provision of miscellaneous services for principals such as printing.

Source: Government of Sri Lanka (1974, pp. 36–37).

to the visiting agent for his recommendations and the visiting agent was an active participant in the budget committee to decide the final estimates.

Unlike in the pre-colonial governance, accounting became more apparent, technical and calculative, and embraced a larger portion of the content of governance. As is seen in Table 2, accounting entailed a range of activities of the Agency Houses from record keeping to planning and control. By and large, it was an isomorphic adoption of western accounting systems and techniques to structure the accountability relationships along the managerial hierarchy to the absentee capital in the London stock market.

However, accounting in colonial governance was mainly confined within the agency relationship between the absentee capital and managerial stewards. Accounting was hardly mobilised to control labour at the point of production. Instead, labour was controlled through a set of paternalistic labour relations and debt bondages, which were centred on an internal contractor known as a *kangani*. A.R. King, the District Judge in a plantation area, has splendidly described the role of the *kangani*

> He is the leader and representative of the coolies composing his gang and artfully binds them to him in every conceivable way. He is their banker and spokesman; and the principal relationship between him and the coolies are of the most complicated nature – a skilfully devised network by which he manages always to exercise a hold upon each coolly, either by virtue of his responsibility to the coolly, or the responsibility of the coolly to him. (Administration Report 1870, Quoted in Moldrich, 1990, p. 61)

Similar to the internal contracting system which prevailed in 19th century Britain (see Buttrick, 1952; Littler, 1980, 1982), a kangani-based system of wage administration and labour control was in operation. In the absence of meticulous record-keeping on labour productivity and control, labour management was effectively delegated to these kanganies. They were paid 'head money' (lump sum payment based on the number of labourers they brought to the estate from South Indian villages) and 'pence money' (a daily payment based on the number of workers turning up to work each day). Kanganies also received large cash advances to cover expenses in recruiting the labour gangs of South Indian villagers. Much of the cash advances were made to the labourers at the point of recruitment and used by them to clear their debts in the village. Planters did not pay wages directly to the labourers but paid the kanganies, who in turn paid the labourers at their own discretion. Millie (1878), for example, stated that

> on pay days the wages went from the pay table into the well bulged out waistcoat of the kangani ... Why was this permitted? ... He (the kangani) had advanced money on the coast (in South India); if the cash went into the hands of the coolly, he would never get it out of him; his wages must be arrested at the pay table before he could possibly touch it ... the kangani was responsible to 'Master' for the whole of the advances and such steps must be taken to secure them. The master would say no more. Visions of refunded 'cost advances' which would no doubt take place tomorrow. (Millie, P.D., 1878, quoted in Moldrich, 1990, p. 83)

In such a system of internal contracting and a rather despotic system of supervision, the need for meticulous record-keeping and accounting for labour was at its minimum. Only a simple ledger book was maintained, where all cash advances were recorded as charges against kanganies. Thus, the managerial line of accountability effectively ended at the point of kanganies, leaving them the discretion of managing their own labour gangs.

As implicated in these historical accounts, the colonial governance structure was one shaped by the supreme dominance of the colonial state and its coalition with mercantile capital. When it found that the native peasantry was non-governable through economic means due to relative independence of the emerging plantation economy, it mobilised its global presence to create a governable workforce through immigration. Then, their governance was ensured largely through a system of internal contracting where administration and accounting for labour were delegated to gang leaders known as kanganies. However, accounting was strongly present, in its modernistic form, to structure the accountability relationships along the managerial hierarchy to the absentee capital in the London stock market.

POST-COLONIAL GOVERNANCE: HEGEMONY CHALLENGING IMPERIALISM

Imperialism was globally challenged in the late 19th century and early 20th centuries. And it was the modernisation in the West itself which provided the early political impetus for challenging imperialism as a global phenomenon (Tucker, 1999). There emerged alternative lines of thought for political possibilities to challenge the imperialism. The exposure of traditional elite classes of the non-settler colonies to the Western education and democracy drew them to agitation for independence in their home countries. Amid fast-growing anti-colonial agitations and the two World Wars, the global power of imperialism was difficult to sustain in its traditional despotic modes and surrendered for a post-colonial regime (Randall & Theobald, 1998).

The constitutional marking of post-colonialism in Sri Lanka was the Independence, which was crucial in the historical evolution of governance structures. It provided the necessary political impetus for the emergence of a political society. The post-colonial episode was a story of converging the political state, civil state and the market economy to form a hegemonic regime of governance. It began with the transfer of political state to the indigenous feudal aristocracy (Jayawardena, 2000). The basic structure of the new political state was set by incorporating the political apparatus of Western modernism: democracy was the organising principle and the universal franchise was the pragmatic. The populace received a political significance through the electoral discourses, which had hitherto never been there. Consent of the masses became a significant factor for the new political elites to sustain their power status in the emerging nation-state. They confronted the need of legitimating themselves before their people (Shils, 1963). These political dynamics of independence resulted in signification of the civil society within the dialectics between the polity, society and the economy. For Gramsci (1971), civil society populates trade unions, political parties, local intelligentsia, other voluntary organisations, kinship networks, and so on, and it constitutes an institutional space between the political state and the economy. It can, on the one hand, spill into the state and, on the other, interpenetrate the market (see also Burawoy, 2003), and thus provides a social space within which governing institutions of economic relations are sited. The post-colonial emergence of a strong civil state was an upset to hitherto existing colonial structures of governance.

The post-colonial formation of the nation-state brought certain contradictory objectives together. First, the political state was confronted with the task of 'organising and maintaining modern political apparatus, that is, rationally conducted administration, a cadre of leaders grouped in the public form of party system, and a machinery of public order' (Shils, 1963, p. 2). Secondly, in contrast to the colonial state, the domain of economic interests of the post-colonial state was not confined to plantations. A larger feudal society was waiting for capitalist penetration and development. Economic progress and welfare of these so far neglected mass was brought to the top of the political agenda. Thirdly, in sharp contrast to the modernisation objectives, the new nation-state was also concerned with upholding the dignity of its traditional cultures and their standing in the world as an independent nation (Shils, 1963). These objectives demanded certain changes in colonial governance structures. The strategy adopted was the 'nationalism' at the frontiers of the political and civil state and 'nationalisation' at the economic front. Nevertheless, neither of them was indigenous invention. Nationalism was the generic political mood of many colonial states even before the independence. Its roots were in the agitations for independence and often decorated by the Marxist political ideologies. Nationalisation was an economic policy programme which the new elites could easily find in its Western counterparts, especially the British nationalisation movement.

The movement of nationalisation and the harbouring of the 'embryo of a democratic socialism' (Burawoy, 2003) can well be conceptualised within the notion of the 'agrarian bloc', which Gramsci used to analyse 'the southern question' of Italy (Gramsci, 1957, 1978). The notion of agrarian bloc specifies a certain mechanism of integrating different social classes and strata into a single structure of governance. This integration is ensured not only by the economic alignment of productive forces possessed by different social strata but also by the 'ideological reproduction of that state of affairs, a reproduction that occurs on many social levels and in many forms of legitimation' (Holub, 1992, p. 158). Thus, agrarian bloc is a main mechanism of hegemonic governance which emphasises consent over coercion. Holub (1992, p. 158) summarises this

> consensus is produced and circulated by the intellectuals of the rural petty bourgeoisie: the pharmacist, the lawyer, the priest, the local newspaper editor, the schoolteacher, and so forth who express, with a few exceptions, a set of values which have a specific function: emotionally, ideally and materially to tie the exploited masses of the peasants to the landed property owners. As mediators between the peasant masses and the big landowners, this group of rural petty-bourgeois intellectuals is extremely important for the survival of the agrarian bloc. Without their multifaceted ubiquitous ideological mediation in the many interstices of what Gramsci will (sic) later call civil society, consent to the status quo could not be maintained.

Thus, post-colonial hegemony, as a wider social structure of governance, is different from the colonial regime in few fundamental ways. First, it is hegemonic rather than despotic: consent prevailed over coercion although coercion never ceased to be used. Application of coercion was indirect and implicated in the structural properties, which constrained the choice of the mass. Secondly, the civil society was dominant over the political state and the economy. Post-colonial democratic politics provided the impetus to awaken the power relations in the civil state, which was largely dormant in the colonial episode, and to integrate with the political state. Thus, consent is manufactured through the patronage structures within which archaic social relations of kinship, caste and ethnicity were the organising principles. Finally, state capitalism was the philosophy of the political state to organise the economy; the state bureaucracy became the principal process of governance, which, however, was made imperfect (in terms of ideal propositions of Western bureaucracy) by the penetration of civil society's power relations.

The convergence of the state and the civil society under the themes of anti-colonialism made nationalisation of plantations politically inevitable. For example, Doric De Souza, then Secretary of the Ministry of Plantation Industries, echoed the political necessity of nationalisation of plantations

> Nationalisation is historically inevitable. This country took the step to recover the lands appropriated by the foreigners in the 19th century. In one way or the other it was inevitable; politically, absolutely necessary. That land had to come back to us. Otherwise

we could not have lifted our heads up and said 'we are independent'. (quoted in Rote, 1986, p. 267)

With the nationalisation, Agency Houses were abolished and all plantations were structured under three state corporations,[4] which in turn came under the monitoring of a cabinet ministry and the Parliament. In addition, a set of supporting institutions such as Tea Research Institute, Institute of Plantation Management (which dealt with the training and development of plantation managers) and Sri Lanka Tea Board (which mainly dealt with the international trading and marketing of the Ceylon Tea) were established as separate wings in the governance of the tea industry.

The governance processes were mainly bureaucratic. As state bureaucracy replaced Agency Houses, an administrative structure across the ministries, state corporations and those supporting institutions was established to institutionalise a western-type bureaucracy. However, political authority intruded and dominated the bureaucracy, institutionalising a line of political patronage within it (see Hettige, 1984; Hettige & Mayer, 2000; Ranuge, 2000; Uyangoda, 2000). Politicians gained the power to recruit, promote and transfer personnel across the state bureaucracy and the bureaucracy was surrendered to the agendas of those in political authorities. Accordingly political patronage became the principal process of governance and control within the structure of state capitalism. The politics of post-colonial governance is portrayed by Ranuge (2000, pp. 55–56).

> While examining the criteria of appointments and promotions to the bureaucracy the affiliation of the candidate to the political party in power is more important especially at higher level of public service ... When there is a vacancy in a scheduled post such as a head of a department, the officer who is qualified for appointment is required to bring a letter of recommendation from a politician of the ruling party. No politician would give such a recommendation to an unknown officer. Hence it is essential for officers to establish hidden alliances with politicians. This kind of relationship keeps the officer concerned under an obligation to serve the political class. Such officers cannot say no to political requests ... Family relationships, caste and personal relationships with powerful politicians are other considerations to get into senior positions of the public service ... Having realised this, many public servants are compelled to build alliances with political parties for their personal benefit.

The infusion of bureaucratic apparatus and political patronage within governance structures and processes had definite implications for the content of governance and accounting. Various legal and administrative tools such as financial and establishment codes, statutory provisions, Government circulars, Central Bank and Treasury guidelines and so on became the official content of governance. However, the ideology of welfarism in state capitalism provided alternative interpretations and usages for them. In contrast to their rational objectives of economic efficiency, impersonality and fairness, these tools were increasingly mobilised to satisfy objectives of political authorities. Political discourses of nationalism and party politics rationalised state enterprises in terms of welfarism, which, however, was to be defined within the political patronage. For politicians, satisfying their political party supporters through mobilising public resources became crucial to sustain their power within the domain of electoral politics. For bureaucrats, helping politicians to do so was crucial to safeguard their positions and their upward career mobility. Reciprocally, politicians needed to ensure that 'their people' were at the right places in the bureaucracy to make it usable for their purposes. This triangular political dependency provided the necessary context within which ideal type content of bureaucratic governance became subordinated to informal political tools such as a 'chit from a politician'.[5]

Accounting was implicated by this particular tension between ideal type rationales of state bureaucracy and the political rationales of the civil state. It was also implicated by the tension between economic objectives of efficiency and profitability, on the one hand, and political objectives of social welfare, on the other. Driven by the accountability frameworks established by the bureaucratic apparatus, there were prototypical accounting activities to provide the basic transactional information upon which financial statements are prepared. For such accounting, every plantation unit was simply a cost centre rather than a profit centre, because all sales and collection of sales proceeds took place at the Colombo Tea Auction and the head office personnel were responsible for them. At the level of individual plantation units, such bookkeeping activities mainly took the form of record keeping on expenditures. As a former superintendent of a state-owned plantation reflected

> As it is the case even now, we had a CC (chief clerk) for every plantation unit. His job was mainly record keeping. There were a set of ledgers and other books and every cent we spent had to be recorded and accounted for in these books with supporting source documents. He was also entrusted with the petty cash administration. All other expenses were to be incurred by the superintendents and CC should be provided with supporting documents for records. But even the superintendent can't spend anything more than the approved allowances under each expense category without a prior approval from the head office ... It was a tedious job indeed because, as I remember now, there were more than eighty expense codes against which those expenses should be classified and recorded. His biggest job was the payroll and he had to compile the weekly payroll based on daily muster attendance records. Every month he had to prepare summary expense sheets and send them to the head office.

This recordkeeping, and subsequent audits, were mainly driven by the public sector accountability doctrine that every cent spent by public officers should be accounted for, and no public officer be allowed to spend public money without the prior consent of the relevant authorities. Periodic 'circulars' and 'instructional manuals' from the Ministry of Plantation became the dominant mode of setting benchmarks against which plantation managers could spend and act. Budgets, which plantation managers used to call 'estimates', especially capital budgets, needed to have ministerial approval. Thus, under this nationalisation regime of governance, plantation managers had effectively become public officers (rather than enterprise managers) whose accountability was driven mainly by political expectations.

Alongside these recordkeeping practices, a set of calculative practices inherited from colonial masters was also in operation. Plantation managers, especially those at the middle and supervisory level, were entrusted with day-to-day routines of collecting, organising and reporting various physical data alongside their day-to-day control rituals. Similar to a typical transaction processing system, these calculative rituals captured and summarised the day-to-day production realities. For example, Field Officers' daily routines were tied up with the compilation of what they called the 'muster card' which contained the names of the workers who attended the day's muster, a system of coding to record the type of work each labourer was assigned to, and the quantity of green tea which pluckers produced at the afternoon and evening weighing sessions. Thus, in addition to the labour attendance data, the muster card provided the 'field weight' of production at each weighing centre. A copy of the muster card compiled by each field officer went to the Assistant Superintendent who then performed what they called 'muster card amalgamation', to calculate the aggregates for the plantation unit as a whole each day (see Ford Rhodes Thornton & Co., 1983 for more details of accounting procedures in plantations).

Interestingly, these calculative procedures, initially established by colonial masters for the purpose of internal controls, were integrated into a system of political reporting during the post-colonial regimes. Periodic summaries were abstracted from these daily-record-keeping rituals and then sent to the Ministry of Plantation and other government agencies for the purpose of compiling national level statistics for the plantation sector. They provided the basis upon which 'political statistics' of the nationalised plantation sector were produced and disseminated to the public at large to legitimise the political ideology of state capitalism. Such political statistics never emphasised the profitability or the economic efficiency of resource utilisation at the level of individual plantation entities. Instead their main focus was on volume of exports, national value added, contribution to the GDP, foreign exchange earnings, employment and such other 'politically meaningful' numbers at the level of national politics (see, e.g., Plantation Sector Statistical Pocket Book published annually by the Ministry of Plantations, and the relevant sections of the annual Central Bank Report). In that way, the role of accounting became rather political: sustaining a set of public accountability doctrines, and most importantly, providing information for legitimating political ideologies.

NEO-COLONIAL GOVERNANCE: REVITALISING THE ECONOMY

The decade of the 1970s witnessed an economic and political crisis[6] which questioned the ideology of state capitalism (Indraratna, 1993). This crisis was coupled with an international economic order which inclined towards liberal economic democratic models vis-à-vis state capitalism (Colambage, 1993). The economic crisis was then strategically used by the right-wing political parties as a basis for attacking the political ideologies of state capitalism. Opposition was also directed at the parameters of governance which emanated from the controlled economy, and which restricted economic freedom of the public (Hettige, 2000). All these forces had shaken the power of hegemony and the regime of governance. The shake-up of the governance was politically symbolised by the new right-wing government which came to power with a 5/6th majority, and was economically justified by opening up the economy to global capital (Indraratna, 1993). The economy revitalised by this political and economic transition coincides with Karl Polanyi's (1957) notion of market economy.

The open economic policy of the new Government bid for the global capital. Soon after the formation of the government, President J.R. Jayawardene visited the United States to revitalise diplomatic relations, which had hitherto been dormant due to Russian favouring of the previous governments. In his first budget speech, Finance Minister Rone de Mel desperately legitimated the need of foreign aid for development (Government of Sri Lanka, 1977). Large-scale development projects were planned to be funded by the World Bank, IMF and ADB (Asian Development Bank) (Central Bank of Sri Lanka, 1978). Programmes of privatisation called for foreign direct investments and the idea of a Free Trade Zone opened the door for multinational corporations (Kelegama, 1993). Imports and foreign exchange restrictions were relaxed for commercial businesses to grow. New forms of export-led industries such as garments were encouraged (Government of Sri Lanka, 1977). The market economy continued to transform the controlled economy dominated by state-owned enterprises. This marked a shift in the relative significance of the forces of governance from civil society (hegemony) to market economy.

The strategy of transforming state capitalism's hegemonic governance was neo-liberalism, on the front of political ideology and privatisation, on the economic front (Cook & Minogue, 1990). Nevertheless, the penetration of this newly emerged political ideology into the plantation industry was delayed as far as it could be owing to the political sensitivity of the plantation industry. After almost all other industries were privatised, as late as 1992, plantations began to be privatized, initially as an interim transition of only the management to the private sector on the basis of a management fee. Full transfer of assets to the private sector took place only in 1995. Plantations, which were hitherto managed under state corporations, were reorganised into 24 Regional Plantation Companies (RPC, public limited liability companies whose shares are traded on the Colombo Stock Exchange). De-politicisation of plantation management was an explicit objective, and it was expected that privatisation would eliminate many managerial problems linked to the political hegemony. It was also expected that transformation of capital structure to corporate capital governed by market dynamics would effectively eradicate inefficiencies associated with political dependency on the state capital (Asian Development Bank, 1995, 1998, 2002; Government of Sri Lanka, 1987, 1992, 1995, 1996a, 1996b; Shanmugathasan, 1997). In this idealised context, it was also anticipated that accounting would ensure transparency, accountability, democratisation and prevention of frauds and corruption (Kaufmann, Kraay, & Mastruzzi, 2003; Potter, 2000). However, privatisation of plantations did not eradicate the political dependency. Instead, a rather complex political mode of governance emerged under the sponsorship of international development funding agencies, especially the World Bank and the ADB, but subject to the continuing political interference of political state, trade union leaders and other political stakeholders.

Present governance structure of the plantation industry consists of a conglomerate of RPCs, the state, international funding agencies, NGOs and trade unions. The plantation industry is a special case because of the peculiarity of its labour force, mainly composed of a special ethnic category known as 'plantation Tamils', whose ancestors were immigrants from South India during the colonial regime. As discussed earlier, the colonial legacy had made the plantation a 'total institution' (Best, 1968; Goffman, 1969) and the current systems of governance have not been totally freed from those colonial legacies. This historical construction of plantations provided them with a 'place identity of ethnicity', which is a critical factor in the electoral politics.[7] Plantations had never been constructed to be economic enterprises, which can be managed solely by the apparatus of private capital and market dynamics, but had always been a socio-political space within which the existential security of a politically powerful ethnic category is constructed through the active engagement of the political state. The result was the emergence of a complex governance structure, within which a certain chemistry of private market capital, state capital and global capital combined with 'social capital' to seek neo-liberal economic rationalities.

Within this new arrangement of the governance structure, formal ownership of the plantations was transferred to private companies, subject to a condition that the State owned a single share of the privatised companies, known as the 'golden share'. The accord of the golden shareholder is required for an RPC to sub-lease land or to amend the Articles of Association. Indeed, the 'golden share' is intended to provide the necessary legislative rights of the State to interfere in company affairs whenever deemed necessary. Similarly, the development of the plantation industry urgently needed a huge investment in the social infrastructure for uplifting the living standards of plantation Tamils, which was strategically important due to their relative position in electoral politics, especially after offering them the universal franchise in 1984. However, private capital had no intention or capacity for participation in these political objectives. This is where the active engagement of international development funding agencies, especially World Bank and ADB, in the privatisation scheme became crucial. As a result, the invested capital in the new plantation industry was a combination of both private and international development capital.

Then there emerged a clear bifurcation of responsibilities in the line of agriculture, production and marketing, on the one hand, and management of labour issues and welfare, on the other. RPCs assumed responsibilities of production and distribution (and also the profits/losses arising from them), while a coalition between Planters' Association (a sort of employers' federation of plantation companies), Government, trade unions and international development agencies assumed responsibility for handling labour politics and welfare, mainly funded by international developmental grants and loans. For example, determination of plantation wages fell beyond the scope of plantation management into the hands of national level tripartite negotiation between trade unions, the Government and the Planters' Association. A senior manager of a plantation company revealed

> When we took over plantations they were in a real mess. No profits recorded for decades. We had to undertake a hell of an investment to make them profitable. We can boast that we turned the situation soon. Now we earn some profits, though they are not to the expectation.[8] At least we are not incurring big losses. We know we can make things better if we continue like this ... Our initial strategy was to concentrate on the agriculture and the manufacture. What we did was reorganising and streamlining agricultural techniques such as fertilising, weeding, replanting, and factory processes. In that way, we were able to gain a reasonable increase in the yield[9] ... Labour discipline is still a big problem. We have lot to do in that respect but we have not touched that area still. They are beyond our control. They are not management but bloody politics. Fortunately or unfortunately, we don't have to bother about them because government and Mr. Thondaman (the leader of the largest plantation trade union and the Minister of Housing and Plantation Infrastructure) take care of them. It is not our business, at least for the moment.

A trade union media officer revealed their political engagement in the new arrangement of governance

> Our main objective is the welfare of our people. We want them to have better housing, education and health facilities. We fight for their citizenship rights. We try to eradicate the poverty they are wrapped in. For that end, we are ready to work together with any party. We are not against privatisation. Companies should make profit otherwise they can't take care of our people. Our people are their employees ... They are doing well now. It is our responsibility to help them achieve their objective, to the extent that they help us.

These emerging ideologies of new governance are processed in a mechanism which we may call a 'welfare state'. The focus of this welfare state is not explicitly on shaping and reshaping regimes of production control and subordination of labour but the distribution of welfare packages such as housing, education and health care which, nevertheless, have certain implications for the construction of collective consent to the interests of capital. The aim of the welfare state is to promote the welfare of its citizens by organised efforts of the state and its associated networks (Byrne, 2003; Chen, 2002; Hobson & Lindholm, 1997). The active agents of the welfare state of the plantation economy are composed of trade union politicians (who are on the other hand part of the political state as cabinet ministers), politicians who represents other non-trade union counterparts of the political state, government bureaucrats, international development funding agencies, NGOs, plantation management and regional political elites.

This welfare state is dependent on funding by international development agencies, especially the ADB, the World Bank and USAID. The Plantation

Development Trust Fund was set up for the overall steering of the welfare state. The Trust Board is represented by Treasury, Central Bank, Ministry of Plantation, Ministry of Housing and Plantation Infrastructure [at the time of fieldwork, the minister was the leader of Ceylon Workers Congress (CWC) – the largest plantation trade union], trade unions and Planters' Association. Trade unions, especially CWC, play a central role in deciding the recipients of welfare benefits. NGOs such as Care International play an active role in the grass roots implementation of the welfare state, which they call capacity building to alleviate poverty and ignorance, by providing human resources for training and awareness programmes. These NGOs are actively supported by plantation management, regional trade union activists and regional political elites.

Implications of this welfare state for governance are straightforward. A coalition between state, capital and labour is constructed by global capital arrangements both at the levels of national policy and individual plantations. Everyone has assumed a common enemy to fight against: 'poverty in the plantations'. Thus, the notion of poverty alleviation is institutionalised within the basic structural antagonism between capital and labour to promote the hegemonic mechanisms embedded in the civil society. In other words, 'poverty alleviation' and its grassroots programmes have provided a material basis for the integration of patronage relations and their hegemonic effects to help revitalise ideologies of profitability and economic rationales. Corporate profits and economic efficiency are discoursed as essential conditions for eradication of poverty. The welfare state promotes communal identities and a network or coalition between labour, trade union activists, plantation management and NGOs at the plantation level, which is the notion of 'social capital' (Putnam, Leonardi, & Nanetti, 1993) or the 'missing link of development' (Carroll, 2001). This resembles 'good governance' as a strategy of managing perpetual tension between civil society and its counterparts: political state and market economy.

Within this emerging framework of governance, 'good governance' initiatives take two interrelated dimensions. First, as already mentioned, they aim at mobilising the capacity of civil society to hegemonise the consent of the labour communities to the profit ideologies and economic rationalities of enterprises. This is yet to be realised through the internal welfare state by offering the poverty ridden plantation communities better conditions of living and fair chances of progress, and seeking their active engagement in the promotion of profit potentials of the plantation industry.

Second, they aim at the transformation of management paradigms from a post-colonial bureaucracy, which retained some of colonial despotic ideologies,[10] to one which operates on the 'new management and organisational rationalities' (see Plantation Reform Project, 1998). Contents of governance within this transforming managerial paradigm were multi-faceted. At one end, there is a series of managerial training programmes and instructional manuals for plantation managers to appreciate and practice 'new' ideologies and techniques of management borrowed from western counterparts. Thereby, managers are compelled to learn a set of new competencies, which are drawn from a set of international competency standard frameworks, namely Competency Standards for Front Line Management – Australia; Management Charter Initiative – United Kingdom; and National Clerical – Administrative Competency Standards developed for the Private Sector – Australia. Accordingly, plantation managers were asked to learn how to (1) manage and develop self, (2) provide leadership in the workplace, (3) establish and manage effective workplace relationships, (4) develop teams and enhance performance and (5) manage operations and opportunities (see Plantation Reform Project, 1998). At the other end, there were certain attempts for rationalisation of accounting.

In respect of financial reporting and auditing, new governance structure demanded proper accounting records and audited financial statements to meet the requirements of the Stock Market, Companies Act and Sri Lanka Accounting and Auditing Standards. Especially, the privatisation of auditing (from the politically dependent government audit and accounting service during the nationalised regime) had a dramatic impact on the streamlining of the financial accounting function. In management accounting, budgeting was streamlined: periodic targets (production and expenditure) are set in monthly budgets followed by reviews for controlling purposes. While expenditure targets are thoroughly controlled within this mechanism, which resulted in enormous reduction of corruption,[11] production budgets were subject to two fundamental constraints: weather and labour discipline. For the plantation level managers responsible for production targets, these constraints were uncontrollable and variations in production budgets are often justifiable on these grounds; for their superiors, these justifications are by and large something yet unverifiable through existing systems of accounting and to be taken for granted. As a one head office manager once sarcastically noted: 'We better have daily meteorological readings for every plantation unit together with production records'.

One remarkable invention during this neo-colonial regime was the establishment of a system of market information for quality control in production. The re-established tea-auction agencies were capable of providing each plantation factory with a new set of information pertaining to the auction prices and factors determining them. As most of these factors were relatively controllable during the factory processes, factory management has now gained enhanced capacity to influence the auction price through quality controls. Not only that, this information is often received in comparative charts which now fill the big factory notice board and even many illiterate factory workers can make sense of them.

Despite these neo-colonial reformations, accounting is still implicated in the perpetual tension (and negotiated harmonies) between civil state, political state and the economy. First, as already noted, accounting has not gained the capacity to penetrate into the control and discipline of labour, which are still left within the patronage institutions of the civil and political states. Secondly, as it was during the nationalised regimes, plantation management is still entrusted with the provision of information for 'political accounts' of the state agencies. This function of providing political information has now been extended towards the international funding agencies on various poverty indicators. Thirdly, in addition to these accounting functions embedded within the day-to-day activities of plantation managers, various NGOs have penetrated into the plantation economy as providers of 'social accounts'. As commissioned agents of international funding agencies, these NGOs account for the 'improvements in the social conditions of plantation communities' through various surveys and so-called community engagement programmes. After all, neo-colonial attempts to liberalise plantations have resulted in constructing a negotiated political order within which governance structures, processes and contents (including accounting) are being tuned to address a multiplicity of economic and political issues but in a rather segmented manner: an attempted decoupling of politics from economics and a bifurcation of enterprise accounting from political accounting. An agenda of 'good governance' in Sri Lankan plantations has thus been implicated in the historical dialectics between economy, polity and the society, and has taken a complex political shape, which, ironically, the good governance initially aimed to escape.

CONCLUSIONS

Accounting research on governance has long celebrated two main streams: the neo-classical economic extensions and the Foucauldian. The former have often operated in a narrow analytical space between corporate ownership and stewardship rather than in the wider structural apparatus of governance. As a result, the analyses have been largely apolitical. The latter, on the other hand, provided rich political analyses linking micro-political deployments of 'technologies of government' to the rise of capitalism. However, their post-structuralist ontology, together with the conception of power as a non-structural phenomenon, failed to capture the significance of wider political structures. So governance was conceived to be the micro-political deployment of technologies for discipline. In contrast, this paper has provided an alternative analysis which conceives the existence of governance in three distinct ontological spectra: structures, processes and contents. We illustrated how governance structures, processes and contents are historically contingent upon the dialectics between market economy, political state and the civil state.

Accounting, as reflected in colonial governance, developed from an articulation of elements of feudal governance with imperial impositions. This regime of governance was largely despotic and the mode of control was inevitably coercive. The despotic governance mode, however, stemmed not only from imperialism, but also from feudalism, because the imperial modes of control were partly made of feudal traditions. Thus, the form of governance was neither purely imperial nor feudal but a combination. Within the non-plantation economy, which prevailed in rural areas, modern accounting never had a role to play. Within the plantation economy, which prevailed in a particular geography, accounting emerged to function for reporting between plantations and absentee-imperial capital. Labour process was controlled by paternalistic coercion and with little accounting.

In the post-colonial governance, the economy became colonised by the civil society. This gave form to state capitalism, an embryonic socialism, rather than the orthodox form, and the resultant governance turned to being hegemonic. There developed consent between labour and capital, especially through the mechanism of trade unions and political patronage. Formal bureaucracy and the legal-rational forms of organisations were developed as ideal models. Sooner or later, however, political patronage penetrated them and subordinated to serve political interests rather than economic rationalities. The roles of accounting bifurcated into two main streams: (1) financial reporting and control for bureaucratic control of expenditures, and (2) adoption of certain calculative practices to generate set of political statistics for the purpose of legitimating ideologies of state capitalism. Labour controls were not subject to accounting, but to the patronage structures across the civil and political state.

Global capital (re)entered the scene at the point of economic deterioration under state capitalism. This marked a colonisation of hegemony by the market economy under the neo-liberal aspirations. In Polanyian terms, this is an imperative unsettling of nation-states and defining a new world order for implementing rules and regulations of global management, and in Faulks' (1999) terms, this is global governance. The ideologies of good governance, privatization, structural adjustments, public sector reforms, productivity improvements and the like constituted the structural and processual elements of neo-colonial governance in which accounting has assumed certain roles.

Accounting in neo-colonial governance, however, did not operate in its ideal forms. The implications of 'good governance' for accounting were different and variable, as our plantation case proved. In plantations, 'good governance' initiatives revitalised accounting roles across managerial agency to strengthening stewardship, and calculative practices made factory processes responsive to market signals. However, accounting could not penetrate into the domain of labour controls, which were put aside by considering them as non-managerial and non-accounting but political. Thus, the hegemonic mechanisms of the civil state rather than accounting persisted in the political apparatus of labour control and welfare. Managerial issues emerged from contradictions between political state, civil state and the economy (enterprise) constructed themselves a distinct political domain within which accounting had little role to play. Accounting was confined to a particular non-political domain, which did not directly manifest contradictions between political state, civil state and economy. These contradictions were manifested in labour politics and welfare, which left out conventional accounting, but gave space to other social actors such as NGOs to provide social accounts on the life conditions of plantation communities. Neo-colonial reformations thus resulted not in de-politicisation of economic enterprises, but in a rather complex negotiated political order within which governance and accounting became multi-trajectory through multiple accountability relations.

The message here is that governance systems and the place of accounting therein cannot be better explained in economic terms where functionalist perspectives are promoted. Historical changes in, and underlying contradictions of, these systems, especially within post-colonial countries, come to outrank the significance of functionalist perspectives. The alternative foregoing political economy analysis not only reveals the path dependence nature of system evolution, but also contradictions and dynamics, which support or hinder ensuing policy agendas and their operational consequences. This framework is thus rather reflexive and revealing, can supplement both post-structural and economic frameworks, and lead to debate current policy-making with respect to governance initiatives, especially in LDCs. We hope that this framework would thrive for further research, especially on how governance systems in other LDCs evolve through the concurrent evolution of hegemonies and accountings.

NOTES

1. World Bank (1992) defines these terms as follows:

- Public management: government must manage its financial and personnel resources effectively through appropriate budgeting, accounting and reporting systems, and by rooting out inefficiency particularly in the para-statal sector.
- Accountability: public officials must be held responsible for their actions. This involves effective accounting and auditing, decentralisation, 'micro-level account-ability' to consumers and a role for non-governmental organisations.
- Legal framework for development: there must be a set of rules known in advance, these must be enforced, conflicts must be resolved by independent judicial bodies and there must be mechanisms for amending rules when they no longer serve their purpose.
- Information and transparency: there are three main areas for improvement (i) information on economic efficiency, (ii) transparency as a means of preventing corruption and (iii) publicly available information for policy analysis and debate.

2. For Foucauldians, power is a post-structural phenomenon, which can exist only in its exercise. Thus, power exists only in the deployment of 'technologies of governance' and thus technologies of governance presuppose the existence of power.

3. Governor Torrington in a despatch to Earl Grey (Colonial Secretary) depicted the state of plantation managers in the very early phase of the plantation establishment

> British Soldiers whose discharges were purchased from the ranks were sent up to the interior to manage plantations on salaries of £300 to £400 per annum; houses for their use were purchased by the agents at excessive prices, and their style of living, wines, and their expenditure of every description were on a scale of the most absurd proportions while the proprietors were mortgaging every security and raising money at 9 or 10 per cent to support this expenditure buoyed by the confident expectation that the first golden harvest would reimburse every outlay and leave them in possession of a splendid and permanent income. (quoted in Moldrich, 1990, p.7)

4. These three state corporations were the State Plantations Corporation (SPC), Peoples' Estate Development Board and Upcountry Co-operative Estate Development Board.

5. 'Political chit' is still a popular political tool in the state bureaucracy. Indeed, this is the principle symbolic tool of the mechanism of political patronage. Bureaucratic officers do not act without a political recommendation, which normally comes to them in the form of such 'chits' (a sort of unofficial recommendation or approval from the relevant politician, often the minister of the relevant ministry).

6. This crisis was manifested in high rate of unemployment, poverty and trade deficiency, etc. which even resulted in a youth insurrection in 1971 (see Abeyratne, 2000; Hettige & Mayer, 2000).

7. These plantation Tamil communities vote enbloc in parliamentary elections on the basis of ethnicity. In national politics, they are represented by their trade unions as their political parties. Due to the majority Singhalese votes being almost equally divided between the two major political parties, support of the plantation Tamil trade unions has become a critical factor for main political parties to establish a government with a majority. When an election comes, there would always be negotiations between major political parties and the plantation trade unions for their support. Such negotiations are typically about the number of ministries for the minority parties in the alliance government. Thus, in the last decade or so, irrespective of government changes, plantation trade union leaders held cabinet ministries and have become an integral element of the political state.

8. According to the aggregate statistics in the Colombo Stock Exchange data, the plantation sector recorded a net profit of Rs.15.8 million in year 2000, compared to a loss of Rs. 16.9 million in 1993. Privatisation of plantation began in 1992, with an interim management contract system, which converted to a full privatisation in 1995.

9. Average yield per hectare after privatisation was 1,515 kg compared to a before-privatisation average of 1,359 (Ministry of Public Administration, Home Affairs and Plantation Industries, 2000).

10. One of the authors participated in a series of workshops conducted by an international consultant for plantation superintendents who stated the objectives of the workshop as transforming 'superintendents', (whom he sarcastically called 'supreme-attendants') into 'managers'. This was officially backed by the adoption of the term 'manager' to replace the traditional term of 'superintendent' in the "Competency Standard Framework for Plantation Sector" (Plantation Reform Project, Ministry of Plantation, 1998).

11. The main source of corruption was that managers appropriated money by inserting fictitious persons in the payroll and by colliding with suppliers to inflate actual expenditures through bogus source documents. These were largely controlled by the new expenditure budgeting system and other internal checks.

REFERENCES

Abeyratne, S. (2000). Policy and political issues in economic growth of Sri Lanka. In: S. T. Hettige & M. Mayer (Eds), *Sri Lanka at cross roads: Dilemmas and prospects after 50 years of independence* (pp. 20–49). New Delhi: Macmillan India Limited.

Asian Development Bank. (1995). *Report and the recommendation of the President to the Board of Directors of a proposed loan and technical assistance to the Democratic Socialist Republic of Sri Lanka for the Plantation Reform Project.* Manila: Asian Development Bank.

Asian Development Bank. (1998). *Report and the recommendation of the President to the Board of Directors of a proposed loan to the Democratic Socialist Republic of Sri Lanka for the Tea Development Project.* Manila: Asian Development Bank.

Asian Development Bank. (2002). *Report and recommendation of the President to the Board of Directors on proposed loan to the Democratic Socialist Republic of Sri Lanka for the Plantation Development Project.* Manila: Asian Development Bank.

Best, L. (1968). Outlines of a model of pure plantation economy. *Social and Economic Studies, 17*(3), 283–326.

Bourdieu, P. (1990). *The logic of practice.* California: Stanford University Press.

Burawoy, M. (2003). For a Sociological Marxism: The complementary convergence of Antonio Gramsci and Karl Polanyi. *Politics and Society, 31*(2), 193–261.

Buttrick, J. (1952). The inside contract system. *Journal of Economic History, 12*(3), 205–221.

Byrne, D. (2003). The new politics of the welfare state. *Work, Employment and Society, 17*(1), 197–205.

Carroll, T. F. (2001). *Social capital, local capacity building, and poverty reduction.* Manila: Office of Environment and Social Development – Asian Development Bank.

Central Bank of Sri Lanka. (1978). *Annual report.* Colombo: Central Bank of Sri Lanka.

Chen, S. (2002). State socialism and the welfare state: A critique of two conventional paradigms. *International Journal of Social Welfare, 11*(1), 228–242.

Chua, W. F. (1986). Radical developments in accounting thought. *The Accounting Review, 61*(4), 601–632.

Colambage, S. S. (1993). *Monetary policy in an open economy.* Colombo: Sri Lanka Economic Association.

Cook, P., & Minogue, M. (1990). Waiting for privatisation in developing countries: Towards the integration of economic and neo-economic explanations. *Public Administration and Development, 10*(4), 389–403.

Cooper, C., Taylor, P., Smith, N., & Catchpowle, L. (2005). A discussion of the political potential of Social Accounting. *Critical Perspectives on Accounting, 16*(7), 951–974.

Covaleski, M. A., Dirsmith, M. W., & Samuel, S. (2003). Changes in the institutional environment and the institutions of governance: Extending the contributions of transaction cost economics within the management control literature. *Accounting, Organizations and Society, 28*(5), 417–441.

Dann, L. Y., & DeAngelo, H. (1983). Standstill agreements, privately negotiated stock repurchases, and the market for corporate control. *Journal of Financial Economics, 11* (1–4), 275–300.

DeAngelo, H., & Rice, E. M. (1983). Antitakeover charter amendments and stockholder wealth. *Journal of Financial Economics, 11*(1–4), 329–359.

de Silva, C. R. (1953). *Ceylon under the British occupation 1795–1833: Its political and administrative development – Volume one.* Colombo: The Colombo Apothecaries Co. Ltd.

de Silva, P. (2001). An overview of ritual theories: Ritualization and human agency. *Pravada – The Journal of Social Scientists' Association, Sri Lanka, 7*(4), 19–22.

de Silva, S. B. D. (1982). *The political economy of underdevelopment*. London: Routledge & Kegan Paul.

Ezzamel, M., & Willmott, H. (1993). Corporate governance and financial accountability: Recent reforms in the UK public sector. *Accounting, Auditing and Accountability Journal, 6*(3), 109–132.

Faulks, K. (1999). *Political sociology: A critical introduction*. Edinburgh: Edinburgh University Press.

Ford Rhodes Thornton & Co. (1983). Financial accounting and control. In: R. L. Wickramasinghe (Ed.), *Aspects of plantation management in Sri Lanka* (pp. 75–102). Colombo: National Institute of Plantation Management.

Foucault, M. (1979). *Discipline and punish: The birth of the prison*. London: Penguin.

Giroux, G., & McLelland, A. J. (2003). Governance structures and accounting at large municipalities. *Journal of Accounting and Public Policy, 22*(2), 203–230.

Goffman, E. (1969). *The presentation of self in everyday life*. London: The Penguin Press.

Government of Sri Lanka. (1974). *Sessional Paper No. XII 1974: Report on the Commission of Inquiry on Agency Houses and Brokering Firms*. Colombo: Government of Sri Lanka.

Government of Sri Lanka. (1977). *Budget speech*. Colombo: Government of Sri Lanka.

Government of Sri Lanka. (1987). *Conversion of public corporations or government owned business undertakings into public companies Act, No. 23 of 1987*. Colombo: Government of Sri Lanka.

Government of Sri Lanka. (1992). *Invitation to tender for management contracts of plantations estates in Sri Lanka – Volume II: Background information and company specific data*. Colombo: Plantation Restructuring Unit – Ministry of Finance.

Government of Sri Lanka. (1995). *Report of the presidential commission on the tea industry and trade 1995*. Colombo: Government of Sri Lanka.

Government of Sri Lanka. (1996a). *Enterprises reforms commission of Sri Lanka Act, No. 1 of 1996*. Colombo: Government of Sri Lanka.

Government of Sri Lanka. (1996b). *Rehabilitation of public enterprise Act, No. 29 of 1996*. Colombo: Government of Sri Lanka.

Gramsci, A. (1957). *The modern prince and other writings*. New York: International Publishers.

Gramsci, A. (1971). *Selections from prison notebooks*. London: Lawrence and Wishart.

Gramsci, A. (1978). *Selections from the political writings (1921–1926)*. London: Lawrence and Wishart.

Hettige, S. T. (1984). *Wealth, power and prestige*. Colombo: Ministry of Higher Education.

Hettige, S. T. (2000). Dilemmas of post colonial society after 50 years of independence: A critical analysis. In: S. T. Hettige & M. Mayer (Eds), *Sri Lanka at cross roads: Dilemmas and prospects after 50 years of independence* (pp. 7–18). New Delhi: Macmillan India Limited.

Hettige, S. T., & Mayer, M. (2000). Introduction. In: S. T. Hettige & M. Mayer (Eds), *Sri Lanka at cross roads: Dilemmas and prospects after 50 years of independence* (pp. 1–6). New Delhi: Macmillan India Limited.

Hobson, B., & Lindholm, M. (1997). Collective identities, women's power resources, and the making of welfare states. *Theory and Society, 26*(3), 475–508.

Holub, R. (1992). *Antonio Gramsci: Beyond Marxism and postmodernism*. London: Routledge.

Hooper, K., & Kearins, K. (1997). The excited and dangerous state of the natives of hawkes bay: A particular study of nineteenth century financial management. *Accounting, Organizations and Society, 22*(3–4), 269–292.

Hopper, T., & Armstrong, P. (1991). Cost accounting, controlling labour and the rise of conglomerates. *Accounting, Organizations and Society*, *16*(5–6), 405–438.

Hopper, T., & Macintosh, N. (1993). Management accounting as disciplinary practice: The case of ITT under Harold Geneen. *Management Accounting Research*, *4*(3), 181–216.

Indraratna, A. D. V. D. S. (1993). *Essays in Asian Economies*. Colombo: Sri Lanka Economic Association.

Jayawardena, K. (2000). *No bodies to somebodies: The rise of the colonial bourgeoisie in Sri Lanka, social scientists*. Colombo: Association – Sri Lanka.

Jenkins, K. (2002). The emergence of the governance agenda: Sovereignty, neo-liberal bias and politics of international development. In: V. Desai & R. B. Potter (Eds), *Companion to development studies* (pp. 485–489). London: Edward Arnold.

Johnson, H. T., & Kaplan, R. S. (1987). *Relevance lost: The rise and fall of management accounting*. Boston, MA: Harvard Business School Press.

Joseph, J. (2002). *Hegemony: A realist analysis*. London: Routledge.

Kaufmann, D., Kraay, A., & Mastruzzi, M. (2003). *Governance matters III – Governance indicators for 1996–2002*. Washington, DC: World Bank.

Kelegama, S. (1993). *Privatisation in Sri Lanka: The experience during the early years of implementation*. Colombo: Sri Lanka Economic Association.

Lambert, R. A. (2001). Contracting theory and accounting. *Journal of Accounting and Economics*, *32*(1–3), 3–87.

Latham, M. (1999). The corporate monitoring firm. *Corporate governance: An international review*, *7*(1), 12–20.

Leftwich, A. (1993). Governance, the state and the politics of development. *Third World Quarterly*, *14*(3), 605–624.

Linn, S. C., & McConnell, J. J. (1983). An empirical investigation of the impact of 'antitakeover' amendments on common stock prices. *Journal of Financial Economics*, *11*(1–4), 361–399.

Littler, C. R. (1980). Internal contract and the transition to modern work systems: Britain and Japan. In: D. Dunkerly & G. Salaman (Eds), *The international yearbook of organization studies* (pp. 157–185). London: Routledge & Kegan Paul.

Littler, C. R. (1982). *The development of the labour process in capitalist societies: A comparative study of the transformation of work organization in Britain, Japan and the USA*. London: Heinemann Educational.

Miller, P. (2001). Government by numbers: Why calculative practices matter. *Social Research*, *68*(2), 379–386.

Miller, P., & O'Leary, T. (1987). Accounting and the construction of the governable person. *Accounting, Organizations and Society*, *12*(3), 235–265.

Miller, P., & Rose, N. (1990). Governing economic life. *Economy and Society*, *19*(1), 1–31.

Ministry of Public Administration, Home Affairs and Plantation Industries. (2000). *Plantation sector statistical pocket book 2000*. Colombo: Ministry of Public Administration, Home Affairs and Plantation Industries.

Minogue, M. (2002). Power to the people? Good governance and reshaping of the state. In: U. Kothari & M. Minogue (Eds), *Development theory and practice* (pp. 117–135). Basingstoke: Palgrave.

Moldrich, D. (1990). *Bitter berry bondage: The nineteenth century coffee workers of Sri Lanka*. Kandy, Sri Lanka: Author's Publication.

Munro, R. (2004). Alignment and identity work: The study of accounts and accountability. In: R. Munro & M. Jan (Eds), *Accountability: Power, ethos and the technologies of managing* (pp. 1–19). London: International Thompson Business Press.

Neimark, M., & Tinker, T. (1986). The social construction of management control systems. *Accounting, Organizations and Society, 11*(4–5), 369–395.

Neu, D., & Heincke, M. (2004). The subaltern speaks: Financial relations and the limits of governmentality. *Critical Perspectives on Accounting, 15*(1), 179–206.

Overseas Development Administration. (1993). *Good governance.* London: Overseas Development Administration.

Pieris, R. (1956). *Sinhalese social organization: The Kandyan period.* Colombo: Ceylon University Press Board.

Plantation Reform Project. (1998). *Competency standard framework: Plantation sector Sri Lanka.* Colombo: Ministry of Plantation Industries.

Polanyi, K. (1957). *The great transformation: The political and economic origins of our time.* Boston: Beacon Press.

Potter, D. (2000). Democratisation, good governance and development. In: T. Allen & A. Thomas (Eds), *Poverty and development into the 21st Century.* Oxford: Oxford University Press.

Putnam, R. D., Leonardi, R., & Nanetti, R. Y. (1993). *Making democracy work: Civic traditions in modern Italy.* Princeton, NJ: Princeton University Press.

Randall, V., & Theobald, R. (1998). *Political change and underdevelopment: A critical introduction to third world politics.* London: Palgrave.

Ranuge, S. (2000). State bureaucracy and development. In: S. T. Hettige & M. Mayer (Eds), *Sri Lanka at cross roads: Dilemmas and prospects after 50 years of independence* (pp. 50–62). New Delhi: Macmillan India Limited.

Roberts, J., & Scapens, R. (1985). Accounting systems and systems of accountability – Understanding accounting practices in their organisational contexts. *Accounting, Organizations and Society, 10*(4), 443–456.

Roberts, M. (1997). Elite formation and elites, 1832–1931. In: M. Roberts (Ed.), *Sri Lanka: Collective identities revisited* (Vol. I, pp. 191–265). Colombo: Marga Institute.

Rote, R. (1986). *A taste of bitterness: The political economy of tea plantations in Sri Lanka.* Amsterdam: Free University Press.

Seneviratne, H. L. (1978). *Rituals of the Kandyan State.* Cambridge: Cambridge University Press.

Shanmugathasan, N. (1997). *Privatisation of tea plantations – The challenge of reforming production relations in Sri Lanka: An institutional historical perspective.* Colombo, Sri Lanka: Social Scientists' Association.

Shils, E. (1963). On the comparative study of the new states. In: C. Geertz (Ed.), *Old societies and New States: The quest for modernity in Asia and Africa* (pp. 1–26). London: The Free Press of Glencoe.

Spekle, R. F. (2001). Explaining management control structure variety: A transaction cost economics perspective. *Accounting, Organizations and Society, 26*(4–5), 419–441.

Tucker, V. (1999). The myth of development: A critique of eurocentric discourse. In: R. Munck & D. O'Hearn (Eds), *Critical development theory: Contributions to a new paradigm* (pp. 1–26). London: Zed Books.

Turner, M. M., & Hulme, D. (1997). *Governance, administration and development: Making the state work.* Basingstoke: Macmillan.

Uddin, S., & Hopper, T. (2003). Accounting for privatisation in Bangladesh: Testing World Bank claims. *Critical Perspectives on Accounting*, *14*(7), 739–774.

Uyangoda, J. (2000). A state of desire? Some reflections on the unreformability of Sri Lanka's post-colonial polity. In: S. T. Hettige & M. Mayer (Eds), *Sri Lanka at cross roads: Dilemmas and prospects after 50 years of independence* (pp. 93–118). New Delhi: Macmillan India Limited.

van den Bogaard, M. A., & Spekle, R. F. (2003). Reinventing the hierarchy: Strategy and control in the Shell Chemicals carve-out. *Management Accounting Research*, *14*(2), 79–93.

Wickramasinghe, D., & Hopper, T. (2005). A cultural political economy of management accounting controls: A case study of a textile mill in a traditional Sinhalese village. *Critical Perspectives on Accounting*, *16*(4), 473–503.

Wickramasinghe, D., Hopper, T., & Rathnasiri, C. (2004). Japanese cost management meets Sri Lankan politics: Disappearance and reappearance of bureaucratic management controls in a privatised utility. *Accounting, Auditing and Accountability Journal*, *17*(1), 85–120.

Williams, G. A. (1960). The concept of 'Egemonia' in the thought of Antonio Gramsci: Some notes on interpretation. *Journal of the History of Ideas*, *21*(4), 586–599.

Williamson, O. E. (1975). *Markets and hierarchies, analysis and antitrust implications: A study in the economics of internal organization*. London: Free Press.

Williamson, O. E. (1991). Comparative economic organization: The analysis of discrete structural alternatives. *Administrative Science Quarterly*, *36*(2), 269–296.

World Bank. (1989). *World Bank report*. Washington, DC: World Bank.

World Bank. (1992). *Governance and development*. Washington, DC: World Bank.

Zaman, M. (2001). Turnbull-generating undue expectations of the corporate governance role of audit committees. *Managerial Auditing Journal*, *15*(5), 5–9.

THE INFLUENCE OF SOCIAL AND POLITICAL RELATIONS ON CORPORATE GOVERNANCE SYSTEMS: THE CASE OF RURAL BANKS IN GHANA

Adom Adu-Amoah, Mathew Tsamenyi and Joseph Mensah Onumah

ABSTRACT

Purpose of paper – *Rural Banks (RBs) are unit banks owned by members of the rural community through the purchase of shares and are licensed to provide financial intermediation in rural areas of Ghana. This paper reports on the external and internal mechanisms through which corporate governance is maintained in these banks.*

Design/methodology/approach – *The findings reported in the paper are based on evidence obtained from a review of relevant documents and interviews with the managers of selected RBs.*

Findings – *The corporate governance system in the RBs is mainly a rational western model recommended by the World Bank and implemented by the Central bank of Ghana. Under this model corporate governance*

Corporate Governance in Less Developed and Emerging Economies
Research in Accounting in Emerging Economies, Volume 8, 311–333
Copyright © 2008 by Emerald Group Publishing Limited
All rights of reproduction in any form reserved
ISSN: 1479-3563/doi:10.1016/S1479-3563(08)08011-0

is expected to be maintained externally through regulatory agencies (the Central Bank of Ghana and the Association of Rural Banks) and internally through the respective Boards of Directors. However, we observe that because of the locations and ownerships of these banks, board appointments and decisions are often embedded in local political and social relations. This affects the independence of the boards and impacts on their role in maintaining corporate governance.

Research limitations/implications – *We argue that any attempt to design corporate governance systems in these banks without taking these social and political factors into consideration is likely to lead to failure. This is particularly important given that the World Bank and other international donors are continuously proposing rational western models of governance to institutions in the developing world, such as the RBs. Given that these organizations operate under different sets of environmental conditions, there is likely to be differences between the actual and the idealized corporate governance systems.*

Originality/value of paper – *The study is important because of the role the rural banks play in the socio-economic development of Ghana. Several other developing countries have established similar institutions to support the development of the informal sector through the provision of microcredit. The research will contribute to the design of appropriate corporate governance systems so as to improve the overall contributions of these institutions.*

1. INTRODUCTION

This paper examines the internal and external mechanisms through which corporate governance is maintained in Rural Banks (RBs) in Ghana. The RBs are unit banks owned by members of the rural community through the purchase of shares and are licensed to provide financial intermediation in rural areas (Addeah, 1989). These banks are important in the socio-economic development of Ghana, as over 60% of the population live in rural areas. The majority of these people are engaged in agricultural activities, which contribute over 40% of the country's GDP and over 60% of employment (Ameyaw, 2001). The RBs play a significant role in the government's poverty alleviation program through the provision of credit to small-scale farmers, fishermen, merchants, industrialists and cooperative farmers. They support development projects and provide employment opportunities in rural areas. The RBs have contributed to improvements in banking culture, access to financial services and household consumption patterns in rural Ghana (Gallardo, 2002; Asiedu-Mante, 2001).

Despite their importance, a significant number of the RBs have been saddled with poor asset quality, unsound banking practices and non-payment of dividends. This has resulted in the closure of some RBs over the years. The lack of effective corporate governance systems has consistently been identified as a major obstacle to the growth and survival of the RBs (Asiedu-Mante, 2001; Hutchful, 2002; Daily Graphic, 2004). As a result, several attempts have been made in the past by the World Bank, other international donors and domestic policy-makers to strengthen the corporate governance systems of these banks (Steel & Andah, 2003). The corporate governance models recommended are largely based on the western models. Under the western models, corporate governance is maintained externally through regulatory agencies such as the Security Exchange Commissions (SEC), Stock Exchanges and the courts of law and internally through the board of directors (OECD, 1999; Monks & Minow, 2004). The board of directors is given a central role in corporate governance, as it is the link between the internal institution of governance and the external institution for governance (Salacuse, 2002; Cadbury, 2002).

The appropriateness of western models of corporate governance to Less Developed Countries (LDCs) has recently been questioned on the grounds that they may be in conflict with the traditional cultures and values pertaining to LDCs (Rossouw, 2005; Qu & Leung, 2006; Uddin & Choudhury, 2008). The RBs are largely located in rural areas of Ghana, with a strong sense of traditional cultures and values. There is evidence to suggest that these traditional cultures and their associated governance systems are different from those imported from the west (Odotei & Awedoba, 2006; Alhassan, 2006; Addo-Fening, 2006). These traditional forms of governance, which evolved out of the history, tradition and culture of the people, rely on the chiefs and the community to enforce accountability. A recent IDRC study on Ghana (IDRC, 2007) reported that: "The advent of colonial rule introduced western forms of governance that, today, with their accompanying political and administrative structures, dominate at the national and regional levels. However, at the district and community levels they share the responsibility of governance with traditional authority, mainly that of the Chiefs. In rural communities, for example, inadequate infrastructure and poverty hamper access to modern or state agencies of security, justice and health".[1]

Given that these banks are located in the rural communities and owned by members of these communities, we wonder how the western systems of corporate governance would function in these institutions. Recent attempts to understand corporate governance systems in LDCs have largely focused on big companies, mostly located in major cities (Ow-Yong & Guan, 2000; Yakasai, 2001, Hussain & Mallin, 2002; Rabelo & Vasconcelos, 2002; Ahunwan, 2002; Vaughn & Ryan, 2006; Krambia-Kapardis & Psaros, 2006; Tsamenyi, Enninful-Adu, & Onumah, 2007; Okike, 2007). As a result, our understanding of how corporate governance operates in smaller organizations, especially those located in areas where traditional culture dominates, is limited. This paper addresses this limitation by exploring the corporate governance systems of rural banks in Ghana. By examining the actual corporate governance systems in the banks the paper assesses the extent to which the recommended western models of corporate governance are applicable to these institutions.

The remainder of the paper is structured as follows. In the next section, we present the approach used in gathering the data for the study. This is followed by a discussion of the evolution and performance of the RBs. This section is also necessary to understand the context of the banks and how this is likely to influence the design and operations of the corporate governance systems. After this, we discuss the external corporate governance mechanisms of the banks. This is essential to understand the various external regulatory regimes of corporate governance in the banks. The results of the case study are presented following this. This is crucial to understand how the corporate governance systems operate in practice in the studied banks. The final section provides some concluding comments.

2. RESEARCH METHODS

Data for the study were gathered from two main sources. First, we reviewed various internal and external documents to understand the history, regulatory environment, operations and performance of the RBs. Documents reviewed included the governmental act establishing the RBs, Bank of Ghana (BOG) regulations and monitoring reports, minutes of board meetings and various annual reports of the RBs.

Second, to understand the role of the boards in corporate governance decisions, we conducted semi-structured interviews with the rural bank managers of nine RBs in 2004. The rural bank managers are effectively the CEOs of these banks. For the purpose of confidentiality, the banks are hypothetically referred to as RB1, RB2 ... RB9. Before the interviews, letters were sent to the BOG, the Association of Rural Banks (ARB) and the Bank Managers requesting assistance in the research, in response to which the Bank of Ghana assisted with a list of RBs in the country. The ARB supplied the dates for the Annual General Meetings of the RBs to enable the researcher to contact the Rural Bank Managers and arrange interviews at these meetings.

To ensure adequate geographical coverage, the RBs were selected from the three major economic and geographical zones of the country, namely the northern, central and coastal zones, to capture any differences that may emerge as a result of geographical differences. Only RBs that were more than five years old and as such had well-developed boards were studied. The sample size was limited to nine to allow in-depth study of the banks.

The semi-structured interviews with each bank manager lasted approximately 2 h. The interviewees were allowed to express themselves freely during the interviews and in so doing brought out some important issues that had not been captured by the original interview guide that we designed for the study. In view of such important observations, the interview guide was updated after each interview to enable those new issues to be captured in subsequent interviews. The interviews were tape recorded and subsequently transcribed and common themes identified through pattern matching (see for instance, Yin, 2002). The pattern matching enabled us to systematically identify and compare the themes that emerged from the interviews. For example, common themes such as local politics, social relations, lack of education, lack of incentives, ineffectiveness of the board, etc. were identified. These were identified based on the frequencies of these terms.

3. THE EVOLUTION AND PERFORMANCE OF RBs IN GHANA

The RBs were set up because of the failure of the traditional banks to provide banking services to the rural community. In other words, financial support in the rural areas has largely been problematic, despite the contribution made by the rural sector to the socio-economic development of the country. Over the years, the few commercial banks that originally had branches in the rural areas have closed these branches due to low profitability and the perceived risk of rural financing. Though the

Agricultural Development Bank was later established by the government to support rural finance, it failed in this role, as it was unable to tailor its programs to suit the rural community in the area of lending to smallholders and peasant farmers (Addeah, 1989; Gallardo, 2002; Ameyaw, 2001). To resolve the problems of low and inadequate rural finance, the BOG initiated the Rural Banking System in 1976 to support saving mobilization and credit for rural economic and social development.

The primary objectives of RBs are to mobilize all available savings within the catchment area, extend credit to rural areas and act as catalysts for rural development by identifying and promoting rural development projects (Gallardo, 2002; Asiedu-Mante, 2001). RBs operate as commercial banks under the Banking Law, except that they cannot undertake foreign exchange operations. Their clientele is drawn from their local catchment areas, and with some collaboration with NGOs, who use microfinance methodologies, they are able to reach the rural communities.

Owing to the low level of income in the rural areas, when the RB scheme started, the BOG permitted banks to be established with as little as US $43,000 capital, provided this amount was raised from the community that the bank was to serve (Steel & Andah, 2003). This amount was based on the start-up needs for expenditure such as fixed assets and the rental of bank premises. The BOG then provided the working capital requirements for the initial six months as preference shares. The acquisition of preference shares, apart from providing financial support for the RB, was also a means of motivating the rural community in which the RB was located to purchase shares in it. The BOG also had a representative on the board of any bank to which it contributed working capital. This enables the BOG to provide guidance on the bank's operations (Ameyaw, 2001). The BOG stopped providing this working capital in 1994 after it decided that the shareholders of the RBs should bear the full cost of the banks' capitalization (Steel & Andah, 2003). The BOG also used to provide services such as cheque clearing and purchase of government securities to the RBs (Asiedu-Mante, 2001). However, the Apex Bank (which is discussed later in the paper) has now assumed responsibilities for these services.

There was a rapid expansion in the number of RBs in the 1980s as a result of the government's decision to introduce a cheque payment system for cocoa farmers. To encourage banking in the rural areas and also to control the fraudulent activities of cocoa purchasing officers, the government introduced a new cheque payment system called the "Akuafo cheque". All cocoa purchasing officers were mandated by law to pay the farmers using "Akuafo" cheques. The creation of these cheques, however, brought difficulties to the farmers in selling their crops because they had to travel long distances to the cities and spend days at banks to cash their cocoa cheques because of the small number of banking outlets in the rural areas. This condition generated a high demand for rural banking services, to the extent that in the 1980s, a number of new RBs and agencies were hurriedly opened to help service areas without banking facilities. These banks began to encounter a number of difficulties and poor financial performance due to a combination of factors, namely rapid inflation, currency depreciation, economic decline, mismanagement of funds and weak supervision by the BOG. The conditions of the banks were so serious that when bank classification was started in 1992, only 23 of the 123 RBs qualified as "satisfactory" (see Addo, 1998).

Owing to the precarious situation of the RBs, the World Bank provided assistance in re-capitalization and capacity building under its Rural Finance Project between 1990 and 1994, which resulted in half of the RBs achieving "satisfactory" status by 1996. In 1998, the number of RBs increased to 133. This number, however, fell to 110 in 1999 as a result of the closure of 23 distressed RBs, which were insolvent because they could not meet the withdrawals of depositors. In that same year, the BOG commissioned one more RB. Since then, five more RBs have been added, bringing the number to 116 at the close of 2004.

4. EXTERNAL CORPORATE GOVERNANCE MECHANISMS OF THE RBs

4.1. Central Bank Regulation

RBs are public companies and as such are required to be registered under the companies' code 1963 (Act 179) and granted licenses to do banking by the central bank. An application for an RB license is made to the BOG by the community requiring the RB.[2] The application should be accompanied by a certified copy of the regulations or other instruments relating to the proposed RB; particulars of directors or persons concerned with the management of the RB; a feasibility report, including a business plan and financial projections for the first five years; and other information including certified assets and liabilities, operating policies and manuals that the BOG may require. If the BOG is satisfied with the information provided, it issues the banking license under the Provisional National Defence Council (PNDC) law 225 to enable the new RB to begin business.

The banking law (1989) (which was passed as part of the banking sector reforms) prescribes that each bank operating in Ghana (including the RBs) must maintain capital adequacy of 6% of its adjusted assets (Asiedu-Mante, 1998). Before the 1989 banking law, the capital adequacy was 5% of total mobilized resources. In terms of liquidity reserve requirements, the BOG regulations require every deposit-taking institution to maintain a proportion of deposits in the form of liquidity reserves made upon primary reserves in the form of cash and balances with other banks and secondary reserves in the form of government and BOG bills, bonds and stocks. In 1996, the primary reserve remained at 10%. The BOG raised the secondary reserve requirement from 20% to 52% as part of the program to improve the solvency of RBs. This directive punished stronger banks, because it limited their capacity to lend, and as such in 2002 the reserve requirements were lowered and varied in accordance with a classification system based on level of loan recovery (Steel & Andah, 2003).

Steel and Andah (2003) identified three additional prudential regulations that apply to RBs. These are: (i) RBs are prohibited from paying dividend for 10 years after commencing business; (ii) RBs are to use the cooperative principle of one shareholder-one vote, irrespective of the number of shares owned and (iii) prior approval from the BOG is required for loans of 2 million Cedis (US$222) or above to a single party, as well as for loans to RB directors or companies in which they have special interest.

BOG monitoring involves both off-site supervision and on-site examination. The off-site supervision entails the review of compliance with seven prudential returns (see Table 1), which the banks are expected to submit to the BOG at varying intervals.

The BOG Supervision Department (BSD) evaluates the performance of the RBs by determining the accuracy and reliability of returns submitted. Through these returns, the BOG is able to monitor the performance of the RBs and ensure that early warnings are picked up by the bank and corrective measures are taken. As a follow-up on the reliability of returns submitted by the RBs, the BSD undertakes on-site examinations, through which it is able to obtain primary data and records. The supervisor is able to obtain clarification from the management of the RB on issues raised in the prudential returns. The examination normally covers: (i) major developments such as board composition, management, agency operations, acquisition of fixed assets and shareholding since the last board meeting; (ii) performance: insolvency and capital adequacy; (iii) asset/portfolio

Table 1. Prudential Returns to BOG.

From	Type	Frequency	Time Limit
BSD 1R	Liquidity return	Weekly	9 days
BSD 2R	Statement of assets and liabilities	Monthly	21 days
BSD 3R	Large exposures-advances and deposits	Monthly	21 days
BSD 4R	Sectoral distribution of credits	Quarterly	21 days
BSD 5R	Capital adequacy ratio	Monthly	21 days
BSD 7R	Advances subject to adverse classification and ageing analysis	Quarterly	21 days
BSD 7R	Positions of facilities extended to directors, officers	Half yearly	2 months

Source: Association of Rural Banks (2002).

quality, which comprises the state of assets, non-performing loans and changes in provisions; (iv) liquidity; compliance status; (v) earnings: adjusted profit and loss and profitability in terms of Return on Assets and Return on Equity; (vi) management; adherence to supervisory issues and regulations and (vii) systems control: risk management and internal control.

A diagnostic study of the RBs sponsored by the World Bank under the Rural Finance Project in 1989 identified the principal operational problems faced by the banks as inadequate capabilities in terms of financial planning and budgeting; weak accounting and management information systems; weak internal control system and fraud and malpractices by staff and some top management (Ameyaw, 2001).

The BOG adopted several measures to address the above problems. To minimize corruption, for instance, the BOG created a pool of managers with relevant skills and practical experience to relieve RB managers who were due to go on their annual leave. Prior to this, a significant number of RB managers had been unable to go on leave, because there were no other managers to relieve them, and this was identified as contributing to fraud and malpractice. To ensure that RBs had the requisite human resources, the BOG directed that recruitment should be based on professional competence, integrity, commitment and loyalty. The BOG directive requested that under no circumstances should an RB employ anyone who had been dismissed from a previous position, and that appropriate references should be sought before all appointments (Asiedu-Mante, 2001). As the majority of the members of the boards of the RBs were judged to lack the expertise to formulate sound and effective policies and execute the boards' monitoring and service roles, the BOG now requires that some of the members of the board should have minimum educational qualifications, professional experience and special expertise (Asiedu-Mante, 2001). At least one of the directors of an RB must be an experienced banker, accountant or lawyer to give the necessary support to the formulation of the bank's strategies and policies. RBs should ensure that budgets are prepared and approved by the board before the beginning of any financial year. The budget should be compared to the actual performance at least once a quarter. Any RB in distress is also required by law to inform the BOG promptly.

4.2. The Association of Rural Banks

Another external monitoring of the RBs comes from the Association of Rural Banks (ARB), which was founded in 1981 as an NGO with voluntary membership, starting with 29 members and reaching 115 at the end of 2001. The association was formed out of the need to promote and strengthen the rural banking concept through advocacy and training. Under the Rural Finance Project, financed with World Bank/International Development Association (IDA) credit in 1991 and with assistance from Danish International Development Agency (DANIDA), the ARB trained 2,341 directors and 2,559 staff members of the RBs in the general areas of governance, leadership, management and operations (Osei-Bonsu, 1998). The ARB has no statutory authority and influences its members through persuasion and training seminars. It will remain an NGO, concentrating on advocacy goals in promoting the rural banking system and maintaining the rural banking network of directors and managers.

One of the achievements of the ARB is the establishment of the ARB-Apex Bank, a proposal supported by the BOG, IDA and DANIDA. The ARB-Apex Bank is a licensed banking institution exclusively owned by the RBs and restricted to servicing them. It was agreed that each RB would contribute 20 million Cedis (USD, 2,200 approximately) to the ARB-Apex Bank, which started operation in July 2002 with initial capital of 2.1 billion Cedis (US$233,000 approximately) contributed by 39 RBs (Steel & Andah, 2003). A significant number of RBs were unable to make the required contribution because this would have brought their capital adequacy below the 6% limit. These RBs were subsequently given ten years to make their contributions.

The ARB-Apex Bank provides specialized services to the RBs, including clearing of cheques, training of both staff and directors, conducting inspections to strengthen operations and internal controls, sourcing domestic and foreign credit for on-lending and instituting deposit insurance schemes to cover depositors. The BOG ceased its cheque clearing services for RBs in 1992, due to abuse by some RBs, and one of the key reasons for the establishment of the ARB-Apex Bank was to take over this role.

5. THE CASE STUDY

Earlier in the paper we identified that rational western models of corporate governance have been implemented in the RBs. We argued that these models place a significant responsibility in the hands of the directors to maintain corporate governance. This section relies mainly on the interviews with the bank managers of the nine RBs to examine how the corporate governance systems operate in practice in these institutions. This analysis is important for us to compare the actual with the idealized corporate governance systems based on the rational western models. Among the issues examined are the qualification, appointments and the roles of the directors.

5.1. Background of the Nine RBs Studied

The nine banks we studied have been in operation for between 6 and 23 years. The average number of employees is 40, with the largest bank employing 109 and the smallest bank employing 16 members of staff. All the banks have agencies and cash mobilization centers.[3] The average number of these agencies is four per bank, with the lowest being one and the highest six.

The managers we interviewed all indicated to us that as the banks are established in rural areas to meet the developmental need of the community, their focus is broader than the narrow goal of profit maximization. According to the manager of RB1, "the board is more focused on community development than creating value for shareholders. The board is always anxious to come out with projects that will benefit the community rather than the individual shareholders".

Table 2 below provides some background information on the nine RBs.

Over the years, financial performance has improved in all the banks in our study. For example, between 2002 and 2003, operating profit increased by 164% and 107% in RB5 and RB6, respectively. BOG regulations prohibit RBs from paying dividends within the first 10 years of their operations. This is necessary to ensure that the banks accumulate enough capital to enable

Table 2. Background Information on the Studied RBs.

RB	No. of Years in Operation	No. of Employees	Profit (Cedis Millions)[a]		No. of Board Members	Directors Allowance per Meeting (Cedis'000)
			2002	2003		
RB1	23	24	340	501	7	120–150
RB2	18	32	149	349	6	200–400
RB3	22	30	n/a	535	5	200–220
RB4	21	29	n/a	n/a	7	n/a
RB5	21	16	80	211	8	200
RB6	17	60	1,500	3,100	11	200–300
RB7	21	109	n/a	1,900	9	350–400
RB8	6	20	n/a	109	9	100–150
RB9	20	n/a	246	318	8	120–150

[a]The Cedi is the currency of Ghana. The exchange rate of the Cedi to the US$ at the end of 2004 was approximately US$1 = 9,000 Cedis. This rate is used to convert the local currency into the US dollar throughout the paper.

them to grow and contribute to the development of the community. With the exception of one bank, all of the banks in our study have met this minimum 10-year requirement (see Table 2). Despite this, some have not been able to pay dividends due to low liquidity. Even among those that have paid dividends, the dividend rate has been considered low. Some RBs have also used the argument that their primary objective is to promote community development rather than shareholder value creation to justify the non-payment or low payment of dividends. The manager of RB4 supported this argument in the following context: "Despite the fact that the bank has been in operation for nearly 20 years, its focus is on the community and not shareholders, and as such it does not dwell so much on dividend payment".

5.2. Qualifications and Roles of the Board Members

The BOG regulations set the minimum board size as 5 and the maximum as 11 for all RBs (ARB, 1997). The 9 RBs in our study have complied with this requirement, as the board sizes varied between 5 and 11. The average age of the board members is 52.6 years. The youngest board member is 48 years old and the oldest is 80. In nearly all the banks studied, the oldest member of the board is the chairman. The manager in RB3 explained the reason for this: "In the Ghanaian society, there is respect for age. This is the reason why you see the oldest member of the board as the chairman". In the majority of the banks, the directors have been on the board for as long as these banks have been in existence. In RB3, for instance, the board chairman was one of the founders of the bank and has served as chairman since the formation of the bank over 20 years ago. It has been pointed out to us by some of the interviewees that while this ensures continuity, a downside is that some directors have stayed on the boards despite under-performance. This was reiterated by the manager of RB5: "One of the reasons for directors staying on for so long is that there is no limit to the number of times a director is subject to re-election after completing each term. As a result, some directors tend to hang onto their positions even if they are not performing well".

A common problem that emerged in all the banks studied is the lack of qualified professionals on the boards. This has been identified by the interviewees as hindering the role of the boards in maintaining effective corporate governance. While the BOG regulation requires that boards should have a significant number of professionals with adequate under-standing of finance and banking, we found that board members are largely teachers, farmers or retired civil servants who have no knowledge of the operation of the banking industry. In RB7, the manager noted that: "The fact that some of the members of the board are not able to understand and appreciate financial statements impedes their monitoring and service role on the board".

The bank managers often become the principal technical consultants to the boards on financial issues. For example, the manager of RB3 indicated that he has to explain technical issues to the members of the board during board meetings because most of the directors are not familiar with the banking business. However, he did recognize the power of the directors: "Though I have better knowledge than most board members, I sometimes seek advice from them because they have the power".

The smallest bank in our sample (RB8) has no professionals on its board and has been one of the poorest performing banks in the country. Nearly all the banks we studied organize little or nothing in the way of training for their board members. Apart from the training program offered by the ARB that we reported earlier, only one of the nine banks in our study had organized a training program for its board members. This was RB7, which had organized a course on corporate governance for its board members in 2003.

The BOG is very concerned about the lack of qualified people on the boards of RBs: hence the law requiring that all boards should have at least one professional member. The BOG has in the past intervened to replace the boards of some RBs. At the time of study, the board of RB2 was replaced with an interim board appointed by the BOG. The original board was replaced because its members were judged to have low educational backgrounds and inadequate knowledge of banking, and as a result could not perform satisfactorily. When the interim board took over, they found that controls were either weak or non-existent. To address this problem, the interim board implemented a number of control measures, including policies on deposit mobilization, investments and expenditure.

Similarly, the first board of RB4 was dismissed by the BOG for being unqualified and grossly mismanaging the bank. The manager we interviewed at RB4 noted that: "The bank became distressed and as such the BOG intervened and formed an interim board to take over from the original board. This interim board was able to mobilize more people to acquire shares in the bank, thereby reviving the bank". Also, RB9 has had three previous boards replaced by the BOG for persistent poor performance.

To comply with BOG requirements, eight of the RBs have various standing committees. The size of these committees varies between three and five members. The most common of these committees are the Local Board committee, Loans Committee, Finance and Audit Committee and Planning and Budget Committee. In addition to the above committees, one bank has a Property Committee (responsible for safeguarding the bank's assets) and a Protocol Committee (responsible for organizing Annual General Meetings). The discussions with the managers suggest that apart from the Loans and Finance and Audit Committees, the other committees are inactive. In RB9, for instance, the reason for the inactivity of the various committees has been explained by the manager as follows: "Most of our committees are not functioning because members of these committees live over 60 miles away from the bank, and because of the rural environment, it is quite difficult to make such journeys to the bank frequently". The bank in our sample that did not have any standing committees had abolished all committees a few years ago when individual committees were found to be abusing their power by granting bad loans.

BOG regulations require boards to meet at least once a month. Eight of the banks we studied have monthly board meetings. Only RB1 holds board meetings every other month, as its directors are not available for monthly meetings. In between the board meetings, some banks use committees to handle issues like loans that need urgent attention. The decisions of these committees are subject to ratification by the main board. The loans committees of the majority of the banks, for instance, are made up of directors who live in the community and can be available whenever the bank needs them, especially for approving loan applications. The manager of RB6 noted that: "We make sure that the majority of the members of our loans committee live in the area. This is important so that they can be called upon anytime they are needed".

In all the banks, materials for board meetings are circulated to board members between one and two weeks before board meetings. On average, board meetings last 6.2 h, with the longest being 8 and the shortest 5 h. Asked how the time of the board is spent at meetings, all the respondents indicated that their boards review previous minutes and prudential returns, review loan reports and approve application for loans.

Nearly all the managers interviewed pointed out that they were dissatisfied with board meetings. Some interviewees indicated that sometimes board meetings are not focused and that most of the board members do not contribute during deliberations due to their inadequate banking/finance knowledge. This was highlighted by the manager of RB9: "A major problem we have is the poor contributions to discussions at board meetings due to the fact that several of our directors have no knowledge in the business of banking". Similarly, the manager of RB1 noted that: "The members who do not have economics, finance or banking background do not normally contribute much to board discussions. Because the board chairman is very strict other members of the board are afraid to influence bank policies". Some managers also suggested that sometimes unnecessary time is spent discussing matters like applications for loans, staff problems and other operational issues instead of focusing on major strategic and financial statements and loan recoveries.

Most local professionals who live in the big cities are unwilling to take on board membership because of low sitting allowances. The manager of RB4 noted that: "The problem the bank has with the appointment of directors is that the catchment areas do not contain people with the requisite qualifications and some of those who qualify are not ready to serve on the board for various reasons". All the managers we interviewed indicated that their board members have regularly complained about the low sitting allowances. Board members are paid sitting allowances ranging from 120,000 to 400,000 Cedis (US$13 to US$44) per meeting (see Table 2). This amount is considered too low to motivate board members to attend meetings, especially given that a significant number of them live and work outside the catchment areas. In RB1, it was pointed out to us during the study that shareholders who have the power to fix directors' fees do not do so with the performance of the bank in mind. Since most of them have poor literacy and are not familiar with banking, they perceive board directorship as a lucrative enterprise, and as such, they are more concerned with the amount they want to share as dividend than the amount taken by the directors as fees.

In RB2, it was reported that there have been times when some bank employees have viewed the director as interfering or probing too much into their work, especially when they visit the agencies. Some of the directors compare their salaries with those of the bank staff and think the bank employees are being overpaid. If employees are sharing bonuses, the directors sometimes become concerned, since they do not have such facilities at their work.

The manager of RB8 indicated that shareholders are mandated to approve the directors' fees, and since most of them have poor literacy, they think that paying a director 100,000 Cedis (US$11) per sitting is too much; as such, it is always difficult for them to accept any increment in fees. In RB3, the manager noted that the bank also gives 'Christmas gifts' to board members as an appreciation of their contribution during the year.

5.3. Why Social and Political Relations are Important in Understanding Corporate Governance in the RBs

It has been argued that traditional rational models of corporate governance may be insufficient in preventing corporate failure because these models ignore social and political behavior, inherent in organizations (Marnet, 2007). This argument is central to our understanding of the corporate governance practices of the RBs. The RBs are located mainly in the rural areas of Ghana where traditional cultural values are considered very important (Odotei & Awedoba 2006; Alhassan, 2006; Addo-Fening, 2006). Social and political relations were identified by the managers we interviewed as being implicated in both board appointments and the subsequent decision-making in the banks. In terms of board appointments, the practice in the banks is that a prospective board member must first be nominated by a shareholder, and the existing board members must accept his/her application before the candidate can contest the board election. The candidate then has to campaign to convince the shareholders before and during the AGM of what he/she is capable of doing on the board. It was pointed out to us that the nomination, campaign and election process is highly politicized, with prospective candidates having to lobby shareholders, existing directors and sometimes influential community leaders. This process discourages a significant number of professionals who do not want to be embroiled in the political process.

The managers we spoke to all indicated that while they are aware of these politics, they try as much as possible to avoid them. The manager of RB3 noted that: "I do not want to get involved in the process of election of any director, since if a director gets to know that I am campaigning against him/ her, I would be in trouble". He gave an instance where a director was removed by the AGM because of poor performance and he, the bank manager, was accused of being the one who had engineered the action taken by the shareholders. This nearly cost him his job. One consequence of the politics, as observed by the manager of RB6, is that eligible and qualified shareholders are very often discouraged from seeking election to board membership, as they do not want to be embroiled in this political process.

In all the banks we studied, every board member comes from the particular community in which the bank is located, although some members may be residing outside that community, for example working in the big cities. The manager of RB1 noted that: "The shareholders do not look at the academic qualifications of candidates: instead, they look at whether the person comes from the community, and whether he/she is in gainful employment and is respected". He further explains that: "Shareholders are not willing to appoint anyone who is not their son to the board to take care of their investments". In effect, shareholders have more confidence in someone who comes from the same community and speaks the same language than someone whom they perceive as alien.

One major problem of appointing only people who come from the community to boards is that some qualified people who could bring a lot of experience and knowledge to board decisions are not appointed, as explained by the manager of RB8: "The problem with the composition of the board is that if one does not come from the community, one will not be appointed as a director, despite the fact that one has the qualifications and experience to serve as a director".

The manager in RB3 reiterated this: "Some directors are not capable, due to their working and educational background. I would like to have directors with business or educational backgrounds, but the shareholders who elect them are not particular about these issues". The manager of RB1 commented that: "Prominent community leaders do not accept the fact that people who have played a considerable role in the establishment of the bank and are shareholders should be excluded from board membership because they have poor literacy in banking or finance. In my view, these people hardly make any impact when they are on the board".

The manager of RB9 explained to us that: "When the bank was being established, the educated in the community did not show much interest in it because they live in the cities, and more to the point, some even are shunning board membership because they do not want to mix with the 'uneducated' guys on the board, who always bring local politics to board meetings. In contrast, the locals were very interested and offered themselves for directorship because it serves as a status symbol". The manager further explained that professionals do not buy shares in the bank because of the non-payment of dividends and those professionals who now want to join the board are finding it difficult because the locals are not ready to accept them.

Social and political relations extend beyond board appointments and are also embedded in the day-to-day management of the banks. Some of the bank managers complained that some of the directors, in their zeal not to be seen as not performing their roles, literally involve themselves in the day-to-day operations of the bank, contrary to what the law requires of them as directors or governors. The manager of RB3 noted that the chairman of the finance committee comes to the bank twice a month and sometimes asks the internal control office to conduct investigations without the knowledge of the bank manager. He stated that: "All that you will know is that a copy of the report has been given to you". He recounted the case of one particular director who visits the bank and sits in the bank manager's office, inconveniencing customers who want to come in and conduct confidential business with him. He concluded: "I am not able to tell the director to leave because he will think that I don't respect him. In the end, I have to accommodate him because I will not do anything that will lead to my dismissal". The manager of RB1 described how "six years ago, the bank manager resigned because the board complained that he was disrespectful and instead of implementing its policies he was rather making his own policies".

Board members are under political pressure to satisfy various interest groups, given that the process of elections to board membership is highly politicized, as explained earlier in this section. Because of this, some board members find it difficult to make decisions independent of the shareholders who elected them. In addition, the influence of the chiefs and community leaders makes it difficult for the boards to make decisions that do not satisfy the interests of these groups. The manager of RB1 observed that: "One problem with the board membership of this bank is that because virtually everybody comes from the same area, there are certain occasions when various pressure groups, clans etc in the community, who think their interest are not being represented on the board, lobby to get their own people, who at times may not even be able to read and write, elected onto the board".

In RB8, the manager identified some of the problems created by the directors, namely that some loan applicants pass their requests through the directors, in the hope that they will be approved even though they know very well that they have not met the conditions. The loan seekers think some directors have the power to grant them loans. According to the manager of the bank, the loan applicants sometimes go to the directors' houses to pursue their loans.

6. CONCLUDING COMMENTS

This paper set out to explore the corporate governance systems of the RBs in Ghana. The RBs are important in the socio-economic development of Ghana, as they provide banking and financial services to the rural areas that the traditional commercial banks have shunned. They play an important role in the government's poverty alleviation strategy. The poor performance and failure of some of these banks over the years have led to the call for improvements in their corporate governance systems. As a result, rational western corporate governance models (Marnet, 2007) were recommended by western institutions such as the World Bank and implemented by the Central Bank of Ghana in the RBs. Under these rational western models, corporate governance is maintained externally through the central bank and the association of rural banks and internally through the boards of directors of the respective banks. The boards are particularly important and are given the power to maintain corporate governance because they provide the link between the internal institution of governance and the external institution for governance (Salacuse, 2002; Cadbury, 2002). It is assumed that the recommended corporate governance systems will improve the accountability and performance of the RBs. The paper was therefore motivated by the need to understand how these rational western corporate governance models operate in environments and organizations that have different character-istics to those that the systems were originally designed for.

Our findings suggest that the design and implementation of the corporate governance systems largely ignore the social and political contexts of the banks. This hindered the effectiveness of the corporate governance systems. Social and political factors are important in understanding how the RBs operate and are managed. In particular, we have demonstrated that appointments and roles of the boards are embedded in local political and social relations. Shareholders only appoint people from the catchment area to serve on boards, even if these people do not have the necessary qualifications and experience. Shareholders trust people from the same area, who speak the same language, to be more loyal and committed to the bank than people from outside the catchment area, no matter how qualified and experienced they are. It can be argued that loyalty supersedes any academic qualification or experience in the appointment of board members. The consequence of this is the lack of qualified people on the boards of the RBs. As we have reported in the paper, this has hindered the strategic and advisory roles of the boards. It has effectively reduced the roles of some boards to routine tasks such as reviewing loan applications. We also reported how board members were under political pressure to satisfy various interest groups in the community, sometimes even being approached at home for loan approvals. This questions the independence and effectiveness of the board (Salacuse, 2002; Cadbury, 2002; Monks & Minow, 2004).

Overall, our study calls for the design of corporate governance mechanism in LDCs in general and in these types of institutions in particular to go beyond the traditional rational western models and to incorporate social and political relations (Marnet, 2007, Uddin and Choudhury, 2008). As suggested by Rabelo and Vasconcelos (2002), the model of corporate governance in developing countries is likely to be different from that of developed countries, due to differences in contextual factors and the structural characteristics of developing countries. While we are not disputing the importance of rational western corporate governance systems to these organizations, we believe that the effectiveness of these systems can be enhanced when their design and implementation incorporate the social and political factors within which the organizations operate.

Social and political issues are imperative in the case of the RBs, as contribution to community development, rather than the traditional shareholder wealth maximization, was identified as the dominant objective of these institutions. Moreover, the rural nature of the environment means that traditional cultural values (Odotei & Awedoba 2006; Alhassan, 2006; Addo-Fening, 2006) permeate these institutions, and as a result, corporate governance systems based primarily on rational western models may miss these social and political issues (Williams, 2004; Marnet 2007). Such an approach will also answer calls for the behavioral aspects of corporate governance to be studied (Huse, 2005). This is particularly important because of the argument that corporate governance systems are socially constructed and as such understanding human behavior is vital for understanding how these systems are designed and operated (Marnet, 2007). In terms of future research, we encourage researchers to examine the extent to which local socio-cultural values and western corporate governance systems could achieve greater complementarity.

NOTES

1. http://www.idrc.ca/en/ev-115665-201-1-DO_TOPIC.html
2. The application is normally made by the community leaders or the District Assembly.
3. The law allows the RBs to operate small agencies and cash mobilization centers in areas that have demand for banking services but cannot support a full-fledged branch. These agencies and cash mobilization centers only provide limited banking services such as deposits and withdrawals.

REFERENCES

Addeah, K. (1989). *The law of rural banking in Ghana.* Accra, Ghana: Amanta Publications.
Addo, J. S. (1998). *A feasibility study and business plan for the establishment of an ARB Apex Bank.* Accra: Revised report for the Association of Rural Banks.
Addo-Fening, R. (2006). Chieftaincy and issues of good governance, accountability and development: A Case Study of Akyem Abuakwa Under Okyenhene Ofori Atta 1, 1912–1943. In: K. Odotei & Awedoba (Eds), *Chieftaincy in Ghana: Culture, governance and development.* Accra, Ghana: Sub-Saharan Publishers.
Ahunwan, B. (2002). Corporate governance in Nigeria. *Journal of Business Ethics, 37*(3), 269–287.
Alhassan, O. (2006). Traditional authorities and sustainable development: Chiefs and resource management in Ghana. In: K. Odotei & Awedoba (Eds), *Chieftaincy in Ghana: Culture, governance and development.* Accra, Ghana: Sub-Saharan Publishers.
Ameyaw, S. (2001). Bank of Ghana and the establishment of rural community bank network. *The Rural Banker* (1), 1–5.
Asiedu-Mante, E. (1998). Financial markets in Ghana. In: *Issues in central banking and bank distress.* Lagos: WAIFEM.
Asiedu-Mante, E. (2001). *Rural Banking in Ghana: Achievements and Prospects. A paper presented at the Financial Stability Institute/Bank of Ghana West and Central Africa Committee for Bank Supervisors Regional Seminar on Current supervisory Issues and Challenges.* Held on 19th February, GIMPA, Accra, and Ghana.
Association of Rural Banks (ARB). (1997). Roles and responsibilities of directors, board room procedures, Annual General Meetings, BSD Returns. Prepared by Association of Rural Banks in Collaboration with Danish International Development Association (Danida), Accra, Ghana.
Association of Rural Banks (ARB). (2002). Annual Report, Accra, Ghana, December.

Cadbury, A. (2002). *Corporate governance and chairmanship: A personal view*. Oxford, UK: Oxford University Press.

Daily Graphic. (2004). *Termination of appointment of managing director of Ghana commercial bank*. Accra, Ghana.

Gallardo, J. (2002). *A framework for regulating microfinance institutions: The Experience in Ghana and the Philippines*. Working Paper, The World Bank, Policy Research, Washington, DC.

Huse, M. (2005). Accountability and creating accountability: A framework for exploring behavioural perspectives of corporate governance. *British Journal of Management, 16*, S65–S79.

Hussain, S. H., & Mallin, C. (2002). Corporate governance in Bahrain. *Corporate Governance: An International Review, 10*(3), 197–210.

Hutchful, E. (2002). *Ghana's adjustment experience, the paradox of reform*. Accra, Ghana: United Nations Research Institute for Social Development, Woeli Publishing Services.

IDRC. (2007). ICTs and Traditional Governance in Ghana, The International Development Research Centre, Canada. Available at http://www.idrc.ca/en/ev-115665-201-1-DO_TO PIC.html

Krambia-Kapardis, M., & Psaros, J. (2006). The Implementation of corporate governance principles in an emerging economy: A critique of the situation in Cyprus. *Corporate Governance: An International Review, 14*(2), 126–139.

Marnet, O. (2007). History repeats itself: The failure of rational choice models in corporate governance. *Critical Perspectives on Accounting, 18*, 191–210.

Monks, R. A. G., & Minow, N. (2004). *Corporate governance* (3rd ed.). UK: Blackwell Publishing.

Odotei, K., & Awedoba, A. K. (Eds). (2006). Introduction. In: *Chieftaincy in Ghana: Culture, governance and development*. Accra, Ghana: Sub-Saharan Publishers.

OECD (Organisation for Economic Cooperation and Development). (1999). *OECD principles of corporate governance*. Paris: OECD.

Okike, E. N. (2007). Corporate governance in Nigeria: The status quo. *Corporate Governance: An International Review, 15*(2), 173–193.

Osei-Bonsu, E. (1998). *The state of rural banks in Ghana*. Paper prepared for the Association of Rural Bank Seminar, Accra, Ghana.

Ow-Yong, K., & Guan, C. K. (2000). Corporate governance codes: A comparison between Malaysia and the UK. *Corporate Governance: An International Review, 8*(2), 125–132.

Qu, W., & Leung, P. (2006). Cultural impact on Chinese corporate disclosure: A corporate governance perspective. *Managerial Auditing Journal, 21*(3), 241–264.

Rabelo, F. M., & Vasconcelos, F. C. (2002). Corporate governance in Brazil. *Journal of Business Ethics, 37*(3), 321–335.

Rossouw, G. J. (2005). Business ethics and corporate governance in Africa. *Business and Society, 44*(1), 94–106.

Salacuse, J. W. (2002). *Corporate governance in the UNECE region*. A Paper commissioned for the Economic Survey of Europe, 2003 No. 1. By the secretariat of the United Nations Economic Commission for Europe.

Steel, W. F., & Andah, D. O. (2003). *Rural and micro finance regulation in Ghana: Implication for development and performance of the industry*. Africa Region Working Paper 49.

Tsamenyi, M., Enninful-Adu, E., & Onumah, J. (2007). Disclosure and corporate governance in developing countries: Evidence from Ghana. *Managerial Auditing Journal, 22*(3), 319–334.

Uddin, S., & Choudhury, J. (2008). Rationality, traditionalism and the state of corporate governance mechanisms: Illustrations from a less developed country. *Accounting, Auditing and Accountability Journal, 27*(7), 1026–1051.

Vaughn, M., & Ryan, L. V. (2006). Corporate governance in South Africa: A bellwether for the continent? *Corporate Governance: An International Review, 14*(5), 504–512.

Williams, P. F. (2004). You reap what you sow: The ethical discourse of professional accounting. *Critical Perspectives on Accounting, 15*(6/7), 995–1001.

Yakasai, A. G. A. (2001). Corporate Governance in a Third World Country with Particular Reference to Nigeria. *Corporate Governance: An International Review, 9*(3), 238–253.

Yin, R. K. (2002). *Applications of case study research, 2nd edition.* Thousand Oaks, CA: Sage.

TOWARDS A THEORETICAL FRAMEWORK OF CORPORATE GOVERNANCE: PERSPECTIVES FROM SOUTHERN AFRICA

Esinath Ndiweni

ABSTRACT

Purpose – *The paper attempts to locate the debate on corporate governance in a social and cultural context.*

Methodology – *It draws on the traditional African philosophy of* ubuntu *and articulates how this might affect corporate governance frameworks. The paper utilises multiple methods that include interviews, a review of documents, and case studies. It analyses incidents from across Southern Africa that demonstrate how notions of* ubuntu *influence corporate practices.*

Findings – *The incidents in selected organisations reveal how multinational corporations are involved in the delivery of social welfare programmes to their employees and local communities. Such practices underscore the differences in perceptions about corporate social responsibility in the West and Southern Africa.*

Corporate Governance in Less Developed and Emerging Economies
Research in Accounting in Emerging Economies, Volume 8, 335–357
Copyright © 2008 by Emerald Group Publishing Limited
All rights of reproduction in any form reserved
ISSN: 1479-3563/doi:10.1016/S1479-3563(08)08012-2

Practical implications – *It highlights the implications of these practices for multinational corporations and auditors who do business in Southern Africa.*

Originality – *The paper argues that* ubuntu *informs corporate practices and influences perceptions on what constitutes* 'good' *corporate governance and ethics in Southern Africa. Finally, it proposes an alternative corporate governance framework informed by* ubuntu, *communitarianism, and stakeholder theories. Arguably, such a corporate governance framework will take into account the social and historical context of Southern Africa.*

Research limitations – *The proposed corporate governance framework might suit only those communities who subscribe to* ubuntu *values and communitarianism.*

1. INTRODUCTION

Globalisation has made it easier for multinational corporations to do business anywhere in the world (Ohmae, 1990; Yeung, 1998). However, this is not without problems due to differences in culture, including perspectives on how to do business. Less developed countries solicit foreign direct investment (FDI) from the developed world, yet they often have weak corporate governance structures and poor accounting systems (CACG, 1999; ADB, 2007). It is against this background that developed countries demand improvements in corporate governance if they are to increase investments in emerging economies (ADB, 2007). A common premise for corporate governance frameworks is a focus on the needs of financial capital markets. For developing countries with least developed financial capital markets 'good' corporate governance practices have been associated with an increase in FDI, if not being a pre-requisite (Markusen & Venables, 1999; Nocke & Yeaple, 2008).

However, coupling the notion of corporate governance with financial capital markets has led to a dominance of neo-classical economics, transactions cost, and agency theories. This has led to a narrow view on corporate governance focused on issues such as best practice for disclosure by listed companies (Cadbury Report, 1992); directors' remuneration (Greenbury Report, 1995); and the role of the board of directors, audit committees; and the effectiveness of non-executive directors (see Financial

Reporting Council, 2003; Higgs Report, 2003). These concerns have resonance in developed capitalist societies, but are yet to be experienced by less developed countries which are grappling with issues of poverty (Fényes & Campbell, 2003), inequitable distribution of resources (Laird, 2004), and sustainable development (Ward & Gaile, 2006). The latter are important issues for less developed economies when contrasted with Western perspectives, which privilege protection of investors in financial markets.

The aim of this paper is to propose a corporate governance framework, which takes into account the historical and social context of Southern Africa. The paper primarily seeks to answer the following question: how does *ubuntu* philosophy influence corporate governance practices in Southern Africa? I address this question through an interrogation of the social context through *ubuntu* and communitarian concepts. The paper utilises incidents from selected organisations to reveal how the social context influences practices, particularly those concerning corporate social responsibility. Through examples, the paper narrates how multinational corporations find themselves implicated in the delivery of social welfare programmes in their communities. It further explores the implication of these social welfare activities for corporate governance, accounting, and audit practices.

The paper comprises seven sections. The next section introduces the concept of corporate governance and demonstrates the fundamental links between it and the socio-economic environment. The third section sets out the theoretical framework that underlies the arguments of this paper, namely the African philosophy of *ubuntu*, communitarianism, and stakeholder theories. It uses selected concepts from these theories to analyse managerial and corporate governance practices in organisations. The argument in this paper is that an understanding of African philosophy, particularly, *ubuntu* may help managers of multinational corporations appreciate the expectations of the communities they serve. The fourth section presents the research methods employed followed by some empirical observations based on incidents from organisations across Southern Africa to demonstrate how the notions of *ubuntu* influence organisational practices. The discussion section highlights the implications of these practices for multinational corporations and auditors. The concluding section, proposes an alternative corporate governance framework modelled on a communitarian stakeholder theory. Such a corporate governance framework is intended to portray fairly the issues underlying corporate social responsibility in Southern Africa including its boundaries and implications for policy makers and governments.

2. CORPORATE GOVERNANCE: CONTEXT

'Good governance' has become a buzzword, yet, its definition is heavily influenced by the Anglo-Saxon model (Meisel, 2004). Corporate governance refers to 'the way a company is directed and controlled' (Cadbury Report, 1992; Rwegasira, 2000; DOH, 2001; Monks & Minow, 2004). However, this definition is problematic because it represents a narrow focus on business enterprises, furthermore it has its roots in the developed countries of the West; thus depicting Western thought on corporate governance (see Cadbury Report, 1992; Hampel Report, 1998; Turnbull Report, 1999; Higgs Report, 2003; OECD, 2004).

Initiatives on corporate governance for emerging, transitional, and developing economies have emanated from the World Bank, OECD (O'Sullivan, 1999), and the African Development Bank (ADB, 2007) and the King Report of South Africa, 1994 and 2002. The Commonwealth Association for Corporate Governance published 15 principles to guide conduct in both private and state-owned enterprises (CACG, 1999). Business responsibility is said to be no longer only about profitability but, rather, incorporates societal objectives and legitimate social concerns (CACG, 1999, p. 3). In Southern Africa, it has become increasingly difficult to separate the business from the community within which it is situated. I discuss this development later in this paper.

The main argument in this paper is that societies interrogate corporate governance issues from different perspectives, and that generally their notions of 'good' corporate governance are rooted in their socio-cultural political values, which might not bear any relationship to the inherited wisdom from the West. This difference in approach has implications for multinational corporations who invest in Southern Africa and for accounting and auditing regimes, which draw on Western ethical corporate codes of practice. Such Western codes have provided the basis for an international code of corporate governance and ethics (IFAC/CIMA, 2004), which often have clashed with non-western business values (see, for example, Versi, 2002; Begley & Boyd, 2003).

This paper adopts a broader view of corporate governance to interrogate practices in organisations. The King Report (1994, 2002) was the first to embrace such a broader concept of corporate governance in the Southern African region by introducing triple bottom line sustainability reporting integrating economic, social, and environmental performance. The Committee recognised that 'a proper balance needs to be achieved between freedom to manage, accountability, and the interests of different stakeholders' (King Report, 1994, p. 3).

Of interest in this paper is what shapes corporate governance practices in different parts of the world, and Southern Africa, in particular. Khoza and Adam (2005) discuss the power of governance in state-owned enterprises in South Africa and stress the importance of aligning corporate governance standards across the globe. Although this might appear to be, a useful tool for benchmarking, we know very little about the social values, which influences corporate governance practices in less developed countries.

This paper elaborates on the social responsibilities of corporations operating in Southern Africa. In native Southern African languages, there is no equivalent notion of corporate governance in a similar vein to the West. Understandably, so, since social and economic activities are organised differently in the associated societies. Governance could be viewed in the context of *ukubusa*,[1] that is, ruling by the King although this is qualified by the saying that *inkosi yinkosi ngabantu* (meaning that a king is a king because of his people) an implication that the King is a servant of the people or at their service. By extension, corporations exist because of the people and their communities. In other words, without people there will be no corporate organisations.

3. THEORETICAL FRAMEWORK

This paper departs from the dominant tradition based on neo-classical economics such as agency theory (Jensen & Meckling, 1976). Instead, it employs social theories to help develop a corporate governance framework that takes into account the historical, socio-cultural contexts of Southern Africa. Its main contribution is to offer new insights drawn from *ubuntu*, which is an African philosophy of the Bantu people who reside mainly in Southern Africa. I argue that *ubuntu* notions influence interactions between multinational corporations and their constituencies, and thus corporate governance.

3.1. African Philosophy of Ubuntu as Institutionalised Behaviours

Ubuntu is a broad African philosophy, which encapsulates a way of social life. Because it touches on all aspects of human lives, it is difficult to define precisely. Forster (2006) posits that it is the primary locus of African notions of human ontology and particularly human identity within the broad sphere. According to Louw (2001, p. 1) *ubuntu* means 'humanity', 'humanness' or even 'humaneness' and the maxim *umuntu ngumuntu ngabantu* (that is, 'a person is a person through other persons') articulates a basic respect and compassion for others (see also Shuttle, 1993, p. 46; Ramose, 1999, p. 49).

Broodryk (2002, p. 31) sums up other core values as

Humanness	Warmth, tolerance, understanding, peace, humanity
Caring	Empathy, sympathy, helpfulness, charity, friendliness
Sharing	Unconditional giving, redistribution, open-handedness
Respect	Commitment, dignity, obedience, order and humility
Compassion	Love, cohesion, informality, forgiveness, spontaneity

All the above are core attributes of *ubuntu*. Each is loaded with deeper meanings that demonstrate the practicalities of exuding *ubuntu*. In a video interview, Mandela (2006) summarised the essence of *ubuntu* as entailing the following: helpfulness, trust, respect, unselfishness, sharing, community, and caring for others. Some of these are similar to Christian values and Kantian notions of moral imperatives (Omari, 2008). It is against these traditional values that society's code of conduct is developed (Ambrose, 2007).

Parts of Southern Africa have institutionalised *ubuntu* values. For example, the South African government gazetted the principle of *ubuntu* as part of its social welfare policy as follows:

> The principle of caring for each other's well-being and a spirit of mutual support for each individual's humanity is ideally expressed through his or her relationship with others and theirs in turn through recognition of the individual's humanity. *Ubuntu* means that people are people through other people. It also acknowledges both the rights and responsibilities of every citizen in promoting individual and societal well-being. (The Government Gazette, 02/02/1996 No. 16943, paragraph 18)

The *ubuntu* concept contrasts with Western thought and reason in that the latter are often detached from culture, community, and natural environment. Under the traditional African view, people are interdependent and co-responsible for each other (Kwamwangamalu & Nkonko, 1999; du Toit, 2004). Recent literature, particularly from South Africa has elevated the concept of *ubuntu* and how it transmits itself through various aspects of life (see Mbigi, 1997, 2000; Roodt, 1997; Shoniwa, 2001; Mbeki, 2001; Nussbaum, 2003; Olinger, 2004).

Some aspects of this complex African philosophy underpins interactions in organisations. Society produces and reproduces rules and routines overtime and constantly modifies its values in the light of other influences (Barley & Tolbert, 1997; Burns & Scapens, 2000; Van Der Bly, 2005). Institutional theory encapsulates this process and posits that numerous aspects of formal organisational structure, policies, and procedures result from prevailing societal attitudes of what comprises acceptable practices and the views of important constituents (Scott, 1987; DiMaggio, 1991; Bealing, Dirsmith, & Fogarty, 1996). Barley and Tolbert (1997) state that organisations and individuals that populate them are suspended in a web of values, norms, rules, beliefs, and taken for granted assumptions, which are partially of their own making. Consequently, there is a reiterative production and reproduction of practices through interactions in organisation as actors draw from a common interpretive scheme. Arguably, *ubuntu* plays a role in shaping organisational practices among the Bantu communities.

Hamilton (1932, p. 84) defined an institution as 'a way of thought or action of some prevalence or permanence, embedded in the habits of a group or the customs of a people'. This definition captures the essence of the influence of *ubuntu*. Burns and Scapens (2000) assert that institutions impose form and social coherence upon human activity, through the production and reproduction of settled habits of thought and action. The institutionalisation process referred to here helps in the reproduction of social values of the Bantu people (Giddens, 1984). The paper refers to institutional theory in order to interpret the influences of *ubuntu* notions in Southern African societies, but also acknowledges that it is not the sole source of influence. Thus, an over-aching aim among African communities is that of achieving social harmony (DeWitt, 2007).

3.2. Communitarianism as a Cornerstone of Ubuntu

Another philosophical understanding that underpins *ubuntu* is communitarianism. Communitarians begin by positing a need to experience our lives as bound up with the good of communities out of which our identity is constituted (Bell, 2001, p. 9). Communitarianism loosely denotes the importance of community values under *ubuntu*. I suggest that communitarianism is a foundation cornerstone of *ubuntu* although it is a broader concept than *ubuntu*. Communitarianism is more of an ideology and is applicable to different societies across the world, rather than just Southern Africa. The key principle is that the interests of the individual are subordinate to that of the group. The Bantu people believe that by ensuring the good of the group, the benefits will flow to each individual member (see also Bell, 2001). Under communitarianism, Mokgoro (1997) suggests each individual realises that s/he is part of a group and that the group depends on their skills, inputs, labour, and loyalty in order to survive. For example, Etzion (1998, 2001) emphasises social responsibility and promoting policies meant to halt the erosion of communal life in the United States.

Furthermore, communitarians believe in democratic participation by all involved at all levels of society (Mokgoro, 1997). Such a development would arguably benefit corporate governance in organisations. This paper proposes a theoretical governance framework that is compatible with the values of *ubuntu*, thereby extending *ubuntu* values to corporations. Such a framework would take into account interests of different stakeholders. Although some corporations already consider contractual stakeholders such as shareholders, employees, suppliers, and customers (Woodward, Edwards, & Birkin, 1996), Stakeholder theory refers to all those affected by the activities of an organisation. In short, stakeholders are 'those groups without whose support the organisation would cease' (Freeman & Reed, 1983, p. 91). Thus, in Southern Africa local communities should also be incorporated (Charkham, 1992) as part of a communitarian stakeholder governance framework. The next section briefly describes the research methods used in this paper.

4. RESEARCH METHOD

The paper utilises multiple methods that include interviews, a review of documents, and case studies to gather evidence about possible influences of *ubuntu* on organisational practices, particularly concerning corporate governance. It gathered evidence from selected critical incidents across organisations in Southern Africa that reflected the influences of *ubuntu* on corporate practices. Interviews were restricted to organisations operating in Zimbabwe while other multiple sources such as case study materials, websites of organisations, magazines, newspaper articles, and academic publications, including unpublished dissertations, provide evidence of corporate practices in Botswana and South Africa. It was not practical to interview managers and employees outside Zimbabwe because at the time of the research I was resident in Zimbabwe. The purpose of the research is not to generalise the results but to highlight particular practices, which affect corporate governance. The findings are coloured by my social values, which are a by-product of *ubuntu* philosophy. In the analysis, I contrast *ubuntu* values with my experiences and professional training, which essentially is

Anglo-Saxon. The insights are part of a reflective account of corporate governance from the perspectives of *ubuntu*.

5. SOME EMPIRICAL OBSERVATIONS

The analysis addresses the major research question of this paper. How does *ubuntu* philosophy influence corporate governance practices in Southern Africa? The presentation focuses on identifying patterns that highlight the impact of *ubuntu* on corporate governance practices. The evidence spans sectors encompassing multinational corporations, educational institutions, non-governmental and other local organisations. I focus on a few attributes of *ubuntu*, such as caring for each other, compassion, and sharing resources in a communal setting. On the basis of the notion that a corporation should exude these characteristics, I also sought to understand how corporations accounted for such activities in their financial statements.

In Zimbabwe, I found that many organisations were engaged in social welfare provision for their employees and their local communities. A similar pattern existed in Botswana. Most of the social welfare programmes addressed education, health, and financial assistance. However, disclosure of these activities was not explicit in the financial statements.

5.1. Educational Assistance

In Zimbabwe, one state-owned university offers free education to children of members of staff if they satisfy entry requirements. A member of staff I interviewed had this to say

> I joined this university two years ago. I had to relocate to this town because I wanted my children to have free education. My daughter is now in the second year of her degree. This has saved me a lot of money, which I would have paid in fees.

From publicly available financial information, it was not possible to determine the total number of beneficiaries under the scheme across the university, which has many faculties. This practice is common even in private, independent schools in the country, for instance a teacher who works for a private primary school had this to say

> I have saved a lot of money on transport since I joined Qhubeka School. It also runs a sister high school where my son attends. I do not have to pay any tuition fees because that is part of my employment package. This has benefited my family. In addition, we live in subsidised accommodation provided by the school where my husband teaches.

Thus, teachers transfer from state schools to private schools in search of perquisites, which benefit their children.

Multinational corporations that operate in the mining sector such as Lonhro, Rio Tinto and Anglo-American have for some time played a role in the education of the children of their staff. They pay tuition fees for the children of their senior staff from pre-school to high school, wherever the parents might wish to send them. On their various sites, they build schools for the children of their junior staff and the local community. The corporations pay teachers and any other workers in their schools.

In addition, the mining corporations provide apprenticeship opportunities for the children of their employees. The children rank first in the recruitment process. Many criticisms levelled against multinational corporations (Deardorff, 2003; Wolf, 2003; Aisbett, 2005) are not obvious to their immediate communities who enjoy such benefits. The corporations also offer subsidised accommodation to their employees and families.

It has been a tradition in Zimbabwe for business corporations, whether local or multinational, to offer scholarships on a competitive basis. For example, an employee of a non-governmental organisation approached the chief executive officer in her organisation for a scholarship for her daughter who had excelled in her examinations. Because most organisations care about social problems facing employees, her daughter got a scholarship to study in the United States of America. Once identified, intellectually endowed children in the community receive assistance with fees from local corporations. Corporations also offer prize moneys or awards for excellence to students at universities and technical vocational institutions across the country. At national policy level, large corporations pay a manpower development levy, which is a percentage of their profit. This money augments budgets for vocational training centres such as polytechnics. Business corporations have for some time had a role to play in the education sector. It is therefore not surprising that before the recent crisis Zimbabwe's literacy rate was 91.9% (World Fact Book, 2005).

In South Africa, educational assistance for the majority of the population is a recent phenomenon, after the demise of apartheid in 1994. Anecdotal evidence shows DaimlerChrysler, a German multinational corporation leading the way. At its plant, it provides literacy classes for the workers. In addition, it has built a school worth R10 million and donated mobile computer vehicles to support 20 rural community schools (Mak'ochieng, 2003). As part of its corporate social responsibility investment, DaimlerChrysler works closely with the Education Department in the

Eastern Province to which it has donated and loaned vehicles to help access rural community schools (Mak'ochieng, 2003).

5.2. Health-Related Assistance

In Zimbabwe, multinational corporations particularly those in the mining sector have built clinics or hospitals on their sites for their staff. These corporations offer free medical services to their employees, their families, and local communities. In addition, they put in place Medical Aid Schemes, whereby both the employer and employee contribute to the fund. The employees obtain medical aid membership cards; covering all dependants including parents. Medical treatment is accessed anywhere in the country or outside, particularly from private hospitals on production of the medical aid card. This makes it easier for employees of corporations to receive medical treatment. This is standard practice for Zimbabwe corporations in different sectors, whether Banks, the Railways or public services. The benefits offered by each medical aid scheme depend on how much the corporations have contributed.

For example, the National Railways of Zimbabwe, a state-owned corporation has one of the best medical aid schemes. It also operates a chain of pharmacies for dispensing medications and prescriptions for its employees across the country. Taking care of the health of the workforce has been a practice in Zimbabwe's business corporations since colonial times. It is not surprising that employees expect corporations to provide for their needs.

Multinational mining corporations in Botswana lead in health-related assistance to their employees and their communities. For example, Debswana was the first private company to provide anti-retroviral treatment for its employees, their spouses, children, and the local community in 2001 (Mukumbira, 2003). Debswana is a subsidiary of De Beers, a diamond mining giant multinational corporation. By embarking on an extensive health programme it acknowledges that its survival is dependent on its employees and community.

As of March 2003, 600 employees and 300 dependants were on the drug treatment. It costs the company P6,000 or US $ 1,200 per year per patient (Sesinyi, 2003 cited in Mukumbira, 2003).[2] Debswana further increased its investment in hospital facilities at one of its mining sites at a cost of US $400,000 and employs resident medical staff including a nutritionist (Mukumbira, 2003). Most of the values of *ubuntu* are evident in this company and its mission statement includes the following values:

Be passionate
We will be exhilarated by the product we sell, the challenges we face, and the opportunities we create.

Pull together
Being united in purpose and action, we will turn the diversity of our people, skills and experience into an unparalleled source of strength.

Build trust
We will always listen first, then, act with openness, honesty and integrity so that our relationships flourish.

Show we care
The people whose lives we touch, their communities and nations and the environment we share, all matter deeply to us. We will always think through the consequences of what we do so that our contribution to the world is real, lasting and makes us proud.

(Debswana, undated)

From its actions and mission statement it is clear that Debswana takes corporate social responsibility seriously and exhibits *ubuntu*.

In South Africa, DaimlerChrysler is tackling HIV/AIDS head on through its corporate social investment fund. It focuses on prevention and care programme for employees and their families, which includes anti-retroviral therapy. Amongst its staff, it has a full-time HIV/AIDS co-ordinator (Kirsten, 2002). In 2002, it received an award from the Global Business Coalition on HIV/AIDS. The former UN Secretary General Kofi Annan presented the award and said the following:

There is no more important sector in this fight than the business community. Increasingly, companies recognise that fighting AIDS is in their interest, that doing so combines good business with doing good. I hope many businesses around the world will be inspired by your example. (The Star, July 2002)

In addition, DaimlerChrysler has donated vehicles to the Department of Health to strengthen its primary care clinics in the rural areas of the Eastern Province (Mak'ochieng, 2003). The World Economic Forum (2002, p. 3) disclosed that DaimlerChrysler's four-year budget for HIV/AIDS project was US $600,000 funded by GTZ (20%) and DaimlerChrysler (80%). In addition, in the same year its Corporate Social Responsibility Initiative contributed US $101,000 to community-based HIV/AIDS projects. The average direct medical costs were US$124 per employee per month. The snippets from these critical incidents across Southern Africa provide evidence of how *ubuntu* notions permeate corporate practices and have implications for how 'good' corporate governance is perceived.

5.3. Financial Assistance

Obtaining financial assistance of one form or another is a common occurrence in Zimbabwean organisations. Providing for one's employees often stretches beyond paying salaries and pension schemes. Extending social welfare provision to employees is now standard practice by organisations in Zimbabwe. I offer some examples of this below.

The university referred to earlier operates a staff revolving loan fund, to cushion employees in case they needed financial help. Members of staff could borrow from this fund and repay through monthly deductions from their salaries. I interviewed a member of staff who had just bought a car from Japan, who said

> I ordered this vehicle from Japan. I borrowed some money from the Staff Revolving Loan Fund to help me pay customs duty. I would not have managed to do this from my personal savings.

Under this facility, the purpose of the loan did not matter. It could have been a deposit on a house or other staff need. The only restrictions were the budget allocated for such assistance in a particular financial year and that the size of the loan could not exceed a certain percentage of the recipient's salary, to ensure affordability. Because of such practices, there were staff debtors in the organisation's balance sheet.

Employees also obtained financial assistance during bereavement. If an employee dies it is common for his employer to give his/her family some financial help towards funeral costs. The corporation provides transport to other members of staff if they wish to attend the funeral.

In another organisation in Zimbabwe forms of assistance varied from free transport to work, to credit facilities for staff in its supermarkets and workshops. I interviewed some of the employees about how their organisation had assisted them during the past financial year. One interviewee had this to say

> I opened an account at the supermarket owned by my organisation. I can take groceries or hardware items as and when required. The accountant deducts what I owe from my salary. I also take my family car for repairs at the workshop and the expenses are deducted from my salary at the end of the month.

These practices reduced the net take home pay but the workers were happy because the organisation could assist them to meet their needs.

Other forms of assistance from the corporations are not likely to occur in Western societies. For example, in another multinational corporation that is a joint venture between Japan and the government of Zimbabwe, employees could buy household items through the Corporation's Buying Office, thus saving through discounts. I interviewed one of the employees who bought a carpet and paint for her house through the corporation. Employees looked upon the corporation as a father who had responsibility for his children, no matter how different their needs were.

I have singled out three areas where several organisations in Southern Africa were heavily involved with their communities as part of their corporate social responsibility projects. There are many other incidents across Southern Africa to demonstrate that organisations care about their businesses, employees, and communities they work with. The findings raise questions of what constitutes 'good' corporate governance, the meaning of ethics, and the relevance of Western/International Codes of Ethics and Corporate Governance to less developed countries of Southern Africa. Do the practices reflect 'good' corporate governance or some version of *ubuntu*?

In the next section, I explore the implications of the findings for multinational corporations, accounting and audit profession, and policy makers.

6. DISCUSSION

Western thought underpins corporate governance frameworks which focus on restoring credibility in financial capital markets. The emphasis in such frameworks is on transparency and accountability for the benefit of shareholders who have invested in corporations. Due to the separation of ownership and management of corporations, agency problems highlight conflicts of interest between providers of capital and managers (Jensen & Meckling, 1976). Remedies to the problem of conflict of interests between directors and providers of capital have resulted in an increase in monitoring costs. The audit function mediates this conflict (Markus, Kals, & Jürgen, 2008). The focus of corporate governance frameworks has been on strengthening the audit function and providing assurance of appropriate use of investors' money. Voluntary disclosures by listed companies enhance transparency. The introduction of audit committees also enhances the audit function and helps in monitoring activities and preventing fraud. However, these frameworks have not been entirely successful judging by the prevalence of financial scandals in the developed world such as Enron and World Com (Stein, 2007).

I argue here that corporations in less developed countries face different problems and their views on social corporate responsibility are different. The incidents chronicled earlier indicate concerns with welfare issues, communal well-being, inter-dependency, poverty alleviation, general survival, and sustainability of the business and its community. Corporate responsibility encompasses all aspects of life and welfare. This thinking resonates with the concept of *ubuntu*, which emphasises sharing and caring for the community.

As explicated through the African philosophy of u*buntu*, participants in organisations view themselves as part of a community, which depends on the corporation for its well-being. In their philosophy of interdependency, concern for each other, they in turn expect corporations to care for them. Their view of a 'good' citizen is that of a person who exhibits characteristics of *ubuntu* that include humanness, sharing, caring for the other, and compassion. Similarly, a 'good' corporation should have a human face and be sensitive to the needs of the community. Biko (1978, p. 46) wrote

> We believe that in the long- run the special contribution to the world by Africa will be in this field of human relationship. The powers of the world may have done wonders in giving the world an industrial and military look, but the great gift still has to come from Africa – giving the world a more human face.

The above mindset persists among Africans; for them an organisation symbolises *ubuntu* hence they do not see the legal artefact but focus on human beings who preside over organisational activities and should exude *ubuntu*. Corporate social responsibility is about an organisation being a 'good' corporate citizen. According to Bantu thinking, the provision of financial capital may not be the sole determinant of ownership. Employees identify themselves with the organisation as if they also were co-owners. In most organisations, employees may work long hours without claiming overtime. Workers think in terms of reciprocity – the organisation is providing their livelihood and they are expending their labour (Song, 2006). For example, in Zimbabwe, corporations award annual bonuses regardless of whether they have made a profit or not. It has nothing to do with either productivity or profitability, but a gesture showing appreciation of a year's service from employees.

6.1. *Implications for Multinational Corporations, Accounting, and Auditing*

The incidents highlighted in the findings have implications for multinational corporations who ply their trade in this globalised village. When African countries solicit for investment, they rarely mention some of the inherent problems that are likely to be encountered. This paper sheds some light on what is going on in regional organisations and does not intend to pass judgment about whether this is good or bad. The practices have been institutionalised in organisations and also impact on accounting and auditing practices. Firstly, the issue of related party transactions is effectively condoned because an organisation is expected to help its employees. In such organisations there is seen to be nothing wrong about giving a loan to the chief executive, because he is just like any other employee, therefore this does not alarm the auditor as long as the transaction is appropriately accounted.

Issuing low interest/zero interest loans to members of staff also does not constitute a conflict of interest, though this reduces funds available for other business, because increasing shareholders' value is just one of the objectives of the corporation, not the only one. In Western circles, this would be tantamount to misuse of resources or even breach of trust. Yet, the communal spirit of sharing affects executives who use different yardsticks. The auditors from the 'Big Four' also factor in the context into the audit reports because they give corporations unqualified audit reports, in spite of the unusual use of corporate resources (see Annual Reports, DaimlerChrysler, Debswana, 2002 and 2003).

The accountants who recorded staff loans are content with the slow recoveries despite the time value of money. Corporations operate as 'one' big family, nepotism is also rife; when vacancies occur preference is given to relatives before outsiders are considered. Such a recruitment policy in an African context leads to an increase in absences when there is a death in the family. There are no attempts to quantify the opportunity costs incurred due to staff absences when several relatives are off to attend a family funeral. A joint research report by the University of Natal and Boston, factored some of the above in their calculation of the estimated costs of HIV/AIDS to DaimlerChrysler, however there was no explicit disclosure in the financial statements (cited in World Economic Forum, 2002, p. 3). The African world-view of community extends to corporations, which become part of their community by virtue of their location. There is seen to be no separation between organisations and their employees. There appears to be an unwritten covenant that an organisation should take care of its workers. According to Rossouw, van der Watt, and Malan (2002), a company is a social institution with responsibilities to those that are normally excluded from the corporate vision, such as the disadvantaged, the natural environment, and future generations.

In view of the incidents that mirror everyday issues in organisations, the challenge is to develop corporate governance frameworks which take cognisance of all the above. The key aspects of 'good' corporate governance are transparency and accountability, but what would be deemed 'good' or 'ethical' would be a situational practice and not universal. Noteworthy is the fact that in most developing countries, there are no public oversights boards such as Public Oversight Board of Accountancy (POBA) in the United Kingdom and the Public Company Accounting Oversight Board (PCAOB) in the United States to strengthen the regulation of corporations. This may be because legislation generally tends to lag behind in developing countries. Considering the influences of culture and influences of philosophies such as *ubuntu*, it is difficult to chart the direction that 'good' corporate governance is to follow.

In this paper, I suggest a corporate governance framework that takes into account the social, historical, and cultural context. More so, because social welfare issues already burden corporations in Southern Africa, yet financial statements do not fully disclose such matters. Critics of globalisation seldom write about the contributions of multinational corporations to social welfare programmes in Africa. I suggest a communitarian stakeholder theory founded on the notions of *ubuntu* of 'good' corporate governance. Most corporations in Southern Africa show that they care for the shareholders, employees, and their communities, but are rather constrained about how to disclose their activities by the Western informed corporate governance frameworks, which have different concerns from theirs. A 'good' contextual corporate governance framework should spell out the corporate objectives for business, employees, and community welfare and the environment. The board of directors should report openly on these to enhance accountability and transparency. If the policies of the corporation are clear, auditing its financial records is made easier. The King Report of 2002 set the groundwork for such reporting under its call for triple bottom line sustainability reporting, integrating economic, social, and environmental performance. However, I found most of the information on corporate social investment in magazines, the local press, but very little in annual reports. The directors should report on the impact of such activities on profits and other stakeholder interests for the sake of transparency to all.

A communitarian stakeholder corporate governance framework should acknowledge the problems facing corporations in Southern Africa. It is apt at this point to evoke the caution raised by the King Report (1994).

> An inclusive approach is fundamental to long-term corporate success in South Africa – but the notion of being accountable to all is rejected because this would result in accountability to none. (King Report, 1994, p. 300)

The communitarian stakeholder model could take the form of a tripartite arrangement, which takes into account the needs of providers of finance capital, the community and employees. The aim should be wealth creation for all stakeholders' not just shareholders (Mosey, 2004). There is some evidence that organisations and multinational corporations operating in Southern Africa are already taking care of their employees and their extended families and the community, but this is not reflected directly in annual reports.

However, the interventions in social welfare provisions by corporations in Southern Africa cannot absolve governments of their responsibility to their populations. If not controlled, they might impinge negatively on corporate profits, particularly in South Africa, because corporate executives are dividing their time between running the corporations and community programmes. Another approach would be to empower communities to run the projects themselves with minimal input from corporate executives. This is where the role of non-governmental organisations is critical in mobilising communities for development and self-reliance (see Doh & Teegen, 2002). Practising *ubuntu* without restraints borders on abuse of corporations' magnanimity, and this should not be an alibi for forcing multinational corporations to pay for the past sins of apartheid and colonialism.

7. CONCLUSION

The search for a theoretical governance framework for Southern Africa should take into account the historical, cultural, and social context in order to achieve social harmony. This paper does not claim that there is a void in governance structures in Southern Africa, but brings to light some of the pressing issues facing corporations. Evidence from company practice shows that the profit motive is not the most dominant objective in the minds of those doing business in that part of the world, but rather making a difference in the lives of communities. However, it is not everyone even in Southern Africa who upholds the values of *ubuntu*; a recent example is that of xenophobic attacks on foreign nationals (NewZimbabwe, 2008, newzimbabwe.com accessed on 24/05/2008). The high crime rate is part of the evidence that the values of *ubuntu* have been eroded by 'deliberate and systematic colonial destruction' (Iya, 1999, p. 9). Historical experiences throughout the apartheid era can explain why it has not been possible for this noble African philosophy to contribute to the betterment of people's lives.

Insights from institutional theory show that societies are not static but are involved in the shaping of their social reality through a reproduction of practices; however, change might be slow (Burns & Scapens, 2000). The power of human agency is vital in the structuration of new systems, in the same way as we have witnessed the fall of apartheid. The views of the dominant groups prevail in the social construction of institutions, they prevail until such time that new understandings emerge (Giddens, 1984). The African philosophy is compatible with practices elsewhere particularly within Christianity. Africans can adopt elements from other existing frameworks of corporate governance if they suit their purpose. The influence of globalisation makes it imperative for those entrusted with resources to be both economically and socially responsible, since the interdependence starts from the local, then spreads to the national and finally the global community.

African scholars should revisit the corporate governance debate by drawing on their own social values so that they can reclaim what has been lost over years of colonisation and apartheid. Furthermore, there is need to lay bare welfare activities of corporations so that there is adequate disclosure in financial statements. For much of the last century, black Africans have not been part of the governance system in corporations. It is apt to caution that without explicit corporate governance frameworks the concept of *ubuntu* is susceptible to abuse because the boundaries of co-ownership and entitlements are blurred in community-oriented societies and could be exploited leading to corruption. Governments should put in place enabling legislation to allow both corporations and individuals to contribute towards societal goals. African governments should not abrogate their responsibilities to provide social welfare to their citizens by shifting responsibilities to corporations. Policy makers should take into account corporate social responsibility investments in their countries and offer incentives such as tax breaks or concessions.

Empowerment of communities cannot be done by business corporations alone, rather by the governments and non-governmental organisations that have invested resources in empowering communities. The communitarian stakeholder theory proposed in this paper envisages full participation by communities rather than inculcating a dependency syndrome but it is only a beginning of the road to a theoretical corporate governance framework that embraces the social values of its constituents.

NOTES

1. Ukubusa – Ndebele language spoken in the South Western part of Zimbabwe.
2. Sesinyi J. was a communications manager at Debswana Mining Company – Botswana.

ACKNOWLEDGMENT

I acknowledge comments from Professor Rebecca Boden and two anonymous reviewers on an earlier draft of this paper.

REFERENCES

African Development Bank. (2007). *Corporate governance strategy* (July 2007). Tunis: ADB.
Aisbett, E. (2005). *Why are the critics so convinced that globalization is bad for the poor?* NBER Working Paper no. W11066. Available at SSRN: http://ssrn.com/abstract = 652363. Accessed on 25/3/2008.
Ambrose, D. (2007). *Ubuntu* from chaos: Lessons from an African tradition. *Synchronicity Magazine*, December/January.
Annual Reports. (2002/2003). Daimler/Chrysler South Africa. Available at http://www.daimlerchrysler.co.za. Accessed on 24/03/2008.
Barley, S., & Tolbert, P. S. (1997). Institutionalisation and structuration: Studying the links between action and institution. *Organization Studies*, *18*(1), 93–117.
Bealing, W. E., Dirsmith, M. W., & Fogarty, T. (1996). Early regulatory actions by the SEC: An institutional theory perspective on dramaturgy of political exchanges. *Accounting, Organisations, and Society*, *21*(4), 317–338.
Begley, T. M., & Boyd, D. P. (2003). Why don't they like us overseas? Organizing U.S. business practices to manage culture clash. *Organisational Dynamics*, *32*(4), 357–371.
Bell, D. (2001). Communitarianism, Stanford Encyclopaedia of Philosophy. Available at http://plato.stanford.edu/archives/win2001. Accessed on 20/3/2008.
Biko, S. (1978). *I write what I like*. London: Heinemann.
Broodryk, J. (2002). *Ubuntu: Life lessons from Africa*. Pretoria: Ubuntu School of Philosophy.
Burns, J., & Scapens, R. W. (2000). Conceptualizing management accounting change: An institutional framework. *Management Accounting Research*, *11*, 3–25.
CACG. (1999). *CACG guidelines: Principles of corporate governance in the Commonwealth*. London: Commonwealth Association for Corporate Governance.

Cadbury, A. (1992). *Report of the committee on the financial aspects of corporate governance.* London: Gee & Co.

Charkham, J. (1992). Corporate governance: Lessons from abroad. *European Business Journal,* 4(2), 8–16.

Deardorff, A. V. (2003). What might globalisation critics believe? *The World Economy, 26*(5), 639–658.

Debswana. (undated). Debswana Diamond Company. Available at http://www.debswana.com. Accessed on 24/03/2008.

DeWitt, M. R. (2007). Tetra sociology: Responses to challenges; Tetra sociology: From sociological imagination through dialog to universal values and harmony; Children's suffrage: Democracy for the 21st century, priority investment in human capital as a way toward social harmony. *International Sociology, 22,* 164–168.

DiMaggio, P. (1991). Constructing an organisational field as a professional project: U.S. art museums, 1920–1940. In: W. Powell & P. DiMaggio (Eds), *The new institutionalism in organizational analysis* (pp. 267–292). Chicago: University of Chicago Press.

DOH (Department of Health). (2001). *NHS Governance Standard.* Leeds: NHS.

Doh, J. P., & Teegen, H. (2002). Nongovernmental organizations as institutional actors in international business: Theory and implications. *International Business Review, 11,* 665–684.

du Toit, C. W. (2004). Technoscience and the integrity of personhood in Africa and the West: Facing our technoscientific environment. In: C. W. du Toit (Ed.), *The integrity of the human person in an African context: Perspectives from science and religion* (p. 33). Pretoria: Research Institute for Theology and Religion, University of South Africa.

Etzion, A. (1998). *The essential communitarian reader.* Lanham: Rowman & Littlefield.

Etzion, A. (2001). *The monochrome society.* Princeton: Princeton University Press.

Fényes, T., & Campbell, W. (2003). Debt relief initiatives and poverty alleviation: Lessons from Africa – 22nd SAUSSC. *Development Southern Africa, 20*(4), 545–549.

Financial Reporting Council. (2003). *Audit committees combined code guidance.* (Smith Report). London: FRC.

Forster, D. (2006). *Self-validating consciousness in strong artificial intelligence: An African theological contribution.* Unpublished Doctoral Dissertation, UNISA, Pretoria.

Freeman, R. E., & Reed, D. L. (1983). Stockholders and stakeholders: A new perspective on corporate governance. *California Management Review, XXV*(3), 88–106.

Giddens, A. (1984). *The constitution of society.* Berkeley: University of California.

Greenbury, R. (1995). *Directors' remuneration: Report of a study group by Sir Richard Greenbury.* Greenbury Report. London: Gee and Company.

Hamilton, W. H. (1932). Institution. In: Seligman, E. R. A. & Johnson, A. (Eds), Encyclopaedia of Social Science (Vol. 73, no. 4, pp. 560–595).

Hampel Committee. (1998). *Report of the committee on corporate governance.* London: Gee.

Higgs Report. (2003). *Review of the role of effectiveness of non-executive directors.* London: Department of Trade and Industry.

IFAC (International Federation of Accountants) and CIMA. (2004). *Enterprise governance – Getting the balance right.* London: IFAC.

Iya, P. (1999). Fraud and the African renaissance. In: G. J. Rossou & D. Carabine (Eds), *Fraud and the African renaissance.* Nkozi, Uganda: Uganda Martyrs, University Press.

Jensen, M. C., & Meckling, W. H. (1976). Theory of the firm: Managerial behaviour, agency costs and ownership structure. *Journal of Financial Economics, 3*(4), 305–360.

Khoza, R. J., & Adam, M. (2005). *The power of governance: Enhancing the performance of state-owned enterprises.* Johannesburg: Pan McMillan and Business in Africa.

King Report. (1994). *Corporate governance for South.* South Africa: Institute of Directors.

King Report. (2002). *Corporate governance for South Africa.* South Africa: Institute of Directors.

Kirsten, C. (2002). DCSA locational social responsibility! Hi-Lite, April 29.

Kwamwangamalu, N. M., & Nkonko, M. (1999). *Ubuntu* in South Africa: A sociolinguistic perspective to a pan-African concept. *Critical Arts Journal, 13*(2), 24–42.

Laird, S. E. (2004). Inter-ethnic conflict: A role for social work in sub-Saharan Africa. *Social Work Education, 23*(6), 693–709.

Louw, D. J. (2001). *Ubuntu* and the challenges of multiculturalism in post-apartheid South Africa. *African Journal of Philosophy, Quest, XV*, 1–2.

Mak'ochieng, A. A. (2003). *A case study of the strategic nature of DaimlerChrysler South Africa's corporate social investment programmes in the local communities of the Border-Kei region in the Eastern Cape Province.* Unpublished Dissertation for Master of Commerce, Rhodes University.

Mandela, N. (2006). *Ubuntu web video.* Available at youtube.com. Accessed on 21/1/2008.

Markus, M. M., Kals, E., & Jürgen, M. (2008). Fairness, self-interest, and cooperation in a real-life conflict. *Journal of Applied Social Psychology, 38*(3), 684–704.

Markusen, J. R., & Venables, A. J. (1999). Foreign direct investment as a catalyst for industrial development. *European Economic Review, 43*(2), 335–356.

Mbeki, T. (2001). Third African Renaissance Festival. Available at http://www.gov.za/president/index.html. Accessed on 24/03/2008.

Mbigi, L. (1997). *Ubuntu: The African dream in management.* Randburg: Knowledge Resources.

Mbigi, L. (2000). *In search of the African business renaissance: An African cultural perspective.* Randburg: Knowledge Resources.

Meisel, N. (2004). *Governance culture and development: A different perspective on corporate governance.* Paris: OECD.

Mokgoro, J. Y. (1997). *Ubuntu and the law in South Africa.* Seminar Report of the Colloquium. Konrad-Adenauer Stifting, Johannesburg.

Monks, R. A., & Minow, N. (2004). *Corporate governance* (3rd ed.). London: Blackwell.

Mosey, P. (2004). *Corporate governance and wealth creation.* Occasional Research Paper no. 37. Certified Accountants Educational Trust, London.

Mukumbira, R. (2003). Mining giant fights workplace, HIV/AIDS. Available at http://www.newsfromafrica.org./newsfromafrica/articles/art_1252.html. Accessed on 24/03/2008.

NewZimbabwe. (2008). Violence spreads to Cape Town, death toll now 42, Online Newspaper. Available at http://www.newzimbabwe.com. Accessed on 24/05/2008.

Nocke, V., & Yeaple, S. (2008). An assignment theory of foreign direct investment. *Review of Economic Studies, 75*, 529–557.

Nussbaum, B. (2003). *Ubuntu* and business: Reflections and questions. *World Business Academy, 17*(3), 1–15.

OECD. (2004a). *Principles of corporate governance.* Paris: OECD.

Ohmae, K. (1990). *The borderless world.* New York: Harper Business.

Olinger, H. N. (2004). *Western privacy and Ubuntu* – Influences in the forthcoming data privacy. Pretoria: Bill School of Information Technology.

Omari, E. (2008). Moral ambitions of grace: The paradox of compassion and accountability in Evangelical faith based activism. *Cultural Anthropology, 23*(10), 154–189.

O'Sullivan, M. (1999). *Corporate governance and globalization.* Working Paper, INSEAD.

Ramose, M. B. (1999). *African philosophy through Ubuntu.* Harare: Bond Books.

Roodt, A. (1997). In search of a South African corporate culture. *Management Today,* (March), 14–16.

Rossouw, G. J., van der Watt, A., & Malan, D. P. (2002). Corporate governance in South Africa. *Journal of Business Ethics, 37*(3), 289–302.

Rwegasira, K. (2000). Corporate governance in emerging capital markets: Whither Africa? *Corporate Governance: An International Review, 8*(3), 258–267.

Scott, W. R. (1987). The adolescence of institutional theory. *Administrative Science Quarterly, 32*, 493–511.

Shoniwa, S. (2001). African imperatives and transformation leadership, *Directorship*, March.

Shuttle, A. (1993). *Philosophy for Africa.* Rondebosch: UCT Press.

Song, F. (2006). Trust and reciprocity in inter-individual versus inter-group interactions: The effects of social influence, group dynamics, and perspective biases. *Experimental Economics, 9*, 179–180.

Star. (2002). Newspaper for the DaimlerChrysler South Africa Group, June 2002.

Stein, M. (2007). Oedipus rex at Enron: Leadership, oedipal struggles, and organizational collapse. *Human Relations, 60*(9), 1387–1410.

The Government Gazette. (1996). Available at http://www.gov.za/whitepaper/index.html, 02/02/1996, No. 16943, paragraph 18. Accessed on 24/03/2008.

Turnbull, S. (1999). *Internal control: Guidance for directors on the combined code.* London: Institute of Chartered Accountants England and Wales.

Van Der Bly, M. C. E. (2005). Globalization: A triumph of ambiguity. *Current Sociology, 53*(6), 875–893.

Versi, A. (2002). Coping with culture clash. *African Business.* Available at http://findarticles.com/p/articles/mi_qa5327/is_200205/ai_n21311895. Accessed on 25 March 2008.

Ward, L. C., & Gaile, G. L. (2006). Exploring sustainable development. *Annals of the Association of American Geographers, 96*(3), 677–679.

Wolf, M. (2003). Is globalisation in danger? *The World Economy, 26*(4), 393–411.

Woodward, D. G., Edwards, F., & Birkin, F. (1996). Organisational legitimacy and stakeholder information provision. *British Journal of Management, 7*(4), 340.

World Economic Forum. (2002). Global health initiative private sector intervention – Case Example, DCSA, South Africa. World Economic Forum, Geneva.

World Fact Book. (2005). Zimbabwe facts and figures. Central Intelligence Agency, Yearbook. Available at encarta.msn.com/fact_631504899. Accessed on 25/5/2008.

Yeung, H. W. (1998). *Capital, state and space: Contesting the borderless world.* Blackwell: Transactions of the Institute of British Geographers.

CORPORATE GOVERNANCE IN INFANCY AND GROWTH – AN INTERVIEW-BASED STUDY OF THE DEVELOPMENT OF GOVERNANCE AND CORPORATE REGULATION IN NIGERIA

Preye Edward Gesiye Angaye and David Gwilliam

ABSTRACT

Purpose – *This paper seeks to contribute to the debate on the role of corporate governance in developing, emerging and transition economies by focusing on the nature and practice of corporate governance in listed companies in Nigeria – a country which has experienced both economic growth and political turbulence over the past three decades and which too has experienced significant corporate failures in particular in the banking and insurance sectors. It does this against a contextual background which discusses issues of ethnicity, gender and power relationships and their relevance to governance in Nigeria.*

Methodology – *Archival and documentary analysis supported and underpinned by semi-structured interviews with 20 stakeholders in governance processes in Nigeria.*

Corporate Governance in Less Developed and Emerging Economies
Research in Accounting in Emerging Economies, Volume 8, 359–407
Copyright © 2008 by Emerald Group Publishing Limited
All rights of reproduction in any form reserved
ISSN: 1479-3563/doi:10.1016/S1479-3563(08)08013-4

Findings – *The analysis of the interviews highlighted the general support of the interviewees for corporate governance procedures and practices in Nigeria to continue to develop in line with those in more developed economies. However, concerns were expressed as to the inadequacies of aspects of the Nigerian governance regulatory infrastructure, in particular in relation to mechanisms for implementation and enforcement within a framework where there was limited confidence that either voluntary adherence to codes of good practice or market-driven regulation and control would be effective.*

Contrary to the researchers' expectations, the majority of the interviewees articulated the perspective that ethnicity, gender and power relationships were not of significance in the determination of the actuality of practice. However, a minority did identify these considerations to be of key importance, albeit frequently not overtly acknowledged or portrayed as such by parties associated with governance practices.

Research limitation(s) – *The interviewees were drawn from a cross section of stakeholders from the business, government, regulatory and academic environment in Nigeria but the exigencies of conducting interview research in Nigeria and the difficulties of obtaining agreement from, and access to, interviewees meant that the potential for self-selection bias has to be considered when evaluating the study findings.*

Practical Implication(s) – *The research paper provides a platform for policy formulation on corporate governance in Nigeria.*

Originality and value of paper – *The paper builds on a number of previous studies of governance in Nigeria (for example, Oyejide & Soyibo, 2001; Yakasai, 2001; Ahunwan, 2002; Okike, 2007) in particular by means of the use of semi-structured interviews to provide a rich field of insight into the actuality of practice.*

1. INTRODUCTION

The academic and professional literature on the role and relevance of corporate governance is dominated by review of its contribution and practice in developed countries. Here the last 20 years have seen significant developments both in institutional arrangements developing from the pathbreaking COSO (Committee of Sponsoring Organisations of the Tread-way Commission) study in North America and the near parallel Cadbury report in the United Kingdom; the Vienot Commission in France and the National Association of Corporate Directors' Blue Commission Report and the Sarbanes-Oxley Act of the United States; and also in the extent of investigation and research into the application of modes and forms of governance and their efficacy in achieving the objectives intended by both regulators and wider stakeholders. Relative to this, corporate governance in developing countries has received less attention, although a number of country-specific studies have emerged for example in relation to Brazil (Rabelo & Vasconcelos, 2002), China (Tam, 2002), Ghana (Mensah, 2002; Tsamenyi, Enninful-Adu, & Onumah, 2007), India (Reed, 2002a, 2002b), Kenya (Gatamah, 2001; Mwaura, 2003), Malaysia (Ismail, Samad, & Zulkafli, 2008), Mexico (Husted & Serrano, 2002), Nigeria (Wallace, 1989, 1990; Okike, 1994, 2000, 2002, 2007; Oyejide & Soyibo, 2001; Ahunwan, 2002, 2003; Ndanusa & Al Mustapha, 2003), South Africa (Gerson, 1992; Barr & Kantor, 1995; Gerson & Barr, 1996; Williams, 2000; Botha, 2001; Rossouw, van der Watt, & Malan, 2002), Tanzania (Mwapachu, 2001), Uganda (Kaheeru, 2001; Rossette, 2002; Matama, 2008), Zambia (Kapumpa, 2002) and Zimbabwe (Tsumba, 2002; Mangena & Tauringana, 2006; Muranda, 2006).

These studies have varied in their emphasis and focus, some concentrating more on the development of institutional rules and requirements, others on the actuality of practice (for example, Wallace, 1990; Okike, 1994, 2007). A number of themes emerge from this and the wider literature. One is the perspective of both national and supranational bodies (including the World Bank and the International Monetary Fund (IMF)) that the adoption by developing countries of Western style governance practices will significantly benefit economic growth and improve welfare in terms of capital market improvement and, in particular, the attraction of foreign direct and indirect investment (McKinsey, 2001; Reed, 2002a, 2002b; Nganga, Jain, & Artivor, 2003); another, almost diametrically opposed to this, is that the direct transfer of western style governance practices to economies with very different political institutions and capital market structures (Briston, 1990; Nobes, 1998; Meisel, 2004), and a diversity of underlying cultural, ethical and religious norms and mores, is likely to be at best cosmetic and ineffective and at worst counter productive (Okike, 1994, 2002; Ahunwan, 2002, 2003; Haniffa & Cooke, 2002; Williams & Ho, 2003; Haniffa & Hudaib, 2006; Kamla, 2007).

This paper seeks to contribute to this debate (and thereby to build on the work of previous studies of governance practice in Nigeria (Wallace, 1989, 1990; Oyejide & Soyibo, 2001; Yakasai, 2001; Ahunwan, 2002, 2003; Nwauche & Nmehielle, 2004; Okike, 1994, 2000, 2002, 2007)) by reporting the findings of an interview-based study into perceptions of the nature, meaning and actuality of practice as it relates to corporate governance in Nigeria. Beyond this short introduction (Section 1) this paper is structured as follows: Section 2 gives an overview of the socio-historical milieu of Nigeria, with specific reference to issues of ethnicity, gender and patriarchy, power relationships against a background of upheaval and turbulence within the post-independence Nigerian polity, before proceeding to discuss economic change post-independence and the civil war; Section 3 sets out the institutional and regulatory background within which corporate governance is placed in Nigeria; Section 4 describes the nature of the research work carried out including the rationale underlying the semi-structured interview methodology utilised in the study; Section 5 reports the results of the interview process analysed thematically within three main headings: wider perceptions of governance; governance in Nigeria and recommendations for change; Section 6 provides an overview and conclusion which draws together the interview findings and relates them to the wider issues referred to above as to the application of western style governance practices to developing countries.

2. SOCIO-HISTORICAL BACKGROUND OF NIGERIA

Nigeria as a country may be considered to be an artificial creation imposed by Britain upon the hitherto independent tribes, ethnic cleavages and peoples of the surrounding lands and waters now amalgamated and called Nigeria – a name first suggested in an essay which appeared in *The Times* on January 8, 1897. The artificiality is emphasised in an observed absence of Nigerian consciousness and pride in the vast majority of the citizenry (Elekwa, Soludo, & Ikpeze, 2004). Following independence in 1960 Nigeria has continued to be a single sovereign state operating within the same geographical framework as that established following the amalgamation of the Southern and Northern protectorates in 1914. However, this apparent stability masks a turbulent post-colonial history which has seen numerous changes in leadership,[1] incessant changes in government and, in the decade after independence, bloody internecine strife with parallels to that of the American civil war as the Eastern state of Biafra sought unsuccessfully to break away from the Nigerian state. Over one million lives were lost in the struggle and the aftermath of the complete victory of the Northern faction has influenced Nigerian political and commercial development to this day.

Nigeria, in common with almost all other countries that were at one time part of the British Empire, inherited a legal system and a system of company legislation and regulation based on the British model (Briston, 1990) and throughout the near 50 years since independence the state has continued to maintain close relations with Britain and the West both politically and economically, as for example in terms of adherence to development and economic programmes prescribed by Western experts through international organisations such as the World Bank and IMF (Held & McGrew, 2002; Monbiot, 2003; Annisette, 2004).

The manner in which post-colonialism has acted to influence the development of business and governance practice in Nigeria is not easy to pin down – but it would be foolhardy not to recognise its importance and indeed the way in which overt colonialism has transformed itself within a wider compass of globalisation and changing international economic and power relationships in line with Bahri's (2001) assertion that "the celebration of independence marks the march of neo-colonialism in guise of globalisation and transnationalism". This paper does not adopt a specific post-colonial perspective (as for example adopted in papers by Said, 1993; Gandhi, 1998; Gray & Bebbington, 2001 – see Wallace, 1990; Okike, 2007 for application of linked concepts and ideas to the Nigerian context) in its analysis of the development and actuality of corporate governance practice in Nigeria, but it does identify three aspects of Nigerian society, each which may be considered to be rooted in Nigeria's pre-colonial, colonial and post-colonial past, specifically: ethnicity; gender and patriarchy and power relationships, aspects which, *a priori*, we considered to be relevant to the manner in which governance practices operate within the Nigerian commercial environment and these are discussed briefly below.

2.1. Ethnicity

Ethnicity is key to understanding Nigeria's pluralistic society (Fafunwa, 1974). Pluralism, a sociological theoretical framework of interaction in which groups show respect and tolerance of each other to ensure fruitful co-existence and interaction without conflict (Haralambos & Holborn, 1990) is clearly relevant in the context of the Nigerian political and commercial environment. The populus of Nigeria is an amalgamation of over 250 different ethnic groups with varying backgrounds, cultures and languages.[2] Nigeria's three largest ethnic groups – the Hausa in the north, the Yoruba in the southwest and the Igbo in the southeast – represent about 70 percent of the population. A further 10 percent consists of substantial minority groups each numbering more than 1 million, the Ijaw, Kanuri, Tiv and Ibibio, and beyond this more than 250 smaller ethnic groups account for the remaining 20 percent of the population. Ethnicity is perceived to be important at all levels of Nigerian society including the conduct of political affairs and private sector activities, and indeed some would claim that public policies emerge from a prism of ethnic and sectional interests rather than from rational consideration of the policies most suited to encourage development and welfare (Elekwa et al., 2004). Individuals in appointive positions in government or in the bureaucracy see themselves largely as representatives of their towns, villages, states or ethnic groups, with a single mission to "get their fair share of the national cake" by whatever means (Angaye, 2002, 2003). Power tussles between the three main ethnic groupings have contributed to a tumultuous political history that has helped stall national economic development.[3] In recent years, smaller ethnic groups in the Niger Delta, where most of the country's oil reserves lie, have become increasingly restive at their neglect and environmental degradation, attacking installations of multinational oil firms operating in their midst (Ndebbio & Ekpo, 1991; Obadina, 1999; Akpan, 2007).

2.2. Gender and Patriarchy

Nigerian society is perceived as functioning in a highly patriarchal fashion, with men exerting broad control over the lives of women (Olubi, 2005).[4] This brings in the concept of feminism which in turn implies a diverse collection of social theories, political movements and moral philosophies, largely motivated by or concerning the experiences of women, especially in terms of their social, political and economic situation. It largely focuses on limiting or eradicating gender inequality and promoting women's rights, interests and issues in society, developments which are seen to be of key importance in the promotion of a fairer, and indeed more productive, society. Against this background, there is a vast and insightful literature on aspects of gender and patriarchy in both developed and developing countries – a perhaps typical example being French (1985) who notes that is the basis on which modern societies have been formed and the necessity and desirability of getting away from this model in order to achieve gender equality and other societal goals.

In Nigeria, discrimination against women is prevalent in almost all sectors of social and economic life whether it be domestic, agricultural, commercial or political and, although the expression of discrimination varies, across almost all ethnic and religious boundaries (Angaye, 1994). There have been endeavours for change, for example the establishment of the "Better Life for Rural Women Programme" in 1986 and subsequent state endorsed programmes such as the "Family Support Programme" in 1993, "Family Economic Advancement Programme" in 1998. These have led to a degree of change in the role and opportunities open to women but some would argue that the pace and reality of change has been very slow (Mazrui, 1991; Angaye, 1994). In the specific context of this study, gender issues are most pertinent in relation to the number of women in senior positions in Nigerian businesses, both in terms of the limited number of board-level appointments and the actuality of their role and contribution.[5] For example, Angaye (2008) records that in a representative sample of 104 listed Nigerian companies only six companies had female representation on their boards of directors.

2.3. Power Relationships

Power relationships, both in the context of interactions between individuals and in the context of wider manoeuvrings between political groups and interested parties for control in terms of resources and influence, are vitally important in the Nigerian commercial environment. This brings in the concepts of power elite and conflict theories. Power elite theory is a sociological analysis of politics based on social-conflict theory that sees power as concentrated along the wealthy. Members of this power elite seek to control all the major sectors of society. The wishes of the power elite tend to prevail to the detriment of the generality of the citizenry (Haralambos & Holborn, 1990).

Corporations exist in a social-cultural milieu governed by legislations emanating from the political set-up characterised by power play and coercion. In Nigeria the interplay between the state with its immense power of patronage and indeed direct enforcement is a very significant factor. Political and commercial power are seen as going hand in hand and failure to maintain this key relationship may have disastrous consequences, as for example in the closure of Savannah Bank of Nigeria (Ezeife, 2005) – where the political perspective and aspirations of the dominant investor may be contrary to those of the government of the day. At the individual level aspects of the paradigm frequently include leadership by a charismatic and powerful (male) individual, a scenario which Wallace (1990) characterises as underpinning much of political and commercial life in post-colonial Africa and may be seen as persisting in Nigerian society today.

At a slight move from, but not necessarily entirely unconnected with, the above discussion there is a widespread perspective, both internally and externally, that levels of corruption in Nigeria are high (Angaye, 2005). Evidence for this is provided in the 2005 transparency international corruption perception index which listed Nigeria as the seventh most corrupt country in the world being ranked 152 out of 158 countries assessed (Transparency International, 2007).[6] There have been efforts to change both the actuality and perception of corruption (for example, the special anti-corruption force – the X Squad in 1973; War Against Indiscipline and Corruption in 1986 and the Independent and Corrupt Practices Commission and the Economic and Financial Crimes Commission (EFCC) in 1999), but these have had limited success and most commentators (Dike, 1999a, 1999b, 2001, 2002, 2008; Ewulu, 2002; Ojo, 2002; Umar, 2008) suggest that it is not possible to consider issues of business practice and governance without taking cognisance of this fact.

Although this study does not make claims to provide a rigorous and detailed analysis from a theoretical sociological perspective as to the influence of these three identified factors – ethnicity, gender and power relationships – on the development of commercial and regulatory practice in Nigeria, it is nevertheless contended that these factors do indeed have relevance to and underpin an understanding of the interview findings – and we return to these themes again in the concluding overview and reflections.

2.3.1. Economic and Business Development – Post-Independence

Notwithstanding access to significant natural resources, in particular oil, statistics show that Nigeria's economic growth performance since independence in 1960 has been disappointing, with little, if anything, to show in terms of significant improvement in living standards (Angaye, 2005; IMF, 2005). Prosperity is now heavily linked to the oil sector rather than agriculture[7], which was the core of the economy under colonial rule. Post-independence the economy has been highly volatile and unstable (Bleaney & Greenway, 2002) and despite the ongoing privatisation and liberalisation efforts since the early 1990s, the public sector's role in the formal economy remains substantial and has undermined the development of the private sector (IMF, 2005). Overall, foreign direct investment and the participation of foreign companies in economic activity outside the oil and gas sectors have been low.

In the immediate post-colonial environment and in the aftermath of the immensely destructive civil war the Nigerian government followed a policy of indigenisation issuing a number of Nigerian Enterprises Promotion Decrees, decrees that barred foreigners from investing in specified enterprises and reserved participation in certain trades to Nigerians. At the time, about 70 percent of commercial firms operating in Nigeria were foreign-owned. In 1975 the federal government bought 60 percent of the equity in the marketing operations of the major oil companies in Nigeria, but full nationalisation was rejected as a means of furthering its programme of indigenisation (Isichei, 1976). Over time there has been a significant shift in both the rhetoric and practice of the Nigerian approach to inward investment and the role of the state in the economy and for many years now Nigeria has been trying to modernise and improve its economy by focusing on macroeconomic stabilisation, and pursuance of a trade and investment liberalisation programme to encourage foreign direct investment in the country (World Trade Organisation, 1998; Soludo, Ogbu, & Chang, 2004). To this end, the country has relaxed restrictions on current and capital transfers, introduced tax relief for multi-nationals willing to invest in the country, and improved access to foreign exchange at near market rates. Another aspect to the liberalisation programme has been the embarkment on a major privatisation campaign of public institutions, again largely to attract foreign investment with the hope that this would help increase economic activity and bring in the much needed revenue (Ariyo, 2004).

Nigeria like most African countries lacks a good and functioning infrastructure such as communications and transportation systems, electricity and water. Comparatively in terms of quality and quantity, the infrastructure is inferior to that in much of the rest of the world and this significantly raises the cost of doing business in Nigeria (Weiss, 1999). Frequent power outages have sharply inflated operational costs through production stoppages, output losses and missed delivery dates (IMF, 2005).

Firms in Nigeria grapple with costly administrative procedures and regulations, and excessive red tape and rent-seeking activities by public officials. To start a business in Nigeria on average a firm must go through at least 10 bureaucratic procedures and wait an average of 44 days (World Bank, 2005). Routine business applications in Nigeria are slow and costly, and firms complain that poor government services add considerably to the cost of doing business.[8] Companies also pay high costs to obtain foreign exchange. All these hurdles and extra payments raise production costs and lower profitability, discourage market entry and weaken competition. The heavy-handed business procedures also imply opportunities for officials to extract bribes and tend to disadvantage small and medium-sized enterprises.[9] However, the government aims to streamline the business registration process. Other constraints on business relate to the inefficiencies of the commercial courts where, for example, resolution of a debt contract takes over 2 years, 23 procedures, and one-third of the debt amount to enforce. Foreclosure procedures are also cumbersome in Nigeria as asset recovery and liquidation come at considerable cost (IMF, 2005).

Overall, the Nigerian financial system has not fostered stability or supported investment and economic development. Banks continue to be plagued by unsound balance sheets and weak governance practices. The 2002 Financial Sector Assessment Program (FSAP) of the IMF noted that misreporting, systemic under provisioning, widespread insider lending and illegal transactions are common. Banks' reluctance to supply loans to the real economy reflects the unstable macroeconomic environment, inefficiencies in the judicial system and shortcomings in corporate governance practices. Furthermore, the World Bank's 2004 Report on the Observance of Standards and Codes (World Bank, 2004) on accounting and auditing also found serious shortcomings in regulations, compliance and enforcement of current national standards and rules.

The combination of macroeconomic fluctuations and weaknesses in economic and corporate structures have contributed over the years to a number of major corporate failures, in particular in the financial services sector, and the loss of confidence occasioned by these collapses with their ongoing impacts in terms of wealth and employment have impacted negatively on the overall Nigerian economy (Aminu & Elueme, 2004; Ezeife, 2005).

3. CORPORATE GOVERNANCE IN NIGERIA – THE INSTITUTIONAL AND REGULATORY FRAMEWORK

In this section we briefly sketch out the institutional and regulatory framework within which commercial entities operate in Nigeria with an especial focus on those that relate to corporate governance. The structure of business organisations in Nigeria is varied and reflects different types of business and ownership patterns (Oyejide & Soyibo, 2001). The regulatory structures applicable to larger corporate enterprises depict an amalgam of UK and US influence. The forerunners[10] of the present Companies Act (The Companies and Allied Matters Act (CAMA), 1990) were directly modelled on UK company law but significant revisions were incorporated in CAMA

(1990) on the basis of recommendations by the Nigerian Law Reform Commission.[11] In particular, CAMA (1990) established a Corporate Affairs Commission (CAC) to administer the Act. Apart from its routine duties with respect to the registration of companies and the receipt of financial statements and other relevant information the Commission has wide-ranging powers of investigation and control. Separate from this is the Securities and Exchange Commission (SEC), which currently operates under the provision of the Investment and Securities Act No. 45 of 1999 and has the primary responsibility for the oversight and management of the Nigerian stock exchange. It has extensive powers to act to preserve the integrity of this market and in respect to the approval of new issues, mergers, etc.

One specific change relevant to the governance framework introduced in CAMA 1990 was a statutory requirement for all listed companies to set up an audit committee (CAMA, 1990, section 359(6)). This section states that the audit committee should assist the board of directors in discharging its oversight responsibilities. This audit committee is required to be made up of three directors (executive or non-executive) and three shareholders.

The specific objectives and functions of the audit committee as stipulated by the Act are to:

- ascertain whether the accounting and reporting policies of the company are in accordance with legal requirements and agreed ethical practices;
- review the scope and planning of audit requirements;
- review the findings on management matters in conjunction with the external auditor and departmental responses thereon;
- keep under review the effectiveness of the company's systems of accounting and internal control;
- make recommendations to the Board in regard to the appointment, removal and remuneration of the external auditors of the company and
- authorise the internal auditor to carry out investigations into any activities of the company which may be of interest or concern to the committee.

(It is noteworthy that this requirement predates the Combined Code requirement in the United Kingdom and that it is enshrined in statute whereas the Combined Code requirement is not (Okike, 2000, 2002, 2007). A further difference is the compulsory inclusion of shareholder representatives on the audit committee, whereas in the United Kingdom the Combined Code requires that only non-executive directors are members of the audit committees. The Act specifically proscribes members of the audit committee receiving remuneration for their work as members of the committee.)

3.1. The Code of Corporate Governance

In addition to the statutory provisions under CAMA 1990 there is a non-statutory Code of Corporate Governance. This emerged as a result of the work of the Committee on Corporate Governance of Public Companies in Nigeria, which finalised its report in April, 2003. The Committee, which was made up of 17 members was inaugurated at the instance of the Nigerian SEC and the CAC. The Committee was composed of members who were selected across all sectors of the Nigerian economy: professional organisations, organised private sector, and regulatory agencies. The terms of reference of the Committee included:

• To identify weaknesses in the current corporate governance practices in Nigeria with respect to public companies.
• To examine practices in other jurisdictions with a view to the adoption of international practices in corporate governance in Nigeria.
• To make recommendations on necessary changes to current practices.
• To examine any other issue relating to corporate governance in Nigeria.

In the course of its work, the Committee identified that the system of corporate governance in Nigeria was still in a developmental stage, noting that principles of corporate governance were not widely appreciated in the commercial sector. A survey sponsored by the Committee revealed that only 40% of quoted companies had specific codes of corporate governance. It pointed out, however, that those without codes were willing to embrace one – emphasising the urgent need for the development of a code of corporate governance for Nigeria. The code which emerged from the work of this Committee essentially followed that developed in various iterations in the United Kingdom[12] with a focus on the role of the board of directors and the importance of both independent non-executive directors and the proper functioning of the audit committee, but there are a number of pertinent differences, for example, in terms of specific requirements for board representation for shareholders in particular significant minority shareholders (Nwauche & Nmehielle, 2004).

4. RESEARCH METHODOLOGY

The methodological approach adopted in this study is that of semi-structured interview. Although the use of such an approach has been commonplace for many years in governance studies there have been few, if any, similar studies conducted in Nigeria. Key players in the Nigerian economic sector are believed to have knowledge, views, understandings, interpretations, experiences and interactions, which are meaningful to obtaining insight into the actuality and practice of governance in Nigeria. Corporate governance issues and practices are intimately related to the environment from which they are drawn and it is therefore conjectured that the use of the semi-structured interview approach that evokes or conjures, as fully as possible, the social experiences or processes surrounding the issues of interest is likely to provide the most meaningful and insightful outcomes.

In compiling the list of prospective interviewees, companies' annual reports, web pages, search engines, Nigerian business and other local newspapers, etc., were explored. At the end of the short-listing exercise, there were 185 names of prospective interviewees who were asked if they were willing to participate. Twenty of these confirmed their willingness. Although the selection process was not strictly a random one, the subjects represented a cross section of stakeholders from the business, government, regulatory and academic environment. Furthermore, subjects came from all of the main regions (north, south, east and west). Clearly the ultimate sample size was in part a reflection of the availability of suitable interviewees and was also conditioned by practical difficulties entailed in obtaining a representative profile of interviewees in a country such as Nigeria with a wide geographical and cultural mix and relatively underdeveloped communication facilities – but nevertheless it is contended that the interviewees were in a position to authoritatively inform on the practice, conduct and overall development of corporate governance in the Nigerian business environment. Brief details of the background and qualifications of the interviewees are included as Appendix 1.[13]

Although acknowledging the limitations of such a study in terms of representativeness of the personnel interviewed – inevitably the background of the interviewees, nearly half of whom were senior managers, will have conditioned the nature of their responses – the number of interviewees and the generic issues associated with interview-based research, as to the veracity or perhaps sub-conscious bias of responses received – the possible desire of the interviewee to be seen to be providing the "correct" or "expected" response, potential interaction effects with the interviewer, the difficulties of analysing the data obtained, etc. – nevertheless we contend that the study has the potential to make a significant research contribution. As noted above, most previous studies of governance in Nigeria have been based on a combination of archival investigation and a priori reasoning. These studies, for example those of Yakassai (2001), Oyejide and Soyibo (2001), Ahunwan

(2002), Okike (2007), have been invaluable – but we seek to build on and add to their contribution by the endeavour to ascertain insights from a wide range of stakeholders in the Nigerian governance process.

Analysis of the interview scripts utilises a synthesis approach, which implies the building of themes emanating from the interview process (Strauss, 1988). There is also some limited use of direct quotes from the interviewees in the reporting of these thematic responses which are discussed below under the following headings:

- *Wider perceptions of governance* – what is corporate governance? governance and performance; regulation and governance and the role of directors;
- *Governance in Nigeria*
    (1) Development – internal influence, external influence, regulatory background
    (2) Process – board appointments, appointments to audit committees
    (3) Audit within governance – roles of audit committee, internal audit and external audit
    (4) Institutional and regulatory structures
    (5) The effectiveness of the legal and regulatory framework;
- *Recommendations for change.*

5. INTERVIEW ANALYSIS AND FINDINGS

5.1. Wider Perceptions of Governance

5.1.1. What is Corporate Governance?
The majority of the interviewees defined corporate governance as encompassing processes, practices, systems and structures aimed at ensuring that the resources of the organisation are well managed to achieve laid down targets and objectives in ethical and lawful ways thereby conforming to standards. The established systems, procedures, etc., spoken about were all targeted at ensuring that investments by shareholders are well rewarded. Encapsulating the views of the respondents as to corporate governance encompassing systems, processes, procedures, principles, etc., one inter-viewee saw corporate governance as:

> the procedures and processes by which an entity is governed that reflects the standards, the values, the principles of the organisation, the controls that are set up within it and the system that establishes the accountabilities and enables the officers who bear responsibilities to be able to give account of their stewardship.

Some respondents conceived of corporate governance in terms of the role and integrity of top management per se. It was opined that corporate governance revolved around the role of board of directors and the top management as regards policy framework, setting up standards and the general framework to keep the organisation in focus entailing oversight functions. It entails the strategic efforts of the top management towards attaining the *raison d'être* of the organisation. The involvement of board committees and other committees towards the successful management of the organisation all constituted corporate governance. Others were of the opinion that it entailed the top management's involvement in the processes, practices, systems and structure. This group of respondents stressed the top management's role in the actual execution of the activities to empower corporate governance ideals and principles. A representative example of this viewpoint was provided by the interviewee who defined corporate governance as

> a system of ensuring that, investments by shareholders or the resources of the company ... are properly managed. By doing that we talk about the managers of the business ... who are executive directors, the CEO and other levels of management and their responsibility towards ensuring that investments by shareholders ... are properly ... equitably deployed to achieve some ... optimum ... returns to the shareholders.

5.1.2. Governance and Performance

Asked about the link between corporate governance and corporate performance, the majority of interviewees considered there to be a link between governance and performance. Few specific examples were provided but rather a general perspective was that if an organisation is well managed in terms of its resources being wisely invested and judiciously utilised, the organisation, *ceteris paribus,* will be expected to make good returns. There was also the belief that good corporate ideals being in practice in an organisation will gradually transform to repeated patronage of the organisation's services and thereby to increased profitability. Furthermore, being corporate governance compliant meant that the organisation was not running foul of the law and was therefore not under threat of incurring fines and penalties. It was also said that a firm that enthrones good corporate governance principles was protective of its shareholders and was almost invariably already achieving performance in that the shareholders were happy and felt safe about their investments in the organisation. A firm that observes good corporate governance practices, it was argued, will be blessed with a board devoid of squabbles which will transcend policy-making, ensuring good profit performance.

For those that saw corporate governance revolving around the top management, it was said that with a good board in place and a favourable environment including absence of undue interference with management by the shareholders that profitability was more likely. A representative view had it that:

> there is a direct correlation ... and it has been proven that where you have efficient and running governance systems you are likely to have better controls ... better accountabilities ... better systems, the organisation itself including the board is likely to have systems for evaluating its own effectiveness and that's bound to highlight areas where there is a development need ... where there is strength and the combination of those is bound to result in improvement in performance whether it is in reliability of the systems but also in the controls ... internally. Beyond that an organisation that has effective governance systems is likely to be able to attract investments, and therefore such investments can power its own growth.

Some were of the opinion that the link was an indirect one but nevertheless were of the opinion that there was a positive relationship in the longer term between good corporate governance and corporate performance. It was opined that in the short run firms could choose to be unethical and follow short-term objectives but that would not be in the long term interests of the firm as eventually the law could catch up with them, whereas the ethical firm would remain "a going concern". It was suggested that appropriate corporate governance creates an environment that could encourage performance. It could also secure goodwill for an organisation that could be relied upon in times of difficulty. With good corporate governance it is believed that an organisation could achieve its objectives in a less risky manner. A number of references were made to the Enron debacle. There is therefore the belief that with the enthronement of good corporate governance an organisation is creating a future for itself that would be sustainable.

The overall environment in terms of values and culture was also a key issue of interest and concern. It was opined that if the value system upheld in the environment did not query the "means by which the end was achieved" but simply appreciated and approved of "the end", then in the short term, organisations engaged in breaching the laws could get away with such behaviour but would have to pay dearly in the longer term. Although the correlation between corporate governance and corporate performance was perceived to be imperfect, it was nevertheless commented that the former enabled firms to guide against certain risks capable of affecting their continued existence and profitability. However, there was not uniformity as to the effectiveness of longer-term sanctions, with one interviewee suggesting that in the banking industry there was evidence to show that institutions had compromised corporate governance – and had been successful in so doing. It was emphasised that the adoption of a good corporate governance regime was not a certain guarantee of profitability and conversely the non-adoption of a good corporate governance regime did not necessarily result in losses. It was however, agreed that when a good corporate governance structure is instituted and it drives the processes and the cultural values of the institution, it makes for a more stable institution that is likely to continue as a going concern and run no (or very low) reputational risk.

Opinions as to whether there are specific linkages between corporate governance and corporate performance in Nigeria different to those found in most Western economies varied. A majority of those interviewed were of the view that there were such differences: the limitation of the rule of law in Nigeria creates a situation where the wrong deeds are not punished. High levels of corruption, disregard and/or disrespect for the law, failure of the regulatory enforcement and police system, the inefficient judicial system, absence of sound regulatory structures, poor infrastructural facilities, instability of government policies all militate against the creation of a corporate governance model similar to that in the United Kingdom and the United States. The representative view was that variations in development and strength of economies significantly impacted corporate governance practices and procedures. But here again, a significant minority felt that such differences if they existed at all were of minor importance. This was summed up by one interviewee accordingly:

> I think ... generally the force(s) governing business is the same all over the world. It's the same forces everywhere ... the laws of economics ... operate like pure science. They are true anywhere you go to ... You can predict ... economic policy that will lead to inflation or something and ... it's true here as it would be true in US.

5.1.3. Regulation and Governance

A majority of the interviewees thought that there was need for intervention by government or regulators in determining the appropriate level and nature of corporate governance. It was felt that just as every game should have an umpire it would be fair practice to have the regulators determine the appropriate nature of corporate governance to avoid chaos. There was the feeling that greed and an unquenching desire for profit maximisation could lead firms without thorough supervision by the regulators to engage in activities that will have adverse social consequences. They believed that firms with inappropriate motives do exist in the Nigerian business environment and therefore made it a need for regulators to be actively involved. The Nigerian aviation industry was given as an example in which failures of control and governance in the industry has resulted in the significant loss of lives and property. This has prompted more direct regulatory interest in the industry, which has been seen as improving safety standards. The banking industry was also identified as having improved since the Central Bank of Nigeria (CBN) became involved in the determination of the nature of corporate governance for banks (Alo, 2003). Failures of individual banks and losses to the depositors prior to the CBNs intervention in the 1990s were seen as having highly negative consequences for the economy.

The attitude of foreign companies operating in Nigeria was also a source of reinforcement of the interviewees' perception as to the need for government intervention. Interviewees suggested that these companies had exploited the country's resources and were enabled to do so by the absence of due government intervention. More recently, setting of standards by the government, such as the minimum wage, has helped curb undue exploitation.

More generally, there was also a perception that in a developing country the free play of market forces will not give rise to the development of appropriate structures and mechanisms which would aid to protect the majority of stakeholders – customers, community residents, employees, suppliers, etc. It was thought that government or regulatory agencies' involvement in the determination of the appropriate nature and level of corporate governance in Nigeria makes the possibility of "weeding out the bad eggs" a real one. Interviewees also identified a role for external intervention and regulation to prevent or limit market abuse, for example, monopolistic or cartel-based pricing – although this function of regulation is at a remove from mainstream governance internal to a company. Again it was pointed out that Nigeria does not have the structures to allow for the determination of corporate governance by the market forces as business ethics and practices and a sound judicial system to speedily adjudicate and resolve potential crisis issues were not yet in place. It is believed that the codes existing were not yet robust enough to permit the market forces to be the sole determinant of the nature of corporate governance in Nigeria.

A smaller number of interviewees commented that both the government and the market forces had roles to play. It is thought that as a third world country the Nigerian government, being a key player in industry and economic development, has to play alongside the market forces in determining the appropriate nature and level of corporate governance. It was suggested that the level of awareness of the stakeholders is low and this could be exploited by the "hawks" – knowledgeable investors who would hijack the entire process of corporate governance determination in the absence of government involvement. The role of the government is thus seen as that of providing for a level-playing ground. It was generally opined that due to the non-existence of an enabling environment and here again – the absence of an efficient legal system being key – there was the need for both the government and the market forces to combine to determine the appropriate nature and level of corporate governance. Moreover, it was opined that due to the fact that markets and governments alike have the potential of failing it was best if there was some "complementarity" by both forces in the determination of corporate governance, believing that both will not fail at the same time. In as much as it would be ideal for the market forces to determine the appropriate nature and level of corporate governance in Nigeria, the government must be a partner as it is the one that would ensure the institution and prevalence of an investor friendly environment. One interviewee suggested that if one of the two dominates, then the system will be at a loss for it.

A still smaller number of interviewees were in favour of the market having an upper hand in the determination of the appropriate level and nature of corporate governance. They thought that the government should interfere and react only when there is clear evidence of market failure. More pervasive regulatory direct involvement would limit companies' freedom of action and possibly limit their access to capital. These interviewees believed that market forces embracing the activities of shareholders, auditors, etc., apart from the government or regulatory agencies could point firms in the right direction. If there was a role for government, it was setting of general principles and ensuring that mechanisms are in place whereby companies that do not abide by these principles are penalised appropriately.

5.1.4. The Role of the Board of Directors
Asked why companies deemed it necessary to have boards of directors, there was a consensus that there was the need to have a structure in place that could be held accountable for the deeds of the company. The board was variously likened to the human heart, brain and spinal cord and as such was seen as the character, credibility and guiding light of the company. It was considered a *sine qua non* for the smooth operation of businesses, without it the company was seen to be lacking goals and visions as well as form and substance. The board of directors was seen as a body that provided direction to the management and the entire organisation. The direction ensured that

the company acted within the law of the land and that any value created was equitably shared amongst all stakeholders. Particular emphasis was placed on the board acting to ensure that one individual does not become all too powerful and dictatorial in the entity. Some interviewees saw the board of directors as a bridge between the owners and the management, existing to protect the interests of the shareholders by setting the ground rules and policies to guide the activities of the executive management and ensuring it acts within the limits of its authority and responsibility towards the attainment of the objectives for which the organisation was formed. These two slightly different versions of the role of board are reflected in the following two extracts from the transcripts. One view was that

> the board of a company makes policies. Supervises management to ensure that those policies are carried out and it monitors ... ensures that management monitors and gives feedback so that policy can be either refined ... to ensure that the company is doing well.

and the other

> Company boards are constituted to give guidance to the company in terms of policy formulation and monitoring management to see to the implementation of such policies and where necessary review of policies based on feedback on the functioning of the policy in terms of the impact it is having on the overall health of the company.

The interviewees identified a number of personal characteristics that make an individual suitable for appointment as a director. They include: knowledge and expertise, honesty, integrity, self respect, objectivity, dedication, willingness to learn, industriousness, independence, experience, competence, influential, mature, discipline, passion and trustworthiness. Knowledge and expertise was a recurring characteristic mentioned by the interviewees and maybe interpreted as basically reaffirming the need to have educated directors with appropriate operational and financial skills. This viewpoint is reinforced by the recommendation of the Nigerian Code of Corporate Governance that directors should be trained at companies' expense before the actual assumption of duty.

5.2. Governance in Nigeria

5.2.1. Development – Internal Influences

It was common ground amongst the interviewees that corporate governance in the Nigerian context was in its infancy and evolving – but that it is now being taken seriously by the business community. Evidence for this and an indication of the penalties attaching to low quality governance procedures was seen in the EFCCs investigation and punishment of prominent Nigerian businessmen, for example, Sir Kingsley Ikpe, the former CEO/MD of Thomas Kingsley Securities Limited; Mr. Bunmi Oni, the former CEO of Cadbury Nigeria Limited, amongst others. Here, the interviewees saw the ongoing privatisation exercise in Nigeria as a particular factor, which has brought corporate governance issues into greater prominence.

From the regulatory angle, the interviewees also referred to the establishment by the SEC, in conjunction with the CAC of a Code of Corporate Governance as giving impetus to the development of governance procedures in Nigeria. Mention was also made of the part played by specific codes of corporate governance for the banking industry published by the CBN. More generally, the interviewees considered that as the Nigerian economy is becoming more liberalised and market oriented basically due to the influence of globalisation, corporate governance issues are of increasing relevance and importance.

Furthermore, some of the interviewees were of the view that corporate failures and scandal within Nigeria leading to loss of trust by would-be investors have fuelled the development of corporate governance. It was said that the collapses of many companies leading to joblessness and insecurity has been an issue necessitating change. The banks were particularly cited as having gone through a number of failure experiences necessitating the recapitalisation order (Atafori, 2007) and the issuance of specific codes of corporate governance relating to the banking sector. That some managers have enriched themselves at the expense of the stakeholders has called into question the effectiveness of regulatory agencies and queried the entire regulatory framework in Nigeria.

Regulatory bodies' insistence on the adoption of best practice together with the establishment of institutions such as the Institute of Directors (IOD) have been seen as basic contributors in advancing the cause of corporate governance. In particular the Nigerian government's economic policy reforms as affecting the business environment were seen as being at the forefront of advancing discourse on corporate governance. Apart from the banking industry reforms mentioned earlier, the insurance industry reforms are ongoing as well as the extractive industry transparency initiative that concerns the oil and gas industries. The ongoing privatisation after the initial Nigerianisation of certain hitherto foreign companies has been viewed as also contributing to the discussion of corporate governance. There is the belief that state-owned enterprises' (SOEs) relatively poor performance as compared to the rising profit profile of privately managed companies has necessitated the ongoing exercise and further strengthened the call for the adoption of good corporate governance practices. One interviewee put it this way:

> I think as privatisation started ... it really has helped to heighten the sensitivity towards governance.

5.2.2. Development – External influences

Enron was referred to on many occasions as a case study for the interest in corporate governance and one with a significant impact on governance in Nigeria. The development of governance codes and regulations in other nations, specifically the Sarbanes-Oxley Act of 2002 in the United States was also seen as a source of influence on the development of corporate governance in Nigeria. A number of interviewees saw the Nigerian government's reforms in line with global developments in modes of doing business and of governance. Globalisation, liberalisation and internationalisation of trade were referred to as influencing the development of corporate governance in Nigeria; and the increasing importance of interaction with the international business community an influence in the adoption of governance practices in Nigeria.

The majority of the interviewees were of the opinion that foreign ownership and management of Nigerian companies had positive impact on the activities of such companies. Furthermore, on the issue of whether corporate governance in a wholly Nigerian company has different characteristics and/or purpose from that in a company with a significant proportion of foreign ownership and management, a majority of the interviewees felt that this was the case. Examples given of these different characteristics attaching to solely Nigerian owned and managed companies are: disregard for standards, local environment and personal characteristics and traits of managers, prevalence of corruption, political interference, mismanagement and waste of resources, low levels of awareness and education, ill-defined company goals, favouritism and nepotism, cultural values, tolerance of malfeasance, external interference, book "cooking" rather than book keeping, poor quality of company management, family control, non-functional boards of directors, etc.

These views were not universally held however with a minority of interviewees perceiving there to be limited differences in governance practices between wholly Nigerian owned and managed companies and those with a significant degree of outside involvement and influences.

There were limited responses and perceptions as to the influence or otherwise of organisations such as the World Bank and the IMF, in the development of corporate governance in Nigeria. The majority that commented on the role of these global institutions were of the opinion that their influence was not directly related to specific issues of corporate governance but rather at national-level issues dealing with accountability, transparency, etc., as concerns national income and resources for overall development – economic and social. However, as businesses and/or commercial activities become increasingly global and internationalised it was expected that these key international institutions would continue to have a role to play in respect to governance – and in particular in relation to banks and other financial institutions.

5.2.3. Development – the Regulatory Background

Asked to what extent the commercial legal and regulatory environment in Nigeria is determined by the country's colonial past and the present day effect of global institutions such as the IMF and the World Bank, a majority of the interviewees were of the opinion that both the colonial past and global institutions were of great influence – although opinion was divided as to which was more important with the majority favouring the colonial past. In the light of this it was said by one interviewee that:

> the country's colonial past has influenced the commercial and regulatory framework. The same can be said of the present day IMF and World Bank. To a great deal the past has influenced. Most commercial laws are modelled after the UK.

Another interviewee noted that:

> the dominant influence is the colonial past. You find that the English law and the English style of doing things is still what direct our own environment to a large extent.

It was said that being a former colony, the English law and style still seem to direct the legal environment to a large extent – although it was noted that there have been conscious efforts over the years to wean the country's legislation away from its colonial antecedents. Interviews noted that the laws have changed due to the various developmental stages the country has gone through (economic doom and boom, military coups, democracy, civil war, etc.). These events and changes in Nigeria have had their impact on business-related legislation in the post-colonial period. Few changes were made to the existing colonial laws immediately after independence in 1960 but over the years changes in government and policies have impacted on the legislation governing businesses. Generally, the particular needs of the Nigerian society, such as desire for an increased flow of foreign investments to boost the economy, create jobs, reduce unemployment, etc., accompanied by its peculiarities in all ramifications – social and cultural (tribal issues, folklores, religious beliefs and perspectives) have necessitated adjustments and amendments of the laws over the years. Two representative views had it that:

> the changes ... it's not because of colonial, the change(s) is because of our dire needs to have more investments.

and that:

> I think the world is becoming a global village so we cannot say whether there is a colonial past or ... whether it is an influence from IMF, World Bank; all of these institutions have become a world institution transcending whether it's Western, Eastern, Northern or whatever, all, it is ... it has transcended all of that, so you cannot localise it.

Again although globalisation and the opening up of the Nigerian economy to outside influences have been important, interviewees also emphasised that the peculiarities of the local traditions and cultures are still very relevant within the Nigerian business environment. One particular example quoted was that in the northern part of the country, some states are under the Sharia law, which is of relevance in terms of taxation, interest and jurisdiction.[14]

Interviewees referred to the banking industry as a specific example where globalisation has been an important factor in the development of the industry and of corporate governance within the industry. The banking industry was particularly said to have modelled its legislations in line with happenings around the world. Global institutions' insistences have been incorporated into the laws governing commerce in Nigeria. There is, however, some level of resistance to global institutions influence with the argument that some of the prescriptions of the IMF and the World Bank have not been considerate of the peculiar Nigerian state. The United States of America was specifically mentioned to have been a great source of influence as regards corporate governance issues in modern Nigeria.

5.3. Process: Appointment of Directors

On the process of appointment to the board of directors, almost all the interviewees were of the opinion that ownership characterised by shareholding was a cardinal determining factor. The board was seen as existing to protect investments of shareholders and in consequence either the majority shareholders or their proxies were normally appointed to sit on boards. New appointments are invariably made at the companies' annual general meetings

(AGMs) in line with the statutory requirement. The CAMA 1990, the Banks and Other Financial Institutions Act (BOFIA) 1991, the individual companies' memorandum and articles of association provide laid down procedures to be followed in the appointments of directors of companies.

Some interviewees noted that in some companies there is a career path arrangement in which after a number of years of diligent service an individual believed to have reached a certain level of competence in technical capability in management and in leadership could merit being invited to serve on the board. It was also said that individuals were also invited to serve on boards of companies on recognition of their personal worth. It is the belief that certain individual's presence on the boards of companies could help boost the corporate image of the company. Such individuals could be filling a knowledge gap, credibility gap or skill gap.

The board of directors was also reported to play a significant role in the appointment of directors. One interviewee said that appointment to the board is:

> spearheaded by the CEO or chairman if the chairman has significant interest ... and any board member that has significant interests ... tend to bring people that they are comfortable with into the board. So they ... suggest the names and request that such persons be made members.

In the same light another interviewee said

> The board has the responsibility for admitting those who join it ... the shareholders will vote on a candidate that is presented by the board.

Some other interviewees also mentioned external factors and government's role as partly influencing the appointment process. It was said that where government had interests or the company depended so much on government's patronage for contracts, the company made it possible for the government to dictate its choice of membership of the board.

A representative view had it that

> But Nigeria being an economy so dependent on the government of the day for contracts and so on, it is common to see government's hand in appointments to the boards of companies.

Summing up the views as to the factors affecting the process of appointment of directors, one interviewee informed that

> Number one shareholding ... two, influence of some strong directors which borders on cronyism and to a very, very insignificant extent someone who really is just viewed as a very good quality material to just come and join the board.

One surprising aspect of the responses was that few of the interviewees clearly distinguished between the appointment of executive and non-executive directors – a key distinction in the modes of governance in Western capitalist economies. This was despite the fact that there is a statutory requirement for audit committees to contain non-executive directors. It was also the case that few of interviewees raised the issue of whether ethnic or gender considerations were relevant in terms of board appointments.

5.4. Process: Appointment of Members of Audit Committees

The interviewees noted both that statute law directed that there should not be more than six members – three directors and three shareholders – and that the Code of Corporate Governance recommended that the chairman of the committee should be a non-executive director. It was reported that the current trend especially as concerns banks in the setting up of the audit committee, was to ensure that there were no executive directors in it. The shareholder representatives on the board are normally nominated before the AGM of the company concerned and voted for on the floor of the AGM, whereas the board appoints its representatives.

Some interviewees felt that the management team including the board of directors was more involved in the process of the appointment of audit committee members, in particular in terms of influencing the appointment of the shareholder representatives. This was seen as having the purpose of heading off the nomination of "mischievous" persons to serve on the audit committees.

> the majority vote at the annual general meeting is already taken care of and in that case you can greatly influence who will come in.

Other interviewees identified factors external to the company as having an influence in the process of appointment. Lobbying by the shareholders' associations to ensure their members are in the committees was referred to as constituting the external factors.

> the only reason why they get on the audit committee is for reasons of blackmail and to hold ... the company to ransom.

One interview contended that shareholders sometimes nominate individuals on the basis of personal characteristics, family relationships, etc., apart from considerations as to whether they are capable of acting for the benefit of the company. Another was of the opinion that even though the statutes are quite clear on how to go about the appointment, it was another challenge altogether to ensure that nominees are truly independent.

5.4.1. Audit Within Governance: The Role of Audit Committees

Asked about the role of audit committees in ensuring appropriate corporate governance within listed companies in Nigeria, a majority of the interviewees were of the view that much work was still to be done before the audit committees played a significant role in ensuring appropriate corporate governance in listed companies in Nigeria. It was said by one interviewee that, the composition of audit committees was not independent as the members were handpicked by the management or the shareholders association without observance of the right procedures. Issues as to the integrity of audit committee members and the possibility of collusion of members of the committee with executive management were raised. There was also reference to the limited scope of work of audit committees, there being an overemphasis on the accounting numbers and insufficient attention being paid to internal controls and internal audit procedures. It was said that the members lacked IT skills to be effective in systems audit.

Furthermore notwithstanding the focus on the financial statement numbers a number of interviewees raised concerns as to how effective the audit committee is in such a monitoring role. Here issues as to the knowledge and commitment of audit committee members were identified. How much financial knowledge the appointees have to effectively function as audit committee members was a concern. It was argued that the effectiveness of audit committees was also hampered by the fact that the legislation setting them up did not look into issues of the right qualifications to be possessed by individuals to be suitable for appointment as members and the absence of remuneration for them. Summing up the fears as to the true contributions of presently standing audit committees to ensuring appropriate corporate governance in Nigeria, one interviewee said:

> What I observed is that yes we have audit committees but ... for a long time my observation is that they are not ... they can do better, maybe in a nut shell. They can do better.

Some other interviewees were however more optimistic about the role of audit committees in ensuring appropriate corporate governance in listed Nigerian companies. The audit committee is considered to be a whistle blower; an audit alarm committee that alerts of some impending danger it was said. The audit committees were also viewed as watchdogs placed to ensure things are properly done, in that basic controls are adhered to. It is believed that they check the records and ensure that the company is fit to face external auditors. The committee was said to have successfully served as a stopgap between management, the shareholders, the board and the external auditors. It is viewed as a vetting committee of the financial reports and taking into account the comments and observations of both the internal and external auditors thereby giving credibility to financial disclosures. The fact that there is a committee exercising oversight responsibilities on which the shareholders are represented and make contributions gives the shareholders confidence that financial information will be compiled and disseminated appropriately.

Perception as to the determinants of the size and membership mix of audit committees in listed Nigerian companies varied amongst the interviewees. A majority saw the companies' legislations – the CAMA 1990, the Banks and Other Financial Institutions Act (BOFIA) 1991 and even the individual companies' articles and memorandum of association as being basic determinants. For some interviewees, the size of the company and amount of work it had to do determined its size. Others considered the matter to be a case of a blend of the above two mentioned determining factors. They felt the statutes as well as the size of the company determined the size and membership mix of the audit committees.

Specifically when asked if ethnic and gender considerations were of relevance in the constitution of committees, a majority of the interviewees were of the opinion that these were not issues of relevance. It was said that geographical representation does not match the real objective of the audit committees – what does matter is that people who have technical competencies, knowledge and experience are appointed. One interviewee considered that though Nigerians were intrinsically conscious of ethnic and gender issues these were of little importance in determining appointments to the audit committees. Another however suggested that companies sought to balance the ethnic mix in particular when companies operated on a national scale. For example it was suggested that at the First Bank of Nigeria, care would be taken to ensure that all its directors do not come from a particular tribe one reason for this being a desire to avoid customer perception of a particular regional or tribal basis. This will be mere sensitivity to the market. A representative view, however, was that ethnic and gender issues are largely irrelevant in the modern Nigerian companies.

A few dissenting voices, however, were of the opinion that gender and ethnic considerations were relevant. It is said that in Nigeria, "societies like our own", there were certain privileges attached to one's ethnic background.

One interviewee suggested that in Nigeria, gender sensitivity is an issue as it is thought that it would be right to ensure that the females are represented in committees. There is also the federal character issue which suggests that there is an implied understanding, though undocumented, that various ethnic groups, states or regions are represented fairly equally in appointments. One interviewee was of the opinion that even though the law did not specifically instruct that gender or ethnic considerations should prevail, that it was part of the "game" to give cognisance to them in appointments – although it was difficult to demonstrate that adequate considerations had been given to an appropriate gender or ethnic balance.

5.4.2. Audit Within Governance: The Role of Internal Audit

Asked about the role of internal audit in the Nigerian corporate governance environment, the majority of the interviewees was positive about its contribution seeing it as a watchdog and an effective tool and additional resource to management. The existence of an internal audit was seen as a further contribution to compliance by management with internal controls and risk management policies and checks instituted by the organisation. Internal audit ensures that due process, transparency and accountability are followed in the operations of an organisation thereby safeguarding its assets. It provides information to guide the management in decision-making and prevents connivance between management and the external auditor. A representative view had it that internal audit exits:

> To ensure basic controls are adhered to. To give comfort that there will be no hasty surprises. Ensure worldwide applicability. Ensure strict compliance by management with internal controls and risk management policies and checks instituted by the organisation.

A minority of those interviewed was sceptical as to its role, in that the effectiveness of internal audit was limited by lack of independence, as the internal auditors are employees who could be fired at will and lack adequate resources, authority and power. Studies have suggested that internal auditors are reliant upon their employers both for their living and also for the scale of resources devoted to internal audit function (Gwilliam, 1987; Gwilliam & Marnet, 2007). The commitment of the internal auditors was also a concern as was the fact that their functions were exercised largely after the event and were less effective thereby. Two representative views are that:

> Internal audit has some significant role to play. Ordinarily with an effective internal audit, external audits are easily carried out because they just try to ascertain few issues. They simply sample items of interest for confirmation. Having said that I still think

> internal audits need to be improved. The expected independence is denied the department. This has negative impact on the overall usefulness of the unit. Internal audits are sometimes seen as an extension of the management. This ought not to be so. Management interferes in its functions that you begin to doubt the usefulness of the department.

and that:

> if they do their work well they would be able to keep people on their toes to ensure that they are doing what they are supposed to be doing as they are supposed to do it. But as I said the leadership of that committee must be at a level that will win the support and respect of the management and board of that organisation ... Again they must have adequate and competent staff. Sometimes they do not have enough staff to be able to cover what they are supposed to cover in a period and at times they do not have enough finance ... So these three things must be there-they must be properly staffed, adequately staffed, headed at a level that is top management because you have top management and they must be adequately financed and they must have independence. If they don't have independence and they have all these then there is no use. It means that if I do something wrong you can ignore it or even if you want to do something you don't have the power to do so. They must also have appropriate powers and authority. If they don't have all that, their job will be compromised ... they are the policeman ... if the policeman is not knowledgeable, is weak, does not have guns, or his guns are out modelled ... he will not be effective.

5.4.3. Audit Within Governance: The Role of External Audit

On the role of external auditors in ensuring appropriate corporate governance in listed Nigerian companies, a majority of the interviewees saw the role of external auditors as very important. External auditors were seen as having strong professional capability to test the organisational system from an external unbiased perspective and that they were committed, fair and systematic in the discharge of their duties thereby ensuring adherence to established regulatory standards of financial reporting. A representative view had it that:

> the external auditors come with strong professional capability to test the ... the system from an external totally unbiased point of view and I think that's ... the value that the external auditor brings. They can totally...have a different perspective in evaluating ... the work of the organisation and they can align those with what they know to be sort of the accounting standards board or the financial regulatory standards to be sure that things work in accordance with what ... the regulations or what the legislation says; and increasingly in areas like revenue recognition, in areas like control mechanisms, in areas like credit control and in areas like management processes. Now those are increasing areas where external auditors can add value to the organisation.

However, again a number of interviewees identified constraints on the exercise of the external auditors' function. These constraints included inadequate and false information/ data provided by companies, length of stay in an organisation, contractual status (being paid by the organisation), connivance with management to ensure reappointment, limited powers of investigation and enquiry, ethical misconduct, deliberate fault finding. Marnet (2004) agrees with some of the observations when he says that:

> Typical to most, if not all, cases of massive corporate fraud cases of the recent past was a clean bill of the firms' financial reports immediately prior to the discovery of the fraud.

Furthermore, some other studies have also suggested that the mere proximity of the client is sufficient to introduce bias in perception, interpretation and judgement by the professional and to result in audit interpretations favourable to the client (Zajonc, 1968; O'Connor, 2002; Bazerman, Loewenstein, & Morgan, 1997; Bazerman, Loewenstein, & Moore, 2002). These constraints were perceived as inhibiting external audit in performing its ascribed role within the overall governance structure. In this light three representative views are that:

> every year you hear a company, they've audited their books and so on, then a couple of years down the line, they die. If the auditors are doing their work ... I have a personal problem with that. If the auditors are doing their work how come they were not able to quickly highlight the problems.

Another is that:

> I'm not sure they are playing that role as much as they should. For many reasons it is difficult to play that role as much as the external auditors should. First the external auditor is appointed by maybe management, of course approved by the board and endorsed by the shareholders so if these people appoint you and you go back and tell them that look your board is too unwieldy, how will they take it? Or you tell them that the way you people function on this board la, la, la, la, la how will they take it? So people get a bit shy, people leave that aspect of what they should as well address and deal with the numbers. That one they probably will do it well and probably would not lie or tell as much lies as they would in telling you, you people are doing ok, the board is nice, because these are numbers; it is difficult to lie with numbers. To an extent they have a strong role to play but I believe they are not playing that role as much as they should.

It was also said that:

> the role of external auditor of course is to give ... precise ... financial position of a company and without ... favour to either the board or the management. The failure of many companies has arisen because the ... auditors in order to ensure that they are reappointed, they try ... to co-operate with the management and they hide things until it's too ... I mean until the situation becomes really bad. I had always thought that the law should be more stringent on the punishment due to auditor who had been auditing the book of a company before they collapse.

In line with the perceptions when asked how well external auditors perform their role, some interviewees were of the opinion that there was need for repositioning and improvement. Concerns were expressed as to whether external auditors had lived up to societal expectations and it was suggested that strengthening of the internal audit units would lead to better quality outcomes. Some interviewees reported their belief that the internationally affiliated external auditors were better performers in that they were more concerned to protect their reputation. Two representative views had it that:

> to a very large extent yes a few had done very well but some others are yet to reposition themselves to do things properly the way it should be done.

and that:

> Well the external auditors in most cases they do well ... as I told you earlier the globalisation has influenced the way things are done in this country even the external auditors are now more professional because a lot of them have international affiliations and they don't want to compromise that. A PWC in Nigeria is a PWC in South Africa, in England in any European country. So if there is a problem here with any of the international auditing firms it affects them internationally. So they wouldn't want to compromise their standards because it would create reputation problems for them.

One dissenting view had it that external auditors were working against the interest of the company – their only concern being to maintain good relationships with management to ensure their reappointment. In this light it was said that:

> I have always had a suspicion that most auditors ... auditing company is ... including expatriate ones, they've not ... been as straight as one would have ... although you see the need to reappoint the auditor from time to time ... can work adversely for the interest of the company because sometimes in order to ensure that they would be reappointed they become complaint with the management.

5.4.4. Institutional and Regulatory Structures

Asked how effective the regulatory agencies in particular the CAC, SEC, CBN were in the enforcement of regulation and ensuring corporate governance in listed Nigerian companies, a majority of the interviewees were of the view that the regulatory agencies were doing their best in an environment constrained by the reality of the influence by government and other external factors. Nevertheless concerns were expressed by the interviewees as to the levels of experience, competence and indeed integrity of employees at all levels of these agencies. Abuse of office was seen as commonplace with some individuals preferring to be seen as "bosses" in charge of regulatory organisations and enforcement was on occasion malicious for political or personal reasons rather than in the interest of promoting compliance more generally. Furthermore, it was mentioned that double standards flourished within the Nigerian regulatory environment. A "favoured" individual or company could be above the law. One interviewee pointed to the circumstances surrounding the sale of Nigerian Telecommunication Limited (NITEL) as an illustrative example. The circumstances for which the first bidder (INTEL London International) lost out were the same that permitted the purchase of the company by the second "favoured" bidder (Transnational Corporation of Nigeria Plc-Transcorp). A representative view had it that:

> these organisations have the capability to be the best they can. But once again the Nigerian factor seems to impact on them quite negatively. In some cases we have the wrong people in positions of trust. They bring in their wrong attitudes to the operations of these ordinarily well organised commissions. The basis for the founding of these commissions was noble but unfortunately the management of these organisations have been the problem in most cases. Appreciate the fact also that some of these organisations are more or less government establishments with the attendant bureaucracies impacting on their performance. The boards are used to satisfy political loyalists. With such a situation where round pegs are in square holes what is expected is nothing other than dismal performance. Summarily, I will like to add that if these organisations are allowed to function based on the establishing ethics they will contribute very positively to the state of corporate governance in Nigeria.

The SEC was given credit for the establishment of the first Code of Corporate Governance in Nigeria – but this was the best it got as it was further suggested that the overall performance of the regulatory bodies was uneven with the CBN being singled out as the most effective and even headed in carrying out its regulatory role. Concerns were also expressed as to the level of resources commanded by the regulatory agencies and indeed levels of internal control and performance evaluation within the agencies.

Weaknesses of monitoring mechanisms as discussed above in the context of the CAMA 1990, were identified as affecting all of the regulatory agencies – and it was also noted that the agencies had to work within an environment in which here was a general disregard for the law and unethical standards in business practices inimical to good conduct of business that would ordinarily not be tolerated in developed economies were allowed to thrive in the Nigerian business environment with impunity. An example given was that the director-general of the Nigerian Stock Exchange is also the chairman of the board of directors of Transcorp, a company with no track record whose shares were allowed to be traded in the stock exchange. This was perceived to be a case of double standards and favouritism. Bureaucracy was also seen to be weighing down the effectiveness of some of the agencies. The fact that Nigerian investors are still not sophisticated in terms of the operations of financial markets is a factor that encourages poor performance; as the investors do not cry foul when they are expected to and when such an outcry would have acted as checks on the regulatory agencies. Fear of individuals in higher positions is also a source of worry. One interviewee said that

> people are scared of doing their job because they are afraid of the powers that be, that nobody sees their face. It's just like a mafia. They can do a lot of things ... and then that's exactly what is impacting negatively on the performance of some of the regulatory authorities because they are scared.

5.4.5. The Effectiveness of the Legal and Regulatory Framework
Asked how effective is the CAMA 1990 as a regulatory framework for the conduct of business in Nigeria and if its implementation and enforcement were adequate, the majority of those interviewed were of the view that the CAMA, 1990 was a well thought through document – but that it suffered from poor implementation and enforcement. Enforcement activities under the umbrella of the CAC are reactive rather than proactive and were heavily reliant upon external sources for information. The interviewees were negative as to the activities of the inspectorate division of the CAC. It was suggested that the CAC engaged itself in mundane activities such as asking companies about absence of information as to the location of the registered office rather than on ensuring that books and other returns are up to date. A representative view had it that:

> I think it's comprehensive and sufficiently robust because it covers every important element. So I'll consider CAMA as adequate. Enforcement? ... Yeah, I think enforcement can be improved, even more compliance could improve.

It was pointed out by one interviewee that the business public's awareness of the Act was poor as many were not aware of its existence or content. The interpretation by Nigerians given to the document was seen to be a problem affecting its successful implementation. Some saw the document as one of the statutes that just exist and really felt that the companies' memoranda and articles of association superseded its authority. One interviewee talked about the fact that since 1990 many things would have changed in the business environment which would have necessitated the review of the Act and since there had not been any such review and update, the law was incapable of addressing the realities of the modern Nigeria business environment with its much more open capital structure and robust stock market. This was summed up by one interviewee accordingly:

> I think it's due for revision ... it has provided a framework but what we are saying is that times are changing, new situations are arising which maybe did not exist at the time those rules were made or like as I said again some of the penalties for non-compliance, they do not make any financial meaning now.

Others, however, opined that CAMA was both adequate and enforceable as those who feel aggrieved could seek reprieve in court. Others considered that updating by means of statutory instrument meant that the Act had changed with times and was quite sufficient. In line with this one interviewee said that:

> I know it's been a veritable tool and since it has guided business so far and such that there are no ambiguities. You have relationships as spelt ... you can align them with provisions on the Companies Allied Act ... Matters Act. And that to a very large extent had helped businesses ... individuals or stakeholders to define their roles in relationship and also be able to define the scope and areas you could go into and ... some conditions and rules that guide them. Yes to that extent the CAMA had done quite well and of course it is enforceable in court ... any person who feels aggrieved and he feels that ... he stuck to the provisions of a section, can seek reprieve in the court. So to that extent it is a legal document that can be enforced. I think it has done well for businesses.

A minority called for more self-regulation by companies, a scenario in which companies will be governed by their internal codes of corporate governance that feeds from the overall code and commercial laws of the state other than outright dependence on the dictates and/or stipulations of the Act.

Other issues not directly related to the issue of governance within publicly listed companies were identified. These are discussed further.

Commercial disputes were also said not to be getting priority attention in the dispensation of justice. The judicial system fraught with bottlenecks was blamed for the poor implementation of the law. It was perceived that the legal system was overly bureaucratic and some interviewees called for the setting up of special and/or industrial courts of law to deal speedily with commercial litigation and such related matters. A particular consequence of the slowness of the judicial system was that banks have had capital tied down for years, capital which otherwise could be put to profitable use. The defaulters go to get court injunctions that paralyse the process of recovery of loans even where there is ample evidence of the existence of a lien, mortgage or collateral from defaulting parties. It was also mentioned that penalties meted out for infraction of the law are very unrealistic in that they are not in tandem with present day economic realities. The monetary penalties consequent to infraction do not reflect the gravity of the offence.

More wide-ranging concerns expressed by interviewees related to the monitoring and enforcement of legislation relating to corporate taxation, the complexity of the law relating to land and property transactions and more prosaically the poor quality of draftsmanship in respect to much commercial legislation and regulation.

5.5. Recommendations for Change

When asked as to the manner in which corporate governance in Nigeria might be enabled to move forward, and, by inference at least, what issues currently held back its development interviewees focused at an overall level on the need for the provision of an enabling environment for business activities to thrive. Key to such an environment were improvements in the economic infrastructure both physical (power, transportation, distribution systems) and in terms of political stability, greater efficiency in the administration of the legal system in particular in relation to commercial transactions and a reduction in the perceived level of corruption both at the individual and the state level.

> Government should also try and provide infrastructure to help corporate outfits. The issue of electricity in this country is creating plenty problems ... government should be able to look into it and improve on our electricity generation and distribution to help corporate outfits to do well.

Another interviewee said that:

> the government should provide the enabling environment so our businesses could move on and that would of course engender the much touted foreign direct investments. Because if the foreigners have confidence in your system definitely capital inflows will just come in and also stimulate the growth, the economic growth we are all yearning for and of course good living for every Nigerian.

Here there was a consensus that the state had a vital role to play in ensuring such developments as there was insufficient confidence that market forces alone would act to bring about the necessary changes. However, this recognition of the importance of the role of the state was balanced by the perspective held by many interviewees that direct interference by the state in business activity should be limited and in particular in respect to political influence on board appointments. A representative view was:

> I think generally government is not expected to be intrusive into companies to the extent
> that it would make things difficult for them.

In line with this perception was support for the ongoing privatisation
exercise of the government and calls for privatisation efforts to be
intensified, albeit proceeding with caution and after proper feasibility
studies and research. This was summed up by one interviewee accordingly:

> the first thing of course is that the private sector should enlarge and most things should
> be done through the encouragement of private investment rather than public ... all
> public something they end up in abuse and ... the future of this country depends upon
> the strong private investment enterprises.

More specific measures endorsed by one or more interviewees included:

5.5.1. Giving Legal Force to the Code of Corporate Governance
One interviewee referred to it as a mere "toothless bulldog" in that
companies are not obliged to comply with the provisions therein. Without it
being compulsory for a developing country such as Nigeria, companies will
prefer to continue to short-change the system. A representative viewpoint
was provided by one interviewee:

> Give weight to the Code of Best Practice. Give it legal backing. Give it teeth.

5.5.2. Development of Sector Codes of Corporate Governance
Here it was suggested that each of the sectors of the economic life of Nigeria
such as the aviation, banking, insurance, automobile, printing and
publication, hotel and tourism, etc., industries should develop codes of
corporate governance to guide business operations and activities within each
of the sectors. This does not however invalidate the necessity of an overall
code of corporate governance but emphasises the peculiarities of each of the
sectors of the economic life of Nigeria. Specific industry codes (other than
those relating to financial services) are not common in developed countries –
but opinion was advanced that the differentials in terms of development,
growth and maturity in the various Nigerian industry and service sectors
meant that serious consideration should be given to specific industry codes:

> every sector should be asked to develop its own code. They should domesticate the code
> of corporate governance.

5.5.3. Revision of Commercial Laws

It was suggested that the framework of commercial law in particular CAMA 1990 should be revised and where necessary updated to reflect and accommodate present day economic realities. One particular aspect was the need for a clearer distinction between companies of different size and consideration of the applicability of legislation to small companies (defined by the interviewees as the informal sector). To require these companies to comply with the disclosure and audit standards designed for much larger companies with significant outside shareholder involvement was seen as unnecessarily burdensome.

A more specific suggestion was that the restrictions contained in the Act on audit committee members receiving remuneration be lifted as it was perceived that this would encourage individuals with appropriate qualifications and training to make themselves available to be audit committee members.

5.5.4. Enhanced Monitoring and Supervision by the Regulatory Agencies

The regulatory agencies, in particular the CAC and the SEC were criticised for their poor performance in relation to effective monitoring and supervision. Examples were given with respect to the quality of disclosures in company annual reports, the failure to ensure appropriate filing of company annual reports, and as to market abuse and irregularity in the Nigerian stock exchange. In this respect the views of many of the interviewees were in line with those expressed by one commentator (Makinde, 2005) that the underlying problems lie not with the formal regulations and associated policy objectives but rather with the methods and manner of enforcement – or lack thereof. It was suggested that attention should be paid both to the possibility of setting up special independent investigation inspectorate units within the regulatory agencies and ensuring that these units, and indeed the agencies themselves were appropriately resourced and staffed.

5.5.5. Training and Education

The importance of training and educating directors on their responsibilities and role in ensuring accountability and transparency was emphasised as vital for the actualisation of the practice of good corporate governance in the Nigerian commercial environment. It was thought that companies should take the training of their directors more seriously. In this context companies were urged to pay for the training of their directors before their actual commencement of their roles as directors. Furthermore, it was suggested that awareness campaigns be organised to educate the investing public on the importance of corporate governance. It was generally agreed by the interviewees that the level of awareness of the public as to corporate governance issues was inadequate. Here, it was recommended that corporate governance be introduced as a subject matter in the business curriculum of institutions. It was also suggested that there was the need for more research to be conducted on corporate governance as concerns the specific Nigerian commercial environment. Two representative views had it that:

> I think a lot of education needs to be put in place, a lot of it, a lot. It hasn't happen and there is an honest desire to actually know what is supposed to be done to improve corporate governance. There are lots of honest people who just don't know ... they are serving on boards but they really don't know what they are supposed to do on those boards.

Another had it that:

> corporate governance should be made a subject matter in business schools ... It should go all the way to suggest what good corporate governance situation can do to our business and a bad corporate governance can do. People will need to understand that a very small and minute issue relating to corporate governance can run down a business or a company.

6. OVERVIEW AND CONCLUSION

The interview responses provided a wealth of detail both as to the manner in which governance is practised in Nigeria and also as to how the interviewees see the direction which governance is, or should be, taking as the Nigerian economy develops and grows. In terms of the dichotomy identified in the introductory section between the perspective that the importation of Western style governance practices will act to benefit growth and welfare in developing countries and that, which suggests that such practices are likely to be ineffective, there is no doubt that the great majority of interviewees, favoured the more positive perspective. Although alert to both failures in implementation and the possibility of cultural dissonance almost all the interviewees were supportive of legislative requirement for audit committees and of the recently introduced Code of Corporate Governance, a Code modelled closely on that developed in the United Kingdom. Furthermore, they provided a number of specific recommendations, for example with regard to: legal backing for the Code of Corporate Governance; the development of sector governance codes; revision and updating of the framework of commercial law; enhanced monitoring and supervision by regulatory agencies and additional commercial training and education.

Perhaps surprisingly, only a minority of interviewees expressed the view that the three factors identified in Section 2 as likely to be of particular relevance to the Nigerian context, specifically ethnicity, gender and power relationships, were of other than marginal importance in terms of their impact on the development and practice of governance and corporate regulation in Nigeria. However, these responses made to explicit questioning were not entirely consistent with those derived more implicitly from the wider interview process. For example, with respect to appointments to board-level positions a number of interviewees were of the opinion that such appointments were frequently determined by factors other than merit alone. Professionalism, experience and qualifications were not always given the highest priority in contrast to considerations of family, friendship, cronyism, ethnicity, religion, associations (social and otherwise). As one interviewee put it:

> I think that people should attach importance to ability of persons appointed into corporate outfits in this country rather than looking at where someone is from ... people should not look so much at the tribe or on the tribe of someone when you want to employ provided the person is able to deliver the goods.

Another possible indicator that cultural issues were of greater importance than might be deduced from the observed responses of interviewees lay in the perception that there were significant differences between the nature and practice of corporate governance as and between "inward facing" businesses, i.e. those owned and managed by Nigerians and catering largely for the domestic market and "outward facing" businesses, i.e. those with a significant overseas ownership and management and whose market was not necessarily solely Nigerian in its composition. Of course given the disparity in size on average between "inward facing" and "outward facing" businesses this might in part be a reflection of the wider phenomenon of the lesser importance accorded to corporate governance in smaller firms and where there is a significant degree of owner management. Nevertheless again the nature of the responses did imply that underlying cultural factors were of greater importance than might be deduced from face value evaluation of interviewees' reactions to more specific questions of this nature – and this is an area, which merits further investigation and study.

NOTES

1. On October 1, 1960, Dr. Nnamdi Azikiwe became the first indigenous governor-general. In 1963, in which year Nigeria became a Republic and adopted the British parliamentary system of government, Abubakar Tafawa Balewa was elected

Prime Minister. On January 15, 1966, junior officers in the military overthrew the government with General T. Aguiyi-Ironsi, an easterner and the most senior military officer, stepping in to restore order as head of state. Following the assassination of Ironsi in a coup d'etat orchestrated by mostly northern officers on August 1, 1966, Yakubu Gowon became head of state. Between 1966 and 1976 military leadership changed twice more before General Olusegun Obasanjo handed over power to Alhaji Shehu Shagari on October 1, 1979. After the over-throw of this civilian administration military rule became the order of the day again as there was one military coup after the other until May 29, 1999, when Olusegun Obasanjo was sworn in as the democratically elected president.

    2. CIA Fact Book (Washington, DC: Central Intelligence Agency, 2003).

    3. Nigeria by Onwudiwe, E. http://unpan1.un.org/intradoc/groups/public/documents/NISPAcee/UNPAN016076.pdf (accessed on 28/09/05).

    4. Chimamanda Adichie's award winning novel 'The Purple Hibiscus' (Adichie, 2003) provides fascinating insights into gender and power issues within a Nigerian domestic context.

    5. http://unpan1.un.org/intradoc/groups/public/documents/NISPAcee/UNPAN016076.pdf (accessed on 28/09/05), The Women's Watch http://iwraw.igc.org/publications/womenswatch/vol%2012-1%20and%202%20December%201998.htm (accessed on 30/10/06).

    6. http://ww1.transparency.org/cpi/2005/cpi2005_infocus.html (accessed on 18/10/05), http://www.guardiannewsngr.com/editorial_opinion/article01 (accessed on 08/11/2005).

    7. http://www.iss.co.za/AF/profiles/Nigeria/Economy.html (accessed on 03/11/05).

    8. World Bank (2002).

    9. Djankov, McLiesh, and Shleifer (2005) and Morriset and Neso (2005).

    10. Companies Ordinance of 1912, The Companies Ordinance 1922 and Companies Act 1968.

    11. See the Nigerian Law Reform Commission Report on Reform of Company Law, 1988, Vol.1, pp.10–11.

    12. The most recent version of the UK Code, issued by the Financial Reporting Council in June 2006, can be found at http://www.frc.org.uk/corporate/combinedcode.cfm (accessed on 04/08/07).

    13. A more extensive set of biographical detail is to be found in Angaye (2008).

    14. For more general references as to the impact of Sharia law on business practices and governance see Sfeir (1988), Zaher and Hassan (2001), Abdalla (2002) and Daly (2005).

ACKNOWLEDGMENTS

This paper is based on research carried out while the first named author was undertaking doctoral studies at Aberystwyth University and the authors would like to acknowledge and thank both Aberystwyth University and Niger Delta University for their support for this research. They would also like to thank two anonymous reviewers for their helpful and insightful comments on earlier drafts.

REFERENCES

Abdalla, R. (2002). The underground banking systems and their impact on control of money laundering: With special reference to Islamic banking. *Journal of Money Laundering Control, 6*(1), 42–46.

Adichie, C. N. (2003). *Purple Hibiscus*. UK: Fourth Estate.

Ahunwan, B. (2002). Corporate governance in Nigeria. *Journal of Business Ethics, 37*(3), 269–287.

Ahunwan, B. (2003). *Globalisation and corporate governance in developing countries: A micro analysis of global corporate interconnection between developing African countries and developed countries*. New York: Transnational Publishers.

Akpan, G. E. (2007). Natural resource control: A market view. *Nigerian Economic Society Journal, 47*(1).

Alo, O. (2003). *Issues in corporate governance*. Lagos: Financial Institutions Training Centre Publication.

Aminu, A., & Elueme, L. (2004). Central Bank of Nigeria to denounce misleading adverts by banks. This day. http://allafrica.com/stories/200412150045.html (accessed on 10/01/05).

Angaye, G. S. (1994). *Socio-economic development in Nigeria*. Port Harcourt: Pam Unique Publishers.

Angaye, G. S. (2002). Who owns papa's land and oil in Nigeria, http://www.nigerdeltacongress. com/garticles/who_owns_papas_land_and_oil_in_nigeria.htm (accessed on 12/05/05).

Angaye, G. S. (2003). Causes and cures of conflicts in Nigeria, http://www.nigerdeltacongress. com/garticles/causes_and_cures_of_conflicts_in.htm (accessed on 27/09/05).

Angaye, G. S. (2005). Poverty amid plenty in Nigeria. *Rivers Journal of the Social Sciences, 1 & 2*, 13–46.

Angaye, P. (2008). *Evaluation of corporate governance in Nigeria*. Unpublished PhD dissertation. Aberystwyth: University of Wales.

Annisette, M. (2004). The true nature of the World Bank. *Critical Perspectives on Accounting, 15*(4 & 5), 303–323.

Ariyo, D. (2004). Small firms are the backbone of the Nigerian economy, www.AfricaEconomic Analysis.org (accessed on 10/10/05).

Atafori, A. K. (2007). Should Ghana emulate Nigeria's banking reforms. *The Statesman*, http:// www.thestatesmanonline.com/pages/news_detail.php?newsid = 3147&section = 7 (accessed on 02/11/07).

Bahri, A. (2001). Introduction to postcolonial studies, http://www.emory.edu/ENGLISH/ Bahri/Into.html (accessed on 12/10/05).

Barr, G. J., & Kantor, B. (1995). Shareholders as agents and principals: The case for South Africa's corporate governance system. *Journal of Applied Corporate Finance, 8*(1), 1–32.

Bazerman, M. H., Loewenstein, G., & Morgan, K. (1997). The impossibility of auditor independence. *Sloan Management Review, 38*(4), 89–94.

Bazerman, M. H., Loewenstein, G., & Moore, D. A. (2002). Auditor independence, conflict of interest and the unconscious intrusion of bias. Harvard NOM Research Paper No. 02-04. Available at http://ssrn.com/abstarct_id = 324261 (accessed on 17/07/07).

Bleaney, M., & Greenway, D. (2002). The impact of terms of trade and real exchange rate volatility on investment and growth in Sub-Saharan African. *Journal of Development Economics, 65*(2), 491–500.

Botha, de Villiers J. H. (2001). Corporate governance in state-owned enterprises: A developmental perspective. Paper presented at the Pan African Consultative Forum on Corporate Governance, Johannesburg, South Africa. 16–18 July.

Briston, R. J. (1990). Accounting in developing countries: Indonesia and the Solomon Islands as case studies for regional cooperation. *Research in Third World Accounting, 1*, 195–216.

Daly, B. (2005). *Islam and the tax code – should Ireland follow the UK's lead?* Tax Monitor, UK: KPMG.

Dike, V. E. (1999a). *Leadership, democracy and the Nigerian economy: Lessons from the past and directions for the future.* Sacramento, CA: The Lightning Press.

Dike V.E. (1999b). *The philosophy of transforming Nigeria into a corruption-free society: Are the probes the solution?* Online Publication, Nigeriaworld.com/feature/article/corruption. html, October 6.

Dike, V. E. (2001). *Democracy and Political Life in Nigeria, Zaria.* Nigeria: Ahmadu Bello University Press.

Dike, V. E. (2002). *The State of education in Nigeria and the health of the nation* (June). Nigeria Economic Summit Group (NESG) periodical, Abuja, Nigeria.

Dike, V. E. (2008). *Corruption in Nigeria: A new paradigm for effective control* (http://www.africaeconomicanalysis.org/articles/gen/corruptiondikehtm.html (accessed on 26/03/08)). Africa Economic Analysis.

Djankov, S., McLiesh, C., & Shleifer, A. (2005). Private Credit in 129 Countries. NBER Working Paper N0. 11078. Cambridge, MA.

Elekwa, N. N., Soludo, C. C., & Ikpeze, N. I. (2004). Nigeria: The political economy of the policy process, policy choice and implementation a continuum. In: C. C. Soludo, O. Ogbu & J. Chang (Eds), *The politics of trade and industrial policy in Africa: Forced consensus?* New Jersey: Africa World Press.

Ewulu, B. (2002). *Why British investors shun Nigeria* (July 9, pp. 7–8). Daily Trust.

Ezeife, D. I. (2005). The Savannah Bank Imbroglio – a critical look, http://www.gamji.com/NEWS1658.htm (accessed on 10/01/05).

Fafunwa, A. B. (1974). *History of education in Nigeria.* London: Allen and Unwin.

French, M. (1985). *Beyond power: On women, men and morals.* New York: Summit.

Gatamah, K. (2001). *Corporate governance in Kenya.* Kenya: CIPE.

Gerson, J. (1992). *The determinants of corporate ownership and control in South Africa.* Unpublished Ph.D Dissertation. University of California at Los Angeles, USA.

Gerson, J., & Barr, G. (1996). The structure of corporate control and ownership in a regulatory environment unbiased toward one-share-one-vote. *Corporate Governance – An International Review, 4*(2), 78–93.

Gray, R. H., & Bebbington, J. (2001). *Accounting for the environment* (2nd ed). London, UK: Sage.

Gwilliam, D. (1987). *A survey of auditing research.* London, UK: ICAEW/Prentice-Hall.

Gwilliam, D., & Marnet, O. (2007). Audit within the corporate governance paradigm: A cornerstone built on shifting sand? Working Paper, University of Exeter, Exeter, UK.

Haniffa, R., & Hudaib, M. (2006). Corporate governance structure and performance of Malaysian listed companies. *Journal of Business Finance and Accounting, 33*(7 & 8), 1034–1062.

Haniffa, R. M., & Cooke, T. E. (2002). Culture, corporate governance and disclosure in Malaysian corporations. *ABACUS, 38*(3), 317–349.

Haralambos, M., & Holborn, M. (1990). *Sociology: Themes and perspectives.* London: Unwin and Hyman.

Held, D., & McGrew, A. (2002). *Globalisation/anti-globalisation.* Cambridge, MA: Polity.

Husted, B. W., & Serrano, C. (2002). Corporate governance in Mexico. *Journal of Business Ethics, 37*(3), 337–348.

International Monetary Fund (IMF). (2005). *Nigeria: Selected issues and statistical appendix.* IMF Country Report No. 05/303. Washington, DC: International Monetary Fund.

Isichei, E. (1976). *A history of the Igbo people.* London: Macmillan.

Ismail, M. I., Samad, M. F., & Zulkafli, A. H. (2008). Corporate Governance in Malaysia, http://www.micg.net/research/CORPORATE%20GOVERNANCE%20IN%20MALAYSIA%20-%20MICG.pdf (accessed on 17/03/08).

Kaheeru, V. (2001). Institute of Corporate Governance of Uganda, Manual, Kampala, Uganda.

Kamla, R. (2007). Critically appreciating social accounting and reporting in the Arab Middle East: A post-colonial perspective. *Advances in International Accounting, 20,* 105–177.

Kapumpa, M. S. (2002). Corporate governance: The role and status of capital and financial markets in Africa. Paper presented at the Pan African Consultative Forum on Corporate Governance, Johannesburg, South Africa, 16–18 July.

Makinde, T. (2005). Problems of policy implementation in developing nations: The Nigerian experience. *Journal of Social Science, 11*(1), 63–69.

Mangena, M., & Tauringana, V. (2006). *Corporate boards, ownership structure and firm performance in an environment of economic and political instability: The case of Zimbabwe stock exchange listed companies* (April 11–13). A paper presented at the BAA National Conference. University of Portsmouth, Portsmouth, UK.

Marnet, O. (2004). Behavioural aspects of corporate governance. *Corporate Governance Advances in Financial Economics, 9,* 265–285.

Matama, R. (2008). Corporate governance and financial performance of selected commercial banks in Uganda. Available online at http://www.crrconference.org/downloads/2006rogers.pdf (accessed on 03/03/08).

Mazrui, A. (1991). *The Black women and the problem of gender: Trials, triumphs and challenges.* Guardian Lecture Series, Lagos: Guardian Publishers.

McKinsey. (2001). Emerging market investor opinion survey: Summary of preliminary findings, London, McKinsey.

Meisel, N. (2004). *Governance culture and development: A different perspective on corporate governance.* Paris, France: Development Centre of the Organisation for Economic Co-operation and Development.

Mensah, S. (2002). Corporate governance in Ghana: Issues and challenges. Paper presented at African Capital Markets Conference, December, Accra, Ghana.

Monbiot, G. (2003). *The age of consent: A manifesto for a new world order.* London, UK: Flamingo.

Morriset, J., & Neso, O. (2005). *Administrative barriers to foreign investment in developing countries,* foreign investment advisory services. Washington, DC: World Bank.

Muranda, Z. (2006). Financial distress and corporate governance in Zimbabwean banks. *Corporate Governance, 6*(5), 643–654.

Mwapachu, J. V. (2001). Corporate governance: Tanzania's experiences and challenges. Paper presented at the Pan African Consultative Forum on Corporate Governance, Johannesburg, South Africa, 16–18 July.

Mwaura, K. (2003). *Regulation of directors in Kenya.* University of Wolverhampton, Wolverhampton, UK.

Ndanusa, S. A., & Al Mustapha, A. (2003). *Preface to code of corporate governance in Nigeria.* Lagos: Securities and Exchange Commission.

Ndebbio, J. E., & Ekpo, A. H. (1991). *The Nigerian economy at the cross-roads: Policies and their effectiveness.* Calabar: University of Calabar Press.

Nganga, S., Jain, V., & Artivor, M. (2003). *Corporate governance in Africa: A survey of publicly listed companies.* United Kingdom: London Business School.

Nobes, C. W. (1998). *Accounting in developing economies: Questions about users, uses and appropriate reporting practices.* London, UK: ACCA Publication.

Nwauche, E. S., & Nmehielle, V. O. (2004). External–internal standards in corporate governance in Nigeria. The George Washington University Law School Public Law and Legal Theory, Working Paper No. 115, Washington, USA.

Obadina, T. (1999). *Nigeria's economy at the crossroads: New government faces a legacy of mismanagement and decay.* Africa Recovery, Lagos, Nigeria.

Ojo, M. (2002). *Corruption and the Nigerian project – issues* (May 26). This Day Sunday Online.

Okike, N. M. E. (1994). Curious auditing regulations in Nigeria: A case study of cultural/political influences on auditing practices. *The International Journal of Accounting, 29,* 78–91.

Okike, N. M. E. (2000). The state of corporate governance in Nigeria. Paper presented at the Annual Conference of the Commonwealth Association for Corporate Governance (CACG), Nairobi, Kenya, 31 October–2 November.

Okike, N. M. E. (2002). Influences on the corporate governance framework and reporting on listed companies in a developing economy: A Nigerian case study. Paper presented at the 3rd International Conference for the British Accounting Association Special Interest Group in Corporate Governance, at the Queen's University Belfast, 16 December.

Okike, N. M. E. (2007). Corporate governance in Nigeria: The status quo. *Corporate Governance, 15*(2), 173–193.

Olubi, K. (2005). Nigerian women in development, http://www.nigeriaonline.com (accessed on 19/01/05).

Oyejide, T. A., & Soyibo, A. (2001). Corporate governance in Nigeria. Paper presented at the conference on Corporate Governance, Accra, Ghana, January 29–30.

O'Connor, S. M. (2002). The inevitability of Enron and the impossibility of auditor independence under the current audit system, Berkeley Centre for Law, Business and the Economy Working Paper. Available at http://www.law.berkeley.edu/centers/bclbe/symposia/postenron/resources.html (accessed on 24/09/07).

Rabelo, F., & Vasconcelos, F. C. (2002). Corporate governance in Brazil. *Journal of Business Ethics, 37*(3), 321–335.

Reed, A. M. (2002). Corporate governance reforms in India. *Journal of Business Ethics, 37,* 249–268.

Reed, D. (2002). Corporate governance in developing countries. *Journal of Business Ethics, 37*(3), 223–247.

Rossette, N. N. (2002). *Board of directors composition, team process and organisational performance of financial institutions in Uganda.* Unpublished MBA Dissertation. Kampala: Makerere University.

Rossouw, G. J., van der Watt, A., & Malan, D. P. (2002). Corporate governance in South Africa. *Journal of Business Ethics, 37,* 289–302.

Said, E. W. (1993). *Culture and imperialism.* New York: Vintage.

Sfeir, G. N. (1988). The Saudi approach to law reform. *The American Journal of Comparative Law, 36*(4), 729–759.

Soludo, C. C., Ogbu, O., & Chang, J. (2004). *The politics of trade and industrial policy in Africa: Forced consensus.* New Jersey: Africa World Press.

Strauss, A. (1988). *Qualitative analysis for social scientists.* Cambridge: Cambridge University Press.

Tam, O. (2002). Ethical issues in the evolution of corporate governance in China. *Journal of Business Ethics, 37*(3), 303–320.

Transparency International. (2007). Corruption Perceptions Index 2005.

Tsamenyi, M., Enninful-Adu, E., & Onumah, J. (2007). Disclosure and corporate governance in developing countries: Evidence from Ghana. *Managerial Auditing Journal, 22*(3), 319–334.

Tsumba, L. L. (2002). Corporate governance country case experience – perspectives and practices: Zimbabwe. Available at www.worldbank.org/wbi/banking/finsecpolicy/ pillars/pdfs/tsumba2.pdf (accessed on 03/03/08).

Umar, A. (2008). For an effective fight against corruption. http://www.saharareporters.com/ colabubakarumar1.php (accessed on 29/03/08).

Wallace, R. S. O. (1989). *Accounting and financial reporting in Nigeria.* Norwich: ICAEW.

Wallace, R. S. O. (1990). Accounting in developing countries: A review of the literature. *Research in Third World Accounting, 1,* 3–34.

Weiss, J. (1999). Infrastructure and economic development. Economic Research, Paper No. 50, African Development Bank, Abidjan, Cote d'Ivoire.

Williams, M. (2000). *Corporate governance diversity and its impact on intellectual capital performance in an emerging economy.* Working paper. University of Calgary, Canada.

Williams, S. M., & Ho, C. A. (2003). International comparative analysis of the association between board structure and the efficiency of value added by a firm from its physical capital and intellectual capital resources. *The International Journal of Accounting, 38,* 465–491.

World Bank. (2002). *An Assessment of the Private Sector in Nigeria.* The World Bank Group September 2002. Washington, DC: World Bank.

World Bank. (2005). *Doing business in 2005, World Bank, International Finance Corporation, and Oxford University Press.* Washington, DC: World Bank.

World Trade Organisation. (1998). Trade Policy Reviews: Nigeria: June 1998, http:// www.wto.org/english/tratop_e/tpr_e/tp75_e.htm (accessed on 15/11/06).

Yakasai, G. A. (2001). Corporate governance in a Third World Country with particular reference to Nigeria. *Corporate Governance, 9*(3), 238–253.

Zaher, T. S., & Hassan, M. K. (2001). A comparative literature survey of Islamic finance and banking. *Financial Markets, Institutions and Instruments, 10*(4), 155–199.

Zajonc, R. B. (1968). Attitudinal effects of mere exposure. *Journal of Personality and Social Psychology Monograph, 9*(2), 1–27.

APPENDIX 1. INTERVIEWEE DETAILS (AS AT THE DATE OF INTERVIEW)

1. Oladimeji Alo, PhD
Dr. Oladimeji Alo, a former President of the West African Bankers Association and a Fellow of the Institute of Personnel Management of Nigeria, is the current Director-General of the Financial Institutions Training Centre, Lagos, Nigeria.

2. Alhaji Garba Yusuf Imam
Mr. Imam is an Executive Director in Sterling Bank Nigeria Plc. and has served on a number of company audit committees.

3. Col. A.A. Peters (Rtd.)
Colonel Peters is a non-executive director of First Inland Bank Plc. and the managing director of Alpha Technologies, a private company with speciality in communications.

4. Mr. Ernest Oji
Mr. Oji is a non-executive director of First Inland Bank Plc and the Managing Director of Ideal Home Finishes and Beta Consortium and Fixtures Limited.

5. Mrs. Cathy Echeozo
Mrs. Echeozo is the General Manager and Group Head, Corporate Banking Group, Guaranty Trust Bank Plc.

6. Prof. Mosobalaje Oyewoye, OON
Professor Oyewoye was the Chairman Board of Directors, Guaranty Trust Bank, Nigeria Plc (1995–2005).

7. Prof. Gesiye Salo Angaye
Professor Angaye is a Professor of Economics at the Niger Delta University. He has previously been chairman of the board of directors of Horicon Construction Company Limited and Radio Rivers Port Harcourt, Nigeria.

8. Alhaji (Dr.) Ayuba Musa
Dr. Alhaji has been a director of the Central Bank of Nigeria and is currently the managing director of a private investment company in Abuja.

9. Mr. Olubunmi Oladapo Oni.
Mr. Oni was previously managing director of Cadbury Nigeria Plc.

10. Chief Emmanuel A.L. Ibanichuka
Chief Ibanichuka was previously managing director of Pabod Investments
Ltd, Port Harcourt, Nigeria. Before that he was the chief internal auditor of
Shell Nigeria Plc. He is a qualified member of the Chartered Association of
Certified Accountants (ACCA).

11. Dr. Clifford Obiyo Ofurum.
Dr. Ofurum is the head of the department of accounting at the University of
Port Harcourt. He is also a private investor.

12. Mr. Peter Amangbo
Mr. Amangbo is an executive director of Zenith Bank Nigeria Plc. He has
previous experience working with PricewaterhouseCoopers.

13. Mr. Bill Laurie
Mr. Laurie was previously the managing director of John Holt Nigeria Ltd.

14. Mr. Paul Okpalo
Mr. Okpalo is the director, finance and supplies, at the University of Port
Harcourt Teaching Hospital. He is a chartered accountant of the Institute of
Chartered Accountants of Nigeria (ICAN).

15. Mr. D.A.N. Eke
Mr. Eke is a deputy director in the Banking Supervision Department of the
Central Bank of Nigeria. He served on the committee that drafted the Codes
of Corporate Governance for Banks in Nigeria.

16. Mr. P.E. Akpala
Mr. Akpala is an assistant director in the Banking Supervision Department
of the Central Bank of Nigeria.

17. Mrs. Ndidi O. Nwuneli
Mrs. Nwuneli is the founder and chief executive of LEAP (Leadership,
Effectiveness, Accountability and Professionalism) Africa, a non-profit
organisation which is committed to inspiring, empowering and equipping a
new cadre of African leaders. She previously worked as a management
consultant with the Bridgespan Group and with McKinsey & Company;
and also as a consultant with Ford Foundation's West Africa Office and the
Centre for Middle East Competitive Strategy in Palestine and Israel.

18. Mr. Nnamdi Okafor
Mr. Okafor is an executive director of May and Baker Nigeria Plc, a leading
Pharmaceuticals company in Nigeria. He is also a private investor.

19. Mr. Luke Uche Azike
Mr. Azike is the managing director of Intercontinental Technical Services Limited, a private company with speciality in the sales and supplies of heavy-duty materials and equipment.

20. Mr. Dan Ogbonna Okereke
Mr. Okereke is a senior executive manager with responsibility for corporate investments in Bank PHB Nigeria Plc. He is also a private investor.

THE CORPORATE GOVERNANCE INERTIA: THE ROLE OF MANAGEMENT ACCOUNTING AND COSTING SYSTEMS IN A TRANSITIONAL PUBLIC HEALTH ORGANIZATION

Mostafa Kamal Hassan

ABSTRACT

Purpose – *The paper explains how internal reporting systems, as embedded practices informing organizational actions and "know-how", contributed to the inertia in implementing a corporate form of governance in a transitional public organization in a developing country – Egypt.*

Design/methodology/approach – *The paper synthesizes an institutional theory framework in order to capture the case study mixed results. Drawing on DiMaggio and Powell's (1983) notions of isomorphic mechanisms, Ocasio (1999) and Burns and Scapens' (2000) notions of organizations' memory, history, cumulative actions and routines, Brunsson's (1994) notion of organizational institutional confusion as well as Carruthers's (1995) notion of "symbolic window-dressing" adoption of new practices, the paper explores the dynamic of a public hospital*

Corporate Governance in Less Developed and Emerging Economies
Research in Accounting in Emerging Economies, Volume 8, 409–454
Copyright © 2008 by Emerald Group Publishing Limited
All rights of reproduction in any form reserved
ISSN: 1479-3563/doi:10.1016/S1479-3563(08)08014-6

corporatization processes. Data collection methods include semi-structured interviews, documentary evidence and direct observation.

Findings – *The case study evidence shows that the interplay between the new form of "corporate" governance and the intra-organizational power, routines and "know-how" created internal organizational confusion and changed organizational members' narrative of risk and uncertainties.*

Research limitations/implications – *The paper does not reveal the role of reformers involved in the public sector "governance" reform in developing countries. Exploring such a role goes beyond the scope of this paper and represents an area of future research.*

Originality/value – *The paper provides a comprehensive account of public sector "governance" reform in a developing nation, while exploring the role of management accounting and costing systems in facilitating or otherwise that reform processes.*

1. INTRODUCTION

Although the term "corporate governance" is a name given to describe how companies control and manage their activities as well as their members' behavior, the last few years have witnessed increasing calls to improve public organizations' governance systems (Lapsley, 1993; Craven & Stewart, 1995; Hodges, Macniven, & Mellett, 2004; Bird, 2001). Different countries are implementing numerous "governance" reforms aiming at improving public organizations' performance in line with the private sector ones (Olson, Guthrie, & Humphrey, 1998; Hodges, Wright, & Keasey, 1996; Vinten, 1998). Accordingly, politicians, public servants and reformers have had to manage and control various activities such as the geographic needs, the delivery speed and the product or service quality. These activities interact together and become more complex in public health organizations (Jones, 1999; Jones & Mellett, 2007; Watkins & Arrington, 2007). Furthermore, governing these activities with the appropriate balance of transparency, efficiency and accountability requires governance and accounting systems that link organizational members' decisions to the organization strategy.

Another key aspect in the corporate governance literature is that it does not highlight the role of Management Accounting and Costing Systems (MACS) during the implementation of a corporate form of governance in transforming public health organizations in developing countries. Some of "corporate governance" studies investigate the governance mechanisms in public organizations (e.g. Ferlie, Fitzgerlad, & Ashburrner, 1995; Craven & Stewart, 1995; Jones, 1999; Harrison, 1998; Clatworthy, Mellett, & Peel, 2000; Freedman, 2002; Giroux & McLelland, 2003; Hodges et al., 2004; Eeckloo, Van Herck, Van Hulle, & Vleugels, 2004), while others stress on the financial reporting as a part of corporate governance systems (e.g. Haniffa & Cooke, 2002; Forker & Green, 2000; Bushman & Smith, 2001; Goodwin & Seow, 2002; Weir, Laing, & McKnight, 2002; Eng & Mak, 2003; Garrod, 2000). Yet few studies explore the role of MACS based on the corporate form of governance in a transitional public organization except for Nor-Aziah and Scapens' (2007) case study that investigates the corporatization processes of a Malaysian public utility.

This paper addresses this research gap and goes further to provide an account of how MACS, as embedded practices informing the organizational members' actions and "know-how", contributed to the inertia of a public hospital-based "corporate governance" organizational change. It seeks to understand how the abstract calls for greater efficiency through the introduction of a corporate form of governance have come to be translated into day-to-day practices of an Egyptian public hospital.

The paper's main contribution is the exploration of linkages between MACS and corporate governance in a transitional public health organization in a developing country undergoing a transition – Egypt, while explaining the role of MACS during the corporate governance, or as Brunsson (1994) states "companization", reform processes. It synthesizes an institutional theory framework that enables the exploration of MACS–corporate governance relationships, while revealing the social and political forces intertwined with the implementation of these MACS. The framework has been synthesized in order to capture the case study mixed findings.

There are various reasons to choose the Egyptian health care sector for this study. First, the Egyptian health sector is undergoing a massive restructuring in which state-based public hospitals are transforming into corporate organizations. Second, public hospitals are pressured to adopt the corporate form of governance while, at the same time, are required to keep the state-based governance systems. Finally, the existence of these two governance structures concurrently does not only drive, as Brunsson (1994) argues, organizational confusion, but also enables hospital members to use each structure to argue against the other as the case study explains.

The remainder of the paper is organized as follows: the theoretical concepts are discussed in section two, followed by a description of the methodology and research methods in section three. Then, the public hospital processes of corporate governance reform, MACS change and organizational response are described, before discussion and conclusion sections.

2. THEORETICAL CONCEPTS

2.1. Corporate Governance and New Public Management (NPM)

The OECD (2004) sets out the fundamental features of corporate governance as:

> involv[ing] a set of relationships between a company's management, its board, its shareholders and other stakeholders ... [and] providing the structure through which the objectives of the company are set, and the means of attaining those objectives and monitoring performance are determined. (p. 11)

The underlying themes of corporate governance deal with issues such as accountability, implementing different mechanisms that ensure good behavior, and protecting and enhancing value to stakeholders (Solomon & Solomon, 2004; Taylor, 2000; Hodges et al., 1996, 2004; Scott & McNamee, 2005; Pesqueux, 2005; Kim, Prescott, & Kim, 2005). The New Public Management (NPM) movement has been characterized as having a number of corporate governance dimensions (Clatworthy et al., 2000). These dimensions include the restructuring of public sector in the line of decentralization and market rationale, the displacement of the bureaucratic administration with new private sector management philosophy and the need for contracts, employee incentive schemes and the quantification as means of demonstrating the achievements of efficiency and high performance levels (Hood, 1995; Parker & Gould, 1999; Watkins & Arrington, 2007, p. 36).

Although the underlying aim of corporate governance is to direct and control organizations in order to maximize value to stakeholders, governance per se can be looked at from two perspectives: a more macro perspective and a micro perspective. This micro/macro distinction coincides with the classification of governance mechanisms into two categories: internal and external mechanisms (see also Mimba, Jan van Helden, & Tillema, 2007; Taylor, 2000; Weimer & Pape, 1999; Pollitt, 2001; Shleifer & Vishny, 1997; Boubakri, Cosset, & Guedhami, 2005).

At the micro level, governance system includes different mechanisms, internal to organizations, that align the interests of various organizational members and organizational objectives while, at the same time, monitoring the performance of these members and specifying the distribution of authorities and responsibilities among them (Solomon & Solomon, 2004, p. 8; Luo, 2005; Kim et al., 2005). At a more macro level, governance is defined as "a set of institutional and market mechanisms", external to organizations, that induce or exert pressures on organizations' managers and members to make decisions that maximize the value to organizations' stakeholders (Lapsley, 1993; Ezzamel & Willmott, 1993; Jones, 1999).

An integral part of corporate governance mechanisms is the MACS (Jones, 1999). Seal (2006) argues that MACS occupy a privilege position in supporting organizations' activities and corporate governance. MACS not only steer public organizations in accordance with organizational constituents/stakeholders' requirements (Power & Laughlin, 1992; Broadbent, 1992; Richardson & Cullen, 2000), but also represent a resolution of a set of social forces, in and around public organizations, that act on shaping these systems in the processes of MACS institutionalization and organizational change (Jones & Mellett, 2007; Dillard, Rigsby, & Goodman, 2004). This paper reveals how MACS, intertwined with social and political forces in and around a public hospital, contributed to the corporate governance reform inertia and created internal organizational confusion.

The case study evidence illustrates how MACS play an intermediate role between public hospitals and the Ministry of Health and Population (MOHP), other ministries and international aid agencies such as International Monetary Fund (IMF), World Bank (WB) and USAID. The case study also shows how MACS restructure organizational members, mainly physicians and accountants, relationships. In this regard, it explores how MACS created organizational tension associated with the "know-how" and "power of control". Finally, the case study clarifies how MACS provoke public hospitals' organizational routines, memory and "know-how" of "free public health institutions". These issues will be explained later in the paper.

With an increasing belief in the superiority of private sector governance practices, Western and European countries tend to implement private sector accounting and control systems in order to improve the performance of public health organizations (e.g. Olson et al., 1998; Doolin, 1999; Jones & Dewing, 1997; Pettersen, 1999; Ballantine, Brignall, & Modell, 1998; Broadbent & Laughlin, 1998; Dillard & Smith, 1999) and Egypt is no exception (Hassan, 2005). The MOHP, in collaboration with the USAID, introduced more profit-oriented and cost controlling systems through the processes of implementing a corporate form of governance to public hospitals. The new MACS systems are assumed to be useful in allocating economic resources, motivating performance and exercising control.

Although MACS are implemented within public hospitals, they were initiated by the MOHP. Public hospitals, because of the MOHP initiatives, have to respond to more macro pressures to change. Although such a macro perspective is crucial to understand the relationship between public hospitals and wider constituents, a micro level analysis is also needed to explore the dynamic processes of MACS based on the corporate form of governance and organizational change that involves intra-organization power, memory and routines. Therefore, it is of importance to combine macro and micro levels of analysis in studying public sector MACS and governance reform (e.g. Modell, 2004; Dillard et al., 2004).

2.2. Governance and Public Sector in Developing Countries

One of the key aspects of governance mechanisms (whether internal/micro or external/macro), Shleifer and Vishny (1997) argue, is that these mechanisms in developing countries, are generally weak and could affect the performance of organizations operating within the context of those countries. Mimba et al. (2007, p. 196) add that developing countries, compared with developed ones, suffer from a limited institutional capacity. Therefore organizations, particularly public sector ones, experience various organizational weaknesses such as vague accountability relationships, administrative inefficiencies, a lack of facilities and insufficient funding (Mimba et al., 2007). These features together with each developing nation local circumstances, such as low level of average income per ordinary citizen, high level of population growth, low stakeholder involvement in decision-making, high levels of corruption and low salaries scales, adversely affect the public sector performance (*ibid.*).

The consequence of these institutional and organizational characteristics, Mimba et al. (2007) argue, institutionalizes practices such as long bureaucratic procedures, a lack of transparency, the production of unsatisfactory products and services, the unfair distribution of these services and products among citizens, the production of little information about public sector performance and the use of weak control systems. In short, they reinforce principles that are in contrast to, what Taylor (2000) calls, "good governance". In response to these characteristics, governments in developing countries reform their public sectors' governance mechanisms in order to enhance those sectors' performance (Boubakri et al., 2005; Mimba et al., 2007).

In this regard, Ocasio (1999) argues that "governance" reform is not only a matter of changing organizations' external and internal mechanisms that direct organizations' members, but also is the processes by which organizations' embedded routines, knowledge and norms are changed and transformed. These routines, knowledge and norms, he argues, are history-dependent rules that are presented in organizational members' actions and mode of thinking. Ocasio (1999) suggests that one of the main aspects to improve governance is the understanding of how history – i.e. cumulative and embedded actions – shapes organizations' routines that mold organizational members' behavior. Such an understanding, he argues, emphasizes the role of actors' cognitive and political interests in the generation and maintenance of organizations' templates or, as Burns and Scapens (2000) argue, "micro institutions".

Likewise, Seal (2006) argues that good governance requires appropriate internal reporting and monitoring practices to be embedded in organizations day-to-day decisions. He adds that linking organizations' routines, which are informed by the practice of management accounting, with external stakeholders is one of the main principles of good governance. Such a link, he argues, connects management accounting practices to the wider political, legal and social processes associated with corporate governance.

Reforming public sector governance systems in developing countries is a multilevel process that develops public organizations' external and internal governance mechanisms as well as reforms those organizations' embedded practices. Fig. 1 presents an institutional theory framework that explores corporate governance reform in public sector in developing countries and the role of MACS during that reform processes. This framework links organizations' routines to organizational structure (internal mechanisms) which, in turn, is linked to the public sector social and institutional environment (external mechanisms).

The framework underscores the characteristics of the public sector "governance" reform in developing countries. First, such a reform is implemented as a part of wider structural adjustment programs. These programs are associated with macro political and economic reforms such as democratization, trade liberalization, bilateral agreements and privatization (Mimba et al., 2007; Boubakri et al., 2005) (see nation-state level in Fig. 1). Second, the government remains the major organizational constituent during the governance reform. Nevertheless, the framework highlights other constituents involved in the governance reform processes (see organizational fields level in Fig. 1). Finally, the framework recognizes that the public sector governance in developing countries is not only an issue of the technical design of governance mechanisms, but also concerned with public organizations' micro routines and institutions that facilitate or otherwise the implementation

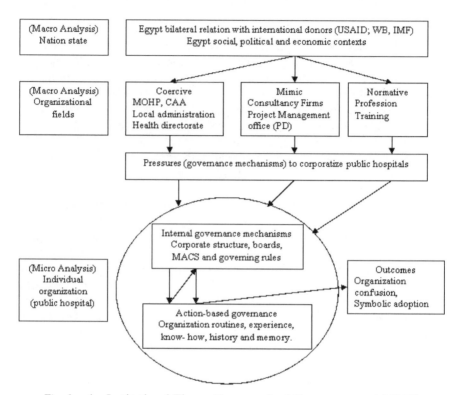

Fig. 1. An Institutional Theory Framework of Governance and MACS.

of these mechanisms (Ocasio, 1999; Jalilian, Kirkpatrick, & Parker, 2006) (see micro organizational level in Fig. 1). The following subsections present the study framework.

2.3. A Synthesized Institutional Framework of Governance and MACS

The paper synthesizes a framework that informs the analysis of the processes of implementing a corporate form of governance in a public health organization. This framework underscores three institutional dimensions of governance. First, the New Institutional Sociology (NIS)-based governance that stresses on organizations' wider environment and constituents' demands and/or pressures to change (DiMaggio & Powell, 1983; Meyer & Rowan, 1977). Second, action-based governance that highlights intra-organizational power, history and routines while stressing on organizations' micro "institutions" which are informed by management accounting practices (Ocasio, 1999; Burns & Scapens, 2000; Yazdifar, Zaman, Tsamenyi, & Askarany, 2007; Seal, 2006). Finally, the paper draws on the prior literature about institutional conflict/confusion wherein individual organizations' micro institutions and routines do not coincide with institutional pressures to change (Brunsson, 1994; Tsamenyi, Cullen, & Gonzalez, 2006; Oliver, 1991; Nor-Aziah & Scapens, 2007; Lukka, 2007). The framework has been synthesized in order to capture the case study mixed results.

2.3.1. Institutional Pressure: New Institutional Sociology

The underlying theme of the NIS is that organizations are pressured to conform with constituents demands (Scott, 1995). It stresses on the processes of obtaining social legitimacy through *isomorphic mechanisms* (Meyer & Rowan, 1977; DiMaggio & Powell, 1983). One can argue that isomorphic mechanisms are governance tools that explain why individual organizations comply with their constituents' demands. Ribeiro and Scapens (2006) argue that the NIS theory acknowledges pressures excreted from a more "macro" level of organizational fields or sectors. Organizational fields include various organizational constituents. Those constituents operate around individual organizations and create institutional pressures that lead individual organizations to adopt specific governance mechanisms including MACS. For instance, the governmental agencies can be a source of *coercive* pressures, professional bodies can contribute to the creation of *normative* pressures and consultants may facilitate the emergence of *mimetic* pressures.

The institutional framework (Fig. 1) suggests that the institutional context around public hospitals can be envisaged as a field in which multiple constituents exert pressures on public hospitals. Those constituents are CAA, MOHP, consultancy firms, and project management office and professional activities (see organizational fields level in Fig. 1). The framework also acknowledges that individual organizations and organizational fields exist in the country economic and political context. This context provides the foundation for institutional practices and, at the same time, exerts pressures on individual organizations through organizational fields' constituents (Dillard et al., 2004) (see nation-state level in Fig. 1). Accordingly, government officials and politicians exercise their influence at the political level (nation-state level), governmental agencies and consultants exercise their influence at the organizational field level (organizational fields level), and managers and organizational members exercise their influence at a more micro organizational level (micro organizational level) (Dillard et al., 2004, p. 513).

The case study highlights that the MOHP, in collaboration with international donors, passed various legislations in order to change public hospitals. These legislations aimed at changing the resources allocation mechanisms, hospitals' organizational structure, accountability relation-ships and rules governing public hospitals' inner lives. The NIS theory enables the exploration of how the government constituents exert pressures on public hospitals to change and, at the same time, reveals the constituents–public hospitals relationships linkages to micro processes of corporatizing public hospitals and MACS change.

The NIS theory has been criticized because of its deterministic nature that stresses on steering and directing organizations (Carruthers, 1995; Abernethy & Chua, 1996; Collier, 2001; Dillard et al., 2004). It explains how organizations are pressured to change through isomorphic mechanisms, but it does not clearly explain how organizations respond to these mechanisms. Accordingly, the NIS theory does not show how the governance mechanisms are accepted, adapted and internalized within the organization. It does not provide an account of how intra-organizational power, history and routines conflict with the constituents' demands that, sometimes, aim at changing the organization's culture and identity (Brunsson, 1994; Tsamenyi et al., 2006).

To this, Ocasio (1999), Burns and Scapens (2000) and Oliver (1991) are primarily concerned with how organizations respond to institutional pressures (whether external or internal). Their views set organizations in a dynamic social context that recognizes the role of organizations routines, history, memory and intra-organizational power during organizational change (e.g. Collier, 2001; Modell, 2002; Tsamenyi et al., 2006; Yazdifar et al., 2007). This recognition is not underscored under the NIS theory. This paper draws on these studies in order to investigate how governance mechanisms (external/internal) interact with organizational routines and how the power in and around accounting routines mould organizational responses.

2.3.2. Organizational Change, Accounting Routines and Power
On the basis of Giddens' (1984) notion of *duality of structures*, Ocasio (1999), Seal (2006) and Burns and Scapens (2000) recognize the role of organiza-tions' micro "institutions" and routines during organizational change. They move beyond the deterministic nature of NIS theory. They stress on organizational members' actions, knowledge and power that are embedded in organizations' routines around which organizational activities are

constructed. In this regard, Ocasio (1999) emphasizes that organizations' practices and routines are both a source of organizational *inertia* and a guide for organizational *adaptation* and change. Accordingly, organizational change occurs not only in response to the interests of organizational constituents through isomorphic mechanisms (macro levels in Fig. 1), but also in accordance with the history, memory, knowledge and experience that are embedded in that organization's practices and institutionalized routines (micro organizational level in Fig. 1).

Therefore, organizational power not only rests on hands of organizational constituents but also exits in organizational practices and routines. These two forms of power are best articulated in Giddens' (1984) structuration theory's duality of domination. On the one hand, power could be a part of the social structure whereby mega actors, or macro institutions such as government institutions, professional institutions and consultancy firms, dominate others through the use of political and economic resources (Cohen, 1989). On the other hand, power is seen in the agency institutionalized actions and routines that shape not only organizations micro "institutions" but also thoughts of organizational members (Burns & Scapens, 2000; Burns, 2000).

MACS, as institutional and organizational practices, could have different frames of power. First, power *in* the MACS, particularly, when those systems shift the organization's knowledge, or as Burns (1997, p. 221) argues "know-how", between groups constituting the organization (Yazdifar et al., 2007). Feinglass and Salmon (1990, p. 240) add that organizational members, who posses the organization's "know-how", which sometimes are embedded in the organization's cumulative actions and routines, have the power to deal with the organization's uncertainties. Therefore, they are more powerful members and can secure their interests at the expense of the less powerful members who do not have access to such "know-how" (Ocasio, 1999; Burns & Scapens, 2000; Burns, 2000). Second, power existing *around* the MACS. This power incorporates broader issues such as the hierarchical authority, the mechanism of allocating economic resources and professionalism (Granlund, 2001; Seal, 2006).

The empirical findings suggest that the MACS based on the corporate form of governance incorporated some of physicians' "know-how". The cost accounting reports incorporated information about: each clinic full cost, clinical episodes and physicians' prescriptions. The implementation of MACS based on the corporate form of governance enabled accountants and accounting "know-how" to penetrate doctors' activities and provides surveillance for all activities of the hospital in financial terms. In other words, physicians' expertise, knowledge and "know-how" become, in part, "taken in" to accounting reports (e.g. Lowe, 2000, p. 195). In this sense, the practice of the MACS merged physicians' practices with the accounting "know-how" since the latter invaded the work of health professional. These issues are explained later in the empirical study.

2.3.3. Interplay between Institutional Pressures and Organizations' Accounting Routines

Because of possible contradictions between organizational constituents' demands and the organizations' practices and routines, various scholars identify different paths of organizational change (Oliver, 1991; Brunsson, 1994; Nor-Aziah & Scapens, 2007; Lukka, 2007). Oliver (1991) suggests that sometimes organizations adopt *acquiescence strategy* where they conform to institutional pressures because of the economic gains and/or positive social legitimacy perceived to be obtainable from such a conformity (see also Carpenter & Feroz, 2001; Shaprino & Matson, 2008).

Brunsson (1994) argues that institutional demands, which move organizations away from their regular routines and practices, may cause organizations to loose their identities or at best to suffer a state of "confusion". Organizational identity, Brunsson (1994, p. 324) argues, is determined by legal systems and rules governing organizations' inner lives. He adds that organizational identity can be labeled as "political" when the organization is a state-based one. Or be labeled as a "company" when the organization freely produces goods in the market place. He (p. 326) emphasizes that resource allocation mechanisms can provide legitimacy for either political or company identity. The former if the organization is able to generate money that has no connection with its products or services – a typical form of such resources are taxation or the centrally allocated resources from the state. Whereas a company identity refers to the organization ability to generate resources in direct connection to the type of services provided by that organization (Scott, 1983, p. 103).

Nor-Aziah and Scapens (2007, p. 213) suggest that organizational members may create a buffer, or as Meyer and Rowan (1977) state to *loosely couple or decouple*, between constituents demands and the organization's activities in order to protect the organization from unwanted institutional disruptions. Loose coupling is an organizational response that attempts to resolve the conflict between institutional demands and the organization's routines (Lukka, 2007). Carruthers (1995, p. 315) adds that when compliance with institutional requirements is essential for survival but there are challenges to actual implementation of institutionally desirable practices, these practices are not embedded in organizational cultures, structures and routines. Instead, these institutional practices are adopted as a kind of, Carruthers (1995) argues, "symbolic window-dressing" for their legitimizing power without necessarily intertwined with the organization activities. This symbolic adoption coincides with Mimba et al. (2007) notion of "informality" that describes the difference between what the organization says it does, and what it is actually doing.

The empirical findings suggest that the coercive introduction of the corporate form of governance aimed at moving public hospitals towards more managerial autonomy, market system and cost sharing concepts. Yet that form of governance kept a remarkable level of the state involvement in the delivery of health care service. Consequently, the corporate governance systems created internal organizational confusion because public hospitals adopt symbols from the business world while still being political organizations relying on the state policies. The public hospital confusion was presented in the hospital members' discussion to issues such as the controllability of some cost elements, whether their hospital is a private or a public one, and the ability to reduce the number of staff working in the hospital. In order to resolve that confusion, the hospital had to comply with the institutional requirements (constituents' demands) even though this compliance might be ritualistic (Pollitt, 2001). These issues will be explained later in the paper.

3. METHODOLOGY AND RESEARCH METHODS

Since the study aims at understanding the processes of MACS based on a public hospital organizational change towards adopting a corporate form of governance, a case study based on interpretative methodology seems as an appropriate approach to proceed (Scapens, 1990; Yin, 1994). The complex interactions between the wider institutional environment and the hospital's micro "institutions" encourage the use of an explanatory case study (Scapens, 1990). The data collection methods included semi-structured interviews, documentary evidence and direct observation. To facilitate access to the public hospital, a formal permission was obtained from governmental officials. Data was colleted during 2000–2001.

Semi-structured interviews were undertaken with two main groups: medical and non-medical staff. Criteria of selecting interviewees were as follows: first, interviewees were chosen to cover a range of the hospital medical and non-medical functions that are associated with the hospital organizational change towards the corporate form of governance. Second, interviewees should be working in the hospital before, or at least joined the hospital during, the move towards the new governance systems. Third, whenever possible interviewees should have had the chance to meet one of the MOHP or the consultancy firms' advisors. Interviews, initially, were undertaken with heads of medical and non-medical departments. Then, heads of departments were asked to name other individuals who are aware of changes that took place in the hospital MACS and governance systems.

Semi-structured interviews allowed interviewees to provide their views through a free-flowing discussion. Accordingly, the order, in which research questions are presented, is altered depending on each interviewee views while keeping the underlying aim of the research "how MACS contributed towards implementing the corporate form of governance". The research questions are presented in Appendix 1. Interviews were undertaken with 31 members of the hospital. It was observable that four members were unwilling to participate. The study successfully interviewed 13 accountants and administrative staff and 14 physicians. Meeting with interviewees took place over a period of 6 months in a single hospital. During this period, the author regularly visited the hospital. Each interview lasted about 50 min on average and was carried out during the normal working hours.

The hospital's "governance" reform processes started in 1997. Therefore, the hospital main entrance had various pictures, with printed USAID logo, showing the installation of new medical equipments and the hospital new corporate/organizational structure (Fig. 2) as well as photos of the "Cost Recovery for Health Project" change team and consultants. Bulletins, published during the hospital organizational change, stated that the hospital was visited by various consultancy firms such as The Health Financing and Sustainability Project of Washington, Abt Association of Cambridge, Massachusetts and Bethesda, The Cambridge Consulting Corporation of Reston (CRHP, 1997).

Although regular visits to the research site helped the author, to large extent, to obtain much data and observe the social reality (Ahrens & Dent, 1998, p. 11), there were some constraints on data obtained from interviews. One of such constraints is that participating interviewees did not like the idea of tape recording. Another constraint is that the hospital was approached when it was at final stages of implementing the corporate form of governance, yet the study investigates the transition from the state-based governance to the corporate form of governance.

What mitigates the second constraint is that most interviewees worked in the hospital before and after the transition, and they observed the

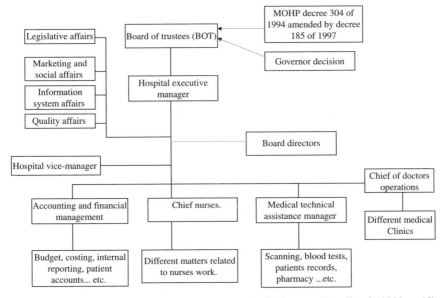

Fig. 2.   Hospital Organizational Structure (Board of Directors Handbook, 1998, p. 12).

pre-corporate and post-corporate form of governance. This enabled the reconstruction of the historical context of the changing public hospital. In other words, a retrospective approach was used. This approach meant to ask interviewees to describe, explain and reflect upon the events that they had experienced during the processes of change. A consequent constraint of approaching the hospital at late stages of change is the inability to interview any of consultancy firms or MOHP advisors. What mitigates this constraint is that selected interviewers should have had the chance to meet some of these advisors as mentioned earlier.

   The study also triangulates data through relying on documentary evidence and direct observation. Documents included materials such as financial regulations, materials of training programs, technical reports; accounting systems' manuals, published bulletins and other financial documents. Some documentary evidence was also provided by some interviewees who wanted to illustrate their work and clarify their points of view. The study of documents also improves the validity of evidence under the "interpretive" methodology (Yin, 1994; Ahrens & Dent, 1998). The use of multiple sources of evidence is justifiable on the grounds that they enable researchers to reach a coherent interpretation of a particular case. Nevertheless, case study approach suffers some limitations such as the limited generalization of findings and the possibility of the author's subjective interpretation (Scapens, 1990).

4. PUBLIC HOSPITALS' MACRO CONTEXT: ORGANIZATIONAL CONSTITUENTS

Since 1952 Egypt had rigid price control systems over all types of products including prices of drugs, medical supplies and treatments. Furthermore, the 1952 constitution gave the right to all Egyptian citizens to have free medical care, free education, guaranteed employment, minimum wages and social insurance for all ages (Samuels & Oliga, 1982; Mansfield, 1969, p. 126). Despite the introduction of the political philosophy known as "*open door policy*", which aimed at liberalizing the Egyptian economy in 1974, the health care policies remained the same. Accordingly, the state budget became loaded by the need to finance public hospitals (Hafez, 1996a). The combination of free health service and the fast growing population created an escalating shortage of resources. This, consequently, resulted in offering substandard health service.

Under the extreme financial shortage, Egypt had to rely on flows of foreign subsidies. In 1987, the government signed an agreement with the IMF and the WB in order to guarantee the supply of the required economic resources (Richards, 1991). A few years later, Egypt subscribed to another agreement with USAID to finance some projects including technical assistance programs (Momani, 2003, p. 88). The government agreed on taking further steps towards the development of market economy institutions. In the mid-1990s, the government took more effective steps to liberalize the economy and reduce the state involvement in providing free social services (Hafez, 1996a, p. 3). Public policy makers believe that:

> Local citizens who once agreed that 'government must provide' now agree that 'we must provide for ourselves'. (Cited in Hafez, 1996a, p. 4)

Despite policy makers' intention to change and develop health care sector in line with the private sector companies, the change processes lagged behind compared to other economic sectors in Egypt. This is due to the fact that health care is a very sensitive issue in all countries and Egypt is no exception (Hafez, 1996a). Nevertheless, policy makers became concerned about the cost of social policies and wanted to reduce public expenditures directed to such policies (Rannan-Eliya et al., 1998, p. 1). They also wanted to reduce possible corruption and increase level of transparency about public sector performance.

Similar to public sectors in developing countries (Mimba et al., 2007), the Egyptian public health sector suffers a gross imbalance between the very comprehensive set of free services that the government aimed to deliver and the financial resources available. This under-financing resulted in low salaries, lack of supplies and therefore delivering substandard services. The combination of these characteristics and the lack of real access to subsidized services created a situation where health care services are provided on a fee paying basis by private providers (Berman et al., 1997, p. xi). Accordingly, the most vulnerable people are those with low-income level. They have to accept either poor quality health services or paying high costs for such services in the private sector. Berman et al. (1997) add that most citizens have accepted the latter solution even though they are entitled to free health services.

Rannan-Eliya et al. (1998, p. 2) argue that the Egyptian public health sector systems do not provide sufficient, accurate and transparent information related to the performance of public medical organizations. They also add that the health sector lacks clear accountability systems that hold public servants, particularly physicians, accountable for their decisions. Public hospitals rely on a budgetary control system that represents the only mechanism to hold hospitals' members accountable. In the absence of any other mechanisms, resources are allocated to different public hospitals without any feedback on these hospitals' performance (*ibid.*).

Under the above-mentioned circumstances, there is a possibility of misusing the economics resources. On the one hand, medical profession and expertise give physicians the right to use the economic recourses without clear accountability. They may misuse these resources in the name of saving patients' life. On the other hand, public hospitals' legal framework institutionalizes the existence of vague accountability systems. Knowles and Hotchkiss (1996) state that public hospitals' legal framework allows physicians to practice their profession in their private clinics as well as to keep their occupations in the public hospitals. They add that it would not be long before physicians practicing their profession in these hospitals would discover that they could accept gifts, in their private clinics, from patients desiring prompt admission to public hospitals that charge no fees. Therefore, the sickest patient would not necessarily get in the hospital first, however, some patients with "good connections", or as Knowles and Hotchkiss (1996, p. 21) state "back door policy", would be admitted before others.

Reforming public hospitals' "governance" systems, in order to offer health service with better quality at affordable prices and reduce possible corruptions, becomes Egypt national requirement. The philosophy behind reforming public hospitals' governance systems is shown in the following:

> [Improving health sector] in Egypt is the overriding goal ... Today's realities: governmental fiscal constraints, rapid population growth with its increased demand for health services and rising cost of medical interventions compel us to implement an urgent and effective transition towards this goal. (Minister of Health and Population, cited in Windows into CRHP, 1995, p. 2)

Despite being Egypt's national requirement, the lack of financial resources and expertise meant that Egypt could not develop the public hospitals "governance" systems alone. Therefore, various international agencies, namely the WB, IMF and USAID together with their consultants firms provided Egypt with the necessary intellectual and monetary support. These agencies recommended the development of better management, accounting and performance systems to improve the health sector efficiency, performance transparency and equality (CRHP, 1993).

As early as 1988 the USAID suggested changing the Egyptian public hospitals in line with private sector organizations. The USAID provided technical and intellectual support through a project that attempted to engender public hospitals to change. This project is known as "Cost Recovery for Health Project (CRHP)" (Hafez, 1996a, p. 17). The USAID contracted specialized expert houses in the area of health care reform (CRHP, 1993, p. 6). These consultancy houses are empowered, only, to provide the MOHP with the needed help to develop its own independent capacity to design, build and operate the components of the CRHP. Few years later, a bilateral international agreement between USAID and Egypt was signed – Project number 263-0170. The project underlying aims are:

> [The conversion] of health care organizations from their current status as free of charge, often under-utilized facilities into high quality service providers with cost recovery capabilities through developing managerial skills, management systems, accounting systems, contracting and training ... at the end of the project it is expected each organization will be capable of generating its needed resources through a fee for services system. (USAID/Cairo Agreement, Appendix 1; CRHP Bulletin, 1997, p. 5)

In 1994, the Egyptian government passed Decree 304 initiating the reforming of public hospitals' governance systems. The new systems required changing the manner in which public hospitals operate in Egypt. The Decree allowed public hospitals to charge patients for the service's full cost or at least recover part of the service's costs. It emphasized management autonomy, more realistic prices, while improving the quality of the health service. Against the background of "free health service" to all *citizens*, public hospitals are to deliver the health service for fee, to make *customers* who have ability to pay share in the health service's costs. Furthermore, hospitals are assumed to mange their financial resources according to market needs. The Decree states:

> [Market is] the basic guideline of hospital operations, thus all the decisions should be in response to market needs ... The hospital is to use revenue collected from affluent patients to subsidize the free-of-charge medical services offered to poor patients. (Executive Regulations of Decree 304 of 1994)

The MOHP, in collaboration with international aid agencies and consultants, organized training programs and conferences aimed at clarifying issues such as health quality control, reducing public expenditures, establishing a relationship between input and output, securing other source of finance via "cost sharing", "fee for services" and the "satisfaction of customers" (Rafeh & Gadalla, 1996; CRHP, 1997). They also aimed at changing public hospitals from being "health care institutions" towards being "multi-products organizations" that face different customers with various choices. This corporate form of governance philosophy is best described during the training programs as follows:

> The paradigm shift in health system

> Health care as an industry may be a new concept for the community at large but not for entrepreneur who invests in health care delivery systems and thinks in terms of product, market and client. (CRHP Bulletin, 1997, p. 4)

The MOHP formed a project management office, known as "Project Directorate" (PD), to manage the implementation of the CRHP systems. The PD incorporated different internal divisions. Each division became responsible for developing certain aspects of public hospitals' administrative functions. The PD included accounting and financial management systems development division, management and human resource development division, marketing and public relation development division, biomedical equipment maintenance division and medical quality standards setting division. Each division had a change team consisting of the MOHP advisors as well as USAID consultant firms' advisors. The PD objectives are expressed in a formal letter sent to public hospitals' managers. The letter states that:

> The cost recovery concept will serve to
> 1. Improve the quality of patient care in terms of both clinical outcomes and patient satisfaction at reasonable prices.
> 2. Increase hospital efficiency by improving management and financial systems.

3. Increase the hospital services' usage and demand through marketing which in turn leads to improving its internal sources of finance. This will release more MOHP funds for other priorities.
4. Channel governmental subsidies to lower income citizens and finance hospital services with fees from those who can afford to pay. Thus, improving equity.
5. Develop different ways to finance health services.

(Letter from Project Director cited on CRHP, 1995)

In this highly political context a new corporate form of governance was introduced within public hospitals. The MACS based on that corporate form of governance emerged as an institutional practice that link public hospitals to the wider social and institutional environment. In terms of Fig. 1, the MACS emerged as a part of the public hospitals' constituents – mainly MOHP, consultancy firms, PD and international aid agencies – demands. Public hospitals are pressured to implement MACS systems together with other desirable institutional practices in order to comply with constituents' pressures exerted from these hospitals' organizational fields.

5. FORMS OF GOVERNANCE AND ORGANIZATIONAL CHANGE

Although several studies investigate different forms of governance in public organizations (e.g. Ezzamel, 1992; Lapsley, 1993; Ezzamel & Willmott, 1993), these studies stress on hierarchies (bureaucratic) and markets as forms of governance. Jones (1999) adds "networks" as a form of governance in public health organizations. In the light of the corporatization processes of the Egyptian public hospitals, this section discusses the state-based governance dimensions. It also analyzes the attitudes of organizational members towards the change to the corporate form of governance that incorporates dimensions such as de-centralization, market control and professional versus managerial control. The section contrasts the attributes of alternative forms of governance with the case study evidence and, at the same time, seeks to reveal how the shift to the corporate form of governance created organizational change and how MACS created stability during the processes of change as will be explained in Section 6.

5.1. The State-Based Governance Systems

5.1.1. Bureaucratic/Hierarchical Control
The public hospital is owned and management by the MOHP and the governorate (Local Administration) where the hospital operates. Fig. 3 presents

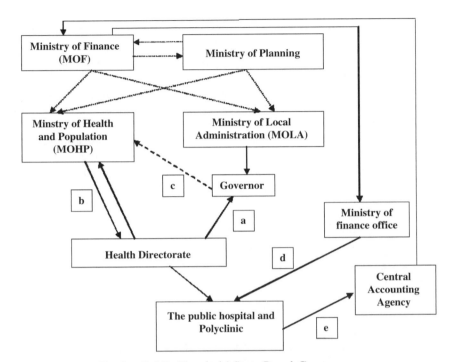

Fig. 3. Public Hospitals' State-Based Governance.

how economic resources are allocated to the public hospital. Each public hospital receives centrally allocated resources from both the MOHP and the Ministry of Local Administration. These ministries budgets are determined after negotiation processes with both the Ministry of Finance (MOF) and the Ministry of Planning (MOP) in the light of the economic resources available to the state (Hassouna & Ali, 1996). The local administration (i.e. governor of the governorate) has an influence on the hospital's management processes. According to different legislations,[1] governors have an authoritative power on public hospitals located in their governorates.

Fig. 3 presents that each governorate has a health directorate, which submits an annual report to the MOHP. This annual report determines the public hospital's financial needs (arrow b refers to this relationship). Following the MOF approval, represented by the MOF office located in the governorate (arrow d refers to this relationship), the hospital use the state allocated resources in accordance with a predetermined line item budget. The MOF-office performs a control, or as accountants say *"before expensing control"*, function each time the hospital uses the state economic resources.

The Central Accounting Agency (CAA) performs *"post expensing control"* function (arrow e refers to this relationship). This mechanism of resource allocation and control is a part of, what Jones (1999, p. 167) describes as, a hierarchical form of governance.

The health directorate also reports to the governor (arrow a) on the hospital operations. The MOHP appoints the director and deputy director of health directorates (arrow b) after consultation with the governor (arrow c) (Hassouna & Ali, 1996, p. 12). The director of health directorate appoints the hospital board of directors and manager after consultation with the governor and the MOHP. Governors have the authority to establish, equip and manage hospitals at their districts within the general policy of the MOHP. That strong influence of governors matches with hierarchical form of governance wherein a person's position affects intra-organizational processes (Jones, 1999).

In the light of this governance structure, the hospital board of directors and the hospital manager are empowered to run the hospital in accordance with the MOHP policies. A Prime Ministerial Decree 3 of 1988 incorporates rules and regulations governing the hospital financial and administrative operations. It describes authorities and responsibilities of the hospital's medical (physicians) and administrative (accountants and others) staff. In sum, there is a detailed formal decision-making system. That system, one can easily state, is in harmony with hierarchy as a form of governance (Jones, 1999).

5.1.2. The Hierarchical-Based Accounting Systems
Since the establishment of the Egyptian public health sector, the budgetary system has been used. The state allocates resources to different public hospitals without measuring the service cost (Rannan-Eliya et al., 1998, p. 2). The budgetary system is organized exclusively according to hospitals' use of resources. In this case, key hospital inputs are salaries, supplies and funding for capital investment. The system is very detailed, regulated and control-oriented as the case of all countries with centrally planned economies (Jaruga, 1996; Bourmistrov & Mellemivik, 1998). In other words, the system supports the functioning of the hierarchical form of governance (Jones, 1999; Weimer & Pape, 1999).

The hospital has to prepare two accounting reports. These reports are (1) balance of budget implementation and (2) a note on specification of fixed assets and materials. The balance of budget implementation is a report showing the balance of resources at the beginning and end of the year. The notes on fixed assets and materials is a supplementary statement, which reports aggregated information at the end of the year concerning values of materials and fixed assets in the public hospital. This statement ensures the physical existence of such assets.

Under this budgetary system, physicians have the rights to do their job without clear financial accountability since they are concerned with "saving patients" lives'. In the light of financial regulations governing the hospital's operations, physicians take decisions regarding the use of the budget's resources. Accountants prepare the paper work supporting physicians' decisions. The budgetary system-based routines separate physicians' decisions from accountants' activities. Nevertheless, both operate in the light of the limited financial resources available to the hospital. A doctor said:

> "Sometimes I need to do what I have to do regardless of what Mrxxx (referring to the financial manager) says. However, at the end I need to compromise to the circumstances and to the limited financial resources. (Doctor No. 1: Head of Dental Department)

This budgetary system established a tradition in which less concern about costs is a norm. Physicians can take whatever decisions provided that these decisions are professionally justifiable and do not breach the financial regulations. The hospital operates as a bureaucratic organization wherein physicians are responsible for the core activities, while accountants' activities are considered as secondary ones. An accountant said:

> Accounting has never been an issue for doctors. (Accountant No. 2: Costing department)

In the same issue, the financial manager said:

> In planning for financial needs, doctors are concerned with the medical materials, supplies of medicines, subscription to medical journals (i.e. supplies item in the budgetary system). Due to limited resources they arrange their priorities and we (accounting department) always try to execute their requirements to the limit granted by the financial regulations. (Accountant No. 1: The Financial Manager)

In addition to the budgetary system, the public hospital legal framework empowers the hospital to provide fee-based service (Hassouna & Ali, 1996, p. 13). By law, the hospital may provide health service and charge nominal fees. The hospital financial regulations set rules to account for and manage fee-based service. According to financial regulations, fee-based services are offered for limited hours (outpatient service) and up to 25% of the hospital occupation capacity (inpatient service). The regulations also state that the hospital calculates fee-based services' surplus through a statement called "surplus to improve service quality".

The statement matches services' fees with services' direct medical materials only. In other words, the service cost does not include some costs that are financed through the state-based budget. These non-calculated costs are cost of doctors' fees (i.e. salaries), cost of equipment, building and fixed assets (i.e. depreciation). One of the accountants explained that:

> The reason behind omitting salaries and depreciation expense under fee-based system is that these costs are free to citizens who demand the hospital services. However, the service price includes the cost of medical materials purchased specifically for that service plus a tiny contribution. (Accountant No. 5: Budgeting and performance evaluation clerk)

The exclusion of some costs, mainly salaries and depreciation, benefits patients and hospitals' members. On the one hand, service cost becomes low and therefore patients will be able to choose a physician s/he likes at affordable price. On the other hand, the fee-based system's surplus will be high and therefore the participating physicians and administrative staff will have a chance to increase their income level. In this regard, an accountant expressed that:

> This system provides patients with an opportunity to choose the physician they like outside the normal working hours. Alternatively they (referring to patients) can wait for the doctor they want until s/he has a hospital duty. (Accountant No. 3: Patients account department)

The financial regulations require the allocation of the fee-based surplus in accordance with the following scheme: the hospital retains 55% to improve the quality of medical services, MOHP receives 10%, the governorate, wherein the public hospital operates, receives 5% and finally 30% assigned to a bonus pool that is distributed to the hospital's members. In this regard, an accountant commented that:

> In comparison to private hospitals, we (referring to the public hospital) almost charge nothing to patients seeking fee-based service from our hospital. However, too many people do not trust the quality of our service and therefore we mostly provide our service to poor people who cannot go to the private hospitals' clinics. This has implications to the amount of bonus distributed to staff participating in the fee-based system. (Accountant No. 4: Patients Account departments)

Public hospitals are perceived as offering substandard services due to the institutional circumstances discussed earlier in Section 4. That perception makes patients, who have ability to pay, reluctant to admit to public hospitals. Instead, these patients prefer to have private hospitals' service, which is perceived as a "better" one. Accordingly, the public hospital's fee-based system does not generate that much surplus. In turn, the amount of bonus, paid to those participated in the fee-based system, would be affected.

5.2. The shift to the Corporate Form of Governance Systems

5.2.1. De-centralization: A Self-Governing Hospital

Due to social, economic and political circumstance described in Section 4, the MOHP introduced a new governance structure (Decree 304 of 1994) that aimed at finding sources of *private* finance in addition to the available *public* funding. The new governance structure is an apparatus to develop the Egyptian public health sector systems or as Ellis, McInnes, and Stephenson (1994, p. 183) argue changing the identity of public hospitals to become increasingly infused with the language of private business, cost sharing and economics. In order to implement the new governance structure, Decree 304 changed the hospital organizational structure (Fig. 2) whereby a new governing board, called the "board of trustees" (BOT), was created. The Decree states:

> The board of trustees may reassess the affordability and suitability of the health services' fees based on the public hospital's social and economic environment. (El-Wakae El-Masria, 1994, Decree 304)

The BOT aims at reducing central authorities, mainly the governorate and the MOHP, involvement in the processes of offering health services. The BOT underlying objective is to move the public hospital from the hierarchal governance to the market governance. It becomes responsible for determining the service's price, controlling costs and retaining any surplus to improve the health service quality. Although these responsibilities existed under the state-based (hierarchical) governance, they were reintroduced under the following principles:

> [BOT executes] the state and MOHP policies through setting different strategies to perform such policies. It executes control over both the quality and efficiency of health service delivery. It guarantees the delivering of affordable services depending on the people's ability to pay: based on actual cost for those who have the ability to pay, subsidizing the service cost for people with limited income and delivering free services for poorest people. However, all three groups are guaranteed the same quality level. (Board of Trustees Manual, 1998, p. 22)

The hospital's Board of Directors and manager implement the BOT policies and report to the board about the hospital operations (Board of Directors Manual, 1998, p. 10). Both run the hospital as a commercial organization and/or as a public organization depending on the patient's ability to pay. This way of functioning fits with, what Jones (1999) argues, "networks" governance wherein organizations' goals are ambiguous. Networks, as a form of governance, also enable to manage cultural diversity that exists in public health organizations (Jones, 1999). In the light of the corporate form of governance systems, public hospitals are free-based bureaucratic and professional organizations, yet they are requested to transform themselves into self-financing business like organizations. Accordingly "networks" governance seems to support the management of diverse and conflict goals introduced under that corporate form of governance.

Although the BOT objective is to run the public hospital as a commercial business, the board also has to accomplish the state health care social policy. The BOT becomes an apparatus to create a balance between the hospital corporate objectives and the MOHP socio-political objectives. BOT members are not nominated based on the public hospital stakeholders' desires. Instead, the governor of the governorate (local administration), wherein the public hospital operates, chooses the BOT members. Decree 304 specifies the BOT members as follows:

> Director of health directorate at the appropriate governorate (local administration), the public hospital's manager, legislative member, the public hospital's vice manager, head of the local council or his representative, people assembly member in the governorate, two businessmen, the chief of doctors' syndicate in the governorate and one of the experts in health care field. (Article 2, Appendix 1, Decree 304, 1994)

According to Decree 304, both the MOHP and the governor have the ultimate power to choose the BOT members. On the one hand, the governor directly appoints four of BOT members, mainly the legislative member, businessmen and expert members. On the other hand, under the state-based hierarchal governance (Fig. 3), the director of health directorate, the public hospital manager and vice manger are appointed in their occupations after consultation between the governor and the MOHP. One can argue that central authorities, mainly MOHP and the governor, remained the ultimate authorities that shape the way in which public hospitals operate under the corporate-based governance system. Although BOT was meant to be an independent board responsible for setting the hospital strategies, the board functioning relied on the pre-existing networks of relationships that existed under the hierarchical governance system.

The consequence of Decree 304 is that the BOT is pressured to fulfill two sets of objectives. First, the BOT must guarantee the availability of free health service to all citizens in order to accomplish the MOHP socio-political objectives. Second, the BOT has to charge customers, patients who have ability to pay, in order to accomplish market system requirements. In contrast to the hierarchical form of governance where hospitals had clear objectives and goals, the new form of governance seems to have too many objectives leading to ambiguity in the public hospitals' goals. Table 1 shows

Table 1. A Comparison Between the State-Based Governance and the Corporate Form of Governance of Public Hospitals.

Main Features	State-Based Governance (Decree 3 of 1988)	Corporate Form of Governance (Decree 304 of 1994 amended by Decree 185 of 1997)
Strategic focus	"Central planning (hierarchy)"	"Central planning combined with market economy (hierarchy and market networks)"
Constituents	MOHP, governorate, health directorate, central accounting agency and MOF	MOHP, governorate, health directorate, central accounting agency, and MOF as well as BOT
Right to health service	Free service to all citizens based on the available resources	Free service to the poorest people while charging customers who have ability to pay
Governance mechanisms	*Administrative devices*: MOHP, governorate and health directorate coordinate public hospital operations *Finance devices*: MOF, MOP, CAA coordinate public hospitals funding mechanisms	*Administrative devices*: MOHP, governorate and health directorates are to provide regulatory framework BOT coordinates and governs the public hospital operations *Finance devices*: MOF, MOP, CAA coordinate public hospitals central funding mechanisms Market system and competition determine level of private finance
Nature of governing bodies	Political	Managerial as well as political
Reliance on governing bodies	Heavy reliance	Mixed
Centrally allocated resources	Cover 75% of the hospital bed capacity (free service)	25% of the hospital bed capacity is financed by fee-based system
Fee-based system (service improvement)	Centrally allocated resources cover 25% of the hospital bed capacity (free service)	Fee-based market system covers 75% of the hospital bed capacity
Managerial Accounting Systems	Budgetary and financial control systems	Business type performance evaluation system, profitability analysis as well budgetary and financial control systems
Cost Accounting Systems	Fee based on marginal costing system (only direct materials)	Fee based on full costing system (direct/ indirect costs – variable/fixed costs)
Organization type	Political bureaucratic public hospital	Political bureaucratic-corporate public hospital

a comparison between the state-based governance (Decree 3 of 1988) and the corporate governance (El-Wakae El-Masria: Decree 304 of 1994 amended by Decree 185 of 1997).

The comparison in Table 1 shows that the public hospital "political" identity was not completely eliminated. The hospital seems to have a dual identity. It is a state-based organization and pressured to comply with the state-based hierarchal governance structure. At the same time, it has incorporated the private business governance characteristics. As a result of the hospital dual identity, the Board of Directors became, as Brunsson (1994, p. 330) argues, "confused". The board is accountable to two governance structures whereby each structure supports one of the identities. That confusion is best described as follows:

> Although I have a full autonomy to work according to the Board of Trustees (BOT) strategies and market system mechanisms, the hospital, including its BOT, is under the full control of central authorities. The governor, director of health directorate and MOHP together formulate BOT. The stated objective of BOT, regardless of decentralization, is to perform the MOHP social policy. (A discussion with Accountants No. 1 and No. 6)

The hospital manager (a doctor) expressed that:

> All the financial matters which we discuss at the Board of Directors' meetings we re-discuss at the BOT ... Mostly BOT gets its information from us (referring to the Board of Directors) ... In fact it is difficult to say what are the differences between the two boards? ... But generally we make decisions for the public benefits. (Doctor No. 3: The Hospital Manager)

5.2.2. The Market Control
In contrast to the hierarchical model of allocating economic resources, a market model was introduced (Decree 304 of 1994). The market model underlying objective is to create a competition among public and private hospitals. Competition, quality enhancement and efficiency improvement are assumed to reduce the health service's cost and price. Accordingly, the demand on the public hospital's service increases from those "customers" who have the ability to pay. Revenues collected from those "customers" will be utilized to improve service quality and subsidize the cost of free services provided to poor citizens who are not able to pay. The MOHP stands behind this market model to guarantee the availability and affordability of the health service for poor citizens. The hospital financial manager expressed the following opinion:

> we (referring to the accounting department) compute the cost of the services, add the required contribution margin, the result is the price. If the price is not competitive

compared with other public and private hospitals, we have to either reduces the contribution margin or eliminate some cost items that are financed by state like salaries. (Accountant No. 1: The Financial Manager)

Although the market model aims at moving the public hospital towards what Jones (1999) calls "the competitive continuum", it is more of "networks" governance. The market model is influenced by deep-seated links between the hospital and other organizations located in the hierarchical model of governance. The market model does not replace the state-based hierarchical model of resource allocation, instead, the former is added to latter. The public hospital is required to transform itself into a self-financing corporation. That self-financing is assumed to contribute in reducing the central resources allocated to the public hospital.

Decree 304 narrows the scope of free health services. Under the state-based governance structure, the hospital was empowered to offer fee-based service up to 25% of the hospital occupational capacity. However, the new governance structure requests, if possible, to offer fee-based service up to 75% of the occupational capacity (see Table 1). Decree 304 states that:

At least 25% of the reformed hospital total beds are assigned to free medical treatments. These treatments are accidents, burning and the poorest people. (Article 17, Appendix 5, Decree 304, 1994)

The Egyptian model differs from the internal/quasi market model introduced in the UK public health sector. In the UK internal market model, health purchasers (i.e. state health authorities) are funded by general taxation and the patient (i.e. customers) does not pay directly for services received from their local trusts. Hence, there is an intermediary, in this case, the health authority who purchases the services on behalf of the patient (Lapsley & Pallot, 2000).

In the Egyptian health care market model, the hospital has a direct relationship with customers (patients). The state does not intervene in this relationship unless the patient is a poor one. The hospital is pressured to comply with two governance structures, first, as a state-owned hospital that provides social services to different citizens, second, as a commercial organization that provides a commodity to customers who have the ability to pay. The Board of Directors and the BOT are assumed to mange the public hospital in a way that fulfills the governance dual requirements.

The Egyptian market model does not correspond to the classic market system where the provision of health services is the result of numerous decisions taken by independent sellers and buyers coordinated by "invisible hand" of market (Powell, 1991; Arviddsson, 1995, p. 69). The Egyptian market model is a hybrid form combined with the need for cooperation and independence. Public hospitals must cooperate with the pre-existing organizations and individuals located in the hierarchical governance as a state-based organization. They also have to be independent in the light of new form of governance requirements. "Networks", as a form of governance, not only suite this hybrid form but also enable those involved in managing the hospital to develop additional skills engendering social and organizational change (Jones, 1999, p. 167).

5.2.3. Professional Versus Managerial Control

Laughlin, Broadbent, and Shearn (1992) argue that professional autonomy allows physicians to commit a significant portion of resources through their clinical decisions, yet they rarely held accountable to the financial consequences of these decisions. Professional autonomy permits physicians to ignore cost and therefore it is targeted as a major reason for raising hospitals' costs (e.g. Thorne, 2002; Abernethy, 1996; Horner, 2000, p. 419). Doctors believe that standard measurements of their performance as well as standardizing costs associated with their medical treatments and surgical interventions do not capture the complexity of their professional work. In this regard, one of the doctors expressed the following opinion about quality standards:

> Although we believe in quality assurance standards, we cannot standardize our medical procedures. For example, if the standards state that a labour takes 4–6 hours, would 3 or 7 hours be inefficient delivery. Each labour has its own circumstances that require professional decisions regardless the standards. (Doctor No. 5: Head of Genecology Clinic)

Physicians' knowledge and expertise provide high levels of autonomy. Physicians rely on that autonomy to explain their decisions. In the name of their professional autonomy and expertise, they do whatever they like without any control. One of the physicians said:

> Although doctors are cost conscious as they practice the profession in their private clinics, they will circumvent and give you a lot of reasons to explain the way in which they behave in certain situations, specially, if someone wants to constrain them. (Doctor No. 3: The Hospital Manager)

Generally hospitals' outputs are difficult to measure since different physicians may describe different treatments, with different costs, for the same illness. Hospitals' outputs depend on physicians' "know-how" and therefore the value of that outputs is not easily measured. Once more "networks" governance seems to suit hospitals' circumstances where implicit, or as Jones (1999) suggests "less overt", control such as professional control is preferred instead of explicitly implementing administrative control procedures and thus being resisted (e.g. Covaleski, Dirsmith, & Michelman, 1993; Abernethy, 1996; Ballantine et al., 1998).

As a part of the hospital organizational change, the hospital's new corporate structure (i.e. Decree 304 of 1994) required the application of *"commercial accounting rules in addition to the budgetary accounting system"*. As a part of these commercial accounting systems, MOHP introduced a full costing system aiming at discussing and defining health problems in terms of cost centers, product costing, standard clinical episode and clinical performance measures (Costing System Manual, 1998; Performance Evaluation Tool Manual, 1998). The costing system is identical to that system applied in the Egyptian public industrial sector. A bulletin, published during the hospital corporatization processes, states that:

> For full hospital autonomy, a commercial financial system is needed. However, public hospitals can start with the public uniform accounting system. (CRHP, 1993, p. 10)

The costing system, applied in public industrial organizations, traces the state's centrally allocated resources (salaries, materials and investment fund) to different cost centers in each of these organizations. Accordingly, the MOHP wanted to extend the public hospital's budgetary control system through including a uniform chart of accounts that show the cost of different clinics within each public hospital. A discussion with one of the hospital members, who was working at a chemical public industrial organization before being transferred to the hospital during the implementation of the corporate form of governance, reveals that:

> Public uniform accounting there (referring to the industrial company) is the state accounting system that helps in running the hospital as a business but under the state control. (Accountant No. 2: Costing Department)

The implementation of cost center based on the corporate form of governance is to engender the public hospital corporatization but within a framework of continuing governmental involvement and control. The aim of that continuing involvement is to avoid the misperception of the hospital change as a "privatization". This is best described as follows:

> Although the hospital has to apply fee for services system, we are a public hospital. The hospital still faces the same type of poor patient who cannot pay a high price for the service. If this privatisation process (referring to the corporate form of the hospital) entailed a completely new accounting system neither I would be here nor that poor patient. (Accountant No. 11: Stock and Inventory Controller)

The introduction of MACS represented a further step towards precision in costing and the measurement of cost efficiency depending on the new corporate form of governance philosophy discussed earlier. Although MACS is a refinement to the budgetary control system, these MACS seem to facilitate the functioning of both the market and hierarchical governances or as Jones (1999) describes a "blend" of different forms of governance. The following section discusses how MACS stabilized the organization rather than engendering organizational change towards the corporate form of governance.

6. MACS AND ORGANIZATIONAL RESPONSE

6.1. Power, Routines, Uncertainty and MACS

One of underlying concerns during MACS and organizational change is the tension that may arise among various organizational members. In public hospitals, it is evident that there is a tension between physicians and administrators regarding the "power of control" (Bowerman, 1998; Thorne, 2002). On the one hand, physicians are classified as the "dominants" because they have the knowledge, the expertise, and the "know-how" to deal with the hospital core activities and uncertainties associated with patients' lives (Feinglass & Salmon, 1990; Broadbent & Laughlin, 1998). On the other hand, administrators are classified as "bureaucratic" since they take decisions in a formal procedural order. The implementation of new MACS did not only raise the tension between the hospital's physicians and accountants regarding the power of control, but also challenges the hospital's micro "institutions" and routines.

Under the state-based hierarchical governance, physicians' knowledge, expertise and "know-how" were, as institutional theorists argue, de-coupled from accounting activities and reports. To recall, accountants said "*accounting has never been an issue for doctors*". The MACS based on the corporate form of governance enabled accountants, through accounting reports, to penetrate doctors' activities and provide surveillance of clinical activities in financial terms such as consultant episodes, performance level and costing. Accordingly, physicians' expertise, knowledge and "know-how" became, in part, "taken in" to the accounting "know-how" through clinical reports (Lowe, 2000, p. 195). MACS re-couple, or as Nor-Aziah and Scapens (2007) argue tightly couple, clinicians' practices to accounting reports since the latter have invaded the work of physicians. The MACS reports incorporated medical judgments and decisions as follows:

> The report prepared by the head of dentist department (a doctor) to the head of the Accounting and Financial Management Department includes professional language concerning types of services offered and each type's revenue and cost. It is difficult to understand the medical language incorporated in that report. However, the Chief accountant easily understands the report's language and explains the difference between different types of services. (A discussion with Accountant No. 1: The Financial Manager)

The tension associated with the professional expertise and "know-how" is best described by a physician who said:

> Doctors have the intellectual abilities to learn and to do anything to run hospital operations even these finance[2] matters, but our major duty is to treat and cure patients. (Doctor No. 2: Radiology Department)

Under the state-based hierarchical governance, physicians manage, or as Feinglass and Salmon (1990, p. 240) argue "cope with", the hospital's medical uncertainties. Physicians are trained to handle patients' illness, medical treatments as well as patients' admission and discharge. The corporate form of governance introduces new forms of business uncertainties such as competition, covering full cost as well as clinics' profitability and performance. These forms of uncertainties place accountants at a higher status since they are trained to cope with such kinds of uncertainties. An accountant expressed the following:

> Things change, if we need to end up having a successful business hospital we have to have managers willing to take risky decisions in order to match market requirements. Although doctors are aware of market system and competition they rarely apply what they know in managing the public hospitals, yet they apply them in their private clinics. (Accountant No. 3: Cost accounting member)

The MACS based on the corporate form of governance aims at tracing the state's budget allocation (salaries, medical requirements and other funding) to each clinic in order to calculate each clinic's service *full cost* and, at the same time, control the escalating costs caused by medical decisions. Accountants believe that such a system is difficult to apply in a public hospital. An accountant said:

> The costing system allows the determination of the exact cost of each type of service the hospital offers. However, the hospital provides its services to large number of patients who do not have the ability to pay the health service cost. (Accountant No. 1: Financial Manager)

Another accountant expressed:

> It is difficult to calculate total costs per service for each centre. We are a public hospital working in a competitive environment. (Accountant No. 3: Costing Department responsible for budgeting)

The implementation of the full costing system increased levels of uncertainty among the hospital members. The system calculates the service full cost, then, charges patients a price that covers the full cost plus a profit margin. The service's full cost incorporates elements such as salaries (i.e. doctors' fees), depreciation as well as medical materials. Under the state-based governance, fee-based service regulations did not require the incorporation of salaries and depreciation as a part of the service cost. In contrast, the corporate form of governance requires the recovery of these costs plus making profit. The hospital should generate sufficient profit from customers, who have ability to pay, in order to subsidize the health service offered to poor citizens.

The hospital measures such a profit through the "statement of improving service quality". That statement existed under the state-based governance structure whereby clinics' revenues are matched with clinics' medical materials only. Under the corporate form of governance, the statement is redefined to match clinics' revenues with clinics' full cost. The inclusion of the service full cost does not only affect the service price, but affects clinics' profit and thereafter the 30% bonus distributed to the hospital members. MACS reports show that the hospital's clinics offer most of health services at high cost. One of the doctors expressed the following:

> We make the hospital's reputation, make patients come to our hospital and thus make the hospital makes revenues not huge costs. (Doctor No. 8: Neurology Department)

In the same manner, the financial manager expressed the following:

> Doctors never accept my explanation or the explanation of any member of my department regarding why their bonus for this month is like that. (Accountant No. 1: The Financial Manager)

MACS based on the corporate form of governance increased physicians' risk and uncertainties. Matching revenues with full cost led various clinics to have operational losses. Physicians refused this situation since their bonuses were affected. Accordingly, they started to hold accountants accountable to this situation. This is best described through the following:

> I'm doing a lot of work with my team, but we feel that what we are doing is useless. Doctors cannot accept that they generate no revenues and there is loss because of costing

rules. Although we (referring to cost team) are not responsible for that, we are not rewarded for the extra workload we do in term of cost allocation, and tracing costs. (Accountant No. 2: Costing Department)

6.2. MACS, Organizational Confusion and Symbolic Adoption

The interplay between institutional pressures and intra-organizational routines led the hospital's members to question their hospital's identity (Brunsson, 1994; Richardson, Cullen, & Richardson, 1996; Bowerman, 1998). MACS based on the corporate form of governance raised concerns about the hospital's identity. The hospital members questioned whether the hospital is a "public" or "private" one. Being a public hospital, the management was unable to make decisions aiming at managing costs.

> Cost elements are controllable if the hospital is a completely independent, but the MOHP hospitals are not independent as there are some factors that affect the hospital revenues and costs beyond the hospital control. (Doctor No. 10: The hospital Vice Manager)

Likewise, an accountant said:

> Are we a public organization or are we a private one where we can execute private sector ideas. (Accountant No. 6: Financial Manager Assistant – head of costing and budgeting section)

Similarly, the hospital manger (a doctor) and the financial manager (an accountant) expressed the following:

> Although the hospital should be having a full autonomy, the hospital is still under the central authorities' control. For example, one of the possibilities to control cost is to reduce the staff number (i.e. salaries) however we cannot do that given the general policy. All what we can do is stop hiring more staff. (A discussion with both Accountant No. 1 and Doctor No. 10)

Furthermore, MACS based on the corporate form of governance contributed to the hospital confusion. The MACS incorporated a costing system similar to that applied in the Egyptian public industrial sector. One of the accountants said:

> How an industrial costing system imposed on a public service hospital? The system needs lots of modification to suit a public hospital. (Accountant No. 3: Costing section)

The public hospital is pressured to comply with constituents' demands. MACS based on the corporate form of governance may increase the hospital members' commitment to Egypt wider social changes such as privatization and liberalization. However, these systems do not substantially serve the hospital's internal decision-making processes. MACS are myths, or as Carruthers (1995) argues "symbolic window-dressing", that reflect the birth of a self-financing corporation. MACS incorporated the hospital "state-based" routines and the "corporate form of governance" rules pressured by the hospital's constituents (e.g. Abernethy & Chua, 1996). MACS kept the "political" identity of the hospital, as a state-based organization, and introduced features of business organizations in order to symbolize the emergence of a modern corporation.

One can also speculate that public hospitals' adoption of "corporate governance" systems was in response to conditions stipulated by the international aid agencies. Pollitt (2001, p. 937) argues that in the world of the public sector "governance" reform, international donors such as WB, IMF or USAID insist on certain types of changes as conditions for granting their assistance. Accordingly, governments comply with these conditions even though this compliance might be ritualistic. MACS based on the corporate form of governance were introduced in the name of a "governance" reform that promotes for de-centralization, cost control and market rationale, yet these systems kept the ultimate power on hands of central authorities mainly the MOHP and the governor (i.e. local administration).

Finally, in the light of the case study evidence presented throughout the paper, one can argue that the corporate form of governance was in line with that of "networks" governance dimensions. The hospital's "corporate governance" is characterized by ambiguity in organizational goals, cooperation and interdependence in resources allocation, difficulty in measuring organizational outputs and the desire to adopt less formal control mechanisms. Institutional pressures, through central authorities, consultancy firms, training programs and international aid agencies, contributed to the hospital's organizational change and governance reform.

Against these institutional pressures to change, the implementation of MACS created counter pressures leading to organizational stability instead of change. MACS enabled organization members to apply the hierarchical governance systems as well as the corporate form of governance systems. MACS also allowed the pre-existing networks (i.e. central authorities), located in the hierarchical governance, to function while promoting for the creation of self-financing independent hospital. MACS intermediation among organizational members created conflict and confusion among physicians and administrators as explained earlier. Finally, MACS were inappropriate for measuring hospitals' output or operations efficiency since these systems were adopted from the Egyptian public's industrial sector. In sum, MACS enabled hospital members to argue against the new form of governance.

7. DISCUSSION

The paper explores the processes of implementing MACS based on the corporate form of governance in a transitional public hospital in a developing country, Egypt. The public hospitals' governance reform aimed at reducing public expenditures and moving public hospitals towards better qualifications in terms of quality, efficiency, market rational and decentralization. These changes evolved through institutional pressures within a framework of continuous control from central authorities. To recall, the changes in the public hospital's governance, or as Brunsson (1994) calls "companization", were added to the bureaucratic rules governing the hospital since 1965. This duality of governance made the hospital's members, as Brunsson (1994) states, "confused".

That confusion has been presented in the hospital members' discussion to issues such as the controllability of some cost elements, whether their hospital is a private or a public one, and the ability to reduce the number of staff working in the hospital. The introduction of MACS based on the corporate form of governance led hospital members' to question their future as well as that of their hospital. To recall, the empirical findings highlighted that some of the hospital members have concerns about the corporate form of governance as a *"privatization process"*. They are also uncertain about the continuity of free public health service as well as their ability to keep their jobs.

The paper also shows how organizational members' knowledge, expertise and "know-how" contributed, as Ocasio (1999) states, to organizational inertia rather than change. It explores how the accounting routines based on the hierarchical governance created a basis for organizational resistance (Burns, 1997; Burns & Scapens, 2000). Despite MACS based on corporate form of governance requirements, accountants deliberately ignored salaries (doctors' fees) and depreciation when they calculated the health service full cost. Accountants justified this deliberate ignorance in the light of the necessity to reduce health service price to poor patients. They felt that this ignorance is legitimate since the eliminated costs are centrally financed by the state under the state-based governance. The paper also reveals how MACS incorporated some of physicians' "know-how". To recall, costing reports incorporated information about physicians' prescriptions and the cost of the prescribed treatments.

MACS enabled accountants to hold the medical staff accountable in terms of the latter's costly practices and performance. To recall, accountants held clinical managers (i.e. doctors) accountable to their clinics' losses. Similar to

Broadbent and Laughlin's (1998) study, this case study reveals that MACS and public sector "corporate" governance reform was seen as unnecessary and inappropriate imposition that undermine the moral values of medical organizations and therefore had to be resisted. Broadbent and Laughlin (1998) point to the possibility of creating what they termed as "absorbing groups" within medical organizations. These groups, they argue, handle the unwanted changes in a way that does not undermine the moral value of their organizations. Whether accountants, physicians or both had acted as "absorbing group(s)" or otherwise is a question that needs a further investigation in future research.

Finally, although the paper stresses on the role of the hospital members during the processes of corporatization, it does not reveal the role of reformers during the hospital organizational change. Therefore, future research is needed to unpack the role of various actors involved in the processes of implementing the corporate form of governance in the public sector. Exploring the role of reformers needs an understanding of how internal and external networks of actors (reformers) interact with the potential health organization that adopts a new form of governance (Jones, 1999; Lapsley & Wright, 2004). That understanding goes beyond the scope of this study and represents an area of future research in developing countries.

8. CONCLUSION

The paper provides a comprehensive account of an Egyptian public hospital corporatization processes. Informed by an institutional theory framework, the paper explores the linkages between the hospital and the wider institutional environment while revealing the tension and confusion during the corporatization processes of a public hospital. The institutional theory framework has been synthesized in order to capture the case mixed findings. The framework has provided a platform to understand how the organization "know-how" and experience, which are informed by management accounting, facilitate or hold back the implementation of a corporate form of governance in a public health organization operating in a developing country. The paper links the theoretical framework to empirical findings while applying an interpretative methodology.

The paper shows how the corporate form of governance was coercively introduced by MOHP to develop the Egyptian health sector. It also reveals the institutional governance mechanisms and arrangements that took place at the Egyptian health care *organizational fields* upon which public hospitals (micro organizations) depend. These arrangements included elements such as providing training programmes, imitating costing systems applied in industrial public organizations, enacting various legislations aimed at changing the resource allocation mechanism, restructuring the hospital clinics into cost centers and changing professional (medical) accountability to an administrative one.

The paper uses an explanatory case study in order to provide an in-depth analysis that shows how MACS based on the corporate form of governance brought physicians' "know-how" into accounting reports. It also presents how the accounting routines based on the state governance created a basis for the hospital resistance to change. The case study reveals how an Egyptian public hospital, which was required to transform itself into a self-financing and profitable organization, is confused as the result of the existence of two governance structures. The case also reveals that the implementation of MACS raised various forms of uncertainties associated with bonus, autonomy and control during the corporatization of the public hospital.

Finally, the issue of public sector "governance" in developing countries is ambiguous and theoretically complex, yet the desire to implement the corporate form of governance in public sector organizations seems to continue. This issue is becoming increasingly complex especially under the pressures to corporatize, or as Brunsson (1994) argues "company-ize", public sector organizations stem not only from the local constituents but also from the interaction between those constituents and international aid agencies that legitimate the need to implement a corporate form of governance in public sector.

NOTES

1. Articles 2 and 26 of Local Administration Law 43 of 1979, hereafter Law 43; and Article 96 of Prime Ministerial Decree 707 of 1979 – the executive regulations of Law 43, Decree 707 (see Hafez, 1996b).
2. For some hospital members, "finance" is an interchangeable term for accounting and budgetary control.

REFERENCES

Abernethy, M. (1996). Physicians and resource management: The role of accounting and non-accounting controls. *Financial Accountability and Management*, *12*, 141–165.

Abernethy, M., & Chua, W. F. (1996). A field study of control system "Redesign": The impact of institutional process on strategic choice. *Contemporary Accounting Research, 13,* 569–606.

Ahrens, T., & Dent, J. F. (1998). Accounting and organizations: Realizing the richness of field research. *Journal of Management Accounting Research, 10,* 1–39.

Arviddsson, G. (1995). Regulation of planned markets in health care. In: R. B. Salltman & C. V. Otter (Eds), *Implementing planned market in health care: Balancing social and economic responsibility.* Buckingham: Open University Press.

Ballantine, J., Brignall, S., & Modell, S. (1998). Performance measurement and management in public health services: A comparison of UK and Swedish practice. *Management Accounting Research, 9,* 71–94.

Berman, P., Nandakumar, A. K., Fere, J., Salah, H., El-Aduay, M., El-Sharty, S., & Nasser, N. (1997). *A reform strategy for primary care in Egypt.* Technical Report no. 9. Partnerships for Health Reform Project, Abt Associate Inc., Bethesda, MD, USA.

Bird, F. (2001). Good governance: A philosophical discussion of the responsibilities and practices of organizational governors. *Canadian Journal of Administrative Science, 18,* 298–312.

Boubakri, N., Cosset, J., & Guedhami, O. (2005). Liberalization, corporate governance and the performance of privatized firms in developing countries. *Journal of Corporate Finance, 11,* 767–790.

Bourmistrov, A., & Mellemvik, F. (1998). Russian local governmental reform: Autonomy for accounting development. *The European Accounting Review, 8,* 675–700.

Bowerman, M. (1998). The public sector financial management reforms: Confusion, tension and paradoxes. In: O. Olson, I. Guthrie & C. Humphrey (Eds), *Global warning! Debating international development in new public financial management* (pp. 400–414). London: Coppellen Akademsik Forlag.

Broadbent, J. (1992). Change in organizations: A case study on the use of accounting in the NHS. *The British Accounting Review, 24,* 343–367.

Broadbent, J., & Laughlin, R. C. (1998). Resisting the "New Public Management": Absorption and absorbing groups in schools and GP practices in the UK. *Accounting, Auditing and Accountability Journal, 11,* 403–435.

Brunsson, N. (1994). Politicization and company-ization on institutional affiliation and confusion on the organizational world. *Management Accounting Research, 5,* 323–335.

Burns, J. (1997). The institutionalization of accounting routines: Keno Ltd. *Proceedings of 1995 Management Control Association Symposium.*

Burns, J. (2000). The dynamic of accounting change: Inter-play between new practices, routines, institutions, power and politics. *Accounting, Auditing and Accountability Journal, 13,* 566–596.

Burns, J., & Scapens, R. (2000). Conceptualising management accounting change: An institutional framework. *Management Accounting Research, 11,* 3–25.

Bushman, R. M., & Smith, A. J. (2001). Financial accounting information and corporate governance. *Journal of Accounting and Economics, 31,* 237–333.

Carpenter, V., & Feroz, E. (2001). Institutional theory and accounting rule choice: An analysis of four US state governments' decisions to adopt GAAP. *Accounting, Organizations and Society, 26,* 565–596.

Carruthers, B. (1995). Accounting, ambiguity and the new institutionalism. *Accounting, Organization and Society, 20,* 313–328.

Clatworthy, M., Mellett, H., & Peel, M. (2000). Corporate governance under 'NPM': An exemplification. *Corporate Governance: International Review, 8*, 166–176.

Cohen, I. J. (1989). *Structuration theory: Anthony Giddens and the constitution of social life.* London: Macmillan.

Collier, P. (2001). The power of accounting: A field study of local financial management in a police force. *Management Accounting Research, 12*, 465–846.

Covaleski, M., Dirsmith, M., & Michelman, J. (1993). An institutional theory perspective on the DRG framework, case-mix accounting systems and health care organizations. *Accounting, Organization and Society, 18*, 65–80.

Craven, B. M., & Stewart, G. T. (1995). Corporate governance, financial reporting and the cost of containing the aids threats in Scotland. *Financial Accountability and Management, 11*, 223–240.

Dillard, J. F., Rigsby, J. T., & Goodman, C. (2004). The making and remaking of organizational context: Duality and the institutionalization process. *Accounting, Auditing and Accountability Journal, 17*, 506–542.

Dillard, J. F., & Smith, H. L. (1999). The effect of prospective payment system on rural health care. *Accounting Forum, 23*, 327–358.

DiMaggio, P., & Powell, W. (1983). The iron cage revisited: Institutional isomorphism and collective rationality in organizational field. *American Sociological Review, 48*, 147–160.

Doolin, B. (1999). Case-mix management in a New Zealand hospital: Rationalization and resistance. *Financial, Accountability and Management, 15*, 397–417.

Eeckloo, K., Van Herck, G., Van Hulle, C., & Vleugels, A. (2004). From corporate governance to hospital governance: Authority, transparency and accountability of Belgian non-profit hospitals' board and management. *Health Policy, 68*, 1–15.

Ellis, R. D., McInnes, K., & Stephenson, E. H. (1994). Inpatient and outpatient health care demand in Egypt. *Health Economics, 3*, 183–200.

Eng, L. L., & Mak, Y. T. (2003). Corporate governance and voluntary disclosure. *Journal of Accounting and Public Policy, 22*, 325–345.

Ezzamel, M. (1992). Corporate governance and financial control. In: M. Ezzamel & D. Heathfield (Eds), *Perspectives on financial control* (pp. 3–26). London: Chapman and Hall.

Ezzamel, M., & Willmott, H. (1993). Corporate governance and financial accountability: Recent reforms in the UK public sector. *Accounting, Auditing and Accountability Journal, 6*, 109–132.

Feinglass, J., & Salmon, J. W. (1990). Corporatization of medicine: The use of medical management information systems to increase the clinical productivity of physicians. *International Journal of Health Services, 20*, 233–252.

Ferlie, E., Fitzgerlad, L., & Ashburrner, L. (1995). Corporate governance and the public sector: Some issues and evidence from the NHS (UK). *Public Administration, 73*, 375–392.

Forker, J., & Green, S. (2000). Corporate governance and accounting model of the reporting entities. *The British Accounting Review, 31*, 375–376.

Freedman, D. (2002). Clinical governance – Bridging management and clinical approaches to quality in the UK. *Clinica Chimica Acta, 21*, 133–141.

Garrod, N. (2000). Environmental contingencies and sustainable modes of corporate governance. *Journal of Accounting and Public Policy, 19*, 237–261.

Giddens, A. (1984). *The constitution of society.* Cambridge, MA: Polity Press.

Giroux, G., & McLelland, A. (2003). Governance structures and accounting at large municipalities. *Journal of Accounting and Public Policy, 22*, 203–230.

Goodwin, J., & Seow, J. L. (2002). The influence of corporate governance mechanisms on the quality of financial reporting and auditing: Perceptions of auditors and directors in Singapore. *Accounting and Finance, 42,* 195–223.

Granlund, M. (2001). Towards explaining stability in and around management accounting systems. *Management Accounting Research, 12,* 141–166.

Hafez, N. (1996a). *Analysis of the political environment for health policy reform in Egypt.* Technical Report no. 5, Vol. V. Partnerships for Health Reform Project, Abt Associate Inc., Bethesda, MD, USA.

Hafez, N. (1996b). *Analysis of the institutional capacity for health policy reform in Egypt.* Technical Report no. 5, Vol. VI. Partnerships for Health Reform Project, Abt Associate Inc., Bethesda, MD, USA.

Haniffa, R., & Cooke, T. (2002). Culture, corporate governance and disclosure in Malaysian corporations. *ABACUS: Journal of Accounting, Finance and Business Studies, 38,* 317–339.

Harrison, J. J. H. (1998). Corporate governance in the NHS – An assessment of boardroom practices. *Corporate Governance: An International Review, 6,* 140–150.

Hassan, M. K. (2005). Management accounting and organizational change: An institutional theory perspective. *Journal of Accounting and Organizational Change, 1,* 125–140.

Hassouna, A., & Ali, A. (1996). *Legal analysis of the health sector policy reform program assistance in Egypt.* Technical Report no. 5, Vol. IV. Partnerships for Health Reform Project, Abt Associates Inc., Bethesda, MD, USA.

Hodges, R., Macniven, L., & Mellett, H. (2004). Governance of the UK NHS, the annual general meeting. *Corporate Governance: An International Review, 12,* 343–352.

Hodges, R., Wright, M., & Keasey, K. (1996). Corporate governance in the public services: Concepts and issues. *Public Money and Management, 16,* 7–13.

Hood, C. (1995). The "New Public Management" in the 1980s: Variations on the theme. *Accounting, Organization and Society, 20,* 93–109.

Horner, J. (2000). Autonomy in the medical profession in the UK – A historical perspective. *Theoretical Medicine, 21,* 409–423.

Jalilian, H., Kirkpatrick, C., & Parker, D. (2006). The impact of regulation on economic growth in developing countries: A cross-country analysis. *World Development, 33*(1), 87–103.

Jaruga, A. (1996). Accounting in socialist countries: The beginnings of reform. In: N. Garrog & S. Mcleay (Eds), *Accounting in transition: The implication of political economic reform in central Europe.* London: Routledge.

Jones, C. S. (1999). Hierarchies, networks and management accounting in NHS hospitals. *Accounting, Auditing and Accountability Journal, 12,* 164–187.

Jones, C. S., & Dewing, I. P. (1997). The attitudes of NHS clinicians and medical managers towards changes in accounting controls. *Financial, Accountability and Management, 13,* 261–280.

Jones, M. J., & Mellett, H. J. (2007). Determinants of changes in accounting practices: Accounting and the UK health service. *Critical Perspectives on Accounting, 18,* 91–121.

Kim, B., Prescott, J. E., & Kim, S. M. (2005). Differentiated governance of foreign subsidiaries in transitional corporations: An agency theory perspective. *Journal of International Management, 11,* 43–66.

Knowles, J., & Hotchkiss, D. (1996). *Economic analysis of the health sector policy reform program assistance in Egypt.* Technical Report no. 5, Vol. II. Partnerships for Health Reform Project, Abt Associate Inc., Bethesda, MD, USA.

Lapsley, I. (1993). Markets, hierarchies and the regulation of NHS. *Accounting and Business Research, Corporate Governance Special Issue, 23*, 384–395.

Lapsley, I., & Pallot, J. (2000). Accounting, management and organizational change: A comparative study of local government. *Management Accounting Research, 11*, 213–229.

Lapsley, I., & Wright, E. (2004). The diffusion of management accounting innovations in public sector: A research agenda. *Management Accounting Research, 15*, 255–375.

Laughlin, R., Broadbent, J., & Shearn, D. (1992). Recent financial and accountability changes in general practice: An unhealthy intrusion into medical autonomy. *Financial, Accountability and Management, 8*, 129–148.

Lowe, A. (2000). Accounting in health care: Some evidence on the impact of case-mix systems. *British Accounting Review, 32*, 189–211.

Lukka, K. (2007). Management accounting change and stability: Loosely coupled rules and routines in action. *Management Accounting Research, 18*, 76–101.

Luo, Y. (2005). Corporate governance and accountability in multinational enterprises: Concepts and agenda. *Journal of International Management, 11*, 1–18.

Mansfield, P. (1969). *Nasser's Egypt*. London: Penguin Books.

Meyer, J., & Rowan, B. (1977). Institutionalised organizations: Formal structure as myth and ceremony. *American Journal of Sociology, 83*, 340–363.

Mimba, N. S. H., Jan van Helden, G., & Tillema, S. (2007). Public sector performance measurement in developing countries: A literature review and research agenda. *Journal of Accounting and Organizational Change, 3*(3), 192–208.

Modell, S. (2002). Institutional perspectives on cost allocations: Integration and extension. *The European Accounting Review, 11*, 653–679.

Modell, S. (2004). Performance measurement myths in the public sector: A research note. *Financial, Accountability and Management, 20*, 39–55.

Momani, B. (2003). Promoting economic liberalization in Egypt: From U.S. foreign aid to trade and investment. *Middle East Review of International Affairs, 7*(3), 88–101.

Nor-Aziah, K., & Scapens, R. W. (2007). Corporatization and accounting change: The role of accounting and accountants in a Malaysian public utility. *Management Accounting Research, 18*, 209–247.

Ocasio, W. (1999). Institutionalized action and corporate governance: The reliance on rules of CEO succession. *Administrative Science Quarterly, 44*, 384–408.

OECD. (2004). *Principles of corporate governance*. Paris: Organization for Economic Co-operation and Development.

Oliver, C. (1991). Strategic responses to institutional processes. *The Academy of Management Review, 16*(1), 145–179.

Olson, O., Guthrie, J., & Humphrey, C. (1998). *Global warning! Debating international development in new public financial management*. London: Coppellen Akademsik Forlag.

Parker, L., & Gould, G. (1999). Changing public sector accountability: Critiques and new directions. *Accounting Forum, 23*, 109–135.

Pesqueux, Y. (2005). Corporate governance and accounting systems: A critical perspective. *Critical perspectives on Accounting, 16*, 797–823.

Pettersen, I. J. (1999). Accountable management reforms: Why the Norwegian hospital reform experiment got lost in implementation. *Financial, Accountability and Management, 15*, 377–396.

Pollitt, C. (2001). Public management convergence: The useful myth? *Public Administration, 79*(4), 933–947.

Powell, W. W. (1991). Neither market nor hierarchy: Networks forms of organizations. In: G. Thompson, J. Frances, R. Levacic & J. Mitchell (Eds), *Markets, hierarchies and networks* (pp. 265–276). London: Sage Publication.

Power, M., & Laughlin, R. (1992). Critical theory and accounting. In: M. Alvessson & H. Willimott (Eds), *Critical management studies*. London: Sage Publication.

Rafeh, N., & Gadalla, S. (1996). The first national conference on quality in health care in Egypt. *International Journal for Quality in Health Care, 8*, 199–200.

Rannan-Eliya, P., Raviandra, P., Nada, K., Abeer K., & Ali, A. I. (1998). *Egypt national health care accounts 1994–1995*. Special initiative Report No. 3. Partnerships for Health Reform Project, Abt Associate Inc., Bethesda, MD, USA.

Ribeiro, J. A., & Scapens, R. W. (2006). Institutional theories in management accounting change: Contributions, issues and paths for development. *Qualitative Research in Accounting and Management, 3*(2), 94–111.

Richards, A. (1991). The political economy of dilatory reform: Egypt in 1980s. *World Development, 19*(12), 1721–1730.

Richardson, S., & Cullen, J. (2000). Autopsy of change: Contextualizing entrepreneurial and accounting potential in the NHS. *Financial Accountability and Management, 16*, 353–372.

Richardson, S., Cullen, J., & Richardson, B. (1996). The story of a schizoid organization: How accounting and the accountant are implicated in its creation. *Accounting, Auditing and Accountability Journal, 9*, 8–30.

Samuels, J., & Oliga, J. (1982). Accounting standards in developing countries. *The International Journal of Accounting Education and Research, 18*(1), 69–88.

Scapens, R. W. (1990). Researching management accounting practice: The role of case study methods. *British Accounting Review, 22*, 259–281.

Scott, F., & McNamee, M. (2005). The ethics of corporate governance in public sector organizations: Theory and audit. *Public Management Review, 7*, 135–144.

Scott, W. (1995). *Institutions and organizations: Foundations for organizational science*. London: Sage Publication.

Scott, W. R. (1983). Health care organizations in the 1980s: The convergence of public and professional control systems. In: R. W. Scott, B. Rowan & T. Deal (Eds), *Organizational environments: Ritual and rationality*. London: Sage Publication.

Seal, W. (2006). Management accounting and corporate governance: An institutional interpretation of agency problem. *Management Accounting Research, 17*, 89–408.

Shaprino, B., & Matson, D. (2008). Strategies of resistance to internal control regulations. *Accounting, Organizations and Society, 33*, 199–228.

Shleifer, A., & Vishny, R. (1997). A survey of corporate governance. *Journal of Finance, 52*, 737–783.

Solomon, J., & Solomon, A. (2004). *Corporate governance and accountability*. London: Wiley.

Taylor, D. W. (2000). Facts, myths, monsters: Understanding the principles of good governance. *The International Journal of Public Sector Management, 13*, 108–124.

Thorne, M. (2002). Colonising the new world of NHS management: The shifting power of professionals. *Health Services Management Research, 15*, 14–26.

Tsamenyi, M., Cullen, J., & Gonzalez, J. (2006). Changes in accounting and financial information in a Spanish electricity company: A new institutional theory analysis. *Management Accounting Research, 17*, 409–432.

Vinten, G. (1998). Corporate governance: An international state of the art. *Managerial Auditing Journal, 13,* 419–431.

Watkins, A. L., & Arrington, C. E. (2007). Accounting, new public management and American politics: Theoretical insights into the national performance review. *Critical Perspectives on Accounting, 18,* 33–58.

Weimer, J., & Pape, J. C. (1999). A taxonomy of systems of corporate governance. *Corporate Governance: International Review, 7*(2), 152–166.

Weir, C., Laing, D., & McKnight, P. J. (2002). Internal and external governance mechanisms: Their impact on the performance of the UK large public companies. *Journal of Business Finance and Accounting, 29,* 579–611.

Yazdifar, H., Zaman, M., Tsamenyi, M., & Askarany, D. (2007). Management accounting change in a subsidiary organization. *Critical Perspectives in Accounting,* forthcoming, doi: 10.1016/j.cpa.2006.08.004.

Yin, R. K. (1994). *Case study research: Design and methods.* London: Sage Publication.

Decrees, Financial Regulations, Manuals and Bulletins

Board of Trustees Manual, CRHP series 1998, manual No. 2. Issued by a co-operation between MOHP/USAID and University Research Corporation by consulting Birch and Davis International, Project Hope and Washington Health Care International Corporation. Financed by USAID/GOE CRHP Project No. 263-0170-C-00-5082-00.

Board of Directors Manual, CRHP series 1998, manual No. 3. Issued by a co-operation between MOHP/USAID and University Research Corporation by consulting Birch and Davis International, Project Hope and Washington Health Care International Corporation. Financed by USAID/GOE CRHP Project No. 263-0170-C-00-5082-00.

Costing System Manual, CRHP series 1998, manual No. 6. Issued by a co-operation between MOHP/USAID and University Research Corporation by consulting Birch and Davis International, Project Hope and Washington Health Care International Corporation. Financed by USAID/GOE CRHP Project No. 263-0170-C-00-5082-00.

CRHP. (1993). Windows into the Cost Recovery for Health Project (CRHP), Issue No. 1, April.

CRHP. (1995). Windows into the Cost Recovery for Health Project (CRHP), Issue No. 4, September.

CRHP. (1997). Cost Recovery for Health Project Bulletin, Issue No. 10, August.

El-Wakae El-Masria. (1994). Ministry of Health and Population, Decree 304.

El-Wakae El-Masria. (1997). Ministry of Health and Population, Decree 185.

Performance Evaluation Tool Manual, CRHP series 1998, manual No. 25. Issued by a co-operation between MOHP/USAID and University Research Corporation by consulting Birch and Davis International, Project Hope and Washington Health Care International Corporation. Financed by USAID/GOE CRHP Project No. 263-0170-C-00-5082-00.

APPENDIX

- How long have you been in the hospital?
- Has the hospital gone through restructuring processes?

- Can you describe the restructuring processes?
- Can you explain why such restructuring processes took place?
- Did you have new accounting systems during the restructuring processes?
- Can you describe these systems?
- Who did recommend the new systems?
- Did you participate in developing the new accounting and/or other systems during the restructuring processes?
- Can you describe the differences between the old and new accounting systems?
- What is your opinion about the new accounting systems associated with the hospital new structure?
- Did the hospital need management accounting and costing information? Why?
- Were there pressures to change the hospital organizational structure and accounting systems? Explain?
- Have you seen new individuals during the hospital restructuring processes?
- Who are those individuals?
- Have you spoken to those individuals?
- Did you rely on the new accounting systems to make decision?
- Do you think that the information obtained from costing system is important?
- What sort of differences that you could observe when you compare between the pre- and post-restructuring systems?
- What is your opinion about the hospital BOT?
- In the light of the hospital restructuring requirements, have you been personally affected by the restructuring requirements (i.e. salaries, office location, position)?
- Generally, can you explain whether the new accounting systems based on the restructuring requirements fit the hospital as a public medical organization?

THE (PERCEIVED) ROLES OF CORPORATE GOVERNANCE REFORMS IN MALAYSIA: THE VIEWS OF CORPORATE PRACTITIONERS

Pik Kun Liew

ABSTRACT

Purpose – *The purpose of this paper is to understand the roles of corporate governance reforms in Malaysia following the 1997/1998 Asian crisis from the perspectives of corporate managers.*

Design/methodology/approach – *The primary evidence used is drawn from a series of in-depth semi-structured interviews with Malaysian corporate managers involved in the overseeing of the governance structures within their companies.*

Findings – *This study shows that most interviewees believed that an appropriate corporate governance system could play a role in resolving the problems associated with the interlocking and concentrated corporate ownership structure in Malaysia. However, the effectiveness of the corporate governance reforms in dealing with this issue is questionable. It also reveals that Malaysian companies 'changed' their corporate governance*

Corporate Governance in Less Developed and Emerging Economies
Research in Accounting in Emerging Economies, Volume 8, 455–482
Copyright © 2008 by Emerald Group Publishing Limited
ISSN: 1479-3563/doi:10.1016/S1479-3563(08)08015-8

*practices predominantly to recover (foreign) investor confidence lost during
the crisis and to fulfil the legal requirements enforced by the government,
where the latter was under pressure from the international community
(especially, the World Bank and IMF) to 'improve' the Malaysian
corporate governance practices after the crisis.*

Originality/value of paper – *This paper adds to the literature on
corporate governance, especially in the context of developing countries.
Prior research investigating corporate governance issues in developing
countries has been limited, particularly the lack of in-depth examination of
corporate governance practices from the perspectives of corporate
managers. This paper will be of great value to researchers and
practitioners seeking to gain a better understanding of the roles of
corporate governance in Malaysia.*

INTRODUCTION

Corporate governance in developing (especially Asian) countries has started
to enjoy a real increase in attention since the 1997/1998 Asian financial crisis
(Singh & Zammit, 2006; Koehn, 2002). 'Poor' corporate governance has
frequently been identified as an important contributor to the 1997/1998
Asian crisis and is sometimes even seen as its main cause. For example, the
World Bank (1998) argued that:

> Corporate governance [in East Asian countries] has been characterized by ineffective
> boards of directors, weak internal control, unreliable financial reporting, lack of
> adequate disclosure, lax enforcement to ensure compliance, and poor audits. These
> problems are evidenced by unreported losses and understated liabilities. Regulators
> responsible for monitoring and overseeing such practices failed to detect weaknesses and
> take timely corrective action. (p. 67–68)

The then President of the World Bank, Wolfensohn (1998, p. 38)
proclaimed that 'poor' corporate governance standards was one of several
factors contributing to the Asian crisis because "rotten national economies
spring from rotten corporations; if business life is not run on open and
honest lines there is little chance that the wider economy can be". Similarly,
the Asian Development Bank (ADB), which launched *A Study of Corporate
Governance and Financing in Selected Developing Member Countries* in
November 1998, found that weak corporate governance was one of the
major contributors to the accumulation of vulnerabilities in East Asia

(including Thailand, Indonesia and Malaysia) that finally led to the economic crisis in 1997 (ADB, 2000). In the same way, the diagnosis of the International Monetary Fund (IMF) was that East Asia had exposed itself to financial chaos because its financial system was riddled with insider trading, corruption and weak corporate governance, which in turn had caused inefficient investment spending and weakened the stability of the banking system (Radelet & Sachs, 1998). International agencies such as the World Bank, IMF and ADB had accordingly called for corporate governance reforms in the Asian crisis affected countries (see ADB, 2000; Aghevli, 1999; Camdessus, 1998; World Bank, 1998, 2000).

The aim of this paper is primarily to understand the roles of corporate governance reforms in one of the developing economies worst hit by the 1997/ 1998 Asian crisis (namely, Malaysia) from the corporate practitioners' perspectives. First, the paper attempts to identify and understand the role of corporate governance reforms in Malaysia. Malaysia is a particularly interesting case in that for a number of years it was seen as a worthy example of a 'tiger economy', experiencing continuous economic growth and social development, and corporate governance issues had not been seen as a matter of concern (see World Bank, 1993). Corporate governance came to be seen as a problem only after the financial crisis, with a range of international agencies and also the Malaysian government itself advocating improved corporate governance practices as a vital reform and a way of making the country resilient to any future financial crises. For example, the World Bank (2000) argued that:

> Deficiencies in corporate governance did not constrain the impressive pre-crisis performance of East Asia's emerging market economies – but they amplified the subsequent downturns. (p. 69)

Malaysia is also of particular interest because the country faces increased pressure for 'good' corporate governance practices, that is to say, meeting the benchmark against the so-called international (essentially Anglo-American) corporate governance code of best practices in view of the growing global competition for foreign investment among developing and developed countries (see Liew, 2007; Shameen & Oorjitham, 1998). Therefore, an analysis of the roles of corporate governance reforms in Malaysia will be of relevance in Malaysia as well as other developing and less developed countries which are increasingly under pressure to reform their corporate governance practices in line with the 'international' standard. The paper also seeks to illustrate how globalisation (or more specifically global capitalism) has (re)shaped corporate governance practices around the world, influenced lives and induced changes that may not be appropriate to a nation/society. Following the Asian crisis, the Malaysian authorities embarked on numerous corporate governance reforms, which were predominantly based on the Anglo-American regimes, aimed at 'improving' corporate governance practices in the corporate sector.[1] The appropriateness of this approach is a matter that needs much consideration, especially at the corporate level – an aspect that is relatively unexplored. The paper through interviews with managers (involved in governance issues within their companies) solicits their views on those reforms. In addition, this paper provides much needed empirical evidence based on the views of 19 managers as to the practical implications of introducing different corporate governance codes and traditions, fundamentally in terms of how they infiltrate and integrate into existing Malaysian business cultures, and their impact on matters of accountability and business performance. The paper offers insights into the significance of the corporate governance reforms in Malaysia and calls for further research to explore the effectiveness of recent corporate governance developments in Malaysia. The paper further contributes to research in developing and less developed countries by stimulating debates about the importance of local peculiarities and cultures.

The paper is structured as follows. The first section develops the theoretical foundation for understanding the spread of worldwide reforms in corporate governance 'converging' towards the Anglo-American model, focusing on the case of Malaysia. This is followed by a discussion on the role of corporate governance in Malaysia after the 1997/1998 economic crisis. The next section describes the research method adopted to assess and explore the role of reforms in Malaysia from the corporate practitioners' perspectives, followed by the results of the interviews. Finally, a number of conclusions are offered in respect of the role of corporate governance reforms in Malaysia in the aftermath of the crisis.

GLOBALISATION AND THE EMERGENCE OF CORPORATE GOVERNANCE REFORMS IN DEVELOPING COUNTRIES

Corporate governance is in a state of transition in most countries in the world, with the strongest force for corporate governance reforms being the liberalisation and globalisation of financial markets (Beeson, 2001). Privatisation, deregulation and open free markets with increased foreign direct investments (FDIs) and trading in recent years have all deepened the role of (local and international) capital markets and the private sector in both the developed and the developing worlds. With the advancement in information technologies and transport, capital is now able to move rapidly around the world in search of profits (Sikka, 2008a; Giddens, 2002). These worldwide trends dictate that investment follows the path to corporations and countries that have 'good' governance standards (Ahunwan, 2003; OECD, 1999). Countries and companies compete on the price and quality of their goods and services, and compete for financial resources in global financial markets. These global market pressures, to a certain extent, are driving many countries (in particular emerging and less developed) to change and conform to the so-called international benchmark of corporate governance practices (predominantly based on the Anglo-American models) (see Uddin & Choudhury, 2008; Lambert & Sponem, 2005; Beeson, 2001; Economist, 2000; Millstein, 2000).

Following substantial changes in the global market, namely, the proliferation of foreign investments, global capitalism and the increasingly internationalised nature of business education, both domestic and multi-national companies have had to respond to new international trading activities, the emergence of new economies and the problems associated with economic downturns. These factors have led to collapses, hostile takeovers and/or restructuring of companies (both domestic and multinational), which have been attributed to ineffective corporate governance (Scott, 1997; Blair, 1995). Owing to these problems, there is an international momentum behind moves for reforming and improving corporate governance practices in recent years, especially in developing and less developed countries.

One of the key events that prompted worldwide corporate governance reforms was the 1997/1998 Asian financial catastrophe (Liew, 2007; Singh & Zammit, 2006; Koehn, 2002; Beeson, 2001). Malaysia and other affected East Asian countries were under pressure from supranational organisations such as the World Bank, IMF and ADB to improve/change their corporate governance practices, especially after the collapse of many large conglomerates in those countries, so as to match the expectations of the international/Western community (Liew, 2007; Glen & Singh, 2005; World Bank, 1998). The recommended 'rescue package' was to adopt the predominantly neo-liberal Anglo-American corporate governance systems – a policy that was not well grounded (Singh & Zammit, 2006; Stiglitz, 1999, 2002). In fact, the then Malaysian Prime Minister, Mahathir Mohamad, pointed out that: "[w]e try to follow [the IMF programmes] not because we think the IMF is right, but because if we don't then there will be a loss of confidence ... So we try to show that we are with the IMF" (Shameen & Oorjitham, 1998, p. 4).

Consequently, the model of governance adopted and implemented in Malaysia after the 1997/1998 crisis was the easily accessible and so-called internationally accepted Anglo-American regimes (Liew, 2007; Ow-Yong & Cheah, 2000). However, it remains open to doubt as to whether the globally favoured Anglo-American corporate governance codes and practices deliver the promised levels of accountability and transparency (Uddin & Choudhury, 2008; Singh & Zammit, 2006; Lambert & Sponem, 2005), let alone whether there is a relationship between such systems and levels or quality of organisational and economic performance (see Moxey, 2004). For example, Lambert and Sponem (2005) argued that the spread of Anglo-American corporate governance model in French companies (with the increase in shareholder pressure) has resulted in a rise in the practice of profit manipulation and a reduction in the relevance of financial statements. Therefore, this paper examines and questions the roles of corporate governance reforms (based on the Anglo-American models) in a developing country like Malaysia.

CORPORATE GOVERNANCE: A NEW ROLE IN MALAYSIA?

Recovery plans for the corporate sector in Malaysia from institutions such as the IMF and the World Bank have come to be based on the need to reform corporate governance, enhance property and minority rights, limit insider-transactions and improve disclosure and accounting practices (World Bank, 1998, 2000) – even though five years earlier, the World Bank had seen no need to mention matters of corporate governance when concluding that Malaysia had the basics right in terms of economic management, and effective public institutions and governance (see World Bank, 1993).

Despite such advocates for reforming corporate governance, there is a substantial body of work challenging the assumption that governance 'failings' were a major contributing factor to the 1997/1998 crisis. Stiglitz and Bhattacharya (2000), for example, claimed that increased transparency in the form of disclosure as would be the case with more extensive corporate governance requirements is unnecessary as markets provide optimal incentives for disclosure. Under certain circumstances, disclosure of corporate information could actually intensify fluctuations in financial markets and trigger an economic crisis. In addition, Furman and Stiglitz (1998) pointed to the fact that even countries with solid legal and regulatory systems and no transparency problems, such as Sweden, have had financial crises. Finally, Singh, Singh and Weisse (2002) suggested the claim that poor corporate governance system was the main cause of the Asian crisis is flawed and argued that countries such as China and India were not affected by the

1997/1998 financial crisis even though their fundamentals were worse than those of Asian crisis countries (Singh et al., 2002).

Notwithstanding the inconclusive evidence for the contentions that corporate governance was a (main) cause of the crisis and that corporate governance in Malaysia was fundamentally flawed, the government focused on reforming corporate governance as an important element in managing the crisis. This raises the issue of what prompted the government and some local professional bodies into introducing 'comprehensive' corporate governance reforms.

One of the factors driving the Malaysian government to improve corporate governance standards is to maintain or ensure the continuity of foreign direct and portfolio investments into the country. For decades, Malaysia has been dependent on FDI to spur economic growth. According to Athukorala (2003, p. 202), net FDI inflows contributed 43% of net capital inflows to Malaysia between 1990 and 1994. For those years, net FDI inflows contributed to almost 20% on average of the country's annual Gross Capital Formation (GCF)[2] and equivalent to over 7% of the country's annual Gross Domestic Product (GDP) (calculated based on World Bank, 2006). The authorities had to take serious consideration of the impact of the 1997/1998 financial crisis on FDI because such investment had played an important role in the country's successful economic development to date, and a substantial drop was likely to have serious consequences for the Malaysian economy.

Among the initiatives undertaken to maintain or attract FDI to the country following the large outflows of foreign capital funds during the crisis period were: improving corporate governance, a call for revamp of the Companies Act 1965 (The Star, 2003) and the introduction of new rules in June 2004 that allowed foreign investors 100% ownership in manufacturing firms that they established (see BizAsia, 2003). The then Malaysian stock exchange[3] executive chairman Mohammed Azlan bin Hashim announced that:

> Enhanced standards of corporate governance and transparency will *increase the attractiveness* of the public listed companies thus making it easier to raise capital ... [and] more attractive as investment options ... [also] the revamped listing requirements are on a par with the rules of other exchanges in developed markets and this should serve to *attract more international investors* ... [and] afford *greater protection to shareholders.* (KLSE, 2001a, [online], accessed on 15 March 2001) [emphasis added]

This is evidence of the significance of FDI in prompting the Malaysian corporate governance reforms.

Furthermore, the Malaysian Securities Commission (SC) argued that emphasis on improving corporate governance was highly significant because globalisation results in increased competition for capital, and investors are factoring corporate governance into their investment decisions (see SC, 1999). For example, following the crisis, CalPERS, the largest United States public pension fund and the third largest in the world, drew up a set of global governance principles and has since tried to ensure that the investments it commits to Asia are not invested in companies that lack 'good' governance practices. In February 2002, it announced its intension to withhold new investment in several emerging markets (including Thailand, Russia, Malaysia and Indonesia) after a review that looked at corporate governance issues such as transparency and shareholder rights in the region. In particular, CalPERS's president, William Crist, claimed that corporate governance reforms in Indonesia and Malaysia still lagged behind other South East Asian emerging markets (Edge Daily, 2002, September 10).

The newly appointed National Economic Action Council's (NEAC) executive director, Mustapa Mohamed (Mohamed, 2002), also proclaimed that corporate governance must not be neglected in an increasingly internationalised economy and that enhancing "corporate governance is an important agenda in any nation's development strategy" (para 3). He argued that for Malaysia to sustain economic competitiveness, apart from sound macroeconomic fundamentals and attractive fiscal incentives, 'good' (or 'improved') corporate governance and effective control systems must be in place to improve and maintain investor confidence thereby drawing investments which will grow the country's economy:

> Any country hoping to attract investors and investments around the world must *demonstrate* that its *corporate culture and governance practices are in line with global best practices* as investors unfamiliar with local business conditions seek to be assured and comforted that their interests are sufficiently safeguarded [emphasis added]. (Mohamed, 2002, para 35)

The need to attract foreign investment to sustain economic growth and pressures from foreign investors and international organisations such as the World Bank and the IMF to 'improve' corporate governance practices so as to align with the so-called global (Anglo-American) best practices could be seen as a major reason for the corporate governance reforms in Malaysia. The question here is that if corporate governance was not a criterion for investors in making their decisions to invest in Malaysia before the crisis, why did it become an issue after the crisis?

On the other hand, it could be that improving corporate governance or adopting 'good' practices of corporate governance in Malaysia was being used as a measure to enhance shareholder protection, in particular protection of minority shareholders (see HLFC, 1999). Zhuang, Edwards, Webb, and Capulong (2000) found that legal protection for shareholders (especially minority shareholders) had always been inadequate in Malaysia. They noted that although laws concerning shareholder rights and the regulatory framework in Malaysia appeared comprehensive and were relatively adequate compared with other countries in their study, shareholder rights were often neglected in practice because of the excessive power enjoyed by controlling shareholders. Furthermore, Fan and Wong (2002) argued that outside investors perceive that controlling owners who oversee the accounting reporting policies have strong opportunistic incentives for self-interested activities; therefore the quality of accounting information will be lower. In another study, they suggested that external independent auditors could be employed as monitors and as bonding mechanisms to alleviate the agency conflicts between controlling shareholders and minority shareholders in Malaysia (Fan & Wong, 2001) – as opposed to the conventional principal-agent problems between managers and shareholders. This implies that corporate governance reforms in Malaysia could contribute to improved minority shareholder protection in the generally concentrated Malaysian businesses[4].

Traditionally, principles of 'good' corporate governance would not be a concern to the family-run or owner-managed companies common in Malaysia. However, the situation may now have changed. Zafft (2002) argues that family-run firms need robust corporate governance structures both to operate the business and to promote business harmony. He notes that the greatest challenge for family businesses is management succession since it is difficult to keep a business going across generations. Family businesses may also fail because of jealousies that emerge, for instance, some family employees hold higher positions than others or work less hard for the same pay, and supervisors find themselves incapable of firing an under-performing subordinate who is related to them. Such businesses should therefore institute decision-making and monitoring procedures that are open and impartial, as well as possibly hiring non-family members as advisors, managers and directors. He concludes that:

> Family-run businesses can represent the work – and the wealth – of several generations. If business owners want to preserve, enlarge and pass on this legacy, they need to make corporate governance a family affair. (p. 19)

The problem here is that the Malaysian corporate management traditions (which are based on concentrated ownership) had certainly contributed to decades of economic success before the crisis, yet these traditions came into question following the crisis. There is therefore a need for further investigation whether corporate governance reform can play a role in the Malaysian family businesses – an issue that will be examined later in this paper.

In addition, the revelation of a few high-profile cases of poor corporate governance relating to companies with political links, notably

Renong-United Engineers Malaysia and Malaysia Airline System (see Ong, 2001) following the economic catastrophe has undermined market sentiment and exacerbated the crisis in Malaysia. Two forms of political favouritism are said to exist in Malaysia (Gomez & Jomo, 1997): the official status awarded to companies that are run by the Bumiputras[5] and the informal ties between leading politicians and companies. The increased government intervention required for implementation of the National Economic Policy (NEP) (since 1971) and privatisation (first introduced in 1983) opened the door to greater political involvement in the financing of Malaysian companies and a number of major conglomerates controlled by Bumiputras, with their close links to the political elite, emerged and developed rapidly during the 1980s and early 1990s. Extensive political nepotism and cronyism had grown with privatisation (Jayasankaran, 2003; George, 2005). Furthermore, these politically affiliated business groups could easily obtain bank loans from government-controlled banks, using their political influence to finance projects (Yoshihara, 1988). Gomez and Jomo (1997) noted that, by 1996, the rise of most leading businessmen in the Malaysian industry was linked to the patronage of influential political actors; wealth creation relied on whether their patrons remained in power. Following the 1997/1998 crisis, the downfall of the then Deputy Prime Minister Anwar Ibrahim and former Finance Minister Daim Zainuddin caused many of their business allies to struggle to protect their corporate interests (see Johnson & Mitton, 2003). Many large conglomerates owned and run by these businessmen collapsed. This raises the question as to whether the corporate governance reforms undertaken so far (essentially based on the Anglo-American models) will be able to capture the political influence in the Malaysian corporate sector because the political elites (who ultimately set the regulatory framework for the corporate sector in Malaysia) and many of the important economic players are mostly the same individuals (see Searle, 1998).

Generally, the fact that Malaysia achieved continuous high growth for nearly a decade raises some issues on whether reforming corporate governance is an appropriate solution to the crisis. First, the global claim that corporate governance in Malaysia was fundamentally flawed has not been definitively established. The question is whether standards of corporate governance in Malaysia were really so poor, or was there a misunderstanding by foreign governments and companies about business practices in Malaysia? For instance, the then chairman of the Malaysian Accounting Standards Board (MASB), Raja Arshad Raja Tun Uda, stated that many foreigners still believe that Malaysian Generally Accepted Accounting

Principles (GAAP) was not based on the International Accounting Standards (IAS):

> The problem with Malaysia is that we do not sell ourselves well enough despite having all the corporate governance, accounting standards and corporate reporting framework the outside world still does not know what we have. (quoted in Yeow, 2002, [online], accessed on 29 October 2002)

This raises another issue: perhaps good fundamentals and policies are not enough if they are not sufficiently visible, and that transparency is essential. However, this is contradicted by the fact that investors invested heavily in the country pre-crisis.

RESEARCH METHOD

The primary aim of this study is to try to understand the roles of corporate governance reforms in Malaysia. An open-ended approach was used to gain data that provided more of an in-depth insight into the research inquiry. Accordingly, the research was conducted using a mix of qualitative research methods, namely, documentary analysis and semi-structured interviews. The reason for using semi-structured interviews as the primary data collection method was that it imposes some structure on the interview situation and therefore assists in framing subsequent analysis. It also allows specific key issues and questions (although these vary slightly from interview to interview) to be discussed in an open-ended manner, with the intention of inviting informants to participate in a dialogue. It is a less restrictive and prescriptive method than structured interviews, in that it permits adjustments to be made and develop further interesting lines of enquiry which arise during the interview itself (Easterby-Smith, Thorper, & Lowe, 2001). Moreover, semi-structured interviews have the potential to elicit in-depth information that is generally difficult to obtain through other approaches (such as questionnaire survey), especially when the subject matter is regarded as complex, confidential or sensitive.

This study draws on the experiences of 19 corporate practitioners gathered from a series of interviews held with them during the summers of 2001 and 2002. The interviews lasted between 30 and 120 mins, with some interviews being tape recorded as permitted by the interviewees while notes were taken throughout all the interviews. These interviews took place shortly after the landmark corporate governance reforms in Malaysia following the crisis, namely, the introduction of the *Malaysian Code on Corporate Governance* in

2000 and the Malaysian stock exchange listing requirement revamp in January 2001. It seemed sensible that collecting interview data close to these events would provide significant and interesting insights into the Malaysian corporate governance reforms.

This research had been designed to interview senior managers who worked in a public listed company and have had direct involvement in the governance issues within their companies. The main reason for choosing senior managers for interviews was that all these interviewees have had some input/workings at different levels of the corporate governance development within their previous/existing companies such as at the operational levels and/or policy development. Moreover, they could be expected to have a broader perspective on corporate governance issues and therefore seemed more likely to be able to provide more detailed accounts of the promotion of corporate governance reform at the corporate level and in Malaysia generally. The issues raised during the interviews covered the importance and benefits of corporate governance reforms to the interviewees' companies and the Malaysian corporate sector in general, the basis for or factors leading to changes, and the changes of corporate governance practices at the corporate level.

FINDINGS

The following sections present and discuss the findings draw from the 19 interviews conducted. The aim was to identify and understand the role of corporate governance reforms (or in other words, what an 'ideal' corporate governance model could have contributed to the Malaysian corporate sector), and the practical implications of introducing a different set of corporate governance code and practices on the corporate shop floor. A number of themes emerged with respect to these matters and they are, to a considerable extent, inter-related.

The (Perceived) Role of the Reforms

Professional Management
A number of interviewees indicated that they supported corporate governance reforms in their companies (and the Malaysian corporate sector in general), on the basis of their beliefs that corporate governance ensures that their companies would have a "better boss" and a team of "better" and "more professional" managers and directors running the businesses. Besides that,

it also promotes "good corporate management", and "the practice of good ethical behaviour" with "no self-interest" on the part of the management (remarks by an audit committee member and the finance director of a family business). Conversations on this matter with the interviewees were linked to the belief that there were many "unprofessional ... [and] irresponsible" corporate directors and senior managers who were "very greedy" and emphasised "too much pure self-interest", and the lack of "integrity and honesty" among them. For example, an interview with the finance director of a family business noted that many individuals took up the job of company director "because of the directors' fees ... [and] they say yes to all" issues raised at board meetings. He also pointed out that many directors did not "even know and understand company law while they were supposed to be responsible". It was argued that corporate governance "is designed to address these issues" and "forces directors to be more aware of their responsibilities". This point of view was also being expressed by the internal auditor of a financial institution, an audit committee member of a family business and the chief executive director of an enterprise with high level of international trading.

In that it could play a role in promoting professional corporate management, along with enhanced transparency and corporate disclosure, many interviewees agreed that corporate governance is "a deterrent to top management and directors mismanagement" and can "reduce the chances of malpractices and abuses of power from happening", because it is the instrument to check and capture "those hanky-panky things ... such as siphoning off of money" (commented by a chief financial officer).

The continuing existence of many corporate abuses and exploitations, and the importance and role of corporate governance reforms to resolve these problems in Malaysia were generally brought into discussion by the interviewees in association with the subject of (widespread) family and concentrated ownership in the Malaysian corporate sector. It was claimed by a number of interviewees that the highly inter-related and concentrated ownership corporate shareholding structure, together with the significant dominance and participation of major shareholder(s) in management in many Malaysian companies, allowed some of them to pursue their self-interest and questionable financial practices:

Most Malaysian companies are dominated by one person – the main shareholder – where this person dictates and commands what should be done. That's the main problem that is always here. (A company secretary)

Most companies in Malaysia are family-controlled with the family members [being] the major shareholders [who] always sit on the board as the managing director or

chairman ... [They] abuse their powers for their personal interests like the chairman's
personal expenses are always charged to the company ... [Besides] their objectives were
different from the management most of the time, and they override the management's
decisions that are inconsistent with theirs ... the management team being the salaried
staff, they have to obey. (A corporate planning manager)

Stressing the importance of corporate governance, a corporate planning
manager stated that effective corporate governance ensures that "no one is
taking control of the company and being able to manipulate company
activities in pursuing their own interests". In other words, and in the context
of the Malaysian corporate sector, corporate governance is seen to be crucial
in preventing controlling shareholder(s) from engaging in activities that are
illegitimate or detrimental to other shareholders or outsiders (especially the
minorities) or other stakeholders. Although most interviewees were positive
about the roles corporate governance can play in their companies in terms of
limiting "owners' ability to 'milk' the company to enrich themselves"
(comments by a finance director), they expressed reservations about its
effectiveness:

The major shareholder always has the control at all levels and is the ultimate
decision maker. At the end of the day, audit committee members will be threatened if
they were not to follow his views. He will tell them that 'you take it or not, if not, I will
give it someone else' – the same applies to the external auditor. (A corporate planning
manager)

Independent directors are important to check upon these [family-based owner] directors
who make all the decisions all the time. Well, it will not necessarily work well because
they are friends [with each other]. (A chief financial officer)

The evidence suggests that corporate governance could potentially play a
role in ensuring corporate accountability to shareholders and possibly
other stakeholders in Malaysia. However, the mindset of controlling
owner-managers is a key to the success of any change and 'improvement'
in corporate governance since it is this group which will largely
determine whether the change is substantive or in form alone. Furthermore,
there appears to be increasing reliance on independent non-executive
directors (NEDs) to play the monitoring role in 'improving' corporate
governance practices in Malaysia without questioning the effectiveness
of NEDs in the local context. For instance, Haniffa and Cooke (2002)
found that non-executive chairpersons in Malaysian companies tend to
keep private information for their own benefits to the detriment of
shareholders.

Economic Importance

The question whether corporate governance will in fact improve corporate performances was raised with some interviewees when they were asked about the benefits corporate governance will bring to their companies. A large number of interviewees argued that corporate governance is "absolutely vital" to their (and any) companies because "with good governance ... profits will definitely be improved", and "if we don't enforce it, it will hit our bottom line" (remarks by a senior manager from a financial institution). Speaking out cynically about existing corporate governance practices, while believing in the potential benefits corporate governance, in terms of enhanced transparency, could bring to her company, the company secretary of a family business noted that:

> If truly practised corporate governance, with proper disclosure and transparency in decision-making compared to the current system of personal self-interests, was in place, it should improve profits.

Similarly, one of the internal auditors interviewed explained that:

> Indirectly, corporate governance would improve profit and performance. For example, with more disclosures and being more transparent, related-party transactions and dishonesties among top management will be limited.

In linking the performance-enhancing role of corporate governance directly with risk management, interviewees also emphasised the importance for their companies of managing all risks involved appropriately. A typical comment was:

> Corporate governance will indirectly help in improving profits because with good internal control and risk management, it will reduce the costs of un-managed risks.

Deeper discussions on this issue revealed their (and many other Malaysian) companies' attitudes towards risk and the state (or rather the lack) of risk management before and during the crisis. For example, most of the planning/ development managers and the senior executive officers interviewed pointed out that companies were "too risk-taking" with a "gambling attitude" before the crisis. It was also noted that many companies "were over-geared", "not prudent enough and too eager for money" where they "grew by extensive borrowings" and were "too diversified into areas in which we have little expertise and are therefore overly exposed to operational risks" and more importantly "the risks attached to all [these] were not assessed and managed accordingly". Indeed, these companies were often regarded as "entrepreneurs during the boom" in virtue of their high (and excessive) risk-taking approach in search for higher returns. Remarkably, it was highlighted that "corporate governance and risks were never in our [corporate and banking] culture" prior to the crisis.

The above evidence implies that corporate governance reforms may play a role (directly or indirectly) in strengthening the performance of the participants' companies. However, an assistant finance manager indicated that "good corporate governance does not translate into good profits. It is not to ensure profitability for us". In a similar vein, while conceding that there may be some indirect association between corporate governance and profitability to their companies, two interviewees specified that "there is no direct linkage between corporate governance and profit". In addition, one of the interviewees who worked for a family business was uncertain about the advantages corporate governance reform will bring to their company in performance terms, stating that "some changes [in corporate governance] have taken place since [the reform]; hopefully there will be some benefits". These four interviewees believed that the main role of corporate governance reforms was to restore (foreign) investors' confidence (will be discussed further in the next section).

The Degree of Reforms in Practice

At the outset, it should be noted that it was not an option for a PLC simply to disregard corporate governance matters because of the changes in the Malaysian stock exchange listing requirements demanding all PLCs to comply with the *Malaysian Code on Corporate Governance* (hereinafter *Code*) (HLFC, 2000). While there were some adjustments to corporate governance, they were to some extent rather ceremonial.

Firstly, most interviewees indicated that "the way the company is run is the same", "nothing is really new in the company", "there is not much change in board composition except those required by the regulations" and "many (corporate governance) matters were mainly 'talking out and acting'" following the crisis. Common changes in corporate governance practices were mostly increases in (more detailed) disclosure and reporting, and not limited to financial information but also other aspects required by the Malaysian corporate governance code of best practices[6] (see HLFC, 2000):

> Last time, we did not need to report much; now with new regulations, everything you do or what has happened and any changes made in the company or members of staffs, etc. need to be reported including attendance of directors at meetings ... [and] the internal auditor is required to report to the audit committee. (A corporate development manager)

> We believe in corporate governance and since the crisis, we have spent a large amount in developing good risk management practices as required by the [Central Bank of Malaysia, stock exchange] and the Securities Commission. (A general business manager)

These comments were echoed by most interviewees as to the main corporate governance changes that their companies had made – increase in disclosure of information and incorporation of new corporate governance rules/regulations implemented by the Malaysian authorities following the crisis.

The interviewees were then questioned as to why their companies had to change in terms of corporate governance practices. All of them answered promptly that "it's the regulations" or more precisely: they had to comply with the new Malaysian stock exchange listing requirements which demand that all listed companies are required to include in their annual reports a narrative statement of how and to what extent they have complied with the principles and best practices set out in the *Code* (HLFC, 2000) and must explain any circumstances justifying departure from such best practices (KLSE, 2001b, para 15.26). While the corporate governance reforms adopted in Malaysia followed the principles-based 'comply or explain' approach, it was evidently being interpreted by interviewees as a requirement to 'comply'. This suggests that the Anglo-Saxon 'comply or explain' concept would be inappropriate in the Malaysian context. Arguably, globalisation (or more specifically, global capitalism) has prompted corporate governance reforms in a nation that may not be suitable in the local context.

Typical elaborations on their initial responses included "the changes in our company in terms of corporate governance practices were quite formal ... being done as required" and "we mainly do only what is required by the KLSE [Malaysian stock exchange] and Securities Commission". Frustrated by the "superficial" change of corporate governance practices at her company, the company secretary of a family business complained that "everything is just being displayed due to the regulations" suggesting that the authorities' actions in legitimising corporate governance reforms had been largely ineffectual and have led to little real practical change in behaviour.

However, when the interviewees were asked whether their companies would make those changes voluntarily if regulations were not in place, instant answers "No" were firmly given by all interviewees, with most arguing strongly that "without regulations, there will be no change for sure", and that "even with regulations, companies are still trying to find ways not to fall within the guidelines" (commented by a legal manager). It was apparent and understandable that the new legal requirements were not welcomed by most interviewees. Interestingly, a chief executive director revealed that "I think there was a lack of regulations that [had] allow[ed] many [governance] problems to exist ... It is important to have the corporate governance rules – it is like all games, there must be some rules", and a legal officer highlighted the necessity to legislate corporate behaviour in Malaysia: "we must be regulated due to the attitudes of Malaysian society and companies ... [They] will only do it when there is a sanction".

Although interviewees claimed that their (and other Malaysian) companies would not voluntarily make the required corporate governance changes, the idea that shareholders' and (especially foreign) investors' expectations of corporate governance practices need to be met in order to maintain easier and cheaper access to capital was brought up by a finance director. He emphasised that failure to implement 'good' corporate governance has a cost beyond regulatory problems and indicated that companies without 'good' governance practices and procedures can pay a (governance) risk premium when competing for scarce capital in the global markets:

> If investors were rational, for a company with better corporate governance, good track record and prudent in decision making as with ours, risk premium will be lower and thus cost of raising capital should improve.

The lack of adequate corporate governance procedures, arising from inadequate timely accurate disclosure of information, leading to the erosion and loss of (foreign) investors' confidence after the disappointment of their expectations in 1997/1998 was raised by other interviewees, for example,

> Foreign investors, sad to say, said that we have not had enough awareness of corporate governance issues ... [and] they had became very reluctant to invest in us. (an internal auditor)

> A lot of foreign investors from the West ... keep on questioning our corporate governance ... saying that we are not transparent. (a chief financial officer)

> Foreign investors demand corporate governance change [after the crisis] ... they said that we don't have good corporate governance, therefore they pulled out their investments ... [then] the local investors followed. (an assistant finance manager)

Most interviewees evidently felt that meeting foreign investors' demands and pressures to 'improve'/reform corporate governance so as to revive and maintain their confidence was paramount, in view of their influence on Malaysian stock market share prices. This knock-on effect had led the interviewees' companies to take steps to 'improve' their corporate governance practices to some extent, or at least, to have reached the point where they were perceived to have done so.

This issue was related directly to the importance of corporate governance in restoring and maintaining shareholders' and investors' confidence after the crisis. A finance director noted that corporate governance is "very critical" to his company's "survival" because it helps in recovering shareholders' and investors' confidence. Expressing it in the same way, the senior corporate planning manager from a financial institution stressed the importance of corporate governance to all financial institutions in "win[ning] the confidence of investors". In addition, a chief finance officer specified that corporate governance reforms in terms of improving transparency and information disclosure is crucial in rebuilding and boosting the confidence of his company's shareholders and potential investors:

> Corporate governance is very much about bringing back and giving more confidence to our shareholders and investors.

This view was echoed by a legal officer who added that his company's corporate governance changes made were essential to "improve the confidence" of investors.

The internal auditor of an enterprise with high level of international trading remarked that "when we have corporate governance in our company, [investors] will have more confidence in us and therefore be more willing to invest in our company". In a similar vein, an executive director pointed out that:

> Good governance provides a good future for us because it enables us to attract long-term external sources of funds by ensuring more confidence from shareholders and investors, both local and foreign.

Similarly, a finance director contended that "we want to attract investors; therefore we must show them that we are disclosing everything to them and not hiding anything". All interviewees except a company secretary mentioned that compliance with corporate governance codes of best practice is important to their companies in securing a "better reputation" or "better corporate rating" to "attract more investors". A legal officer also argued that "companies with full compliance stated in their corporate governance statements will be regarded as good companies" and therefore it was essential for companies to have the corporate governance changes "so that we will be able to sell ourselves better".

Sitting uncomfortably with the development of corporate governance in the country where many companies "unethically" strive to be seen to have 'good' corporate governance rather than actually to have it in order to attract investors, the senior corporate planning manager of a financial institution voiced his concern that corporate governance "has turned into a sort of business". He illustrated his point with an event that happened in the Malaysian corporate sector (at the time of the interview) where "some companies financed or provided businesses to some magazine publishers, which produce rankings of companies' corporate governance practices, to make sure that they were being ranked highly". This suggests that companies recognise the benefits of being seen to be practising 'good' corporate governance; while, arguably, genuine changes were still avoided.

Apart from that, many interviewees raised the issue of difficulties encountered in integrating the recommended corporate governance principles and practices into their companies. At a specific level, some interviewees claimed that the continuous changing of the corporate governance rules by the regulators had "confused companies in terms of what should be done ... the government should not change a rule suddenly without careful and public discussion" (a corporate development manager). This may imply that the recommended corporate governance practices (and rules) were implemented on an ad hoc basis that may lead to some undesirable consequences at a later stage. At a broader level, the practicality of the Malaysian corporate governance guidelines and the effectiveness of the approach used in reforming corporate governance were criticised:

> We have the framework in place, but we didn't have the follow-through procedures to ensure the effectiveness of corporate governance principles. (A senior corporate planning manager)

> Not all of the corporate governance recommendations and regulations enforced are particularly applicable ... The problem is that one country's corporate governance doesn't mean that it is applicable to us. In the US and UK, there are differences in culture, environment and attitudes towards managing a company. The current corporate governance code is 90% of the US/UK corporate governance code; that's the reasons many provisions [of the promoted corporate governance code] are inappropriate to us. We cannot simply put a ready made system into a country. (An internal auditor)

The above discussion clearly indicates that global capitalism and pressures from foreign investors had pushed Malaysia to adopt (the Anglo-American) corporate governance practices that may not be appropriate to domestic firms because of differences in history, traditions and social relations. Furthermore, although not a widely shared view among interviewees, it was pointed out by five interviewees that the corporate governance reforms implemented in Malaysia neglected the idea of corporate social responsibility:

> Corporate governance should be for everyone in the society, not just for companies and shareholders but also the employees, the public and other [stakeholders] ... basically [the promoted corporate governance] is mainly for shareholders.

In general, the Malaysian corporate governance reforms appear to be a direct attempt to please an even more limited set of stakeholders than 'company shareholders' – namely, foreign investors. For example, the Malaysian corporate governance code of best practice was introduced in recognition of the crucial role that enhanced standards of corporate governance can play in boosting international investor confidence (HLFC, 1999). Significantly, the views of corporate practitioners interviewed presented above indicated that foreign investors certainly play a role in advocating corporate governance changes in their companies and Malaysia in general. Globalisation and pressures from foreign investors had played a part in highlighting that the Malaysian corporate governance reforms should focus on company shareholders and foreign investors. However, the issue of whether the reforms *should* favour shareholders/investors or minority shareholders and other stakeholders has not yet been clearly raised.

During and after the crisis, those who were badly affected were the minority shareholders and other stakeholders such as employees, creditors, suppliers and society (especially the poor) rather than large shareholders. Should the former therefore be given more protection compared to the latter? The corporate governance reforms undertaken have noticeably not given sufficient attention to protecting minority shareholders and other stake-holders (see HLFC, 1999) and this was clearly highlighted by the interviewees. It appears therefore that the newly emerging corporate governance philosophy of Malaysian enterprises may not fully promote public accountability, social responsibility or any strong commitment to good corporate citizenship and truly sustainable growth. Implementing the 'new' (globally promoted Anglo-American) corporate governance practices that privileges (foreign) shareholder accountability, rather than focusing on minority shareholders and corporate social responsibilities, may ultimately end up being damaging to Malaysia. Arguably, globalisation has induced corporate governance reforms (which are based on the globally accepted Anglo-American regimes) that may not be suitable to a nation because of the existence of local peculiarities, cultures and traditions.

In addition, the corporate governance reforms do not seem to have had the desired effect of sustaining Malaysia's competitiveness in terms of attracting foreign investment. Five years after the national promotion of corporate governance, the FDI in Malaysia had not returned to its pre-crisis level. The annual average net inflows of FDI as a percentage of GDP in Malaysia between 1990 and 1997 was more than 6%, a figure that has constantly decreased over the years since the crisis to just over 3% between 1998 and 2005 (World Bank, 2006). This implies that the corporate governance reforms have not been sufficient for Malaysia to improve its attractiveness to foreign investors, as opposed to the belief advocated extensively by the international community, especially intergovernmental organisations such as the World Bank, IMF and OECD.

CONCLUDING REMARKS

Based on material gathered from the 19 interviews conducted, this paper has presented an analysis of the roles and the extent of corporate governance reforms in Malaysia. It was found that the interviewees shared the view that the promotion of corporate governance reforms in Malaysia was primarily to fulfill the legal requirements enforced by the regulators. This has implications for the degree of genuine corporate governance changes in practice. According to the interview data, it seems that companies tend to focus on the form rather the substance or spirit of corporate governance practices. It could also be argued that there was substantial hesitancy about, and resistance to, corporate governance reforms aimed at improving accountability and responsibility. Nevertheless, on the positive side, the reforms appear to have made the Malaysian corporate board members and top management more cognizant of their accountability and responsibility in their decision-making processes.

The complex system of interlocking, concentrated and family ownership structure prevalent in Malaysian companies and problems in relation to this were brought up and discussed extensively among many interviewees. They expressed the view that corporate governance could play a significant role in solving the problems (corporate misconduct) associated with the Malaysian corporate ownership structure; however, the effectiveness of the corporate governance reforms initiated by the government was doubted. The inference from the analysis is that the degree of corporate governance reforms depends largely on controlling shareholders' (for family-run concentrated and politically-connected businesses) and top managements' (for professional-run companies) willingness to change, and the extent of the (external) pressures to which their companies are exposed (see Liew, 2007). The corporate governance reforms undertaken do not seem to have resolved the issues raised by the interviewees: the recent study by Tam and Tan (2007) concluded that shareholders' rights protection, especially protection of minority shareholders, remains an issue to be dealt with in Malaysia, since large shareholders continue to exert dominant control via ownership concentration and representation on company board. The self-seeking and self-gratifying attitudes of companies' owner-managers and/or those charged with governance appeared to be the main obstacle to fundamental reform of corporate governance practices in Malaysia. It specifically highlights the need to strengthen minority shareholder protections in Malaysia – an issue that may also need to be dealt with by other East Asian and developing countries where corporate ownership structure is relatively concentrated.

Hitherto, it seems that Malaysian companies and the country in general had striven to reform corporate governance as a response to deflect and pacify negative publicity and criticism from the international/'Western' community in the aftermath of the 1997/1998 Asian crisis[7] while not making any substantive change (as pointed out by many interviewees). Globalisation and the apparently growing global reach of Anglo-American corporate governance regimes have certainly played a central part in pushing the approach adopted by Malaysia, to the extent that the Malaysian authorities and institutions established to ensure sound corporate governance feel obliged to align Malaysian corporate governance standards with the widely accepted Anglo-American standards (see Liew, 2007), with little opportunity to seriously consider the economic and social consequences that the approach could have. Arguably, the promotion of (essentially neo-liberal Anglo-American) corporate governance reforms in Malaysia is questionable and has not seemed to be providing solutions and targeting the specific local (political) problems in the corporate sector and country. This is similar to the findings of other studies based on developing and less developed countries. For instance, Uddin and Choudhury (2008), Liew (2007) and Beeson (2001) argue that the Anglo-American forms of capitalism are not necessarily suitable to emerging and less developed countries especially that the reforms undertaken are likely to be resisted by local powerful vested interests.

This research raises a number of issues that need further consideration with regards to the appropriateness of the corporate governance reforms implemented in Malaysia following the crisis. First, the focus of corporate governance reforms in Malaysia could have been on minority shareholder protections, as commented by some of the interviewees, rather than the conventional principal-agent problems (conflict of interests between owners and managers) in Anglo-American businesses. Furthermore, the reforms could have placed more emphasis on corporate social responsibility to stakeholders and wider public interests – something that is very much needed in Malaysia and other countries in the era of global capitalism. The Malaysian economic, political and social settings have resulted in undue state and detrimental political influence on businesses, yet the corporate governance reforms undertaken seemed to not be able to resolve this matter – this may be due to the fact that the adopted globally favoured Anglo-American corporate governance models were based on economic, political and corporate settings that mainly exist in the UK and the USA. It would perhaps be beneficial for Malaysia to have more independent regulatory authorities representing a wide variety of stakeholders as well as improvement in their accountability and transparency to ensure that the rules and regulations are effectively enforced without any political influence. It is also evident that the Malaysian corporate governance reforms have concentrated on amending rules and regulations, and advocating self-regulatory mechanisms. This may not be sufficient to create change and securing accountability as witnessed in the UK and the USA (see Sikka, 2008b, Arnold & Sikka, 2001), and certainly had not been effective in practice from the interviewees' perspectives. Legal institutional reforms may therefore be needed to improve the structure, capacity and performance of the Malaysian judicial system. A radical overhaul of the existing regulatory, institutional and corporate governance framework that is capable of capturing the domestic (especially political) problems and promoting public accountability is needed in Malaysia. This paper calls for further research to explore the effectiveness of the more recent corporate governance developments in Malaysia.

The findings of this research have significant implications for improving the overall corporate governance practices in Malaysia in that they highlight the inappropriateness of adopting the so-called international (predominantly Anglo-American) corporate governance regime. Unlike most studies on corporate governance issues in Malaysia and East Asian countries which are quantitative based, this research has provided a more in-depth insights and understanding of corporate governance practices, using a qualitative interview based approach: Haniffa and Hudaib (2006, p. 1057) suggest that "future research ... using ... semi-structured interviews with those involved in the overseeing of the governance structures within the company may enhance our understanding of governance structures appropriate for adoption".

This study may also have implications for other East Asian and developing countries' corporate sector regulators and reformers who are striving to improve corporate accountability, governance practices and social responsibility in their countries.

NOTES

1. See Liew (2007) and Cheah (2005) for a more detailed account of corporate governance reforms initiated by the Malaysian government after the Asian crisis.

2. GCF is a measure of the net new investment by businesses in a domestic economy in capital assets during an accounting period. According to the World Bank (2006), GCF is outlays on additions to the fixed assets of the economy plus net changes in the level of inventories. Fixed assets include land improvements (fences, ditches, drains and so on); plant, machinery and equipment purchases; and the construction of roads, railways and the like, including schools, offices, hospitals, private residential dwellings and commercial and industrial buildings. Inventories are stocks of goods held by firms to meet temporary or unexpected fluctuations in production or sales and work in progress. According to the 1993 System of National Accounts, net acquisitions of valuables are also considered capital formation.

3. The Malaysian stock exchange has changed its name from Kuala Lumpur Stock Exchange (KLSE) to Bursa Malaysia Berhad on 20 April 2004 (see Bursa Malaysia Berhad, 2004). To avoid confusion, this paper therefore does not use either of these names but rather the term 'Malaysian stock exchange'.

4. Malaysian businesses are characterised by the high level of (family) ownership concentration, pyramiding and significant participation of owners in management (Liew, 2007; Tam and Tan, 2007; Claessens et al., 1999; La Porta, Lopez-de-Silanes, Shleifer, & Vishny, 1998; Lim, 1981).

5. The Malay term 'Bumiputra' means 'sons of the soil', i.e. the indigenous people. In Malaysia, Bumiputras are entitled to preferential treatment in many respects, e.g. education, business opportunities and so on.

6. Although increased disclosure of information such as directors' attendance might be useful, the impression of director effectiveness might just be an illusion.

7. This phenomenon was also noted by Clark, Wójcik, and Bauer (2005) study on the case of Royal Ahold. They found that due to the dramatic loss of international investor confidence following the crisis at Ahold, the company's management had responded quickly by improving transparency and governance standards consistent with the expectations of global investors.

ACKNOWLEDGMENTS

The author is grateful to the two anonymous reviewers, Harro Hopfl, Stuart Manson, Prem Sikka, David Owen, Josephine Maltby and the Journal Editors for their invaluable comments and suggestions to the previous versions of this paper.

REFERENCES

Aghevli, B. B. (1999). The Asian crisis: Causes and remedies. *Finance and Development, 36*(2), [Online], Available at http://www.imf.org/external/pubs/ft/fandd/1999/06/. Accessed on 13 October 2002.

Ahunwan, B. (2003). *Globalization and corporate governance in developing countries.* New York: Transnational Publishers Inc.

Arnold, P. J., & Sikka, P. (2001). Globalization and the state-profession relationship: The case of the bank of credit and commerce international. *Accounting, Organizations and Society*, *26*(6), 475–499.

Asian Development Bank (ADB). (2000). Corporate Governance and Finance in East Asia – A Study of Indonesia, Republic of Korea, Malaysia, Philippines, and Thailand Volume One (A Consolidated Report), ADB Publications, Manila.

Athukorala, P. (2003). Foreign direct investment in crisis and recovery: Lessons from the 1997–1998 Asian crisis. *Australian Economic History Review*, *43*(2), 197–213.

Beeson, M. (2001). Globalization, governance, and the political-economy of public policy reform in East Asia. *Governance: An International Journal of Policy and Administration*, *14*(4), 481–502.

BizAsia. (2003). Malaysia Allows Foreign Investors More Leeway (June 23). [Online], Available at http://www.BizAsia.com. Accessed on 30 June 2003.

Blair, M. M. (1995). *Ownership and control: Rethinking corporate governance for the twenty-first century*. Washington, DC: The Brookings Institution.

Bursa Malaysia Berhad. (2004). CEO Yusli: KLSE is Now Bursa Malaysia. Media Releases, April 20 [Online], Available at http://www.klse.com.my/website/mediacentre/mr/2004/20040420b.htm. Accessed on 30 April 2004.

Camdessus, M. (1998). The IMF and Good Governance, an address to the Transparency International, January 21, Paris, France.

Cheah, K. G. (2005). Corporate governance reforms in Malaysia: Issues and challenges. In: K. L. Ho (Ed.), *Reforming corporate governance in Southeast Asia* (pp. 85–101). Singapore: Institute of Southeast Asian Studies Publications.

Claessens, S., Djankov, S., & Lang, L. H. P. (1999). *Who controls East Asian corporations?* World Bank Discussion Paper, No. 2054, The World Bank, Washington, DC, USA.

Clark, G. L., Wójcik, D., & Bauer, R. (2005). *Corporate governance, cross-listing and managerial response to stock price discounting: Royal a hold and market arbitrage – Amsterdam and New York, 1973–2004*. Economic Geography Working Papers, Working Paper No. 05-07, School of Geography, Centre for the Environment, University of Oxford, UK.

Easterby-Smith, M., Thorper, R., & Lowe, A. (2001). *Management research: An introduction* (2nd ed.). London, UK: Sage Publications Ltd.

Economist. (2000). Survey of European business: Lean, mean, European. The Economist, April 27.

Edge Daily. (2002). CalPERS: Malaysia lags in governance. The Edge Daily, September 10.

Fan, J. P. H., & Wong, T. J. (2001). *Do external auditors perform a corporate governance role in emerging markets? Evidence from East Asia*. Paper presented at the Third Annual Financial Market Development Conference, March, Hong Kong.

Fan, J. P. H., & Wong, T. J. (2002). Corporate ownership structure and the informativeness of accounting earnings in East Asia. *Journal of Accounting and Economics*, *33*(3), 401–425.

Furman, J., & Stiglitz, J. (1998). Economic crises: Evidence and insights from East Asia. *Brookings Papers on Economic Activity*, *2*, 1–135.

George, K. (2005). Re-nationalise these profiteering firms: Mahathir's Malaysia Inc. and privatisation have burdened the people and bred corruption. *Aliran Monthly*, *25*(7), 7.

Giddens, A. (2002). *Runaway world: How globalisation is reshaping our lives*. London, UK: Profile Books.

Glen, J., & Singh, A. (2005). Corporate governance, competition and finance: Re-thinking lessons from the Asian crisis. *Eastern Economic Journal*, *31*(2), 219–243.

Gomez, E. T., & Jomo, K. S. (1997). *Malaysia's political economy: Politics, patronage and profits.* Cambridge: Cambridge University Press.

Haniffa, R., & Cooke, T. E. (2002). Culture, corporate governance and disclosure in Malaysian corporations. *Abacus, 38*(3), 317–349.

Haniffa, R., & Hudaib, M. (2006). Corporate governance structure and performance of Malaysian listed companies. *Journal of Business Finance & Accounting, 33*(7 & 8), 1034–1062.

High Level Finance Committee on Corporate Governance (HLFC). (1999). *Report on Corporate Governance (February),* Kuala Lumpur: Securities Commission.

High Level Finance Committee on Corporate Governance (HLFC). (2000). *Malaysian code on corporate governance (March).* Kuala Lumpur: Securities Commission.

Jayasankaran, S. (2003). Lasting achievements. *Far Eastern Economic Review, 166*(40), 32.

Johnson, S., & Mitton, T. (2003). Cronyism and capital controls: Evidence from Malaysia. *Journal of Financial Economics, 67*(2), 351–382.

Koehn, D. (2002). Overview of Issues in Corporate Governance. [Online], Available at http://www.stthom.edu/cbes/daryl_koehn.html. Accessed on 12 August 2002.

Kuala Lumpur Stock Exchange (KLSE). (2001a). *Listing requirements strengthens capital market, securities industry, media releases (January 22).* Kuala Lumpur: KLSE.

Kuala Lumpur Stock Exchange (KLSE). (2001b). *Kuala Lumpur stock exchange listing requirements for main board and second board (January).* Kuala Lumpur: KLSE.

La Porta, R., Lopez-de-Silanes, F., Shleifer, A., & Vishny, R. (1998). Law and finance. *Journal of Political Economy, 106*(6), 1113–1155.

Lambert, C., & Sponem, S. (2005). Corporate governance and profit manipulation: A French field study. *Critical Perspectives on Accounting, 16*(6), 717–748.

Liew, P. K. (2007). Corporate governance reforms in Malaysia: The key leading players' perspectives. *Corporate Governance: An International Review, 15*(5), 724–740.

Lim, M. H. (1981). *Ownership and control off the one hundred largest corporations in Malaysia.* Kuala Lumpur: Oxford University Press.

Millstein, I. (2000). Opening Remarks at Global Conference on Corporate Governance. July 10, Southern Connecticut State University. [Online], Available at http://www.gcgf.org/library/speeches/Millstein710.doc. Accessed on 15 September 2002.

Mohamed, M. (2002). Corporate governance as a source of global competitiveness. Keynote Address at the International Conference on Corporate Governance in Asia (April 2), Kuala Lumpur.

Moxey, P. (2004). *Corporate governance and wealth creation.* ACCA Occasional Research Paper, No. 37, Certified Accountants Educational Trust, London, UK.

Ong, L. (2001). Corporate Malaysia: Falling from Grace. *Asia Times Online,* December 22.

Organisation for Economic Co-Operation and Development (OECD). (1999). *OECD principles of corporate governance.* Paris: OECD.

Ow-Yong, K., & Cheah, K. G. (2000). Corporate governance codes: A comparison between Malaysia and the UK. *Corporate Governance: An International Review, 8*(2), 125–132.

Radelet, S., & Sachs, J. D. (1998). The East Asian financial crisis: Diagnosis, remedies, prospects. *Brookings Papers on Economic Activity, 1,* 1–74.

Scott, J. (1997). *Corporate business and capitalist classes.* Oxford: Oxford University Press.

Searle, P. (1998). *The riddle of Malaysian capitalism: Rent seekers or real capitalists?* Sydney: Allen and Unwin.

Securities Commission (SC). (1999). *Disclosure-based regulation – What directors need to know.* Kuala Lumpur: The SC.

Shameen, A., & Oorjitham, S. (1998). I've lost my voice. *Asiaweek, 24*(12), 4.

Sikka, P. (2008a). Globalization and its discontents: Accounting firms buy limited liability partnership legislation in Jersey. *Accounting, Auditing and Accountability Journal, 21*(3), 398–426.

Sikka, P. (2008b). *Corporate governance: What about the workers?* University of Essex AFM Working Paper, Working Paper no. 2008/1, University of Essex, UK.

Singh, A., Singh, A., & Weisse, B. (2002). *Corporate governance, competition, the new international financial architecture and large corporations in emerging markets.* ESRC Centre for Business Research Working Papers, Working Paper no. 250, University of Cambridge, UK.

Singh, A., & Zammit, A. (2006). Corporate governance, crony capitalism and economic crises: Should the US business model replace the Asian way of "doing business"? *Corporate Governance: An International Review, 14*(4), 220–233.

Stiglitz, J. E. (1999). Reforming the global financial architecture: Lessons from recent crises. *Journal of Finance, 54*, 1508–1522.

Stiglitz, J. E. (2002). *Globalization and its discontents.* London: Penguin.

Stiglitz, J. E., & Bhattacharya, A. (2000). Underpinnings for a stable and equitable global financial system: From old debates to a new paradigm. *Proceedings of the World Bank Annual Conference on Development Economics 1999.* The World Bank, Washington, DC.

Tam, O. K., & Tan, M. G. (2007). Ownership, governance and firm performance in Malaysia. *Corporate Governance: An International Review, 15*(2), 208–222.

The Star. (2003). Revamp on Act may boost FDI. The Star, March 20.

Uddin, S., & Choudhury, J. (2008). Rationality, traditionalism and the state of corporate governance mechanisms: Illustrations from a less-developed country. *Accounting, Auditing and Accountability Journal, 21*(7), 1026–1051.

Wolfensohn, J. D. (1998). *"A battle for corporate honesty", The world in 1999.* New York, USA: The Economist Newspaper Limited.

World Bank. (1993). *The East Asian miracle.* Oxford, UK: Oxford University Press.

World Bank. (1998). *East Asia: The road to recovery.* Oxford, UK: Oxford University Press.

World Bank. (2000). *East Asia: Recovery and beyond.* Washington, USA: The World Bank.

World Bank. (2006). *World Development Indicators Online.* Available at http://go.worldbank.org/6HAYAHG8H0. Accessed 2 December 2006.

Yeow, J. (2002). Malaysia should promote strength of corporate governance, accounting. The Edge Daily, October 29.

Yoshihara, K. (1988). *The rise of ersatz capitalism in South-East Asia.* Singapore: Oxford University Press.

Zafft, R. (2002). When corporate governance is a family affair. OECD Observer 234, October, 18–19.

Zhuang, J., Edwards, D., Webb, D., & Capulong, V. A. (2000). Corporate governance and finance in East Asia: A study of Indonesia, Republic of Korea, Malaysia, Philippines and Thailand: Volume One (A Consolidated Report). The Asian Development Bank, Manila.

CORPORATE GOVERNANCE AND INTERNATIONAL FINANCIAL REPORTING STANDARD (IFRS): THE CASE OF DEVELOPING COUNTRIES

Ronita D. Singh and Susan Newberry

ABSTRACT

Purpose – *Corporate governance requirements imposed internationally as part of the New International Financial Architecture (NIFA) include compliance with International Financial Reporting Standards (IFRS). The appropriateness of applying IFRS in developing countries has long been controversial. Recently, the International Accounting Standards Board (IASB) extended its project on IFRS for Small and Medium Entities (SMEs) to include developing countries. This paper provides a history of the controversy over IFRS in developing countries and examines the SMEs project as it affects developing countries.*

Design/methodology/approach – *This paper uses an agenda-setting theoretical framework and document analysis to analyse IASB's published documents as part of its formal due process.*

Corporate Governance in Less Developed and Emerging Economies
Research in Accounting in Emerging Economies, Volume 8, 483–518
Copyright © 2008 by Emerald Group Publishing Limited
All rights of reproduction in any form reserved
ISSN: 1479-3563/doi:10.1016/S1479-3563(08)08016-X

Findings – *The controversies surrounding the application of IFRS in developing countries seem likely to continue. The public submission process may be ineffective and too late for those seeking to influence IFRS developments. The findings suggest that those seeking IFRS for developing countries may need to both devise an acceptable solution and obtain inside access to the standard-setting process to achieve this aim.*

Research limitations – *The research is limited to literature review and documentary analysis and therefore subject to the known limitations of published project documentation in accounting standard-setting.*

Originality/value – *Contributes to understanding of international accounting standard-setting, including why developing country issues seem likely to continue.*

Since the Asian financial crisis of 1998, increased efforts have been devoted internationally to strengthening the international financial system. A New International Financial Architecture (NIFA) has emerged that consists of multiple sets of rules and procedures devised by various international regulators. The International Monetary Fund (IMF) and World Bank use their considerable international surveillance powers to ensure countries comply with the NIFA via their Reports on Observance of Standards and Codes (ROSCs) (Soederberg, 2002).

The political implications of technical developments and processes have long been recognised (Herring, 1938). Although the NIFA is promoted as essential for strengthening the global financial system (a seemingly technical objective), it is intended to facilitate the political objective adopted by major developed countries of global financial integration and globalised capital markets (Jordan & Majnoni, 2002; Soederberg, 2002). Its applicability in developing countries is debated, Soederberg (2002), for example, criticising it as a means of coercing developing countries into this globalised capital market economy, regardless of their own preferences. With 71% (149) of the world's 209 countries categorised as developing countries, the NIFA and its impact on developing countries is not a trivial matter (World Bank, 2008).[1]

The NIFA includes a corporate governance unit that is advocated as necessary, not just for good corporate governance, but for the economic development of developing countries (Claessens, 2006, p. 92). This unit specifies "best practices" to protect investors' rights and facilitate the long-term supply of capital necessary for sustained economic growth

(Soederberg, 2003, p. 17). These best practices require effective means for corporate boards to monitor performance of enterprises, and specify accounting and auditing practices to facilitate this. Compliance with international financial reporting standards (IFRS) promulgated by the International Accounting Standards Board (IASB) represents best accounting practices, thus making compliance with IFRS integral to the NIFA via the corporate governance unit.[2] Controversies surrounding the suitability of the NIFA for application in developing countries also surround the suitability of the individual sets of best practices it contains. This paper reviews issues surrounding the suitability of IFRS for application in developing countries and examines the IASB's latest effort to address the issues arising.

Accounting practices and financial reporting have long been linked by some with this desire for economic development (see, for example, Enthoven, 1965) and with the World Bank's early economic development efforts (McNamara, 1973; Enthoven, 1983; Mould, 1983).[3] This linking reflects ideas that accounting may be used as a policy tool to develop "a country's industry, its capital market, and thus its economy in general" (Anon, 1974, p. 80; Mahon, 1965, p. 34). On this basis, "effective accounting techniques are a necessary prerequisite to the efficient use of capital", and help to build "investor confidence to stimulate the flow of [private] investment capital" into developing countries (Enthoven, 1965, pp. 30–31).

The establishment in 1973 of the International Accounting Standards Committee (IASC) was "the organized accountancy profession's most important and enduring response to the growing internationalization of capital markets following the Second World War" (Camfferman & Zeff, 2006, p. 1). The IASC's role was to develop international accounting standards (IAS), but after restructuring in 1999 that function is now performed by a board of the IASC known as the IASB, with the standards known as IFRS. Almost from the time of the IASC's establishment, the suitability of its standards for application in developing countries has been debated, recent concerns about this issue echoing that debate (UNCTAD, 2007). The issue of developing countries has been on the international standard-setters agenda twice and subsequently dropped. Most recently, the IASB proposed an IFRS for small and medium entities (SMEs) that would also "provide emerging economies with an internationally recognised basis for financial reporting" (IASB, 2007c, p. 4).[4] This paper uses an agenda-setting theoretical framework to examine background and how the IASB has addressed the developing country issues in the proposed standard.

The research reported here analyses the IASB's proposals and the public responses to those proposals published as part of the IASB's due process. The IASB's project is not yet concluded, and this paper reports only initial results from a larger ongoing research project. This analysis shows that responses made as part of the formal due process do not seem influential in the standard-setting process. The findings suggest that developing countries may need to develop a solution and obtain more direct involvement in the standard-setting process for their concerns and needs to be addressed in the IFRS.

The next section outlines the theoretical perspective and research method adopted, and identifies the documentary sources obtained. This is followed by background information on international accounting standard-setting and the controversy surrounding application of such standards in developing countries before presenting the findings from examination of the documents as they relate to developing countries. The final section discusses the findings and identifies matters requiring further research.

THEORETICAL PERSPECTIVE AND RESEARCH METHOD

The history of the NIFA initiative reflects an agenda that is political as much as, or more than, it is technical. Accounting standard-setting is also known as a political, rather than merely a technical activity (Gerboth, 1987). The adoption of a political agenda-setting theoretical perspective is well-recognised as useful for studying accounting standard-setting and has been adopted for this research project (for examples of agenda-setting research in accounting, see Klumpes, 1994; Walker & Robinson, 1994; Jones, Rahman, & Wolnizer, 2004).

Agenda-setting "is the process by which problems and alternative solutions gain or lose public and elite attention" (Birkland, 2001, p. 106). It provides a useful way to understand policy debate and outcomes: "The likelihood that an issue will rise on the agenda is a function of the issue itself, the actors that get involved, institutional relationships, and, often, random social and political factors that can be explained but cannot be replicated or predicted" (Birkland, 2001, p. 131).

To understand how issues enter a policymaker's agenda for consideration and policy response, Cobb, Ross, and Ross (1976) differentiate between the policymaker's public agenda and its formal agenda. Public agenda issues are those generating public interest and visibility, while formal agenda issues are those that policymakers have formally accepted for serious consideration (Cobb et al, 1976). Cobb and Elder (1972) identify three phases of an issue's career: issue creation, issue expansion, and issue entrance. Issue creation raises an issue on the public agenda, while issue expansion is the means used to generate wider public support.

The fact that an issue is on the public agenda does not necessarily mean it will be addressed by the policymakers. The issue would need to be placed on the formal agenda for that to occur. Issue entrance occurs when the issue is placed on the policymaker's formal agenda. This may occur after an issue has gained sufficient support on the public agenda, or it may occur directly if insiders, such as political leaders or those with direct access to the policymakers can influence agenda entry. If the issue is not already on the public agenda, or not on the agenda in a particular form, and is placed on the formal agenda directly, issue expansion may follow formal agenda placement, especially if the desired policy will require "widespread, voluntary compliance" (Cobb et al., 1976, p. 132). Sometimes the issue may be placed directly on the formal agenda without prior or subsequent expansion to the public agenda. The potential for this to occur is greater if the issue risks defeat from public opposition (Cobb et al., 1976).

The agenda building framework assists with understanding the forces that move policy formation processes in one direction or another (Cobb & Elder, 1972, p. viii). Placement of an issue on the policymaker's formal agenda, however, does not necessarily mean the issue will stay there or be addressed. Kingdon's (1984) three-stream approach (problem, policy, and politics) to understanding policy development helps to illuminate the policy issue's career on the formal agenda. The problem stream recognises a problem exists and must be addressed; the policy stream identifies alternative solutions; and the politics stream acknowledges the need for political support to bring the proposal on to the policymakers' formal agenda at the right time. These three streams are not necessarily consecutive and may be independent of each other. For example, solutions may precede the problems to which they eventually represent the policy response (Kingdon, 1984). Whether the policy response is appropriate for the particular problem is another matter. Kingdon (1984) further argued that if a solution is not available, or if a problem is not sufficiently compelling or support is not forthcoming from the political stream then the issue's career on the formal agenda will be short-lived.

The issue of IFRS and their applicability in developing countries has remained on the public agenda throughout the IASC's existence.

Twice (1989 and 1998) it was placed on the IASC's formal agenda but was in the problem stream and was subsequently dropped and public agenda calls for attention continued. This study provides background history of the issue of accounting standards in developing countries, and the two prior entrances onto, and exits from, the IASC's formal agenda before examining the most recent agenda placement. The research reported here is part of a larger study into a current project on the IASB's formal agenda, initially known as the small and medium entities (SMEs) project but renamed in May 2008 as the private entities project. In 2005, during its career as the SMEs project, the stated objectives of the project were extended to include developing countries. The documentary material published by the IASB allows analysis of the IASB's proposals as they relate to developing countries, and the public responses of those commenting on developing countries.

The IASB documents obtained cover events from the IASB's establishment in March 2001, through to the IASB Board meetings in mid-2008. General documentary material includes IASB Annual Reports 2001–2006, the IASB's *Insight* publication series and its updates issued from 2002 to 2007. Documents specifically related to the SMEs project consist of:

- Discussion paper: *Preliminary Views on Accounting Standards for Small and Medium-Sized Entities* (IASB, 2004a);
- 121 public submissions in response to the discussion paper (IASB, 2004b);
- IASB staff questionnaire: *Staff Questionnaire on Possible Recognition and Measurement Modifications for Small and Medium-sized Entities (SMEs)* (IASB, 2005b);
- 101 public submissions in response to the staff questionnaire (IASB, 2005c);
- Exposure draft: *Proposed IFRS for Small and Medium-Sized Entities* (IASB, 2007a);
- Basis for conclusion: exposure draft (IASB, 2007b);
- 162 public submissions in response to the exposure draft (IASB, 2007f);
- Field test questionnaire: IFRS for SMEs (IASB, 2007e);
- Summarised results of the field tests (IASB, 2007g); and
- IASB Board meeting papers January 2006–May 2008.

Documentary analysis does not tell the complete story, but it does provide a useful means to build understanding of the issues and identify matters that can be pursued via other means, such as interviews (Hodges & Mellett, 2008; Howieson, 2008). The findings from the documentary analysis presented here illustrate the limitations of published project documentation when attempting to understand any accounting standard-setting effort. Those making submissions are not necessarily influential and the number of public submissions on a particular matter does not necessarily indicate the importance of the issue raised (Howieson, 2008). Further, in the non-public "black box" process that typifies standard-setting, influential parties may use alternative, non-public processes to exert their influence (Hodges & Mellett, 2008). Even so, analysis of the published documents and comparison with the project outcome may assist with identifying what has come through that "black box" process (Hodges & Mellett, 2008).

The larger research project will include interviews with key participants, but the interviews are yet to be conducted and the research reported here relies on published documentary sources. While these findings are, therefore, interim, they are sufficiently interesting to warrant wider publication in the context of continued interest in seeking IFRS adapted for developing countries and in improving governance in developing countries by strengthening the NIFA. Further, these findings provide analysed material for other researchers interested in this initiative as it affects developing countries.

INTERNATIONAL FINANCIAL REPORTING STANDARDS AND THEIR APPLICATION IN DEVELOPING COUNTRIES

The growing internationalization of capital markets prompted the establishment of the IASC and an effort, now spanning 35 years, to develop IFRS. Throughout that time, one controversial issue has been whether one set of IFRS is appropriate for application in all countries of the world, or whether instead, because those standards have been devised by those from developed countries, largely for use in a capital market environment, they are not necessarily relevant or appropriate for application in developing countries (Scott, 1968; Briston, 1978; Samuels & Oliga, 1982; Perera, 1985).

One view from the outset, not necessarily shared by the IASC, was that IFRS, along with the "existing and potential accounting systems, techniques, procedures and data [would] enhance economic development within a nation and among nations" (AAA, 1977, p. 20).[5] This was the view of some seeking "economic development accountancy" evidently assuming that the underlying objective of accounting in developing countries is, or should be, the enhancement of economic development and that this would benefit the developing countries (Wallace, 1990).

Many developing countries are so different from the developed countries, and from each other, that the applicability of the accounting technologies of developed countries for application in at least some developing countries is debatable (Briston, 1978; Hoarau, 1995; Points & Cunningham, 1998).

> In the case of developing countries where socio-political, economic and cultural differences tend to be not only highly pronounced but also in a highly dynamic and fluid state, the relevance of international accounting standards becomes even more questionable. (Samuels & Oliga, 1982, p. 69)

SyCip (1979, p. 19) recommended that the international accounting standard-setters consider the circumstances of developing countries because, "Certain standards or principles that may seem logical and appropriate from the viewpoint of a western developed country may be inappropriate or may work undue hardships ... in a developing country".

Summarised, these contrasting views are that one set of IFRS (and, thus, the systems and practices required to support compliance) is suitable for all countries and, indeed, will support economic development in developing countries, while the contrary view is that developing countries have special needs and circumstances that should be allowed for and therefore that the financial reporting standards of developed countries are not necessarily appropriate for application in developing countries.

The view that one set of IFRS is suitable for all has been imposed almost by default through the gradual importation into developing countries of the accounting practices and standards of developed countries, often via overseas aid conditions and colonialism (Nobes, 1998). Overseas aid may include exchanges of staff, provision of scholarships for local students and grants of textbooks from developed countries, thus contributing to the importation of the accounting practices of developed countries (Briston, 1978). Adding to this impetus has been the World Bank and IMF, both of which have long insisted on international accounting firms auditing the projects they finance, thus indirectly requiring the use of developed country accounting systems and practices (Hove, 1986, p. 91; Perera, 1989). Indeed, the World Bank has for many years promoted efforts in developing countries to "develop the accounting profession, install IASC and auditing standards, and prepare students and members of the accountancy profession to use them" (Camfferman & Zeff, 2006, p. 441). As one of the largest users of financial statements from developing countries, the World Bank has, over time, become a "major force" in efforts to impose one set of IFRS (Walton, 1998):

> We have 5,000 sets of audited financial statements coming in every year. It is in our interests to have a common basis for accounting. We also did not want to see developing countries go through the business of evolving a standard-setting process, which is handled very well by the IASC. There is no need to reinvent the wheel. (Randolph Andersen, World Bank, cited in Walton, 1998, p. 10)

The desire is also reflected in the World Bank's accounting manual, first published in 1995:

> In the absence of any superior national standards, the Bank requires the use of IASs in the preparation of financial statements because their use facilitates comparability between projects and countries, ensures consistent presentation of financial statements, and facilitates their interpretation. (Camfferman & Zeff, 2006, p. 442)

From the time of its establishment in 1973, the IASC was perceived to be focused on gaining recognition of its standards for use by multinational businesses in a globalising capital market. Its early standard-setting efforts, however, were more accepted in developing than in developed countries, the standards being flexible and the IASC promoting them as a lower cost alternative for countries than developing their own standard-setting infrastructure. Even so, criticisms mounted that the IASC issued standards without regard to the circumstances of developing countries (CAPA, 2003; Camfferman & Zeff, 2006, pp. 1, 190).

Various events and arrangements seemed to affect some developing countries differently from developed countries, examples including inflation, devaluation and foreign exchange losses, consolidation of subsidiary interests, transfer pricing and capitalisation of interest (SyCip, 1967, 1981). In 1983, when inflation in Latin America was a particular issue, interest from the World Bank and requests from developing countries prompted the IASC to commence a project on hyperinflation and it issued IAS 29, *Financial Reporting in Hyperinflationary Economies* in 1989 (Camfferman & Zeff, 2006, p. 288).

By this time, the IASC had adjusted its direction by sharpening its focus on standards for capital markets more typical of the advanced developed countries and began to "improve" its standards accordingly. This led to less flexible and increasingly complex standards (Camfferman & Zeff, 2006). Arguments mounted that a country's accounting principles should suit its local conditions (Talaga & Ndubizu, 1986) and that, especially in those developing countries without sophisticated capital markets, or with relatively large local and national governments and a smaller private sector, the main users of financial statements may differ from those in the developed countries (Hove, 1986). At the IASC meeting that approved IAS 29, the IASC agreed to form a steering committee that would conduct "a comprehensive review of the financial reporting needs of developing and newly industrialized countries" (Camfferman & Zeff, 2006, p. 289). The issue of developing countries thus entered the IASC's formal agenda, albeit as a research project in the problem stream.

The steering committee comprised members from both developed and developing countries, as well as from international organisations such as the United Nations and the World Bank. The committee employed R. S. Olesegun Wallace as an international research fellow. Wallace's (1990) comprehensive literature review about developing countries' accounting practices from the early 1960s identified a shortage of skills in developing countries to cope with sophisticated imported accounting technologies, and concluded this shortage resulted in deficient accounting, poor internal control, lack of management accounting concepts, unauditable systems, and late, incomplete, inaccurate, and irrelevant financial reporting.

The steering committee produced and submitted to the IASC a comprehensive project proposal and a draft working programme that included promulgation of separate financial reporting standards for developing countries. Members of the IASC, however, were unconvinced that "developing countries had reporting needs that should be addressed by separate standards", although they did accept that "small countries or specific industries might have reporting needs where the IASC could play a useful role" (Camfferman & Zeff, 2006, p. 290). The steering committee's proposal was replaced by a proposal to establish an advisory board on the reporting needs of the developing countries, and the steering committee's chairman resigned. The IASC's "staff resources were withdrawn to concentrate on the Improvements project" for gaining international capital markets recognition, and the project made no progress until it was terminated in 1993 (Camfferman & Zeff, 2006, p. 290). Thus, over the four years the issue was on the IASB's formal agenda, the issue of financial reporting standards appropriate for use in developing countries did not get past the "problem stream" stage. Wallace, the steering committee's research fellow observed that:

> Developing countries continue to adopt foreign accounting and educational systems. This is often expensive, and the adopting country has little control over the relevance of imported accounting ... The main issue is whether the objectives of the assistance granting country (or aid agency) and receiving country are congruent ... The biggest

problem developing countries have is that of too many foreign "experts" marketing half-baked solutions to problems that neither they nor the recipient nations understand. (Wallace & Briston, 1993, pp. 216–217)

The next entry of accounting in developing countries onto the IASC's formal agenda was prompted in 1997 by a World Bank donation to the IASC restricted to purposes "linked to work on developing countries and countries in transition" (Camfferman & Zeff, 2006, p. 404). The IASC formed a preparatory committee on developing country issues, following this with the formation of a steering committee in November 1998. This committee "included, for the first time, representatives from the People's Republic of China and the Russian Federation" (p. 406). By this time, the Asian financial crisis had prompted the World Bank's "increasing recognition that a sound basis of financial reporting is essential" and, it seems, increased desire for application and enforcement (via the ROSCs) of IFRS in developing countries (Walton, 1998, citing Andersen). The idea that IFRS should be applied in developing countries, however, remained controversial, because of problems caused by overly-sophisticated technologies (Hassan, 1998, p. 74), the expense imposed by requiring full scale IFRS (Nobes, 1998), and because the intended major user group served by the IASC's conceptual framework is users/investors in public companies. In developing countries, however, economic planners (Hassan, 1998) and other user groups require consideration:

The main users/use combinations for accounting in developing countries are; (1) decisions by investors in public companies, (2) decisions (including on accountability) by owners and others in private companies, (3) reporting to tax authorities, (4) decision by managers. (Nobes, 1998, p. 5)

Little emerged from the steering committee's deliberations. In 2000, the steering committee decided to study barter transactions, thus presumably, using the World Bank's donation for the specified purposes because when the IASC transferred its standard-setting responsibilities to the IASB "developing countries were not mentioned in the IASC's 'legacy document'" for the IASB (Camfferman & Zeff, 2006, p. 406). Again, the developing countries issue dropped from the formal agenda without getting past the problem stream stage.

The IASC's report to the newly formed IASB advised that, "A demand exists for a special version of International Accounting Standards for Small Enterprises" but this legacy document did not mention developing economies (IASB, 2004a, IN5). Although the IASB acknowledged the issue of SMEs as a matter for future research, its main focus initially was on the need:

> to develop in the public interest a *single* set of high quality understandable and enforceable global accounting standards that require high quality, transparent and comparable information in financial statements and other financial reporting to help participants in the various capital markets of the world and other users of the information to make economic decisions. (IASB, 2004a, para 8, emphasis added)

The case for this single set of standards was further emphasised following the collapse of Enron in 2001, and renewed efforts were made to bring the NIFA into force while the IFRSs became increasingly complex as the IASB attempted to respond to the problematic issues raised by Enron's collapse and the similarly high profile collapse of other companies. In July 2002, both the European Commission and Australia announced they would adopt IFRS from 2005 (Camfferman & Zeff, 2006, pp. 432, 435) and other countries soon followed with announcement of their intentions to adopt IFRS.

The World Bank, the Asian Development Bank, the IMF, and other lending organisations continued to push for the adoption of IFRS internationally, Pakistan and Bangladesh (both developing countries) doing so in response to those pressures (Mir & Rahaman, 2005; Ashraf & Ghani, 2005). Whether this really has improved financial reporting in Pakistan (Ashraf & Ghani, 2005), and whether IFRS are relevant in developing countries remains a matter of debate. Mir and Rahaman (2005), for example, reporting on Bangladesh observed that IFRS provide no guidance for such major sectors as jute, tea, garments, and oil and gas.

THE IASB's AGENDA PROJECT ON SMEs

Soon after the IASB's establishment in 2001, it commenced discussion on "Accounting by Small and Medium Entities and in Emerging economies" seeking to:

> explore whether there is a need for special guidance to clarify financial reporting requirements in the context of financial reports used in emerging economies or for certain types of enterprises, for example, for small enterprises or for privately-held enterprises. (IASB, 2001, p. 8)

Its major efforts were focused on the single set of enforceable global accounting standards, but various international bodies were lobbying the IASB for "accounting guidance" for SMEs, the World Bank, and

European Commission being especially prominent in these lobbying efforts (Walton, 2007).

Some IASB members questioned whether the IASB had, or should have, a role beyond financial reporting for listed companies in capital markets but, in 2002, the Trustees of the IASC Foundation reported their support for "efforts by the IASB to examine issues particular to emerging economies and to small and medium-sized enterprises" (IASB, 2004a, IN5). The IASB decided in mid-2002 to prioritise financial reporting by SMEs (IASB, 2002a, 2002b), but anticipated asking:

> its staff and members of the advisory panel with experience in emerging economies to highlight those issues that are specific to emerging economies and need to be addressed by the IASB. (IASB, 2002b, p. 15)

The IASB issued a 45 page discussion paper, *Preliminary Views on Accounting Standards for Small and Medium-sized Entities* in 2004 (IASB, 2004a, 2004c). This discussion paper invited comments on nine major SME issues prior to developing proposals (Table 1). Although the discussion paper acknowledged both the IASC's transitional report to the board about the need to address SMEs, and the IASC Foundation Trustees' encouragement

Table 1. Major Issues in the Discussion Paper Preliminary Views on Accounting Standards for Small and Medium-sized Entities.

Major issues in the discussion paper
1. Should the International Accounting Standards Board (IASB) develop special financial reporting standards for SMEs?
2. What should be the objectives of a set of financial reporting standards for SMEs?
3. For which entities would IASB Standards for SMEs be intended?
4. If IASB Standards for SMEs do not address a particular accounting recognition or measurement issue confronting an entity, how should that entity resolve the issue?
5. May an entity using IASB Standards for SMEs elect to follow a treatment permitted in an IFRS that differs from the treatment in the related IASB Standard for SMEs?
6. How should the Board approach the development of IASB Standards for SMEs? To what extent should the foundation of SME standards be the concepts and principles and related mandatory guidance in IFRSs?
7. If IASB Standards for SMEs are built on the concepts and principles and related mandatory guidance in full IFRSs, what should be the basis for modifying those concepts and principles for SMEs?
8. In what format should IASB standards for SMEs be published?
9. Are there any other matters related to how the Board should approach its project to develop standards for SMEs that you would like to bring to the Board's attention?

Source: Reproduced based on the discussion paper.

to examine issues relating to both emerging economies and SMEs, all of the nine issues related to SMEs (IASB, 2004a, IN5, 2004d, p. 1).

The 120 responses to the discussion paper generally supported the IASB developing an IFRS for SMEs, rather than leaving the issue for local standard-setters to address (IASB, 2007b, BC7). Fourteen respondents commented on developing countries, six of those coming from respondents in developing countries: Africa, Brazil, Malawi, Malaysia, Mozambique, and Pakistan. The other eight respondents commenting on developing country issues were from Australia (2), International Federation of Accountants (IFAC), United Nations Trade Cooperation and Develop-ment-Intergovernmental Working Group of Experts on International Standards of Accounting and Reporting (UNCTAD-ISAR), the United Kingdom (3) plus one IASB advisory panel member on SMEs. Table 2 summarises the developing country issues identified by these respondents.

Table 2. Summary of Issues Identified by Responses Commenting on Developing Countries.

Response #	Organisation	Issue Raised
		From respondents in developing countries
CL 16	Susela Devi, University of Malaya, (Malaysia)	Provide comprehensive guide to SMEs as in most instances, the accounting personnel of SMEs are not qualified professional accountants. Provide web-published volume of SMEs standards for easier access if possible. It should be recognised that developing countries require the IASB's assistance and that there is a greater need for SME standards in such countries.
CL 21	KPMG (Mozambique)	In developing countries, it is not practical for most companies to meet the complex reporting requirements of IFRS.
CL 52	Accounting and Auditing Standards Committees of the Institute of Chartered Accountants of Pakistan (ICAP) (Pakistan)	Given that economic conditions between countries differ, the criteria to determine which entities are SMEs should be left with individual jurisdictions. For example, a large company in a developing country may be a SME in a developed country.
CL 70	Accounting Federal Council & IBRACON-Brazilian Institute of CPAs (Brazil)	IFRS for SME completely tuned to IASB pronouncements and interpretations, will provide easier way to full adoption of IFRS in future.
CL 94	Eastern Central and Southern African Federation of Accountants (ECSAFA)	Accessibility of IFRS in developing countries is an issue.

Table 2. (*Continued*)

Response #	Organisation	Issue Raised
CL 99	Society of Accountants in Malawi	The IASB should consider where the need for SME is coming from and active involvement in SME project of member bodies of developing countries and regional bodies. *From respondents in developed countries/ international bodies*
CL 4	Chartered Institute of Public Finance and Accountancy (UK)	Proposed IFRS for SMEs are too onerous for SMEs in developing countries.
CL 36	International Federation of Accountants (IFAC)	Due to high costs of compliance with IFRS, many countries especially smaller developing countries, seek less onerous set of accounting standards.
CL 38	Institute of Chartered Accountants in Australia (ICAA) (Australia)	IFRS for SMEs project gives the opportunity to create something simpler to be used by SMEs and developing countries.
CL 65	United Nations Trade Cooperation and Development – Intergovernmental Working Group of Experts on International Standards of Accounting and Reporting (UNCTAD-ISAR)	Special circumstances of SMEs in developing countries should be considered when developing IFRS for SMEs. IFRS is difficult to apply in developing countries.
CL 78	Institute of Chartered Accountants of Scotland (UK)	IFRS for SME should be updated annually or else it would be costly for developing countries to keep up with the changes. Also provide updated translations if IFRS for SMEs is translated into other languages.
CL 92	Institute of Chartered Accountants in England & Wales (ICAEW) (UK)	If in a less developed economy, a small listed entity is permitted to use the new standards and complies fully with its requirements; "its financial statements should be described as in compliance with IASB standards for SMEs".
CL 97	Raggy, David Member, IASB Advisory Panel on Small and Medium-sized Entities	Given that developing countries lack active markets, sufficient guidance is requested to be provided for the SMEs.
CL 101	CPA (Australia)	IFRS for SMEs provides a migration path for developing countries to move to full IFRS.

Source: Based on submissions to the discussion paper.

In summary of the comments about developing countries, two respondents (CPA Australia, and the Brazilian respondent) regarded the proposed IFRS as providing a transitional path to full IFRS. The other respondents all identified particular issues of accessibility, comprehensibility and language, applicability and circumstances within some countries. There was also a call to involve developing country bodies in the project.

The IASB's next step was to develop terms of reference for proceeding with the project. For completeness, this is reproduced in full to show that SMEs remained the focus of attention (IASB, 2005a, p. 12):

- IASB Standards for SMEs should focus on financial reporting by those non-publicly accountable entities that have external users of their financial statements (i.e. users other than primarily owner-managers). Jurisdictions could, of course, choose to permit or require them for all SMEs, including very small ones.
- The IASB should not develop detailed guidelines on which entities should or should not be eligible to use the IASB Standards for SMEs. That is a matter to be decided by national jurisdictions.
- The IASB agreed that the *Framework for the Preparation and Presentation of Financial Statements* should apply to all entities. However, the IASB should consider recognition and measurement simplifications for SMEs, as well as disclosure and presentation simplifications – based only on user needs and cost-benefit considerations as provided for in the *Framework*. There should be no preconceived objections to such changes.
- If a recognition or measurement issue is addressed in an IFRS, but not in SME Standards, the entity should be required to apply that IFRS to the issue. This "mandatory fallback" should be implemented by including IFRSs at the top of the accounting policy hierarchy in the SME equivalent of paragraph 11 of IAS 8 *Accounting Policies Changes in Accounting Estimates and Errors*.
- An entity following IASB Standards for SMEs should follow those standards in their entirety and should not have a choice of reverting to IFRSs on a standard-by-standard or principle-by-principle basis.
- If an entity follows IASB Standards for SMEs, the basis of presentation note and the auditor's report should make that clear so that the user understands that full IFRSs are not being followed.
- When published in printed form, IASB SME standards should be organised topically.
- The composition of the Advisory Group should be broadened to include more preparers and users of SME financial statements.
- Staff should develop a project plan that includes roundtable – table meetings with preparers and users of SME financial statements.

In April 2005, a *Staff Questionnaire on Recognition and Measurement Simplification* was issued for public comment and sent to the respondents to the discussion paper seeking further insight on two recognition and measurement matters (Table 3).

Table 3. Questions in the Recognition and Measurement Simplification Questionnaire.

Questions in the Recognition and Measurement Simplification Questionnaire
Question 1: What are the areas for possible simplification of recognition and measurement principles for SMEs? In responding, please indicate:
• The specific accounting recognition or measurement problem for an SME under IFRSs; • The specific translations or events that create the recognition or measurement problem for an SME under IFRS; • Why it is a problem; and • How that problem might be solved.
Question 2: From your experience, please indicate which topics addressed in IFRS might be omitted from SME standards because they are unlikely to occur in an SME context. If they occur, the standards would require the SME to determine its appropriate accounting policy by looking to the applicable IFRSs.

Source: Reproduced based on the Recognition and Measurement Simplification Questionnaire.

Eight of the 101 responses to the questionnaire commented on developing country issues, three of these coming from respondents in developing countries (Table 4).

In summary of the comments about developing countries, one respondent pointed out that in many developing countries compliance with full IFRS was, or was about to be, required of all entities. Problems anticipated and emerging from this requirement included the lack of capacity to cope with such complex standards. Seven of the eight respondents reported recognition and measurement requirements arising from fair value accounting requirements because the developing countries lacked active markets, expertise, and resources.

Expansion of the SME Project to Include Developing Countries

In July 2005, as enforceable IFRS began to take effect internationally, the Trustees of the IASC Foundation went further than merely expressing support for the IASB to extend its focus, as they had done in 2002. The trustees changed the constitution, extending its mandate to require the IASB to recognise and take account of "as appropriate, the special needs of small and medium-sized entities and emerging economies" (IASB, 2007b,

Table 4. Summary of Issues Identified on Developing Countries in the Recognition and Measurement Simplification Questionnaire.

Response #	Organisation	Developing Country Issues Identified
		From respondents in developing countries
CL 4	Ministry of Finance, People's Republic of China	Developing countries would have difficulties in using fair value accounting because they often lack active market prices.
CL 35	Institute of Certified Public Accountants of Kenya (ICPAK)	Developing countries have resource constraints and it is not cost-effective for them to invest in the expertise needed to produce financial statements that fully comply with IAS. Since the bulk of SME provide information for short-term stewardship purposes, rather than for long term investment decision making, the use of fair value is "likely to cloud rather than improve comprehension" (pp. 1–2).
CL 96	Susela Devi (Malaysia)	In most developing countries, all entities are required to prepare financial statements in accordance with national standards which are now converged to IFRS. SMEs in most developing countries lack technical expertise in complying with complex standards.
		From respondents in developed countries/international bodies
CL 26	CFA Institute (global organisation)	Disagrees that the IASCF objective should include the need to address challenges facing SMEs. In emerging and developing countries, problems are anticipated for some preparers, auditors and regulators where accounting expertise are in short supply, but this does not warrant the development of SME standards.
CL 44	IFAC	SMEs operating in jurisdictions with less developed capital markets will often lack access to observable market data. SMEs in developing countries face difficulty in calculating present value, where there is limited availability of market data.
CL 79	Interamerican Accounting Association	Many developing countries lack current and precise market information, and this should be considered in the development of the standard.
CL 85	UNCTAD	The situation of SME in developing countries should be considered in the development of SME standards. UNCTAD is of the view that special efforts need to be made to ensure the participation of users and preparers of the financial statements of SMEs in developing countries and countries with economies in transition in conducting the public roundtable–meetings. Fair value estimates are difficult to obtain in developing countries.

Table 4. (*Continued*)

Response #	Organisation	Developing Country Issues Identified
CL 97	CAPA	Many developing countries are in great need of separate SME standards. Given that SMEs in most developing (as well as developed) countries lack technical expertise, it might be appropriate to consider providing a consistent set of financial statements containing information relevant to assessing management stewardship and instilling a notion of accountability to the stakeholders.

Source: Based on submissions to the Recognition and Simplification Questionnaire.

para 54c). With the IASB already working on IFRS for small and medium enterprises (SMEs), while the title of the project remained the same, the IASB expanded its stated objectives to include specific mention of emerging economies.

In February 2007, the IASB released for public comment its 254-page *Exposure Draft of a Proposed IFRS for Small and Medium-Sized Entities* (ED), accompanied by a 48-page *Basis for Conclusions.* The IASB's Staff Overview of the project stated that the proposed standard would be "based on full … IFRS developed primarily for listed companies" and, in addition to assisting SMEs, it would "provide emerging economies with an internationally recognised basis for financial reporting" (IASB, 2007c, p. 4). The IASB's Chairman, Sir David Tweedie, however, suggested the proposed IFRS would assist SMEs internationally and therefore assist SMEs in developed and developing countries alike:

> The IASB's goal has been to produce a standard for use by smaller and unlisted companies that offers the comparability of full IFRSs while reducing the burden on the preparing company. When completed, the SME standard will make the accounting requirements more accessible to smaller preparers in both developed and *emerging markets.* (IASB, 2007d, p. 1, emphasis added)

The ED and the accompanying basis for conclusions were issued in English, with responses due by 1 October, thus allowing some eight months for responses. Translated versions of both documents were issued subsequently to facilitate broader consultation, this becoming the first IASB exposure draft to be translated into a language other than English: Spanish was issued in April 2007, French in May 2007, German in June 2007, and Romanian in September. A Polish translation of the ED, but not the basis for conclusions, was issued in September 2007 (IASB, 2007g). The deadline for public responses was extended from 1 October 2007 to 30 November 2007.

Scrutiny of the ED and the basis for conclusions suggests that Sir David Tweedie's explanation of the project is the more apt description. The ED mentions emerging economies once, to acknowledge the IASB's amended constitution (IASB, 2007a, P2 (c)). The basis for conclusions mentions emerging economies four times, three times to acknowledge the IASB's amended constitution (see IASB, 2007b, para BC 3 and 54 (c)), and once to state the views of one Board member[6] who disagreed with the need to develop SME standards (IASB, 2007b, AV 6).

The ED is organised according to accounting topics, and reduces the volume of guidance applicable to SMEs by more than 85 per cent when compared with the full IFRS "by removing choices for accounting treatment, eliminating topics that are not generally relevant to SMEs and simplifying methods for recognition and measurement" (IASB, 2007d, p. 1). The basis for conclusions explains that the ED omits hyperinflation, equity-settled share-based payment, agriculture, interim financial reporting, lessor accounting for finance leases, earnings per share, segment reporting, and insurance because these topics are not relevant to SMEs. In the event that any SMEs encounter such matters reference to the relevant IFRS is necessary (IASB, 2007b).

The ED sought responses to 11 questions (Table 5), none of which mention developing countries or emerging economies.

Submissions on the Exposure Draft

The ED prompted 161 submissions from 51 countries. Forty one submissions came from 29 developing countries, and 101 submissions from 22 developed countries, with the largest number of submissions coming from the United Kingdom (21 responses) and Germany (17 responses). The number and distribution of responses is summarised in Table 6.

Although the ED did not seek responses on developing country issues, 22 submissions mentioned developing country issues. Five of these submissions were from developing countries, 13 from developed countries, two from international organisations and two from international accounting firms. Table 7 provides further information about those identifying developing country issues and categorises the particular issues identified into developing countries' needs (five responses), small entities (six responses),

Table 5.   Questions in the Exposure Draft IFRS for SMEs.

Questions in the Exposure Draft

---

1. Stand-alone document
   With the objective of a stand-alone document in mind, are there additional transactions, other events or conditions that should be covered in the proposed standard to make it more self-contained? Conversely, is there guidance in the draft standard that should be removed because it is unlikely to be relevant to typical SMEs with about 50 employees?
2. Recognition and measurement simplification that the Board adopted
   Are there other recognition or measurement simplifications that the Board should consider? In responding, please indicate:
   a) the specific transactions, other events or conditions that create a specific recognition or measurement problem for SMEs under IFRSs;
   b) why it is a problem; and
   c) how that problem might be solved.
3. Recognition and measurement simplification that the Board considered but did not adopt
   Should the Board reconsider any of those and, if so, why?
4. Whether all accounting policy options in full IFRSs should be available to SMEs
   Do you agree with the Board's conclusions on which options are the most appropriate for SMEs? If not, which one(s) would you change, and why?
   Should any of these options that would be available to SMEs by cross-reference to the full IFRSs be eliminated from the draft IFRS for SMEs and, if so, why?
5. Borrowing costs
   Do you agree or disagree with the proposal to allow SMEs to choose either the expense model or the capitalisation model for borrowing costs, and why?
6. Topics not addressed in the proposed IFRS for SMEs
   Should any additional topics be omitted from the IFRS for SMEs and replaced by a cross-reference? If so, which ones and why?
7. General referral to full IFRSs
   Are the requirements in paragraphs 10.2–10.4, coupled with the explicit cross-references to particular IFRSs in specific circumstances, appropriate? Why or why not?
8. Adequacy of guidance
   Are there specific areas for which SMEs are likely to need additional guidance? What are they, and why?
9. Adequacy of disclosures
   Are there disclosures that are not proposed that the Board should require for SMEs? If so, which ones and why? Conversely, do you believe that any of the proposed disclosures should not be required for SMEs? If so, which ones and why?
10. Transition guidance
    Do you believe that the guidance is adequate? If not, how can it be improved?
11. Maintenance of the IFRS for SMEs
    Is this approach to maintaining the proposed IFRS for SMEs appropriate, or should it be modified? If so, how and why?

Source: Reproduced based on ED.

Table 6.   Analysis of the Submissions to the ED by country.

Developing Countries	No. of Submissions	Developed Countries	No. of Submissions
Argentina	1	Australia	7
Brazil	1	Austria	4
Cameroun	1	Barbados	1
China	1	Belgium	1
Colombia	2	Canada	5
Costa Rica	2	Denmark	2
Ecuador	1	Finland	2
El Salvador	1	France	9
Fiji	1	Germany	17
India	2	Hong Kong	2
Indonesia	1	Ireland	3
Iran	1	Israel	1
Jamaica	1	Italy	8
Kenya	2	Japan	1
Korea	3	Netherlands	3
Malawi	1	New Zealand	1
Malaysia	1	Norway	2
Mexico	1	Spain	3
Pakistan	2	Sweden	1
Philippine	1	UK	21
Poland	1	United Arab Emirates	1
Russia	2	US	6
South Africa	5	*Submissions from developed countries*	101
Tanzania	1		
Thailand	1	*Submissions from Global /International Organisations*	13
Tunisia	1	*Submissions from European Bodies*	5
Uruguay	1	*Submission from unknown location*	1
Venezuela	1		
Zambia	1	Total submissions received	161
Submissions from developing countries	41		

Source: Based on submissions received on the ED.

lack of market (eight responses), lack of expertise and resources (six responses), language barrier (one response), and access to IFRS (two responses). The following comment about each of these issues commences with the broader concerns about the idea of developing countries using IFRS to more specific ones about particular accounting techniques.

Table 7. Summary of Responses to ED Commenting on Developing Countries.

Sub No.	Organisation	Country	Affiliation	Developing Countries' Needs	Small Entities	Lack of Market	Lack of Expertise/ Resources	Language Barrier	Access to IFRS
Responses from developing countries									
CL 15	University of Cape Town	South Africa	Academic				X		
CL 25	Fiji Institute of Accountants (FIA)	Fiji	Professional Body				X		
CL 68	South African Institute of Chartered Accountants (SAICA)	South Africa	Professional Body				X		
CL 84	Malaysian Accounting Standards Board(MASB)	Malaysia	Standard Setter			X			
CL 131	Federacion Argentina de Consejos Profesionales de Ciencias Economicas	Argentina	Professional Body	X		X			
Responses from developed countries									
CL 20	InterAmerican Accounting Association	Canada/ America	Professional Body			X			
CL 24	Institute of Chartered Accountants of Scotland (ICAS)	UK	Professional Body	X					
CL 35	New York Society of CPA's (NYSSCPA)	US	Professional Body			X			
CL 46	Certified General Accountants Association of Canada	Canada	Professional Body	X					
CL 86	Ernst & Young	Global	Accounting Firm						X
CL 92	Grant Thornton International	Global	Accounting Firm						
CL 93	Consiglio Nazionale dei Dottori Commercialisti and the Consiglio Nazionale dei Ragionieri	Italy	Professional Body			X			

Table 7. (*Continued*)

Sub No.	Organisation	Country	Affiliation	Developing Countries' Needs	Small Entities	Lack of Market	Lack of Expertise/ Resources	Language Barrier	Access to IFRS
CL 110	British Accounting Association's Financial Accounting and Reporting Special Interest Group	UK	Professional Body						
CL 118	Association of Chartered Certified Accountants (ACCA) (UK)	UK	Professional Body		X				X
CL 124	International Network of Accountants and Auditors (INAA)	UK	Professional Body			X	X		
CL 125	European Accounting Association (EAA) FRSC	EU	Regional Body	X	X				
CL 129	C. Hecht, D&L GmbH, BPG GmbH, Treuh.-ges. Herrmann GmbH	Germany	Corporation						
CL 134	The Confederation of Asian and Pacific Accountants (CAPA)		Regional Body		X		X	X	
CL 140	Hong Kong Institute of Certified Public Accountants	Hong Kong	Professional Body		X				
CL 142	International Federation of Accountants (IFAC)		International Body		X	X			
CL 150	Institute of Chartered Accountants of Barbados	Barbados	Professional Body	X		X	X		
CL 156	London Society of Chartered Accountants	UK	Professional Body		X				
Total				5	6	8	6	1	2

Source: Based on submissions to ED which commented on developing countries.

The Confederation of Asian and Pacific Accountants (CAPA), high-lighted the language barrier developing countries face. The publication of documents in languages other than those used in the developing countries means the imposition of translation costs and increased difficulties to understand and apply the standard. The translated version of the ED (in Spanish, French, German, Romanian, and Polish) would not have lowered the language barriers in the Asia-Pacific region and CAPA reporting received few responses from developing countries in the region. Language barriers and other challenges, including lack of resources, were thought to be contributing factors (CL 134):

> If the medium of communication within these emerging economies is not English, there is also the added challenge of the need to have a translated version of the full IFRS when the SME IFRS is adopted so as to enable the cross-referencing. This may effectively be beyond the technical and financial means of many emerging countries whose population does not speak one of the common languages of the world. (CL 134, p. 3)

The cost of access to IFRS presented another barrier, two respondents arguing that the "IASB should make the text of the standard freely available for download from its website" (CL 118, p. 2).

Several submissions called for specific consideration of developing countries' needs. The ED had omitted simplifications of several matters including hyperinflation and agriculture because these were deemed not relevant for SMEs, and cross reference to the full IFRS was proposed should SMEs encounter such issues. Five respondents argued that those matters are relevant in developing countries, and therefore that simplified accounting guidance on accounting in hyperinflationary economies and on agriculture is necessary (CL 86; CL 131). Consequently, some doubted that the proposed IFRS would assist the developing countries. For example, the Institute of Chartered Accountants of Barbados noted that:

> The SME project initially included consideration of issues peculiar to emerging economies but this objective seems to have been removed at some point. The burden of complying with full IFRS is clearly greater for SMEs in developing markets operating in emerging economies. The SME standards as drafted do very little to reduce this burden. The Board's concern in the SME accounting project should be to develop standards for those jurisdictions where the need is greatest and not for jurisdictions which already have their own standards and standard-setting bodies. (CL 150, p. 2)

The European Accounting Association (EAA) questioned whether the proposed IFRS did consider the "needs and circumstances of [developing] countries" and urged the IASB to wait for the results of the field tests before promulgating the final standard (CL 125, p. 13). The Institute of Chartered

Accountants of Scotland (ICAS), however, thought the simplified standard proposed would provide a sound basis for financial reporting in developing countries (CL 24).

Six respondents suggested developing countries may lack the resources, expertise and access to the information necessary to prepare financial reports in accordance with full IFRS (CL 124). The ED's cross-references to full IFRS would, therefore, increase the burden on those in developing countries because they would need to know the full IFRS to apply the SME requirements (CL 134). A self-contained, easy to apply, and understandable standard was therefore recommended (CL 124).

Eight respondents advised that developing countries lack active markets to allow fair value determinations of most of their assets (for example, CL 84; CL 124). Neither do some developing countries have the specialist support needed to assist in fair value determination, thus potentially undermining the credibility and reliability of information through lack of precision and excessive subjectivity (CL 68; CL 150; CL 142).

Six respondents commented on the applicability of IFRS for SME to small entities in developing countries, some arguing that the proposed IFRS was not for small entities at all, but rather was directed at medium-sized non-publicly accountable entities (CL 118; 140; 142). Because the needs of small entities had been overlooked, there was potential for the proposed IFRS to be rejected, especially in developing countries (CL 118, p. 2) because it was:

> ill-suited on cost-benefit grounds for application by the great majority of small entities that produce GPFS for external users, especially those operating in developing nations. (CL 142, p. 4)

Field Tests and Field Test Questionnaire

In June 2007, four months after it first published the ED in English, but five months before responses were due, the IASB issued a field test questionnaire for those trialling the ED. This questionnaire was published in English, French, and Spanish (IASB, 2007e).

The IASB reported it had "worked with a number of organisations, including the International Federation of Accountants, national and regional professional accountancy bodies as well as accounting standard-setters and auditing firms to identify field test companies and to help them to apply the draft IFRS for SMEs and to respond to the field test questionnaire" (IASB, 2007g).[7] The IASB also encouraged auditing firms to assist their clients with the field tests (IASB, 2007e) and announced it would work with IFAC's SMP Committee, Developing Nations Committee, Transitional Auditors Committee, and Professional Accountants in Business Committee in field testing the draft IFRS for SMEs.

According to the field test questionnaire, the IASB sought the participation of two groups of entities: "(1) entities with between 10 and 50 employees and (2) entities with fewer than 10 employees" (IASB, 2007e, p. 4). The IASB sought to field test the proposals in a wide range of countries, and "especially encourage[d] entities in emerging and developing economies to field test the draft IFRS for SMEs" and submit their findings to the IASB by 30 November 2007, the same date as for the responses to the ED (IASB, 2007e, p. 4).

The IASB reported that the responses to the field tests would be treated confidentially, although "a report summarising and explaining the findings, without individual company data, will be made publicly available" (IASB, 2007g). The field test companies were asked to provide:

> background information about the company, submit their most recent annual financial statements under their existing accounting framework, prepare financial statements in accordance with the proposed IFRS for SMEs for the same financial year (though without presenting comparative prior year information), and respond to a series of questions designed to identify specific problems to field test company encountered in applying the draft IFRS for SMEs. (IASB, 2007g)

The IASB reported the participation of 115 SME field test companies from 20 countries, 11 of which are developing countries (Argentina, India, Kenya, Malawi, Malaysia, Nigeria, Poland, South Africa, South Korea, Tanzania, and Tunisia). The nine developed countries involved are Australia, Barbados, Denmark, France, Germany, Italy, Netherlands, United Kingdom, and United States. Information is not available, however, on how many of the companies were from each country, the IASB reporting that information only on a regional basis as 56 companies from Europe, 36 from the Asia-Pacific region, 23 from Africa and three from America[8] (IASB, 2008b).

This field testing was intended to help the IASB to assess understandability, scope, burden, impact, users' needs, accounting policy choices, small entity, and developing country problems and adequacy of implementation guidance (IASB, 2007g). Preliminary results of the field tests were presented to the IASB's Standards Advisory Council (SAC)'s meeting held on the 14th February 2008. The preliminary observations from the field test results were that:

- Few companies had problems applying the ED
- Main issues were:
  - Determining fair values
  - Computing deferred taxes
  - First time: Equity and cash flow statements
- Minimal incremental cost (IASB, 2008a, p. 14).

The further information "explaining the main issues" issued for the April meeting stated that a goal of the field testing was to assess problems arising for micro-entities (defined as those with fewer than ten employees) and those entities in developing economies (IASB, 2008c, p. 2). Numerous issues are explained, although none are specifically identified as related to developing countries.

The report identifies only 12 of the field test entities as "full IFRS reporters", with more than half of those in developing countries (IASB, 2008c, p. 3). Discussion of some fair value problems comments on the lack of market data that would normally be available "in more advanced or developed countries" (IASB, 2008c, pp. 8, 16, 20). For those fair value requirements that depend on whether a market is active or inactive, it was noted that "the stock market in certain countries is generally inactive, so fair value measurements may not be reliable even for 'quoted' instruments" (p. 13). Further, it was noted that in the absence of simplified requirements for agriculture, the ED's cross-referencing to the IASB's full standard on agriculture requires determination of fair values for biological assets (including plants and animals) and agricultural produce (harvested). This was a source of difficulties.

IASB staff had encountered some challenges in the field testing from "financial statements that were … in foreign languages" which made it difficult for IASB staff to determine how thoroughly the ED requirements had been applied (IASB, 2008a, p. 5). Responses to the questionnaires that were submitted in foreign languages had been translated for IASB staff use.

The nature of some issues identified in the report implies difficulties for the IASB attempting to address known issues encountered by SMEs and developing countries when the conduct of business activities globally includes the conduct of some significant activities through developing countries and, possibly via smaller entities in developing countries. In May 2008, the IASB changed the title of the project to IFRS for Private Entities, and announced its intention to re-deliberate the proposals in the ED. The IASB's summary of this project now explains that full IFRS were designed to "meet the needs of equity investors in companies in public capital markets". The users of the financial statements of private entities do not have the same needs as investors in public capital markets and, as "IFRS have become more detailed", private entities have increasingly come to regard compliance with full IFRS as a burden. Accordingly the IASB seeks reporting requirements that "meet user needs while balancing costs and benefits from a preparer perspective", and the objective of this project now is to "develop an IFRS expressly designed to meet the financial reporting needs of entities that (a) do not have public accountability and (b) publish general purpose financial statements for external users" (IASB, 2008d). The argument is similar to that made about the applicability of IFRS to SMEs and to developing countries. It is not yet clear whether, with this re-titled project, the IASB has abandoned the earlier objectives or is now attempting to address them from a different angle.

DISCUSSION AND CONCLUSION

The question of IFRS appropriate for application in developing countries has been on the IASC's and then the IASB's public agenda throughout their existence (from the early 1970s). Throughout that time, the importation into developing countries of the accounting and financial reporting practices of developed countries has continued.

The NIFA is intended to bring about the political objective of global financial integration and globalised capital markets. Although the NIFA has become prominent only recently, the use of accounting as a political tool to bring about "economic development" has long been promoted. While this view is not necessarily shared by the IASC/IASB, the international standard-setter does seem to be involved in the NIFA. As the NIFA is imposed on developing countries, ostensibly to strengthen the international financial system and support good governance, and IFRS become increasingly complex in the IASB's effort to address financial reporting issues in the major capital markets, the problems facing developing countries seem to magnify. The evidence presented here suggests a tension between the IASB seeking to devise IFRS for use by those already operating in capital markets, and those pursuing the NIFA seeking one approach for all, evidently on the basis it will bring about globalised capital markets.

Kingdon's (1984) three stream approach to understanding the career of an issue on a policymaker's agenda recognises the need for political support to bring an item onto the formal agenda at all, and asserts that the problem and policy streams need to be coupled before an issue on the policymaker's agenda will be addressed. If one element is missing the issue's career on the formal agenda will be short-lived. The issue of developing countries has been placed on the standard-setter's formal agenda twice previously (1989 and 1998) and subsequently dropped. The first placement (1989) seemed to be the most concerted attempt to produce a solution, but the policy solution proposed (which included promulgating special standards for developing countries) was unacceptable to the policymakers. Standards promulgated to address particular issues affecting developing countries may help, but it should be noted that the standard on agriculture with its fair value requirements seems to add to the difficulties rather than alleviating them. On commencement, this agriculture project was supposed to assist developing countries (Camfferman & Zeff, 2006, p. 402).

The findings presented here suggest that when the developing countries issue was added to the IASB's agenda in 2005, the SMEs project was well-advanced with a policy solution already devised. There is little evidence that the IASB sought to deal with specific issues facing developing countries but rather, as Kingdon (1984) suggests may occur when a policy solution emerges, offered the pre-existing policy solution for SMEs, possibly regarding that as a partial solution for developing countries.

The history of this issue suggests that an acceptable policy solution for developing countries is yet to be devised. Whether the IASB possesses the knowledge and resources required to address financial reporting matters that go beyond a capital market environment is not clear. Neither is it clear that the issues facing developing countries can be addressed by simplifying standards devised for use in capital markets, although such an approach may provide a transitional path, as some respondents noted. An IFRS for SMEs was thought to provide little if any relief for developing countries partly because the simplified versions of IFRS that it contained were only those deemed significant for SMEs. Other issues, however, went beyond that omission.

Some respondents worried about the complexity of IFRS and that language barriers may impose disproportionate costs on developing countries. These barriers could easily be under-estimated, but the IASB staff report on the field tests of the ED does at least acknowledge the costs arising and difficulties encountered by IASB staff because some field test material was returned in languages other than English. The ED for this project was the first for which the IASB translated versions in five other European languages, but those languages may not assist in some regions of the world. Obtaining well-translated and up-to-date versions of highly complex technical material is costly, and if those imposing compliance with IFRS on developing countries do not bear the cost, then that cost is imposed on all those required to comply.

Those respondents who raised developing country issues did so on their own initiative, and the IASB's analysis of the responses and of the field tests omits specific mention of developing country issues. The "black box" nature of the standard-setting process and the need to look beyond the public processes to understand standard-setting developments is well-recognised and is a matter for future research as this project proceeds (Howieson, 2008; Hodges & Mellett, 2008). The involvement of major insiders, such as the World Bank, is not apparent. The World Bank, having long sought attention to developing country issues is directly involved in the project, but did not take part in the public submissions process. The documentary evidence presented here suggests that the public submission process may be too late and ineffective for those seeking to influence policy, and the power of insiders largely escapes notice if attention is confined to the documents published as part of the IASB's due process.

The continued imposition and strengthening of the NIFA means that controversies surrounding the application of IFRS in developing countries will continue. This research suggests that those seeking a solution for developing countries may need to both devise an acceptable solution and obtain inside access to the standard-setting process, in order to influence an acceptable policy response.

NOTES

1. The World Bank classifies the 209 countries of the world into three categories: high income (60 countries); middle income (96 countries) and low income (53 countries). The middle income and low income countries (a total of 149) are regarded as "developing" countries (World Bank, 2008). Some developing countries are well-recognised today as significant participants in world trade (for example, China (lower middle income) and India (low income), while others are less so (for example, Kiribati (lower middle income) and Yemen (low income)).

2. Camfferman and Zeff (2006, p. 443) observe that the IASB's international stature has been enhanced by the inclusion of IFRS in the NIFA and the IASB's involvement with the Financial Stability Forum (FSF) which conducts meetings of the international regulators.

3. Compliance with financial reporting standards is not a superficial activity. Adoption of IFRS will necessitate the use of accounting practices and systems designed to facilitate such compliance (Walton, 2006, p. 27). Accounting practices and financial reporting standards are, therefore, tightly linked.

4. The project title and objectives changed in May 2008. At the time of writing, it remains unclear whether this earlier objective has been abandoned.

5. Camfferman and Zeff (2006) describe the IASC's early standard-setting efforts as "tinged with idealism" and conducted from a public interest perspective.

6. One IASB Board member voted against the publication of the ED-IFRS for SMEs. The board member argued that "the proposed IFRS for SMEs is neither necessary nor desirable, because the vast majority of accounting policy decisions of SMEs are straightforward and extensive reference to IFRS to will not be required and, when required, not burdensome" (IASB, 2007b, AV2). The board member also argued that "the Exposure draft is inconsistent with the Constitution of the International Accounting Standards Committee Foundation and the Preface to International Financial Reporting Standards. Those documents set out an objective of a single set of accounting standards taking account of the special needs of small and medium-sized entities and emerging economies" (IASB, 2007b, AV6). The board member accepts the objective, but does not believe that there should be separate sets of standards for entities in differing circumstances.

7. The regional organisations and groupings the IASB reported it planned to work with included: Eastern, Central and Southern African Federation of Accountants (ECSAFA); InterAmerican Accounting Association (IAA); European Federation of Accountants (FEE) and other European organisations; Confederation of Asian and Pacific Accountants (CAPA); South Asian Federation of Accountants (SAFA); European Financial Reporting Advisory Group (EFRAG).

8. These figures (56 companies were from Europe, 36 from Asia-Pacific, 23 from Africa and 3 from America) add up to 118 and not 115 companies. However, this is how it was presented in the IASB Agenda Paper 3. Also no further analysis is given of which American countries the field tests were conducted in, given that some countries in America may be developing countries.

REFERENCES

American Accounting Association (AAA). (1977). Report of the 1975–76 committee on international accounting operations and education. *Accounting Review, 52*(Suppl.), 65–132.
Anon. (1974). Towards an international accounting profession. *Journal of Accountancy* (June), 80–82.
Ashraf, J., & Ghani, W. I. (2005). Accounting development in Pakistan. *The International Journal of Accounting, 40*, 175–201.
Birkland, T. A. (2001). *An introduction to the policy process: Theories, concepts, and models of public policy making*. Armonk, N.Y: M. E. Sharpe, Inc.
Briston, R. J. (1978). The evolution of accounting in developing countries. *International Journal of Accounting Education and Research, 14*(Fall), 105–120.
Camfferman, K., & Zeff, S. A. (2006). *Financial reporting and global capital markets: A history of the international accounting standards committee 1973–2000*. New York: Oxford University Press.
Claessens, S. (2006). Corporate governance and development. *The World Bank Research Observer, 21*(1), 91–122.

Cobb, R. W., & Elder, C. D. (1972). *Participation in American politics: The dynamics of agenda-building.* Boston: Allyn and Bacon.

Cobb, R. W., Ross, J., & Ross, M. H. (1976). Agenda building as a comparative political process. *The American Political Science Review, 70*(1), 126–138.

Confederation of Asia and Pacific Accountants (CAPA). (2003). *A Framework for Differential Reporting: A Response to ISAR's Accounting and Financial Reporting Guidelines for Small and medium-Sized Enterprises (SMEs),* June, http://www.capa.com.my/article.cfm?id = 125, accessed on 5 January 2007.

Enthoven, A. (1965). Economic development and accountancy: The accounting approach can accelerate the economic development which the less developed nations so urgently require. *The Journal of Accountancy* (August), 29–35.

Enthoven, A. (1983). The socioeconomic and international significance of current cost accounting. In: A. Enthoven (Ed.), *Current cost accounting: Its aspects and impacts, proceedings of April 1983 conference* (pp. 93–104). Dallas.

Gerboth, D. (1987). The conceptual framework: Not definitions but professional values. *Accounting Horizons, 1*(3), 1–8.

Hassan, N. A. (1998). The impact of socioeconomic and political environment on accounting system preferences in developing economies. *Advances in International Accounting* (Suppl. 1), 43–88.

Herring, P. (1938). The politics of fiscal policy. *The Yale Law Journal, 47*(5), 724–745.

Hoarau, C. (1995). International accounting harmonisation: American hegemony or mutual recognition with benchmarks? *The European Accounting Review, 4*(2), 217–233.

Hodges, R., & Mellett, H. (2008). *Investigating outside the black box of accounting standard setting.* Sydney: Accounting and Finance Association of Australia and New Zealand (AFAANZ) Conference.

Hove, M. R. (1986). Accounting practices in developing countries: Colonialism's legacy of inappropriate technologies. *International Journal of Accounting Education and Research, 22,* 81–100.

Howieson, B. (2008). *Agenda formation and accounting standards setting: Lessons from the standard setters.* Sydney: Accounting and Finance Association of Australia and New Zealand (AFAANZ) Conference.

International Accounting Standards Board (IASB). (2001). *Press Release: IASB Announces Agenda of Technical Projects,* 31 July, http://www.iasb.org/, accessed on 20 May, 2007.

International Accounting Standards Board (IASB). (2002a). IFRSs and smaller entities. *IASB Insight* (January), 15–16.

International Accounting Standards Board (IASB). (2002b). Accounting and reporting by small and medium-sized entities. *IASB Insight* (October), 15–16.

International Accounting Standards Board (IASB). (2004a). *Discussion Paper: Preliminary Views on Accounting Standards for Small and Medium-Sized Entities,* June, http://www.iasb.org/Current + Projects/IASB + Projects/Small+and+Medium-sized+Entities/Small+and+Medium-sized+Entities.htm, accessed on 15 March 2006.

International Accounting Standards Board (IASB). (2004b). *Archive IASB Project-Comment Letters: Discussion Paper Preliminary Views on Accounting Standards for Small and Medium-sized Entities,* 6 October 2004: http://www.iasb.org/Archive/Archive+IASB+Project+-+Comment+Letters.htm#sme, accessed on 5 October 2007.

International Accounting Standards Board (IASB). (2004c). Standard for small and medium-sized entities. *IASB Insight* (January), 1–15.

International Accounting Standards Board (IASB). (2004d). Comments invited on proposals for standards for SMEs. *IASB Insight* (July), 1–17.
International Accounting Standards Board (IASB). (2005a). Accounting Standards for Small and Medium-Sized Entities (SMEs). *IASB Insight* (January), 1–16.
International Accounting Standards Board (IASB). (2005b). *Staff questionnaire on possible recognition and measurement modifications for small and medium-sized entities (SMEs)*, http://www.iasb.org / NR / rdonlyres / A6BB4F8C - 1866-4FB6-94A4-AB04575884DB/0/ SMEquestionnaire.doc, assessed on 10 February 2008.
International Accounting Standards Board (IASB). (2005c). *SME questionnaire*, http:// www.iasb.org/Current+Projects/IASB + Projects/Small+and + Medium-sized+Entities/ SME+Questionnaire.htm, assessed on 10 February 2008.
International Accounting Standards Board (IASB). (2007a). *Exposure draft of a proposed IFRS for small and medium-sized entities*, February, http://www.iasb.org/NR/rdonlyres/ DFF3CB5E-7C89-4D0B-AB85-BC099E84470F/0/SMEProposed26095.pdf, accessed on 15 March 2007.
International Accounting Standards Board (IASB). (2007b). *Basis for conclusions on exposure draft*: *IFRS for small and medium-sized entities*, February, http://www.iasb.org/ Current + Projects/IASB + Projects/Small + and + Medium-sized + Entities/Exposure + Drafts+for+Small+and+Medium-sized+Entities/Exposure+Drafts+for+Small+and+ Medium-sized+Entities.htm, accessed on 15 March 2007.
International Accounting Standards Board (IASB). (2007c). *A staff overview; exposure draft of a proposed IFRS for small and medium-sized entities*, February, http://www.iasb.org/ NR/ rdonlyres / 17150CAC-08DB-4B74-90CE-DBB2CF540167 / 0/SMEs_Overview.pdf, accessed on 15 April 2007.
International Accounting Standards Board (IASB). (2007d). IASB publishes draft IFRS for SMEs December. *IASB Insight* (March), 1–19.
International Accounting Standards Board (IASB). (2007e). *Field test of SME exposure draft*, http://www.iasb.org / NR / rdonlyres / 2A33A8EE-6665-45A4-987A-16CE8FB8888F / 0 / FieldTestDocument.doc, assessed on 5 February 2008.
International Accounting Standards Board (IASB). (2007f). *Exposure draft for IFRS for small and medium-sized entities: Comment letters*, http://www.iasb.org/Current+Projects/ IASB + Projects / Small + and+Medium-sized+Entities/Exposure+Drafts+for+Small+ and+Medium-sized+Entities/Comment+Letters/Comment+Letters.htm, accessed on 16 December 2007.
International Accounting Standards Board (IASB). (2007g). *International financial reporting standard for small and medium-sized entities (IFRS for SMEs)*, December, http://www. iasb.org/NR/rdonlyres/BBF5F938-93E7-44D1-85FD-A87D35415F03/0/SMEprojectup dateDec07.pdf, accessed on 23 February 2008.
International Accounting Standards Board (IASB). (2008a). *SAC meeting agenda 3*, http:// www.iasb.org/NR/rdonlyres/C71BBC36-8FBA-42F6-9F4D-286E433E9695/0/AP3.pdf, accessed on 22 February, 2008.
International Accounting Standards Board (IASB). (2008b). *Information for observers: IFRS for small and medium-sized entities – overview of key issues raised in comment letters and project plan (agenda paper 4)*, 12 March, 2008, http://www.iasb.org/Meetings/ IASB+Board+Meeting+12+March+2008.htm, accessed on 03 March, 2008.
International Accounting Standards Board (IASB). (2008c). *Information for observers: IFRS for small and medium-sized entities – summary of issues raised in the field tests (Agenda Paper 6)*, 6 April 2008.

International Accounting Standards Board (IASB). (2008d). *IFRS for private entities,* http://
www.iasb.org/Current+Projects/IASB+Projects/Small+and+Medium-sized+Entities/
Small+and+Medium-sized+Entities.htm, downloaded on 25 July 2008.

Jones, S., Rahman, S. F., & Wolnizer, P. W. (2004). Accounting reform in Australia:
Contrasting cases of agenda building. *Abacus, 40*(3), 379–404.

Jordan, C., & Majnoni, G. (2002). *Financial regulatory harmonisation and the globalisation of
finance.* World Bank Policy Research Working Paper 2919. World Bank.

Kingdon, J. W. (1984). *Agendas, alternatives, and public policies.* Boston: Little, Brown and
Company.

Klumpes, P. J. M. (1994). The politics of rule development: A case study of Australian pension
fund accounting rule-making. *Abacus, 30*(2), 140–159.

Mahon, J. (1965). Some observations on world accounting. *The Journal of Accountancy*
(January), 33–37.

McNamara, R. (1973). *One hundred countries, two billion people: The dimensions of development.*
London: Praeger Publications.

Mir, M. Z., & Rahaman, A. (2005). The adoption of international accounting standards in
Bangladesh: An exploration of rationale and process. *International Journal of Accounting,
18*(6), 816–841.

Mould, M. (1983). International aspects of current cost accounting. In: A. Enthoven (Ed.),
Current cost accounting: Its aspects and impacts, proceedings of April 1983 conference
(pp. 83–86). Dallas.

Nobes, C. (1998). *Accounting in developing economies: Questions about users, uses and appropriate
reporting practices.* London: The Association of Chartered Certified Accountants.

Perera, M. H. B. (1985). *The relevance of international accounting standards to developing
countries.* Working Paper 85-8, School of Financial Studies. Scotland: University of
Glasgow.

Perera, M. H. B. (1989). Accounting in developing countries: A case for localised uniformity.
British Accounting Review, 21, 141–158.

Points, R., & Cunningham, R. (1998). The application of international accounting standards in
transitional societies and developing countries. *Advances in International Accounting*
(Suppl.), 3–16.

Samuels, J. M., & Oliga, J. C. (1982). Accounting standards in developing countries.
International Journal of Accounting Education and Research, 18(1), 69–88.

Scott, G. M. (1968). Private enterprise accounting in developing nations. *International Journal
of Accounting Education and Research,* (Fall).

Soederberg, S. (2002). On the contradictions of the New International Financial
Architecture: another procrustean bed for emerging markets? *Third World Quarterly,
23*(4), 607–620.

Soederberg, S. (2003). The promotion of 'Anglo-American' corporate governance in the South:
Who benefits from the new international standard? *Third World Quarterly, 24*(1), 7–27.

SyCip, W. (1967). Professional practice in developing economies. *Journal of Accountancy*
(January), 41–45.

SyCip, W. (1979). The role of CAPA in achieving harmonization. *Accountant's Journal
(Philippines Institute of Certified Public Accountants), 29*(3/4), 14–22.

SyCip, W. (1981). Establishing and applying standards in diverse economic and social
environments. In: J. C. Burton (Ed.), *The International World of Accounting: Challenges
and Opportunities (1980 Proceedings of the Arthur Young Professor's Roundtable)*
(pp. 85–96). Virginia: The Council of Arthur Professor, Reston.

Talaga, J. A., & Ndubizu, G. (1986). Accounting and economic development: Relationships among paradigms. *International Journal of Accounting Education and Research*, *21*(2), 55–68.

United Nations Conference on Trade and Development (UNCTAD). (2007). *Report of the Intergovernmental Working Group of Experts on international standards of accounting and reporting on its twenty-third session, TD/B/COM.2/ISAR/35/*, 9 January, 2007. http:// www.unctad.org/en/docs/c2isard35_en.pdf, accessed on February 2008.

Walker, R. G., & Robinson, S. P. (1994). Competing regulatory agencies with conflicting agendas: Setting standards for cash flow reporting in Australia. *Abacus*, *30*(1), 18–43.

Wallace, R. S. O. (1990). Accounting in developing countries: A review of the literature. *Research in Third World Accounting*, *1*, 3–54.

Wallace, R. S. O., & Briston, R. (1993). Improving the accounting infrastructure in developing countries. *Research in Third World Accounting*, *2*, 201–224.

Walton, P. (1998). There's more to it than just lending $20bn. *Accounting and Business*, (April), 10, 12, and 16.

Walton, P. (2006). Boardroom battles. *The Financial Regulator*, *10*(4), 25–30.

Walton, P. (2007). *Technical report: Draft SME standard*, http://www.essec-kpmg.net/fr/ recherche/pdf/projet-normes-pme.pdf, accessed on 30 July 2008.

World Bank. (2008). *Country classification*, http://web.worldbank.org/WBSITE/EXTERNAL/ DATASTATISTICS/0,,contentMDK:20420458~menuPK:64133156~pagePK:64133150 ~piPK:64133175~theSitePK:239419,00.html, accessed on 10 January 2008.

THE BANKS' USES OF SMALLER COMPANIES' FINANCIAL INFORMATION IN THE EMERGING ECONOMY OF VIETNAM: A USER'S ORIENTED MODEL

Son Dang-Duc, Neil Marriott and Pru Marriott

ABSTRACT

Purpose – *The aim of this study is to provide insights into the factors affecting the banks' use of financial information in financial statements of small- and medium-sized enterprise (SME) which has implications for the governance of these important organizations. Specifically, this study assesses the views of bank lending officers on their demand for and use of financial information relating to SMEs.*

Design/methodology/approach – *The study uses the data collected from a quantitative study in the form of a postal questionnaire survey. The model is constructed based on the data collected and the use of structural equation modelling (SEM).*

Findings – *The research finds that the main factor affecting the use of financial information is the directors' perceptions of the role of accounting. Bank lending officers tend to use a great variety of sources*

Corporate Governance in Less Developed and Emerging Economies
Research in Accounting in Emerging Economies, Volume 8, 519–548
ISSN: 1479-3563/doi:10.1016/S1479-3563(08)08017-1

of information to make lending decisions and do not rely on financial information provided by SMEs. Direct contacts with the SMEs were extensively used and were perceived as having a significant effect on the utility of information.

Research limitations/implications – *The limitation of the study lies in the relatively small sample of respondents and the response rate.*

Practical implications – *The model is important as it can aid the banks' understanding of the business activities of the smaller company sector. This leads to improved relationships between the banks and smaller companies and more positive lending decisions.*

Originality/value –*The model is of interest to the banks and other parties. The model may also be of interest to accounting regulators and standard setters to clarify the issue of how financial information of smaller companies is used. The model implies the revision of the current reporting frameworks to improve the transparency of the corporate governance in SMEs in the context of the less developed reporting environment of transitional economies.*

1. INTRODUCTION

Previous studies suggest that the improvement in information flows between banks and businesses were crucial for small- and medium-sized enterprise (SME) to improve governance mechanisms, therefore increasing firm's accountability and reducing the pressure on collateral requirements to access to bank finance. For example, Le, Venkatesh, and Nguyen (2006) argue that SME growth constraints were usually associated with informational constraints, the need for support services and the inefficient information exchange between SMEs and financial providers. Tagoe, Nyarko, and Anuwa-Amarh (2005) also argue that small firms perceived access to finance as their most significant constraint on meeting their business objectives.

It is argued that the information constraints are not only the fault of companies, but also users of the information are also to blame. Banks, as the principal in the credit relationship, have power to exert corporate governance over firms, especially small firms that have no direct access to financial markets. However, this depends extensively on the amount and quality of financial information provided. In a survey on the finance gap in small- and medium-sized firms in Eastern European countries, Lloyd-Reason, Marinova, & Nicolescu (2000) argue that in transitional economies, banks, which had poorly developed risk assessment skills, had little understanding of the SME sector and the financial instruments available were often inappropriate to the needs of the SMEs. Small firms face difficulty in accessing finance because their governance regime, including information and managerial system, is not transparent enough for potential investors to rely on when making an investment decision (Sarapaivanich & Kotey, 2006). Poor accounting records in SMEs also made it difficult for information users, such as banks, to assess risks and future returns and therefore created funding problems for the companies and high risks for lenders (O'Connor, 2000).

The relationship between banks and smaller companies are important for the economic growth of transitional economies where banks and SMEs have little history of working together (Nguyen, Le, & Freeman, 2006). Small and medium companies comprise the majority of the number of registered companies in Vietnam.[1] The Statistics Year Book 2004 supplied by the General Statistics Office shows that small- and medium-sized enterprises account for more than 90% of total number of firms and more than 89% of job creation. Further analysis on the data shows that about 2.5% of these small businesses are companies contributing roughly 18% of the Vietnam's GDP. SMEs also have been reported to be the fastest growing sector in the economy with the annual growth rate in the number of companies about 30% each year for the last 10 years (GSO, 2006). However, smaller companies in Vietnam are characterised as operating in an under-developed institutional environment which has a profound effect on governance and on to the availability of their financial choices. Owing to the effect of the former socialist economic model, the financial regulations seem to be more 'rule based' rather than 'principle based' (Yang & Nguyen, 2003). The Vietnamese accounting system is a mixture of a uniform chart of accounts with detailed guidance and a new system of the Vietnamese Accounting Standards (VASs) which are very similar to the international standards (VAC-Deloitte, 2003). The Vietnamese accounting system for SMEs is a simplified model of the Vietnamese accounting system which was primarily designed for large state-owned enterprises. However, as Nguyen and Bryant (2004) argues, the disclosure requirements might not cover certain aspects of a company's operations and might not present all the information needed for the decision-making process of external users. As a result, SMEs may have to pay a higher rate in less competitive lending markets (Blackwell and Winters, 2000).

This paper contributes to this research area by developing a structural model of the banks' uses of financial information provided by SMEs in the context of the transitional economy of Vietnam. The main purpose of the study is to provide insights into the factors affecting the utility of financial information in financial statements of SMEs. Practically, the study attempts to assess the views of bank lending officers on their demand for and use of financial information of SMEs. The study provides empirical evidence to extend the findings of previous work in terms of the banks' uses of financial information of SMEs in developed countries (e.g. Berry, Faulkner, Hughes, & Jarvis, 1993; Deakins & Hussain, 1994) and transitional countries (Le et al., 2006). The investigation uses the data collected from a quantitative study, namely a postal questionnaire survey. The model is based on the use of structural equation modelling (SEM) of quantitative evidence to test the results derived from a qualitative study (Dang, Marriott, & Marriott, 2006). The model reveals that the main factor affecting the use of financial information is the directors' perceptions of the role of accounting and bank lending officers tend to use a great variety of sources of information to make lending decisions. Direct contacts between the bank lending offices and the companies were widely used and were perceived as having a significant effect on the utility of information.

2. LITERATURE REVIEW ON BANKS AND THEIR USE OF FINANCIAL INFORMATION

The theoretical framework of the study stems from the decision-usefulness theory. This theory, as argued by Gray, Owen, and Adams (1996), attempts to describe accounting as a process of providing the relevant information to the relevant decision makers. Staubus (2000) introduced the decision-usefulness theory as a base for making accounting choices. He argues that the theory was based on the decision-usefulness objective which specified investors as the defining class of the user of financial statements. As a consequence, the investors' cash-flow oriented decisions had a profound impact on the choices of measurement and reporting.

As the banks are the main external source of finance for small businesses, they are one of the main users of company financial information. In a study comparing the uses of lending officers of financial information of small versus large companies, Page (1984) identifies that the intensity of use of financial reports was likely to be different between small and large companies. Danos, Holt, and Imholff (1989) found that the quality of the accounting data of small business borrowers is very inconsistent and was sometimes of limited use to lenders. In addition, the quality of information tends to increase in accordance with the size the business.

The information relationship between banks and smaller companies has been a topic of discussion and debate in developed countries. In a study on bank lending behaviour, Berry, Crum, and Waring (1993) identified that financial reports played a significant role within the lending process. However, the poor accounting records of SMEs made institutional creditors and the government reluctant to lend the needed amounts. In addition, the study reveals that while credit references and transaction history were important in making lending decisions, only a limited amount of the information was approved to reduce potential risks and to assure the returns. It is also notable from the study that financial information in financial statements was not used directly, but converted to a standard evaluation form to access loan applications. Deakins and Hussain (1994) examined bank manager assessments of small firm propositions under conditions of uncertainty and asymmetric information. Their study reveals that bank managers relied on a narrow range of financial information on the business and personal assets and income generation such as forecast balance sheets and profit and loss accounts. However, their study also admitted that little discussion was given to the information on the appropriateness of the risk assessment of small firm propositions. Kent and Munro (1999) found that the judgments of bank loan officers' assessment of the repayment ability are not significantly affected by differential reporting. However, bankers request additional information from borrowers when non-GAAP financial reports are presented. In a similar study, Berry, Grant, and Jarvis (2003) state that there are two main types of banks' approach to lending decisions, namely going concern approach and gone concern (liquidity) approach and the use of different approaches affect to their use of financial information.

The relationship between banks and SMEs has been the subject of much research effort in less developed countries. For example, in another study on the relationship between banks and small firms in the post-socialist economy of Poland, Feakins (2001) argues that the solutions to financial problems of SMEs in developed countries were not available in transitional economies. Based on these findings, he concluded that "SMEs in the post-socialist transformation context experience particular problems and solutions that are specific to their own circumstances" (p. 6). The findings were supported by Ronnas and Ramamurthy (2001) and Kokko and Sjoholm (2005) that shortages of capital emerged as the most frequent and serious constraint in the development of small non-state enterprises. It can be argued that research and other work published in the area of banking and smaller companies does not attempt to make any comparisons between those in developed and less developed countries.

Like other transitional countries, Vietnam has a bank dominated financial system where banks account for more than 90% of financial intermediation and informal credit such as private lending and informal financial markets remain significant. The financial sectors consist of a central bank with many affiliates whose main functions were to dispense credit to state-own enterprises and there was little evidence on the relationship between the general purpose of financial statements and the uses by external users (O'Connor, 2000). Le et al. (2006) surveyed small firms to identify how the firm owners persuaded banks to make needed loans. They noted that firm legitimacy, growth stages and business networks positively affect the accessibility of Vietnamese small firms to bank financing. However, it is implied from this study that a user perspective also needed to be taken into account. In another empirical study, Nguyen et al. (2006) interviewed 23 bankers and found that financial information was critical for making lending decisions of the banks. However, banks had to make lending decisions in the absence of business data. They also argued that banks employed a combination of uncertainty avoidance and reliance on trust in lending to their private business clients. However, as this work is purely qualitative, Nguyen et al. (2006) indicated a need for quantitative evidence to verify their findings, which is the content of this current work.

3. RESEARCH METHODOLOGY AND DATA

3.1. Research Hypotheses

The study is a research attempt to provide answers to one main research question:

What factors affecting the banks' uses of financial information of SMEs?

The review of the relevant literature and the results of the preliminary interviews conducted in the earlier stage of the study (Dang et al., 2006) identified seven factors that might have an impact to the use of the information, including the purpose of the use of information, the methods of communication between the preparers and users, the attitude of the directors towards accounting, the quality of financial information, the role of the auditor's report and of the Vietnamese accounting standards and the perceptions of the cost-benefit relationship. Based on these conclusions, seven hypotheses were constructed:

Hypothesis H1

H_0. There is no association between the usefulness of information and the purposes of the use of information.

Previous studies (Dang et al., 2006) have indicated that users had different purposes of using information and these specific purposes had an impact on their perception of the usefulness of information. Therefore, this hypothesis is constructed to provide evidence on whether a specific purpose of users has an impact to the usefulness of the information.

Hypothesis H2

H_0. There is no association between the method of the communication and use of financial information.

This hypothesis concerns the main methods of communication of financial information between the company and outside parties in terms of the content, method and frequency of communication. The hypothesis is based on the assumptions that there were alternative ways to the traditional method of providing financial statements. The alternative methods were perceived important in communication between SMEs and the bank lending officers.

Hypothesis H3

H_0. There is no association between the directors' perceptions of the role of accounting and the use of the information in the financial statements.

This hypothesis is constructed to provide evidence for the assumption that the directors' perceptions of the role of accounting had a strong effect on the quality of information provided.

Hypothesis H4

H_0. There is no association between the quality and the utility of financial information provided by SMEs.

This hypothesis is about the users' perceptions of the quality of information in terms of four major characteristics that make financial information useful to the users: reliability, relevance, timeliness and comparability. The findings from previous studies demonstrated that the quality of information was a major concern of the users about the financial information provided by SMEs.

Hypothesis H5

H_0. There is no association between the auditor's report and the use of financial information of SMEs.

This hypothesis is about the role of audit in the use of financial information. The issue focused on audit costs and the potential benefits the company might received from audit services.

Hypothesis H6

H_0. There is no association between the application of accounting standards and the use of financial information of SMEs.

This hypothesis considers the role of accounting standards in the use of financial information of SMEs. As the national accounting standards were intended to be applied to all companies regardless of their size and industry, more research is needed on their application to SMEs and how the bank lending officers perceive the role of accounting standards in their use of financial information.

Hypothesis H7

H_0. There is no association between the perceptions of cost–benefit perceptions and the use of financial information.

This hypothesis considers the awareness of the banks about the cost–benefit considerations of the provision of financial information. There was evidence from the qualitative study (Dang et al., 2006) that there was a lack of cost–benefit considerations among users of information and the relationships between the costs and benefits were also not well perceived.

3.2. Data Collection and Analysis

Surveys seem to be appropriate once the hypotheses and their corresponding variables have been developed. Oppenheim (1992) suggests that the survey questionnaire is suitable for respondents to answer a large number systematic questions. It is also appropriate to explore the perceptions and opinions of respondents upon specific research issues. Roberts (1999) suggests that the survey method is the most common approach to provide empirical evidence on characteristics and sociological variables. The construction of the hypotheses and variables for the study was followed by the development of the questionnaire. The questions were structured in a way which enables the subsequent analysis to provide the support or otherwise for the hypotheses. The respondents were asked to provide responses to 25 specific questions.

It is recognised that SMEs, especially those in transitional economies, are notorious for low response rates to questionnaire surveys and for providing limited comments. Therefore, many standard response enhancing techniques were adopted to improve the response rates of the survey. The questionnaire was designed with clear and simple formats and instructions were provided at the beginning of all sections and on the top of every answer box (see appendix). In addition, as Dillman (2000) suggested, each questionnaire was accompanied by a covering letter explaining the purpose and significance of the research and emphasising the contribution the respondents would make to the research by filling out the questionnaire. The respondents were guaranteed anonymity and confidentiality of their answers and the research findings were available to the respondents if requested. The questionnaires were also sent with a self-addressed free-post envelope to facilitate the return of the questionnaires. Furthermore, follow-up letters were sent to all respondents approximately three weeks after the first request.

The most appropriate database for sampling frame is the Business Information Centre Database (VietBic) which is the most up-to-date and comprehensive sources of information. A search on VietBic produced a list of 812 banks including bank branches, credit institutions and the People Credit Funds. On average, each institution had 6 credit officers. Therefore the population was equivalent to $812 \times 6 = 4872$ bank lending officers. Random sampling was employed at the 1:20 scale. This method produced a sample of 244 bank lending officers. Copies of the questionnaire were sent to all members of this sample. Data collection involved sending out the questionnaires in early March 2006 resulting in 68 questionnaires returned.

Although the postal survey produced low response rates (i.e. 27.8%), this was expected (e.g. William & Dennis, 2003). A review of literature has shown that similar studies in developed countries have experienced low response rates. For example, Poutziouris, Chittenden, and Michaelas (1998) experienced a very low response rate of 11.5%, Collis (2003) also experienced a response rate of 17%. It is also recognised that business size and response rates are positively related in that greater response rates can be expected from larger businesses (Marriott & Marriott, 1999; Curran & Blackburn, 2001) and low response rates "do not mean results are unrepresentative" (Curran, 2000, p. 40).

Since the study involved in a number of variables, factor analysis is used to reduce the number of variables and to interpret the meaning of the correlations. Factor analysis is used in combination with SEM to construct and to test the fitness of the model with the data collected. The reason to perform SEM rather than traditional regression is that SEM is the advanced development of traditional multiple regression. The true power of SEM is to allow the researcher to construct the model and test it with the data many times until the model is fitted to the data (Byrne, 2001). In this way the researcher can make full control and deep understanding of the process. However, as an obstacle for SEM is its difficulty in handling categorical variables (Skrondal & Rabe-Hesketh, 2005); the general approach of SEM is modified to accommodate dichotomous and categorical variables. To facilitate the use of SEM, an endogenous variable (USEFUL) was created by summing the individual scores and dividing by the number of variables ($n = 15$). This variable is used with factors extracted from factor analysis to build and test the models using AMOS software (version 6.0).

4. RESULTS

4.1. Factor Analysis

Exploratory factor analysis was used with five groups of variables in indicating the impact of different factors to the usefulness of financial information. The variables and their corresponding components were presented in Table 1.

Before factor analysis was used, all the variables in Table 1 were screened to look for correlation among the variables. The tests showed that correlation existed among the variable in each group. Therefore factor analysis could be used to reduce the number of the variables.

All the variables in Table 1 were included in factor analysis resulting in 11 factors extracted. It is recognised that input variables loaded highly in their corresponding factors. Where the factors were extracted, the absolute coefficient values were of more than 0.65 with all the variables. Table 2 presents the results of factor analysis.

Table 1. Factors Affecting the Use of Financial Information – Factor Analysis.

Components	Loading Variables
The purpose of the use of information (FACPUR)	Taxation purpose (USETAX)
	Government control (USEGOV)
	Lending decisions (USELEND)
	Investment (USEINVE)
	Business contracts (USECON)
The use of alternative methods of communication between users and preparers (FACCOM)	Direct submission (ACCEDIRE)
	Financial advice (ACCEADV)
	Database (ACCEDATA)
	Colleagues (ACCECOLE)
	Internet (ACCEINTE)
	Direct contact (ACCEDIAC)
	Rumour (ACCERUM)
The role of statutory audit in improving the quality of financial information (FACAUD)	Fulfil legal requirements (AUDLAW)
	Verify business performance (AUDCONF)
	Strengthen the control system (AUDCNTL)
	Provide recommendation/advice (AUDRECO)
The role of accounting standards in financial reporting process (FACVAS)	Increase reporting costs (INCCOST)
	Increase the complexity (INCCOM)
	Increase quality of information (INCQLTY)
	Increase the uniformity (INCUNIF)
Other factors (FACOTH)	Educational background (EDUBAGR)
	Management skills (MGNTSKI)
	Directors' perceptions (MGNTPER)
	Capability of accountants (CABLACT)
	Role of audit (ROLEAUD)

It should be noted from Table 2 that the variable representing the purpose of using information for investment (USEINVE) loads highly on two factors (FACPUR11 and FACPUR12) with coefficients of 0.670 and 0.427, respectively, indicating that there is significant correlation between these variables. Therefore, as suggested by Field (2005), an oblimin rotation was employed to maximise the correlation among variables while recognising the association between these two factors.

Apart from the variables generated from factor analysis, two other variables measuring the perceptions of the cost–benefit relationship (COSBEN) and an improvement in quality of information (IMPQLTY) were included in the test of the structural model.

Table 2.   The Factors Affecting the Utility of Financial Information.

Factors	Description	Measure	Eigenvalue		Loading Variables[c]
			Value	% Variance	
FACOTH11	The directors' ability and perceptions of accounting	Ratio	2.525	50.502	EDUBAGR, MGNTSKI, MGNTPER
FACOTH12	The alternative sources for improvement in the quality of information	Ratio	1.419	28.384	CABLACT, ROLEAUD
FACPUR11[a]	Financial information is used to meet legal requirements and economic transactions	Ratio	2.596	51.925	USETAX, USEGOV, USEINVE, USECON
FACPUR12[a]	Financial information is used for making lending decisions	Ratio	1.230	24.607	USELEND
FACCOM11	Indirect methods of access to financial information	Ratio	2.528	36.111	ACCECOLE, ACCEDATA, ACCEINTE, ACCEADV
FACCOM12	Direct contact with the company in the utility of financial information	Ratio	1.245	17.789	ACCEDIRE, ACCEDIAC
FACCOM13	Other methods of communication: rumour	Ratio	1.047	14.956	ACCERUM
FACAUD11	Fulfil legal requirements and improve internal management	Ratio	1.958	48.958	AUDLAW, AUDCNTL, AUDRECO
FACAUD12[b]	Verify business performance	Ratio	0.888	22.188	AUDCONF
FACVAS11	The impact of accounting standards on increasing quality and uniformity of information	Ratio	1.917	47.914	INCQLTY, INCUNIF
FACVAS12	The impact of accounting standards on increasing costs and complexity of financial reporting	Ratio	1.567	39.164	INCCOST, INCCOM

[a]Rotation method: Oblimin with Kaiser normalization.
[b]Eigenvalue is of less than 1.
[c]Variables are loaded on each factor with absolute coefficient values of more than 0.65.

4.2. The Structural Model

All the variables were included in AMOS to perform analysis and to test the appropriateness of models. A model is acceptable when it fits relatively well to the data. The statistics of regression estimates and their corresponding probabilities are represented in Table 3.

Table 3 shows that the model relatively fitted to the data with the ratio of χ^2/degree of freedom (CMIN/DF) of between two and five (i.e. 2.068) which is indicative of an acceptable fit (Carmines & McIver, 1981). The directors' ability and perceptions of accounting (FACOTH11), direct contact with the company in the utility of financial information (FACCOM12), the impact of accounting standards on increasing costs and complexity of financial reporting (FACVAS12) are the most important factors affecting the banks' perceptions of the usefulness of financial information with coefficients being significant at $p < 0.01$. The role of audit in verifying business performance (FACAUD12) and the purpose of using financial information to meet legal requirements and economic transactions (FACPUR11) have the least influence on the utility of information. The regression weights in the model provide significant evidence to reject hypotheses H1, H2, H3, H5 and H6 while there is no significant evidence to reject the hypotheses H4 and H7. The summary of the seven hypotheses in the study is presented in Table 4.

Table 3. Model of Factors Affecting the Use of Information – Regression Weights.

		Estimate	SE	CR	P
USEFUL	← FACOTH11	.156	.041	3.807	.000
USEFUL	← FACOTH12	.045	.046	.981	.327
USEFUL	← FACCOM11	.036	.046	.770	.441
USEFUL	← FACCOM12	.117	.043	2.702	.007
USEFUL	← FACCOM13	−.092	.046	−1.999	.046
USEFUL	← FACPUR11	−.032	.041	−.769	.442
USEFUL	← FACPUR12	.318	.130	2.445	.015
USEFUL	← FACAUD11	.120	.050	2.392	.017
USEFUL	← FACAUD12	.037	.053	.694	.488
USEFUL	← FACVAS11	−.047	.047	−1.005	.315
USEFUL	← FACVAS12	−.132	.046	−2.869	.004
USEFUL	← IMPQLTY	−.121	.148	−.816	.414
USEFUL	← COSBEN1	.188	.108	1.734	.083
FACPUR12	↔ FACPUR11	.034	.047	.731	.465

Model fit summary (default model): χ^2: 159.231; degree of freedom: 77, CMIN/DF: 2.068.

Table 4.   Hypotheses on the Factors Affecting the Utility of
Information.

Hypothesis	Null Hypothesis (H_0)	Accepted/ Rejected
H1	There is no association between the usefulness and the purpose of the use of information	Rejected
H2	There is no association between the methods of communication and the utility of information	Rejected
H3	There is no association between the director's perceptions of the role of accounting and the usefulness of information.	Rejected
H4	There is no association between the quality of information and the utility of information	Accepted
H5	There is no association between the auditor's report and the utility of information	Rejected
H6	There is no association between the accounting standards and the utility of information	Rejected
H7	There is no association between the perceptions of cost–benefit and the use of financial information	Accepted

It is notable that the regression coefficients of the five variables (FACCOM13, FACPUR11, FACVAS11, FACVAS12 and IMPQLTY) are negative. These indicate that there is a negative impact of these factors on the use of information. The negative impact of the use of information (FACPUR11) may indicate that the users perceive a 'less decision-usefulness' perspective in the use of information for their duties. The results also suggest that the perceptions of the role of accounting standards (FACVAS11 and FACVAS12) also have less impact on the use of information. The negative significant impact of the need for improvement in the quality of data (IMPQLTY) on the utility of information means that there is concern over the quality of information provided by SMEs. The impact of the above variables on the use of financial information is depicted in Fig. 1 and the section that follows provides a deeper insight into the structural model.

4.3. Discussion on the Structural Model

The model reveals that the main factors affecting the use of financial information is the directors' perceptions of the role of accounting (FACOTH11) with correlation coefficient at 0.156 (0.16), followed by the direct contact with the company in the utility of financial information (FACCOM12) with correlation coefficient at 0.117 (0.12) and the impact of

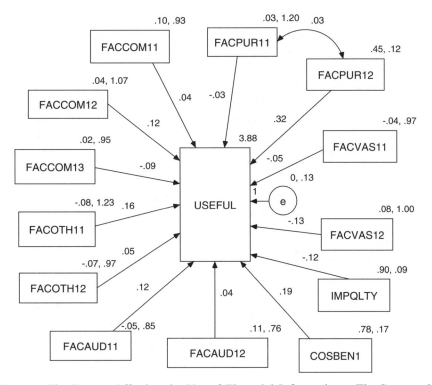

Fig. 1. The Factors Affecting the Use of Financial Information – The Structural Model.

accounting standards on increasing costs and complexity of financial reporting (FACVAS12) with correlation coefficient at −0.132 (−0.13). As addressed above, these coefficients are significant with $p < 0.01$.

The model tends to support the findings of Le et al. (2006) that management practices have a positive impact on the accessibility to bank financing. More specifically, the model indicates that small scale and close managerial structure of the companies result in the sizeable impact of the director's view of the accounting information to the banks' use of financial information.

Nguyen et al. (2006) argue that banks in Vietnam had to make lending decisions in the absence of small business data. As a result, they had to rely on trust and had to face considerable uncertainties. The model tends to support this argument. The model reveals that many of the items in the financial statements are not useful to the banks and banks have to rely on the alternative sources of financial information such as site visits, rather than the information in the financial statements, to assess the financial position of the companies. However, they have to face uncertainties and cope with the low quality of information, such as the lack of comparability of information. This leads to the banks' perceptions of smaller companies as 'high risk' and in many cases, leads to the suspension of making appropriate lending decisions.

In contrast to the findings of Berry (2006), the study found that direct communication between the banks and their clients play an important role in the bank–small company relationship. Bank lending officers tended to use direct contact such as site visit to smaller clients to obtain the information they needed.

It should be noted that while national accounting standards are applied to all companies regardless of their size and industry, the model presented in Fig. 1 reveals that the banks perceived them as regulatory burdensome. Current accounting standards were perceived as increasing the cost and complexity of accounting regulations. This result tends to support of the establishment of a differential reporting regime for small and medium companies in Vietnam. The model also reveals that there is a lack of the banks' perceptions of the costs and benefits of the provision of financial information. It is recognised that a better understanding of the cost–benefit relationship is not only useful for the preparers but also for the users of information to evaluate the quality of the information.

5. CONCLUSION

Key stakeholders in SME are the banks, who are their main providers of debt finance. The governance of SMEs in terms of verifying performance and managing expectations is affected by the quality of the information they provide to their banks. The information exchange between banks and SMEs is also instrumental for the bank to exert corporate governance over SME clients. This study examines the banks' perceptions and uses of financial information of smaller companies in a transitional economy. The study is based on the postal survey with a sample of bank lending officers in Vietnam. Factor analysis and SEM were employed to construct a model of the factors affecting the utility of financial information.

The model reveals that the main factor affecting the use of financial information is the directors' perceptions of the role of accounting. Supporting the findings of the previous studies, this study provided evidence that bank lending officers tend to use a great variety of sources of information to make lending decisions. In addition, direct submission such as site visits, were widely used and these had a significant effect on the utility of information. Audit was seen as having less importance than other factors in the utility of information.

The limitation of the study lies in the sample of the respondents and response rate. The researchers were challenged by small sample sizes, low response rates and a large number of missing variables. In addition, the narrow focus of a user group suggests that more research should be conducted on another transitional economy to arrive at appropriate conclusions.

In spite of the above limitations, the model is of interest to the banks and other parties. Banks and other institutional creditors may use this model as a reference for their current perceptions and use of financial information of SMEs. The model is important to aid the banks' understanding of the business activities of the smaller company sector. This leads to improved relationships between the banks and smaller companies and more positive lending decisions. As most of the banks in transitional economies lack necessary experience in dealing with small private companies, the model is critical to them to improve their current lending practices. The model may also be of interest to accounting regulators and standard setters to clarify the issue of how financial information of smaller companies is used. The model implies the revision of the current reporting frameworks to improve the transparency of the corporate governance in SMEs in the context of the less developed reporting environment of transitional economies.

NOTE

1. SMEs are defined as independent companies with less than 300 employees or registered working capital of less than 10 billion VND (equivalent to US$620,000) (VieGov, 2001).

ACKNOWLEDGMENTS

The authors are grateful to the respondents who participated in the interviews as well as to those that commented upon the presentation at the Financial Reporting & Business Communication-Eleventh Annual Conference, Cardiff Business School, Cardiff, 5–6 July 2007 and the presentation at the British Accounting Association Annual Conference, Imperial Hotel, Blackpool, 1–3 April 2008. They are also grateful for the comments and suggestions made by reviewers and editors.

REFERENCES

Berry, A. (2006). *Banks, SMEs and accountants-an international study of SMEs' banking relation-ships*. Research Report No. 95, The Association of Chartered Certified Accountants.

Berry, A., Faulkner, S., Hughes, M., & Jarvis, R. (1993). *Financial information, the banker and the small businesses*. Occasional Research Paper No. 14, University of Brighton Business School, Brighton.

Berry, A., Grant, P., & Jarvis, R. (2003). *Can the European banks plug the finance gap for UK's SMEs?* ACCA Research Report No. 81, The Association of Chartered Certified Accountants.

Berry, R. H., Crum, R. E., & Waring, A. (1993). *Corporate evaluation in bank lending decision*. London: CIMA.

Blackwell, D. W., & Winters, D. B. (2000). Local lending markets: What a small business owner/manager needs to know. *Quarterly Journal of Business and Economics*, *39*(2), 62–79.

Byrne, B. (2001). *Structural equation modeling with AMOS – Basic concepts, applications, and programming*. New Jersey: Lawerence Erlbaum Associates.

Carmines, E. G., & McIver, J. P. (1981). Analysing models with unobserved variables. In: G. W. Bohrnstedt & E. F. Borgatta (Eds), *Social measurement: Current issues*. Sage: Beverly Hills.

Collis, J. (2003). *The utility of the statutory accounts to the directors of small private companies in the UK*. PhD Thesis, Kingston Business School, Kingston University.

Curran, J. (2000). What is small business policy in the UK for? Evaluation and assessing small business policies. *International Small Business Journal*, *18*(3), 36–50.

Curran, J., & Blackburn, R. A. (2001). *Researching the small enterprise*. London: Sage Publications.

Dang, D. S., Marriott, D. N., & Marriott, P. (2006). Users' perceptions and uses of financial information of small and medium companies (SMEs) in transitional economies: Qualitative evidence from Vietnam. *Qualitative Research on Accounting and Management*, *3*(3), 218–235.

Danos, P., Holt, D. L., & Imholff, E. A. (1989). The use of accounting information in bank lending decisions. *Accounting, Organisation and Society*, *14*(3), 235–246.

Deakins, D., & Hussain, D. (1994). Financial information, the bankers and the small businesses: A comment. *British Accounting Review*, *26*(4), 323–335.

Dillman, D. A. (2000). *Mail and internet surveys: The tailored design method* (2nd ed.). New York: Wiley.

Feakins, M. (2001). *Access to capital for small and medium-sized enterprises in Poland: Bank, decisions and economic development in post-socialism*. Oxford: Oxford University.

Field, A. (2005). *Discovering statistics using SPSS for windows* (2nd ed.). London: Sage Publications.

Gray, R., Owen, D., & Adams, C. (1996). *Accounting and accountability*. London: Prentice-Hall.

GSO. (2006). *The real situation of enterprises through the results of surveys conducted from 2002 to 2005*. [Online] General Statistics Office, Available at http://www.gso.gov.vn/default_en.aspx?tabid = 479&idmid = 4. Accessed on 1 August 2006.

Kent, P., & Munro, L. (1999). Differential reporting and the effect on loan evaluations: An experimental study. *Accounting Forum*, *23*(4), 359–377.

Kokko, A., & Sjoholm, F. (2005). The internationalization of Vietnamese small and medium-sized enterprises. *Asian Economic Papers*, *4*(1), 152–177.

Le, N. T. B., Venkatesh, S., & Nguyen, V. T. (2006). Getting bank financing: A study of Vietnamese private firms. *Asia Pacific Journal of Management, 23*(2), 209–227.

Lloyd-Reason, L., Marinova, M., & Nicolescu, O. (2000). Financing entrepreneurial development in Centre and Eastern Europe in the new millennium: Some lesson from Bulgaria. 22nd ISBA National Small Firms Conference.

Marriott, N., & Marriott, P. (1999). *The provision of financial information to smaller companies.* London: Institute of Chartered Accountants in England & Wales.

Nguyen, V. T., & Bryant, S. E. (2004). The study of the formality of human resource management practices in small and medium-sized enterprises in Viernam. *International Small Business Journal, 22*(6), 595–618.

Nguyen, V. T., Le, N. T. B., & Freeman, N. J. (2006). Trust and uncertainty: A study of bank lending to private SMEs in Vietnam. *Asia Pacific Business Review, 12*(4), 547–568.

O'Connor, D. (2000). Financial sector reform in China and Vietnam: A comparative perspective. *Comparative Economic Studies, 42*(4), 45–66.

Oppenheim, A. N. (1992). *Questionnaire design, interviewing and attitude measurement.* London: Continuum.

Page, M. J. (1984). Corporate financial reporting and the small independent company. *Accounting and Business Research, 12*(47), 271–282.

Poutziouris, P., Chittenden, F., & Michaelas, N. (1998). *Financial management and working capital practices in UK SMEs.* Manchester: Manchester Business School.

Roberts, E. S. (1999). In defence of the survey method: An illustration from a study of user information satisfaction. *Accounting and Finance, 39*, 53–97.

Ronnas, P., & Ramamurthy, B. (2001). *Entrepreneurship in Vietnam: Transformation and dynamics.* Norway: Nordic Institute of Asian Studies and Institute of Southeast Asian Studies.

Sarapaivanich, N., & Kotey, B. (2006). The effect of investment readiness in accessing external finance of SMEs in Thailand. 29th Institute for Small Business and Enterpreneurship Conference, Cardiff, 31st October to 2nd November.

Skrondal, A., & Rabe-Hesketh, S. (2005). *Entry for the encyclopedia of statistics in behavioral sciences.* Wiley.

Staubus, G. J. (2000). *The decision-usefulness theory of accounting: A limited history (new works in accounting history).* New York: Garland Publishing.

Tagoe, N., Nyarko, E., & Anuwa-Amarh, E. (2005). Financial challenges facing urban SMEs under financial sector liberalisation in Ghana. *Journal of Small Business Management, 43*(3), 331–343.

VAC-Deloitte. (2003). Vietnam Accounting Standard vs Current Accounting Regulations. [Online] Vietnam Auditing Company-Deloitte Toche Tohmatsu. Available at http://www.iasplus.com/resource/vas.pdf. Accessed on 16 October 2004.

VieGov. (2001). *Supporting the development of small and medium-sized enterprises.* Decree No. 90/2001/CP-ND, Vietnam Government.

William, J., & Dennis, J. (2003). Raising response rates in mail surveys of small business owners: Results of an experiment. *Journal of Small Business Management, 41*(3), 278–295.

Yang, D. C., & Nguyen, A. T. (2003). The enterprise accounting system of Vietnam and United States general accepted accounting principles: A comparison. In: J. T. Sale, S. B. Salter & D. J. Sharp (Eds), *Advances in International Accounting* (Vol. 16, pp. 175–204). Oxford: JAI.

APPENDIX

[This appendix is included for reviewers' use only. However, it is also available to other interested parties by contacting the authors of the paper].

QUESTIONNAIRE

The users' needs and uses of the information of small and medium sized companies in Vietnam

Your participation in this research is greatly appreciated.
Your responses are anonymous and no attempt is made to identify you.

SECTION I - GENERAL INFORMATION

Instructions **: In this section we would like to know about your general awareness about a small and medium sized enterprise (SME). You are required to circle, to fill in or to tick the box(s) that most represents your opinion about the issues. Please treat each question separately.**

1.   **Do you know the official definition of a SME issued by the government**

Yes ☐   No ☐

2.   **To classify a company as a SME, which criteria would you use?**

*(Please **tick** all that apply)*

Number of employees   ☐
Average annual revenues   ☐
Total balance sheet assets   ☐
Other (please specify)   ☐
....

3.   **Please indicate the specific threshold(s) you use to classify a company as a SME**

*(Please **enter** the values for all that apply)*

Number of employees   (No. of employees) ☐
Average annual revenues   (million dong)   ☐
Net balance sheet assets   (million dong)   ☐
Other (please specify)   (   )   ☐
....

4. **Do you make a distinction between the financial statements of a SME and those of larger entities?**

Yes ☐ No ☐

(If __yes__, please indicate to what extent agree with the following statements. If __no__, please go to Q 5.)

*(For each item, please **circle** the number that most represents your opinion)*

	Strong agree		Of some agreement		Disagree
SME's format contains less information	5	4	3	2	1
SME's format contains more information	5	4	3	2	1
SME's format is easier to understand	5	4	3	2	1
SME's format is more difficult to understand	5	4	3	2	1
Other (please specify)					
………………………………………………..	5	4	3	2	1

5. **Who should be the main user(s) of the financial statements of a SME?**

*(Please **tick** all that apply)*

The directors/managers of your enterprises	
The shareholders/owners	
Employees	
Banks and credit institutions	
Tax authorities	
Statistics offices and other government agencies	
Institutional investors	
Private investors	
Financial analysts/advisors	
Business contacts	

Other (please specify)

………………………………………………………………………………………

End of section I

Please go to the next section

SECTION II - USERS' NEEDS AND USES OF INFORMATION

Instructions: **In this section we would like to know about what information you need and how you use the information of an SME. You are required to circle, to fill in or to tick the box(s) that most represent your opinion about the issues. Please treat each question separately.**

6.   **Please indicate how you currently access the information of a SME?**

*(Please **tick** all that apply)*

By receiving financial reports directly from the company

By receiving advice from financial experts

By retrieving information in databases/information centres

By discussing with your colleagues

By looking for information on the Internet

By paying site visits to the company

By getting tips and rumours

Other (please specify)

....

7.   **How many sets of financial statements do you read annually?**

*(Please tick **one box** only)*

1-5

5-10

10-30

More than 30

8.   **For what purpose do you use the information about a SME?**

*(Please **tick** all that apply)*

To serve taxation collection

To gather information for administrative/statistics purposes

To make lending decisions

To make investment decisions

To tender for business contract/project

Other (please specify)

....

9. How many weeks after the end of the financial year do you receive the financial statements of a typical SME?

(Please tick __one box__ only)

0-30 days
30-60 days
60-90 days
More than 90 days

10. How much time do you spend reading each of the following financial statements?

*(For each report, please **tick** the box indicating the estimated time you typically spend on reading it)*

(minutes)	0-15	15-30	30-60	60-120	>120	Do not read
Balance sheets						
Income statements						
Cash flow statements						
Notes to the financial statements						
Trial balance of accounts						
Auditors' report						
Other (please specified)						

11. To what extent do you use the following information?

*(For each information section, please **circle** the number that most represents your opinion)*

	Always		Sometimes		Never
Current/fixed assets	5	4	3	2	1
Liabilities	5	4	3	2	1
Owners' equity	5	4	3	2	1
Revenues	5	4	3	2	1
VAT amounts	5	4	3	2	1
Cost of sales	5	4	3	2	1
Expenses	5	4	3	2	1
Profits	5	4	3	2	1
Income tax amounts	5	4	3	2	1
Declarations of accounting policies	5	4	3	2	1
Obligations to state budget	5	4	3	2	1
Trial balance of accounts	5	4	3	2	1
Cash flow information	5	4	3	2	1
Forecasts	5	4	3	2	1
Auditors' report	5	4	3	2	1

12.   How useful do you find each of the following information of a SME?

*(For each item, please **circle** the number that most represents your opinion)*

	Very useful		Of some use		Not useful
Current/fixed assets	5	4	3	2	1
Liabilities	5	4	3	2	1
Owners' equity	5	4	3	2	1
Revenues	5	4	3	2	1
VAT amounts	5	4	3	2	1
Cost of sales	5	4	3	2	1
Expenses	5	4	3	2	1
Profits	5	4	3	2	1
Cash flow information	5	4	3	2	1
Income tax amounts	5	4	3	2	1
Declarations of accounting policies	5	4	3	2	1
Obligations to state budget	5	4	3	2	1
Trial balance	5	4	3	2	1
Forecasts	5	4	3	2	1
Auditors' report	5	4	3	2	1
Other (please specify)					
....	5	4	3	2	1

13.   Please indicate how well you understand each of the following information

*(For each item, please **circle** the number that most represents your opinion)*

	Understand very well		Some understanding		Not understand at all
Current/fixed assets	5	4	3	2	1
Liabilities	5	4	3	2	1
Owners' equity	5	4	3	2	1
Revenues	5	4	3	2	1
Cost of sales	5	4	3	2	1
Expenses	5	4	3	2	1
Profits	5	4	3	2	1
Cash flow information	5	4	3	2	1
VAT amounts	5	4	3	2	1
Income tax amounts	5	4	3	2	1
Declarations of accounting policies	5	4	3	2	1
Obligations to state budget	5	4	3	2	1
Trial balance	5	4	3	2	1
Forecasts	5	4	3	2	1
Auditors' report	5	4	3	2	1
Other (please specify)					
....	5	4	3	2	1

14. <u>In addition to</u> the information in the financial statements, do you need other information to fullfil your duties?

Yes ☐   No ☐

(If <u>yes</u>, please indicate the <u>type</u> of information you need and how <u>important</u> it is to you. If <u>no</u>, please go to the next section.)

*(Please **indicate** the information and **circle** the number that most represents your opinion)*

Information	Very important		Of some importance		Not important
……………………………………………………	5	4	3	2	1
……………………………………………………	5	4	3	2	1
……………………………………………………	5	4	3	2	1
……………………………………………………..	5	4	3	2	1

End of section II

Please go to the next section.

SECTION III - THE FACTORS AFFECTING THE USE OF INFORMATION

Instructions**: The questions in this section cover a range of information about the factors that affect your utility of the information of a SME. You are required to fill in, to circle or to tick the box(s) that most represent your opinion about the issues. Please treat each question separately.**

15. **Is there a need to improve the quality of information in the financial statements?**

Yes ☐   No ☐

(If yes, please answer Q 16. If no, please go to Q 17)

16. **Please indicate to what extent the following characteristic(s) of information needs to be improved**

*(For each characteristic, please **circle** the number that most represents your opinion)*

	Major improvement		Some improvement		No improvement
Reliability	5	4	3	2	1
Relevance	5	4	3	2	1
Timeliness	5	4	3	2	1
Comparability	5	4	3	2	1
Other (please specify)					
………………………………………………..	5	4	3	2	1

17. **How important are the following factors to the quality of information provided by SMEs?**

*(For each factor, please **circle** the number that most presents your opinion)*

	Very important		Of some importance		Not important
The educational background of the directors	5	4	3	2	1
The management skills of the directors/managers	5	4	3	2	1
The perceptions of the directors about accounting functions	5	4	3	2	1
The capability of accountants	5	4	3	2	1
Statutory audit	5	4	3	2	1
Other (please specify)					
……………………………………………………..	5	4	3	2	1

18. **How significant is each of the following items in terms of the costs of preparing and disseminating financial information?**

*(For each item, please **circle** the number that most represents your opinion)*

	Great significant		Of some significance		Not significant
Salary and wages of accounting staff	5	4	3	2	1
Costs of legal and accounting regulation update	5	4	3	2	1
Costs of accounting software license and maintenance	5	4	3	2	1
Costs of computers/office tools	5	4	3	2	1
Costs of stationery	5	4	3	2	1
Costs of information dissemination	5	4	3	2	1
Other (please specify)					
…………………………………………………..	5	4	3	2	1

19. **What benefits do you think a SME will have from providing information in financial statements?**

*(For each item, please **circle** the number that most represents your opinion)*

	Very beneficial		Of some benefit		Not beneficial
To fulfil tax declaration	5	4	3	2	1
To serve administrative/statistical purposes of the government	5	4	3	2	1
To support borrowing applications	5	4	3	2	1
To tender for business contracts/projects	5	4	3	2	1
To meet your internal management	5	4	3	2	1
To join business associations	5	4	3	2	1
To achieve better public image	5	4	3	2	1
Other (please specify)					
…………………………………………………..	5	4	3	2	1

20. **What do you think about the relationship between the costs and the benefits an SME may receive from the preparation and provision of information?**

*(Please tick **one box** only)*

The benefits outweigh the costs

The benefits fit with the costs

The costs outweigh the benefits

No idea

Other (please specify)

………………………………………………………………………………………….

546 SON DANG-DUC ET AL.

21. How important is the auditors' report in terms of the following roles?

*(For each item, please **circle** the number that most represents your opinion)*

	Very important		Of some importance		Not important
To fulfill the requirements of law	5	4	3	2	1
To confirm and verify the data	5	4	3	2	1
To strengthen internal control system	5	4	3	2	1
To provide more consultant/recommendations	5	4	3	2	1
Other (please specify)					
....	5	4	3	2	1

22. Do you agree that SMEs should have their financial statements audited?

Yes ☐   No ☐

Please provide the reason to support your choice:

....
....

23. What do you think about the role of accountants in the preparation and provision of accounting information?

*(For each function, please **circle** the number that most presents your opinion)*

	Very important		Of some importance		Not important
Inputting accounting data and prepare the financial reports	5	4	3	2	1
Providing financial advice to management	5	4	3	2	1
Increasing the reliability of accounting information	5	4	3	2	1
Providing statutory audit	5	4	3	2	1
Other function (please specify)					
....	5	4	3	2	1

24. Do you think that current national accounting standards are suitable with SMEs?

Yes ☐   No ☐   No idea ☐

25. **What is your opinion about the following statements of the influence of current national accounting standards on SMEs?**

*(For each item, please **circle** the number that most represents your opinion)*

	Strong agree		Of some agree		Disagree
They increase the costs of financial reporting	5	4	3	2	1
They make the accounting regulations more complex	5	4	3	2	1
They help improve the quality of accounting information	5	4	3	2	1
They make the accounting activities more uniform	5	4	3	2	1

End of section III

Please go to the next section.

SECTION IV - DEMOGRAPHIC INFORMATION

Instructions: **This section asks for some demographic information. Any information given will be only used for the purposes of this research. Anonymity will be preserved at all times. The information about you and your organization will not be published under any circumstances. Please treat each question separately.**

26.   Would you please describe your job fuction?

Position:...

Main job functions:

....

....

Working experience:......year(s)......month(s).

Your highest educational qualification..

27.   Would you like a summary of the findings of the research?

Yes ☐   No ☐

If yes, please provide the following information:

First name ....Surname:.......................................

Postage address: ....

Tel:..Post code:..............

Email address:...

Thank you for completing the questionnaire.
Please return the questionnaire to the following address by using the enclosed stamped envelope

Dang Duc Son
Faculty of Accounting and Finance, University of Commerce
HoTung Mau St, Cau Giay Dist, Ha noi, Vietnam
Tel: +844 8347686
Fax: +844 7643228